ENGLISH G

| Abschlussband |

access 5

Lehrerfassung

W0337439

Vokabel Trainer
Cornelsen

Vokabeltrainer-App

Verfügbar für: iOS, Android und Windows Phone

Cornelsen

English G Access · Band 5

Abschlussband für die 5-jährige Sekundarstufe 1

Lehrerfassung

Im Auftrag des Verlages herausgegeben von
Prof. Jörg Rademacher, Mannheim

Erarbeitet von
Laurence Harger, Wellington, Neuseeland
Cecile Niemitz-Rossant, Berlin

unter Mitarbeit von
Dr. Annette Leithner-Brauns, Dresden; Birgit Ohmsieder, Berlin; Mervyn Whittaker, Bad Dürkheim

in Zusammenarbeit mit der Englischredaktion
Dr. Philip Devlin (koordinierender Redakteur), Gareth Evans, Bonnie Glänzer (Lehrerfassung), Stefan Höhne (Projektleitung), Dr. Christiane Kallenbach, Meike Kolle, Thomas Schulze, Uwe Tröger *und beratend* Filiz Bahsi, Ulrike Berendt, Solveig Heinrich, Renata Jakovac *und* Lothar Teworte (digitales Schülerbuch)

Beratende Mitwirkung
Friederike von Bremen, Hannover; Peter Brünker, Bad Kreuznach; Anette Fritsch, Dillenburg; Uli Imig, Wildeshausen; Bernd Koch, Marburg; Thomas Neidhardt, Bielefeld; Wolfgang Neudecker, Mannheim; Dr. Andreas Sedlatschek, Esslingen; Sieglinde Spranger, Chemnitz; Marcel Sprunkel, Köln; Sabine Tudan, Reichenau; Harald Weißling, Mannheim

Illustrationen
Tobias Dahmen, Utrecht/NL; Burkhard Schulz, Düsseldorf, Michael Fleischmann, Waldegg *sowie* Eric Gira, Berlin

Umschlaggestaltung und Layoutkonzept
kleiner & bold, Berlin
hawemannundmosch, Berlin
klein & halm, Berlin

Layout und technische Umsetzung
Eric Gira, Ungermeyer, Berlin

Legende zur Lehrerfassung

12	Tracknummern
school	Lernwortschatz (produktiv)
°spy	Situativer Wortschatz (nicht produktiv)
Box "when", Voc, S. 197	Verweis auf Wortschatzbox im *Vocabulary*
+wife	Hinweis auf zusätzl. Wortschatz im *Vocabulary*
were used by them	Grammatische Strukturen
YT	Übungen, die zur Lernaufgabe hinführen
FöFo 1.1 • KV 1 • …	Verweise auf Begleitmedien
www 1.1	Verweis auf interaktive Übungen
[ˌtʃerəˈkiː]	Aussprachehinweis
Die S können …	Lernfelder, didaktische Hinweise, Alternativen, KV
learned • sat	Lösungen (geschlossene Aufgaben)

www.cornelsen.de
www.englishg.de/access

1. Auflage, 2. Druck 2019

Alle Drucke dieser Auflage sind inhaltlich unverändert und können im Unterricht nebeneinander verwendet werden.

Druck und Bindung: Livonia Print, Riga

ISBN 978-3-06-033751-4
ISBN 978-3-06-033769-9 (E-Book)

PEFC/12-31-006

PEFC zertifiziert
Dieses Produkt stammt aus nachhaltig bewirtschafteten Wäldern und kontrollierten Quellen.
www.pefc.de

English G Access 5 enthält folgende Teile:

Units	die vier Kapitel des Buches
Text challenge	Vorbereitung auf die Oberstufe
Text File (TF)	eine Sammlung englischer Gedichte, Geschichten und Sachtexte
Skills File (SF)	eine Beschreibung wichtiger Lern- und Arbeitstechniken
Grammar File (GF)	eine Zusammenfassung der Grammatik jeder Unit
Vocabulary	das Wörterverzeichnis zum Lernen der neuen Wörter jeder Unit
Dictionary	alphabetisches Wörterverzeichnis zum Nachschlagen

In den Units findest du diese Überschriften:

Background file	Informationen über Land und Leute
Looking at language	Beispiele sammeln und sprachliche Regeln entdecken
Language help	Hilfe in Form von sprachlichen Regeln
Practice	Aufgaben und Übungen
Access to words	Wortschatz systematisch ausbauen
Speaking course	nützliche sprachliche Hilfen beim Sprechen
The world behind the picture	vom Bild in den Film – Videoclips mit Aufgaben

Du findest auch diese Symbole:

	Texte, die du dir anhören kannst: *www.englishg.de/access*
www	zusätzliche Materialien, die du unter *www.englishg.de/access* finden kannst
	deinen Alltag mit der Alltagskultur anderer Länder vergleichen
	Übungssequenz: neue Grammatik intensiv üben und dann anwenden
Early finisher	zusätzliche Aktivitäten und Übungen für Schüler/innen, die früher fertig sind
More help	zusätzliche Hilfen für eine Aufgabe
You choose	eine Aufgabe auswählen
EXTRA	zusätzliche Aktivitäten und Übungen für alle
My Book	schöne und wichtige Arbeiten sammeln
Study skills	Einführung in Lern- und Arbeitstechniken
Your task	Was du in einer Unit gelernt hast, kannst du in einer Lernaufgabe zeigen.
	Hören Sprechen Lesen Schreiben Hör-Seh-Verstehen
	Mediation (zwischen zwei Sprachen vermitteln)
	Partnerarbeit Partnercheck Gruppenarbeit Kooperative Lernform

Inhalt

Skill in focus: Listening

Skill in focus: Reading

Inhalt

Die hier und auf den Folgeseiten aufgeführten Angebote sind nicht obligatorisch abzuarbeiten. Die Auswahl der Übungen und Übungsteile richtet sich nach den Schwerpunkten des schulinternen Curriculums.

Describe the picture and discuss what ideas it expresses.

Say how you think these ideas are linked to the topics of Units 1-4.

Australia, country and continent

A
Western Australia

Tasmania
E

New South Wales
F

YT 1 Australia and me

a) Write a list of ten words you think of in connection with Australia.

b) In a double circle, use your list to tell your partners your ideas.

c) Imagine you took the photos on these pages. Describe two of the photos to your partner and the situation when you took them (noise, smells, temperature etc).

- This photo shows …
- I took it when we were in / we were travelling through / …
- You can see …
- It's a tropical/coastal/… region.
- I took this photo because …

bush · coral · desert · kangaroo · outback · palm tree · rainforest · spider · wildlife

coastal · exotic · humid · lonely · marine · remote · rocky · sandy · stunning · tropical · urban

+the tropics *(pl)*

→ Workbook *Wordbank 1*

Die S geben bekanntes **Wissen über Australien** wieder, identifizieren Merkmale typischer australischer Symbole und beschreiben die **landschaftliche Vielfältigkeit des Kontinents**. Sie können einem Hörtext **landeskundliche Informationen** über Australien entnehmen.

Text File: Zu Unit 1 passt **Text 1**.

2 Uncle Ozzie's fun facts 02

a) Say what these words mean before you listen.

Aboriginal · camel · convict · koala · poisonous snake

b) Decide if Uncle Ozzie's "facts" are true or false. Then check your answers. ➜ p. 134

c) Did Uncle Ozzie manage to fool you? Say which fact you found most surprising.

Die S können aufgefordert werden, vor dem Hören Zahlen von 1–10 zu notieren und hinter diesen beim Hören jeweils einen Haken (für richtig) oder ein Kreuz (für falsch) zu setzen. Bei Bedarf kann L den Hörtext nach jeder Quizfrage kurz stoppen.

3 EXTRA A road trip

Länge: 04:03

Watch the film.
Which landscape/scene made the biggest impression on you?
Describe it to your partner and explain why.

Your task

At the end of this unit:
Find good reasons for a six-month exchange visit to Far North Queensland.

Die S lernen Australien besser kennen, indem sie verschiedenen Quellen Informationen über **Attraktionen, Sehenswürdigkeiten** und **Freizeitziele** entnehmen.

1 On the way to Sydney

Skim the text. Say what kind of information it gives, who it is written for, and where you might find it.

Hinweis: Rosella (Plattschweifsittich) ist eine in Australien vorkommende Papageienart.

Rosella In-Flight Tips

A ferry at Circular Quay.

Flying in to Sydney?
Here's how to make your stay a great one!

Stay in **The Rocks**, the lively historical quarter where the first convicts settled in the 1790s. Or in the trendy suburb of **Woolloomooloo** with its beautiful wharf. From there, it's a short walk through the **Royal Botanic Gardens** into the city, to the crowds and skyscrapers of the Central Business District (CBD). On the way, you'll see the flying foxes hanging from the trees and, of course, the world-famous **Sydney Opera House**.

+fox

The best way to see Sydney's **stunning harbour** is to head for **Circular Quay** and jump on one of the ferries going to **Manly**. At the end of the half-hour ride, a five-minute walk through Manly takes you to its beautiful ocean beach.

Box "a half-hour ride, …", Voc, S. 197

After an ice cream in one of the cafés at Circular Quay, wander round the waterfront and enjoy all the street performers, like the great **Aboriginal didgeridoo players**. Or head for the **Museum of Contemporary Art** and go on a teen-guided tour to get a young person's fresh and honest take on the museum's works.

If you've still got some energy, don't catch the ferry back – walk the **Manly Scenic Walkway** along the water, across the northern harbour beaches and through **Sydney Harbour National Park**. Watch the sailing boats, wind and kitesurfers along the route and then catch a bus back to the city from **Spit Bridge**.

If it's night and winter and the **VividSydney** festival is on, look out across the water from the museum and watch the light show transforming the Opera House and other Sydney landmarks into magical, colourful works of art changing from minute to minute.

DID YOU KNOW?

Sydney has more than 100 beautiful, sandy beaches along its harbour and waterfront. So, if you're looking for the perfect wave to surf or a kitesurfing paradise, calm water for a relaxing swim, a quiet corner to read a book or a busier place to watch the people, you'll find the right spot in Sydney.

Kitesurfers at Botany Bay

2 Discovering Sydney

Say which of the tips you would most like to follow. Give reasons.

Find out more about other Australian cities.

3 Leon's testimonials

HOME | ABOUT US | PROGRAMS | DESTINATIONS | TESTIMONIALS | GALLERY | HOW DO I APPLY | BLOG | CONTACT US

Leon, 16, Germany

Six months ago I was on the plane flying to Sydney. I was going to spend half a year at an Australian high school and live with a family I didn't know, 16,000 km from home. From morning till night I would have to speak English. Back then I was nervous. But now I know there was nothing to worry about.

There was just one problem at first. Before I heard Australians talking, I thought I understood English. But Aussies use words I had never learned and their accent was strange, so in the first few weeks my favourite phrase was *Sorry, can you say that again, please? Slowly.* They did – and it helped. Now I sound like an Aussie myself.

Box "Group nouns", Voc, S. 198

My host family are great and they immediately made me feel at home. My host dad, Brian, tells a lot of jokes, though it was hard to get some of them at first. He cooks a lot, especially on the barbie. I love the way families here eat outside together in hot weather, and I have to say Brian makes absolutely ripper snags (Aussie for "great sausages").

My host mum, Elvira, and host brother, Nick, taught me how to surf at Manly Beach, which is five minutes from their house. I fell off the board a lot at first and swallowed tons of salt water. But I'm better now … and I love it.

[el'vɪərə]

At school I felt a bit lonely in the beginning. It was a private school – boys only – and sport was so important. Playing rugby is the easiest way to get accepted into a group, but it wasn't my game. But Australian kids are talkative and friendly and I soon made some great friends.

At school I was able to do subjects we don't have in Germany, like photography and drama. In the end, I even liked the uniform – when everyone wears the same, you don't have to think about what to wear every morning.

I only got homesick once, at Christmas. It was fun to celebrate it in summer but I really missed my family and the presents on Christmas Eve.

This has been the best six months of my life and I can't believe it's almost over. I'm much more self-confident now and have learned how to do everything on my own. Sydney is fantastic and I love the easy-going Aussie way of life.

Me and a mob of kangaroos hang out near the beach

4 Six months in Sydney

a) Make notes on
- what Leon likes about his stay in Sydney
- difficulties or problems he has experienced

b) Write down questions you would ask Leon.
- Leon, when did you first see …
- Have you eaten … since you arrived?
- …

c) Partner A: Ask your questions from b). Partner B: You're Leon. Use your imagination to answer A's questions. Swap roles.
- Actually, I saw a … on my very first day.
- Yes, I've often eaten … – it's really tasty!
- …

1 REVISION Have you packed your bags yet? (Simple past or present perfect)

a) Look at these sentences.

Have you **packed** your bags yet?
– Yes, I **packed** them yesterday.

Make two similar question and answer examples.

b) Agree on answers to the questions below. Check your results in class.

1 When do you use the simple past and when do you use the present perfect?
2 How do you form them?
3 What are typical signal words for each?

➜ *GF 1.3: The past (p. 164)*

c) Put the sentences in the right order. Choose the correct form of the verbs in brackets.

1 (I · be) too tired and anyway (I · not decide) exactly what to take with me yet.
2 Not all. (I · pack) my big rucksack last night, but (I · not start) to pack my two travel bags yet.
3 Why (you · not pack) the bags last night too?
4 (you · pack) all your bags yet?

1 Yes, (I · buy) it. (It · not be) very expensive.
2 Well, (I · be) in town last Saturday and (I · see) this book about German baking - in English!
3 (you · find) a present for your host family yet?
4 Wow, (I never · see) a German cookbook in English before. (you · buy) it?

Dialogue 1: 4 Have you packed …? · 2 … I packed … I haven't started … · 3 Why didn't you pack …? · 1 I was … I haven't decided … · Dialogue 2: 3 Have you found …? · 2 Well, I was … I saw … · 4 Wow, I have never seen … Did you buy it? · 1 Yes, I bought it. It wasn't …

More help ➜ p. 114

More help: Die Signalwörter sind farbig markiert.

2 REVISION Leon in Sydney (Simple present and present progressive)

a) Look at this sentence:

Leon usually **lives** in Germany, but at the moment he **is living** with a family in Sydney.

Make two more sentences about
- what Leon ***usually*** does at home and
- what he is doing differently ***at the moment***

b) Agree on answers to the questions below. Check your results in class.

1 When do you use the simple present and when do you use the present progressive?
2 How do you form them?
3 What are typical signal words for each?

➜ *GF 1.2: The present (p. 163)*

c) Put the verbs in brackets into the correct form: simple present or present progressive. Compare answers and make corrections. Then act out the dialogue.

A: [1] Are you enjoying (you · enjoy) your stay in Sydney?
B: Yes, [2] … (I · enjoy) it a lot.
A: What part of Sydney [3] … (you · stay) in?
B: I [4] … (I · stay) with a family in Manly. [5] … (They · have) a nice house near the beach.
A: So [6] … (you · learn) to surf at the moment?
B: Yes, [7] … (my host mum · teach) me right now.
A: What sports [8] … (you · play) back in Germany?
B: Well, [9] … (I · not live) on the coast, so [10] … (I · not do) water sports. But [11] … (I · play) football a lot.
A: What [12] … (you · think) of the weather here in Oz?
B: You get a lot of sun. As you see, [13] … (I · wear) a hat today. In Germany, [14] … (people · not worry) so much about the sun. Not like here, where [15] … (everyone · wear) sunscreen all the time.

2 I'm enjoying · 3 are you staying · 4 I'm staying · 5 They have · 6 are you learning · 7 my host mum is teaching · 8 do you play · 9 I don't live · 10 I don't do · 11 I play · 12 do you think · 13 I'm wearing · 14 people don't worry · 15 everyone wears

KV 1A/B: **Australian abbreviations** bietet Wortschatzarbeit zu *Australian English*.

Access to cultures

Like American English, Australian English is different in some ways from British English. But *no worries, mate*. Here's some help with Aussie words and Aussie pronunciation.

a) Look at these Australian words and phrases. Say what you think some of them might mean.

03 b) Listen to someone explaining Australian English. Note down words and phrases you hear and what they mean. Compare your results.

G'Day = good day · Godzone = God's own country · Oz = Australia · arvo = afternoon · barbie = barbecue · mozzie = mosquito · roo = kangaroo · Pom = British person · Yank = American · chook = chicken · esky = portable cooler · bush = countryside · stations = cattle or sheep farms · outback = further in the bush, where the country is drier · walkabout = a long walk in the outback · no worries = Don't worry about it. · She'll be right = It will be OK.

3 Sounds Australian (Pronunciation of Australian English)

04 a) Australian English isn't just about words; it's also about sounds. Listen to the same ten sentences spoken by British and Australian speakers. Say what sounds different in AusE.

05 b) Listen to eight short dialogues. Decide if the people are British or Australian. (Be careful: in two dialogues *only* AusE is spoken.) After each dialogue, say which sounds helped you to recognize AusE.

1 BE / AusE · 2 BE / AusE · 3 AusE / BE · 4 AusE / AusE · 5 AusE / BE · 6 AusE / BE · 7 AusE / AusE · 8 BE / AusE

LISTENING TIP

Some consonants, e.g. [l] and [t], sound different in Australian English. These BE vowel sounds also sound different in AusE:

[aɪ] tried · [eə] hair · [ɪ] village · [e] text · [ɑː] car · [iː] tea

4 The Rocks

Die S können einem Audio-Guide Informationen über eine konkrete Sehenswürdigkeit entnehmen und diese ins Deutsche übertragen.

06 a) Listen to an audio guide to The Rocks, an old area of Sydney.
Partner A: Take notes on the area today.
Partner B: Take notes on the area's history.

b) **Partner B:** You are A's parent. You phone A in Sydney and ask about his/her plans.
Partner A: Say that you're going to The Rocks and what you can do and see there today.

c) **Partner A:** You're a German tourist in Sydney. You see B waiting to start a city tour. Ask in German what the tour is about.
Partner B: Say that you're going on a tour of The Rocks and what you expect to see about Sydney's past.

Early finisher → *p. 122*

Early finisher: Die S ordnen Sehenswürdigkeiten ihren Beschreibungen zu.

→ Workbook *4–6 (p. 4)*

5 REVISION Around Sydney (Relative clauses: *who* or *which*)

Use who or which to complete these sentences. Then explain when to use who and when to use which.

1 It's Sydney's great atmosphere ... attracts millions of tourists.
2 When you arrive in the city, it's good to have someone ... can show you around.
3 The Rocks is the part of Sydney ... convicts used to live in.
4 The harbour is a big attraction for visitors ... like sailing or swimming.
5 Anyone ... is planning to learn surfing should head for Bondi or Manly.
6 There you will find experienced teachers ... know the waves.
7 The ferry ... is just leaving the quay is going to Manly.
8 The Manly Scenic Walkway is a 10-km route ... takes you along the coast to Spit Bridge.
9 When you're out in the sun, always wear a hat ... protects your face, neck and ears.
10 Most people ... visit Sydney can't wait to come back again.

➜ *GF 9.1: Relative clauses (p. 183)*

1 which • 2 who • 3 which • 4 who • 5 who • 6 who • 7 which • 8 which • 9 which • 10 who •
'who' is used for persons, 'which' is used for things

6 REVISION The Sydney Harbour ferry (Participle clauses instead of relative clauses)

Relative clauses give more information about a person or thing:
anyone *who is planning to learn surfing*
the **ferry** *which is leaving the quay*

If the verb is in the progressive form, you can also use a participle clause.
anyone ~~who is~~ *planning to learn surfing*
the **ferry** ~~which is~~ *leaving the quay*

➜ *GF 10.2: Participle clauses (p. 185)*

Use a participle clause to make one sentence out of two.

1 There are a lot of people on the ferry. The ferry is crossing Sydney Harbour.
There are a lot of people on the ferry crossing Sydney Harbour.
2 On the top deck there is a group of tourists. They're taking photos of the view.
3 One man is filming the seagulls. They're following the ferry.
4 A woman is standing next to him. She's looking at a tourist brochure.
5 On board there are several school kids. They're going home from school.
6 On the bottom deck we met a German boy. He was carrying a surfboard under his arm.

2 On the top deck there is a group of tourists taking photos of the view. • 3 One man is filming the seagulls following the ferry. • 4 A woman looking at a tourist brochure is standing next to him. • 5 On board there are several school kids going home from school. • 6 On the bottom deck we met a German boy carrying a surfboard under his arm.

7 REVISION I saw the ferry arriving (Participle clauses after verbs of perception)

You can also use participle clauses after verbs of perception like *see, notice, ...* ➜ *GF 10.3: Participle clauses (p. 186)*

a) Use the verbs to make sentences about the pictures.

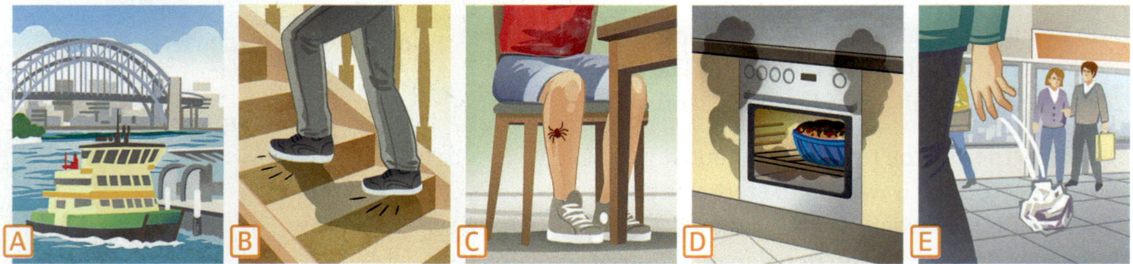

A see – arrive | B hear – come | C feel – climb | D smell – burn | E notice – throw

b) Imagine you are in Sydney. Describe what you see, hear, smell and feel.

More help ➜ p. 114
Early finisher ➜ p. 122

a) 1 I saw the ferry arriving. • 2 I heard someone coming upstairs. • 3 I felt something climbing up my leg. • 4 I smelled something burning in the oven. • 5 I noticed someone throwing litter on the ground.

More help: Die Sätze sind vorgegeben; die Verben müssen nur in die korrekte Form gebracht werden.

Early finisher: Rätsel, bei dem die S spielerisch weitere Partizipialsätze bilden.

 ➜ Workbook *7–9 (p. 5)*

Die S können einen **argumentativen Essay inhaltlich planen, vorbereiten** und **schreiben**. Sie können einem Partner konstruktives Feedback dazu geben.

YT 8 Study skills: Argumentative writing

Box "(to) argue – argument – argumentative", Voc, S. 199

Your topic is: *An exchange year in Australia is a good idea.* **Now work through the following steps.**

- In an argumentative text you present arguments in writing for and against a topic.
- Before you write, it is important to collect ideas, form your opinion and structure your content.
- There are special expressions and phrases that can help you to structure and present your arguments.

STEP 1

Brainstorm ideas and put them in a table.

For	Against
- students can learn about Australian culture - ...	- it costs a lot of money - ...

STEP 2

Think about

- any examples to support your arguments e.g. A year in Australia would cost about ... euros.
- which arguments are stronger
- whether to support or oppose the topic

Then write down your opinion in one or two sentences.

STEP 3

Look at the argumentative text structure and the expressions that start each paragraph.

i Introduction	You introduce the topic without giving your opinion. Use one paragraph.	Students often ask whether they should spend ...
ii Main body 1 paragraph	a) You present the arguments you oppose. Use one paragraph.	One of the main reasons why people think a year abroad ...
1 or 2 paragraphs	b) You present the arguments you support. Use one or two paragraphs.	There is, however, another way of looking at the question.
	(second paragraph)	In addition, people argue ...
iii Conclusion 1 paragraph	You state and explain your opinion briefly. Use one paragraph.	Personally, I believe that ...

How else could you start each paragraph? Choose an alternative.

After looking at both sides of the argument, ... · A question that people often discuss is ... · Furthermore, you could argue that ... · In my opinion/view, ... · It is often said that ... · I would first like to look at the reasons why ... · On the one hand, some people think that ... · On the other hand, people say that ... · Some people take a different view. · Some people think ...

STEP 4

Now write your text. You may need language to

- talk about advantages or disadvantages: · A big advantage/disadvantage of ... is ... · Another/The biggest advantage/disadvantage is ...
- make comparisons: · ... is much more important than ... · ... isn't quite as important as ...
- give examples: · For example, ... · This is clear because ...
- order arguments and examples: · To start with, ... · Firstly,/Secondly,/Thirdly, ... · Finally, ...
- explain your conclusion: · Although I understand the other side of the argument, I still think ...

STEP 5

Read your partner's text and give feedback. → *p. 272 Giving feedback*

KV 2: Giving feedback on a text hilft den S bei ihren Rückmeldungen.

Die S lernen **eine Region in Australien** und deren **geographische und klimatische Besonderheiten** kennen.

YT 1 Far North Queensland (FNQ)

Say what impressions Emily's pictures give you of FNQ.

°CAPE TRIB KID
Hi, I'm Emily. I'm 15 and I live in Cape Tribulation – Cape Trib as we call it in FNQ. This is a great place for the outdoor life with the world's oldest rainforest (the Daintree) and biggest coral reef (the Great Barrier Reef) at our front door. I'm posting some stuff you only know about if you live up here.

Two school kids … out in the wet

Folk at home … in the wet

Being tropical, FNQ is always very warm and has two seasons – the "dry" and the "wet". In the wet, it rains a lot, sometimes flooding the roads. While these guys were determined to get to school, most of us (like me) were in bed, listening to the radio. But it doesn't always help to stay inside. You can also get wet while hanging out at home if an FNQ°cyclone has torn your roof off.

The ants escape the water …

… and a frog comes to visit.

Insects aren't keen on wet weather either. While waiting for the flood waters to go down, the ants headed for this big stone. But green tree frogs love wet weather. So why was this guy here, sitting on the living room floor, when he could have been out enjoying the rain?

Beau Peberdy with a visitor …

… and another cool visitor.

So maybe that frog wanted to hide from the python our neighbours found in the garden. °Amethyst pythons ['æmɪθɪst ˌpaɪθən] are the biggest Australian snakes and one of the longest in the world, growing to over 5 m long. Luckily, they prefer frogs, °possums, birds and small kangaroos to a snack of humans.
The beach is a great place for unexpected visitors too. °Cassowaries are another of our exotic animals. They are the third tallest and second heaviest birds in the world. They live in FNQ's rainforest, feeding mainly on fruit. But don't provoke them – they can injure or even kill dogs or humans.

Some of our animals just look scary …

… some of them really are.

FNQ's (and Australia's) largest moth, the Hercules, might make you nervous when flying round your bedroom lamp, but don't worry – it hasn't got a mouth so it can't bite you.
Crocodiles live in rivers, right? Yes, but the monster crocs in FNQ are known as "salties" because they don't mind salt water. They often swim out of rivers into the sea. So watch out at the beach. You don't want to bump into a 6-m-long, 1-ton saltie while enjoying FNQ's warm, tropical waters.

341 comments

YT 2 Tropical life

a) Read the texts. Take notes about the climate, wildlife, dangers, … Then say how your first impression of FNQ has changed.

b) My Book Write a comment to post on Emily's site. Say if you like her post. Use your notes.

www Find out more about life in FNQ.

➔ Text File 1 (pp. 104–106)
Text File: In the outback

3 Have a go

Die S verwenden vorbewusst ***participle clauses***.

a) Make sentences about what Emily was doing at the beach. Use these ideas.

look out for salties · snorkel with a friend · build a sandcastle · play frisbee · lie in the sun · watch the waves

1 Emily was at the beach, looking out for salties.
2 Emily was at the beach …

b) Make sentences about yourself.

1 I'm at school, thinking about the weekend.
2 I'm in my English lesson, …

a) 2 …, snorkeling with a friend. • 3 …, building a sandcastle. • 4 …, playing frisbee. • 5 …, lying in the sun. • 6 …, watching the waves.

➔ Workbook 11 (p. 6)

Die S üben **Partizipialkonstruktionen**.

Looking at language

a) Find sentences on pp. 18–19 with the same meaning as these. Write them down.
1 It rains a lot and sometimes floods the roads.
2 So why was this guy here and why was he sitting on the living room floor?
3 Amethyst pythons are one of the longest snakes in the world and grow to over 5 m long.
4 Cassowaries live in FNQ's rainforest and feed mainly on fruit.

b) Look at your sentences. Say what form of the verb is used there instead of "and … "

c) Now say this sentence another way:
We scanned the text and looked for participle clauses.

We scanned the text, looking for participle clauses.

➜ *GF 10.4: Participle clauses (p. 186)*

a) 1 (…) it rains a lot, sometimes flooding the roads. • 2 So why was this guy here, sitting on the living room floor (…)? • 3 The Amethyst python is the biggest Australian snake and one of the longest in the world, growing to over five metres long. • 4 They live in FNQ's rainforest, feeding mainly on fruit.

1 Two school kids walked through the water … (Participle clauses)

Rewrite the sentences, using a participle clause.
1 Two school kids walked through the water and pushed their bikes.
Two school kids walked through the water, pushing their bikes.
2 A cyclone hit the house and tore off the roof.
3 Everyone stood in the kitchen and discussed what to do next.
4 A frog looked up at the sky and hoped for rain.
5 We picked up the python for the photograph and held it as carefully as we could.
6 The cassowary walked across the beach and wished it could fly.
7 The crocodile moved quietly through the water and looked for food.
8 Bruce swam for his life and escaped from the crocodile.

2 A cyclone hit the house, tearing off the roof. • 3 Everyone stood in the kitchen, discussing what to do next. • 4 A frog looked up at the sky, hoping for rain. • 5 We picked up the python for the photograph, holding it as carefully as we could. • 6 The cassowary walked across the beach, wishing it could fly. • 7 The crocodile moved quietly through the water, looking for food. • 8 Bruce swam for his life, escaping the crocodile.

2 Everyone was outside … (Participle clauses)

Match the sentence beginnings to the pictures. Then finish each sentence with a participle clause.

A

B

C

D

E

F

1 Everyone was outside …
2 Fluff is walking along the piano …
3 Jake was standing in the greenhouse …
4 Mum was in the car …
5 Have you seen the photo of Rover …?
6 This is Ella on her way to a party …

1C waiting to go in / waiting to buy tickets / … • 2E playing music / trying to play / … • 3D smiling for the camera / holding a box of tomatoes / … • 4A relaxing in the front seat / … • 5A playing in the park / playing frisbee / … • 6B wearing a beard/glasses/etc. / carrying presents / …

More help ➜ *p. 115*

More help: Die Sätze sind den Bildern bereits zugeordnet. Eine Box bietet Hilfe beim Vervollständigen.

 ➜ Workbook 12 (p. 7)

3 While waiting ... (Participle clauses with *while* and *when*)

TIP
Clauses with ***while*** or ***when*** can use a participle instead of subject and verb. Compare:
- *While waiting for the flood waters to go down, the ants headed for this big stone.*
- *While they were waiting for the flood waters to go down, the ants headed for this big stone.*

Using a participle clause shortens your sentence.
This style is common in formal texts.
➔ GF 10.5: Participle clauses (p. 187)

Use participle clauses to join each pair of sentences. You can use when or while in the participle clause. Sometimes you must change sentence a) into a participle clause, sometimes sentence b).

1 a) I waited for my flight to Sydney. b) I read my guide to Australia.
While waiting for my flight to Sydney, I read my guide to Australia.
2 a) I often went surfing. b) I lived in Sydney for six months.
3 a) I attended school in Sydney. b) I made a lot of new friends.
4 a) I took photographs of Sydney Harbour. b) I took the ferry to Manly.
5 a) I got a lot of information on the internet. b) I planned a trip to Far North Queensland.
6 a) We visited Cape Tribulation. b) We saw a cassowary on the beach.
7 a) We looked out for crocodiles. b) We swam in the sea near Cape Tribulation.

2 While living in Sydney for six months, I often went surfing. • 3 While attending school in Sydney, I made a lot of new friends. • 4 While taking the ferry to Manly, I took photographs of Sydney Harbour.
5 When planning a trip to Far North Queensland, I got a lot of information on the internet. • 6 When visiting Cape Tribulation, we saw a cassowary on the beach. • 7 When swimming in the sea near Cape Tribulation, we looked out for crocodiles.

4 A trip that went wrong

a) **Write a short text (about ten sentences) about a trip that went wrong.**
Think about how you could use participle clauses (to improve your style, to describe something you saw happening, e.g.:

While packing my bag, I forgot ... A dog ran out in front of the airport bus, forcing it to stop suddenly.

b) **Hang up all your stories around the classroom for everyone to read and enjoy.**

More help: Als Hilfe sind einige Formulierungsvorschläge vorgegeben.
More help ➔ p. 115 Early finisher ➔ p. 123
Early finisher: Rätsel

YT 5 EXTRA Being new in Australia ... (Participle clauses to give reasons)

TIP
You can use participles to give a reason. The participle clause usually comes first.
Being tropical, FNQ is always warm. (Because it is tropical, FNQ is always warm.)
➔ GF 10.6: Participle clauses (p. 187)

Use participle clauses to explain the reasons.

1 I'm new in Australia. That's why I don't understand Aussie English very well.
Being new in Australia, I don't understand Aussie English very well.
2 We know all about floods because we live in the tropics.
3 I saw a python in the garden. I pulled out my camera to take a photo.
4 I knew that pythons are dangerous. That's why I was careful not to get too close.
5 We arrived late at the cinema, so we missed the first twenty minutes of the film.
6 I felt really tired, which is why I fell asleep in the middle of the movie.

2 Living in the tropics, we know all about floods. • 3 Seeing a python in the garden, I pulled out my camera to take a photo. • 4 Knowing that pythons are dangerous, I was careful not to get too close. • 5 Arriving late at the cinema, we missed the first twenty minutes of the film. 6 Feeling really tired, I fell asleep in the middle of the movie.

Die S können ein **ein-minütiges Kurzreferat über eine Region (Land, Landschaft, Städte) in Australien** halten.

On this page you will work with words that help you to talk about a country, its landscape and towns. Then you will give a one-minute talk about Australia – the whole continent, or just a region or town.

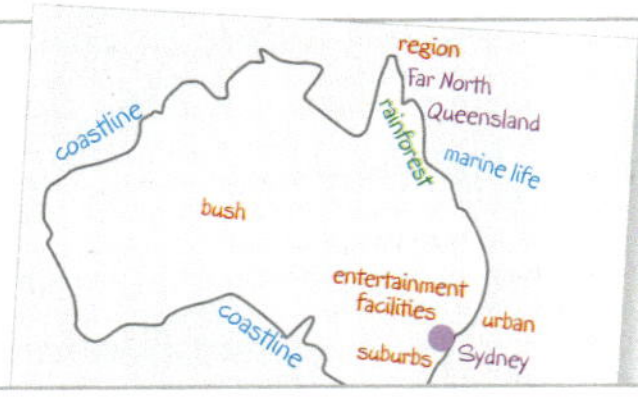

YT 1 Word field: Country and town (Structuring vocabulary)

a) Structure the vocabulary in the box. Add other words you know.

amazing · botanic gardens · bush · business district · central · centre · cinema · climate · +coastline · crocodile · desert · +dramatic · entertainment +facilities · harbour · outback · +overcrowded · rainforest · region · regional · river · +rural · shopping area · sports facilities · street · stunning · suburb · +suburban · +vast

+ = new words

TIP
Use a map to structure geography vocabulary. Or use one of the other ways you have learned, e.g. tables or mind maps.
➜ *SF 31: Ordering and structuring vocabulary (p. 160)*

KV 3 enthält zur Zeitersparnis die Box und eine Umrisskarte Australiens, mit der die S den Wortschatz strukturieren können.

b) Compare your methods for structuring the words. Say why you chose your method.

YT 2 Adjectives (Opposites)

Pairing words with opposite or contrasting meanings can make them easier to learn. Make as many pairs as you can with words from boxes A and B. Sometimes you can pair a word with two others. Sometimes it will not be possible to find pairs

A
humid · +inland · +mild · +mountainous · nearby · northern · +old-fashioned · rural · vast · wide

B
busy · coastal · dry · +flat · modern · narrow · remote · southern · suburban · tiny · tropical · urban

rural	urban, suburban
humid	...

humid – dry · inland – coastal · mild – tropical · mountainous – flat · nearby – remote · northern – southern · old-fashioned – modern · vast – narrow · wide – narrow

YT 3 Collocations (Adjectives and nouns)

a) Which adjectives from 2 go well with these nouns: *business district, climate, coastline, rainforest, region, sports facilities, street?*
Write phrases with your ideas.
- a mountainous region, a modern business district

b) Write six sentences on what you like or dislike about a place you know, e.g.
What I like about ... is the long rocky coastline.
One thing I hate about ...

More help ➜ *p. 115*

EXTRA **In a double circle, share your ideas from b).**

TIP
Collocations are groups of two or more words that sound right together, e.g. *a tall tree*, but *a high mountain*.
When we use two descriptive adjectives, size adjectives usually come first:
a small coastal town, a vast tropical rainforest
Opinion adjectives usually come before descriptive adjectives:
a nice suburban park, lovely wide streets

More help: Als Hilfe sind einige Adjektive vorgegeben.

Prepare your talk about Australia. Make a list of ten words or phrases you want to use.
Ask for a copy of your partner's list. While listening to his/her talk, tick the words that you hear.

KV 4: Giving feedback on a presentation hilft den S bei Rückmeldungen zu Präsentationen.

➜ Workbook 16 (p. 8)

YT Agreeing and disagreeing with people's opinions

On this page, you will practise agreeing and disagreeing with somebody's opinion.

STEP 1 Giving your opinion

When giving your opinion, you can say
- In my opinion, …
- In my view, …
- I'd say …
- Personally, I think …
- If you ask me, …

STEP 2 Agreeing with an opinion

To agree, you can use expressions like
- I agree.
- That's just how I feel.
- I couldn't agree with you more.
- That's so true.
- You're right.

Listen to the five phrases in short dialogues. Say which three phrases you think sound the strongest. Give reasons. 07

Practise different ways of expressing the opinion from the cartoon.
In my view, red is …

Practise giving opinions and agreeing.
A: In my view, red is …
B: You're right.

STEP 3 Disagreeing with an opinion

Say which three expressions are the strongest.
- I don't share your view.
- That's nonsense.
- That's not how I see it.
- I totally disagree.
- I don't agree.
- I think that's rubbish!

08 Listen and say what effect the words in orange have on the sentences.

- Sorry, I don't agree.
- I'm afraid I don't share your view.
- Actually, I think that's rubbish.

Access to cultures

In English, people are usually less direct than in German when they disagree with someone. So be careful: being very direct when you disagree could seem rude or be hurtful.
Try not to give short answers like "No".
Be careful with strong expressions like *That's nonsense* or *I think that's rubbish!* Only use them if you're sure they won't seem rude.
Be careful too when listening to someone's views. They might say what they think politely, and then you might not notice how strongly they disagree with you.

Showing understanding for someone's opinion before you disagree helps you to sound polite.
When you disagree, it is polite to give your own view and explain it.
- I see what you mean, but I don't quite agree. Personally, I think blue is nicer. It's a friendly colour.
- Actually, you have a point there, but …
- You're right about that, but …

Take turns to disagree with these statements.
- Living in the country must be fun.
- Short hair looks nicer than long hair.
- It's OK to borrow something from a friend without asking.
- A gift voucher is a good birthday present.

→ Workbook 17 (p. 9)

Die S lernen mehr über die **Geschichte und Kultur der Aboriginal people** und können sich dazu äußern.

Gujingga songline

[guːˈdʒɪŋgə]

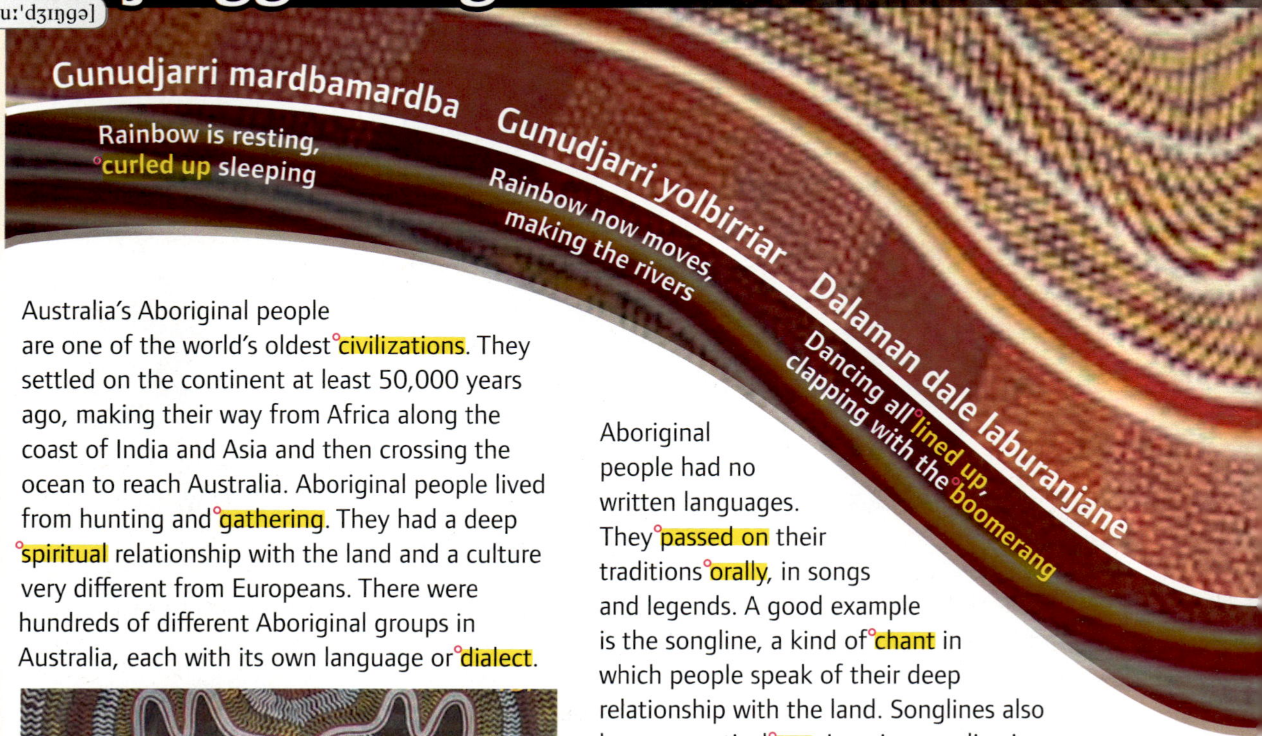

Australia's Aboriginal people are one of the world's oldest civilizations. They settled on the continent at least 50,000 years ago, making their way from Africa along the coast of India and Asia and then crossing the ocean to reach Australia. Aboriginal people lived from hunting and gathering. They had a deep spiritual relationship with the land and a culture very different from Europeans. There were hundreds of different Aboriginal groups in Australia, each with its own language or dialect.

Kangaroo people dancing, making the springs.

Aboriginal people had no written languages. They passed on their traditions orally, in songs and legends. A good example is the songline, a kind of chant in which people speak of their deep relationship with the land. Songlines also have a practical use. Imagine you live in open country, with no roads or buildings to help you know where you are. But you need to move around, and sometimes travel long distances, to hunt, find waterholes, gather food, or trade with your neighbours. How can you find the way?

The oppression of Aboriginal Australians: A timeline

1788

British colonists settle the area of present-day Sydney – 250 free persons and 750 convicts.

The Aboriginal population is estimated at between 300,000 and 1,000,000.

1790 – 1900

British colonists take possession of the Australian continent and divide it into six colonies: New South Wales, Queensland, Victoria, South Australia, Western Australia and Tasmania. The colonial economy grows, with wool, minerals and food as the main exports. The colonists build towns in coastal regions, and roads and railways across the country. More and more colonists arrive and the population grows to about four million.

At the same time, the Aboriginal population falls to 90,000. British colonists kill tens of thousands of people, forcing entire communities off their lands. Many more die from diseases which the Europeans brought, like smallpox and measles. Although the Aboriginal people try to resist, their weapons cannot match the colonists' firepower. Without land, the traditional way of life is impossible and most Aboriginal people are forced to become farm workers or live in poverty in the cities.

1901

With a new constitution, the six colonies come together as federal states and Australia becomes a single country. 98% of the people are white. The new parliament passes a law allowing immigration from Europe only. This is the beginning of the "White Australia Policy".

The new constitution does not recognize Aboriginal people as citizens.

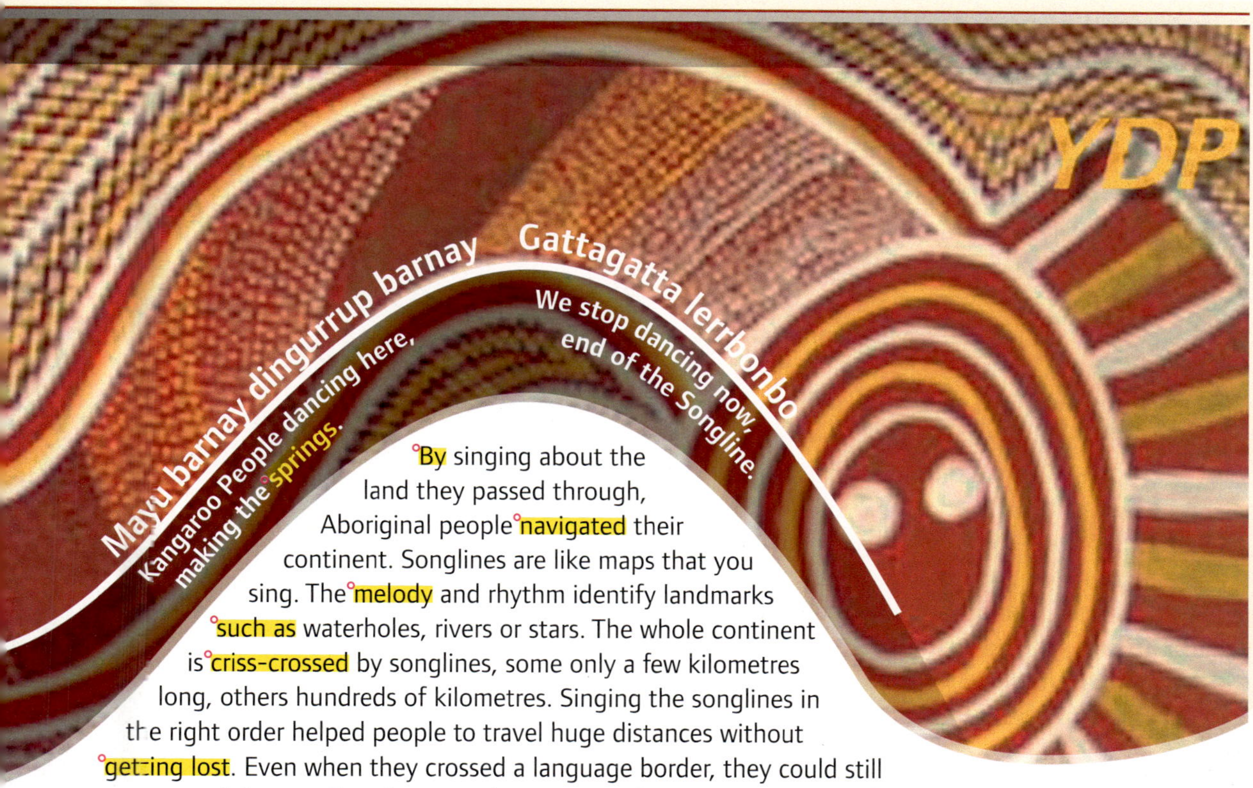

By singing about the land they passed through, Aboriginal people navigated their continent. Songlines are like maps that you sing. The melody and rhythm identify landmarks such as waterholes, rivers or stars. The whole continent is criss-crossed by songlines, some only a few kilometres long, others hundreds of kilometres. Singing the songlines in the right order helped people to travel huge distances without getting lost. Even when they crossed a language border, they could still understand the songlines because the message about the landscape is contained in the melody and rhythm. This knowledge of the landscape is also expressed in the paintings of Aboriginal artists.

Länge: 04:01

a) Watch the film and follow the words of the songline. Imagine there were no signs or street names. Write a songline for your way home from school. Read your songline to a partner.

b) Say what you learn about the Aboriginal people of Australia. How and why did their lives change after 1788?

1901 – 1971

For about 70 years, the "White Australia Policy" is in force. More and more Europeans arrive in Australia, as the government encourages immigration, especially from Britain. At 12 million, the population of Australia in 1971 is three times as large as in 1901.

The Aboriginal population grows too, but only to 115,000 in 1971. The new Australian state continues to discriminate against Australia's native people. Until 1962, they cannot vote in federal elections. Between 1910 and 1970, the government takes some 50,000 Aboriginal and mixed-race children from their families, forcing them to live in institutions where they may not use their own languages. These children are now called the "Stolen Generations".

1976

The Australian parliament passes a law giving Aboriginal communities the right to reclaim land that was once theirs.

1998

A movement of Australian citizens starts a National Sorry Day to remember the suffering of the Stolen Generations.

2008

A decade later, Australia's parliament also apologizes to the Stolen Generations. Government support for Aboriginal culture is now well established.

2016

People from all over the world, many of them from Asia, emigrate to Australia. The total population is 25 million. About 700,000 people identify themselves as Aboriginal.

➜ Workbook 18–19 (p. 10)

Die S können **ausgewählte Aspekte und Handlungen eines Textes** erfassen und dabei ggf. **Unterschiede zu ihrer Kultur und Lebenswelt** identifizieren.

1 A young Aboriginal person's story

Find Kintore on the map on the inside cover. Describe its location and say what life might be like there.

09

Coreen, 15, Kintore

I'm from Kintore in the Northern Territories and I'm 15. Kintore is the home of the Pintupi group and I've lived here with my family all my life. We all speak Pintupi and this is our home. [pɪn'tu:pi]

I have a big family. There's my mum, four brothers and two sisters. I'm the oldest. I also live with my gran, most of my uncles and aunties and lots of cousins! I never feel alone. We don't do everything together, but we all go out bush. That's an important part of learning about our culture and it's also a lot of fun. Box "English "so"", Voc, S. 202

Out in the bush, men and women have different jobs. I go out with Mum to look for goannas and dig up witchety grubs and so do all the other women. My older brothers go with the men and hunt kangaroos and bush turkeys. We camp out, cook and eat outside and then we tell stories around the fire.

Gran likes to tell us dreamtime stories, especially the Honey Ant dreaming. It's a story about the past, a long time ago. All the kids sit close to Gran so we don't miss any part of her stories. Gran is also an artist – she makes paintings with sand, rocks and plants when we're out in the bush, but she also makes paintings for people's walls. They come from Alice Springs and buy her work for a lot of money. I love my gran – and I love listening to her stories under an open sky. That's the way I learn about my culture.

Of course I learn a lot at school too, although it's a different sort of learning. In class we study different countries and languages, and do writing and maths. I've got great classmates – I feel like I've known them forever. Sometimes there are seven or eight of us, other times fewer than that. At school, I also play soccer and volleyball.

Through my teacher I had the opportunity to get work experience at the health clinic in our town where I help take care of the patients. I enjoy the work, but I actually want to be a teacher when I'm older, or maybe an artist like Gran. That way I can keep passing on my culture and learn more.

Box "German "Möglichkeit"", Voc, S. 202

An example of typical Australian Western Desert art

2 Life in the community

a) Describe what happens when Coreen goes out bush with her family.

b) In what way is going out bush different from learning at school?

c) Think of three questions you would ask Coreen if you met her.

Digging for witchetty grubs. Yummy!

A goanna

3 Australia debates racism +racist

The story of Adam Goodes [gudz]

Adam Goodes was born in Wallaroo, South Australia in 1980 to a white father and Aboriginal Australian mother. Between 1996 and 2015, he was a professional Australian Rules Football player, playing for the Sydney Swans. During that time he played a total of 372 games, scored 464 goals and was twice winner of the Brownlow Medal, the award for the fairest and best player of the year.

During his career Goodes has stood up for Aboriginal rights and has worked a lot with Aboriginal youth. In 2014, in recognition of his stand against racism, Goodes was named 'Australian of the Year'. But Goodes has also been criticized for speaking out.

In May 2013, during a football match watched by tens of thousands, a fan of the opposing team called Goodes an ape. Goodes heard the jeer, turned around and pointed out the fan: a 13-year-old girl seated in the first row. The stadium police led the girl out of the stadium. Goodes was so upset by the insult that he couldn't take part in his team's victory celebrations. When interviewed the next day, Goodes had the following things to say in reaction to the girl's comments:

"It's not her fault. She's 13, she's still so innocent. I don't put any blame on her. Unfortunately it's what she hears, in the environment she's grown up in, that has made her think that it's OK to call people names."

"I felt like I was in high school again being bullied, being called all these names because of my appearance. I didn't stand up for myself in high school. I'm a lot more confident, I'm a lot more proud about who I am and my culture, and I decided to stand up last night, and I'll continue to stand up because racism has no place in our industry. It has no place in society."

The debate about racism provoked by this event continued for well over a year. Some people supported Goodes' reaction, many others attacked him, saying that the girl was innocent and had not meant anything hurtful with her comment.

After this incident, Goodes was loudly booed at every game. When interviewed after he had left the team in 2015, he said the booing during his final season was "one reason" he gave up professional football.

4 A great career

Say what the text tells you about
- Adam Goodes' achievements
- what the girl said and what happened to her
- how Goodes felt about the incident
- the public reaction to the incident
- what Goodes decided to do in 2015

5 Our view

Neigungsdifferenzierung: Die S diskutieren eine der angebotenen Fragestellungen.

You choose a) or b).

a) Discuss this question:
- Is the 13-year-old girl a racist?

b) Think of examples of racism.
Say what people can do if they want to do something against racism.

1.8 · FöFo 1.5 · VAS 1.1, 1.2

1 Sports news

Die S können die **Informationen einer Sportsendung zusammenfassen und ins Englische übertragen**.

10 a) You are exchange students in Australia.
You listen to a sports programme on German radio.
Later you tell an Australian classmate what you heard.
Partner A: Listen and take notes on women's sports.
Partner B: Listen and take notes on Australian sports.

b) Take turns to talk about what you heard.
Partner A: Talk about what you heard about women's sports.
Partner B: Talk about what you heard about Australian sports.

2 Sports and sportspeople (Past participle clauses)

Language help

You already know how to use present participle clauses.
- *A boy carrying a surfboard appeared on the beach. (= who was carrying ...)*
- *Always wear a °wetsuit when surfing in cold water. (= when you are surfing ...)*

You can also make participle clauses with past participles.
- *I scored in a match watched by thousands of people. (= which/that was watched ...)*
- *When interviewed the next day, he talked about his feelings. (= When he was interviewed ...)*

→ *GF 10.2, 10.5: Participle clauses (p. 185, p. 187)*

a) Rewrite these sentences with past participle clauses.

1 Australian Rules Football (ARF) is a game that is played between two teams of 18 players.
Australian Rules Football is a game played between ...
2 The Sydney Swans are an ARF team which was founded °originally in the 19th century.
3 Swans player Adam Goodes twice won the Brownlow Medal, an award which is given °annually to the fairest and best AFR player.
4 When he was asked how he felt about winning twice, Goodes said he was happy because his mum was proud of him.
5 Goodes became Australian of the Year at a ceremony which was held in Canberra in January 2015.
6 In a speech that was reported in most papers, Goodes spoke about his Aboriginal °identity.
7 When he is criticized for his strong stand against racism, Goodes replies that speaking out is better than saying nothing.

2 The Sydney Swans are an ARF team founded originally in ... · 3 ... an award given annually to the fairest and best AFR player. · 4 When asked how he felt ... · 5 ... a ceremony held in Canberra in January 2015. · 6 In a speech reported in most papers, ... · 7 When criticized for his strong stand against racism ...

b) Choose the correct participle: present or past.

Cathy Freeman, Atlanta 1996

1 When (choose) for the Australian team in 1992, Cathy Freeman was the first Aboriginal woman to take part in the °Olympic Games.
2 She took part again in 1996, (win) a silver medal in the Atlanta Olympics.
3 In Sydney in 2000, she lit the Olympic Torch in a ceremony (watch) around the world.
4 She was first in the 400 metres, (become) the second Aboriginal Australian to win gold.
5 After winning, she ran round the stadium (carry) the Australian and Aboriginal flags.
6 Her grandmother was one of the children (take) away from her family – the Stolen Generations.

1 chosen · 2 winning · 3 watched · 4 becoming · 5 carrying · 6 taken

Early finisher → p. 123

Early finisher: Rätsel zum Thema Sport

 → Workbook 20–22 (p. 11)

1 Double Trouble: A television series

Die S können ***Film stills*** nutzen, um vorab **Vermutungen zum Inhalt einer Szene anzustellen** und diese beim Schauen zu überprüfen.

a) Yuma, a girl from Sydney, visits Alice Springs with her father. ['juːmə]
On her first day she has some strange encounters.
Look at these stills from episode 1 and describe each situation.

A

B

C

D

b) Now watch part of episode 1. Say how Yuma feels when she meets the other girl, Kyanna. [ki'ænə]
What do you think their relationship is? Länge: 03:53
Explain the reactions of the women sitting on the bench and the boy to Yuma.

c) Watch another part of episode 1. Say what plan the girls make. Länge: 02:14
What problems could they have if they go ahead with their plan? What tips would you give them?

2 Making the film: Setting

Die S lernen die **Bedeutung des *Settings* als filmisches Mittel** kennen. Sie können verschiedene Settings unterscheiden und deren unterschiedliche Wirkungen identifizieren.

a) Look at these two places shown in the film.
Describe each place. In what ways are they different?

b) 👥 Where did Yuma and Kyanna meet? Say why you think the film-maker chose that place.
Was it the best place for their meeting? Give reasons for your opinion.

Workbook Checkpoint 1 (pp. 12–15)

Your task

Step 1 und **2** können gut von den S zu Hause als vorbereitende HA gemacht werden.
Step 3–6 werden dann in den Folgestunden gemeinsam in der Klasse gemacht.

Six months in Far North Queensland

The Queensland government is offering $5,000 to students from Germany to help them to finance a six-month exchange in Far North Queensland. Applicants have to write and say why they think FNQ is the best place to spend six months in Australia.

Your task is to prepare good arguments for your application to the Queensland government.

Work at separate tables in groups of four.

STEP 1

Say which photos remind you of what you have learned about FNQ. Explain why.

A *Exploring the Great Barrier Reef*

B *Rainforest in Barron Gorge National Park* [ˌbærən ˈgɔːdʒ]

C *Celebration in Cairns, FNQ*

D *Aboriginal Australians in FNQ*

STEP 2

Think of arguments for staying in FNQ (climate, landscape, wildlife, marine life, sports and other free-time activities, towns and cities, etc).
Decide which of your arguments is the strongest.
Find photos (in this unit, on the internet, ...) to support your strongest argument.

➔ *p.22 Access to words*

STEP 3

Each student takes one large sheet of paper.

On your sheet of paper, write down a statement with your strongest argument for going to FNQ.

I think the strongest argument for going to FNQ is the marine life because ...

Then pass your sheet of paper to another member of your group.
Read the statement on the sheet you get and write down your comments.

I see what you mean about marine life in FNQ, but in my view ...

Then pass the sheet on again so that the other people in the group can add their comments.
You can comment on the original statement or on the other comments.

I agree with the statement!

I don't quite agree with the statement, but I don't agree with Alex's comment either.

➜ p.23 *Agreeing and disagreeing politely*

STEP 4

Compare all four sheets of paper. Choose the two sheets with the most positive comments.
Hang them up on the classroom wall.

STEP 5

Walk around and read what the other groups have written.
Write down any good ideas that you don't already have. Then return to your table.

STEP 6

Discuss the arguments of the other groups. Are they similar or different, stronger or weaker?
Then decide on the four best reasons for going to FNQ.
Review all the photos you have looked at.
Try to decide on a good photo to go with each point.

I think this would be a good picture. It shows a group of people exploring a tropical rainforest.

This is a photo of ... I think it goes very well with our second argument.

In the Oberstufe, you will often have to analyse English non-fictional texts: **reports** or **news articles** written to inform you about the world around us, or **comments** or **reviews** that try to influence you. When analysing a text you will need to

- understand and summarize it (comprehension)
- study how it is written and what effect that has on the reader (analysis)
- give an opinion (comment)

Now read this newspaper article, making sure that you understand it.

Experience: I am 16 and live alone in the wilderness

I have an open fire and spend my evenings tanning animal and fish skins, and carving wood

Zeki Basan: 'I've had a few hairy moments."
Photograph: Murdo Macleod for the Guardian

I live alone on the Isle of Skye in a tipi almost impossible to find without detailed directions. It might seem unusual for someone of 16, but I love my own company and I'm passionate about preserving wild spaces. I grew up with my mum, Ghillie, and older sister, Yazzie, in the wilds of the Cairngorms, in a remote and sometimes inaccessible home, using cross-country skis to haul food and supplies to the house.

Mum, a cookbook writer, taught us about possible dangers and how to cope with them, then let us run wild from an early age. We also travelled abroad regularly, visiting remote tribes and cultures, where we lived for weeks as Mum studied food and recipes to write about. I spent so much time with tribes who rely on the land that this became second nature to me. When I gained a place at the School of Adventure Studies on Skye last year, I decided to live in a tipi, practising what I preach.

I sleep on an ancient canvas camp bed my grandfather gave me, with two old army blankets and some skins I tanned myself from roadkill for warmth. I have an open fire and spend my evenings tanning animal and fish skins, and carving wood. I store clothes and books in an old metal trunk of my mum's – it's covered in stickers from her travels. I wash my clothes in the river and dry them in the wind or in the heat from the fire. I have a bush shower using water from the river.

I wake at 6am and get the fire on straight away using flints and steel. There's usually a good bed of embers from the previous day, so the fire is soon blazing while I have cereal or bannock, which I bake myself, for breakfast. I collect kindling for later in the day, then I wash at the river. Sometimes I just jump in, especially when there's frost on the ground. When I rush back to the tipi, it's like a sauna.

I get my backpack organised, including any food and kit I need for the day, bank the fire (by covering it, which keeps it low, but alive) and walk 30 minutes to the school. There are 12 of us on the course, of all ages, and we've just finished mountaineering, focusing on practical navigation in the Red Cuillin. We're about to start whitewater kayaking.

review *(Buch-, Film-)*Kritik **influence** beeinflussen **tan skins** Häute gerben **passionate** leidenschaftlich **preserve** erhalten **inaccessible** unzugänglich **supplies** *(pl)* Vorräte **rely on** sich verlassen auf **preach** predigen **flints and steel** Feuersteine und Stahl **embers** *(pl)* Glut **bannock** *schottische Art Fladenbrot* **kindling** Anmachholz

My friends used to love coming to our home and running wild with me, so they are used to the way I live. I hope some of them will visit me soon. People ask if I miss the internet, but I never used to use it much, or watch television. I am sociable, but I have always enjoyed my own company.

I use my mobile every few weeks to catch up with friends and my mum, who I usually see once a month when I go back to the Cairngorms. I work with a bushcraft expert, Willow Lohr, teaching wild skills to others. I also visit a small tribe of bushmen in Namibia. We show each other our ancestral skills to keep them alive.

What I'm doing isn't for everyone, but it makes me happy. I'd like to see more people look after the land and not be scared of getting outside, getting wet, learning how to survive. I'd like to learn western riding (horse riding like a cowboy), because my ambition is to run my own wilderness school, travelling on horseback. When my studies are over, I'll move the tent back to Mum's house and use it to tan skins. Until then, I'm happiest sitting by the flickering fire, carving a spoon in perfect silence and watching the northern lights through the open tipi door.

• As told to Joan McFadden. The Guardian, 29 April 2016; downloaded 30.04.2016

KV 5 bietet den S eine Checklist zu ***Writing a summary***.

STEP 1 Comprehension

Task: Summarize how Zeki lives now.

- Read the task carefully. The word *now* shows that you needn't cover the past or future.
- Scan the text to identify the relevant content.
- Only summarize the main points.

➜ *SF 8: Writing a summary (p. 141)*

Zeki lives by himself in a lonely spot .... He leads a ... life ...
On a typical day he ... In addition to this, ...

STEP 2 Analysis

Task: Explain how the text expresses Zeki's feelings about his way of life.

- Refer to the text's structure and how it affects our understanding of the writer's choices.
  At the beginning, Zeki describes how he experienced outdoor life ... This shows ...
- Look at the language the writer uses.
  He uses simple/descriptive/... sentences such as ... • He uses everyday language, which ...
- Look at the way he presents himself.
  Zeki describes himself as passionate /... • He refers to how he feels about ...
- Support your analysis with quotations.
  It seems clear that he really enjoys ... /is very relaxed about/... when he says "... ... ...".

STEP 3 Comment

Task: *"… practising what I preach"* (l.18) Comment on Zeki's choices from his perspective and yours.

- Explain what the quotation says about Zeki.
  By "practising what I preach" Zeki means that... /wants to express how ... /...
- State your view of Zeki's choices, giving reasons.
  To me, such a life seems quite attractive/hard/ ... because.../although.../... Another reason is ... •
- Say if you could imagine living in a similar way and explain why/why not.
  Personally, I would choose a different/similar/... path. This is because ... / The reason for this is ...

be used to gewöhnt sein an **sociable** gesellig **catch up with friends** sich von Freunden auf den neuesten Stand bringen lassen **bushcraft** Survival-Skills **ambition** Ehrgeiz **carefully** sorgfältig **express** ausdrücken **affect** beeinflussen **comment on sth.** etwas kommentieren **perspective** Perspektive

Relationships

A

1

2

3

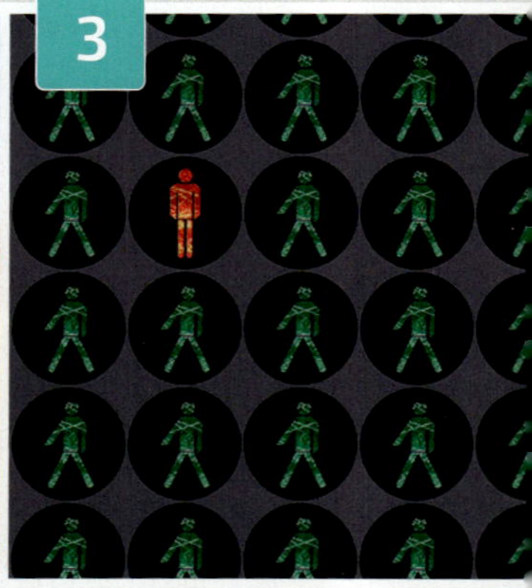

Alternativer Einstieg zur Aktivierung von Vorwissen und bereits bekanntem Wortschatz: L schreibt das Wort *relationships* an die Tafel und die S assoziieren dazu kurz in PA *(buzz group)*. Anschließend Austausch der Assoziationen im Plenum.

YT 1 Explaining images

a) **Think:** What might the photographer's message be in photos A–C?

b) **Pair**: Describe photos A–C and explain your ideas about the photographer's message.

- This photo shows …
- In the foreground / On the left/… you see …
- I think the photo was taken at/in/while …
- The photographer probably wanted to …

→ *SF 25: Describing and interpreting images (p. 156)*

c) **Share**: Imagine photos A–C are stills from documentaries. In your group, discuss what each documentary might be about.

Unit 2

Die S können sich zu **Freundschaft und Beziehungen** in Fotos und Texten äußern. Dabei können sie verschiedene Perspektiven einnehmen.

Text File: Zu Unit 2 passt **Text 2**.

B

C

4

5

6

YT 2 Connecting images

a) Look at photos 1–6. Choose two with a connection to the photo you described in 1.

b) Explain the connections you see. Discuss your ideas with the group.

More help → p. 116

More help bietet sprachliche und inhaltliche Hilfen.

EXTRA In which of the photos A–C could you most easily imagine yourself? In which could you least imagine yourself? Explain why.

Your task

At the end of this unit:
Make a short video about yourself.

→ Text file 2 *(pp. 107–108)*

Text File: Three poems

Die S können über die **Beziehungen von Charakteren** in einem Romanauszug sprechen. Sie können Szenen aus einem Roman in einer anderen Perspektive schreiben und dabei feststellen, was sich bei dem **Perspektivwechsel** ändert.

1 Coast to coast (from the novel by David Fermer)

Think of different reasons why people go to the beach.
Say why you like going to the beach and what activities you do there.

11

When I was a kid, Dad used to say heaven is an Australian beach, and I reckon he's right. The beaches around Darwin are beautiful: the endless sky, like the promise of adventure, the breeze of the salty air, the soft sand against your feet, the border between land and sea.

We have two beaches in Darwin: Mindli ['mɪndli] and Casuarina [ˌkæzjuə'riːnə]. Mindli is where you go to party. Casuarina is where you go when you want to be alone. I go there when life is °getting me down, when school is shitty, or something is bugging me – or when I have an argument with my dad.

"When are you gonna stop treating school like a goddam holiday camp, Cooper?" (I've heard that a hundred times.) "Get a haircut!" (At least I've got hair, Dad.) "If you wanna throw your life away that's fine by me, but let me give you one word of advice: stop hanging around with losers like Graham Barton!"

Just some of the things he said to me when he got back from work yesterday.

12

Of course, I had answers like: "If Graham is a loser and his parents voted for you at the last aldermen elections, what does that say about the people who vote for you, Dad?"

Get Dad onto the subject of politics, he backs off faster than a dog caught napping by a snake. He's campaigning to become mayor of Darwin, and politics is a sensitive issue between us.

Once I've had enough of hearing about what a waste of space I am, I go to the beach to clear my head. One more year of school, then I'm out of this place. Sydney, Melbourne, Perth. There's no town north of Darwin.

I was walking along the beach as the sun went down. An orange blaze cut through the clouds, sending golden °shimmers onto the water. How could anyone not feel good here? You can be at rock-bottom, the worst day of your life, but when you look at the °sundown over the Timor Sea ['tiːmɔː], you just know everything's going to be all right.

It was then that I saw him: a brown °lump on the sand, dark against the orange of the sun. At first I didn't know what it was. A baby croc? A tree trunk? It was only when I took a few steps closer that I saw it was a person. He was °huddled up like

bug sb. jn. ärgern **treat** behandeln **vote (for)** (für jn./etwas) stimmen **aldermen elections** Stadtratswahlen *(Ältestenrat)* **subject** Thema **back off** klein beigeben **a dog caught napping** ein Hund, der beim Schlafen erwischt wird **campaign** kämpfen *(im Wahlkampf)* **a sensitive issue** ein heikles Thema **once** sobald, sowie, wenn **a waste of space** eine Platzverschwendung **blaze** lodernde Flamme **rock-bottom** Nullpunkt, Tiefpunkt **tree trunk** Baumstamm a baby, his knees under his chin, his arms around his legs. his T-shirt torn and dirty. I had to walk around him to get a look at his face: black hair °speckled with white sand; °slender, Asian eyes. He looked around my age.

"Hey! Are you all right?" I put my hand on his back. He didn't move. I shook him harder. "Hey! Wake up, mate!"

No reaction.

I panicked. Jesus, this guy is °friggin' dead!

I already had my phone in my hand, ready to call Triple Zero, but my fingers froze on the keys.

I was shaking.

13

I put my phone away and got down to my knees. I took a deep breath and tried to °focus. I've done a lot of First Aid courses in my time. I know the °routine. First check to see if he's breathing. If not, do CPR. I bent down and put my face up to his nostrils. I could feel his breath on the skin of my cheek.

"Hey, mate, can you hear me?"

I tried to check his pulse, but I couldn't find it.

I rolled him onto his back and grabbed his legs. I started shaking them like I was trying to °rip them off. Get some blood back into that head of his! The brain needs oxygen!

It was then that he opened his eyes. He stared straight up at me, me standing above him, holding his feet under my arms, shaking his legs. He didn't seem °in the least bit surprised.

I dropped his legs. "Are you all right?"

He turned his head and looked from left to right. "Where I?" he asked – two words that sounded like a distant dream.

"You're in Australia, mate. You're gonna be fine."

14

His name was Bashir, that much he could tell me. He came from Afghanistan. He spoke a few words of English, not much, but enough to say he'd been on a boat and that the boat had sunk in a storm. He'd held onto a life jacket and must have drifted around in the sea for hours. It's a miracle the sharks didn't get him. Or the crocs on the beach.

We sat there together on the sand for a while, watching the sun disappear behind the sea, and I knew from the moment I met him that I liked this guy. There was something intelligent in his eyes. He didn't say much, but I understood him. Occasionally he smiled, a dreamy smile, as if he couldn't quite believe what was going on, as if he was surprised to be alive. A couple of his front teeth were missing. He looked like a little kid or an old homeless guy. His face kept changing, sometimes young, sometimes old, like two people moving between two different worlds. I figured he was both at the same time – young and old. I guessed that was why he was here.

...

15

What now? I kept thinking. What am I going to do with this guy? What do you do with an illegal immigrant °washed up on a beach in Australia?

"Are you hungry?" I asked him.

He didn't understand. I used my hands to show him what I meant.

He nodded. "Yes. Hungry," he said.

I took him to Joey's near the university and bought him some spare ribs and chips with lots of ketchup. He ate the stuff like he hadn't eaten for days. I guess he probably hadn't.

People kept looking at us.

"°Slow down, Bashir," I told him. "°Take it easy."

He seemed to understand. He saw the people staring.

After he'd finished his meal, we headed back to Rapid °Creek. It was getting late. I told him to wait for me on the °footbridge. "I'll be back in fifteen minutes." I gave him my watch and showed him when I'd be back.

I walked home and took the back door into the house. I went upstairs quietly, making sure no one

torn zerrissen **triple zero** 000 *(australische Notrufnummer)* **key** Taste **First Aid** Erste Hilfe **CPR** kardiopulmonale Reanimation *(Herz-Lungen-Wiederbelebung)* **nostril** Nasenloch **skin** Haut **cheek** Wange **brain** Gehirn **occasionally** gelegentlich **figure** glauben, annehmen **spare ribs** Spareribs *(gegrillte Schweinerippchen)*

saw me. Dad was out. Mum was in the living room, working on her laptop with the TV on. My little sister was in bed.
I put some fresh clothes into a bag, took some soap and deodorant out of the bathroom. A toothbrush, toothpaste, my old sleeping bag. I went back downstairs and took some milk out of the fridge, a can of spam, a tin opener, some biscuits. Don't ask me how I did it without Mum seeing me, but I did. I guess I can be pretty sneaky at times.
I was back on the footbridge in no time. Bashir looked relieved to see me.
"Come with me," I told him.

16 I took him to the hut where Dad keeps his canoe and fishing gear. It's around the back of the Surf Life Saving Club on Casuarina beach where Dad is a member. They let him build it when I was a kid, back in the days when we used to go canoeing together. It's not really official, but they let him build it anyway. It's kind of hidden away in the mangroves. No one in the Club has ever really noticed it. You can't even see it from the beach. It was the perfect place for Bashir.
I opened the hut and told Bashir he could stay here. I gave him the sleeping bag and showed him what I'd brought with me. He didn't say anything. He just nodded and flashed that dreamy smile of his that was fast becoming familiar to me.
It was hard to leave him there that night alone, but I guess anything was better than lying half-dead on a beach. I told him I would come around after school the next day. I told him not to go out. "You have to be careful," I said. "No one can see you here." I think he understood.
I went home and slipped back into the house. Dad was home. I could hear him talking to Mum in the living room. I called out to them, saying I was going to bed. I didn't want them asking any awkward questions.
Up in my room I realized how tired I was. I went straight to bed, but I couldn't sleep. My mind was racing, a thousand questions shooting through my head like a pinball machine. It was strange. Bashir and I were complete strangers, but now we were connected: me in my bed, the TV humming downstairs, my sister fast asleep in the room next door, and Bashir down at the beach, sleeping on the floor of our hut.
I was still awake when my parents turned off the TV and came upstairs. I heard them walk past my

Box "anyway", Voc, S. 206

2 Understanding the text

a) Explain who Bashir is and say what Cooper does to help him.

b) Discuss what Cooper means in these lines:

1. Get Dad onto the subject of politics, he backs off faster than a dog caught napping by a snake. *(ll. 26–27)*
2. I figured he was both at the same time – young and old. *(ll. 101–102)*
3. Kate is straighter than the Stuart Highway. *(ll. 223–224)*

3 Cooper's relationships

a) Read lines 1 – 34 and 141 – 147. Say what they tell us about Cooper's relationship with his dad now <u>and</u> as a kid.

b) Describe the ways in which Cooper's and Bashir's lives have been different. Then read lines 167 – 175. Say why you think Cooper feels connected with Bashir.

c) Explain why you think Cooper decides to tell Kate about Bashir and what that tells you about their relationship.

---

soap Seife **fridge** Kühlschrank **can of spam** Dose Frühstücksfleisch **pretty sneaky** ziemlich raffiniert **relieved** erleichtert **familiar** vertraut **awkward** peinlich, unangenehm **pinball machine** Flipper(automat) door. One of them stopped, I guess Mum, to listen for a moment. I didn't move a muscle until I heard her walk away.

17 School next day was like a waiting game. Waiting for the day to end, waiting to get to the beach. I'd left my watch with Bashir the night before, so I spent all day discovering clocks on the walls that I'd never even seen before, watching their hands creep slowly by, checking my phone under the shadow of desks. Time can be your worst enemy when you want it to go by quickly.
I couldn't concentrate on anything that day. The teachers' voices sounded like °faraway echoes. Everything I wrote was like someone else was writing it for me. Me? I was somewhere else.
The only person I spoke to was Kate.
"I need to talk to you," I told her in the morning.
"Sure. What's up?"
"Not now. At break. Alone."
I didn't mean to scare her, but I know I did. God knows what she thought. Trouble with my dad? Trouble with the law? Trouble was written all over my face. She kept looking at me during lessons, sneaking glances between heads and shoulders, trying to read what had happened from my eyes, but I know how to keep my face °blank.
We met at break around the back of the school. It °stinks around there because of the trash cans, so you can usually count on being alone.
"What is it?" Kate asked me.
I've known Kate all my life. We went to the same kindergarten, the same primary school, now we attend the same secondary school. We're like brother and sister.
I told her about finding Bashir the night before, about how I'd given him food and let him sleep in the °hut. I told her the few things I knew about him, that he came from Afghanistan, that his family lived in Pakistan, that he was on the boat that had sunk °off the coast near Darwin. Kate listened to me with that listening face of hers, the way she does when things are serious. When I finished, she turned to me and said, "Are you crazy?"
It wasn't quite the response I was expecting, but it didn't surprise me. Kate is straighter than the Stuart °Highway.
"You have to talk to your dad," she said.

4 Telling a story

Coast to coast is a first-person narrative.

TIP

First-person narrative

If one character tells a story from his/her point of view, we call this a first-person narrative.
We see this character's world and the whole story through his/her eyes.

a) In groups of three, each student takes one of these sections and rewrites it from Bashir's point of view:
ll. 60–81 · ll. 82–103 · ll. 141–161

b) **Read out each narrative.**
Say what changes when the story is told from Bashir's point of view (e.g. the focus on key events, emotions, impressions, language, …). Give reasons for your opinion.

My Book **Keep a copy of your narrative.**

hand Uhrzeiger **creep by** vorbei-, vorankriechen **somewhere else** anderswo **sneak glances** einen schnellen Blick werfen **primary school** Grundschule **secondary school** weiterführende Schule **serious** ernst **response** Antwort, Reaktion **straight** gerade, geradlinig

→ Workbook Wordbank 2

2 Part A Practice

2.3 · FöFo 2.2

Die S können verschiedene **Höflichkeitsformen in formellen und informellen Situationen** verwenden.

1 REVISION Between friends *(must be/can't be; must have been/can't have been)*

You can use *must be*, *can't be* etc. to stress that you are sure about something: *You must be thirsty.*

a) Say something to a friend in the situations below. Use *must be* or *can't be* with a word from the box.

cold · disappointed · excited · hungry · serious · tired · wet · worried

Your friend …

1 didn't get chosen for the school team.
You must be … disappointed.

2 orders a third hamburger. You're very surprised. You must be very/can't still be hungry.

3 had no umbrella when the rain started.

4 wants to borrow a pullover. It's 25 degrees.

3 You must be wet. • 4 You can't be cold.

5 wants to go to bed. You're surprised – it's only 7 pm. 5 You can't be tired!

6 is going to New York for the weekend.

7 can't find her new mobile.

8 tells you he's moving to England. You don't believe it.

6 You must be excited. • 7 You must be worried. • 8 You can't be serious.

b) Act out the short dialogues. Swap roles after 4.
Use *must have* or *can't have* with the correct form of the verb in brackets.

	A:	B: *… must have lost …*
1	I can't find my keys – I've looked everywhere.	Oh no, you … (lose) them.
2	Why didn't you answer the phone yesterday?	Sorry, I … (fall) asleep.
3	I'm glad I passed that test. I was so worried.	Well done! It … (be) easy.
4	I'm so upset. Grandma didn't send me a birthday card.	That's a pity. She … (forget).
5	Yes, I'd like to go out. Don't sound so surprised.	You … (finish) your homework already!
6	Guess what! A dog tried to bite me – in the park.	That's awful. You … (be) scared.
7	Who's Harry Potter? I've never heard of him.	But you … (see) some of the films!

1 Oh dear. You must have lost them. • 2 Sorry, I must have fallen asleep. • 3 Well done! It can't have been easy. • 4 That's a pity. She must have forgotten. • 5 You can't have finished your homework already! • 6 That's awful. You must have been scared. • 7 But you must have seen some of the films!

→ *GF 4.3: Modal auxiliaries (p. 174)*

2 It mustabin … *(Compression: must be/can't be; must have been/can't have been)* 18

a) Listen to ten short statements and complete the sentences below.

1 Jake was ill in bed yesterday, so you can't have seen him. *It …* must have been someone else.

2 20, you think? *No, he …* can't be older than 15.

3 I'm glad you found your phone again. You must have been worried about it.

4 I like your bag. It must have cost a lot.

5 I wasn't waiting long – it can't have been more than 10 minutes.

6 Sorry I didn't hear my phone – I must have turned it off.

7 Where are Jo and Tim? They can't have gone already, can they?

8 Their house is huge – they must be really rich.

9 Who's that girl with John? She must be his new girlfriend.

10 He only started 5 minutes ago. He can't be finished already!

LISTENING TIP
When people speak at normal speed, they link words and leave consonants out, e.g. they say *mustabin* instead of *must have been*.
You need to practise listening to understand normal English in the real world.

b) Listen again. Then read the sentences to each other. Try to join words in the same way.

→ Workbook *2–5 (pp. 16–17)*

YT 3 REVISION Do you think you could …? (Asking people to do things: *can, could, would*)

a) Look at the people in the pictures and say who wants to ask who to do what.

b) Imagine the people are good friends. Write down the requests in different ways.
Hey Jack, could you …

c) Imagine the people are strangers. Write dialogues for each request.
Practise your dialogues together.
A: Sorry, but could I ask you to …
Say what was different about the language you used in each situation.

Access to cultures

When we ask family or friends to do something, we often use *Can you (do) …? Could you (do) …?* or *Would you (do) …?*

When speaking to people we aren't so close to (teachers, shop assistants, strangers), we usually use more indirect expressions like:
(Sorry, but) do you think you could (do) …?
(Excuse me, but) could I ask you to (do) …?
(Sorry, but) would you be able to (do) …?

→ *GF 4.3: Modal auxiliaries (p. 174)*

4 REVISION Can we fish here? (Talking about permission: *can* and *be allowed to*)

a) Compare the two dialogues and say which words are used to talk about permission. Say what else is different in the way the people speak.

Informal *(friend, family, etc.)*
A: Hey, Jake.
B: Yeah, what?
A: Do you think we can fish here?
B: I've no idea. Let's ask someone.

Formal *(stranger, official, etc.)*
A: Excuse me.
B: Yes?
A: Can you tell me if you're allowed to fish here?
B: I'm sorry, but you aren't allowed to fish here. (or: I'm sorry, but fishing isn't allowed.)

b) Make similar dialogues for these questions:
Can you …
- bring meat and sausages into the UK?
- take photos in the museum ?
- put up a tent on the beach?
- ride bikes in this park?

TIP
In the **present** tense you can use *can* or *be allowed to* to talk about permission.
be allowed to is common in formal situations.
In the **past** tense, we use *be allowed to* in formal and informal situations.

c) Read the text message on the right. Then write text messages for two of the situations from b).
Use a form of *be allowed to* in each message.

Jake and I were in the countryside. There was a nice river, but we weren't allowed to fish there. So we went swimming instead.

→ *GF 4.2: Modal auxiliaries (p. 172)*

Early finisher → p. 124

Early finisher: Die S entschlüsseln die Aussage australischer Verkehrsschilder.

Die S können den Wortschatz zum Thema **Gefühle und Beziehungen** in verschiedenen Situationen anwenden.

On this page you will work with words that help you talk about relationships and feelings. Then you will write a short text about the relationship between two people.

YT 1 Word field: Relationships (Structuring vocabulary)

a) Order the phrases in the box in a sequence in which they might occur.

1 be attracted to sb. 2 ...

+be attracted to sb. · +be seeing sb. · +fall in love · +date sb. · get back together · give sb. a second chance · go out with sb. · +break up (with sb.) · +get to know sb.

b) Comment on each other's sequence.

Zusatz: Die S verfassen eine kurze Geschichte, in der sie alle *phrases* verwenden.

YT 2 Adjectives (Feelings)

a) Group these words in two lists.

Box "hopeful – hopefully", Voc, S. 207

afraid · angry · +annoyed · +confused · +cross · disappointed · +frightened · glad · glum · happy · +hopeful · nervous · optimistic · +pessimistic · +pleased · sad · scared · shocked · unhappy · upset · worried

negative feelings	positive feelings
afraid angry, annoyed, confused, cross, disappointed, frightened, glum, nervous, pessimistic, sad, scared, shocked, unhappy, upset, worried	glad, happy, hopeful, optimistic, ... pleased

b) Make a table like this:

afraid	angry	happy	sad
confused, frightened, nervous, pessimistic, scared, worried	annoyed, cross, ... glum, upset	glad, hopeful ... optimistic, pleased	disappointed, shocked, unhappy

Then find words in a) with a similar meaning and add them to your table.

c) afraid – terrified · angry – furious · happy – thrilled · sad – heartbroken

c) Adjectives can be normal or strong. Match a strong adjective to each normal adjective.

normal afraid · angry · happy · sad

strong +furious · +heartbroken · +terrified · thrilled

TIP

Words like very, +absolutely or really make adjectives stronger. Use

- very only with normal adjectives:
  I was very happy to see him again.
- absolutely only with strong adjectives:
  I was absolutely thrilled to see him again.
- really with normal or strong adjectives.
  I was really happy/thrilled to see him again.

d) Write sentences about how you felt when

- you were lost in a dark forest · your cat died
- you won a race · your bike was stolen

YT 3 Collocations (Relationships)

Choose one word from each box to make a collocation for each underlined name. Then rewrite the sentences using the collocation you've made.

1 Jake has just started going out with Sarah.
Sarah is Jake's latest girlfriend/new girlfriend.
2 My family knows Mr Green, but not very well.
Mr Green is ...
3 Dad knew Sally well years ago at school.
4 Jane isn't seeing Max anymore.
5 Helen is one of the few girls Mike is friendly with.
6 Pete is almost the only person I can talk to about this.

family · school · +ex- · old · new · latest · +male · +female · close · good · great · best · special · true

+acquaintance · friend · mate · boyfriend · girlfriend

2 Mr Green is a new family acquaintance. · 3 Sally is an old (school) friend of Dad's. · 3 Max is Jane's ex-boyfriend. · 4 Helen is one of Mike's few female friends. · 5 Pete is my best friend.

Write a short text about the relationship between two characters (from a book, film, TV series ...) Use eight words from 1, 2 and 3.

Read each other's texts and comment. Which new words/phrases has your partner used?

➔ Workbook 8 (p. 19)

1 Noah

Die S können den **Inhalt einer Filmsequenz zusammenfassen** und dabei auf die Gefühle und Beziehungen der Personen eingehen.

a) Say what the film still shows you.

b) Watch the film and say what happens.
These phrases may help you:
· visit a website · open a window
· log in/out · enter a password
· post sth. · send a message
· update your status/profile
· hack sb's account/texts
· end a call

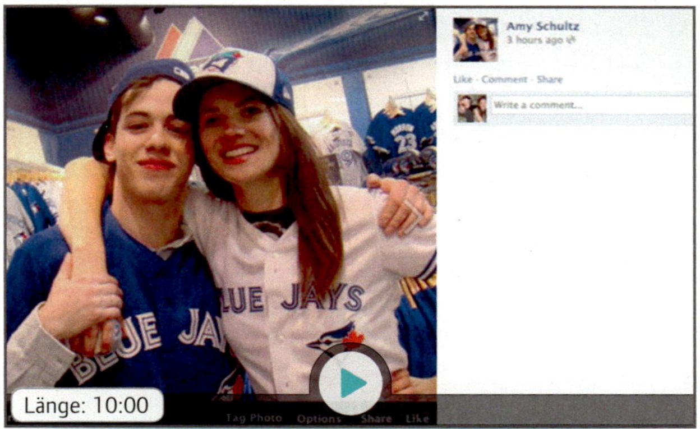

Länge: 10:00

c) Write a summary of the film in about five sentences. KV 5 bietet den S eine Checklist zu ***Writing a summary***.
Comment on each other's summaries and revise yours if necessary.

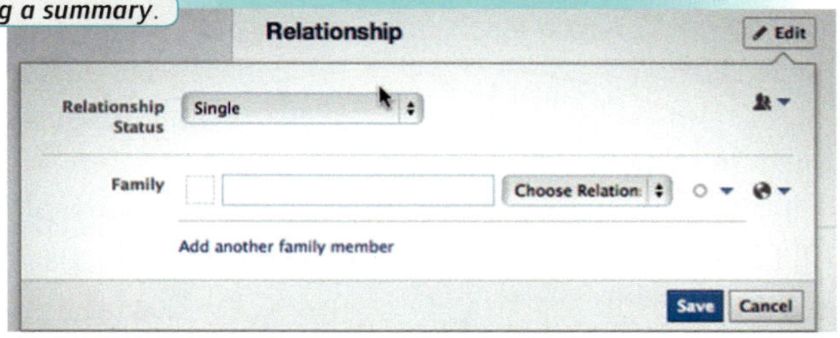

d) Say if you think Noah listens to what Amy says while they're chatting.
Give reasons for your opinion.

e) Look at the still on the right.
Say how you think Noah feels at this moment in the film.
How might Amy feel when she finds out what has happened?

EXTRA How might the situation at the end of the film have been different if Noah and Amy had spoken face to face?

YT 2 Making the film: Sounds

Die S können den **Sound** einer Filmszene in Kontext zum Geschehen setzen und seine Wirkung beschreiben.

a) Say what kind of sounds you can hear in films.
Think of voices, music and other sounds, including background noise.

b) Listen as Noah chats to three girls on webcam later in the film (sound only).
Make a table like this and take notes to describe the sounds you hear. Länge: 01:25

	Voices	Music	Other sounds
I can hear	girls: excited voices ...	...	...

c) Now watch the scene and say what it is about. Länge: 01:25
Then use your notes to link the sounds to the scene.
- You hear the excited voices when three girls …
- …

Say what effect all the different sounds have on the viewer.
- The voices/music/… give you the impression that /make you think that …

2 Part B

FöFo 2.4

Die S nutzen ***skimming*** und ***scanning***, um sich Texte zu erschließen. Sie können **einem Text Pro- und Contra-Argumente entnehmen**.

1 Family arguments

a) Skim the text and decide what it is about.

b) Scan the article to find out what it says about tofu.

➜ *SF 1: Skimming and scanning (p. 137)*

Not so quiet on the Auckland food war front

by Nicola Wright, September 15

There's been no peace in our dining room since our teenage daughter became a vegetarian

The food war started when my 15-year-old daughter Zoe posted a "meat is murder" poster on her social media site. Her brother Jacob showed me his reaction, a photo of a T-shirt slogan: *Vegetarians! I love animals too – they're yummy.*

Meat or no meat?

Adult friends sometimes tell us we shouldn't eat meat but they don't get as angry about it as a teenager who has declared war on the meat-eaters of this world.

"They're destroying vast areas of rainforest to grow food for animals so that Jacob can have a cheeseburger every evening," she tells us during breakfast.

+wife

At lunch, while my husband Paul is enjoying a plate of roast beef, she says, "You ought to stop eating meat. So many people are hungry. We ought to grow food for them, not for animals."

Jacob doesn't take his sister seriously. "If we aren't supposed to eat animals, why does meat taste so good?" he laughs. But Zoe doesn'tlaugh back. "Humans are supposed to taste good too," she replies. "So you had better be quiet, although I wouldn't want to eat you for lunch."

"Rabbit!" says Jacob and holds up a sausage on his fork.

Rabbit food?

Crowded kitchen

Personally, I have no problem with Zoe's new diet, though I was worried at first that she wouldn't get enough protein. How would she if she just stopped eating meat? She has never really liked many vegetables, especially healthy green ones. But she has bought a vegetarian recipe book and is now into beans and tofu. Tofu is supposed to be full of protein and other good stuff.

This means preparing family meals in our tiny kitchen has become practically impossible.

Our children used to be busy with their smartphones while Paul or I were cooking. Now we have to make room in the kitchen for Zoe to cook at the same time.

Zombies and rabbit food

Parents are supposed to keep the peace but it's hard sometimes. At the weekend, I made an Italian pasta dish I found in the Sunday magazine. Paul ate it but Jacob didn't touch it, shouted something about "rabbit food" and then went out to get a takeaway with his own pocket money. When he got back, Zoe declared that meat was for zombies, while Paul watched jealously as Jacob bit into a double baconburger.

2 The people and the issues

You choose a) or b).

Neigungsdifferenzierung: Die S wählen zwischen zwei Aufgaben.

a) Write ten lines on the relationship between Zoe and Jacob. Read your text to the class.

b) List the arguments used for/against eating meat. Explain which you agree with.

Early finisher ➜ *p. 124*

Early finisher: Buchstabenrätsel um *food words*.

3 Have a go

Die S verwenden vorbewusst verschiedene englische *phrases* für das deutsche **sollen**.

Imagine a vegetarian is coming to dinner. Say what you should and shouldn't do.

· We ought to · We'd better · We'd better not	look for a vegetarian recipe. buy some green salad. talk about meat. ...

Die S verwenden unterschiedliche englische Entsprechungen für das deutsche **sollen** ***(should, ought to, had better, be supposed to)***.

YT

Looking at language

German *sollen* has different meanings. In English, we use different expressions for these meanings.

a) You already know *should* for giving advice or for telling people what we think they should do:
Friends sometimes tell us we *shouldn't* eat meat.

Find two synonyms for *should* in 1 on p. 44.
1 You ... stop eating meat, Dad. · 2 So you ... be quiet, ...

1 ought to · 2 had better

b) German *sollen* has two other meanings. Look at these sentences:
1 Tofu soll voll von Protein sein. · 2 Eltern sollen für Frieden sorgen.
Now find the sentences in English in 1 on p. 44 and write them down.

1 Tofu is supposed to be full of protein. · 2 Parents are supposed to keep the peace.

Complete these explanations and match them to the English sentences 1 and 2.
- We use ... to say that we expect people to follow rules, traditions, laws, etc. ought to, should, be supposed to
- We also use ... to say what people say or think. had better, be supposed to

→ GF 4.3: sollen (p. 175)

YT

1 We'd better use the bridge (German *sollen: should, ought to, had better*)

Imagine you're in the countryside in New Zealand. What should/shouldn't you do in these situations? Make as many different sentences as you can for each situation.
Then comment on each other's sentences.

We should We ought to We'd better We'd better not	· be very careful · check the map · find out ... · fish here	· go back · go straight on · look for ... · try to cross here	· turn left/right · wait until ... · walk around/through ... · use the bridge

1 A: We should try to jump over the water. – B: No, we ought to ...

YT

2 Auckland is supposed to be a great city (German *sollen: be supposed to 1*)

We often use a form of *be supposed to* **+** *be* **to support advice we give.**
Use the correct form to complete these sentences.

1 You should visit Auckland. It ... a great city.
It's supposed to be a great city
2 You should ask Jane for some tips.
She ... an expert on the city.
3 You should read this guide. It ... very helpful.
4 You should buy one of these big rucksacks.
They ... really good.
5 You should go sailing there. It ... be great fun.
6 You should ask Jack to give you lessons.
He ... a great teacher.

1 It's supposed to be a great city. · 2 She's supposed to be an expert on the city. · 3 It's supposed to be very useful. · 4 They're supposed to be really good. · 5 It's supposed to be great fun. · 6 He's supposed to be a great teacher.

→ Workbook 9–10 (p. 20)

3 Life away from home (Giving advice)

You have a friend who is going to spend time in New Zealand as an exchange student. You want to give this friend some advice on how to get on well with his/her host family.

Partner A: Go to p. 130.
Partner B: Go to p. 134.

TIP
Here's one way to make your advice sound friendlier: Instead of just saying
You ought to / should / shouldn't do this.
you could also say
I think / I don't think you ought do this.
How else could you sound friendlier?

YT 4 You aren't supposed to ride bikes here (German *sollen: be supposed to* 2)

Read each pair of sentences. Then complete them using a form of *be supposed to* and *had better*. Use *be supposed to* when talking about general rules. Use *had better* for specific situations.

1 You (not · ride) bikes in this park. We (get) off and push them.
You aren't supposed to ride bikes in this park. We'd better get off and push them.
2 I (buy) some apples and bananas today. You (eat) lots of fruit.
3 You (not · put) bananas in the fridge. You (take) them out again.
4 You (not · wear) shoes in the living room. You (take) them off now.
5 We (turn) down the music. We (not · make) noise after ten in the evening.
6 You (not · use) a dictionary in the test. So you (leave) it outside.
7 You (pick) up that paper bag. You (not · leave) any rubbish here.
8 We (hurry). We (be) at the airport 90 minutes before the flight leaves.

2 I'd better buy … You're supposed to eat … · 3 You aren't supposed to put …You'd better take … · 4 You aren't supposed to wear … You'd better take … · 5 We'd better turn … We aren't supposed to make … · 6 You aren't supposed to use … you'd better leave · 7 You'd better pick … You aren't supposed to leave · 8 We'd better hurry. We're supposed to be a …

More help → p. 116

More help: Als Hilfe sind *general rules / specific situations* farblich unterschieden.

5 New Zealand and Germany (Cultural differences)

Länge: 04:30

a) Watch *Lifeswap*, a Skype chat between a German and a New Zealander. Then describe
- the mistake Jörg made and Duncan's reaction
- what Duncan thinks about the German expressions he has learned

b) Read the information in *Access to cultures*. Then watch the film again and take notes on Duncan's advice to Jörg and Jörg's reaction. Comment on how Jörg reacts.

Access to cultures

Talking about problems
There are different styles of communication in different countries. In Germany, people are usually very direct. If there is a problem, they say exactly what it is. Other people expect this, and don't usually find it rude.
In English-speaking countries, people prefer to talk about problems indirectly. If you are too direct, you may sound rude and even hurt someone's feelings.
If a problem is very small, sometimes it can be better not to speak about it at all. But if you must say something, try to use words and phrases that make your message sound softer.

www Find out more about New Zealand.

6 Explaining the situation

Work in groups of three.
A German student is hosting a guest student from New Zealand. In three situations, the German student helps the New Zealander by explaining what another German has said.

Go to pp. 132–133.
You will take turns to play the German student.

→ Workbook 11–13 (pp. 20–21)

Die S können **Diagramme und Statistiken** beschreiben und ihre Inhalte mündlich und schriftlich darlegen.

7 Study skills: Talking about statistics

On this page you'll learn to identify different kinds of statistics and talk about what they tell you.

a) Choose the right word for each way of presenting statistics.

bar chart · pie chart · table

1 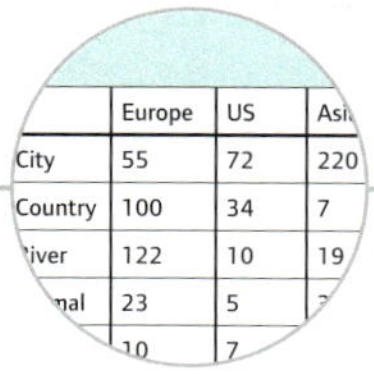

2 

3 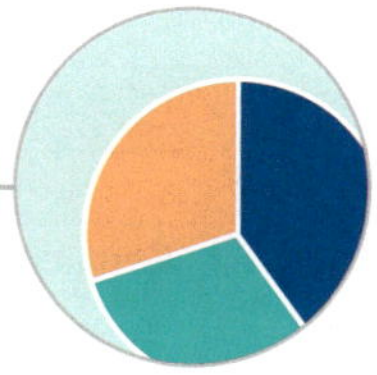

b) In groups of three, each student chooses one chart or table. Use phrases from the box to tell your partners what information it gives.

1 Family arguments in the UK

Number of arguments per year	1095
Average length of arguments	5 minutes
Time spent arguing per year	91.25 hours

2 Who starts family arguments?

Number of every 10 arguments started

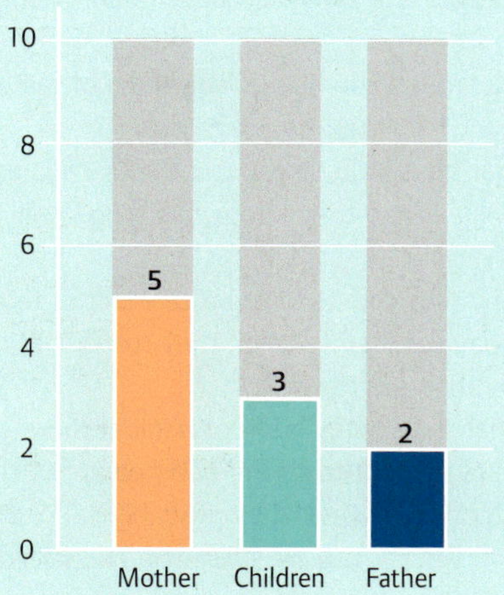

Based on different internet sources, *September 2016*

TIP Useful language

The table / bar chart / pie chart is about …

It gives us information about …
- *the percentage of / the number of …*
- *who / what / how many / what percentage of …*

The chart / table shows that …
- *most / more / fewer …*
- *a high percentage of / 25 per cent of …*
- *twice as many / three times as many …*

If you compare …
- *the percentage of / the number of …*

… you can see …

3 Causes of family arguments

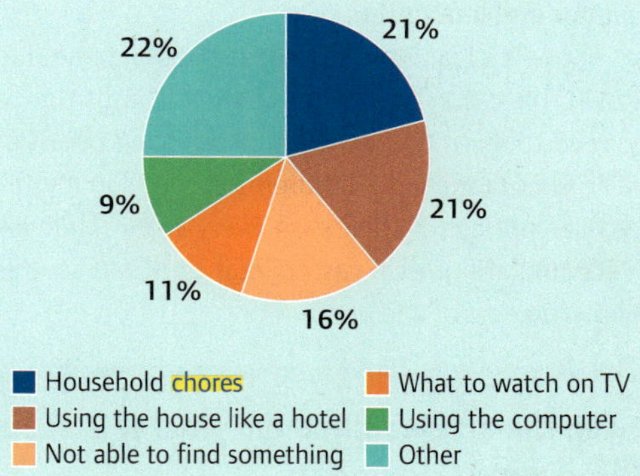

c) Finish with a conclusion about what you have found out.

My main conclusion is that …

The most important thing I've learned is that …

One thing that I hadn't realized is …

→ *SF 26: Talking about statistics (p. 157)*

8 Statistics from different countries

a) Look at the table and say what kind of information is given. Compare the three countries with each other and with the European average. Agree on the four most interesting facts and write them down in a short text.

The table shows how much pocket money kids of different age groups in Germany, Turkey, the UK and on average in Europe get.

EUROPEAN STATISTICS: AMOUNT OF POCKET MONEY PER WEEK*

Age	Under 5	5 to 10	10 to 15	15-plus
Germany	1.00	4.00	10.00	20.00
Turkey	1.50	3.25	6.50	16.00
UK	2.50	6.00	6.00	12.00
European average	2.00	4.75	9.50	20.00

Source: ING International Survey, September 2014 — ** figures in euros*

b) Swap texts with another group. Check the language and suggest corrections if necessary. Comment on the other group's four most interesting facts. Are they different from yours?

9 Advice to parents

Solving the Pocket Money Problem

By: Merryn Somerset-Webb

Should you give your children pocket money? If you do, should you insist that they do household chores in return?

The answer to the first question is clearly yes. All children should have small amounts of their own money from a young age – it teaches them the value of money, and hopefully a bit about basic budgeting.

The answer to the second is trickier. I interviewed people in Cardiff on this very subject just a few weeks ago. Most people told me that they only gave their children pocket money in exchange for work around the house. And if they wanted more money, they had to do more chores. I was mildly shocked by this. Why? Because I don't think this is the way it should be.

Instead, children should be keeping their bedrooms tidy and helping around the house regardless of family cash flow. Doing so is simply part of being a member of a family.

Start giving them a small and regular amount every week. The regular bit is vital. If you want your children to be able to budget and save, they need to get the same amount every week - then they know how long it will take them to save for any one thing.

Next, make it clear what expenses should come out of pocket money. And you need to be careful not to override your own rules; don't buy your children things they are supposed to pay for themselves if they run out of money. They need to learn how to balance out their needs and their wants by themselves.

Box "(to) run out", Voc, S. 209

Finally, encourage your children to save. You might perhaps insist that their piggy bank or bank account gets a certain percentage of their cash every week. That way not only will they get in the saving habit early but they might even accumulate quite a cash pile: if they can save £3 a week - which on £6 a week they probably can - they'll have £156 by the end of the year.

Source: Channel 4 (original article abridged)

a) Skim the article to find out what it is about.
Compare your ideas.

The article gives advice to parents on how to deal with giving pocket money.

b) Read the article. Take notes on the author's opinions about whether
- children should work for pocket money
- pocket money is good for children

Then say if you agree with her.

Children shouldn't work for pocket money because housework should be a regular duty and not be paid. • Pocket money is good for children because it teaches them the value of money and how to budget it.

TIP

Try to guess the meaning of new words on your own before you look them up in a dictionary.

→ *SF 29: Dealing with unknown words (S. 159)*

Early finisher → *p. 125*

Early finisher: Die S vervollständigen Redewendungen zum Thema Geld.

Die S lernen, wie sie eine **sinnvolle Diskussion** führen.

KV 6 bietet ***discussion tickets*** – nützliche Redewendungen für eine Diskussion.

YT Having a discussion

On this page, you will practise having a discussion and trying to reach agreement.

STEP 1 Starting a discussion

At the beginning of a discussion, you express an opinion and agree or disagree with someone else's view.
Say what expressions you know for doing this. ➜ *Speaking course, p. 23*

STEP 2 Continuing a discussion

During a discussion you may want to
- give reasons for your opinion
- support your argument with examples
- stress that your arguments are strong
- interrupt another speaker
- answer when somebody interrupts you

Let me explain why …

Let me give you an example of what I mean.

I feel very strongly that …

I think … because …

Sorry, but can I say something here?

A good example is …

Let me remind you that …

Yes, of course. Go ahead.

I'm quite sure that …

Sorry, but could I just finish what I was saying?

a) Match the speech bubbles to the points above.

b) Continue this discussion.

Worm *I really don't think you should eat me.*
Hen *I'm not sure if I share your view.*
Worm *Let me explain why it isn't a good idea.*
Hen *Go ahead, then.*
Worm *Well, …*

"Can't we discuss this?"

STEP 3 Ending a discussion

a) Prepare to bring your discussion from step 2 to an end.
First look at these strategies and phrases and think about how the discussion could finish.
- point out what views you have in common
- concentrate on areas where you still don't agree
- state your conclusions …
  … or accept that you aren't able to agree

So we both agree that …

I think we'll have to agree to differ.

There's one point we still need to discuss.

To sum up, we decided …

b) Now try to reach a conclusion.

Worm *So we both agree that a hen …*
Hen *Yes, but …*

STEP 4 Discuss another topic

a) In groups of four discuss this topic:
Kids should only get pocket money if they work round the house.

Note down your arguments before you start:
Partners A and B: You are for the topic.
Partners C and D: You are against the topic.

b) Tell the class your conclusion.

Die S beschäftigen sich mit Menschen in anderen Lebenssituationen und befassen sich mit dem Thema **Diskriminierung/Anti-Diskriminierung**.

1 Building community: RefugeeYouth London

Do you know any organizations that help young refugees? Say what kind of help they offer.

RefugeeYouth is an organization which supports young refugees trying to make London their new home. It is run for refugees by refugees, who make decisions and organize projects themselves. One project was publishing a book, Becoming a Londoner, which 117 young people worked on together. You can read parts of it below. ›

› Fun, food and friendship

Still from documentary on RefugeeYouth (I am)

is the °basis of everything we do. We build relationships, and start to feel at home by cooking and eating together, exploring London and creative arts work. … Our regular "°Mix it up" events (big all-day youth-led arts festivals) bring together young people from across our °network in celebration. We don't offer any formal advice or °guidance services, but "we walk the path" with people, whether that's helping someone to fill in a form or write a letter, °accompanying them to a scary °court case, or listening when they need to talk.

› London life

We will travel long distances to be with people who share our language, culture or interests. However, London is a big city and travelling around is really expensive. Access to °affordable transport is really important for us.

› Education

Young refugees face °a host of problems when we come to London. If you don't speak English, you need to learn the language – and quickly:

"I remember the first day of school crying, because I didn't know how to say I wanted to use the toilet."

It is extremely difficult to find a place at a school and to fit in when you get here:

"I used to say I was a refugee from Guinea but I felt like no one wanted to be my friend. In Richmond, people are very white. I had to °get into it and act a certain way to fit in: you adapt and get used to it."

› Family pressures

Young refugees often end up taking many adult responsibilities within their families and communities:

"We end up becoming translators, legal advisors, °housing advisors and carers for the whole community."

All young people in every community make change by challenging their °elders, but this is harder if parents are lonely and dependent on their children:

"Parents don't get to experience this culture like we do. I don't know anywhere I can take my mum where she can explore things like I can in my youth group. Parents need new experiences too."

Source: www.refugeeyouth.org

YT 2 Our everyday lives

Länge: 02:09

a) Say what problems young refugees have and what kind of help RefugeeYouth offers.

b) Say how your life may be different from a young refugee's. Think about school, your social life, family relationships and transport.

c) Watch the RefugeeYouth video *I am* and write down three things people say that impressed you. Then think about yourself and complete the sentence *I am …, or I want to, … I like … or I love …*

3 Building community: Über den Tellerrand, Berlin

Always Cook on the Bright Side of Life

by Melanie Tomkins

Behind a shop window on a corner in Berlin, about ten people wearing aprons were dancing around a kitchen island. I was in a hurry, so normally I would have walked on. But I just had to find out what was going on. So I rang the bell.

Cooking It all started when a group of university students were given an assignment to found a small business in eight weeks. They came up with the idea of publishing a book filled with the stories, photos and recipes of refugees in their city. It was a great experience but the eight weeks were soon over. If they had stopped there, *Über den Tellerrand* would never have been born.

The group planned their next project: cooking lessons. Rafael Strasser, who was on the planning team, said: "We hoped to attract people who don't know any refugees, and might even be a bit afraid of them. We wanted to offer an environment where they can meet some of those who have found a safe place in Berlin."

The cooking lessons, taught by a refugee, were stiff and quiet at first, but cooking together totally changed the atmosphere. "In the end we had to force people out the door because they were having such a good time!" said Rafael with a smile.

Next projects The team didn't stop there. With lots of help from local people, refugees and friends, they organized community events with a cultural theme: their Syrian, Egyptian and Halloween nights attracted up to 150 people. The key ingredients? "Food, music and dance are all activities which connect people. At one point in the evening, the music gets louder and people start dancing – it's really very powerful."

The *Über den Tellerrand* team also organized smaller special interest groups that meet once a week, including a soccer team and language tandems, in which two people teach each other their language.

Working together To be successful, projects need partners. Strasser points to their new 'Kitchen Hub' with its freshly painted walls and handmade furniture that can be used for all sorts of occasions. It was designed and built by a team of student architects and refugees.

The word 'hub' usually describes a place where transport routes come together. *Über den Tellerrand*'s 'Hub' is a place where people from many different cultures meet and share.

English is essential The English language is also a key ingredient in everything they do. As Rafael explains, "English is the most important language for us. Many people we meet and work with speak English and Arabic. Personally, if I hadn't learned English at school, I would have found it much harder to talk to people from so many countries."

And then, Strasser explains, there is the creative process: "In the work I do, I want to be creative. *Über den Tellerrand* is a platform for people to try out their ideas. We want to move others to be creative."

YT 4 From idea to project

KV 7 enthält eine ***Placemat*** zum Befüllen.

a) Describe the different ways in which *Über den Tellerrand* helps refugees.

b) Explain why Rafael thinks English is the most important language for the project.

EXTRA Imagine you are members of *Über den Tellerrand*. Use a placemat to brainstorm ideas for a project.
Discuss the ideas, agree on one and develop it.
Present your project idea to the class.

Die S können ausdrücken, was in der Vergangenheit hätte passieren können *(Conditional 3)*.

Language help

a) **The would have-form (*would have* + past participle) is used to talk about situations in the past that were *possible*, but *didn't* happen:** I was in a hurry, so normally I would have walked on.
Read lines 1–3 in 3 on p. 51 again. Say what happened: The person walked on / didn't walk on.

b) **Sentences in the would have-form can be combined with an *if*-clause in the past perfect to make conditional 3 sentences:**
If they had stopped there, *Über den Tellerrand* would never have started up.
If I hadn't learned English at school, I would have found it hard to talk to people …
Say what happened: The person *found it hard* / *didn't find it hard* to talk to people.
Say why: The person *learned* / *didn't learn* English at school.

➜ GF 8: Conditional sentences (pp. 182–183)

1 REVISION I would have done it differently (*would have*-form)

Use the *would have*-form to complete the dialogues.

1 A: Jens broke up with his girlfriend by text.
B: That's cruel. I (meet her and tell her).
I would have met her and …
2 A: Do you like my new profile photo?
B: Well, to be honest, I (use another one).
3 A: I asked Tim to be my friend on social media.
B: Tim? No way! I (not ask him).
4 A: I met someone really nice at the weekend, but I don't know how to °contact them.
B: I (ask for their phone number).
5 A: Leonie changed my social media profile.
B: Wow! I (never give her my password).
6 A: I clicked on this °link and I got a °virus.
B: It's your fault. I (not click on a strange link).

1 I would have met her and told her. • 2 I would have used another one. • 3 I wouldn't have asked him. • 4 I would have asked for their phone number. • 5 I would never have given her my password. • 6 I wouldn't have clicked on a strange link.

2 If I had seen a bear, … (Conditional 3)

a) Imagine these things happened yesterday. Write sentences about what you would have done.

1 (see) a bear in the park · (call) the police
If I'd seen a bear in the park, I would have …
2 (lose) my key · (climb) through a window
3 (be) late for class · (say) sorry to our teacher
4 (feel) tired · (not go) out with my mates
5 a dog (follow) me to school, …
If a dog had … , I would have …
6 there (be) metre of snow during the night, …
7 my dad (speak) Chinese to me at breakfast, …
8 my friend (fall) into a river …

b) Compare your ideas for sentences 5–8. Choose your two best ideas and tell the class.

a) 1 … called the police. • 2 If I'd lost my key, I would have climbed … • 3 If I'd been late for class, I would have said … • 4 If I'd felt tired, I wouldn't have gone … • 5 If a dog had followed me …, I'd have … • 6 If there'd been …, I'd have … • 7 If my dad had spoken …, I'd have … • 8 If my friend had fallen …, I'd have …

3 If I had been you, … (Conditional 3)

a) Read the text. Then write as many sentences as you can about what you would have done differently.
If I'd been you, I would have got up at …
If I'd been late, I wouldn't …

More help ➜ p. 117
More help: Es sind mögliche Satzteile vorgegeben.

7:30. Mum and Dad were away. It was cold, so I stayed in bed till 8. Now I was late. I had breakfast really fast, but I still missed the bus. I could have used my bike, but … While I was waiting for the next bus, a dog came up to me. I could tell he was hungry – I was sure he hadn't eaten for days. So I bought some dog food and took him back home to feed him. He was so happy and didn't want to leave. So I never got to school.

b) Read your partner's sentences and correct them if necessary.

Early finisher ➜ p. 125
Early finisher: *Matching puzzle* zu Fragen und Ratschlägen

Die S können die **Aussagen von Plakaten erläutern** und ihre **Wirkung analysieren**.

YT In a double circle, discuss these points:

- the message of the posters
  I think this poster …
  - is about … /… makes a statement about …
  - symbolizes … /is a metaphor for …
  - uses the image/symbol/… of … to show …
- whether the message comes across well, and why
  - The message is strong/powerful/… because …
  - The message isn't really clear because …
- which of the posters you would hang up, where, and why.
  - I would hang up … in … because …
  - I wouldn't hang up any of them because …

→ *SF 25: Describing and interpreting images (p. 156)*

Workbook Checkpoint 2 (pp. 26–29)

Your task

Es bietet sich an, mit dieser Lernaufgabe im Unterricht zu beginnen (**Step 1**). **Steps 2** und **3** sollten dann von den S am Nachmittag durchgeführt werden, bevor **Steps 4** und **5** wieder im Unterricht stattfinden.

Welcome to my world: A video about me

In teams of four, you will make a video in which *one* of the team members introduces him/herself to English-speaking viewers. Your teacher will tell you when your videos need to be finished. After making and presenting your videos, you will evaluate your teamwork.

STEP 1 Plan your roles

Agree who will introduce him/herself. Then share out the other roles.

Presenter

Think of what to tell your viewers. Perhaps start with some facts about yourself and then concentrate on any of the following topics:

- people – family, special friends, groups – that are important to you
- places and activities you like
- your lifestyle choices (food, clothes, music)
- your experience of other cultures and your own

IMPORTANT: Make a draft script and give it to your partners before your meeting in Step 2.

Other roles

1 Language watchdog
You will need to check the draft script before shooting and suggest corrections.

2 Camera
You will need to read the presenter's script and think of ideas for where and how to shoot the video.

3 Timekeeper
You will need to make sure that everything (draft script, discussion, preparation. shooting) happens on time.

STEP 2 Prepare for the shoot

a) **Discuss the draft script. Decide:**
- whether to change any of the content
- the best order for the content
- possible settings (where to shoot)

➔ *Speaking course (p. 49)*

b) **Make a final version of the script. Maybe make a storyboard (an outline of the different parts of the video). Remember to get the language checked before the shoot. Make corrections, if necessary.**

evaluate [ɪ'væljueɪt] bewerten, beurteilen **shoot** [ʃuːt] Dreharbeiten; drehen, filmen

STEP 3 Make a video

a) The timekeeper arranges the time and place for the shoot and makes sure that everyone knows when and where to appear.

b) Now you're ready to shoot.

TIP

- You can use smartphone camera apps to make simple videos.
- Make sure the light is good and hold the camera still while filming.
- If you have editing software, you can shoot different scenes separately and join them later.

STEP 4 Watch

Present your video to another group and watch theirs.

TIP

If you like your video a lot and are thinking of putting it online, remember:

- It's not always a good idea to put very personal information on the internet. Think carefully about what you want strangers to know about you.
- Respect other people's rights. Never put anything about your classmates on the web without their permission.

STEP 5 Evaluate

a) Your teacher will give you an evaluation target. Look at the criteria in each section and say how well you think they will help evaluate your teamwork. Change some criteria if you wish.

b) Each student evaluates the team's work by putting one dot in each section:
target centre = most successful
target edge = least successful.

c) Look at each section of your target. Think about the position of the dots and what it says about your teamwork. Make notes for a discussion.

d) Discuss what went well and what you could do better next time. Write down ideas on how your teamwork could be improved.

KV 8 bietet ein ***Evaluation target*** für das ***teamwork***.

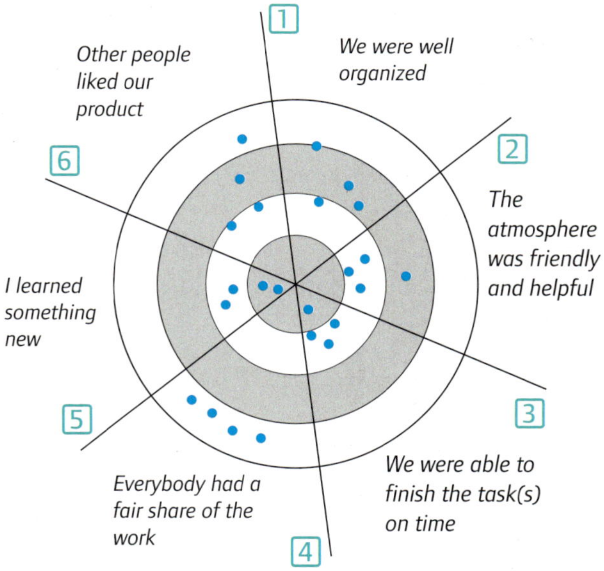

➜ *SF 23: Teamwork (p. 154)*

EXTRA Make a video to introduce another member of the team.

criterion [kraɪ'tɪəriən], *pl* **criteria** Kriterium **dot** [dɒt] Pünktchen **evaluation** [ɪˌvælju'eɪʃn] Bewertung, Beurteilung
target ['tɑːgɪt] Ziel, Zielscheibe

KV 9 bietet ein ***Evaluation target***, mit dem die S die Unit evaluieren können.

Text challenge 2

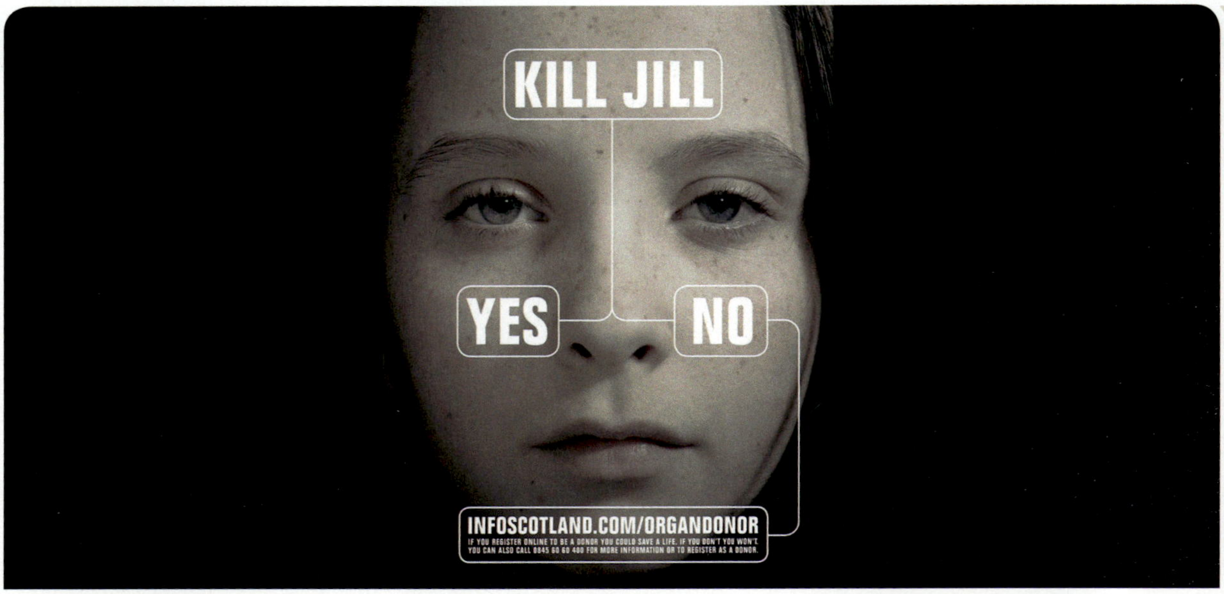

In the *Oberstufe*, you will be asked to interpret texts that combine words and images. Interpreting ***image-based texts*** is similar to interpreting ***non-fictional texts*** (➜ *Text challenge 1, pp. 32–33*). There are three important steps:

- ***comprehension*** You describe the content of the image-based text: What is it about? This is a skill you have often used, for example when describing images like photos or posters.
- ***analysis*** You study how the content is presented and what effect that has on the viewer.
- ***comment*** You react with a critical or personal comment in written or spoken form.

STEP 1 Comprehension

Task: Describe one of the posters to your partner. ➜ *SF 25: Describing and interpreting images (p. 156)*

STEP 2 Analysis

Task: Discuss how the two posters convey their message about organ donation.

- Refer to the kind of **image** used, e.g. photo, drawing, etc. Also mention qualities such as colour or size, how realistic or unrealistic the image is, etc.
  - ***The use of a*** *photo/illustration/ …* ***makes the message*** *clearer/more emotional/…*
  - ***The*** *dark/bright/different/…* ***colours*** *make it easier to understand/reinforce/…* ***the message.***
- Refer to the kind of information the **text** contains, e.g. emotional, humorous, facts, statistics, etc. You can also mention the amount of text, the colour/size of the letters, the use of capital letters, etc.
  - ***By asking*** *a short/an emotional/…* ***question****… /* ***By including statistics, the poster …***
  - ***The use of*** *only a few words/capital letters/larger and smaller letters/…* ***makes the message*** *…*
- Explain how well the **image** and **text** fit together.
  - ***By depicting*** *different organs/… ,* ***the poster*** *focuses on/highlights/…* ***the message of the text.***
  - ***The*** *image of a face/girl's facial expression/… complements/reinforces/…* ***the text.***

---

organ donor Organspender/in **convey** übermitteln, vermitteln **donation** Spende **mention** erwähnen **reinforce** verstärken, untermauern **contain** enthalten **capital letter** Großbuchstabe **depict** darstellen, abbilden **complement** ergänzen, komplementieren

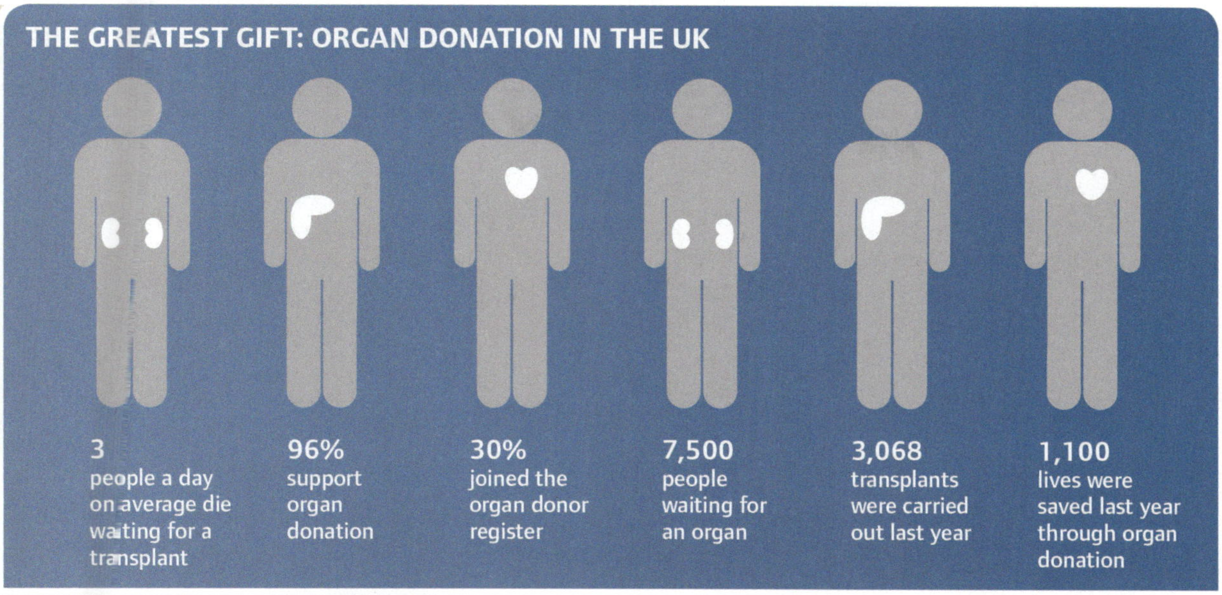

STEP 3 Comment

Task: Compare the two posters and comment on how effective they are.

- Compare the message and goal of the posters.
  - *In my view, the message of the two posters is similar/different/…*
  - *Although … focuses on a single person/on statistics …, it seems to me that they both want to …*
- Refer to points you covered in your analysis.
  - *In general I think a photo/statistics/facts/… move/influence/… people more than …*
  - *In this case, I feel/don't feel that the illustration/photo/colours/… work very well.*
  - *In my opinion a shorter/longer/more detailed/… text is more/less effective because …*
- You may also wish to give your own opinion on the issue.
  - *I feel/don't feel very strongly about transplants because …*

EXTRA FUTURE CHALLENGES

In the *Oberstufe*, you can expect to be given just <u>one</u> single instruction (*Operator*) for a task. In addition, you may be asked to use a specific format (e.g. discussion) or text type.

Neigungsdifferenzierung: Die S wählen zwischen zwei unterschiedlich ausgerichteten Schreibaufgaben.

You choose a), b) or c)

a) Write a story showing the effect that receiving an organ can have on somebody's life.

b) In a short article, comment on the relevance of organ donation to young people.

c) In a discussion of the two posters, assess how effective campaigns of this kind can be.

KV 6 bietet ***discussion tickets*** – nützliche Redewendungen für eine Diskussion.

gift Geschenk **carry out** aus-, durchführen **single** einzelne(r, s) **in general** generell; im Allgemeinen **influence** beeinflussen **in this case** in diesem Fall **instruction** Anweisung; Operator **specific** spezifisch, speziell **receive** erhalten, empfangen

Big dreams - small steps

1 What's the message?

a) Describe the pictures and explain how they relate to the unit title.

b) Say what you think this saying means:
A goal is a dream with a deadline.

YT 2 Achieving my goal

a) **Think**: Choose a phrase from p. 59 which you could imagine as a life goal.
Note down the first steps you could take to achieve this goal.

b) **Pair**: Use your notes to explain your goal and your ideas for achieving it.
Brainstorm ideas for other steps you can take.

c) **Share**: Describe your goals and compare your ideas for achieving them.
Say how similar or different your ideas are.

Early finisher Discuss this quote with your partners. Say what you think it means and how it might be relevant to you.

"Ever tried. Ever failed. No matter. Try again. Fail again. Fail better." *Samuel Beckett, Worstward Ho, 1983*

KV 6 bietet ***discussion tickets*** – nützliche Redewendungen für eine Diskussion.

→ Text file 3 *(p. 109)*

Text File: Roar

Die S wählen ein eigenes **Ziel** und erklären, wie sie dieses **umsetzen** könnten.

Text File: Zu Unit 3 passen **Text 3** und **4**.

go skydiving
learn lots of languages have a quiet life make a scientific discovery
make a difference become a doctor make films
build the longest bridge help others become an artist
stop global warming make people laugh
learn how to fly get a girlfriend/boyfriend get rich
start a business become a teacher live a long life go to university
become a computer programmer be happy repair old furniture work in a team
become a professional athlete play in a band become an actor
travel the world lead an exciting life work with animals
travel to the moon work for peace get good marks
become a celebrity become rich start a family
protect the environment
join the army

Your task

At the end of this unit:
Prepare an application and do an interview for a volunteer summer job abroad. +apply (for)

Die S können einem **Romanauszug** entnehmen, welche Beziehungen die Hauptfiguren zueinander haben und Aussagen zu Atmosphäre und Charakteren treffen.

1 The Crossover

Excerpts from a novel in verse by Kwame ['kwɑːmeɪ] Alexander

Twins Josh and JB go to a school where their mother is vice-principal. Thanks to training by their father, a former basketball professional, the twins are stars on the school basketball team. They get on well, but their relationship is about to be tested.

a) Look at the titles of the first four verses and say what you think might happen.

JB and I

19

are almost thirteen. Twins. Two basketball goals at
opposite ends of the court. Identical.
It's easy to tell us apart though. I'm

an inch taller, with dreads to my neck. He gets
his head shaved once a month. I want to go to
Duke, he flaunts Carolina Blue. If we didn't love
each other,

we'd HATE each other. He's a shooting guard.
I play forward. JB's the second
most phenomenal baller on our team.

He has the better jumper, but I'm the better
slasher. And much faster. We both
pass well. Especially to each other.

To get ready for the season, I went
to three summer camps. JB only went to
one. Said he didn't want to miss Bible school.

What does he think, I'm stupid? Ever since
Kim Bazemore ['beɪzmɔː] kissed him in Sunday school,
he's been acting all religious,

thinking less and less about basketball,
and more and more about
GIRLS.

Girls

20

I walk into the lunchroom with JB.
Heads turn.
I'm not bald like JB,
but my hair's close enough
so that people sprinting past us
do double-takes.
Finally, after we sit at our table,
the questions come:
Why'd you cut your hair, Filthy?
How can we tell who's who?
JB answers, *I'm the cool one*
who makes free throws,
and I holler,
I'M THE ONE WHO CAN DUNK.
We both get laughs.
Some girl who we've never seen before,
in tight jeans and pink Reeboks,
comes up to the table.
JB's eyes are ocean wide,
his mouth swimming on the floor,
his clownish grin, embarrassing.
So when she says,
Is it true that twins
know what each other are thinking?
I tell her you don't have to be his *twin*
to know
what *he's* thinking.

b) Say how you could tell the twins apart in a basketball game.

Josh: an inch taller • has dreadlocks • plays forward • is faster than JB • …
JB: shaves his head once a month • plays shooting guard • better jumper • …

crossover Crossover (*schneller Handwechsel beim Dribbeln*) **be caught by surprise** völlig überrascht sein **vice-** Vize- **court** Spielfeld **tell sb. apart** jn. auseinanderhalten **dreads** Rastalocken **shave** (sich) rasieren **Duke** *Duke University in Durham, North Carolina* **flaunt** zur Schau stellen, protzen mit **Carolina Blue** *Wappenfarbe der University of North Carolina, Chapel Hill* **bald** kahl, glatzköpfig **do a double-take** stutzen; zweimal hinschauen müssen **holler** brüllen, schreien

How Do You Spell Trouble? 21

During the vocabulary test
JB passes me a folded note
to give to
Miss Sweet Tea,
who sits at the desk
in front of me
and who looks
pretty tight
in her pink denim capris
and matching °sneaks.

Someone cracks a window.
A cold breeze whistles.
Her hair dances to its own song.
In this moment I forget
about the test
and the note
until JB hits me in the head with his No. 2.
Somewhere between
camaraderie and *imbecile*
I tap her beige bare shoulder
with the note.
At that exact moment
the teacher's head °creeps
up from his desk, his eyes directly on me.
I'm a fly caught in a web.
What do I do?
Hand over the note, embarrass JB;
or hide the note, take the heat.
I look at my brother,
his forehead a factory of sweat.
Miss Sweet Tea smiles,
gorgeous pink lips and all.
I know what I have to do.

Bad News 22

I sit in Mom's office
for an hour,
reading
brochures and °pamphlets
about the °Air Force and the °Marines.

She's in and out
handling principal stuff:
a parent protesting her daughter's F;
a pranked °substitute teacher crying;
a broken window.

After an hour
she finally sits
in the chair next to me
and says, *The good news is,*
I'm not going to suspend you.

The bad news, Josh,
is that
neither Duke nor any other college
accepts cheaters. Since I can't
seem to make a decent man out of you
perhaps the Air Force or Marines can.
I want to tell her I wasn't cheating,
that this is all JB and Miss Sweet Tea's fault,
that this will never happen again,
that Duke is the only thing that matters,
but a water pipe bursts in the girls' bathroom.

So I tell her I'm sorry,
it won't happen again,
then °head off to my next class.

c) Describe what happens in these three excerpts.
Explain how it might affect the twins' relationship with each other.

d) Imagine how the twins might have talked about the day's events a little later. Write a short dialogue between them.

tight *(infml)* stylisch **denim capris** Caprihose **crack a window** ein Fenster einen Spalt öffnen **No. 2** Bleistift *(der Härte 2)* **camaraderie** Kameradschaft **imbecile** Schwachkopf **fly** Fliege **web** Spinnennetz **take the heat** den Kopf hinhalten **sweat** Schweiß **gorgeous** hinreißend **handle sth.** etwas erledigen **F** ungenügend *(Schulnote)* **pranked** angeschmiert **suspend sb.** jn. vom Unterricht ausschließen **neither … nor …** weder … noch … **cheat** mogeln **since** weil **decent** anständig **matter** von Bedeutung sein **a water pipe bursts** ein Wasserrohr platzt

Die S können Charaktere einer Geschichte mithilfe von Adjektiven schriftlich und mündlich beschreiben.

School's Out

23

Mom has to work late,
so Dad picks us up.
Even though JB's
still not talking to me
Dad's °cracking jokes
and we're both laughing
like it's the good ol' times.
What are we getting for Christmas, Dad? JB asks.
What we always get. Books, I reply,
and we both laugh
just like the good ol' times.
Boys, your talent will help you win games, Dad
says, *but your intelligence, that will help you win*
at life. Who said that? I ask.
I said it, didn't you hear me?
Michael Jordan said it, JB says,
still looking at Dad.
Look, boys, you've both done good
in school this year, and your mom and I appreciate
that.
So you choose a gift, and I'll get it.
You mean no books? I ask. Yes!
°*Nope. You're still getting the books, player.*
Santa's just letting you pick something extra.
At the stoplight, JB and I look out
the window
at the exact moment
we pass by the mall
and I know exactly
what JB wants.
Dad, can we stop
at that sneaker store
in the mall? *Yeah, Dad, can we?* JB °echoes.
And the word *we*
never sounded
sweeter.

e) Describe the atmosphere in the car and the mood of the three characters.

2 The twins' characters

a) Say if you think these words describe the character of each twin. Give reasons.

brave · competitive · crazy about girls · cruel · easy-going · friendly · funny · honest · jealous · kind · loyal · self-confident · serious

b) Choose one twin each and write a short description of his character.
Then read your partner's text and comment.

3 EXTRA Showoff

a) Read this verse from *The Crossover* aloud.

Showoff
UP by sixteen
with *six seconds*

showing, **JB** smiles,

then **STRUTS**
side
steps
stutters
Spins, and
S
I
N
K
S
a sick **SLICK SLIDING**
SWeeeeeeeeeT
SEVEN-foot shot.
What a showoff.

b) Now listen to a recording of it. 24
Practise reading the verse aloud again.

c) Describe the layout of this verse and the way some of the words are written. Say what effect this has.

www Find out about books for teenagers.

→ Text file 4 (pp. 110–111)
Text File: 7 Years

showoff Angeber/in **up by sixteen** mit sechzehn Punkten vorn **strut** stolzieren **sidestep sb.** jm. ausweichen; jn. ausspielen **stutter** *von* **stutter step** *= ein schneller Verzögerungs- oder Trippelschritt zur Verwirrung des Gegners* **a slick shot** ein raffinierter/gekonnter Wurf **gift** Geschenk

→ Workbook 3 (p. 31)

Die S strukturieren Wortschatz zum **Beschreiben von Charakteren und Gefühlen**.

On this page you will work with words that help you to describe a person's character.
Then you will write a short character description.

1 Word field: Character and emotion (Structuring vocabulary)

a) Copy the table. Then read the tip and add these adjectives: brave · loyal · thrilled

Character	Character/Emotion	Emotion
easy-going	nervous	annoyed
...	...	...

TIP
Character adjectives tell us about someone's qualities. He's an easy-going guy.

Emotion adjectives describe people's feelings at a particular time: She felt really annoyed.

Some adjectives refer to character or emotion. He's a nervous kind of guy. / He felt nervous.

Mit **KV 10: Character profiles** wird das Vokabular zum Wortfeld ***character and emotion*** nochmal umgewälzt.

b) Think about the meaning of these adjectives and add them to your table.
Then compare and discuss your results. Try to add other words you know.

calm · cruel · excited · +generous · +hard-working · jealous · kind · +lazy · +mean · natural · negative · old-fashioned · optimistic · patient · practical · relaxed · rude · self-confident · shy · surprised · +tolerant · tough · weird · wise

2 Prefixes and suffixes (Understanding new words)

Prefixes like *dis-*, *un-*, *im-*, etc. give a word the opposite meaning, e.g. *polite* - *impolite*.
Suffixes like *-ness*, *-ance*, *- ence*, *-y* are used to make nouns out of adjectives.
Recognizing prefixes and suffixes can help you to understand a lot of words you haven't met before.

a) Choose five words from the box and write sentences to show their meaning.

+dishonest · +disrespectful · impatient · impolite · impractical · +intolerant · irresponsible · +unkind

A dishonest person is someone who ...

b) Compare your sentences in class.

c) Group the nouns in the box by their suffixes. Write down the adjective in a second column.

kindness	kind
laziness	...

-ness: .../lazy, liveliness/lively, meanness/mean, politeness/polite, rudeness/rude
-ance: tolerance/tolerant
-ence: patience/patient, impatience/impatient
-y: honesty/honest, jealousy/jealous

+honesty · +impatience · +jealousy · +kindness · +laziness · +liveliness · +meanness · +patience · +politeness · +rudeness · +self-confidence · +tolerance

Together think of one figure from a book or film. Then write separate character descriptions. Refer to personal qualities you like or dislike. Use eight words from this page.
Read your partner's text. Comment on what is similar or different.

More help → p. 118 **Early finisher** → p. 126

More help: Als Hilfe sind Ideen und Satzteile vorgegeben.
Early finisher: Gegensätze bilden mit Hilfe von Präfixen

→ **Workbook** 4 (p. 31) **Workbook** *Wordbank 4*

Die S können Vorhersagen mit ***will, might*** und ***going to*** formulieren.

Language help

YT Making predictions

a) You already know that the *will*-future is used to make predictions. You've also learned verbs like *may* and *might*.

A *Do you think Josh will join the Air Force?*
B *No, I think he'll probably go to college.*
A *But his mom might not allow him to go.*

b) We use the *going to*-future for predictions when we can see from a situation that something is about to happen:
Look at those clouds. It's going to rain.

We often use *going to* in warnings:
Be careful! You're going to fall.

➜ *GF 1.5: The future (pp. 166–168)*

YT 1 REVISION Summer camp (Predictions with *will* and *might*)

a) Look at the camp application form. What do you think your partner will/will not choose, and why? Make notes.

Choose one activity from each category.

Category 1	*Canoeing*	*Tennis*	*Riding*
Category 2	*Photography*	*Cooking*	*Gardening*
Category 3	*Dance*	*Singing*	*Juggling*
Category 4	*Chess*	*Crosswords*	*Poetry*

Choose your diet

Regular	*Vegan*	*Vegetarian*	*Other**

** Please give details*

b) Say what you think your partner will do and react to their predictions about you. Try to use each of these phrases once.

1 I think you'll ...
2 I don't think you'll ...
3 You'll probably ...
4 You probably won't ...
5 I'm sure you'll ...
6 Maybe you'll ...
7 You might ...
8 You might not ...

I don't think you'll choose riding, but you might ...

Why don't you think I'll choose riding?

Well, you ...

YT 2 It looks like there's going to be a storm (Predictions with the *going to*-future)

A

B

C

D

E

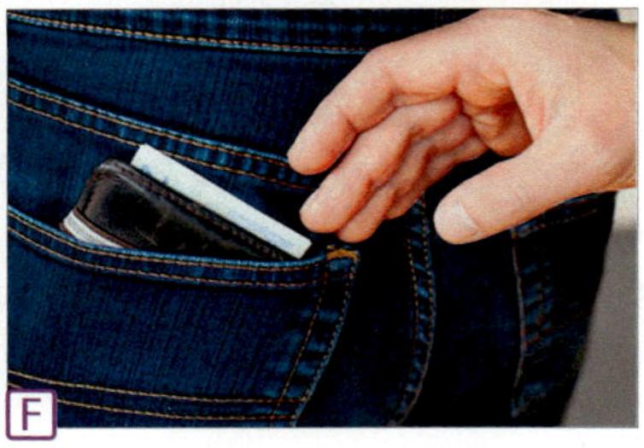
F

a) Say what's going to happen in each picture.

A *I'm sure it's going to rain.*
It looks like there's going to be a storm.

b) Choose one picture and write a short dialogue to warn others about what's about to happen.

More help ➜ *p. 118*

More help: Einige Ideen sind vorgegeben.

➜ **Workbook** *5–6 (pp. 31–32)*

Die S können einem Text **landeskundliche Informationen zu einem bildungsrelevanten Thema** entnehmen, Vor- und Nachteile sammeln und sich eine Meinung bilden.

A passport to college *by US correspondent Jane Eliot*

College costs

At 17, high school student Wes Young is thinking about university. "I'm applying to different colleges," Wes explains, "but my dream is Ohio State. I'm hoping I'll be offered a sport scholarship." For Wes and for thousands of other American students, a sport scholarship is a passport to an education they couldn't otherwise afford. "With college fees and living costs I'd need over $20,000 a year. There's no way my mom and dad could pay money like that."
A college education in the US is expensive, and Ohio State is at the cheaper end of the scale. At leading private universities like Princeton or Harvard, the annual costs would be closer to $60,000, three times as much as at top English universities.
"A good scholarship would cover the costs of teaching, room and board, and books," Wes explains. "That's a good deal."

Good chances

How does Wes rate his chances? "Well, I've been crazy about basketball since I was a little kid. In high school I really started perfecting my skills in the game and I've gone to basketball camp nearly every summer. That's paid off because I'm now one of the stars of our high school team."
"Wes's chances are good," says coach Marvin Aston. "Colleges all over the US are competing to find the best athletes. They need people like Wes. That's how college sport works."

Big business

In the United States, sport at college is more than just keeping fit while you're at university. Across the country, millions of fans follow college sporting events – in huge stadiums, on TV, in the newspapers and on social media. With ticket sales, merchandise and especially TV contracts, college sport is big business. For America's universities, success in sport improves their public profile, and they share in the profits too.

Wes Young – Future celebrity?

A scholarship will make Wes one of 450,000 student athletes in the US. Although he won't earn any money in college sport, it could be the ticket to a professional career. Tiger Woods, Michael Jordan and Mia Hamm were all once student athletes. Wes is planning to take things step by step. "My hope is to play well at college, get noticed by the pro-teams, and finally get onto an NBA team. But I have a whole lot more hard work to do first."

Full house at Ohio State football stadium

a) Make a list of the advantages of sport scholarships. Then think of possible disadvantages and add them to your list.

b) Compare your ideas. Then say if you would apply for a sport scholarship.

Mit Hilfe von Rollenkarten auf **KV 11: A debate about sport scholarships** führen die S eine Debatte zu den Vor- und Nachteilen von *sport scholarships* durch.

➜ Workbook 7 (p. 32)

Die S erschließen sich einen Text mittels *true/false statements*. Sie setzen sich schriftlich mit Kerngedanken des Textes auseinander.

1 A student's idea for saving lives

Say what you know about science competitions in your school, region or country.

['hæləsi]

In Olivia Hallisey's 10th-grade research science class, each student was asked to do their own experiment. When Olivia couldn't come up with an idea, her teacher suggested that she investigate something really important to her. It was then that she read about how the Ebola virus was spreading through communities in African countries, killing thousands of people. Shocked and upset, she knew she wanted to help. What was needed, Olivia realized, was a faster way to diagnose the Ebola virus. The sooner treatment started, the better the chance of helping a patient. The test available at the time was not only expensive; it was also dependent on refrigeration, impractical in rural Africa. A cheaper and more practical test would save lives.

Olivia spent long hours in the lab, often working at weekends. She faced many challenges. Some companies refused to sell her the chemicals she needed for her tests. She also had to travel to meet scientists and ask for advice. This meant waking early, traveling to New York or Boston from her home in Connecticut, and returning the same day in time for her other big passion: swimming. Hallisey says that traveling has taught her good time management skills, while in competitive swimming she has learned to keep going in difficult situations. Skills like these have helped her through the project.

Thanks to her hard work, Olivia developed a new test for the Ebola virus, with big advantages. It gives faster results: the virus can be diagnosed in only 30 minutes, compared with the 12 hours it takes with the current test. It will be much cheaper: $25 instead of the current $200. Finally, the test is not temperature-dependent, which means that no refrigeration is necessary. Olivia submitted her test to Google Science Fair, and won the 2015 Grand Prize which included $50,000.

For the future, Olivia has many plans. She is going to do more work on her test. Her hope is that it will soon be ready to use in the field and also in tests for other diseases.

She will also be traveling the country to talk to kids, and especially to girls about playing a bigger role in science. After high school, she wants to study medicine and work for an international health organization such as Doctors Without Borders. Although she plans to be busy, swimming will still be an important part of the picture: Olivia is determined to join the swim team at whatever university she attends.

Box "German "je …, desto …"", Voc, S. 215

Olivia Hallisey with Laura Erikson and Barbara O'Neill (chair and vice-chair of Greenwich Public Schools Board of Education)

2 Olivia and her project

a) Write 5 true/false statements about Olivia's test, the prize she won and her future plans.

b) Read each other's statements and decide if they are true or false.

c) Describe the character traits and skills which helped Olivia reach her goal.

YT 3 Skills and motivation

You choose a) or b).

Neigungsdifferenzierung: Die S wählen zwischen zwei Themen.

a) My Book Olivia investigated a topic "that really mattered to her". In a short text, explain what project you would do and why.

b) My Book In a short text, explain how skills learned in sport can help you to reach other goals.

Die S erschließen sich einen Text, indem sie *summarizing sentences* diskutieren.

4 Learning to learn

MICE AND MORE – An evolution project and a bigger lesson

Ashley Gaines, Los Angeles, 8 Dec.

Students at Palo Canyon High School don't worry about getting things wrong. Why not? Because they know that they learn better by making mistakes while tackling problems.

[ˌpæləʊ ˈkænjən]

I sat with a group in a 9th-grade biology class. They were doing a project on evolution and one of their tasks was to work out why the mice in a park changed color over time. At first there were equal numbers of white and gray mice, but after some time there were more gray mice. Why was that?

The students got no help to start them off. They simply began with a brainstorming session. "Gray fur protects mice better against the cold," suggested Juan. "It's thicker. So when the temperature falls, more white mice die."

[hwɑːn]

"Sounds weird to me," said Taylor. "Is it true?"

"I'm not sure," said Juan. "I'll look it up."

Taylor had a different idea. "White mice are easier to see," he argued, "so their enemies can find them and eat them."

Interesting ideas – but they couldn't all be right. So weren't students being sent down a blind alley, I wondered. Later, I spoke to teacher Jennifer Levitzky. "Of course students can travel down blind alleys," she told me. "But if they try to work out answers themselves, they'll understand a topic better than if they just have it explained right at the beginning. And in the long term they'll remember what they learned, even if they get it wrong the first time. Hey, why don't you come again tomorrow. I'll show you how we do it."

Next day I began to see what Jennifer meant. The students already had a good understanding of the principle of evolution and were keen to hear whether they had come up with the right ideas.

After the lesson I talked to students. "Taylor was right," said Juan. "Predators do eat more white mice."

Box "do/does/did in positive statements", Voc, S. 217

"But it's not just the fact they get eaten," Taylor pointed out. "It's about how many babies they have. Gray mice live longer because their predators can't see them. And that means they will have more babies. I hadn't realized that."

"And it's not just the total number of babies," added Juan. "Gray mice have more gray babies than white babies, so, over time, there will be more gray mice. It's how evolution works."

I reminded Juan of his idea from yesterday, about white mice dying from the cold.

"Right," he replied. "We talked about that in class. I understand now why this idea was wrong. And understanding that helps me to understand the whole topic better."

YT 5 If at first you don't succeed, …

Discuss the sentences below. Decide which best sums up the article and explain why.

- Grey and white mice can help you to learn.
- Learning is a blind alley.
- Getting things wrong can help you to learn.

EXTRA Write about an example from your own life where you learned from a mistake.

6 Have a go

Die S verwenden vorbewusst das ***will-future***, um spontane Pläne und Entscheidungen auszudrücken.

a) Look at how Juan answers Taylor.

Taylor: Is it true?

Juan: I'm not sure. I'll look it up.

b) Decide what to do in these situations:

- you don't know an English word *I'll …*
- you lose your friend's book *I'll …*
- somebody knocks on the door
- something falls onto the floor

Die S können **spontane Entscheidungen und Pläne** mithilfe von ***will-future*** oder ***present progressive*** ausdrücken.

YT Looking at language

Plans and decisions

a) You already know how to use the *going to*-future to talk about plans and decisions that somebody has already made: *Olivia is going to do more work on her test.*

You also know the present progressive for talking about appointments (diary future): *Is Olivia meeting her friends this weekend?*

b) If you announce a decision as you make it (spontaneous decision), you use the *will*-future.

Look at these two sentences from p. 69. Say which one is a spontaneous decision.
In the long term they'll remember what they learned. (l. 26)
Hey, why don't you come again tomorrow. I'll show you how we do it. (l. 28) spontaneous decision

Say what tense is usually used in German for spontaneous decisions. present tense ➔ *GF 1.5: The future (pp. 166–168)*

YT 1 I'll help you (Spontaneous decisions: *will*-future)

a) Complete B's reactions to A. Use I'll … or I won't … in each sentence.

	A:	B:
1	I can't do this exercise. I don't understand it.	Just a moment. I'll help you if I can.
2	Would you like something hot to drink?	Yes, please. I'll have … a hot chocolate/cup of tea/…
3	Don't forget it's your grandma's birthday tomorrow.	Don't worry, … I won't forget/I'll remember/…
4	The dog's barking. He wants to come back inside.	OK, … I'll let him in/open the door/…
5	I can't have lost my phone. I had it a minute ago.	What's your number? … I'll call your phone/…
6	No, you can't use my bike. You always give it back dirty.	Please, I promise … I'll clean it/I'll be careful/…
7	We're going into town. Are you coming with us?	No, thanks. I … 'll take a nap/I'll do my homework/…
8	Can you keep this money in a safe place for me, please?	Of course. … I'll take care of it/…

b) Check each other's sentences. Suggest improvements if necessary.

YT 2 Maybe I'll go as a ghost (Spontaneous *will* or *going to*)

Choose the correct future form to complete the dialogues: will or going to.

A: Are you going to Jan's Halloween party?
B: Yes, I … (dress) up as a pirate. And you? I'm going to dress up
What … you … (dress) up as? are … going to dress up
A: I'm not sure. Maybe I … (go) as a ghost. I'll go

A: Do you have plans for the weekend?
B: Yes. I … (play) my new computer game. I'm going to play
Do you want to play too?
A: Uh … I'm not sure. I … (let) you know later. I'll let

A: It's much too hot in here.
B: Is it? OK, I … (open) a window. I'll open
A: But it's so loud outside.
B: OK, if you prefer, I … (not open) it. I won't open

A: Can I borrow your good camera?
B: Sure, I … (give) it to you tomorrow. What do you need it for? I'll give
A: I have to take photos for a project I … (do). I'm going to do

 ➔ Workbook 9–10 (pp. 33–34)

3 Text messages (Spontaneous *will* or present progressive)

Read the text messages and use the notes below to write a reply to each one. Use the *will*-future or the present progressive for the coloured verbs.

Mit Hilfe von **KV 12A/B: Future tenses** wiederholen oder vertiefen die S die Verwendung der Zeiten des Futurs.

1 Hey! What's up? Can we meet this evening?
Sorry • play football • phone you • weekend
Sorry mate, but I'm playing ...

2 How's it going? What are you doing in the holidays?
OK • visit uncle New York • send card when there

3 Hi. We need someone to feed the cat this weekend. Do you think Jack could do it?
not sure • I ask • but think he go • London

4 My computer isn't working – again! Can you help me please?
OK I have a look • not do anything else this evening

1 … football tonight. I'll phone you at the weekend. • 2 I'm OK, thanks. I'm visiting my uncle in New York. I'll send a card when I'm there. • 3 I'm not sure. I'll ask him but I think he's going to London. • 4 OK, I'll have a look. I'm not doing anything else this evening.

More help ➜ p. 119 Early finisher ➜ p. 126

More help: Die S müssen die Sätze nur vervollständigen.
Early finisher: Buchstabenrätsel

YT 4 Youth competitions

Die S können einem deutschen Text Informationen zu Jugendwettbewerben entnehmen und sie auf Englisch wiedergeben.

You are at an international summer school. You have been asked some questions about competitions for young people in Germany. The information you should give is about

- why the competitions take place
- who can take part
- the topics on which the young people can focus
- what successful competitors can win

a) Partner A: Go to p. 131 and take notes.
Partner B: Go to p. 135 and take notes.

b) Use your notes to tell your partner what you found out about the four points above.

Two prize winners at *Jugend forscht*

Alternative: Diese Aufgabe kann auch schriftlich durchgeführt werden, indem die S aus den gesammelten Informationen kurze Informationstexte verfassen.

5 EXTRA Have your hair cut … (*have something done*)

Why don't you have your hair cut …

… and clean your shoes!

a The woman says "Clean your shoes", but not "Cut your hair". Explain why.

b) Say what you or your family would usually do in these situations.

- Your hair is too long.
  I always have my hair cut. I'd never cut it myself. I wouldn't be able to do a good job.
- Your bike/phone/TV is broken.
- You need a new key / a passport photo.
- Your bedroom/kitchen needs painting.

a) I can clean my shoes myself, but I can't cut my own hair. So, if I have something done, that means I get somebody else to do that for me.

More help ➜ p. 119

More help: Es sind Satzteile vorgegeben.

➜ Workbook 11–13 (pp. 34–35)

Die S können eine **Internetrecherche** durchführen, bei der sie die besten Suchresultate auswählen, die Information sichern und die Zuverlässigkeit von Quellen überprüfen.

YT 6 Study skills: Internet research

You need to find out about UK national science competitions similar to Germany's *Jugend forscht*. On this page you focus on three internet skills that will help you to get information you need.

1 SEARCHING FOR A TOPIC

- An internet search can bring thousands of results. So try to limit your results to relevant websites.

a) Explain in what way the search engine settings in A will limit your results.

b) Assess the three searches in B. How effective are the keywords for your topic?

c) Write down three tips for effective searching.

SF 28: Internet research (p. 158)

A

Sprache:	**Englisch**
Land:	**Vereinigtes Königreich**

B

- science competitions
- national school science competitions UK
- competition like Jugend forscht

2 CHOOSING THE BEST SEARCH RESULTS

- When you search, you get a list of site descriptions. Read site descriptions carefully before opening a site. Even good keywords do not always produce the results you need.

d) Compare the top two site descriptions from your search. Say which site you would click first, and why.

Competitions - SchoolScience.co.uk
www.schoolscience.co.uk/competitions ▾ Diese Seite übersetzen
The National Women in Engineering Day is taking place again on 23 June 2016 ... The competition aims to: Encourage an interest in biology beyond the school ...

National Science + Engineering Competition
www.nsecuk.org/ ▾ Diese Seite übersetzen
The National Science + Engineering Competition is open to all 11-18-year-olds living in the UK and in full-time education. The Competition aims to recognise ...

- When you open a website, skim the first page to check that it has the information you need.
  SF 1: Skimming and scanning (p. 137)
- Check where information comes from before you decide to use it.

e) Say where you would click to check who is behind the website you're using.

NEWS | GET STARTED | HOW TO ENTER | PRIZES | SUCCESS STORIES | ABOUT US

f) Suggest other ways to check if a website is reliable.

SF 28: Internet research (p. 158)

3 SAVING INFORMATION YOU FIND

- Finding information can take time. So add websites to your bookmarks if you wish to use them.

TIP
Saving a website will also make it easier for you to name your sources when you write a text.
If you use information from a website, always give the URL at the end of your text.
When you write a text using information from the internet, always use your own words unless you want to quote something. When you quote, use quotation marks ("…") and give the URL.

1 Bruce Lee played badminton too

Die S können einen *film still* nutzen, um vorab Vermutungen zum Inhalt einer Szene anzustellen. Sie können die Aussage und Charaktere eines Films beschreiben.

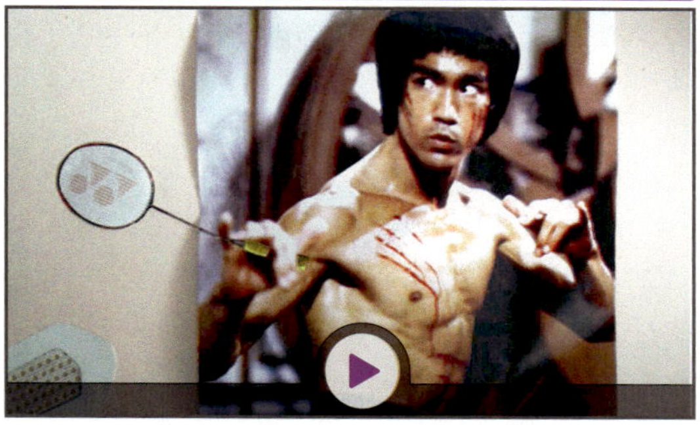

a) Form a buzz group. In two minutes, describe the poster in the still on the right and say what you think its message is. Refer to

- the man's appearance
- the expression on his face
- the different sports that are shown

Now say what you think the film might be about.

I think the film is probably about …

I'm not sure if I agree. In my view, …

b) Watch the first 60 seconds of the film (Part 1). Describe the characters and say what happens. Then compare the still on the right with the poster in a). What do they have in common?

Länge: 01:24

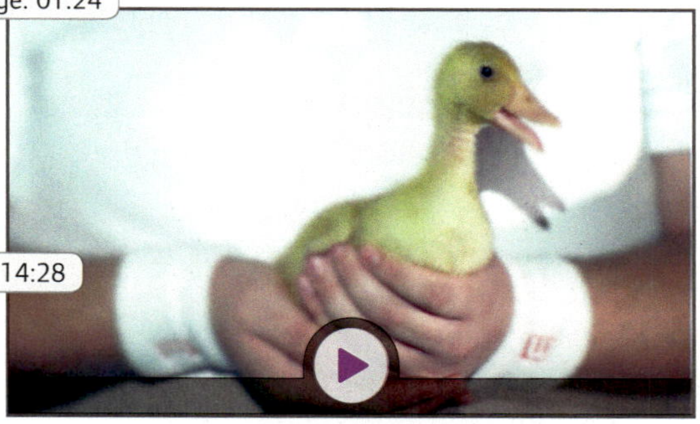

c) Watch the rest of the film (Part 2). Explain what Nic's goals are and if he achieves them.

Gesamtlänge: 14:28

d) Which of Nic's parents gave this advice?

- *Sometimes you're just not good enough.* his father
- *Being a champion – it's not about being the best in the game.* his mother

Say which piece of advice you think was more helpful to Nic. Give reasons.

Alternative: Der zweite Teil von ***d)*** kann auch als kurzer schriftlicher Kommentar in HA erledigt werden.

2 Making the film: Setting and effects

Die S befassen sich mit ***setting* und *effects* als filmischen Stilmitteln** und erläutern deren unterschiedliche Wirkungen.

a) Watch the two different scenes again and describe what happens.

b) Say what the film-maker does differently. Refer to

- the setting
- the use of light
- the use of sound and music

Explain what effect these differences have.

EXTRA Watch Nic's two matches again. Each student concentrates on one aspect:

- editing and cuts
- close-ups
- body language and gestures

Describe the effect of the aspect you focused on.

Die S können einen **Lebenslauf (CV)** auf Englisch verfassen.

YT 1 Volunteer

a) Say what kind of work you think volunteers might be able to do in each of these contexts.

British mascot race

A historical cemetery

b) Read the two job adverts and say which one interests you more. Give reasons.

Mascot marathon volunteer

If you're good at sewing, this may be the volunteer job you're looking for.
The Hathaway Sports Charity organizes one of Lancashire's biggest attractions: the Morecambe Mascot Marathon which takes place every year. For this major event, we are looking for a mascot "doctor". You will be responsible for repairing any costumes that get torn before or during the marathon. You will need to be good with people, creative and able to work well under pressure. Over 90 mascots will be competing in this year's event and relying on the services of our volunteer doctor. If you're interested, contact Sue Hancock at our Morecambe office.

Become a gravestone cleaner

Pollution and weather are damaging Britain's historical cemeteries, where gravestones can be over a thousand years old. The Historical Cemeteries Trust is looking for volunteers to clean and restore gravestones in a number of cemeteries in the South West. Some volunteers will work in teams, while others may work alone on single gravestones with the help of an expert. No experience is necessary, but volunteers must take a training course to learn how to clean gravestones without damaging them.
Applicants should be fit and ready to work outside in all weather. If you think this is a job for you, please contact Brian Hill.

YT 2 Your CV in English

a) Daniel Koch wants to volunteer while spending his summer holidays in the UK. Look at his CV on p. 73 and say which position he should apply for. Give reasons.

b) You want to apply for one of these two jobs. Write your CV in English. Read the *Access to cultures* box and use Daniel's CV as a model.

c) Swap CVs and use the tips to give each other feedback.
Think about the information your partner has given and say which job they're interested in.

Access to cultures
Writing a CV in English

When you write a CV, remember that the same information may not be expected in every country. If you apply for a job in the UK,

- stress your relevant strengths and interests in a personal statement
- suggest why you are the right candidate
- list dates in reverse order (i.e. with the latest date at the top)
- do not include a photo or give personal information (e.g. married or single)

It is also helpful to explain German terms like *Abitur*. And check your CV carefully and have it proofread by a good English speaker.

YT 3 Daniel's CV

Examine Daniel's CV. Say what is similar to, or different from, a German CV.

CURRICULUM VITAE
Daniel Koch

Muellerstrasse 70, 70178 Stuttgart, Germany
Telephone: +49 (0) 711 287 560 95 Mobile: +49 (0) 172 786 0xxx
Email: danko55@gmx.de

Personal statement
I have always loved working with other people, in team projects at school or volunteer projects in my neighbourhood. I like to give 100 percent of my energy to the project.

My favourite subjects are history and art and I have always looked for ways to increase my knowledge in these two areas.

Education

2010 to date	Karls-Gymnasium, Stuttgart (secondary school)
2006-2010	Römerschule Stuttgart (primary school)

Qualifications/Skills

Felt craft	Successful completion of felt craft course at the Volkshochschule (evening classes)
IT Skills	Good knowledge of MS Word, PowerPoint, Excel and Adobe Photoshop
Languages	German native speaker; good spoken and written English; some Latin

Work experience

2016 to date	Photographer for school yearbook
May 2015	Placement: two weeks working at Roman ruins with Mainhardt Walking Tours
2014 to date	Volunteer work: once a month park clean-up

Hobbies and interests
Felt craft; member of school photography club; I play volleyball in an after-school club; I make short videos of sport events.

➔ Workbook 14 (p. 35)

Die S können auf Englisch eine **Bewerbung für einen Job** schreiben und dabei auf angemessenen Inhalt und Stil achten.

YT 1 Writing a letter of application

KV 13: A letter of application erleichtert den S die Bearbeitung der Aufgabe.

a) Daniel is applying for the job as mascot doctor.
Look at the letter layout (1–8) and choose the best modules (a-y) for each point.

1a, d · 2f · 3h · 4i · 5l · 6o, q, r · 7v · 8w

Letter layout:

1. Your address
2. Name and address of the person/organization you're writing to
3. Heading: what the letter is about
4. Date
5. Start. *Dear …*
6. Main body of letter
   Paragraph 1: Say why you are writing.
   Paragraph 2: Describe your qualifications.
7. Conclusion
8. °Finish

(a) Muellerstrasse 70
(b) Müllerstraße 70
(c) 70178 Stuttgart BRD
(d) 70178 Stuttgart Germany

(e) Hathaway Health Charity, 25 Wise Street, Morecambe, UK
(f) Ms Sue Hancock, Hathaway Health Charity, 25 Wise Street, Morecambe LA4 5HX, United Kingdom

(g) **Your advert**
(h) **Volunteer mascot doctor**

(i) 20th February 2016
(j) Feb 20, 2016

5
(k) Hi Sue
(l) Dear Ms Hancock,
(m) Dear Sir or Madam,

6
(n) Hey great, I found this °ad on the internet, and I love fun activities. That's why I want to work for you this summer.
(o) I am writing about your advert of 13th January on the internet. I would love to volunteer as a mascot doctor this summer.
(p) I'm writing about the mascot job in Morecambe. I'll be in England this summer so I could easily do it.

(q) As you can see from my CV, one of my hobbies is felt craft, which I have also done a course in. This experience will help me to repair the mascot costumes. I am a good team player and I always try to give my best.
(r) I am 16 years old and have a good °level of English, so communication should not be a problem. One of my favourite subjects is art. I feel I have the °artistic skills to be a good mascot doctor. I have a younger brother who also likes art.
(s) I've included my CV so you'll be able to see everything I can do. I'm one of the best in my class at English, so language really won't be a problem. I love working in teams and I'm sure I'll get on with everyone.

7
(t) It would be great if you choose me for the job. Please let me know.
(u) Please let me know as soon as possible if I get the job.
(v) Thank you for °considering my application. I am looking forward to hearing from you.

8
(w) °Yours sincerely, Daniel Koch
(x) Bye, see you this summer. °Yours, Alex
(y) Your Daniel Koch

b) Compare and explain your answers.
Refer to both content and style.
Using a placemat, make a list of tips on how to write a good letter of application.

c) Go to p. 131 and choose a summer job.
Then write your own letter of application.

Early finisher → p. 127

Early finisher: Die S beschäftigen sich mit Korrekturen in einem Bewerbungsschreiben.

YT 2 Check your spelling

a) Copy the table and add the words from the box.

same spelling	different spelling	difference
argument	address	Adresse
...		

Adresse · akzeptieren · Architekt · Argument · Autor · britisch · Broschüre · Computer · Dezember · diskutieren · emotional · exakt · Figur · Film · Fotografie · Galerie · Industrie · Meter · national · negativ · Problem · Produkt · Prozent · separat · Situation · sozial · speziell · Struktur · Symbol · Szene · Temperatur · Telefon · Tipp

TIP
Some words are spelled the same in German and English:
e.g. *Information – information*
Some words are similar, but have small spelling differences:
e.g. *Musik – music*

It's easy to make spelling mistakes with words like these, so when you're checking a text, pay special attention to words that are similar in both languages.

b) Compare your tables. Examine the differences between English and German and say what patterns you see. a) same spelling: argument, computer, emotional, film, meter (AE), national, problem, situation, symbol · different spelling: address, accept, architect, author, British, brochure, December, discuss, exact, figure, photography, gallery, industry, metre (BE), negative, product, percent, separate, social, special, structure, scene, temperature, telephone, tip (Unterschiede sind in der Box unterstrichen)

Early finisher → p. 127
Early finisher: Worträtsel

3 Voice messages (Words that sound the same)

25

a) Look at the words below. For each one, you know another word that sounds the same but is spelled differently. Write it down.

1	guest	guessed	6	piece	peace
2	knew	new	7	here	hear
3	key	quay	8	nose	knows
4	weather	whether	9	meet	meat
5	right	write	10	hole	whole

LISTENING TIP
Different words often sound the same, e.g. *aloud* and *allowed*, *side* and *sighed*. So a sound you hear *can* make you think of more than one word.

If something you hear doesn't °make sense, ask yourself if you've matched a sound to the "wrong" word.

b) Listen to ten voice messages. Each one contains *either* the word from a) *or* the alternative. Write down the word that goes with the message.
1 guessed · 2 knew · 3 quay · 4 whether · 5 right · 6 peace · 7 here · 8 knows · 9 meet · 10 whole

Die S können einer Aufzeichnung eines **Job-Interviews** wichtige Informationen entnehmen.

YT 4 Phoning to make an appointment

26

a) Alicia Jessop has applied for a summer job in the design department of a fashion company. She gets a letter asking her to make an appointment. Listen and find out:
- the date and time of the interview
- where the interview will take place
- who Alicia should ask for when she arrives
- if she needs to take anything to the interview

Date: Wednesday, 15th June · Time: 4.30 pm · Place: 3 Molyneux Street · Who: Matt Irving, Personal Assistant · What: nothing

b) Say who used these phrases, and at what point in the telephone conversation. Then listen again and check.
- *Could I ask you to spell that?*
- *Could you °put me through to …?*
- *Is there anything else I can help you with?*
- *How can I help you?*
- *Hold on, please.*
- *Just one more thing.*
- *Sorry, °I didn't catch that.*

c) Prepare and act out a short conversation in which someone phones to arrange a job interview. Use phrases from b). Swap roles.

b) 1 Alicia, when she noted down the street name · 2 Alicia, when a man at Fashion Friends picked up · 3 Lilly Ellis, after they had talked about the details of the interview, i.e. place and time · 4 the man who picked up the phone at the beginning of the call · 5 the man before he tried to put Alicia through to Ms Ellis · 6 Alicia, towards the end of the call · 7 Alicia, when she didn't understand the assistant's name

→ Workbook 17–19 (pp. 37–38)

Die S können ein **Bewerbungsgespräch** durchführen und dabei sowohl die Rolle des Interviewers als die des Bewerbers einnehmen.

YT A job interview

On this page, you will practise getting ready for, and taking part in, a job interview.

Möglicher Einstieg: In einem *Brainstorming* sammeln die S an der Tafel typische Fragen, die in einem Bewerbungsgespräch gestellt werden können.

STEP 1 °Evaluate an interview

a) Watch a job interview and take notes on
- the applicant's clothes
- his body language
- the way he answers questions
- his interaction with the interviewer

b) Say what impression you think the student made, and what you think he could do better.

STEP 2 Think of tips

You'll give a better interview if you remember the 4 Ps: Prepare – Practise – Present – °Participate.
Think of more tips for each of the 4 Ps and make lists.

Before the interview
- PREPARE
  - 1: Find out what you can about the job and °employer.
  - 2: ...
- PRACTISE
  - 1: Think of possible questions and answer them aloud.

At the interview
- PRESENT
  - 1: Think about the right clothes for the occasion.
- PARTICIPATE
  - 1: Introduce yourself at the beginning.

More help → p. 119

More help: Als Hilfe sind mehr Ideen vorgegeben.

STEP 3 Prepare

Think of a job you'd like to apply for. Then read the questions below. Decide
- what information you might need about the job you're applying for
- what answers you will give

Personal questions	Questions about you and the job
• Tell me about yourself.	• Why should we °hire you?
• What are your strengths/°weaknesses?	• What can you do that other candidates can't?
• What are your goals?	• Why do you want this job?
• Where do you see yourself five years °from now?	• Do you have any questions about the job?

STEP 4 Practise

a) Partner A: You are the interviewer. Decide what questions you are going to ask.
Partner B: You are the applicant. Read your tips from Step 2 and think about what you'll say.

b) Now practise. You may need language to …
- start your answers: *Well, I'm 16 years old and …* • *Actually, one of my main strengths is …*
- explain what you mean: *What I mean is …* • *What I'm really trying to say is …*
- move to another point: *Another point I should °mention is …* • *There's something else I'd like to say.*
- show you are following the other person: *I see.* • *Right.* • *Uhuh.*
- show you don't understand something: *Sorry, I don't quite understand.* • *Sorry, but do you mean …*

c) Swap roles.

Mit Hilfe von **KV 14: A job interview: assessment** können die S das Bewerbungsgespräch evaluieren.

Workbook Checkpoint 3 (pp. 40–43)

 → Workbook 20–21 (p. 39)

Your task

Die komplette Lernaufgabe sollte im Unterricht durchgeführt werden.

Mit Hilfe von **KV 14: A job interview: assessment** können die S das Bewerbungsgespräch evaluieren.

Role-play: Applying for a volunteer job

Work in groups of six. Three students will play an applicant. Three will play an interviewer.

Applicants	Interviewers
STEP 1: The application	
a) Read the advert. Invent a character who is suitable for the job. Think of their name, address, school etc., and about their interests, skills and experience.	a) Read the advert. Brainstorm the qualities, skills and experience that the successful applicant will need.

Park and aquarium volunteers
Aquariums accept volunteers as office helpers to clean the park. We also encourage volunteers to do more unusual jobs. For example, volunteers work at the aquarium to feed the fish and clean the tanks and habitats. We also allow older volunteers with dive training to swim with the fish, examine them for injuries, just to play with them from time to time.

Applicants	Interviewers
b) Together, write one CV for your character. Make a copy for each member of the group. ➜ pp. 74–75	b) Agree on criteria for choosing the right candidate. Make a checklist.
c) Alone, each member of the group should write their own letter of application for your character. Give a letter and CV to each interviewer. ➜ p. 77	c) Alone, each member of the group should think of their own questions to ask the candidates and write them down.
STEP 2: The interview	
d) Prepare for the interview. Imagine questions the interviewers might ask and practise answering them.	d) Discuss the CV and letters of application. Make notes on what you think is interesting, well done or less well done.
e) Take turns to go to the three interviewers for your interview.	e) Interview the applicants. All three interviewers should ask each applicant questions and take notes.
STEP 3: Evaluation	
f) Note down what you did well. Discuss how you could improve your performance.	f) Discuss the interviews. Use your checklists and notes to decide who should get the job.
g) Join up with the interviewers. Together, say what you have learned from the task.	g) Join up with the applicants. Together, say what you have learned from the task.

dive [daɪv] tauchen **encourage** [ɪn'kʌrɪdʒ] ermutigen **suitable** ['suːtəbl] geeignet

Mit **KV 9** können die S diese Unit wieder evaluieren.

Titus and Sym (from the novel *The White Darkness* by Geraldine McCaughrean)

a) Read these quotations and put them into your own words. Say which one you like better and why.

- "Your mind can be either your prison or your palace. What you make it is yours to decide." *Bernard Kelvin Clive*
- "When reality is a prison, your mind can set you free." *Zack Snyder*

b) Now look at these quotations from the excerpt below. Speculate on what the story might be about.

- "It's true that none of my teachers knows much about Antarctica."
- "The day I came to school and said my dad had died, I heard Maxine say to Nats, "Don't worry. I expect she just *imagined* it."
- "I was powerless to rewrite the past—to change the outcome of the story; …"

Chapter One "Titus"

I have been in love with Titus Oates for quite a while now—which is ridiculous, since he's been dead for ninety years. But look at it this way. In ninety years I'll be dead, too, and then the age difference won't matter.

Besides, he isn't dead inside my head. We talk about all kinds of things. From whether hair colour can change spontaneously to whether friends are better than family, and the best age for marrying: 14 or 125. Generally speaking, he knows more than I do, but on that particular subject we are even. He wasn't married—at least, he wasn't when he died, which must have substantially cut down his chances.

Uncle Victor says I shouldn't marry at all. Uncle Victor knows about these things and he says that "marriage is a bourgeois relic of Victorian sentimentality". That suits me. No one would match up to Titus. And we have a kind of understanding, Titus and I.

Uncle Victor is marvellous: he's done so much for us—for Mum and me, I mean. And anyway, he's just so clever. Uncle Victor knows a fantastic amount. He knows at what temperature glass turns to liquid, and where Communism went wrong and how the Clifton Suspension Bridge was built and just what the Government ought to be doing: you can't fault him. He's read books about everything: history, geography, politics, astrology, animals … The Fount of All Knowledge, Dad used to call him.

I would get stuck doing my homework, and Dad would say, "Ask the Fount of All Knowledge." And I'd telephone Victor and he would tell me.

either … or … entweder … oder … **speculate** spekulieren **outcome** Ausgang **even** gleich(auf), ausgeglichen **a bourgeois relic of Victorian sentimentality** ein bürgerliches Relikt viktorianischer Sentimentalität **suit sb.** jm. recht sein, jm. passen **fault sb.** etwas an jm. auszusetzen haben; Fehler an jm. finden **fount** Quelle

Quite often he knew more than the teachers, so they'd think I'd got my homework wrong, but as Victor says, "What teachers don't understand is that the body of learning is still growing. They reckon it stopped the day they came out of college. That, or they're bog ignorant. Lot of ignorance in yon schools."

It's true that none of my teachers knows much about Antarctica. When Dad and Victor and I went to Iceland, one of the teachers had been, too, and knew all about Dettifoss and the hot springs and people having stinking saunas in their back gardens. But none of the teachers at school has been to Antarctica. Some of them know about Scott of the Antarctic going to the South Pole and not coming back. But they mostly mean John Mills in the movie. I don't.

In the general way of things, I don't know much about anything. Uncle Victor says I'm "the victim of a shoddy education system'. But I do know about the Polar Regions. The bookshelves over my bed are full of books about the North and South Poles. Ice-bound almost. A glacial cliff-face teetering over my bed. I remember: the night after Dad had been rushed into hospital, one of the shelves sheared off and crashed down on me. I woke up thinking the house was collapsing—books gouging at my head, bouncing off the bed-frame, slapping flat on the floor. I looked at the hole in the wall and the rawlplugs on the pillow and I didn't know what to do.

About the shelf. About anything.

So I went back to sleep, and dreamt I was sailing towards the Ross Ice Barrier, and that crags were splitting off its face, plunging down, massive as sea-going liners foundering.

...

If we ever did a project at school on Antarctica, I could shine. Like Mount Erebus in midsummer, I could, I could shine!

Except that I don't think I would choose to. It's all bound up with Titus, and I know better than to mention Titus at school. I do now, anyway. I made that mistake once. I won't do it again.

"Symone has a pretend friend! Symone has a pretend friend!"

It was the conversation about snogging. Like the ant nest in the larder: you think you've done everything to be rid of it—that it can't possibly come back again—but there it is: "How many boys have you snogged?" There is no right answer. You say "None" and you're sad and frigid or they know someone whose brother would be willing to snog you for a quid. You refuse to answer and you are sadder still—or hiding something, or prefer girls, or ... It's not that they care; they only want to tell you how many they've snogged—chiefly because they like saying the word. It makes them feel as if they are wearing red underwear. But on and on they go: "How many boys, Sym? How many boys have you snogged?"

Why is it that all the words to do with sex are ugly? Words to do with love aren't. No wonder Titus thought women were a nuisance. No wonder he died without ever ... getting mixed up with all that.

Anyway, I said that I could do without it. (At least that's what I tried to say. I don't explain things very well out loud.) I tried to say that I was happy to stick with imagining for the time being, thanks all the same. Later, maybe. If I ever met anyone who could compare with Titus ...

And after that I was the mad girl—sad, frigid, and mad; all three—the retard who had an imaginary friend: "Like little kids do, oo-hoo. Like little kids do!"

The day I came into school and said my dad had died, I heard Maxine say to Nats, "Don't worry. I expect she just *imagined* it."

So that's when I sealed myself inside. Laced up the tent, so to speak. Filled the locks with water so that they would freeze. That's when Titus and I looked at one another and decided we could do without them, so long as we had each other. *"You and me now, Sym."*

"You and me now, Titus."

...

spring Quelle **victim** Opfer **shoddy** schäbig, lausig **ice-bound** im Eis gefangen **a glacial cliff-face** eine eisige Klippenwand **teeter** schwanken, wanken **rawlplug** Dübel **pillow** (Kopf-)Kissen **crag** Fels **liner** Schiff, Dampfer **founder** *(fml)* sinken **mention** erwähnen **snog** knutschen, schmusen **larder** Speisekammer, Vorratsschrank **be rid of sth.** etwas los sein **quid** *(infml)* Pfund (£) **underwear** Unterwäsche **ugly** hässlich **nuisance** Ärgernis **retard** Vollidiot/in **seal** versiegeln, verriegeln **lace up** zuschnüren **lock** Schloss

Chapter Two Freeze Frame

I remember the day Titus arrived in my head—not when I first heard of him, I don't mean, but the day he arrived, like some distant cousin you've heard tell of but who suddenly comes to visit. I remember. Uncle Victor had given me the box-set DVDs for my birthday: The Last Place on Earth—an old TV series made before I was born.

I had the house to myself, because Dad was bad in hospital and Mum had gone to see him. So I plugged the DVD player into the TV, turned the sound right up and I sat down and I watched all the episodes straight off, one after another—six hours—the cellophane wrapping still scrunched up in my hand, my breakfast bowl on the table.

I knew this story—thought it held no surprises for me. But I was seeing people that I'd read about, so already I felt I knew them. I was like one of those relatives on the dockside waving the men goodbye, minding about whether or not they came home again.

And then it came real.

I watched so intently—concentrated so hard that there was no sofa, and no screen, no chime from the clock, no traffic outside, no whine from the fridge or thump from the central heating. And it came real. So real. So real. So real. So real. So real.

When one disc came to an end, I suppose I must have put in another, but I don't remember doing it. I knew this story: it shouldn't have held any surprises for me. Five men trekked to the South Pole. A Norwegian expedition made it ahead of them, so they didn't even have the joy of being first. And then they didn't quite get home.

If he had been there, Dad would have said, "What do we want to watch this for? We know how it turns out."

Mum would have said, "I wonder where they filmed it? Wasn't he in something else?"

Even Uncle Victor would have spotted an inaccuracy in somebody's cap badge or the rigging on the *Terra Nova*.

But me, I didn't think anything. I let it soak into me like water into salt, until I was invisible, absorbed. It blew me away. That's what people say, isn't it? It blew me away—like wind ripping a tent loose of its guy-ropes, or the blizzard submerging a man in powdery, edgeless Death.

And there, at the heart of it, was Captain Oates: so sublimely beautiful that his image passed clean through my retina and scorched itself on my brain. And his voice flowed into me, so sensuous that I was wading across the River Jordan, up to my ears and deeper in milk and honey, towards Paradise on the other side. He was perfect—as I've always known he would be if ever the blurred photographs, the expedition portraits, were to come to life. Like everything perfect, he set up a ferocious pain inside me—a flickering, griping sort of pain, because nothing so marvellous is ever within reach, is it? Nothing so beautiful can ever last. I was powerless to rewrite the past—to change the outcome of the story; to save Oates from dying—in the film—in real life ... The DVD-player grew hotter and hotter in my lap, so that after Oates got up, and went outside into the blizzard, and crawled away into the snow to die, his body warmth was still there in my lap, slow to cool. He lingered in my lap.

And then the phone rang.

And it was Mum to say that Dad had died.

I thought there was really bad static on the line, but it was only the cellophane clenched in my hand, crackling by the receiver. And all I could say was "Oh', because it had been on the cards for weeks. I had been half-expecting the call all day. The news held no surprise for me.

And besides, Dad never liked me.

freeze frame Standbild **wrapping** Verpackung **relative** Angehörige(r) **dockside** Kai **make it ahead of sb.** es vor jm. schaffen **joy** Freude **how it turns out** wie es ausgeht **inaccuracy** Ungenauigkeit **badge** Abzeichen **rigging** Takelage **invisible** unsichtbar **guy-rope** Zeltschnur, Abspannseil **blizzard** Schneesturm **submerge** bedecken, versenken **sublimely** außergewöhnlich **retina** Netzhaut **sensuous** sinnlich **a ferocious pain** ein heftiger Schmerz **marvellous** wundervoll **within reach** erreichbar **last** (an)dauern **lap** Schoß **linger** (ver)weilen; nachklingen **static** Rauschen **line** Leitung **receiver** (Telefon-)Hörer **be on the cards** zu erwarten sein **besides** außerdem

In the *Oberstufe*, you will be asked to interpret ***fictional texts***. These include *novels*, like *The White Darkness*, as well as *short stories, poems*, and *plays*.
As with ***non-fictional*** and ***image-based texts*** (➜ *pp. 32–33, 56–57*) there are three important steps:
comprehension You state what the text is about.
analysis You study how the text is written and what effect that has on the reader.
comment You react to the text with a personal comment or with a creative text.

STEP 1 Comprehension

Task: Summarize the excerpt of the novel.

KV 5 bietet den S eine Checklist zu ***Writing a summary***.

➜ *SF 8: Writing a summary (p. 141)*

STEP 2 Analysis

Task: Analyse how the author tries to create interest in the story.

a) Look at these narrative techniques. Say if they were used in the excerpt you read. Give examples.
foreshadowing: The author gives a clue about something that will happen, but doesn't go into detail.
flashback: The story goes back in time.
narrative gap: The author leaves out a key event.
cliffhanger: The author creates a situation so exciting, often at the end of a chapter, that the reader can't wait to continue reading.

b) **Discuss the effect which the passages you identified in a) had on you as a reader.**

c) **Now write a paragraph analysing the author's storytelling techniques.
You can use phrases from the table below.**

In the first few lines/... In lines ... On one occasion, ... On several occasions, ... As the chapter ends, ...	when Symone when the author ...	says ..., describes ..., refers to ..., ...	she it this ...	gives us a clue that ... makes us think that ... tells us something about ... makes us wonder if ... make us impatient to ... ...

By using this technique / these two/... techniques, Although there are no cliffhangers, ...	the author tries to .../wishes to ...

STEP 3 Comment

You may be asked to comment on how the **story** develops or on one of the **characters**.

You choose **a), b) or c)**

Neigungsdifferenzierung: Die S wählen zwischen unterschiedlichen Schreibaufgaben.

a) **Write about Symone's relationship with her uncle and his role in the story.**

b) **Relate one of the quotations from a) on p. 78 to the excerpt you've just read.**

c) **Imagine your are Symone. Write a diary entry in which you speak about your relationship with your classmates.**

comprehension Verständnis **create** schaffen, erzeugen **narrative technique** Erzähltechnik **foreshadowing** Vorausdeutung **flashback** Rückblende **gap** Lücke **chapter** Kapitel **on one occasion** bei einer Gelegenheit **relate ... to ...** einen Zusammenhang herstellen zwischen ... und ...

It's up to you

1

Taipei, Taiwan - The message reads: "Save the Antarctic. Young people rise up."

1 Collective action

a) Look at photos 1 and 2.
Describe what the people are doing and compare the settings for each action.

Then discuss
- what audience they want to reach
- what effect their action might have

b) Compare your ideas with another pair and then present them to your class.

2 A flashmob

Länge: 02:28

a) Try to define the term flashmob.
Then watch a video about the action in photo 2 and describe how it develops.

At first, there are a few cyclists standing on a pavement.

Then …

b) Say what impression the flashmob makes on you, and why you think it was put online.

c) Write a short text about the advantages and disadvantages of actions like this.

Zusatz: Hier kann wieder **KV 2: Giving feedback on a text** eingesetzt werden, wenn die S einander Rückmeldungen zu ihren Texten geben.

Die S können über **Protestaktionen** oder **Kampagnen** sprechen, schreiben und sie zusammen mit Dingen, die ihnen selbst wichtig sind, reflektieren.

Text File: zu Unit 4 passen **Text 5** und **6**.

2

Manchester, UK, Oxford Road

YT 3 Bringing about change

a) Make a list of issues you care about (local, national or global) and explain why they are important. Then agree on one issue you would like to take action on.

b) Look at the ideas in the box and discuss which action(s) you would take on your issue.

> make a poster
> start an initiative on social media
> start/sign a petition
> take part in a sit-in
> organize/go to a flashmob/demonstration/…
> go on a march · go on strike
> boycott a product/company …

c) Present your ideas to the class.

EXTRA Tell the class about any experience of collective action you have had (e.g. flashmob demonstration, protest, …).

Your task

At the end of this unit:
Give a short talk or presentation about an issue of public interest and explain your opinion about it.

→ Workbook 1 (p. 44)

Die S können Fotos und Videos von unterschiedlichen **Protestaktionen** (Installation, Street Art) beschreiben, ihre Aussage erläutern und ihre Wirkung reflektieren. Sie können in einem Text kritische Fragen (z.B. über Street Art und Graffiti) diskutieren.

YT 1 The Standing March, Paris 2015

Look at the pictures on pp. 84–85 and say what they all have in common. Give your first reaction (e.g. how they make you feel, questions you would like to ask, etc.).

November 2015: World leaders arrived in Paris for the United Nations COP 21 climate conference. The goal of the conference was to reach an agreement that would slow down global warming. As the conference was taking place, a huge video installation created by French artist JR and filmmaker Darren Aronofsky was projected on six public buildings. 500 people from all over the world had volunteered to be part of this installation called "The Standing March".

YT 2 Art and its message

a) Describe the video projections above and say what you think their message is.

b) Say if you would have taken part in the installation and explain why or why not.

EXTRA Say what images you would use in a video installation with a political message.

3 The street is a gallery

Read the text about the face and say what you think the artist's message is.

THE LAKOTA IN MANHATTAN

Just a few months ago, Layla Cohen was spending the afternoon in Upper East Side, Manhattan. She was walking along the High Line when all of a sudden she saw a huge face. "Who created this?" she wondered. "And why?"
Back home Layla checked the internet for information about the face she had just seen.
"I had been searching for less than a minute when I found the answer. The face was the work of a French street artist ... "

LISTEN ▶

Die S können ein aufgezeichnetes Interview verfolgen, sich Notizen machen und mit deren Hilfe Fragen auf Deutsch beantworten.

4 JR's projects

27

a) A German friend has asked you about the artist JR. Listen to the radio interview. Take notes to help you answer the questions.

Partner A: Your friend has asked you about JR's ideas on street art.
Partner B: Your friend has asked you about examples of New York projects involving JR.

b) Take turns to answer your friend's questions. Use German.

5 My ideas

Neigungsdifferenzierung: Die S wählen zwischen einer eher kreativen und einer eher argumentativen Aufgabe.

You choose a) or b).

a) My Book Take a photo to upload to the Inside Out project. Write a short text explaining where you would put the poster, and why.

b) My Book Write a short text and discuss one of these topics:
- Street art and graffiti make cities better
- The gallery, not the street, is the place for art

Zusatz: Hier kann wieder **KV 2: Giving feedback on a text** eingesetzt werden, wenn die S einander Rückmeldungen zu ihren Texten geben.

→ Workbook 2–3 (p. 45) Workbook Wordbank 6

Die S verwenden ***narrative tenses*** und ***linking words***.

4.2 · FöFo 4.2

Box "Narrative tenses", Voc, S. 220

Language help

a) To tell a story or to report on past actions or events, you use the narrative tenses. You already know the simple past (the tense most often used), the past progressive and the past perfect.
Say which tense the green verbs are in and match them to the explanations on the right.

Layla Cohen was spending the afternoon in Upper East Side. She was walking along the High Line when all of a sudden she saw a huge face. She jumped back.
Back home Layla checked the internet for information about the face she had just seen.

The ... tense is used to
- describe a finished action /event — simple past (saw, jumped, checked)
- describe an action/event in progress when another, shorter action happened — past progressive (was walking)
- set the scene or context for a story — past progressive (was returning)
- describe an action/event that happened earlier than another action/event — past perfect (had just seen)

b) For actions that were in progress before a point in the past, you need the past perfect progressive.
I had been searching for less than a minute when I found the answer.

➔ *GF 1.3: The past (pp. 164–165)*

1 REVISION A flashmob on the river (Simple past, past progressive or past perfect)

Put each verb in the correct form.

Last month, my older brother and I [1]... (decide) to spend a week in London. We [2]... (save) a lot of money, so we [3]... (choose) a really cool hostel near the London Eye. On our first day, we [4]... (walk) along the Thames when my brother [5]... (suggest) taking a boat tour down the river. A few minutes later we [6]... (sit) up on deck enjoying the fantastic views. Then all of a sudden I [7]... (see) hundreds of people dancing on the Millennium Bridge. Nearly all of them [8]... (hold) open umbrellas in their hands. It [9]... (be) an amazing sight! So I [10]... (pull) out my phone and [11]... (start) photographing them. By the time the dancers [12]... (disappear) from view, I [13]... (take) hundreds of photos.

1 decided · 2 saved · 3 chose · 4 were walking · 5 suggested · 6 were sitting · 7 saw · 8 were holding · 9 was · 10 pulled · 11 started · 12 disappeared · 13 had taken

YT 2 After the boat tour (Linking words)

Write a paragraph continuing the story of the trip to London.
Use your own ideas or the ideas below.
Show the sequence of events by using linking words.

- look for a restaurant
- visit the Tower of London
- take the Underground to ...
- go to a demonstration ...

After the boat tour was over, we ...

More help ➔ p. 120

More help: Es sind *linking words* in einer Box vorgegeben.

TIP
In a narrative, linking words like *First of all ..., Then ..., Next ..., Finally ..., By the time ..., All of a sudden ...* show the order of actions or events.

3 We had been walking for hours (Past perfect progressive or simple past)

Match the sentence halves. Decide which verb should be simple past, which past perfect progressive.

1 We had been walking (walk) for hours, so we
2 I ... (have) a sore throat because I
3 The grass ... (be) very wet because it
4 Dad ... (work) hard all year, so he really
5 Mum ... (have) mud on her shoes because she
6 I ... (train) for months so I

a ... (talk) for hours.
b ... (need) a holiday.
c ... (work) in the garden.
d decided (decide) to take a break.
e ... (feel) confident about the race.
f ... (rain) for days.

2a I had a sore throat because I had been talking for hours. · 3f The grass was very wet because it had been raining for days. · 4b Dad had been working hard all year, so he really needed a holiday. · 5c Mum had mud on her shoes because she had been working in the garden. · 6e I had been training for months so I felt confident about the race.

Early finisher ➔ p. 128

Early finisher: Rätsel

Die S können **Cartoons** beschreiben und interpretieren.

YT Interpreting images

**Photos, posters, adverts or cartoons often contain an important message.
You have practised *describing* images before. This page will also help you to *interpret* them.**

Partner A: Do steps 1–3 with cartoon A.

A

Gentlemen, it's time we gave some serious thought to the effects of global warming.

from the New Yorker

Partner B: Do steps 1–3 with cartoon B.

B

I'm starting to get concerned about global warming.

from the New Yorker

STEP 1 Describe

a) Start with a general description.

- In this cartoon you can see an office / a street scene / …
- This cartoon depicts a scene in …
- This is a black and white / colour drawing of …

b) Give the position of the main elements.

- In the foreground / … there's a group of people / men / … walking … / sitting …
- In the background / On the left / … you see …

c) Say what (you think) is happening.

- They're talking about … / discussing … / looking at …
- I think they're probably talking about / …
- It looks like they're talking about …
- They seem to be looking at …

d) Refer to captions, speech bubbles, etc.

- The caption reads "…"
- One of the characters / The person at the desk / … says / comments that …

STEP 2 Analyse

Say what you think the message is.

- The cartoon treats an environmental / a political / … issue.
- I think its message is …
- It focuses on the issue by showing a cactus … / water …

Early finisher → p. 128

Early finisher: Cartoon captions

STEP 3 Comment

Say if/why the cartoon is effective for you.

- It's effective because it's funny / dramatic / …
- What made me laugh / smile is the fact that …
- The message comes across well because …
- The message would come across better if …

Box "make sb. do sth. – let sb. do sth.", Voc, S. 220

EXTRA **Find an English-language cartoon about an important topic. Bring a copy to school. Describe and interpret your cartoons for each other. Then hang them up for a gallery walk.**

Die S können einen Text erschließen und die Hauptaussagen wiedergeben.
Sie können über **Ziele und Methoden einer Kampagne diskutieren**.

YT 1 Taking a stand

Skim the short articles and say what you think they are about.

A

Hackers in dolphin threat

The Tokyo Times reported yesterday that the hacker organization "Anonymous" had hacked a number of Japanese government websites including the prime minister's office and several ministries. The group told the Japanese government to stop the slaughter of dolphins immediately or they would face the group's anger. They said they would hack another 22 websites.
Every year about 18,000 dolphins are killed for their meat off the northern coast of Japan while in the Taiji cove around 2,000 are either killed or taken to aquariums.

Hacker organization Anonymous

B

Youth group fights for tougher laws

Following the death of 17-year-old Aaron Lewis in a fight between teenagers drinking in a local bar, a high school youth group in Glen Falls, Wisconsin, decided to oppose teenage drinking in their city. After learning that stores that sold alcohol to teens only lost their license after their third strike, the youth group said they would campaign for zero tolerance. "We want to increase fines on bar owners for selling alcohol to teenagers," Logan Schultz told us. The group attended a council meeting and presented their ideas. Councillor Amy Dorn said the students had given a great presentation. Although city bar owners and license holders denied selling alcohol to under-21s, the city council passed the new law. Stores that break the law can now get a $2000 fine and risk losing their license for 60 days.

Box "a campaign for/against", Voc, S. 221

Box "(to) pass", Voc, S. 221

High school campaigner Logan Schultz, Glen Falls, Wisconsin

YT 2 Their opinions, your opinions

KV 6 bietet ***discussion tickets*** – nützliche Redewendungen für eine Diskussion.

a) In groups of four, each partner reads one of the above articles and takes notes on:
- who has taken a stand
- their goals and how they try to achieve them

b) Use your notes to explain the key facts to your group. Answer any questions.

c) Discuss the goals and methods of the four campaigns.
- I like/agree with / disagree with ... because ...
- I'm not sure if I agree with ...
- In my view, the campaign goal is OK/..., but ...
- I think / don't think campaigners should ...
- It's all right/wrong/illegal/... to ...

C

Not equal yet

In a piece written for the Shriver Report, Beyoncé said people needed to stop buying into the myth about gender equality.
"It isn't a reality yet," she explained, pointing out that the average U.S. working woman earned only 77 percent of what the average man made. She said that if men and women accepted this situation, nothing would change. Men had to insist on more money for their wives, daughters, mothers and sisters – dependent on their qualifications and not on their gender. She argued that equality would only be a reality when men and women had equal pay and equal respect.

American singer-songwriter Beyoncé

C

Success for British teenagers' safety campaign?

Last September, 16-year-old Katie Butterworth from Harrogate was hit by a car while cycling to school. She wasn't hurt, but the accident made her realize the dangers cyclists face. Together with friends Simon O'Neill and Liza Faulkner, Katie started a campaign for a bike path along the route to their school. Students and teachers had a right to cycle safely, Katie insisted. But many were worried about using their bikes.
Katie, Simon and Liza did a survey at school, and asked students and teachers if they supported their bike path plan. Over 90 percent said yes. The three friends also started a petition and worked out how much the project would cost. They then asked local MP Susan Lewis if she could help.
Ms Lewis, who signed the petition, also contacted Harrogate council and asked when they were going to take action on cyclist safety. The council admitted that the cycling °infrastructure wasn't perfect and is to announce a solution soon. "We'll certainly consider the students' research," they told us.
Ms Lewis said the students had asked the right questions and refused to give up, and were an example to their community.

Harrogate schoolgirl Katie Butterworth

Box "(to) be to do sth.", Voc, S. 221

+consider doing sth.

3 Have a go

Die S verwenden vorbewusst die **indirekte Rede**.

Report what Katie said.

1 Everyone has a right to cycle safely.
2 Hundreds of students in Harrogate cycle every day.
3 Over 90 percent of students and teachers support our idea.
4 Your local MP can help you a lot.
5 It's great that the council wants to use our research.

1 Katie said that everyone had a right … to cycle safely. • 2 Katie said hundreds of students in Harrogate cycled every day. • 3 Katie said over 90 per cent of students and teachers supported their idea. • 4 Katie said their local MP could help them a lot. • 5 Katie said it was great that the council wanted to use their research.

Die S üben und verwenden die **indirekte Rede**.

Looking at language

a) Read the direct statements and questions below. Then complete the indirect sentences. You can find the indirect sentences in texts B and D on pp. 88–89.

Direct	Indirect
"We'll campaign for zero tolerance."	The youth group said they ...
"The students gave a great presentation."	Councillor Amy Dorn said ...
"Do you support our bike path idea?"	They asked students and teachers if ...
"Can you help?"	Then they asked their local MP if ...
"When are you going to take action on cyclist safety?"	They asked the council when ...

b) Compare the verbs in direct and indirect speech. Describe what changes.

➜ *GF 7: Indirect speech (pp. 180–182)*

YT 1 My questions for an interview (Indirect speech: Questions)

You interviewed your local councillor on his position on cycling. Use indirect speech to report the questions you asked.

1 Are you planning to build more cycle paths?
I asked my councillor if they were ...
2 When will the council make more parking spaces for cyclists?
3 Are you for or against a law on cycle helmets?
4 Will you make it legal to cycle in the pedestrian zone?
5 Should children be allowed to cycle on pavements?
6 How much money has the council spent on cycling infrastructure this year?
7 Are you going to talk about cycling at the next council meeting?

1 … planning to build more cycle paths. • 2 I asked him if the council would make more parking spaces for cyclists. • 3 I asked him if he was for or against a law on cycle helmets. • 4 I asked the councillor if he would make it legal to cycle in the pedestrian zone. • 5 I asked him if children should be allowed to cycle on pavements. • 6 I asked him how much money the council had spent on cycling infrastructure this year. • 7 I asked him whether he was going to talk about cycling at the next council meeting.

YT 2 My report on the interview (Indirect speech)

Use the notes on the right to complete your report on your interview.

When I phoned Councillor Brown, she told me she was a cyclist herself and would be happy to give me an interview. We had planned to meet at ...

More help ➜ *p. 120*

More help: Die S vervollständigen den bereits formulierten Text.

- cyclist herself: happy to give me interview
- 4 pm - town hall
- Cllr Brown late: a lot of traffic
- offered me tea/coffee
- asked reason for interview -> cycling in town dangerous
- council is hoping to do more for cyclists BUT: bike paths expensive, roads in town centre too narrow, shops against bike paths (fewer parking spaces for cars)
- will ask the next council meeting to consider the issue

… at 4 pm at the town hall, but Councillor Brown was late: she told me later that there had been a lot of traffic. She asked me if I wanted some tea or coffee. Then she asked me why I wished to interview her. I replied that I thought cycling in town was dangerous. She insisted that the council wanted to do more for cyclists. But she also explained that bike paths cost a lot of money and that the roads in the town centre were too narrow. She also said that many shops disliked bike paths because it meant fewer parking spaces for cars. However, she promised that she would ask the next council meeting to consider the issue.

YT 3 Reporting on a demonstration

Die S können einen **Bericht über eine Demonstration** schreiben und dabei Fakten und ggf. Zitate einbauen.

a) Describe the scene in the photo. Say why you think the people are wearing these costumes.

+weak (adj)

Protest at Marble Arch, London, by animal rights activists.

b) Write a report about the demonstration. Use the facts from box A.
You should also imagine you interviewed some of the demonstrators. In your report, include some statements from box B. Remember you can use indirect speech.

More help → p. 120

More help: Die S vervollständigen Lückentext.

A

When:	August 6th
Where:	Marble Arch, central London
Who:	Almost 100 people
What:	Demonstration
Why:	To protest against planned laws to make it easier for laboratories to use cats and dogs in animal testing

B

1 "I travelled 100 miles. It's a huge issue."
2 "I'm a cat owner. It could be my cat."
3 "Animal testing isn't necessary."
4 "We don't want our animals to be in pain."
5 "We have to make the government listen."
6 "I hope we'll be able to prevent these new laws."

Early finisher → p. 129

Early finisher: Worträtsel

4 "Raise your voice"

Box "(to) raise", Voc, S. 223

Die S entnehmen einem auf Deutsch geführten Gespräch Informationen und geben diese auf Englisch wieder.

a) Your class has taken part in a song competition about children's rights. Your song has got through to the final round. There is now an online vote to choose the winner. You have contacted students at your American partner school and asked for their votes.

Stimme für KINDERRECHTE

Partner A: You received this text message from a friend at your partner school.

> Hey!
> Sure I'll vote for you. Sounds like a cool competition. How many other songs are there? And what kind of music? I hope there are good prizes. What can you win?

Go to p. 130 to get the information you need.

Partner B: You received this text message from a friend at your partner school.

> Hi to you all in Germany!
> I don't usually do online voting, but maybe this time. What's this thing with children's rights? Why's that so important? And why are they doing a song competition?

Go to p. 135 to get the information you need.

b) Partner A: Phone your friend and answer their questions. Partner B plays the American friend.

c) Partner B: Phone your friend and answer their questions. Partner A plays the American friend.

Die S üben **Verb + *gerund***.

Language help

When you use two verbs together, the second verb is often an infinitive.
A youth group decided to oppose teenage drinking. They wanted to increase fines on bar owners.

But be careful! After some verbs, the second verb must be a gerund.
Bar owners denied selling alcohol to teenagers. They now risk losing their license for 60 days.

There are no rules about which verbs take a gerund. You need to learn them. They include: *admit · consider · discuss · enjoy · fancy · feel like · give up · imagine · keep (on) · miss · regret · risk · suggest*

Remember! Verbs following a preposition must also be a gerund.
Katie said many people were worried about using bikes.

➜ *GF 5: The gerund (pp. 176–178)*

YT 5 Let's protest (Verb + gerund)

Choose one verb from each box to complete each sentence. Use the gerund form for the second verb.

1: discuss · enjoy · feel like · give up · imagine · risk · suggest

2: get · hang out · join in · paint · spend · take · try

Dan really enjoyed hanging out at his school's afternoon youth club. He couldn't ... [2]... his free time anywhere else and was very upset when the school decided to close the club. So he met some friends to ... [3]... action to protest the decision. Unfortunately, most of them didn't ... [4]... . Some didn't want to ... [5]... into trouble. Others just weren't interested. Disappointed, Dan ... [6]... to get their support. Only Jenny offered to help. She ... [7]... a big slogan that everyone would be able to see.

Box "anywhere", Voc, S. 223

2 imagine spending · 3 discuss taking · 4 feel like joining in · 5 risk getting into trouble · 6 gave up trying · 7 suggested painting

More help ➜ *p. 121*

More help: Das erste Verb ist jeweils vorgegeben.

YT 6 Dan and Jenny take action (Verb + gerund or infinitive)

Complete the news report. Choose the right form for the verbs in brackets: gerund or *to*-infinitive.

Police have managed [1]... (identify) the students responsible for giant graffiti at Newton school. Dan Blake (16) and Jenny Miles (15) admitted [2]... (spray) SAVE OUR CLUB on the school wall. Earlier, school managers had decided [3]... (close) the club, but Blake and Miles refused [4]... (accept) the decision. "We just didn't fancy [5]... (have) nowhere to go after lessons," they said. "We'd have missed [6]... (see) the other kids." They now regret [7]... (damage) the wall and have promised [8]... (clean) it. However, they are determined to keep on [9]... (protest).
Head teacher Sue Burns says the school needs [10]... (save) money but has offered [11]... (ask) managers to consider [12]... (keep) the club open after all.

1 to identify · 2 spraying · 3 to close · 4 to accept · 5 having · 6 seeing · 7 damaging · 8 to clean · 9 protesting · 10 to save · 11 to ask · 12 keeping

YT 7 Legal graffiti

Die S können über Entscheidungen diskutieren und anschließend den Inhalt der Diskussion wiedergeben ***(indirect speech)***.

a) **In many cities around the world people can spray graffiti legally on some walls. In your group discuss**
- whether to have a legal graffiti wall at your school, which wall …
- rules for using the wall (e.g. who can use it and when, how long graffiti can stay, standards, OK to have slogans? …)

b) **Join up with another group. Tell them about your discussion.**
- *We considered/discussed/…*
- *Jana offered to …*
- *I suggested …*
- *We didn't want to risk …*
- *Some of us were against …*
- *We agreed to/decided to …*

Die S strukturieren und verwenden Wortschatz aus dem **Wortfeld *Social and political involvement***.

The focus on this page is on words that help you to talk about involvement in political and social issues. Then you will talk about taking a stand on an important issue.

YT 1 Word field: Social and political involvement (Structuring vocabulary)

Box "involvement", Voc, S. 223

a) Make mind maps using words from the box and words or phrases from pp. 88–89.

civil/animal/human rights · demonstration · MP · law · petition · discrimination · parliament · president · government · nation · +senator · vote · +activist · +immigration · +citizen · strike · campaign · +congress · protester · elections · +democracy · prejudice · racism · +activism · border · flashmob

Partner A: start with the words *get involved*.

get involved – actions – issues – people

Partner B: start with the word *nation*.

nation – government – people – citizens

b) Comment on each other's mind maps and suggest ways to improve them. Then make a copy of your partner's mind map.

YT 2 Verb and noun collocations (Political and social involvement)

a) Form as many collocations as you can with a verb from the box on the left and a noun from the right.
TIP You can find many of these collocations on pp. 82–83 and 88–89.

1: attend · become · contact · join · organize · sign · start

2: activist · demonstration · march · movement · MP · petition · sit-in · strike

- attend a demonstration …
- join a movement …

b) Compare lists. Add to or correct your list if necessary.

YT 3 Collocations with prepositions (Political and social involvement)

a) Write five sentences using the prepositions below to link the verbs and the nouns.
It's illegal to discriminate against people because of their colour.

campaign demonstrate discriminate go protest take a stand take part	against for in on	• a campaign / protest • a demonstration • discrimination / racism / prejudice • the government • people who … • strike

b) Comment on each other's sentences.

Tell your partner about an issue that's important to you and how you'd like to get involved. Use at least ten of the words and phrases you've practised on this page. Take notes on what your partner says and give him/her feedback.

KV 4: Giving feedback on a presentation kann den S dabei helfen.

4 Background file EXTRA Taking part: UK and US

Die S können Texten **Informationen zu Wahlsystemen** entnehmen und mit anderen vergleichen (hier: **Wahlsystem USA und UK**).

YT Two political systems

Länge (UK): 06:06 Länge (USA): 06:12

Before you read, watch two short clips on the American and British political systems.
Take notes on the main political °institutions in both countries and the powers they have.
Use your notes to compare the two systems.

Voting

Elections

In the **US** you can vote from age 18:
- in local elections (e.g. for mayor)
- at state °level (°Governor, state Senators and °Representatives)
- at °federal level (President, Senators and Representatives in Congress)

In the **UK**, you can vote from age 18 (in Scottish elections from 16):
- in local elections (e.g. for mayor)
- for regional parliaments (in Northern Ireland, Scotland and Wales)
- in UK-wide elections to the °House of Commons

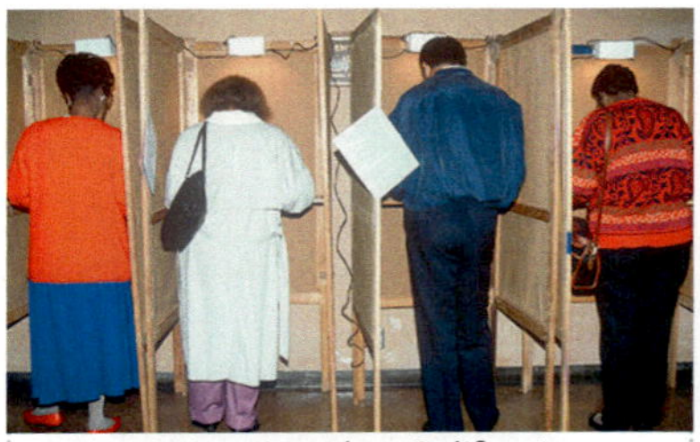
Voting in Los Angeles, California.

The °House of Lords is not °elected, most members are °appointed.
And of course, people cannot choose their °head of state, the Queen (or King), who is born to the job.
°Opinion polls show that most Britons would like a more °democratic House of Lords. However, the °monarchy is very popular, with between 70 and 80 percent of the people wanting to keep it.

°Referendums and initiatives

In a referendum, the people are asked by the °legislature to vote on a single issue.
In an initiative, citizens who want to change the law collect °signatures. If they collect enough, a °vote is held.

In the USA, referendums and especially initiatives are very common and are held in about half of the 50 states. Examples of initiatives include votes on °cigarette taxes, on the °minimum wage and on °banning the °death penalty. There are no referendums or initiatives at federal level.

In the UK, there are no initiatives, and referendums are only held on big issues.
In the last 50 years, there have been three nationwide referendums.
- 1975 Britons voted by 67 to 33 percent to join the EEC (later the European Union).
- 2011 The people voted against introducing a °proportional system for House of Commons elections.
- 2016 °Voters decided by 52 to 48 percent to leave the European Union.

°Supporters of °Remain in the 2016 EU referendum.

Supporters of Leave in the 2016 EU referendum.

There have also been a small number of special referendums in Scotland, Wales and Northern Ireland. In 2014, for example, the Scots voted against Scotland becoming an independent country.

Compare the right to vote in Germany with that in the UK and the USA.
www Find out more about the British and American voting systems.

Getting involved

Joining a °party

If you join a political party, you can °shape its °policies and help to get its candidates elected. In the USA, there are two big parties: °Republicans and °Democrats. Smaller parties exist, but their candidates have little chance at federal level.
Traditionally, the UK has also had a two-party system. Even today, the two big parties, the °Conservatives and °Labour, hold 550 of the 650 seats in the House of Commons. About 70 are held by regional parties from Scotland, Northern Ireland and Wales.

Young members supporting their party's election campaign in the UK.

You can join a party from the age of 15 or 16. In the UK, there are about 1 million party members (less than 2 percent of the population). °By contrast, the two big parties in the US have over 70 million members (about a quarter of the population). One reason for this is you often need to °register with a party to vote in °primaries (the first °round in an American election).

Standing for election

If you're a party member, you could try to get elected yourself.

Look at the table and say how well young people are represented.*

	House of Commons (UK)	*House of Representatives (US)*	*°Senate (US)*
Average age	51	57	61
Members under 30	13 (of 650)	0 (of 435)	0 (of 100)
Youngest member	21	32	39
Minimum candidate age	18	25	30

**Figures for August 2016*

Mhairi Black, youngest MP ['mæri]

Fighting for °causes

If you prefer to support a particular cause, you can join a °pressure group. °Unlike political parties, pressure groups do not usually put up candidates in elections. Instead they try to °win over public opinion with petitions, demonstrations or other activities. Many of the big pressure groups like Greenpeace or Amnesty International °operate in different countries. However, some groups fight for local causes, e.g. saving a °historic building.

2015: °Demonstrators wait for the °Supreme Court decision on °same-sex °marriage.

Say how you have got involved in the past or could imagine getting involved in the future.

➜ Text File 5 (p. 112) ➜ Text File 6 (p. 113)
Text file 5: The US president; **Text file 6:** The UK monarch

Die S können einem längeren **Auszug aus einem Theaterstück** Informationen entnehmen und sich zu den Inhalten äußern.

Glasgow Girls

excerpt from a musical about a true story, based on a book by David Greig

CAST

Mr Girvan – *bilingual-learning teacher*
Agnesa – *a Roma girl from Kosovo*
Roza – *a °Kurdish girl from Ira*
Amal – *a girl from Somalia*
Ewelina – *a Roma girl from Poland*
Emma and **Jennifer** – *two Scottish girls*

Agnesa, Roza, Amal and Ewelina have left their own countries to escape violence and war. Glasgow is now their new home and the four girls, who all attend Drumchapel School, have become close friends. With the support of their teacher Mr Girvan, they work hard at school, have big dreams for the future and finally have the security to live like "normal teenagers". That is, until one Sunday morning at dawn, when something happens that has the °potential to change everything …

Setting: The bilingual support room.
The girls and Mr Girvan all gathered round a speakerphone.

All Aggie!!!!
Agnesa Oh my God! Guys …
Amal Aggie, are you ok, what happened?
Agnesa It was horrible, Amal, we were sleeping, right, and we just heard this really loud banging on the door. When my dad went to °get it, like 14 immigration just pushed him °aside and runned in. Then they came into my room, and I screamed, I was mental. And my mum crying and they wouldn't let her pack anything, and I can see they are handcuffing my dad, and he's not even fighting or struggling or nothing, he's just trying to reason with them and no one is listening.
…
Amal Aggie, what happened next?
Agnesa They took us outside, and I'm still in my pyjamas and I'm crying and they said don't cry, you know, if you cry you're gonna be the first to go … They took my phone, they wouldn't let us call anyone, not even Mr Girvan. And I said I can't leave school, I have my exams and everything. Then they put my dad in a separate van and then drove along at 100 miles per hour!
Roza Aggie, are they gonna deport you?
Agnesa They're saying they're going to put us on a plane. We don't even know when. I've got to get out of here, man. I don't feel safe here.
Ewelina We're gonna get you out, Agnesa. Agnesa?
Phone goes dead
All Aggie? Aggie?
Amal Can we call back, sir?
Mr Girvan I'll try …
Silence.
Mr Girvan The line's dead. It's no good.
Phone line dead. A moment.
Amal Mr Girvan, how can they do this to her?
Roza Agnesa's been here five years.
Ewelina This is her home.
Amal What about her exams?
Roza There must be an appeal?
Ewelina They don't have anywhere else to go. Their village was cleansed. What on earth is she supposed to do?
Mr Girvan I know. Ewelina. I know. It's horrible. You girls wait here. I'm going to go see Mr Blakey and see what I can find out.
A moment – hesitation.
Ewelina Poor Aggie. What do we do now?
Amal Don't worry. We're going to get her back.
Ewelina How? This is so unfair.
Amal I'm not going back to class.
Ewelina Me neither.
Roza Me neither.
Roza We could go on strike.
Amal A strike?
Roza If Agnesa can't be in school –
All We won't be in school either.
Emma and Jennifer arrive.
Emma Hi.

Roma *(pl)* Roma **escape** (ent)fliehen **violence** Gewalt **dawn** Sonnenaufgang **gather round a speakerphone** sich um ein Telefon mit Freisprechanlage versammeln **14 immigration** *hier* 14 immigration officers **mental** (total) ausgerastet **handcuff** Handschellen anlegen **reason with sb.** vernünftig mit jm. reden **deport sb.** jn. abschieben, ausweisen **line** Telefonleitung **appeal** Berufung, Revision **cleanse** säubern **hesitation** Zögern

Amal Hi.

Roza What are you doing here?

Jennifer We heard about Agnesa …

Emma It's just not right. It's cruel. I can't believe this is happening in Scotland!

Jennifer We want to help.

Amal You want to help?

Emma Look, I know we don't know you guys that well, but Agnesa's one of us now. We can't just let folk take her away.

Both If you're on strike for Agnesa – we're on strike too.

…

Mr Girvan Girls! Where do you think you're going?

Amal We're marching!

Mr Girvan Where to?

Emma To see Mr Blakey.

Mr Girvan But Mr Blakey hasn't got Agnesa.

Roza Our demand is that Mr Blakey calls the Home Office.

Mr Girvan Don't you think he's already done that? He's been on the phone since half past eight this morning. As soon as we got word, he was on to the education department, the council, everyone.

Amal We're going on strike. We have to march somewhere.

Jennifer We can't just march round and round the playground.

Ewelina Agnesa's in prison – somebody has to do something.

Mr Girvan Look, girls, I understand you want to help your friend, but a strike's the wrong tactic in this situation.

Amal Agnesa has to know we're out here fighting for her.

Mr Girvan She does know.

Emma And it isn't just the asylum kids, the other kids are angry too.

Jennifer We could have a riot?

Mr Girvan I don't think a riot's a good idea Jennifer.

Jennifer A sit in – a sit down?

Mr Girvan No.

Ewelina What then?

Mr Girvan The home office say Kosovo's designated safe. They say there's UN soldiers there now keeping the peace.

Ewelina It might be safe if you're Kosovan – it's not safe if you're Roma.

Jennifer I don't understand.

Emma What's the difference?

Ewelina Aggie's Roma. The Roma aren't part of the civil war. They're a minority. Both sides are against them.

Mr Girvan Exactly, Ewelina. She's not safe – the government have got that wrong. That has to be our focus.

Ewelina But the government? How do we get them to change their minds?

Emma We persuade them.

Roza We make them take notice.

Amal We make it impossible for them to ignore.

Mr Girvan We do all of those things, but first we have to make a plan of action. What skills do you have?

Ewelina Skills?

Mr Girvan What talents can you use to help you draw attention to Agnesa's case?

Box "attention", Voc, S. 225

Roza I don't know.

Mr Girvan Just think.

Emma I can do broadcasting … media stuff.

Amal Oh yeah, you're the girl that does the school radio. You're brilliant!

Mr Girvan That's a start. Roza?

Roza I'm good at arguing.

Amal I can argue as well.

Roza Yeah, but I can argue things from a more legal perspective.

Amal Yeah, but I know what's right and what's wrong, which I think you'll find is a better way of arguing.

Roza That's so naïve …

Mr Girvan Ewelina?

Ewelina I like to bake.

---

demand Forderung **Home Office** britisches Innenministerium **asylum** Asyl **riot** Aufruhr, Aufstand **designate** erklären **minority** Minderheit **persuade** überreden **take notice** aufmerksam werden **draw attention to sth.** auf etwas aufmerksam machen **case** Fall **broadcast** senden, ausstrahlen *(Rundfunk, Fernsehen)*

Roza Baking? What use is that for a political struggle?

Mr Girvan If I've learned one thing in all my experience of political campaigning, Roza, it's this: you can never have too many macaroons. Jennifer?

Jennifer Me?

Mr Girvan What's your special skill?

Jennifer My special skill is … ninja moves.

Emma Don't be daft, Jennifer. Your special skill is persuading people.

Jennifer No, it's not.

Emma Yes, it is. You persuaded Mr Girvan to dress up as Cher for Children in Need.

Mr Girvan I don't think we need to be reminded of that, Emma.

Emma She got loads of people to sign your sponsorship form, though.

Mr Girvan An ability to make people sign things. I wonder in what way we could use a talent like that?

A moment.

Emma A petition!

All A petition!

Music starts

Jennifer Listen up, Drumchapel. They've taken Agnesa away. And we're going to get her back! Sign the petition!

Song

What kind of country do you want this to be?
One that abandons good people? Is this what you really believe?
Put yourself in their shoes – why should you help?
Well, there's your clue …
Just imagine you were them – and they were you
Chorus

Jen and Emma

Sign the petition – support your fellows now
Let one of us turn into two – then become a crowd
Ready to stand – sign, sign, and say it loud
Let's show the world what Scotland's about …

1 Understanding the play

a) Take notes on
- what Amal, Roza, Ewelina and Agnesa have in common
- what has happened to Agnesa and her family
- how this affects her friends

b) Compare your results.

c) Copy the table. On the left, list the Glasgow girls' ideas for taking action. On the right comment on how effective you think those ideas would be.

Ideas for taking action	Comment

d) Report your ideas to the class.

EXTRA If the girls manage to get a lot of people to sign their petition, what action should they take next? Brainstorm ideas in your group.

2 Understanding the background

Read lines 116–130 and the information below. Then explain the sense of danger that Agnesa's friends feel about her situation.

Access to cultures: The Roma

The Roma are a traditionally nomadic people living in communities in many parts of Europe. They have been victims of persecution since the 13th century. During the 17th and 18th centuries many attempts were made to forbid their nomadic way of life.
The persecution of the Roma increased dramatically during the Holocaust when over a million Roma people were murdered by the Nazi government. The Roma still face widespread racism and discrimination across Europe and most of their communities in Kosovo have been destroyed.

struggle Kampf **macaroon** Makrone **ninja moves** Ninja-Bewegungen **daft** albern **sponsorship** (finanzielle) Förderung **though** aber; jedoch **abandon** im Stich lassen **fellow** Kamerad/in

→ Workbook 15 (p. 52)

1 *From A to B and back again*

Die S können *Film stills* nutzen, um vorab Vermutungen zum Inhalt einer Szene anzustellen und diese beim Schauen zu überprüfen.

These four stills are from a short film in which a young girl called Rachel tells her story.

1
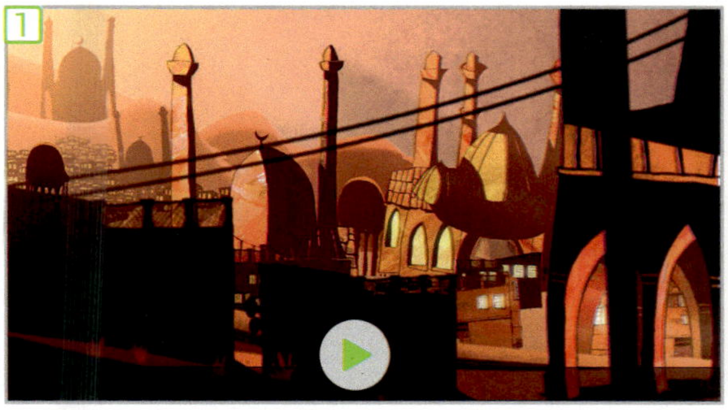

2

3

4

a) In groups of four, each partner chooses one still and describes it to the others.

b) Share your ideas about what Rachel's story might be about.

I think the story begins in …

It looks as if the people are …

I have a different idea. I think …

Then say what you expect the film will tell you about the settings and characters.

c) Now watch the film and check all your ideas. Länge: 06:14

d) Together think of different ways you could finish these sentences:
- Rachel must feel …
- If I were Rachel, I would …

2 Making the film: Atmosphere

Die S setzen sich mit **Atmosphäre im Film** auseinander und erkennen, wie in Filmen Atmosphäre erzeugt wird.

a) In groups of four, watch the film again. Each student focuses on one of these techniques:
- light (and darkness), colours
- music and sounds
- shots (long, middle, close-up …)
- the changing sizes of people and things

As you watch, note down examples of how the film-maker uses the technique you're focusing on.

b) Using your notes, share your impressions with your group.
Discuss how the different techniques affect the atmosphere in the film.

EXTRA *From A to B and back again* is an animated film. Would prefer to watch an animated film or a live-action film (film with real actors) about Rachel's story? Discuss your reasons.

Die S üben und verwenden die **indirekte Rede** bei Vorschlägen, Ratschlägen und Versprechen.

4.7 · FöFo 4.5

Language help

Reporting verbs

When we report what someone said, we don't always repeat everything word for word.
Instead we use verbs which show the speaker's intention, e.g. *promise, suggest, advise*.
Remember: Different verbs take different sentence patterns.

Ewelina	*"We're gonna get you out, Agnesa."*	*Ewelina promised to get Agnesa out.* (infinitive)
Jennifer	*"We could have a riot?"*	*Jennifer suggested having a riot.* (gerund)
Mr Girvan	*"I don't think a riot's a good idea, Jennifer."*	*Mr Girvan advised Jennifer not to have a riot.* (object + infinitive)

➔ *GF 7.3: Indirect speech (pp. 181 – 182)*

YT 1 Supporting Agnesa (Indirect speech: *advise, promise, suggest* …)

Use a suitable verb from the box to report what the people said. Use each verb only once.

1 Amal: "Don't worry, Ewelina, we're going to get her back."
Amal told Ewelina not to worry.
2 Amal: "We won't forget you, Aggie."
3 Amal: "I'm not going back to class."
4 Roza: "We could go on strike."
5 Mr Girvan: "I wouldn't go on strike. It's the wrong tactic."
6 Ewelina: "Roza, shall I bake you a cake."
7 Jennifer: "Would you like to sign our petition to get our friend Agnesa back?"

2 Amal promised not to forget Agnesa.
3 Amal refused to go back to class.
4 Roza suggested going on strike.
5 Mr Girvan advised not to go on strike.
6 Ewelina offered to bake a bake.
7 Jennifer invited students to sign their petition to get Agnesa out.

advise
invite
offer
promise
refuse
suggest
tell

YT 2 A radio discussion (Indirect speech: *advise, promise, suggest* …) 28

Listen and take notes on what Sam Meyer and Jessie Rosen say in a radio discussion. Then complete the sentences below.

1 Mr Meyer denied … He then described …
2 Ms Rosen insisted that … She then told listeners …
3 She also advised listeners not to …
4 Mr Meyer again denied …
5 He invited … and promised …
6 But then he refused … after Ms Rosen …
7 Finally Ms Rosen suggested …

More help: Die S wählen aus vorgegebenen Möglichkeiten die richtige aus.

More help ➔ *p. 121*

Happy or not?

1 … that the conditions were bad. … the 200-year history of his farm. • 2 … the video showed the truth … that the chickens couldn't move. • 3 … eat meat from these factories. • 4 … that there was anything bad at his farm. • 5 … Ms Rosen to his farm …to show her everything. • 6 … to continue the discussion …said the tour didn't show everything. • 7 … visiting the website www.CAAC.org

YT 3 An argument on a train 29

You're travelling on a train in Germany with a friend from the USA.
The people sitting opposite you have an argument. Then they get up and leave.
Your American friend asks you some questions. Listen. Then answer your friend's questions.

What was that argument about?

Why was the man so angry?

Why did the woman speak to us?

Why did the man suddenly calm down?

What did the man say when they were walking away?

Die S können eine ansprechende **Präsentation** halten (mit Opener, Ending, dem Eingehen auf Fragen und Kommentare).

YT 3 Study skills: Refining your presentation techniques

You've already learned skills that help you to introduce, develop and summarize the topic of your presentation effectively. This page focuses on two special techniques that will help you to refine your introduction and summary.

1 STRONG OPENERS

If you grab your audience's attention at the very beginning of your talk, there's a good chance they will listen more carefully. The following techniques will help you to make a stronger first impression.

Tell a joke or a funny story that has something to do with your theme.
"Proof of global warming: One early summer's day, a farmer goes out to the fields check on her corn crop. What does she find? 150 acres of popcorn."

Begin with a relevant quote.
"Barack Obama recently said, 'Climate change is no longer some far-off problem; it is happening here, it is happening now.' Today I'm going to explain why …"

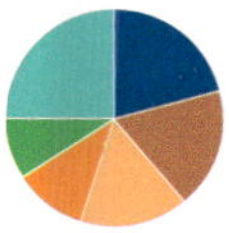

Begin with a surprising or shocking statistic or statement.
You love chicken? You're not the only one. In the USA 24 million chickens are killed for meat every day, 17,000 each minute, or 285 every second.

Challenge your audience with a question.
Animal rights – I don't have a pet, so why should I care?
Is that what you think?

a) Write openers, one of each type above, for a presentation on global warming or animal testing.

b) Take turns to read out your openers. Give each other feedback.

2 ENDING WITH A BANG!

Find a special way of ending. This will help your audience to remember the message of your presentation.

Propose a plan of action or solution to the issue you raised in your introduction.
"It couldn't be clearer what action we all have to take.
The way forward is this: …"

Ask a question that will make your listeners go on thinking about the issue.
"The question you need to ask yourself is: Would you want to live on this planet a hundred years from now?"

Use a memorable image.
"These eyes sum up what I've been saying. They speak more than a thousand words."
"Do I need to add anything to this? It's time to stop allowing animals to suffer."

c) For each of your openers from a) think of a good "ending with a bang" and write it down.

d) Work in the same group. Share your ideas and give each other feedback.

Early finisher → p. 129

Early finisher: Wortgitter mit Präsentationstipps

Workbook Checkpoint 4 (pp. 54–57)

Your task

Steps 1–3 können als länger angelegte vorbereitende HA durchgeführt werden. Steps 4 und 5 finden dann im Plenum statt.

Presentation: An issue I care about

**Your school has organized an online forum with your English partner school.
You have agreed to give a short presentation on an issue you care about. You are to talk about**
- **why the issue is important to you**
- **what action you could take to win public support for your position**

After your presentation listen and respond to comments from the audience.

STEP 1 Select a topic

a) Think about which issues are important to you and decide the topic for your presentation.

STEP 2 Collect information

**a) Use the internet to search for facts you need for your presentation.
For local issues, you might wish to talk to people affected or to ask an expert.**

➜ *Study skills: Internet research (p. 70)*

b) Check that you have all the special vocabulary you need.

➜ *Access to words: Social and political involvement (p. 93)*

**c) Find informative visuals you can use in your presentation – photos, graphs or other illustrations.
Don't forget to quote the sources of the images you use.**

Animal rights protesters march in Düsseldorf

A flashmob in Berlin protesting the death of a cyclist

STEP 3 Prepare your presentation

You have already learned a lot of basic presentation skills. The new skills you have learned this year will help you to make your presentation even more effective.

- A *good opener* and a *good conclusion* will help your audience to remember your message.
  - ➜ *Study skills: Refining your presentation skills (p. 101)*
- In a presentation, you often *quote what other people have said.*
  - ➜ *Study skills: Refining your presentation skills (p. 101)*
- The language you have learned for *interpreting images* and *speaking about statistics* may be useful.
  - ➜ *Speaking course: Describing and interpreting images (p. 87)*
  - ➜ *Study skills: Talking about statistics (p. 47)*

Don't forget to practise your presentation with a friend, family member or in front of the mirror.

STEP 4 The presentation

Presenter · While giving your presentation, remember to look at your audience.
· Speak as freely as possible, clearly and not too fast.

Audience · Take notes, especially on points you'd like to ask about or comment on.

Presenter · When you have finished, invite your audience to ask questions or make comments.

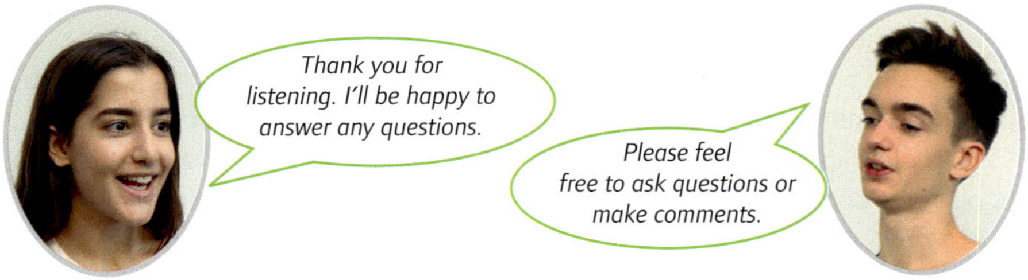

➜ *SF 24: Giving a presentation (p. 155)*

STEP 5 Questions and comments

Audience · When you ask a question or make a comment, refer to something the speaker said.

Presenter · Try to answer questions from the audience and respond to comments.

EXTRA Use a feedback sheet to evaluate your classmates' presentations.

KV 4: Giving feedback on a presentation hilft den S bei Rückmeldungen zu Präsentationen.

➜ *SF 27: Giving feedback to your classmates (p. 158)*

Text 1

In the outback

(adapted from the novel A prayer for Blue Delaney *by Kirsty Murray)*

Read the introduction and look at the photo. Then say what you imagine a journey through the outback might be like.

It's the 1950s. British orphans are being sent to children's homes in Australia. One, Colm McCabe, is at a home so cruel that he runs away. When the police come after him, an old man, Bill, offers to take Colm with him as he drives through the outback in his old ute, Tin Annie. Together with Bill's dog, Rusty, they set off. Bill is hoping for work repairing the Dog Fence that runs across Australia.

It was slow and hot travelling along the Dog Fence. There was nothing to see except scrub and tough little grasses in the rock and sand, and the fence stretching like a thin grey scar across the landscape.

"What if we break down?" asked Colm.

"Don't you worry about that. They used to do the fence on camel, but these days they use jeeps. Tin Annie here, she's part camel part jeep, so she'll be fine."

Bill stopped next to the fence where an emu had crashed into it. They both climbed out of the ute. Bill shook his head. "She's hit the fence very fast, this one. Looks like she broke her neck."

In the distance another emu was running across the desert. "See, they're so fast. They can go 30 miles an hour but they don't see the fence until they've hit it."

Colm helped Bill as he looked for the tools he would need for the job and then climbed back into Tin Annie to wait while Bill repaired the fence. Later they stopped to fill in a hole made by a wombat. The day dragged on. They drove so slowly that Colm got tired looking at the fence. When he closed his eyes he saw the endless fence moving along in his head. Despite the flies and the heat, he fell asleep. When he woke up, it was to the sound of Bill repairing a fencepost.

Colm's shirt was wet with sweat. He went round to the back of the ute and took a long drink from the billycan. The water was as warm as tea, but it was good to wet his throat. Flies buzzed around his face and although he tried to swat them away, they came back. Colm felt as if he was inside a strange and frightening dream.

The days dragged on, long and boring. Colm's neck was sore from always turning his head one way to watch the fence. After a few days he took over the job of filling the wombat holes while Bill repaired the holes in the fence. They filled up the billycans at every dam or tank, and ate tins of beef and vegetables until Colm felt he couldn't take another mouthful of them. The nearest town was hundreds of miles away.

One morning, Rusty wasn't in camp when they woke up. Colm helped Bill to pack up the breakfast dishes, and all the time he scanned the scrub and looked for a sign of movement.

"Where is that dog?" said Bill. He put two fingers in his mouth and whistled. Nothing moved.

"I'll find her," said Colm. He walked out into the scrub. If he closed his eyes and willed it, then he should be able to feel Rusty wherever she was. He was sure she was quite close.

When he opened his eyes he saw something move in the dust. Rusty was lying under a bush: she was shaking violently.

"Bill," called Colm. "Bill, here, I've found her! But something's wrong! Hurry!"

Bill knelt beside the dog. When he touched her body, Rusty shook even more violently.

"What is it?" asked Colm.

---

orphan Waise **ute** *(AusE) kleiner Geländewagen* **scrub** Gebüsch, Gestrüpp **scar** Narbe **break down** eine Panne haben **tool** Werkzeug **drag (on)** sich hinziehen **despite the flies** trotz der Fliegen **heat** Hitze **fencepost** Zaunpfahl **sweat** Schweiß **billycan** Kochtopf **frightening** erschreckend **will sth.** etwas herbeiwünschen **shake violently** stark/heftig zittern **beside** neben

"Snakebite, maybe. Then again, maybe not." Rusty started shaking uncontrollably, as if there was electricity running through her. Colm was cold with fear.

"What's wrong?" he cried, feeling tears in his eyes.

"I think she's taken dingo bait. Poison. It might be better for her if we killed her."

Colm walked beside Bill as he carried Rusty over to the ute and put her on her blanket in the back. Bill picked up the knife he used to kill rabbits.

"No! What are you doing!" Colm grabbed Bill's hand. "We have to save her."

"Get out of my way," said Bill. He pushed Colm away and held Rusty's head. Quickly he made cuts on the side of Rusty's ears. Blood poured down.

"Now go and fill the billycan." Bill pushed it at Colm and then looked for something in the food bag.

When Colm returned, Bill threw two handfuls of salt into the water. He took Rusty in his arms. "Now I'll keep her mouth open. I want you to pour the salty water straight down her throat."

The salt water made Rusty throw up. When Bill put her down, she staggered around the ute, and threw up again and again. As soon as they could, they poured more water down her throat. Finally, when she'd finished, Bill carried her over to a bush and put her on her old blanket. Bill and Colm knelt beside her and massaged her.

"Here, you need a break," said Bill. "Go get yourself a drink and sit in the car. I'll call you if I need you."

Colm walked back to Tin Annie, fighting back tears.

The morning grew hotter. Colm fell asleep and then, when he woke, he prayed as hard as he could. He was still praying when he heard Rusty bark – a weak bark, but a bark. He ran across to where she lay.

"I prayed for her," said Colm. "Maybe it helped."

"Maybe it did," said Bill. "Between your prayers and my hard work, she'll be better quite soon."

❖

"C'mon. I've got a job to do. Can't just sit around and talk all day. A wild boar's been making trouble just south a bit."

They drove out into the landscape where the old trees looked like burnt bones. Tin Annie struggled over the dry creek beds and Rusty put her head out the open window, watching the fine red dust fly up around the sides of the ute.

"This is the place. We'll look for the bugger on foot from here. You stay close by me."

Colm followed Bill through the scrub. A hot, foul smell was in the air. As the smell got stronger, Rusty put her head down and walked in front, as if she was following something. She led them to what was left of a steer. A cloud of flies flew up in the air.

Bill knelt down beside the dead steer. "He's had a great time with this steer. He hasn't been gone long."

They climbed up a nearby hill and scanned the countryside. Apart from a family of wallabies, they could see nothing.

"Damn, he heard us coming and left."

Bill turned to walk back to the steer. There was a noise in the scrub and the black boar was on them. Colm jumped behind a rock as the boar hit Bill and sent him flying. It ran at the old man with its tusks, tearing his boot and ripping open his leg. Bill let out a cry of pain.

Blood poured from Bill's leg as the boar attacked again, and the old man struggled free. Rusty sank her teeth into the boar's leg, but it turned and tore her with its tusks. Rusty yelped and fell.

Colm jumped out from behind the rock. He had to do something.

Bill's face was scared. "Run, Colm, get out of here," he shouted. "Get help!"

Colm turned and ran down the path. He had nearly got to Tin Annie when he heard a terrible cry, more animal than human. He stopped and turned. What if Bill was killed before he could get help? What should he do? Run back to Tara Downs? Try to save Bill himself? Suddenly he realized there was only one answer and there was no time to lose.

---

bait Köder **poison** Gift **throw up** sich übergeben, sich erbrechen **stagger** torkeln **weak** schwach **wild boar** Wildschwein **bone** Knochen **creek** *(AusE)* Bach **bugger** *(infml, rude)* Kerl **steer** junger Ochse **apart from** außer **wallaby** Wallaby *(kleine Känguruart)* **send sb. flying** jn. zu Boden schicken **tusk** Hauer *(Eckzahn eines Wildschweines)* **tear, tore, torn** (zer)reißen **pain** Schmerz(en) **yelp** aufjaulen

He ran back to Bill. On the way he picked up a stick. As he came over the hill, he ran at the boar, hitting it again and again. It turned to face Colm. There was blood on its tusks.
Bill tried to pull himself away, leaving a trail of blood behind him. Colm raised the stick high and brought it down on the boar's head. The boar snorted, but instead of running at Colm, it turned back to Bill.
Colm threw the stick down and grabbed Bill's gun. He was shaking as he raised the gun to his shoulder. Colm knew that if he shot the animal in the back, it would only make it wild. He let out a scream, a long, loud scream. The boar turned round. For a moment it stared at him with its small black eyes. Then it lowered its head and ran towards him. Colm aimed straight between the eyes.
The kickback from the gun made Colm stagger. He fell in the sand beside Rusty.
"Colm, my mate," said Bill. He held out one bloodied hand and smiled. Then he lay back in the red dust and passed out.
Suddenly, everything was quiet. Blood soaked into the dry earth around Bill in a dark circle. Colm could see the bones of his leg where the boar had ripped open the flesh. He would have to stop the blood flow or Bill would bleed to death. Colm ran back to the ute and grabbed an old shirt to tie up the wound. Then he took off his own shirt and tore it up for Bill's hands. When he was sure the bleeding was slower, he sat back and tried to think. He had to get help, but how? The flies were collecting. He would have to get Bill into the car. Colm took Bill's arms and put one over each of his shoulders and then tried to pull the old man up. It was almost impossible. He'd never be able to go far like this. He laid Bill down again and ran to Tin Annie. Colm took a deep breath and turned the key. Tin Annie started. He had no idea how to drive backwards, so he moved forwards carefully, bringing the car as close to Bill as he could. Somehow he found the strength to pull Bill back on his shoulders and put him into the car. Then he ran and picked Rusty up. He could just hear the dog's heartbeat and it gave him hope.
The dust flew up around the car as Colm raced along the track. Every time they hit a stone Bill cried out with pain, but at least that meant he was still alive.
When they drove across a dry creek bed, Tin Annie first struggled, then stopped. Colm tried to start her up again. But even as his foot pushed to the floor, he knew it was a mistake. The old ute died completely.
They were just at the top of the hill and he could see Tara Downs, but there was still at least a mile to go. He tried to start the car again and again, but it was no good. He would have to go on foot and leave Bill and Rusty in the car.
Colm wished the old man was conscious and could tell him what to do next. Then he began the long run to Tara Downs.
Colm's heart pounded and his head hurt, but the ground flew beneath him. He took the steps up to the house two at a time.
"It's Bill. An accident. He's bleeding, real bad. A boar ripped him up."
Then Colm sank down on his knees. People appeared from nowhere. They ran, a car started up and strong arms helped Colm to his feet and took him into a bedroom. For a moment he struggled against them. "I have to be with Bill."
"It's all right."
"Bill needs me," said Colm.
"They're getting the Flying Doctor out here. We don't know if the old man will make it if we have to drive him down to the hospital in Katherine. Best to fly him to Darwin."
Colm felt the blood drain from his face. "He will make it. He has to make it."

a) Make a network with the names of the characters from the excerpt. Then describe the relationship between them and their feelings for each other. Give examples.

b) Agree on adjectives that best describe each character (e.g. *brave*, *easy-going*, *honest* ...). Support your ideas with examples from the text.

snort schnauben **gun** Waffe, Gewehr **lower** senken **aim** zielen **pass out** ohnmächtig werden **tie up** verbinden **wound** Wunde **conscious** bei Bewusstsein **pound** (wild) pochen **beneath** unter **brave** mutig

Text 2

I Come From by Dean Atta

30

I come from shepherd's pie and Sunday roast
Jerk chicken and stuffed vine leaves
I come from travelling through my taste buds but loving where I live

I come from a home that some would call broken
I come from D.I.Y. that never got done
I come from waiting by the phone for him to call

I come from waving the white flag to loneliness
I come from the rainbow flag and the union jack
I come from a British passport and an ever-ready suitcase

I come from jet fuel and fresh coconut water
I come from crossing oceans to find myself
I come from deep issues and shallow solutions

I come from a limited vocabulary but an unrestricted imagination
I come from a decent education and a marvellous mother
I come from being given permission to dream but choosing to wake up instead

I come from wherever I lay my head
I come from unanswered questions and unread books
Unnoticed effort and undelivered apologies and thanks

I come from who I trust and who I have left
I come from last year and last year and I don't notice how I've changed
I come from looking in the mirror and looking online to find myself

I come from stories, myths, legends and folk tales
I come from lullabies and pop songs, Hip Hop and poetry
I come from griots, grandmothers and her-story tellers

I come from published words and strangers' smiles
I come from my own pen but I see people torn apart like paper
Each a story or poem that never made it into a book.

Dean Atta:
- *born 1988*
- *studied English and philosophy*
- *2012: Winner of the London Poetry Award*
- *2013: published poetry collection,* I Am Nobody's Nigger
- *lives in London*

Jigsaw

a) Form groups of three. Some groups work on verses 1–3, some on 4–6, some on 7–9. Read and discuss your group's verses and take notes on what they mean.

b) Form new groups of three with students who read the other verses. Use your notes to explain what your verses were about. Discuss what the message of the poem is.

c) Think about how to read the poem aloud to best express its message:
- which words to stress, where to pause, where to read loudly, softly, etc.
- how to share the reading: each student reads one line, one verse, the whole poem …?

d) Write your own poem in as many lines as you like. Each line should begin with *I come from* …

---

jerk chicken mariniertes Hühnchen **stuffed vine leaves** gefüllte Weinblätter **taste buds** Geschmacksknospen **D.I.Y. (do-it-yourself)** Heimwerken **wave the flag** die Fahne hochhalten **suitcase** ['suːtkeɪs] Koffer **jet fuel** [fjuːəl] Flugzeugtreibstoff **issue** ['ɪʃuː 'ɪsjuː] (Streit-)Frage **shallow solutions** oberflächliche Lösungen **unrestricted imagination** grenzenlose Phantasie **decent** ['diːsnt] anständig **marvellous** wundervoll **effort** ['efət] Anstrengung **undelivered apolgies** [ə'pɒlədʒiz] nicht ausgesprochene Entschuldigungen **trust** (ver)trauen **folk tale** Volksmärchen **griots** *(pl)* ['griːəʊz] *Bezeichnung f. afrik. Sänger* **tear apart** [teə], **tore, torn** zerreißen

Veggie Panini is the Answer to Everything

by Sara Holbrook and Allan Wolf

I don't know what makes
two people "just friends" on Thursday
and "more than friends" on Friday.
But today was Friday.
The one-hundredth look
was different from the first ninety-nine.
Today's "Hi" was different
from every "Hi" that came before.

I swear I wasn't smitten,
but then . . . the lunch bell rang.
And there you are:
sitting at our usual lunchroom table
(has she always sat like that?)
and we look at each other
(has she always looked like that?)
and we say "Hi"-
(has she always talked like that?)
eating what looks like
(has she always chewed like that?)
just a sandwich but what you inform me
is actually a "veggie panini."

"A veggie what?" I ask and smile
as wide as a door on well-oiled hinges.
And you smile back the same and answer,
"Paah-NEE-nee. Paah-NEE-nee. A veggie panini."
In English class I even look it up

"Paah-NEE-nee. Paah-NEE-nee. A veggie panini."
I whisper it into the electric air and picture
your lips, your smile, your look, your lunch, your hair.
I mutter it all the way home:
"Veggie panini. Veggie panini."
I hug my mom (first time in like a year).
"And how was your day?" my mother asks.
"Veggie paah-NEE-nee" is my answer.

Veggie panini is the answer to everything.

Taking One for the Team

by Sara Holbrook

We practiced together,
sweat and stained.
We pummeled each other
and laughed off pain.
Teams may disagree,
may tease,
may blame.
Teams may bicker and whine,
but get down for the game.

You had my back.
We fought the fight.
And though our score
was less last night,
we're walking tall.
Our team came through
and stuck together like Crazy Glue.
I'm proud to say
I lost with you.

Sara Holbrook:
- *born 1949*
- *studied English*
- *author of several poetry books for adults and children*
- *now a full-time poet*
- *lives in Ohio, USA*

Allan Wolf:
- *born 1963*
- *studied English*
- *writes and performs poems*
- *author of book on writing poems*
- *lives in North Carolina, USA*
- *lives in Ohio, USA*

a) Read both poems. Say what kind of relationship is being described in each one.

31–32 33–34 b) Listen to the poems being read by two different readers. Compare the readers' speed, where they pause, and which words they stress. Then read one of the poems for your partner.

swear [sweə] schwören **smitten** verknallt **chew** [tʃuː] kauen **hinge** Scharnier **picture** sich vorstellen, vor sich sehen **mutter** murmeln **sweat** [swet] Schweiß **stained** fleckig **pummel sb.** auf jn. einschlagen **pain** Schmerz **tease** [tiːz] hänseln, ärgern **bicker** sich zanken **whine** jammern **get down** zur Sache kommen **have sb.'s back** jm. Rückendeckung geben **walk tall** erhobenen Hauptes gehen **stick together** zusammenhalten

Text 3

Roar

35

Text and music by Katy Perry and others

I used to bite my tongue and hold my breath
Scared to rock the boat and make a mess
So I sat quietly, agreed politely
I guess that I forgot I had a choice
I let you push me past the breaking point
I stood for nothing, so I fell for everything

You held me down, but I got up (hey!)
Already brushing off the dust
You hear my voice, your hear that sound
Like thunder, gonna shake your ground
You held me down, but I got up
Get ready 'cause I've had enough
I see it all, I see it now

I got the eye of the tiger, a fighter
Dancing through the fire
'Cause I am the champion, and you're gonna hear me roar
Louder, louder than a lion
Cause I am a champion, and you're gonna hear me roar!

Chorus
Oh oh oh oh oh oh oh oh
Oh oh oh oh oh oh oh oh
Oh oh oh oh oh oh oh oh
You're gonna hear me roar!

Now I'm floating like a butterfly
Stinging like a bee I earned my stripes
I went from zero, to my own hero

Repeat verses 2 and 3

Repeat chorus twice

Roar, roar, roar, roar, roar!

Repeat verse 3
Repeat chorus

a) The singer speaks about her past and insists that her future will be different.
Say in what ways you think she wants to change.

b) The song uses imagery to express the writer's feelings. Make a list of the images used.

> **TIP** Imagery
> **Similes** and **metaphors** are two kinds of imagery. They are used to make a statement more visual and therefore stronger.
>
> A simile compares two things with each other.
> It uses the words *like*, *as* or *than*:
> *His words were like a knife.*
> *His words were sharper than a knife.*
>
> A metaphor is a word or phrase which is used in a different context from its usual one.
> *His words were a knife in my heart.*
> *His words cut me to pieces.*
> Here, words are not just compared with a knife. Instead they are a knife. This is why a metaphor is more powerful than a simile.

c) Compare your results. Think of other similes or metaphors you could use to express the same ideas.

d) Now listen to the song and comment on how strongly the singers ideas come across.

roar [rɔː] brüllen **I bite my tongue** [tʌŋ] ich beiße mir auf die Zunge; ich halte den Mund **rock the boat** Ärger machen **make a mess** *etwa:* Mist bauen **fall for sth.** auf etwas hereinfallen **brush sth. off** [brʌʃ] abbürsten, abklopfen **float** schweben **sting** stechen **bee** Biene **stripe** (Ärmel-)Streifen *(milit. Rangabzeichen)* **imagery** ['ɪmɪdʒəri] Bildsprache, Metaphorik **simile** ['sɪməli] Vergleich **metaphor** ['metəfɔː, 'metəfə] Metapher **visual** ['vɪʒuəl] bildhaft; sichtbar **therefore** daher

Text 4

7 Years

36

by Lukas Forchhammer and others

Once I was seven years old, my mama told me,
"Go make yourself some friends or you'll be lonely."
Once I was seven years old

It was a big big world, but we thought we were bigger
Pushing each other to the limits, we were learning quicker
By eleven smoking herb and drinking burning liquor
Never rich so we were out to make that steady figure

Once I was eleven years old, my daddy told me,
"Go get yourself a wife or you'll be lonely."
Once I was eleven years old

I always had that dream, like my daddy before me
So I started writing songs, I started writing stories
Something about that glory just always seemed to bore me
'Cause only those I really love will ever really know me

Once I was twenty years old, my story got told
Before the morning sun, when life was lonely
Once I was twenty years old

I only see my goals, I don't believe in failure
'Cause I know the smallest voices, they can make it major
I got my boys with me, at least those in favor
And if we don't meet before I leave, I hope I'll see you later

Once I was twenty years old, my story got told
I was writing about everything I saw before me
Once I was twenty years old

a) Read the lyrics of the song.
Say what advice the narrator's parents give him and whether he follows it.

b) Explain the narrator's dream and whether or not he realizes it.

liquor ['lɪkə] Spirituosen, Alkohol **make a steady figure** ['stedi] ein regelmäßiges Einkommen erzielen **glory** Ruhm, Ehre **bore sb.** jn. langweilen **failure** ['feɪljə] Versagen, Scheitern **make it major** ['meɪdʒə] groß rauskommen **those in favor** die, die für mich sind/die mich unterstützen **lyrics** *(pl)* ['lɪrɪks] Liedtext **narrator** [nə'reɪtə] Erzähler/in

Soon we'll be thirty years old, our songs have been sold
We've traveled around the world and we're still roaming
Soon we'll be thirty years old

I'm still learning about life
My woman brought children for me
So I can sing them all my songs
And I can tell them stories
Most of my boys are with me
Some are still out seeking glory
And some I had to leave behind
My brother, I'm still sorry

Soon I'll be sixty years old, my daddy got sixty-one
Remember life, and then your life becomes a better one
I made a man so happy when I wrote a letter once
I hope my children come and visit once or twice a month

Soon I'll be sixty years old, will I think the world is cold
Or will I have a lot of children who can warm me?
Soon I'll be sixty years old

Soon I'll be sixty years old, will I think the world is cold
Or will I have a lot of children who can warm me?
Soon I'll be sixty years old

Once I was seven years old, my mama told me,
"Go make yourself some friends or you'll be lonely."
Once I was seven years old

Once I was seven years old

c) Listen to the song. Use these lines to write your own lyrics about your life:
- Once I was seven years old, my mama told me ...
- Once I was seven years old, my mama told me ...
- Once I was ... years old ...
- Soon we'll be ... years old ...
- Soon I'll be ... years old ...

roam [rəʊm] umherziehen, durch die Gegend ziehen **seek** *(fml)* suchen, streben nach **leave sb./sth. behind** jn./etwas zurücklassen **realize sth.** etwas verwirklichen

Text 5

1 The US president

a) Name the American presidents in the pictures. Is the current president among them? Say what you know about them or any other presidents.

b) Make notes on what you know about the job of the US president. Share your ideas in class.

George Washington

Abraham Lincoln

Barack Obama

Donald Trump

2 The president's job

Read the outline of a US president's roles and responsibilities. Then read the weekly schedule. Match the president's activities on each day to the correct role. Compare your answers in class.

1 Chief of State – ceremonial head of USA; welcomes ambassadors and leaders from abroad.
2 Chief Legislator – usually proposes major policy initiatives such as health care reform and immigration policy reform and signs laws.
3 Chief Executive – head of the executive branch of government.
4 Chief Diplomat – spokesperson for the USA in all kinds of meetings with foreign governments.
5 Commander in Chief – head of the military with control over the use of nuclear weapons. The president can decide to send the army, the air force and the navy into a conflict.

THE WHITE HOUSE Office of the Press Secretary

The President's schedule for next week

- *On Tuesday, the President will announce new policies on gun ownership. This proposal will then come before Congress.*
- *On Wednesday morning, the President will receive the Presidential Daily Briefing in the Oval Office. Later, mid-morning the President will make a televised statement on the number of American troops currently stationed abroad and on plans for the coming year.*
- *On Thursday, the President will announce the name of the new Head of the Environmental Protection Agency.*
- *On Friday morning the President will meet the Presidents of the European Council and the European Commission to discuss US-EU cooperation in fighting terrorism, supporting economic growth, and addressing the global refugee crisis. In the evening, the President will participate in a NATO family photo and attend a working dinner with NATO leaders.*

Research the main differences between the roles of the American and German presidents. Then write a short text to present your results.

outline Übersicht **ambassador** Botschafter/in **legislator** ['ledʒɪsleɪtə] Gesetzgeber/in **propose** vorschlagen **major** ['meɪdʒə] bedeutende(r, s) **policy** Politik, politische Linie **health care reform** Gesundheitsreform **the executive** [ɪɡ'zekjətɪv] die Exekutive **branch** Zweig **Commander in Chief** Oberbefehlshaber/in **nuclear weapon** [ˌnjuːkliə 'wepən] Atomwaffe **air force** Luftwaffe **press secretary** Pressesprecher/in **gun violence** Waffengewalt **ensure** sicherstellen **receive** erhalten **improvement** Verbesserung **act** Gesetz, Verordnung **access** zugreifen auf **growth** Wachstum **address (a problem)** (ein Problem) angehen **participate** [pɑː'tɪsɪpeɪt] teilnehmen

Text 6

Moments in the history of the monarchy

The UK is a monarchy ruled by a king or a queen. The word monarchy comes from the Greek *monos* (alone) and *arkhein* (to rule). Today the British monarch does not rule alone. In fact, he or she plays no active part in government. Their role is ceremonial. For over 900 years, however, monarchs were powerful figures whose conflicts with people and parliament have shaped modern Britain.

1066: The Norman invasion

For hundreds of years in Anglo-Saxon England, different parts of the country had different kings. However, by the 10th century, all England was united under one king, who wanted to make the monarchy a stronger power in the country. A key moment was the 1066 invasion of England by the Duke of Normandy (in France), who defeated the last Anglo-Saxon King at the Battle of Hastings. As the new king, supported by a strong army, William I increased royal power all over the country.

1215: King John and the Magna Carta

King John's reputation is so bad that no king of England has used that name for over 800 years. To pay for his wars in France, John took land from the church and castles from the barons, stole from peasants and raised taxes. In 1215, some of England's barons rebelled against John, forcing him to accept the Magna Carta (Great Charter). The Magna Carta stated that everyone, including the king, had to respect the law, and that the king could not take away anyone's freedom or property unless they had broken the law.

King John accepts the Magna Carta

1649: The execution of Charles I

In 1603, James VI of Scotland became James I of England, uniting the two countries for the first time. James and his son Charles, who ruled from 1525, believed in the divine right of kings, the idea that God had given the monarch absolute power. For eleven years Charles ruled without parliament, becoming unpopular with the people. A civil war broke out in 1642 and the king was defeated by supporters of parliament. After a trial for high treason, he was executed in 1649. The country became a republic until 1660, when parliament restored the monarchy. Charles I's son became King Charles II.

1690: The Battle of the Boyne

On the death of Charles II, his younger brother came to the throne as James II. As a Catholic in Protestant Britain, James soon clashed with parliament. When in 1688 a son was born to the king, a group of British Protestants offered the throne to the Dutch ruler, William of Orange. James fled from Britain. Supported by parliament in 1690, William defeated King James at a battle at the River Boyne in Ireland. This was the last time that a monarch and parliament settled a conflict in armed battle.
The monarch continued to exercise power well into the 19th century, but parliament had become the more important political player in Britain.

"The people in Britain have always been happy with their monarchy."
Comment on this statement, referring to the text.

rule (be)herrschen **shape** gestalten, formen **duke** [dju:k] Herzog **defeat** besiegen **reputation** [ˌrepju'teɪʃn] Ruf, Ansehen **peasant** ['peznt] Bauer/Bäuerin **rebel** ['rebl] rebellieren **charter** Urkunde, Charta **divine** [dɪ'vaɪn] göttlich, gottgegeben **civil war** Bürgerkrieg **trial** ['traɪəl] Prozess **high treason** ['tri:zn] Hochverrat **Catholic** ['kæθlɪk] Katholik/in; katholisch **Protestant** ['prɒtɪstənt] Protestant/in; protestantisch **Dutch** holländisch, niederländisch **flee, fled, fled** fliehen **exercise** ausüben **well into the 19th century** weit ins 19. Jahrhundert

Part A Practice

1 REVISION Have you packed your bags yet? (Simple past or present perfect)

p. 14

Choose the correct form of the verbs in brackets. The signal words can help you.

1 (you · pack) all your bags yet?
2 Not all. (I · pack) my big rucksack last night, but (I · not start) to pack my two travel bags yet.
3 Why (you · not pack) the bags last night too?
4 (I · be) too tired and anyway (I · not decide) exactly what to take with me yet.

1 (you · find) a present for your host family yet?
2 Well, (I · be) in town last Saturday and (I see) this book about German baking - in English!
3 Wow, (I never · see) a German cookbook in English before. (you buy) it?
4 Yes, (I · buy) it. It (not be) very expensive.

7 REVISION I saw the ferry arriving (Participle clauses after verbs of perception)

p. 16

You can also use participle clauses after verbs of perception like *see*, *notice*, ...

→ *GF 10: Participle clauses (p. 186)*

a) Use the given verbs to make sentences about the pictures.

A I (see) the ferry (arrive) in Sydney Harbour.

B I (hear) somebody (come) up the stairs.

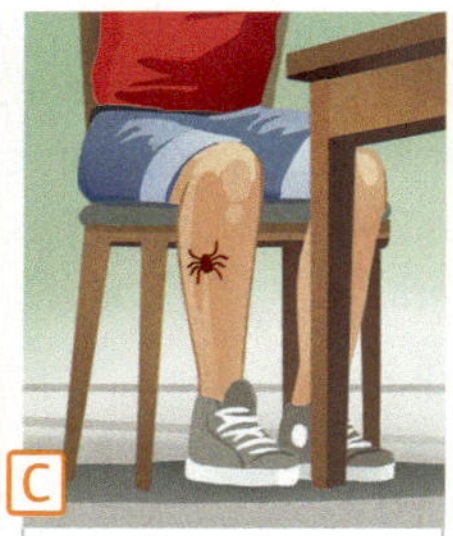

C I (feel) a spider (climb) up my leg.

D I (smell) a cake (burn) in the oven.

E I (notice) a person (throw) rubbish on the ground.

b) Imagine you are in Sydney. Describe what you see, hear, smell and feel. Here are some ideas:

see: people – climb – Sydney Harbour Bridge · tourists – walk – the Rocks
hear: Aboriginal man – play – didgeridoo · seagulls – call – each other
smell: meat – be cooked – barbecue
feel: sun – shine – my face · waves – hit – legs

Part B Practice

2 Everyone was outside

p. 20

Complete sentences A–F with ideas from the box, using a participle clause.

A

Have you seen the photo of Rover … ?

B

This is Ella on her way to a party …

C

Everyone was outside …

D

Jake was standing in the greenhouse …

E

Fluff is walking along the piano …

F
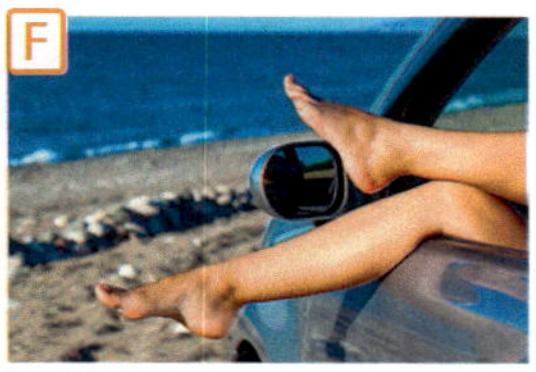
Mum was in the car …

carry some presents · catch a Frisbee · hang her feet out of the window · hold a box of tomatoes · make an awful noise · play in the park · play interesting music · relax in the front seat · smile for the camera · stand in a queue · wait to go in · want to buy tickets · wear a beard

4 A trip that went wrong

p. 21

a) **Write a short text (about ten sentences) about a trip that went wrong.**
Using a participle clause where it fits can improve your style. This overview may help you.

While	packing my/his/… bag waiting for the train …	I he/she …	noticed … dropped … …
The girl Somebody …	sitting opposite me wearing a blue cap …	(suddenly)	looked at me angrily. asked me a question. …

I he/she …	heard noticed …	a boy a dog …	running towards me/down the street/… standing at the corner. …

Access to words

3 Collocations (Adjectives and nouns)

p. 22

b) **Say what you like or dislike about places you know. Try to use one adjective from each box.**

What I like about *One thing I hate about*	*Berlin* *my village* *where I went on holiday last year* …	*is the*	*boring · little · lovely · narrow · nice · old-fashioned · small · tiny · ugly · vast ·* *busy · coastal · new · old · open · rocky · overcrowded · suburban · tropical · wide*	*blocks of flats.* *parks.* *pedestrian zone.* *streets.* …

Lead in

2 Connecting images

p. 35

a) Look at photos 1–6 on p. 22. Choose two with a connection to the photo you described in 1. Here are some ideas:

I'd say In my view, In my opinion,	there's a connection between … and … … is connected to …	because	the theme of both photos is friendship/… the idea of community/… can be seen in both. both photos show … the hands/… is/are a symbol of …

Here are some ways to react to your partners:

- Yes, I agree. I can see that connection.
- That's just how I feel.
- That's so true.
- You're right.
- Oh, I see. I'd never thought of it like that before.

- No, sorry, I just don't get it.
- I can't follow you – … has nothing to do with …
- I don't share your view.
- That's nonsense/rubbish.
- That's not how I see it.
- I totally disagree.

Part A Practice

4 You aren't supposed to ride bikes here (German *sollen: be supposed to 2*)

p. 46

In each pair of sentences, decide what is correct, ***be supposed to*** or *had better*.
Use *be supposed to* when talking about general rules. Use ***had better*** for specific situations.

1 You (not · ride) bikes in this park. We (get) off and push them.
You aren't supposed to ride bikes in this park. We'd better get off and push them.
2 I (buy) some apples and bananas today. You (eat) lots of fruit.
3 You (not · put) bananas in the fridge. You (take) them out again.
4 You (not · wear) shoes in the living room. You (take) them off now.
5 We (turn) down the music. We (not · make) noise after ten in the evening.
6 You (not · use) a dictionary in the test. So you (leave) it outside.
7 You (pick) up that paper bag. You (not · leave) any rubbish here.
8 We (hurry). We (be) at the airport 90 minutes before the flight leaves.

Part B Practice

8 Statistics from different countries

p. 48

a) Look at the table and say what kind of information is given.
Compare the three countries with each other and with the European average.
Agree on the four most interesting facts and write them down in a short text.

EUROPEAN STATISTICS: AMOUNT OF POCKET MONEY PER WEEK*

Age	Under 5	5 to 10	10 to 15	15-plus
Germany	1.00	4.00	10.00	20.00
Turkey	1.50	3.25	6.50	16.00
UK	2.50	6.00	6.00	12.00
European average	2.00	4.75	9.50	20.00

Source: ING International Survey, September 2014 — ** figures in euros*

Use these ideas to help you:

The table gives us information about	pocket money in Europe. three countries in Europe. …

The table shows that children	under 6 between 10 and 15 …	get	more less the same	…

If you compare	Germany and the UK, the EU average with …, …	you can see	…

Part C Practice

3 If I had been you … (Conditional 3)

p. 52

a) Read the text. Then write what you would have done differently. Use the table to help you.

7:30. Mum and Dad were away. It was cold, so I stayed in bed till 8. Now I was late. I had breakfast really fast, but I still missed the bus. I could have used my bike, but … While I was waiting for the next bus, a dog came up to me. I could tell he was hungry – I'm sure he hadn't eaten for days. So I bought some dog food and took him back home to feed him. He was so happy and didn't want to leave.
So I never got to school.

If	I you the dog	had hadn't	(be) you, (be) late, (stay) in bed until 8, (leave) without breakfast, (come) up to you,	I you	would have wouldn't have	(get) up at 7:30. (have) breakfast (be) late. (miss) the bus. (use) the bike. (see) he was hungry.

If I'd been you, I would have got up at … *If I'd been late, I …*

Access to words

1–2

p. 63

Together think of <u>one</u> figure from a book or film. Then write separate character descriptions. Refer to personal qualities you like or dislike. Use words from p. 63 and/or the ideas below.

One thing I find	attractive horrible interesting	about	Harry Potter …	is	her his	self-confidence. liveliness. rudeness. …

On the one hand,	I	like love …	the way	she he	is	always never sometimes …	brave. tough. …	You can see this when …
On the other hand,		dislike hate …					negative. old-fashioned …	You can see this in the way he/ she …

To sum up, …

Read your partner's text. Comment on what is similar or different.

Part A Practice

2 It looks like there's going to be a storm (Predictions with the *going to*-future)

p. 64

a) Say what's going to happen in each picture. Here are some ideas:

A *there – be a storm • it – rain • we – get wet*

B *cat – play with / kill mouse • mouse – eat*

C *police – photograph/stop a fast car*

D *fire – start • firefighters – be busy*

E *someone – fall • hurt themselves*

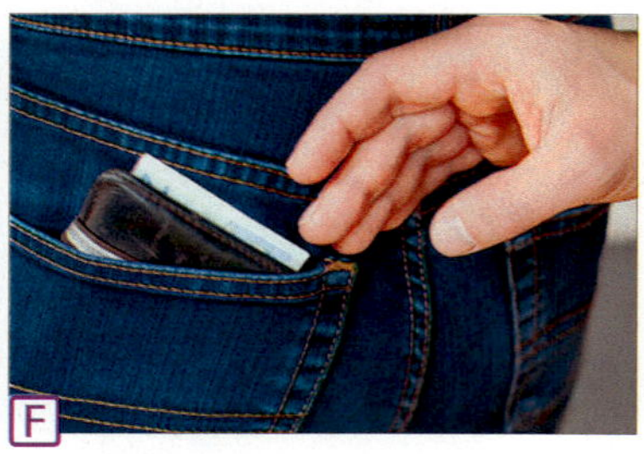

F *thief – steal • someone – money – be stolen*

Part B Practice

3 Text messages (The future: *will* or present progressive)

p. 69

Read the text messages and complete the replies with the correct forms of the verbs.

1
Hey! What's up? Can we meet this evening?
Sorry mate, but (I · **play**) football tonight. (I · **phone**) you at the weekend, OK?

2
How's it going? What are you doing in the holidays?
I'm OK, thanks. (I · **visit**) my uncle in New York. (I · **send**) you a card when I'm there.

3
Hi. We need someone to feed the cat this weekend. Do you think Jack could do it?
I'm not sure. (I · **ask**) him, but I think (he · **go**) to London.

4
Can you help me, pleeease? My computer isn't working – again!
OK (I · **have**) a look. (I · **not do**) anything else this evening.

5 EXTRA Have your hair cut … (*have something done*)

p. 69

b) **Say what you or your family would usually do in these situations and give reasons.**

- Your hair is too long.
- Your bike/phone/TV is broken.
- You need a new key/a passport photo.
- Your bedroom/kitchen needs painting.

I'd *We'd*	*always* *never* *sometimes*	*have*	*my* *our* *a*	*hair* *bike/phone/TV* *new key* *passport photo* *bedroom/kitchen*	*cut* *repaired.* *made.* *taken.* *painted.*	*I wouldn't be able to do it myself.* *We don't know how to do it ourselves* *It's really easy.*

Speaking course

A job interview STEP 2 Think of tips

p. 76

You'll give a better interview if you remember the 4 Ps: Prepare – Practise – Present – Participate

In which of the 4 Ps would you put these tips?

Before the interview		At the interview	
PREPARE	PRACTISE	PRESENT	PARTICIPATE

Arrive on time. • Ask for a glass of water. • Ask how much money you will get. • Ask if you can bring your dog to work. • Ask lots of questions. • Be honest. • Do a roleplay with a friend. • Don't interrupt the interviewer. • Expect to be surprised. • Find out about the job and employer. • Go to the toilet. • Have a look at the employer's building. • Have your hair cut. • Introduce yourself. • Plan your clothes. • Sell yourself well. • Smile a lot. • Think of possible questions and prepare answers.

Part A Practice

2 After the boat tour (Linking words)

p. 86

Continue the story of the trip to London. Show the sequence of events by using these linking words:

after · all of a sudden · by the time · so · so · then · when · when

When the boat tour was over, we were really hungry, ... we went to a little restaurant in Chinatown. ... our meal, we took the Underground to visit the Tower of London.
... we got there, it was already 4:30 pm and there were only 30 minutes until closing time, ... we decided just to photograph the building from outside. ... we walked along the river taking funny selfies as we went.
... we saw the flashmob with the umbrellas again. ... we asked them what they were doing, they told us it was a demonstration for rain! In London!

Part B Practice

2 My report on the interview (Indirect speech)

p. 90

Use verbs to complete your report on your interview.

TIP When you report what someone said, think of their exact words, e.g. *"I am a cyclist myself"*.
When you use <u>indirect speech</u>, remember the backshift. e.g. *<u>She told me</u> she was a cyclist herself.*

When I phoned Councillor Brown, she told me she (be) was a cyclist herself and (be) would be happy to give me an interview. We had planned to meet at 4 pm at the town hall, but Councillor Brown was late: she told me that there (be) lot of traffic. She asked me if I (want) some tea or coffee. Then she asked me why I (wish) to interview her. I replied that I (think) cycling in town (be) dangerous.
She insisted that the council (want) to do more for cyclists. But she also explained that bike paths (cost) a lot of money and that the roads in the town centre (be) too narrow.
She also said that many shops (dislike) bike paths because it (mean) fewer parking spaces for cars. However, she promised that she (ask) the next council meeting to consider the issue.

3 Reporting on a demonstration (Indirect speech)

p. 91

b) Complete this report about the demonstration. Add verbs from the box and use indirect speech where necessary.

be (x3) · can · have · make · not want · say · take (x2) · tell · travel

Anti-lab protest 7 August

A demonstration ... place in central London yesterday against government plans on animal testing.
Almost 100 people ... part in the protest at Marble Arch. The planned laws ... it easier for laboratories to use cats and dogs in animal testing.
A 73-year-old activist from Plymouth said that she ...a cat owner and that the animal in the laboratory ... be her cat. She insisted that animal testing ... not necessary.
One protester from Cambridge ... that he ... 100 miles to be there, because "it ... a huge issue".
A young woman from Scotland ... me that she ... the animals to be in pain. She added that the protesters were there because they ... to make the government listen to them.

5 Let's protest (Verb + gerund)

p. 92

Remember, the verbs in orange in the text below are always followed by a gerund (e.g. hanging). Complete the text using the correct form of the verbs in the box.

~~hang out~~ · get · join in · paint · spend · take · try

Dan really enjoyed hanging out at his school's afternoon youth club. He couldn't imagine ... his free time anywhere else and was very upset when the school decided to close the club. So he met some friends to discuss ... action to protest the decision.

Unfortunately, most of them didn't feel like ... . Some didn't want to risk ... into trouble. Others just weren't interested. Disappointed, Dan gave up ... to get their support. Only Jenny offered to help. She suggest ... a big slogan that everyone would be able to see.

Part C Practice

2 A radio discussion (Indirect speech: *advise, promise, suggest* ...)

p. 100

Listen and take notes on what Sam Meyer and Jessie Rosen say in a radio discussion. Then choose the correct alternative a) or b) to finish the sentences below.

	a)	b)
1 Mr Meyer denied	that the conditions were bad.	that the chickens were really bad.
2 He then described	the 200-year history of his farm.	the happiness of his chickens.
3 Ms Rosen insisted	that the factories were clean.	that the video showed the truth.
4 She then told listeners	that the chickens couldn't move.	that the chickens were thin.
5 She also advised listeners not to	worry about their health.	eat meat from these factories.
6 Mr Meyer again denied	that there was anything bad at his farms.	that the world was a good and kind place.
7 He invited	the presenter to his farm.	Ms Rosen to his farm.
8 But then he refused	to continue the discussion ...	to get his facts right ...
9 ... after Ms Rosen said	that the tours didn't show everything.	that journalists arrange tours for the public.
10 Finally Ms Rosen suggested	that it was all a trick.	visiting the website www.CAAC.org.

Die S können ihre Antworten selbstständig mit den Lösungen auf S. 266–267 abgleichen.

Which place in Sydney?

p. 15, The Rocks

In these dialogues, people are talking about some of the places you read about on p. 12. Read them and try and work out which place.

Hornby Lighthouse

1 A: Actually, if you're going there, make sure you see Hornby Lighthouse.
B: Hornby Lighthouse?
A: It's a historic building, built in 1858, and a great place to watch whales too.
B: Whales! I've never a whale before.
A: They pass by on their way to the coast. And of course, there's also a great view of everyone out on the water enjoying themselves.

A detail of Utzon's building.

2 A: The architect was Danish, a guy called Jørn Utzon.
B: Oh, right. Isn't the building on the World Heritage List?
A: Yes, since 2007.
B: I bet he felt proud.
A: I'm sure he did. He was actually the first person ever who was still alive when their work was added to the list.

The world's largest wooden building?

3 A: It was built between 1911 and 1915 and it's still one of the world's largest wooden buildings.
B: I bet those apartments are really expensive.
A: Yes, but back when it was built, they used to export wool from here. Then the building was empty for years before they changed it into apartments. Of course, the whole area is really trendy now.

Photo captions

p. 16, I saw the ferry arriving

Complete the captions with a participle. If you get all the right words, the highlighted letters will give you the name of place in Sydney that you've read about.

1

We stopped for this kangaroo _ _ [ ] _ _ _ _ across the road.

2

This is a photo of a kookaburra _ [ ] _ _ _ _ _ _.

3

Even a mile away, we could smell the forest _ _ _ [ ] _ _ _.

4

This is just one of the koalas I saw _ [ ] _ _ _ _ _ _ a tree.

5

This is a cool pelican _ _ [ ] _ _ _ over the water.

Whose tent?

p. 21, A trip that went wrong

Copy the nine tents into your exercise book. Then read the sentences below. Under each tent, write the name of the person staying there.

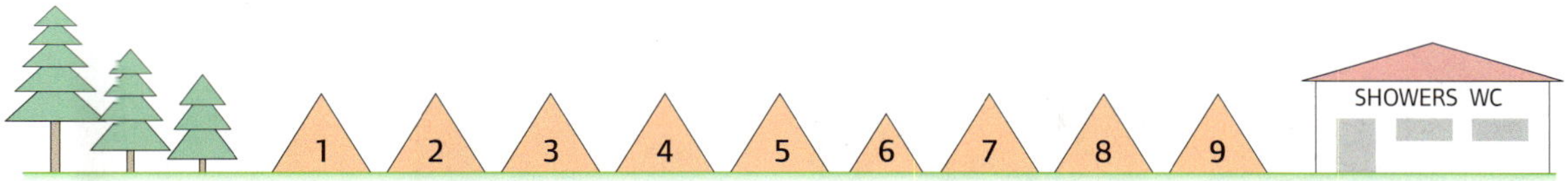

Amy My tent is so far from the toilets – it's a long way in the night. OK, Cara has to go the furthest, but it's still awful.

Bob The guy two tents away from me snores so loudly – it's terrible.

Cara I'm afraid of the wild animals in the forest – I wish I was at the other end. The guy next to me would never hear me if there was a problem because he snores so loudly.

Doris I wish my tent wasn't next to the showers and toilets – everybody stands outside talking while they're waiting.

Eddy My tent is smaller than all the others. It's not fair.

Fiona The guy next to me borrowed my torch and lost it. How can you lose a torch in such a small tent?

Gary Nobody here seems very friendly. The girls on the left and the right never speak to me. And that guy Bob complains about my snoring.

Hal It's awful being in the middle – it's so noisy! It would be OK if I had girls next to me, but …

Isabel I wish I was nearer the forest – it would be better than being near the toilets and showers. Of course, it's worse for Doris. But if there is a long line of people, they stand outside my tent too.

Which sports?

p. 28, Sports and sportspeople

Read the clues and write the name of each sport in a list in your exercise book. Then highlight the letters to get the name of another sport.

1	Germans call it *Fußball*. The British call it *football*. Americans call it … (6)	
2	A ball sport. Six players per team. Or just two per team if you play on a beach.	
3	One against one or two against two. Played on grass <u>or</u> on a harder surface.	
4	If you're good at this sport, you can wear a black belt.	
5	American professional players of this game are about 2 metres tall on average.	
6	A sport loved by the English and Australians, but hardly known in Germany.	
7	Exercises which show that the body is strong and flexible.	
8	Impossible to keep dry in this sport.	

Australian sign language

p. 41, Can we fish here?

What do these signs tell you? In two or three sentences, write down the message of each sign and say what could happen if you don't follow it.

1

2

3

4

5

6

7

8

Example: 1. There are crocodiles is the area. You aren't allowed to swim here. If you do, you could be eaten!

Find the food

p. 44, The people and the issues

Unscramble the letters to find the food words. Write them down in your exercise book.

chicken

1	I'd really prefer a cheese to a check in cash wind.
2	Would you like some cool cheat cause with your ice cream?
3	You can have chips or taptoo as lad with your sausages.
4	I feel like a tapas dish, maybe lasagne or the pig sat.
5	If you don't have any jail cup pee, I'll just drink art we.
6	I like to start the day with clean forks and milk but no ragus.
7	This vegetarian sue saga is just as tasty as a tame one.
8	I eat lots of ray id products like cheese and ugh tory.

Sayings about money

p.48, Advice to parents

Complete the sayings with a word from the box. Then match the meanings of 1–6 to definitions a–f.

burn · grow · hand · leg · mouth · song

a) be really cheap.
b) be really expensive.
c) have just enough money to survive, but no extra.
d) The available amount of money is limited.
e) come from a rich family background
f) have much more money than you need

1 That's too expensive for us. Money doesn't ... on trees!
2 Times were hard and the family was living from ... to mouth.
3 That won't be a problem for him. He has money to ...
4 I got new jeans in that trendy shop. They cost me an arm and a ...
5 I found this old picture at a flea market – I got it for a ...
6 You can tell that he was born with a silver spoon in his ...

Tina's advice for teens

p. 52, If I had been you

Match the advice on the right to the letters to Tina. There is one piece of advice you don't need.

1 *Dear Tina, I've asked my parents several times to give me more pocket money, but they always say no. They don't realize how much a teenager needs today. My dad has a good job and spends a lot of money on his hobby – golf. Why can't they give me more? What can I do?* **Dan, Bristol**

2 *Dear Tina, On Saturdays, my friends and I always go to a disco in the next town, but I have to leave early to get the last bus home. And my dad always comes to the bus stop to meet me – I hate that! My friends are allowed to stay till the end and get a taxi. My parents say we don't have the money for a taxi. It's so unfair – my dad smokes and he has the money for his cigarettes!* **Sue, Liverpool**

3 *Dear Tina, I'll be 16 next month and I want to have a party in the evening with ten of my friends. My parents say it will be too noisy with music in the evening and we have to think about our neighbours – we live in a block of flats. But their kids are often noisy. For example the baby in the flat under us cries a lot.* **Nicky, Glasgow**

4 *Dear Tina, I've been learning to play the guitar for two years and my teacher says I'm really good. But of course I have to practise a lot. My mum says I can't play after ten in the evening because she goes to bed then. But that's so early and I need to practise. What can I do?* **Matt, Belfast**

a You ought to try to see things through your parents' eyes. They clearly care about you. Money doesn't grow on trees! OK, you don't like your dad's 'hobby', but it's his life and health. Maybe if you offer to pay out of your pocket money, your parents will let you stay later sometimes.

b I'm sure the situation isn't easy, but it is important to think about other people. How would you feel if you couldn't sleep? And remember – not everyone likes the same music. Can't you start earlier, so you don't need to play so late?

c I think you should talk to your parents and explain the situation. Have you thought about getting a Saturday job to earn some extra money? If you show that you know how expensive things are, your parents might give you more pocket money.

d Your mother is right, you know. You can't just eat vegetables. It is important to eat enough protein. And it is a lot of work for her if she has to cook two different meals every evening. Why don't you find some good vegetarian recipes on the internet and offer to cook a meal for the whole family?

e You should think about an alternative and ask your parents again. Maybe you could plan something with just four or five friends. If you start early, then there won't be a problem with music in the evening. Or could you meet at a local youth club?

Cartoon captions

p. 63, Prefixes and suffixes

Use prefixes (*dis-*, *un-*, *im-* etc) to make the opposite of the word in the box.

honest · kind · patient · polite · practical · responsible · respectful · tolerant

Then write captions for the cartoons below. Use one of the opposites you made in each caption.

Change one letter

p. 69, Text messages

Change one letter of each word to get a word that matches the definition.
Write the new words on a piece of paper and underline the changed letters.
The underlined letters make up two words. What are they?

1	CHEAP	get something by being dishonest
2	WISH	understanding thanks to experience
3	TEST	words that make up a book, magazine, etc.
4	ADVERB	message that helps to sell a product
5	CATCH	look well together
6	TENTH	hard white things used to bite
7	NIGHTS	what you go to see when you visit a place
8	PAST	hit or kick a ball to players on your team
9	SWEET	get wet skin when you are hot
10	STATE	place in theatre where actors act
11	STOP	a surface you put your foot on when going up or down

Check the corrections

p. 74, Writing a letter of application

There are 12 mistakes in this letter. But the person who corrected it has underlined 16!
Decide which of the underlined words really are mistakes, and why (grammar, spelling, wrong word…?).
Make a list in your exercise book.

Dear Ms Anderson,

I am writing about the announcement on your website. I would love to work at your hotel this summer.

As you can see from my CV, I am 16 years. I am learning english since eight years and it would be great to have the chance to practise my language skills at your Kids Club. I have many experience with childrens. For example I babysit for my neighbours kids every weekend and I have two younger brothers. Sport is one of my hobbys, so I would be happy to help to organize sport aktivities for the older kids. I love working in teams, so I am sure I'll get on well with everyone.

I look forward to hear from you soon.

Yours sincerly,

Colour phrases

p. 75, Check your spelling

Match sentences 1–6 with sentences A–F.
To complete the colour phrases in A–F, choose the right colour from the box and solve the word puzzles.

black · green · green · red · white · white

1 We don't often get snow here.	A He's the … P E E S H of the family.
2 It's OK to start with the project.	B He looked as … as a T H O G S.
3 His mum and dad are so disappointed in him.	C It's time he was given the … A R C D.
4 Something must have scared him an awful lot.	D Somebody really has got … N E G R I F S.
5 He just doesn't play fairly.	E So a … M A C S H I R T S is really very unusual.
6 Their garden looks so beautiful.	F We've been given the … G L I T H at last

An airport incident

p. 86, We had been walking for hours

Work out what happened at the airport. Put the paragraphs of a newspaper report in the right order.

A Immediately Ms Brown grabbed her microphone: "May I have your attention, please, may I have your attention, please," she began – her voice heard clearly throughout the terminal.

B Ms Brown kept calm and smiled at the passenger. "I'm very sorry, sir. I'll be happy to try to help you, but these people are before you in the queue. Please be patient – I'm sure we'll be able to work something out."

C The man was not happy. He asked loudly, so that the passengers behind him could hear, "DO YOU HAVE ANY IDEA WHO I AM?"

D At London's busy Heathrow airport yesterday, Cheryl Brown, who works at the check-in desk of Grey Arrow Airlines, faced a difficult situation.

E "We have a passenger here at Desk 14 who does not know who he is. If anyone can help him find his identity, please come to Desk 14."

F A flight had been cancelled because of technical problems, and there was a long line of travellers hoping to get onto another flight. Suddenly an angry passenger pushed his way to the check-in desk. He slapped his ticket down on the counter and said, "I HAVE to be on this flight and it HAS to be FIRST CLASS".

Cartoon captions

p. 87, Describing and interpreting images

Find another early finisher and discuss the message of each cartoon. Then write captions for each one.

Definitions

p. 91, Reporting on a demonstration

Write down the correct word for each definition.
Use the given letter for each word to make another word. Then write a definition for that word.

1 show that you disagree strongly with something (7) *LETTER 1*

2 the group of people responsible for controlling a country (10) *LETTER 4*

3 an event when people come together to oppose or support something (13) *LETTER 7*

4 the process of choosing people for a public or political (8) *LETTER 6*

5 stopping work to try and get better pay or conditions (7) *LETTER 2*

6 a number of activities planned to achieve a goal (8) *LETTER 6*

7 make your choice in an election (7) *LETTER 2*

8 the group of people who are elected to make laws (10) *LETTER 9*

Presentation tips

p. 101, Study skills: Refining your presentation techniques

Match two boxes to make a presentation tip. Write the tips in your exercise book.

PRESENTATION TIPS
5, 21 Practise as often as you can.
...

1 MAKE EYE 2 OPENER 3 EARLY

4 END WITH 5 PRACTISE AS OFTEN 6 SMILE AT

7 A SCRIPT 8 USE A STRONG 9 DON'T READ OUT 10 ARRIVE

11 DON'T SPEAK 12 YOUR AUDIENCE 13 TEST ALL 14 NOTES

15 A BANG 16 KEEP IT 17 USE 18 AUDIENCE

19 EQUIPMENT 20 CONTACT 21 AS YOU CAN

22 TOO FAST 23 FACE YOUR 24 SIMPLE

3 Life away from home (Giving advice)

p. 46

Partner A: Give your partner some tips on how to get on well with your host family Use some of the ideas below and think of some of your own.

- Have a small present to give your family when you arrive, maybe something German.
- Join in family activities whenever you can.
- Offer to help with jobs around the house.
- Always keep your room clean.
- Get up early sometimes and make everyone breakfast.
- …

Then swap roles. Listen to your partner's advice and react to it.

That sounds like a good idea.

That's a great suggestion!

Do you really think I should do that?

I'm not sure if I agree with that idea.

4 "Raise your voice"

p. 91

Partner A: Read the leaflet and note down the information you need for your American friend.

RAISE YOUR VOICE

ALLE WICHTIGEN INFOS ZUM SCHÜLER-SONG-CONTEST

WIE KANN MAN MITMACHEN?

Die Schülerinnen und Schüler sollen einen eigenen Song zum Thema Kinderrechte erstellen. Was sie inhaltlich genau darin behandeln und ob sie als Chor, Schulband oder Hip-Hop-Projekt auftreten, bleibt ihnen selbst überlassen – der kreativen Freiheit sind keine Grenzen gesetzt. Wichtig ist nur, dass der Song als Video oder Musik-Stream für den Contest aufbereitet wird.

WER KANN MITMACHEN?

Teilnehmen können alle Schülerinnen und Schüler der Jahrgangsstufen 9 bis 13, die das Einverständnis ihrer Eltern haben und gemeinsam als Team, zum Beispiel als Klasse, Stufe, Kurs oder AG, mit ihrem Lehrer/ihrer Lehrerin einen Beitrag einreichen.

WIE LÄUFT DER WETTBEWERB AB?

Die Songs können für den Contest auf www.raise-your-voice.de hochgeladen werden. Vom 10. bis 20. April wählt eine Jury, bestehend aus Vertretern des Deutschen Kinderschutzbundes, von ROLAND Rechtsschutz, aus der Politik, der Musikbranche und Ado Kojo, die zehn besten Songs aus. Ab dem 20. April wird dann online per Voting entschieden, wer die absolute Nummer 1 wird. Abschließend werden die Gewinner benachrichtigt und erhalten ihre Preise.

WAS GIBT ES ZU GEWINNEN?

Auf die Erstplatzierten warten ein exklusives Schulkonzert mit Ado Kojo sowie eine Musikausrüstung im Wert von 3.000 Euro für die Schule und Bluetooth-Boxen für jeden Schüler aus dem Gewinnerteam. Die Plätze 2 und 3 erhalten je ein Tablet und 1.000 Euro für die Klassenkasse, die Plätze 4 bis 10 werden mit je 500 Euro für die Klassenkasse belohnt.

4 Youth competitions

p. 69

Partner A: Read this text on and takes notes on the information you have been asked to find.

BUNDESWETTBEWERB FREMDSPRACHEN

Wer in fremden Sprachen die richtigen Worte findet, dem steht die Welt offen.
Beim Bundeswettbewerb für Fremdsprachen stellen sich Schüler und Auszubildende jedes Jahr Aufgaben, die Kreativität und Sicherheit im Umgang mit Sprachen erfordern.
Wer beim Wettbewerb gewinnt, reist in ferne Länder – zum Beispiel nach China.

Beim Bundeswettbewerb für Fremdsprachen treten jedes Jahr 15.000 Jugendliche an. Er ist einer der traditionsreichsten Schülerwettbewerbe in Deutschland. Schon seit 1979 fördert er junge Leute, die Spaß an fremden Sprachen und Kulturen haben. Ausgetragen wird der Wettbewerb vom Zentrum für Begabungsförderung „Bildung & Begabung".
Besonders begabte Sprachenkünstler qualifizieren sich mit einer guten Platzierung beim Wettbewerb für die Aufnahme in die Studienstiftung des deutschen Volkes. Aber auch für alle anderen ist die Teilnahme ein Gewinn – schon allein durch den Austausch mit Sprachenfans aus ganz Deutschland. Antreten kann man in den beiden Kategorien SOLO und TEAM.

SOLO:
Hier gibt es zwei Jahrgangsgruppen, zum einen für die achten und neunten Klassen, zum anderen für Schülerinnen und Schüler ab der zehnten Klasse. Während die Jüngeren in einer der sieben Wettbewerbssprachen – zum Beispiel Englisch, Spanisch oder Altgriechisch – antreten, kommt bei den Älteren eine zweite Fremdsprache hinzu. Die Besten aus der jüngeren Altersgruppe fahren jedes Jahr zum „Sprachenturnier", wo es ebenfalls viele Preise und tolle neue Erfahrungen zu gewinnen gibt.

TEAM:
In dieser Kategorie kommt es darauf an, in der Gruppe kreativ zu werden. Mitmachen können Schülerinnen und Schüler der Klassen 6 bis 9. Die Zweier- bis Zehnerteams drehen zum Beispiel Filme, erfinden Bühnenstücke, erstellen Multimedia-Präsentationen oder erfinden Spiele und Web-Anwendungen. Die besten Gruppen aus jedem Bundesland präsentieren ihre Kreativbeiträge dann vor großem Publikum auf dem „Sprachenfest".

1 Writing a letter of application

p. 74

We are a small international summer camp in Essex for children aged 6–11. We are looking for a responsible and creative camp helper in August. You will need to have good English and feel comfortable organizing activities for children, including a day trip to London. You will also be expected to help at meals and bedtimes.
Salary £500. Meals free. Please apply to
Jake Welch
Fingringhoe International Camp
Fingringhoe CO5 3FH

Edinburgh public libraries are offering work experience to volunteers age 14–18.
No qualifications are needed.
The work experience will last for four weeks from mid-July to mid-August and is unpaid.
Students who would like to discover what a career in a library can offer are invited to apply to
Maura McPherson
Capital Libraries
Edinburgh EH35 2BT

5 Explaining the situation

p. 46

**Choose one situation each and read your dialogue carefully.
Work out when you should speak English or German and what you should say.**

**Then act out your dialogue. Try not to sound too direct or unfriendly when speaking English.
Your two partners should take turns to play the New Zealand student and the German speaker.**

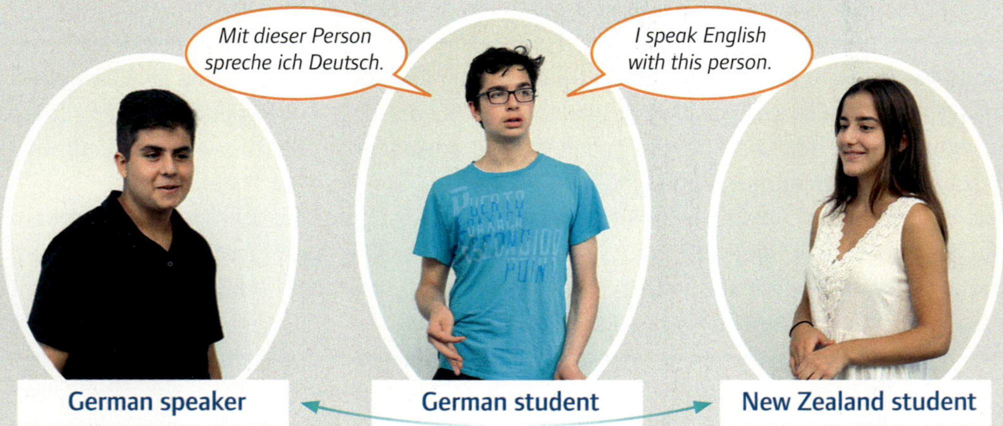

When you play the German student, you are the mediator. In other words, you help people who don't have a common language to understand each other.

SITUATION 1

New Zealand student: *I think I need to make an appointment with a doctor.*
You: *…*
New Zealand student: *I'm not feeling great. I've been getting headaches and not sleeping so well.*
You: *…*
Arztpraxis: *Praxis Dr Koppe. Guten Tag. Was kann ich für Sie tun?*
You: *…*
Arztpraxis: *Wie heißt der Gast, und worum geht es genau?*
You: *…*
Arztpraxis: *Verstehe … und wie lange leidet er/sie schon an Kopfschmerzen?*
You: *…*
New Zealand student: *For the last three or four days.*
You: *…*
Arztpraxis: *Ich kann Ihnen nächste Woche Dienstag um 15 Uhr 10 einen Termin anbieten.*
You: *…*
New Zealand student: *Not till next Tuesday afternoon? But the headache is really bad.*
You: *…*
Arztpraxis: *Im Moment sind wir sehr voll … Warten Sie mal. Wie wäre es Freitag um 12.20?*
You: *…*
New Zealand student: *Friday would be much better, thanks.*

SITUATION 2

Kontrolleur(in): Guten Morgen, die Fahrausweise bitte.
New Zealand student: Hey, what does this guy want?
You: …
New Zealand student: Oh right, one minute. **(looks in backback)** *Hey, I can't find my ticket.*
You: …
Kontrolleur(in): Dann werden 60 Euro fällig. Gehören Sie zusammen?
You: …
Kontrolleur(in): Dann steigen Sie mit mir am nächsten Bahnhof aus.
You: …
New Zealand student: But why do I have to pay 60 euros? I have a student's ticket. It's just that I've forgotten to put it in my backpack.
You: …
Kontrolleur(in): Dann muss er/sie die Schülerkarte innerhalb von 7 Tagen im Kundenbüro vorlegen.
You: …
Kontrolleur(in): Nein, dann kostet es keine 60 Euro. Es gibt aber eine Bearbeitungsgebühr von 7 Euro.
You: …
New Zealand student: Well, I suppose 7 euros is better than 60.
Kontrolleur(in): So, jetzt bitte aussteigen. Er/Sie muss noch seine/ihre Personalien angeben.
New Zealand student: Sorry, what does he/she want us to do now?
You: …

SITUATION 3

Bibliotheksangestellte(r): Wie kann ich Ihnen helfen?
You: …
Bibliotheksangestellte(r): Dann brauche ich erstmal den Personalausweis oder Reisepass.
You: …
New Zealand student: Oh right. Actually, we don't have ID cards in New Zealand, and I never thought of bringing my passport. I have my student travel card, though. It has a photo, so it should be OK.
You: …
Bibliotheksangestellte(r): Leider nicht. Ein Fahrausweis ist doch kein amtliches Dokument.
You: …
New Zealand student: I suppose we'll have to go back home and get my passport then.
Bibliotheksangestellte(r): Und weil er/sie aus dem Ausland kommt, brauche ich auch noch die Meldebescheinigung.
You: …
New Zealand student: Actually, I don't think there is an English word for it. New Zealand doesn't have a register of where people live. But I know where my Meldebescheinigung is. It's with my passport.
You: …
New Zealand student: Well, maybe you could ask how much it's going to cost. And how long can I borrow things for?
You: …
Bibliotheksangestellte(r): Für Schüler und Schülerinnen ist die Bibliotheksbenutzung kostenlos. Die Ausleihzeit ist für Bücher, CDs und Video-Spiele unterschiedlich. Es steht alles in diesem Infoblatt. Leider nur auf Deutsch.
You: …

2 Uncle Ozzie's fun facts

p.10

1 **There are three times as many sheep in Australia as people.**
True: 23 million people, 75 million sheep.

2 **One in three Australians speak Japanese.**
False: However, there are about 43,000 people living in Australia who speak Japanese at home.

3 **There are over 750,000 wild camels in Australia's deserts.**
True: Camels were introduced to Australia in the mid-19th century. They were used to transport building materials in dry and desert areas.

4 **About 750,000 people live in the outback.**
False: Fewer than 500,000 people live in the outback. Most of Australia's population live in or close to a few cities on the east, south and south-west coast.

5 **People arrived in Australia before they arrived in the Americas.**
True People arrived in the Americas at least 20,000 years later.

6 **17 out of 26 of the world's most poisonous snakes are found in Australia.**
True Australia has 140 different kinds of snake. About 5 people die from snake bites each year.

7 **The 'selfie' is an Australian invention.**
True The Oxford English Dictionary says the word "selfie" was first used by an Australian in 2002.

8 **A kangaroo is only one centimetre long when it is born.**
True A female kangaroo is fully grown after 14–20 months, a male kangaroo after 2–4 years.

9 **Koalas eat insects, grass and birds' eggs.**
False: Koalas only eat leaves. An adult koala eats between 200 to 500 grams each day.

10 **One in five Australians has somebody in their family who was once in prison.**
True Many of the ancestors of today's Australians arrived as convicts. The UK sent convicts between 1788 and 1868.

3 Life away from home (Giving advice)

p. 46

**Partner B: Listen to your partner's advice and on how to get on well with your host family.
React to the advice your partner gives you.**

That sounds like a good idea.

That's a great suggestion!

Do you really think I should do that?

I'm not sure if I agree with that idea.

**Then swap roles. Give your partner some tips
Use some of the ideas below and think of some your own.**

- Show your host family photos of your family and where you live in Germany.
  Make sure they know what food you can't/don't eat.
- Talk to them if you feel homesick.
- Always ask before you bring a friend home.
- Never borrow money from your host family. Contact your parents if you need money.
- ...

4 Youth competitions

p. 69

Partner B: Read this text and takes notes on the information you have been asked to find.

Jugend forscht

Jugend forscht ist Deutschlands bekanntester Nachwuchswettbewerb. Ziel ist es, einerseits Jugendliche für Mathematik, Informatik, Naturwissenschaften und Technik zu begeistern und andererseits Nachwuchswissenschaftler/innen zu finden und zu fördern. Pro Jahr gibt es bundesweit mehr als 100 Wettbewerbe. Teilnehmen können Jugendliche ab der 4. Klasse bis zum Alter von 21 Jahren. Die große Herausforderung ist, dass sich alle Teilnehmer/innen selbst eine interessante Fragestellung für ihr Forschungsprojekt suchen müssen. Die Gewinner/innen erhalten attraktive Geld- und Sachpreise.

Jugend forscht wurde von dem damaligen STERN-Chefredakteur Henri Nannen im Jahr 1965 ins Leben gerufen. Er startete eine gesellschaftlich breit angelegte Initiative, um den qualifizierten Nachwuchs an jungen Wissenschaftlerinnen und Wissenschaftlern in der Bundesrepublik Deutschland zu fördern.

Die Bandbreite möglicher Themen bei Jugend forscht ist praktisch unbegrenzt. Die jungen Forscher/innen können Lösungen für Probleme aus ihrem Alltag finden, oder sie wagen sich an Probleme, die die Wissenschaft zur Zeit beschäftigen. Fragestellungen lassen sich auch aus dem Unterricht ableiten. Meist werden die Jugendlichen von ihren Lehrern und Lehrerinnen oder von Beratern von Jugend forscht bei ihrer Arbeit unterstützt. Eine Wettbewerbsrunde dauert ungefähr ein Jahr von der Themensuche und dem Beginn der Projektarbeit an. Es folgen Regional- und Landeswettbewerbe bis zum Bundesfinale. Einer der Preise kann auch die weiterführende Teilnahme an internationalen Wettbewerben sein.

4 "Raise your voice"

p. 91

Partner B: Read the leaflet and note down the information you need for your American friend.

Kinderrechte sind wichtig. Sie schützen Kinder und Jugendliche und machen aus ihnen starke Persönlichkeiten, die für sich selbst und andere eintreten können. Die Tatsache, dass es überhaupt Kinderrechte gibt, ist jedoch leider den wenigsten Erwachsenen und Kindern bekannt. Daran möchten wir mit der Aktion „Raise Your Voice“ etwas ändern. Der Deutsche Kinderschutzbund und ROLAND Rechtsschutz rufen im Rahmen eines bundesweiten Schüler-Song-Contests gemeinsam mit dem Paten der Aktion, Future-R&B-Sänger Ado Kojo, Schüler/innen der 9. bis 13. Klasse sowie Lehrer/innen dazu auf, sich aktiv mit dem Thema auseinanderzusetzen.

Gerade Musik ist in der jungen Zielgruppe von großer Bedeutung. Deshalb sollen die Schüler/innen im Rahmen eines Song-Contests mit einem selbst verfassten Lied ausdrücken, welche Kinderrechte ihnen wichtig sind und wo sie verletzt oder aktiv gelebt werden. Um das Thema zur Ergänzung des Lehrplans zu machen und es auch im Schulalltag zu verankern, bieten wir über den Wettbewerb hinaus zusätzlich Anregungen, Broschüren und Unterrichtsmaterial an. Alle Infos finden sich auf der Aktions-Website www.raise-your-voice.de.

Skills File – Inhalt

Im **Skills File** findest du **Lernhilfen und Methoden,** die dir z. B. beim Schreiben von eigenen Texten oder bei der Sprachmittlung helfen oder Tipps zum Vorbereiten von Präsentationen geben. Techniken, die du in den Units gelernt hast, werden hier aufgenommen und erläutert, ebenso wie solche, die du schon aus früheren Bänden kennst.

Du kannst das Skills File auch nutzen, um Methoden nochmal nachzuschlagen, wenn du z. B. einen Text schreiben sollst.

READING SKILLS

SF 1 Skimming and scanning

Skimming *(reading for gist)* und Scanning *(reading for specific information)* sind Lesetechniken, die viel Zeit sparen, v. a. beim Lesen von langen Texten.

SKIMMING

Skimming hilft, schnell zu sehen, ob ein Text für deinen Zweck geeignet ist.

Step 1: Sieh dir diese Textteile an, um zu sehen, worum es im Text geht:
- Überschrift und Unterüberschriften
- Bilder und Bildunterschriften
- den ersten Satz jedes Absatzes – dieser Satz ist meist der *topic sentence*, der die Hauptidee des Absatzes nennt
- den letzten Absatz des Textes, der oft eine Zusammenfassung des Textes enthält

Step 2: Fasse für dich selbst den Text in ein paar Worten zusammen. Wenn dir das ohne Probleme gelingt, dann weißt du, um was es in dem Text geht – und dass dein Skimming erfolgreich war.

TIPP
Mach dir um unbekannten Wortschatz erstmal keine Gedanken – dafür ist Zeit, wenn du feststellst, dass der Text für dich geeignet ist.

SCANNING

Scanning hilft, in einem Text schnell nach bestimmten Informationen zu suchen.

Step 1: Überlege dir *keywords*. Suchst du z. B. die Öffnungszeiten eines Museums, könnten das Wörter sein wie *open, hours* oder *days*.

Step 2: Überfliege den Text und suche nach den *keywords*. Du kannst dabei mit dem Finger in einer "S-Form" durch den Text gehen.

Step 3: Lies die Textstelle, die dein *keyword* enthält, um zu sehen, ob sie die gewünschten Informationen enthält. Wenn nicht, scanne weiter.

TIPP
Wenn du mit Texten im Internet arbeitest, kann dein Browser dir viel Arbeit abnehmen.
Mit Strg+F (Cmd+F am Mac) kannst du nach deinen *keywords* suchen und nur die Textstellen lesen, in denen ein *keyword* markiert ist.

SF 2 Marking up a text

Auf Kopien von Texten kannst du Informationen markieren, um sie einfacher wiederzufinden, z. B. wenn du eine Zusammenfassung schreiben sollst.

Step 1: Lies die Aufgabe genau und überlege, welche Informationen du zur Beantwortung brauchst. Behalte dies beim Lesen des Textes im Kopf.

Step 2: Markiere nur Informationen, die wichtig sind (z. B. durch Unterstreichen, Einkreisen oder Markieren mit einem Textmarker). Oft reicht es, nur ein oder zwei Wörter in einem Satz zu markieren.

Step 3: Mach dir kurze Notizen am Rand – z. B. kurze Überschriften oder Stichwörter –, die den Inhalt kurz zusammenfassen. (➜ *SF 33*)

TIPP
1. Verwende unterschiedliche Farben für unterschiedliche Aufgaben/Fragestellungen.
2. Markiere wirklich nur Stichwörter, sonst wird es unübersichtlich.

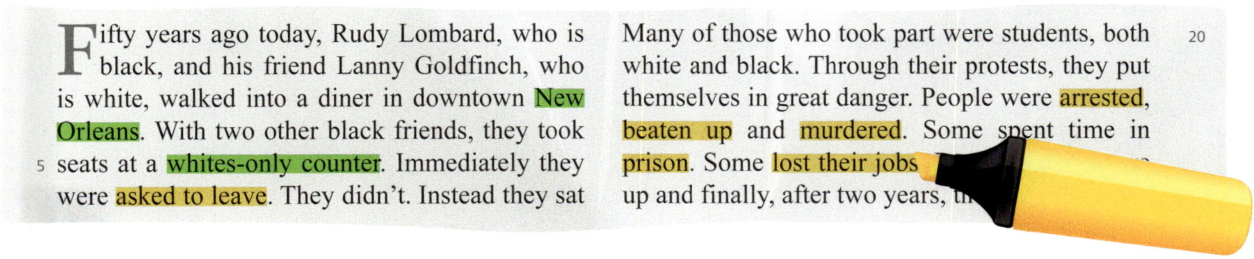
Fifty years ago today, Rudy Lombard, who is black, and his friend Lanny Goldfinch, who is white, walked into a diner in downtown New Orleans. With two other black friends, they took seats at a whites-only counter. Immediately they were asked to leave. They didn't. Instead they sat

Many of those who took part were students, both white and black. Through their protests, they put themselves in great danger. People were arrested, beaten up and murdered. Some spent time in prison. Some lost their jobs … up and finally, after two years, …

WRITING SKILLS

SF 3 The stages of writing

Wenn deine Texte präzise und gut lesbar sind, machst du es deinen Lesern leichter, deinen Gedanken zu folgen. Dabei spielt es keine Rolle, welche Art von Text du schreibst – ob Bericht, Zusammenfassung oder eine Geschichte. Du solltest ihn stets gut planen und zuerst einen Entwurf erstellen, den du dann überarbeitest, bis das Ergebnis so ist, wie es sein soll – gut lesbar, leicht zu verstehen und ohne Fehler.

Dieses Vorgehen braucht Zeit, aber es macht deine Texte besser.

PLANUNGSPHASE

Step 1: Plane ausreichend Zeit ein und denke über folgende Fragen nach:
- Über welches Thema willst du schreiben?
- Was sollst du tun (beschreiben, erläutern, zusammenfassen ...)?
- Welche Dinge musst du für den geforderten Text beachten?

Step 2: Dann solltest du
- alle nötigen Informationen für dein Thema recherchieren (➔ *SF 28*),
- Ideen/Argumente sammeln und sortieren
- und eine Gliederung (Outline) für den Text (z. B. einen Bericht) machen. (➔ *SF 6*)

ENTWURFSPHASE

Jetzt schreibe deinen ersten Entwurf:

- Füge deiner Gliederung linking words (➔ *SF 5*) und topic sentences hinzu (➔ *SF 4*).
- Beginne für jede neue Idee einen neuen Absatz.
- Führe deine Ideen aus und gib Beispiele (wenn das die Textsorte erfordert).
- Denk über das Ende deines Textes nach. Wenn du weißt, wie dein Text endet, ist es leichter, eine gute Einleitung zu schreiben, die darauf hinführt. (➔ *SF 4*)

ÜBERARBEITUNGSPHASE

Wenn der Entwurf fertig ist, bist du mit deiner Arbeit am Text leider noch nicht durch – jetzt beginnt die Überarbeitung. Am besten ist es, wenn du oder jemand anderes deinen Text mehrmals liest, jedes Mal mit einem anderen Schwerpunkt:

- Liest sich der Text gut? Ist er logisch aufgebaut? Hat er eine gute Struktur? (➔ *SF 4*)
- Prüfe die sprachlichen Aspekte deines Textes: Grammatik, Rechtschreibung, Zeichensetzung, Ausdruck, *linking words, time markers* etc. (➔ *SF 5, SF 11*)
- Schreibe deinen Text noch einmal ab. Verbessere alles, was im ersten Entwurf noch nicht ganz gepasst hat. Wenn du Feedback von jemand anderem bekommen hast, sieh es dir genau an und entscheide dann, was davon du für deinen Text übernehmen möchtest.

TIPP
Mehr Informationen zum Verfassen guter Texte findest du auch auf folgenden Seiten:
- SF 4: Structuring texts
- SF 5: Writing good sentences
- SF 6: Making an outline
- SF 7: Writing a report
- SF 8: Writing a summary
- SF 9: Argumentative writing
- SF 10: Writing a formal letter or email
- SF 11: Revising texts
- SF 28: Internet research

SF 4 Structuring texts

STRUKTUR

Ein guter Text besteht in der Regel aus drei Teilen:

- Einleitung *(introduction)*:
  Hier steht, worum es in dem Text geht. An dieser Stelle kann auch ein Problem genannt werden, das in dem Text erörtert werden soll.
- Hauptteil *(main body)*:
  Dieser Teil ist in mehrere Absätze gegliedert und präsentiert die Details (Fakten, Beispiele etc.) zu deinem Thema.
- Schluss *(conclusion)*:
  Hier gibst du deinem Text ein passendes Ende.

ABSÄTZE

Längere Texte sind einfacher zu lesen und schneller zu verstehen, wenn sie in Absätze eingeteilt sind. Dabei solltest du folgende Dinge beachten:

- Fange für neue Aspekte einen neuen Absatz an.
- Beginne mit einem interessanten *topic sentence*.
- Beende deinen Text im letzten Absatz mit einer Zusammenfassung oder etwas Persönlichem.

EINLEITUNGSSÄTZE

Jeder Absatz sollte mit einem Einleitungssatz beginnen. Dieser topic sentence beschreibt, worum es in dem Absatz geht. Wichtige Dinge, die du in einem *topic sentence* ansprechen kannst, sind z. B.

- ***Orte:*** *My trip to Berlin was exciting.*
- ***Personen:*** *The Beatles are a famous band.*
- ***Aktivitäten:*** *Lots of people ride their bike every day.*

My Trip to Wales

Last summer I wanted to go to Wales because I like the mountains.

First I had to find some information on Wales. So I went to the library and looked for books about Wales. I found a book with some interesting information on hiking tours and I also found a camping guide for Wales. I went home with three books under my arm.

At home I started to plan for my trip. I read all the books and took notes on hiking trails, the weather and the equipment I would need for camping and hiking. After a few days I knew where I wanted to go and what I wanted to do there.

I did not want to go to Wales alone, so I had to find someone to go with me. I called most of my friends and told them about my plan. Some of them did not want to go hiking and others had no money for the trip. But my friend Judith agreed to go with me. We decided to go in late August.

Judith and I spent two lovely weeks in Wales. We went to Snowdonia and enjoyed the fantastic mountains. We stayed in a lovely bed and breakfast and met lots of really nice people. Before we went home we spent two very interesting days in Cardiff.

This was one of the best summer holidays I ever had. Go to Wales – it's fantastic!

SF 5 Writing good sentences

Interessante Texte bestehen aus guten, abwechslungsreichen Sätzen. Die folgenden Techniken helfen dir, dich variabel auszudrücken und damit den Stil deiner Texte zu verbessern.

ADJEKTIVE

Verwende Adjektive, wenn du Dinge, Orte und Menschen beschreiben möchtest:

- *a bright face*
- *a fantastic trip*

Stell aber sicher, dass du die Adjektive good, bad and nice nicht zu häufig einsetzt. Ersetze sie durch andere Adjektive mit einer ähnlichen bzw. genaueren Bedeutung:

- *a nice teacher: a friendly teacher, a helpful teacher, …*
- *a good book: an interesting book, a funny book, …*

ADVERBIEN

Verwende Adverbien, um Handlungen näher zu beschreiben:

- *They walked home slowly.*
- *She talked quietly.*

Verwende Ausdrücke wie really, very, a bit etc., um Aussagen zu verdeutlichen oder zu verstärken:

- *It was a really sad story.*
- *The houses are very high.*

KONJUNKTIONEN

Konjunktionen wie and, but oder because geben deinen Sätzen eine klare, gut nachvollziehbare Struktur:

- *We went to the London Eye, but it was very expensive.*

RELATIVSÄTZE

Relativsätze verbinden Sätze oder geben mehr Informationen zu einer Sache oder einer Person:

- *This is the shop which sells the best ice cream in Berlin.*

ZEITANGABEN

Time markers / adverbiale Bestimmungen der Zeit helfen dem Leser, sich in einem Text oder einer Geschichte zeitlich zurechtzufinden. Verwende *time markers*, um …

- die Reihenfolge von Ereignissen zu verdeutlichen:
  at first, next, finally, …
- zu zeigen, wie viel Zeit zwischen einzelnen Ereignissen vergeht:
  for half an hour, just two minutes later, …
- zu verdeutlichen, wie langsam oder schnell etwas passiert:
  immediately, it took hours, faster than I could look, …
- zu sagen, wenn etwas zeitgleich passiert:
  while I was waiting, during the lesson, as we came round the corner, …
- die Ereignisse eines Textes/einer Geschichte zeitlich einzuordnen:
  two summers ago, last Halloween, on my way home from school yesterday, …

SF 6 Making an outline

Jede Art von Text profitiert davon, wenn du dir vorab überlegst, was du in welcher Reihenfolge schreiben willst.

- Wenn du einen Bericht schreiben sollst (➔ *SF 7*), kann es helfen, die wichtigsten Punkte schon in der Gliederung zu berücksichtigen: eine gute Struktur und die Beantwortung der *wh*-Fragen.
- Bei einer Zusammenfassung (➔ *SF 8*) kannst du hier die wichtigsten Punkte festhalten.
- Für eine Erörterung (➔ *SF 9*) kannst du in deiner Outline schon die Argumente sortieren, die du im Text bringen möchtest.

Damit leistest du schon eine Menge Vorarbeit und erleichterst dir das Schreiben.

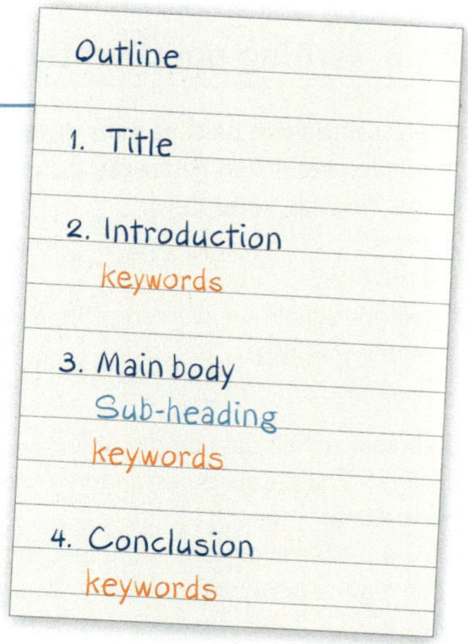

SF 7 Writing a report

In einem Bericht geht es darum, dem Leser übersichtlich und gut verständlich Fakten darzustellen, z.B. zu einem Ereignis oder einem Vorfall.

STRUKTUR

Wie jeder Text sollte ein Bericht aus einer Überschrift, einer Einleitung, einem Hauptteil und einem Schluss bestehen. (➔ *SF 4*)

In einer Gliederung (➔ *SF 6*) kannst du diese Struktur schon anlegen und für jeden Textteil eine Überschrift notieren sowie Stichwörter dazu ergänzen. Wenn du viele Informationen im Hauptteil unterbringen möchtest, verwende auch Unterüberschriften.

STICHWÖRTER

In der Einleitung eines Berichtes sagst du kurz, was passiert ist. Dabei kannst du schon knapp die wichtigsten *wh*-Fragen beantworten, bevor du im Hauptteil näher darauf eingehst.

In deiner Gliederung (➔ *SF 6*) solltest du deswegen für die Einleitung deine Stichworte auf die Fragen Who?, What?, When?, Where? und Why? konzentrieren.

Im Hauptteil eines Berichtes stehen dann die Details des Ereignisses, meist in chronologischer Reihenfolge. Hier werden also die *wh*-Fragen genauer beantwortet, deswegen solltest du in der Gliederung für den Hauptteil weitere Stichworte zu den einzelnen Fragen sammeln.

Im Schlussabsatz bringst du deinen Bericht zum Abschluss, indem du z.B. kurz das Ergebnis oder die Folgen des beschriebenen Ereignisses darstellst.

TIPP

Ein Bericht soll objektiv sein und Fakten darstellen. Konzentriere dich bei deinen *keywords* in der Gliederung darauf, die 5 *wh*-Fragen zu beantworten:

- What happened?
- Who did what?
- When did it happen?
- Where did it happen?
- Why did it happen?

Denk daran, dass ein Bericht im *simple past* geschrieben wird. Du solltest also deine Stichworte auch gleich so notieren.

SF 8 Writing a summary

Wenn du eine Zusammenfassung schreiben sollst, ist es wichtig, den Text gut zu kennen. Erst dann kannst du entscheiden, welche Aspekte so wichtig sind, dass sie in deiner Zusammenfassung erwähnt werden sollten – und welche nicht. Die folgenden Schritte können dabei helfen:

PLANUNGSPHASE

Step 1: Lies den Text genau. Mach dir Notizen (➔ *SF 33*) oder markiere wichtige Stellen im Text (➔ *SF 2*).

Step 2: Beantworte die *wh*-Fragen Who? What? Where? When? Why? zum Text. Du kannst dir dazu Stichworte am Rand machen.

Who?	Who does something? Who is the text about?
What?	What happens? What does person X do?
Where?	Where does it take place?
When?	When does it take place?
Why?	Why does person X act this way? Why does something happen?

Step 3: Entscheide, welche Textteile wichtige Informationen enthalten. Beispiele, Vergleiche, direkte Rede oder Zahlen und Ähnliches gehören nicht in eine Zusammenfassung.

TIPP

Du kannst Teile, die für deine Zusammenfassung überflüssig sind, im Text einklammern.

SCHREIBPHASE

Step 1: Schreib einen ersten Entwurf.

- Beginne mit der Einleitung, in der wichtige Informationen wie Titel, Autor/in, Thema und Hauptaussage des Textes stehen. Wenn du einen Artikel zusammenfasst, solltest du hier die Quelle nennen.
- Verwende immer das simple present.
- Kopiere nicht den Text, sondern benutze deine eigenen Worte.
- Wichtig: gib nie deine eigene Meinung oder Wertung.

Step 2: Überarbeite deine Zusammenfassung.

- Hast du alle wichtigen Aspekte genannt? Hast du unwichtige Details weggelassen?
- Ist der Text durchgängig im *simple present*? Sind die Textteile gut verbunden? Ist der Text logisch aufgebaut und gut zu verstehen?
- Vergiss nicht, Rechtschreibung/Grammatik zu prüfen. (➜ *SF 11*)

LANGUAGE HELP

Folgende *phrases* können dir bei der Einleitung helfen:

- The story/text is about …
- The text deals with …
- The topic of the text is …
- The article/text shows …

SF 9 Argumentative writing

Wenn du eine Erörterung schreibst – also schriftlich für oder gegen etwas argumentierst – solltest du deinen Text gut strukturieren und deine Argumente klar und schlüssig präsentieren, um deine Leser zu überzeugen.

PLANUNGSPHASE

Step 1: Lies die Aufgabe sorgfältig durch.

Step 2: Sammle Ideen und mache erste Notizen. Schreibe alle Argumente pro *und* contra auf, die dir einfallen.

Step 3: Ordne deine Argumente, z.B. in Form einer Outline. (➜ *SF 6*) Hebe das Argument hervor, das deine Position am besten unterstreicht – damit solltest du deinen Hauptteil beenden, denn das merken sich die Leser am ehesten.

SCHREIBPHASE

Step 1: Schreibe deine Einleitung: sage kurz, um welches Thema es geht, ohne deine eigene Meinung dazu zu äußern.

Step 2: Im Hauptteil präsentierst du die Argumente, die du dir überlegt hast. Dabei helfen folgende Redemittel:

- Presenting arguments:
  One of the main reasons why … • It is often said that … • Some people think … • In addition to these points …
- Ordering arguments:
  To start with, … • Firstly,/Secondly,/Thirdly, … • Finally, … • First of all …
- Contrasting arguments:
  On the one hand – on the other hand • Contrary to what most people believe, … • While / Although … • …
- Giving examples:
  For example, … • This is clear because …

Outline / Notes

1. Introduction
   introduce the topic

2. Main body
   1. paragraph: arguments contra
      - argument 1
      - argument 2 etc
   2./3. paragraph: arguments pro
      - argument 1
      - argument 2 etc
      end with strongest argument!

4. Conclusion
   sum up your arguments
   give your opinion

Step 3: Am Schluss fasst du deine Argumente nochmal kurz zusammen und erklärst deine Schlussfolgerung:

- Summing up arguments:
  To sum up, … • In conclusion, … • All in all, … • I would like to finish by pointing out again that …
- Explaining your conclusion:
  After looking at both sides of the argument … • Although I understand the other side of the argument, I still think … • Personally, I believe that …

TIPP
Deine Argumente wirken überzeugender, wenn du:
- dich wo möglich auf deine eigenen Erfahrungen berufst,
- Fakten (Quellen, Experten, Statistiken usw.) präsentierst:
  It can't be denied that …, It's a fact that …, It goes without saying that …

SF 10 Writing a formal letter or email

Wenn du einen Brief an eine Organisation, einen potenziellen Arbeitgeber oder eine Universität schreibst, sollte dein Brief gewissen formalen Regeln folgen.

Schreibe deine Adresse (ohne Namen) oben rechts. Verwende keine typisch deutschen Buchstaben wie ä, ö, ü oder ß.

Schreibe die volle Anschrift (mit Namen, wenn du ihn weißt) des Adressaten auf die linke Seite.

Schreibe das Datum auf die rechte Seite.

Sage kurz im Betreff, worum es im Brief geht.

Beginne deinen Brief mit *Dear Sir or Madam* wenn du keinen genauen Ansprechparntner hast. Ansonsten schreibe *Dear Mr/Mrs/Ms …* (ohne Komma danach!). Fange danach immer groß an.

Nenne den Grund des Schreibens im ersten Absatz.
- Ergänze weitere Informationen in den folgenden Absätzen.
- Verwende Langformen *(I am/We are/I would)* statt Kurzformen *(I'm/We're/I'd)* und Abkürzungen.

Wenn du den Adressaten um etwas bittest (z.B. Informationen), bedanke dich im Voraus.

Beende den Brief mit *Yours faithfully* wenn du den Namen des Ansprechpartners kennst; ansonsten schreibe *Yours sincerely*. Tippe deinen Namen am Ende des Briefes, aber lasse ausreichend Platz für deine Unterschrift.

Kruemelstrasse 12
12345 Berlin
Germany

John Keats
Donne House
Ipswich IP3 4BA
United Kingdom

3 March 2016

Enquiry about exchange programme

Dear Mr Keats

I am writing to enquire about the exchange programme which I saw advertised in The English Magazine.

I have been studying English at school for five years now and I would like to take part in an exchange programme to improve my English.

Could you please tell me if you offer any exchange programmes for one month in the summer? It would be helpful to know about dates, application procedures and the cost such an exchange. Any additional information would be very welcome.

Thank you for your help. I look forward to hearing from you soon.

Yours sincerely,

Paul Panther

Paul Panther

TIPP
Bei einer formellen E-Mail brauchst du Datum und Adressaten nicht zu nennen. Ansonsten gelten dieselben Regeln wie bei einem formellen Brief. Liste am Ende der Mail deine Kontaktdaten auf (Name, Adresse, ggf. Telefonnummer). Ganz wichtig: verwende auf keinen Fall Emoticons oder Smileys.

SF 11 Revising texts

Egal, ob du eine Rückmeldung von jemandem zu deinem Text bekommen hast oder nicht – du solltest ihn auf jeden Fall noch einmal selbst gut prüfen, bevor du ihn an den Adressaten übergibst.

TEXTÜBERARBEITUNG

1. **Stimmt die Struktur?** (➡ SF 4)
   Jeder Text braucht
   - eine Einleitung, die in das Thema einführt,
   - einen Hauptteil, der das Thema ausführt,
   - einen Schluss, der alles auf den Punkt bringt.

2. **Stimmt der Aufbau der Absätze?** (➡ SF 4)
   Jeder Absatz
   - befasst sich mit einem zusammenhängenden Gedanken,
   - beginnt mit einem *topic sentence*, der diesen Gedanken einführt.

3. **Stimmen die Verknüpfungen?** (➡ SF 5)
   Gute *linking words*
   - schaffen Verbindungen zwischen Sätzen oder Satzteilen,
   - helfen, Zusammenhänge besser darzustellen und verständlich zu machen.

4. **Sind die Zeitangaben richtig gesetzt?** (➡ SF 5)
   Time markers
   - helfen, sich z. B. in einer Geschichte zurechtzufinden,
   - machen das Geschehen anschaulicher.

5. **Enthält der Text Adjektive und Adverbien?** (➡ SF 5)
   Adjektive und Adverbien
   - erlauben nähere Beschreibungen von Personen und Dingen,
   - machen Texte anschaulicher.

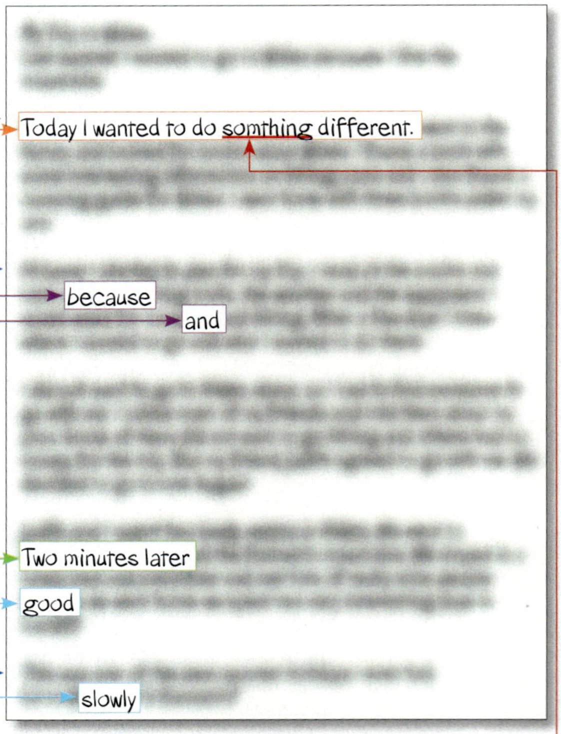

6. **Hat der Text sprachliche/grammatikalische Fehler?**
   Überprüfe deinen Text
   - auf Rechtschreibung,
   - auf grammatische Formen, z. B. Verbformen, Satzbau *(word order)* usw.

FEHLERPROTOKOLL

Deine Fehler in einem Text zu korrigieren ist eine Sache, aber besser wäre es natürlich, dieselben Fehler nicht zu wiederholen.

Dabei hilft ein Fehlerprotokoll. Darin notierst du Fehler, die du immer wieder machst. Dieses Fehlerprotokoll kann ein Heft sein, ein Karteikasten oder auch eine Sammlung von Notizzetteln, die du dir über deinen Schreibtisch hängst.

Hauptsache, es ist etwas, das du immer schnell zur Hand hast, wenn du zu Hause einen Text schreiben oder überarbeiten sollst.

TIPP

Häufige Fehlerquellen sind z. B.
- Groß-/Kleinschreibung
- Wörter, die gleich klingen, aber unterschiedlich geschrieben werden: *your/you're, their/they're/there*
- Verwendung des Apostrophs
- Bildung der Zeitformen der Verben: *stop* ⟶ *stopping, try* ⟶ *tries*
- Wörter mit "stummen" Buchstaben: *walk, talk, know*

MEDIATION SKILLS

SF 12 Mediating written or spoken information

Nicht jeder spricht und versteht sowohl Deutsch als auch Englisch; daher kann es vorkommen, dass du in bestimmten Situationen für Andere zwischen den Sprachen vermitteln musst – das nennt man dann Mediation.

Wie und was genau du vermitteln musst, hängt von der Situation ab und auch davon, ob du den Inhalt eines geschriebenen Textes wiedergeben oder zwischen zwei Sprechern vermitteln sollst.

Sprachmittlung bedeutet nicht Übersetzen (von Texten) oder Dolmetschen (bei Unterhaltungen), sondern das sinngemäße Übertragen von Inhalten in die andere Sprache.

MEDIATION VON SCHRIFTLICHEN ODER MÜNDLICHEN INFORMATIONEN

Wenn du Informationen in einer anderen Sprache wiedergeben sollst, geht es nicht darum, alles zu übersetzen, sondern es kommt darauf an, die wichtigsten Informationen herauszusuchen. Oft stellt dir die Person, für die du die Informationen wiedergibst, gezielte Fragen – so weißt du, worauf du achten musst.

Schriftliche Informationen

- Scanne den Text gezielt nach den geforderten Informationen. (➜ *SF 1*)
- Mach dir keine Sorgen, wenn du nicht jedes Wort verstehst. Das ist oft nicht nötig, um die wichtigen Punkte zu verstehen und wiederzugeben.
- Wenn der Text länger ist und du viele Informationen im Blick behalten musst, markiere die wichtigsten Textstellen. (➜ *SF 2*)
- Mach dir Notizen in deinen eigenen Worten. (➜ *SF 33*)

Mündliche Informationen

- Achte beim Hören gezielt auf die gesuchten Informationen. (➜ *SF 22*)
- Mach dir Notizen. (➜ *SF 33*)
- Überlege, wie du deine Notizen am besten in der anderen Sprache wiedergeben kannst.

TIPP
Bei Mediation im Unterricht hast du in der Regel eine Aufgabenstellung, die dir sagt, worauf du beim Lesen oder Hören achten musst bzw. welche Stellen du wiedergeben sollst. Konzentriere dich beim Lesen des Textes auf diese Stellen *(scanning)* bzw. mache dir gezielt zu diesen Stellen Notizen.

TIPP
Wenn du den Inhalt eines Texts schriftlich in einer anderen Sprache wiedergeben sollst, achte darauf, dass deine Mediation nicht länger ist als ca. 35-40% des Originaltextes, ähnlich wie bei einer *summary*. (➜ *SF 8*)

SF 13 Selecting relevant information

Manchmal gibt es keine gezielten Fragen oder Aufgabenstellungen, die dir sagen, welche Informationen du aus einem Text heraussuchen und wiedergeben sollst. In der Regel hast du aber trotzdem Anhaltspunkte, die sich aus der Situation ergeben oder aus dem, was dir dein Gegenüber erzählt hat.

Wenn du in einer solchen Situation bist, helfen folgende Hinweise:

- Analysiere die Situation, um abzuschätzen, um welche Informationen es gehen könnte (Restaurant, Bahnhof, Flughafen usw.).
- Wenn du unsicher bist, frage nach.
- Übersetze wichtige Stichworte direkt, wenn du die Wörter kennst.
- Umschreibe Begriffe, die du nicht kennst. (➜ *SF 14*)

TIPP
Wenn du Informationen wiedergibst, kannst du oft Details zu einem Begriff zusammenfassen. Wenn z. B. in einem Text twitter, facebook und Pinterest vorkommen, kannst du *social media* sagen anstatt alle aufzuzählen.

SF 14 Paraphrasing

Es fällt dir eventuell manchmal schwer, Informationen in Englisch wiederzugeben, z. B. weil

- dein Wortschatz nicht ausreicht
- dir bekannte Wörter in der Situation nicht einfallen
- oder spezielle Fachbegriffe auftauchen.

Wenn dir das passiert, dann solltest du versuchen, diese Wörter zu umschreiben, z. B. mithilfe von Relativsätzen wie:

It's somebody/a person who …
It's something that you use to …
It's an animal that …
It's a place that/where …

LANGUAGE HELP
Oft helfen beim Umschreiben auch Synonyme (gleiche Bedeutung) oder Antonyme (gegenteilige Bedeutung). Wenn du die weißt, kannst du z. B. sagen:
- It's the same as …
- It's the opposite of …

SF 15 Cultural differences

Wenn du anderen Menschen hilfst, Texte oder Gehörtes zu verstehen, kann es neben Wortschatzproblemen auch noch andere Schwierigkeiten geben. Diese sind häufig in kulturellen Unterschieden begründet. Um hier helfen zu können, musst du dir beim Sprachmitteln bewusst machen, dass dein Gegenüber evtl. bestimmte Dinge nicht weiß, die für dich selbstverständlich sind, oder dass er/sie dich nicht sofort versteht, obwohl du den Inhalt korrekt übertragen hast.

Dinge, die häufig zu Missverständnissen führen, sind z. B.
- Temperaturen: 30 Grad bei uns sind heiß, in den USA eher kalt, weil in den USA Temperaturen in Fahrenheit angegeben werden, nicht in Celsius.
- Längenangaben/Geschwindigkeit: Bei uns wird das metrische System verwendet (Meter, Kilometer usw.), in den USA das *imperial system* mit *inch*, *yard* und *mile*. Das kann auch bei Geschwindigkeitsangaben zu Verwirrung führen, denn 75 *mph* (Meilen pro Stunde) sind z. B. ca. 120 km/h.

Am besten ist es, wenn du immer noch mal höflich nachfragst, ob dein Gegenüber alles verstanden hat. Wenn du dann feststellst, dass es zu einem Missverständnis gekommen ist, dann kannst du folgende Dinge probieren:

- Frage höflich nach, wo das Missverständnis ist. (➜ *SF 16*)
- Versuche, das Missverständnis durch eine neue Erklärung zu beseitigen.
- Ergänze deine Erläuterung evtl. mit Hintergrundinformationen: Es kann sein, dass du bestimmte Dinge, die für dich völlig normal sind, erklären musst (wie z. B. Mülltrennung oder das Benutzen des Nahverkehrs).
- Sei auch offen für die Erklärungen, die du evtl. im Gegenzug bekommst – hier kannst du Dinge über das Land deines Gegenübers lernen.

TIPP
Es hilft, wenn du versuchst, mögliche "Stolperstellen" schon im Vorfeld vorauszusehen. Frage dich, was dein Gegenüber evtl. nicht oder anders verstehen könnte und erkläre diese Stellen besonders genau und evtl. auf unterschiedliche Arten.

SPEAKING SKILLS

SF 16 Communicating in everyday situations

Es ist nicht immer einfach, sich mit Menschen aus anderen Ländern zu unterhalten. Neben der Sprachbarriere gibt es oft auch kulturelle Unterschiede (➡ *SF 15*), wie das folgende Beispiel zeigt.

Lies dieses Gespräch zwischen Paul, einem deutschen Schüler, und seinem Austauschpartner Jack in den USA:

Jack: How's your school at home?
Paul: It's okay.
Jack: Oh … good. What are your favorite subjects?
Paul: Er, I don't know.
Jack: Oh, well. Maybe you'll enjoy our school too.
Paul: Maybe.
Jack: Er … want to play a game?

Das Gespräch kommt nicht so richtig in Gang, und Jack gibt irgendwann auf. Wenn man aber einige Regeln beachtet, werden Unterhaltungen einfacher und für beide Parteien erfreulicher. Vergleiche das folgende Gespräch mit dem obigen:

Jack: How's your school at home?
Paul: I like it … but of course I don't like all my teachers.
Jack: Yeah, I think that's normal. What are your favorite subjects?
Paul: I'm not sure. I like history and maths, but art and German are okay too.
Jack: Ah, my favorite subject is English. Anyway, I'm sure you'll enjoy our school too. Our history teacher is pretty cool. Have you met any of the teachers yet?
Paul: No, not yet, but I think …

Die folgenden Schritte helfen dir, wenn du dich freundlich und flüssig unterhalten willst:

Step 1: Beginne freundlich, z. B. mit etwas, was beide Gesprächspartner verbindet (der Ort, die Situation usw.).

Step 2: Halte die Unterhaltung am Laufen:
- zeige dein Interesse, indem du Fragen stellst
- vermeide einsilbige Antworten, um nicht desinteressiert oder unfreundlich zu wirken
- wenn du etwas nicht verstehst, frage nach
- wenn du etwas nicht sagen kannst, versuche es zu umschreiben oder bitte deinen Gesprächspartner um Hilfe

Step 3: Beende das Gespräch so freundlich, wie du es angefangen hast:
- bedanke dich, wenn du um Hilfe gebeten hast
- verabschiede dich freundlich

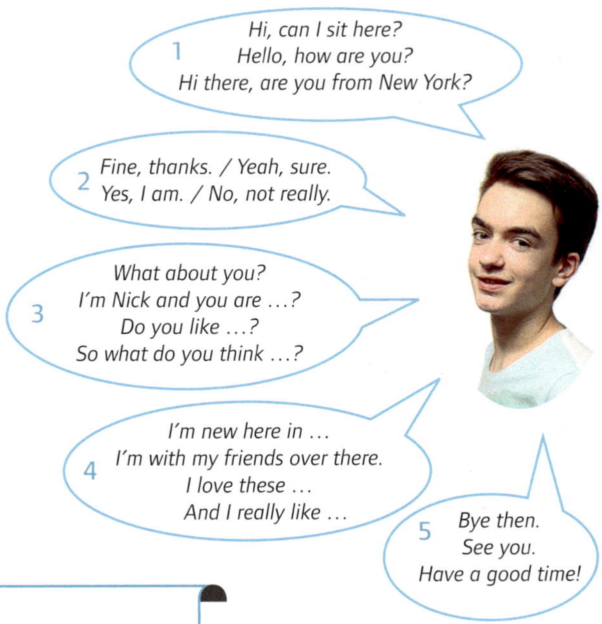

TIPP
Mach dir vor dem Gespräch klar, mit wem du redest. Mit anderen Jugendlichen kannst du häufig viel informeller sprechen als mit älteren Menschen. Überlege auch, ob es kulturelle Unterschiede gibt (➡ *SF 15*) und ob es Dinge gibt, die du deswegen beachten musst.

SF 17 Having a discussion

In einer Diskussion tauscht man Meinungen und Ideen zu einem bestimmten Thema aus.

VORBEREITUNGSPHASE

Step 1: Bereite dich auf das Thema vor: Recherchiere Fakten und Beispiele und überlege, was deine Meinung zu dem Thema ist. Mache dir Notizen.

Step 2: Halte deine Notizen für die Diskussion bereit – z.B. auf kleinen Zetteln – damit du darauf zugreifen kannst, falls du sie brauchst.

Step 3: Überlege dir vorher ein Statement, das deine Meinung zum Thema gut ausdrückt; das erleichtert den Einstieg in die Diskussion.

TIPP
Bei Rollenspielen musst du manchmal eine Meinung vertreten, die anders ist als deine eigene. Dann kannst du in deinen Notizen z.B. versuchen, Argumente und Gegenargumente einander gegenüberzustellen, um dann in der Diskussion schnell und gut reagieren zu können.

DISKUSSION

Step 1: Starting the discussion: Sage deine Meinung (z.B. mithilfe der Eröffnung, die du dir überlegt hast).

Step 2: Continuing the discussion: Tausche deine Meinung mit anderen aus. Bleibe höflich und sachlich. Hör den anderen zu und lass sie ausreden.

- Wenn du sprichst, beziehe dich auf die Anderen und sage, weshalb du ihren Argumenten zustimmst (oder nicht).
- Stütze deine Meinung mit Fakten und Beispielen.

Step 3: Ending the discussion:

- Fasse deinen Standpunkt noch einmal knapp zusammen.
- Versuche, Gemeinsamkeiten festzustellen (v.a. wenn es darum geht, sich auf etwas zu einigen) oder einigt euch darüber, dass es nicht *eine* gemeinsame Lösung gibt *(agree to disagree)*.
- Falls gefordert, einigt euch auf eine Lösung oder einen Kompromiss.

TIPP
Im Englischen ist man häufig weit weniger direkt als im Deutschen. Das bedeutet, dass du bei Diskussionen
- besonders gut zuhören musst, weil du sonst evtl. nicht genau mitbekommst, ob man dir zustimmt oder widerspricht;
- kurze, zu direkte Antworten wie *"No."* vermeiden solltest, weil die unhöflich wirken.

SF 18 Agreeing and disagreeing with people's opinions

Wenn du mit Anderen diskutierst, wirst du anderen Gesprächsteilnehmern zustimmen oder widersprechen. Wie im Deutschen, gibt es dafür auch im Englischen bestimmte Redewendungen, die du dafür gut verwenden kannst.

LANGUAGE HELP
Es ist bei Diskussionen hilfreich, einige Standard-Redewendungen parat zu haben. Wenn du die beherrscht, kannst du dich mehr auf deine Argumente konzentrieren. Folgende Phrasen solltest du dir aufschreiben und sie lernen:

Stating your opinion
- In my opinion …
- Well, I'd say …
- It's a fact that …
- Personally, I think…
- If you ask me …
- I think/feel/believe …
- First of all, I'd like to point out…
- I'm certain that …

Agreeing
- I agree …
- Exactly./Absolutely./…
- You're quite right.
- I think so too.
- You've got a good point there.
- That's exactly how I see it.
- That's true/right.
- I couldn't agree with you more.

Disagreeing
- I'm afraid I don't quite agree …
- I'm not sure about that.
- Do you really think so?
- I'm not convinced that …
- I doubt that (very much).
- I don't agree with you at all.
- I disagree (completely).
- It's not as simple as that.

SF 19 Taking part in an interview

Interviews sind häufig Bestandteil von Prüfungen oder Bewerbungen. Es ist wichtig, gerade wenn es um Bewerbungsgespräche oder Prüfungen geht, dass du dich gut darauf vorbereitest.

Bei Bewerbungsgesprächen helfen die folgenden 4 Ps:

PREPARE

- Finde so viel wie möglich über den Job und den Arbeitgeber heraus.
- Notiere mögliche Fragen, die du dem Arbeitgeber stellen kannst.
- Überlege dir aber auch, welche Fragen man dir stellen könnte und bereite Antworten darauf vor.

PRACTISE

- Übe das Bewerbungsgespräch mit einem Partner/einer Partnerin.
- Gib deinem Übungspartner die Fragen, die du von deinem Arbeitgeber erwartest und beantworte sie. Sage deinem Übungspartner auch, dass er/sie dir ruhig unerwartete Fragen stellen soll. So übst du, auf unvorbereitete Fragen zu antworten.

PRESENT

- Überlege dir im Vorfeld, was du zu dem Bewerbungsgespräch anziehen möchtest. Besprich das ruhig auch mit einem Freund/einer Freundin oder deinen Eltern. Die Auswahl der Kleidung hängt vom Arbeitgeber ab.
- Stelle sicher, dass du pünktlich bist. Suche dir vorher heraus, wie du zum Ort des Gespräches kommst. Plane Zeit für Unvorhergesehenes ein. Es ist immer besser, zehn Minuten zu früh als zu spät zu sein.

PARTICIPATE

- Stelle dich am Anfang vor, am besten mit einem freundlichen Lächeln.
- Lass dir Zeit, Fragen zu beantworten, besonders wenn es unerwartete Fragen sind. Antworte nicht mit "Yes." oder "No.", sondern versuche, Fragen ausführlich und höflich zu beantworten.
- Wenn du eine Frage nicht verstehst, frag nach.
- Am Ende des Gespräches, verabschiede dich mit einem freundlichen Lächeln und bedanke dich für das Gespräch.

TIPP
Achte auch auf deine non-verbale Kommunikation – wie du stehst, gehst, sitzt – und siehe deinem Gegenüber in die Augen.

LANGUAGE HELP
Es ist bei Diskussionen hilfreich, einige Standard-Redewendungen parat zu haben. Wenn du die beherrscht, kannst du dich mehr auf deine Argumente konzentrieren. Folgende Phrasen solltest du dir aufschreiben und sie lernen:

Stating your opinion
- In my opinion …
- Well, I'd say …
- It's a fact that …
- Personally, I think…
- If you ask me …
- I think/feel/believe …
- First of all, I'd like to point out…
- I'm certain that …

Agreeing
- I agree …
- Exactly./Absolutely./…
- You're quite right.
- I think so too.
- You've got a good point there.
- That's exactly how I see it.
- That's true/right.
- I couldn't agree with you more.

Disagreeing
- I'm afraid I don't quite agree …
- I'm not sure about that.
- Do you really think so?
- I'm not convinced that …
- I doubt that (very much).
- I don't agree with you at all.
- I disagree (completely).
- It's not as simple as that.

SF 20 Preparing for a speaking exam

Auf Sprechprüfungen/Kommunikationsprüfungen kannst du dich ebenso vorbereiten wie auf schriftliche Prüfungen.

WIE SIEHT DIE PRÜFUNG AUS?

Step 1: Als erstes solltest du herausfinden, um welche Art von Prüfung es sich handelt. Es gibt zwei Formen: monologisches Sprechen oder dialogisches Sprechen (oder eine Kombination von beidem, z.B. zuerst ein Monolog, gefolgt von einem Dialog zu einem bestimmten Thema).

Monologisches Sprechen (p. 150)
- Präsentation/Mündlicher Vortrag als Reaktion auf einen Impuls
- Präsentation/Mündlicher Vortrag zu einem Thema (spontan oder vorbereitet)

Dialogisches Sprechen (p. 151)
- Gespräch mit einem Lehrer oder der Prüfungskommission
- Gespräch mit einer/m oder mehreren Partnern/Partnerinnen

Step 2: Informiere dich über weitere Aspekte:

- Partner: Kannst du eine/n Partner selbst wählen oder wird er/sie zugeteilt? Könnt ihr vor der Prüfung gemeinsam üben?
- Format: Welche Form hat die Prüfung? Freies Sprechen zu einem Thema oder bekommst du einen Impuls (Text, Bild etc.)?
- Dauer: Wie lange dauert die Prüfung/die einzelnen Teile?
- Vorbereitung: Wann erfährst du das Thema? Kannst du dich zu Hause vorbereiten oder erst direkt vor dem Test?
- Medien: Sollst du Medien (Computer, Folien etc) verwenden? Wieviel Zeit hast du, diese vorzubereiten?
- Benotung: Wie wird die Prüfung benotet? In der Regel setzt sich die Note aus Inhalt und sprachlicher Kompetenz zusammen.

Step 3: Sammle alle Informationen wie z.B. auch Musterprüfungen und Informationen zur Benotung in einem Ordner, so dass du schnell darauf Zugriff hast.

MONOLOGISCHES SPRECHEN
PRÄSENTATION/MÜNDLICHER VORTRAG ZU EINEM IMPULS

Wenn du in deinem mündlichen Vortrag auf einen Impuls reagieren sollst, kann das z.B. ein Bild oder Text sein, aber auch ein Zitat, eine Statistik, ein Cartoon oder eine oder mehrere Fragen. Oft erfährst du das erst kurz vor oder in der Prüfung selbst.

Aber auch wenn du nicht genau weißt, mit welcher Art von Impuls du konfrontierst wird, kannst du dich vorbereiten:

- Erstelle eine Mindmap oder Liste für jede Art von möglichem Impuls.
- Sammle darin Wörter oder ganze Sätze, um über die verschiedenen Impulse zu sprechen. Dies hilft dir, deinen Vortrag zu strukturieren, und deinem Gegenüber, ihm zu folgen. Lerne diese Redewendungen – wenn du sie sicher beherrschst, kannst du dich in der Prüfungssituation auf die Inhalte konzentrieren. (➜ *SF 16, SF 23, SF 24*)

PRÄSENTATION/MÜNDLICHER VORTRAG ZU EINEM THEMA

Wenn du für deine Prüfung eine Präsentation/einen mündlichen Vortrag zu einem Thema vorbereiten sollst, gehe dabei vor wie bei anderen Präsentationen auch (➔ *SF 24*). Einige Punkte solltest du aber besonders beachten:

- Struktur: Stelle sicher, dass die Zuhörer deiner Präsentation gut folgen können. Lerne und verwende Redewendungen wie *first of all, finally, next, I would like to finish by saying …*
- Medien: Bereite alle Medien (Bilder, Präsentationen etc.) gut vor. Dazu gehören z.B. auch deine Notizen, am besten auf Karteikarten.
- Zeitmanagement: Halte dich an die vorgegebene Zeit. Das schaffst du am besten, wenn du deine Präsentation ein paar Mal laut übst, z.B. vor einem Partner/einer Partnerin oder deiner Familie.
- Vortrag: Sieh die Prüfer an, wenn du sprichst, nicht deine Notizen. Sprich langsam, deutlich und lass dir ruhig Zeit, zwischendurch mal tief Luft zu holen, besonders wenn du nervös bist. Mach das auch schon beim Üben.

DIALOGE – AN GESPRÄCHEN TEILNEHMEN

Oft beinhaltet eine mündliche Prüfung auch einen dialogischen Teil, in dem du mit einem Partner oder den Prüfern kommunizierst.

Dies kann z.B. ein Gespräch zu einem Thema sein, aber auch eine Diskussion, ein Interview oder ein Rollenspiel. Auch wenn du nicht genau weißt, mit was du in deiner Prüfung konfrontiert wird, kannst du dich auf die Situation vorbereiten.

Step 1: Überlege dir, evtl. mit einem Partner/einer Partnerin, im Vorfeld für jede der möglichen Formen – Gespräch, Diskussion, Interview, Rollenspiel – worauf du dabei achten musst.

Step 2: Notiere dir, was du an Phrasen und Redewendungen für die einzelnen Phasen eines Dialoges brauchst und lerne sie.
(➔ *SF 16, SF 17, SF 18, SF 19*)

- Anfang einer Diskussion: Today we're talking about … • Let me start with … • …
- Zustimmen/widersprechen: What a great idea. • My point exactly. • … / That's not how I see it. • I don't agree with … (➔ *SF 16*)
- Nachfragen: Can you give an example of that? • Do you mean …?
- Eine/n Partner/in einbeziehen: How about you? • What do you think/How do you feel about that?
- Unterbrechen: May I interrupt? • Excuse me, can I just say that …?
- Zeit zum Überlegen gewinnen: Can I repeat what we said before? • Well, now let me see … • Let me think about that for a second.
- Zusammenfassen: We've seen that … • To come to a conclusion …

TIPP

Beachte auch diese allgemeinen Tipps für die Prüfungssituation:

- Erstelle deine Notizen so, dass du sie schnell finden und auf einen Blick entziffern kannst.
- Sei gut ausgeschlafen. Trage angemessene Kleidung, in der du dich auch wohlfühlst. Sei pünktlich.
- Sei höflich und freundlich. Bedenke auch, dass du in einer dialogischen Prüfungssituation nicht für deine eigene Note arbeitest, sondern auch für deine/n Partner/in.

VIEWING SKILLS

SF 21 Viewing

Wenn du verstehst, wie Filmtechniken eingesetzt werden, um beim Zuschauer z.B. Angst, Freude, Spannung oder Lachen auszulösen, bekommst du ein besseres Verständnis dafür, wie Filme funktionieren. Es gibt viele verschiedene Elemente, die die Atmosphäre und die Wirkung eines Filmes beeinflussen:

- Genre: Handelt es sich um einen Dokumentarfilm (documentary), einen Spielfilm (feature film) wie z. B. thriller, science-fiction/sci-fi movie, comedy oder ein drama? Oder ist es ein Videoclip oder ein Werbefilm?
- Story: Wo und wann spielt der Film (setting)? Besetzung der Rollen (cast), Schauplatz (location), Handlung (plot).
- Camera: Erst durch die Bilder der **Kamera** ist der Zuschauer in der Lage, einen Film wahrzunehmen. Die Kamera stellt das Blickfeld her und begrenzt es gleichzeitig, z. B. hinsichtlich der Beziehung der Charaktere zueinander. Auch die Stimmung oder Spannung in einer Szene wird von der Kameraführung beeinflusst. Dafür gibt es z. B. folgende Mittel:
  - Shots: Die **Kameraeinstellung** beeinflusst, wie man Szenen wahrnimmt, ob z. B. Personen oder Objekte als Nahaufnahme (close-up), aus der mittleren Distanz (medium shot) oder als Totale (long shot) gefilmt sind.
  - Editing: Filme werden in der Regel nicht chronologisch gedreht und auch nicht nur mit einer einzigen Kamera, d. h. am Ende der Dreharbeiten müssen viele einzelne Shots zu einem Film zusammengefügt werden. Dieser **Filmschnitt** bestimmt, wie eine Szene wirkt. Er bestimmt den Rhythmus – lange Einstellungen mit wenigen Schnitten wirken eher ruhig, können aber auch große Spannung erzeugen, während schnelle, harte Schnitte eher actiongeladen wirken. Wie genau eine Szene wirkt, hängt oft auch vom Zusammenspiel von Schnitt und Musik ab.
- Soundtrack: Die **Musik**, die für eine Szene gewählt wird, hat großen Einfluss darauf, wie man die Szene wahrnimmt. Eine Actionszene wird meist mit schneller, lauter Musik unterlegt, eine romantische Szene eher mit ruhiger, leiser Musik. Dies geschieht, um die Wirkung des Gesehenen zu verstärken.

long shot

medium shot

close-up

FILMTAGEBUCH

Wenn du eine Szene oder einen ganzen Film sehr intensiv analysieren möchtest, hilft es, ein Filmtagebuch (viewing log) anzulegen, in dem du die Handlung oder einzelne wichtige Szenen sowie deine Reaktion darauf festhältst.

Das Filmtagebuch kann z. B. eine simple, zweispaltige Tabelle sein:
Spalte 1: What you noticed – images, sounds, dialogue, lighting, costumes, mood, characterization, plot, etc.
Spalte 2: Your reaction – What did you think? How did the scene make you feel?

LANGUAGE HELP

Wenn du über Filme sprechen möchtest, können dir folgende Redewendungen helfen:

- The film is about … / shows … / tells the story of …
- The music creates/builds/supports tension/suspense/joy …
- The actor's body language helps to create a feeling of happiness/joy/anger/suspense …
- In this scene the music/effects/camera angle … supports the plot /mood of the scene / …
- The camera movement creates a feeling of …
- The camera work/soundtrack helps to …
- The close-ups show his/her feelings.

LISTENING SKILLS

SF 22 Listening strategies

Wenn du Englisch hörst, kann es sein, dass du entweder Details heraushören musst (listening for detail), z. B. bei Ansagen am Bahnhof, oder generell verstehen musst, um was es geht (listening for gist) wie z. B. bei einem Film. Dazu kannst du verschiedene Hörverstehenstechniken anwenden.

HÖRVERSTEHENSTECHNIKEN

Es gibt zwei verschiedene Herangehensweisen:

- Top-down-Technik – das Verstehen beginnt von der Gesprächssituation her:

  Beim Hören eines englischen Textes hilft es, sich bewusst zu werden über den Kontext, den Sprecher und seine Rolle, wie gesprochen wird (Emotion, Tempo, Sprachebene, ...) und was dabei das Thema ist.

  Solche Informationen helfen dir oft mit einiger Treffsicherheit zu erraten, was im Gespräch gemeint ist, selbst wenn du nicht jedes gesprochene Wort verstehst.

- Bottom-up-Technik – die Erschließung der Bedeutung beginnt beim Gesprochenen selbst:

  – Die Dekodierung der Laute, die du in der Fremdsprache hörst, ist eine Frage der Übung. Achte möglichst genau darauf, *was* gerade gesagt wird und beachte dabei z.B. die Besonderheiten verschiedener Akzente.

– Chunks: Im Englischen spricht man oft mehrere Wörter als Einheit aus, bei der Wortgrenzen verschwinden. Das findet man verstärkt bei
  - Ausdrücken mit Modalverben: she'd've told me · you shouldn't've bought it · you mustabin asleep
  - häufigen Alltagsphrasen: Whatcha think o'that? · Howdju feel? · Dincha see it?

– Wörter, die gesprochen gleich klingen, sich in der Bedeutung aber unterscheiden:
We'd like ice in our drinks. – We like ice in our drinks.
I can't see them now. – I can see them now. (besonders im AE)
Hier schafft im Gespräch gezieltes Nachfragen Sicherheit: Sorry, was that *can* or *can't*?

TIPP
Es gibt dir Sicherheit, wenn du dich von vornherein auf typische Missverständnisse durch Akzente einstellst.
Versuche, dir folgende Beispiele mal mit britischen und dann mit amerikanischem oder australischem Akzent vorzustellen: can't · stop · pretty · student · main · text · tea

TIPP
Um sich auf die Chunks im Gespräch einzustimmen, kannst du die häufigsten Wendungen, die beim Sprechen verkürzt ausgesprochen werden, einmal in voller Länge aufschreiben.

ANFORDERUNGEN AN DAS HÖRVERSTEHEN

LISTENING FOR DETAIL

- Überleg dir vorher, auf welche Informationen du achten musst.

  – Bei einem Wetterbericht sind das z. B. Beschreibungen wie sunny, cloudy, chance of rain etc., bei Bahnhofsansagen z. B. Wörter wie platform oder Orte und Zeiten.

  – Höre dann gezielt auf solche Wörter und notiere sie. (➔ *SF 33*)

TIPP
- Oft kannst du die Menschen um dich herum fragen, wenn du nicht alles richtig verstanden hast – z.B. bei Durchsagen am Bahnhof.
- In einer Unterhaltung kannst du deinen Gesprächspartner bitten, Sachen zu wiederholen oder zu erklären.

- Manchmal können auch Signalwörter helfen, dem Inhalt zu folgen und dich auf die Details zu konzentrieren:
  - Gründe, Folgen: because, so, so that, …
  - Vergleiche: larger/older/… than, as … as, more, most, …
  - Reihenfolge: before, after, then, next, later, …

LISTENING FOR GIST

- Mache dir keine Sorgen, wenn du nicht jedes Wort verstehst – das brauchst du nicht, um der Grundaussage folgen zu können. Überlege dir vorher, um was es gehen könnte (z. B. anhand des Themas) und konzentriere dich darauf.
- Versuche, von den Sachen, die du verstehst, auf Inhalte zu schließen, die noch kommen könnten.

TIPP
Im **Unterricht** kannst du Texte oft zweimal hören und hast weitere Hilfen:
- Sieh dir die Aufgabenstellung an: Was sollst du heraushören?
- Sieh dir Titel und Bilder an.
- Vergleiche nach dem Hören mit einem Partner, was ihr verstanden habt.
- Vervollständige deine Notizen sofort.

PROJECT AND PRESENTATION SKILLS

SF 23 Teamwork

Bei Projekten arbeitet ihr oft im Team. Dabei solltet ihr eure unterschiedlichen Fähigkeiten und Talente einbringen und bestimmte Regeln beachten. Folgende Schritte können helfen, die Arbeit zu organisieren:

Step 1: Legt Regeln für die Arbeit in der Gruppe fest, z. B. gegenseitige Unterstützung, pünktliches und zügiges Arbeiten, einander zuhören oder verschiedene Lösungen diskutieren usw.

Step 2: Sammelt Ideen für die Bearbeitung eures Themas (z. B. in einer Mindmap). Wählt gemeinsam Unterthemen aus und legt die Arbeitsschritte fest, die für die Bearbeitung nötig sind.

Step 3: Verteilt Rollen und Aufgaben nach euren Interessen und Fähigkeiten. Wenn ihr euch nicht einigen könnt, hilft Auslosen oder Würfeln. Folgende Rollen solltet ihr auf jeden Fall verteilen:
- coordinator
- writer
- researcher

Step 4: Macht einen Zeitplan für eure Arbeiten, an den sich alle halten.

Step 5: Am Ende der Arbeit sollte ein Rückblick stehen: Besprecht, was gut war und wo ihr Verbesserungsmöglichkeiten seht.

SF 24 Giving a presentation

Ob in der Schule oder später im Beruf, es ist wichtig, eine gute Präsentation halten zu können, z.B. um andere über ein Thema zu informieren oder um sie von einer Idee oder einem Projekt zu überzeugen. Dabei ist die Vorbereitung genauso wichtig wie das eigentliche Halten, denn eine gut vorbereitete Präsentation ist eine gut strukturierte und überzeugende Präsentation.

Die folgenden Schritte helfen dir bei beiden Schritten:

VORBEREITUNG DER PRÄSENTATION

Step 1: Recherchiere dein Thema (➔ *SF 28*) und mach dir Notizen, am besten gleich auf Englisch (➔ *SF 33*).

Step 2: Strukturiere die Informationen, z. B. mit einer Gliederung. (➔ *SF 6*)

Step 3: Wähle eine Form der Präsentation aus, die das Thema gut veranschaulicht (Poster, Folie, ...). Gestalte dein Poster/deine Folie und beachte dabei die Grundsätze für ein gutes Poster.

Step 4: Bereite deine Notizen für die Präsentation vor, z. B. auf nummerierten Karteikarten. Verwende keine ganzen Sätze, sondern Stichworte, Symbole oder Halbsätze. Notiere dir z.B. auch schwierige Wörter und ihre Aussprache.

TIPP
Um ein gutes Poster zu gestalten, solltest du folgendes beachten:
- Wähle eine passende Überschrift.
- Schreibe groß und für alle gut lesbar.
- Ergänze passende Bilder, um den Text/die Inhalte zu veranschaulichen.

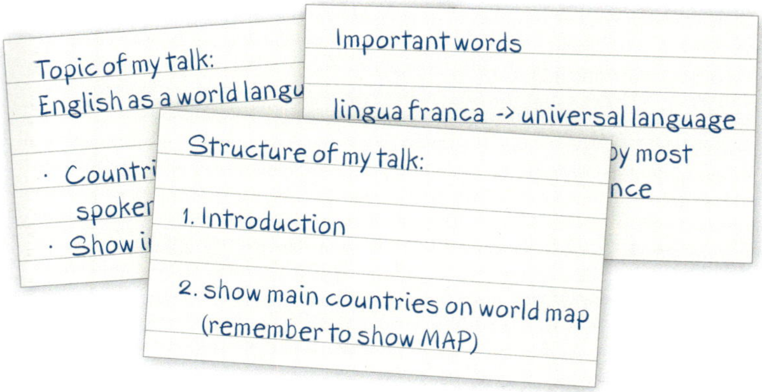

Step 5: Wenn du in einem Team arbeitest, entscheidet gemeinsam, wer welchen Teil der Präsentation übernimmt. (➔ *SF 23*)

Step 5: Übe deine Präsentation zu Hause vor einem Spiegel oder vor einem kleinen Publikum (Eltern, Großeltern, Freunde).

HALTEN DER PRÄSENTATION

Step 1: Warte, bis es ruhig ist. Schau die Zuhörer/innen an. Erkläre, worüber du sprechen wirst und wie deine Präsentation aufgebaut ist.

Step 2: Sprich langsam und deutlich und möglichst frei. Lies nicht von deinen Notizen ab.

Step 3: Beende deine Präsentation mit einer kleinen Zusammenfassung der wichtigsten Punkte. Bedanke dich fürs Zuhören und beantworte Fragen zu deinem Vortrag.

SF 25 Describing and interpreting images

Manchmal sollst du im Unterricht ein Bild (Fotos, Cartoons etc.) beschreiben und interpretieren. Hier sind ein paar Hilfen dazu:

BESCHREIBUNG

Step 1: Stelle das Bild vor und sage, woher es kommt.

Step 2: Beschreibe das Bild:

- Sage, was wo zu sehen ist: at the top/bottom · in the foreground/background · in the middle · on the left/right
- Geh bei der Beschreibung in einer bestimmten Reihenfolge vor, z. B. von links nach rechts oder von oben nach unten.
- Diese Präpositionen sind auch hilfreich: behind · between · in front of · next to · under · above
- Beziehe dich – v.a. bei Cartoons – auch auf Bildunterschriften, Sprechblasen etc.:
  The caption reads …
  One of the characters says/thinks …

1 *I'd like to talk about this photo of …/cartoon … I found it online/in a magazine/…*

2 *In the foreground you can see … I think the people in the photo/cartoon are talking about …*

3 *I really like/don't like the photo/cartoon because … It's interesting/boring/ … because …*

4 *Thank you for listening. Do you have any questions?*

INTERPRETATION

Step 1: Sage, was deiner Meinung nach die Botschaft des Bildes/Cartoons ist:
This is a political/environmental/educational/… photo/cartoon.
I think the message is …
It's about …
… shows that …
The fact that there is … means …
The picture/cartoon may be meant to show …

Step 2: Sage, weshalb du das Bild/den Cartoon wirksam/witzig findest (oder nicht):
The picture/cartoon clearly shows …
The message is made clear by showing/saying …
I really laughed at the cartoon because it …
I don't find the cartoon funny because …
The picture/cartoon speaks to us directly by …

Wenn du das Bild/den Cartoon in einer Präsentation vorstellst, musst du evtl. genauer erklären, weshalb du es ausgewählt hast oder was daran witzig ist:
I chose this picture because …
The joke is that …
It's funny because …
The picture/cartoon is criticizing/making fun of …

"Now don't forget to go on social media and rate today's lesson plan."

SF 26 Talking about statistics

Statistiken können auf unterschiedliche Weise dargestellt werden: Tortendiagramm (pie chart), Säulendiagramm (bar chart), Kurvendiagramm (line graph) oder in einer Tabelle (table). Wenn du Statistiken analysieren und vorstellen sollst, gehst du am besten wie folgt vor:

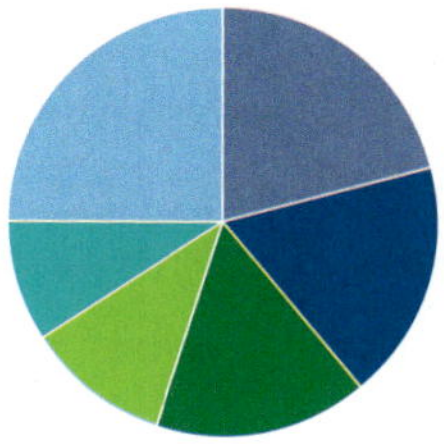

pie chart

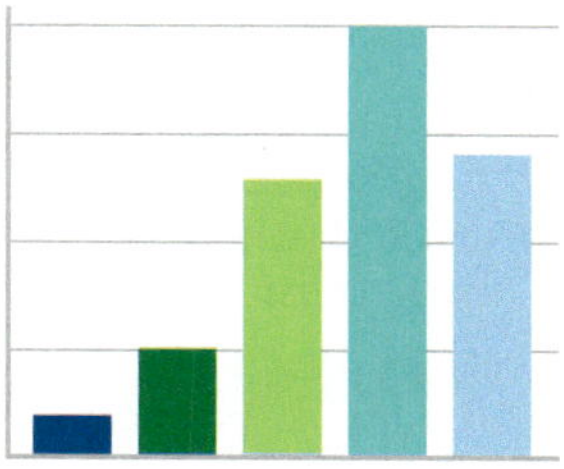

bar chart

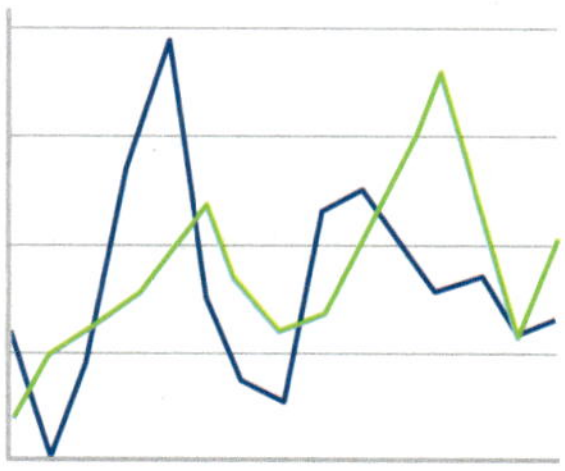

line graph

Step 1: Identifiziere, welche Art von Diagramm du vor dir hast – pie chart, bar chart, line graph oder Tabelle – und sieh dir die Quelle an:

- Ist die Quelle verlässlich?
  Ist der Herausgeber z.B. ein Ministerium/eine Behörde oder eine Organisation wie *amnesty international*?
- Sind die Angaben/Zahlen im Diagramm aktuell?
  Wenn du z.B. eine Statistik zu Kinderarmut in Großbritannien vor dir hast, ist es ein wichtiger Unterschied, ob die Zahlen von 1973 oder 2013 sind.

Step 2: Beschreibe das Diagramm/die Tabelle:

- Worum geht es? Welche Informationen gibt das Diagramm?
  The bar chart / pie chart / line graph / table … shows the different … / compares the size/number of … / is about … / contrasts … with …
- Zeigen die Daten eine Entwicklung oder werden verschiedene Zeitpunkte miteinander verglichen?
  It shows … in contrast to…
  The chart gives us information about who/what/how many/…
- Werden absolute Zahlen oder Prozentangaben verwendet?
  The chart/table shows us the number of/percentage of …
  It shows which percentage of …

Step 3: Ziehe deine Schlussfolgerungen aus dem Diagramm/der Tabelle:
My main conclusion is that …
The most imporant thing I've learned is that …
One thing that I hadn't realized before is …

LANGUAGE HELP

Wenn du über Diagramme sprichst, können dir folgende Redewendungen helfen:

Pie chart
- The pie chart is divided into … segments, which show/represent …
- The smallest/biggest segment …
- The segments representing … and … constitute the majority …
- A huge majority/minority is …

Bar chart
- The bars are arranged horizontally/vertically.
- There are big/vast/surprising differences between …
- At the top/bottom of the ranking comes…
- … is first/last in rank
- … has the largest / second largest …

Line graph
- The graph shows the relationship between … and …
- … is twice/three times as high as …
- There are more than / nearly twice as many … as there are …
- … increase/decrease / reach a high point / rise/fall/drop/ grow steadily

SF 27 Giving feedback

Gegenseitige Rückmeldungen sind für dich und deine Partner wichtig, damit du siehst, was dir gut gelungen ist und woran du noch arbeiten musst. Wenn du eine Rückmeldung gibst, solltest du grundsätzliche Regeln beachten, die für einen geschriebenen Text genauso gelten wie für eine mündliche Präsentation.

Diese Dinge solltest du beachten:

- Lies den Text sorgfältig durch oder höre der Präsentation gut zu.
- Bei Feedback zu einer Präsentation mach dir Notizen zu den Punkten, auf die du achten sollst, z. B. Inhalt, Struktur, Sprache, Verständlichkeit des Vortrags. Wenn du einen Feedbackbogen hast, kannst du deine Notizen gleich darauf festhalten.
- Bei Feedback zu einem Text lies den Text noch einmal genau und achte dabei besonders auf Inhalt, Struktur, Wortwahl, Grammatik und Rechtschreibung. Wenn du einen Feedbackbogen hast, mach dir darauf Notizen (siehe rechts).
- Begründe deine Einschätzungen.
- Gib dein Feedback mit Respekt – niemand soll sich angegriffen fühlen. Nenne erst Gelungenes und mache dann Verbesserungsvorschläge zu Punkten, die aus deiner Sicht noch nicht so gelungen sind.
- Wenn du Feedback bekommst, überdenke die Vorschläge gut. Korrigiere die Fehler, die andere gefunden haben, und arbeite an den Stellen nach, wo du eventuell Probleme hattest.

PEER FEEDBACK CHECKLIST

	☺☺	☺	😐	☹
Content				
Lena's text is:				
· interesting			✓	
· exciting				✓
· funny				✓
· ______				
· easy to understand.		✓		
Language				
You connected short sentences with linking words.		✓		
You connected short sentences with relative clauses.		✓		
You used different adjectives in your description of places, people and things.			✓	
You used time phrases to show the order of events.		✓		
You chose interesting words.				✓
You used adverbs.			✓	

SF 28 Internet research (Finding information for a presentation)

Das Internet ist voller Informationen, und es ist nicht einfach, genau das zu finden, was du benötigst.

Step 1: Überlege dir gute Stichwörter für dein Thema und gib sie in eine Suchmaschine ein. Je besser die Suchbegriffe sind, desto genauer sind die Ergebnisse. Die Infografik rechts hilft dir, wenn du ganz spezielle Informationen suchst.

Step 2: Nutze die Erweiterte Suche. Dort kannst du nicht nur festlegen, in welcher Sprache deine Ergebnisse sein sollen, sondern auch das Land eingrenzen (z.B. nur Ergebnisse aus den USA) oder die Domäne (z.B. .edu, .gov, .org).

Step 3: Sieh dir mehrere Suchergebnisse an, um zu sehen, ob sie passen (➔ *SF 1*).

Step 4: Achte darauf, wer die Webseite erstellt hat, um die Qualität der Suchergebnisse einzuschätzen.

Step 5: Speichere die besten Ergebnisse als Lesezeichen ab, damit du schnell darauf zugreifen kannst. Ordne deine Lesezeichen thematisch zur besseren Übersichtlichkeit.

Step 6: Setz dir ein Zeitlimit für deine Recherche und ordne dann dein Material. Prüfe, ob etwas fehlt, und suche dann ggf. gezielt nach diesen Informationen.

Step 7: Wenn du einen Text oder eine Präsentation vorbereitest, kopiere nicht einfach Inhalte von Webseiten. Mach dir Notizen und verwende deine eigenen Worte, um die Inhalte wiederzugeben. (➔ *SF 33*)

Internet research
Tipps und Tricks

Wenn du ganz spezifische Informationen suchst, helfen diese Tricks:

Was du suchst: Artikel aus dem *Guardian* von 2000–2014 über den Liverpool FC in der Champions League.

Wie du danach suchst:

site:theguardian.com "Liverpool FC" "champions league" 2000..2014

site:	**" "**	**..**
sucht nur auf der genannten Seite	sucht den exakten Begriff	zeigt nur Ergebnisse aus diesem Zeitraum

Was du suchst: Einen englischsprachigen Bericht, am liebsten als PDF, über den Lebensraum von Füchsen.

Wie du danach suchst:

filetype:pdf intitle:habitat of *fox

filetype:	**intitle:**	*****
sucht nur diesen Dateityp (pdf, doc, jpg usw.)	zeigt nur Ergebnisse, in denen dieses Wort im Titel auftaucht	sucht auch Worte wie Red Fox, Black Fox, Desert Fox usw.

STUDY SKILLS

SF 29 Dealing with unknown words

Nachschlagen kostet Zeit und ist nicht immer nötig. Diese Tipps können dir helfen, unbekannte Wörter auch ohne ein Wörterbuch zu erschließen:

- Sieh dir die Überschrift, die Zwischenüberschriften und Bilder sowie den Kontext an. Beispiel: *Let's hurry. The train* ***departs*** *in ten minutes.*
- Wenn du einen Teil des Wortes kennst, kannst du oft die Bedeutung erschließen, z.B.
  knowledge = things someone knows
  bottle opener = something you use to open bottles
- Viele englische Wörter haben eine Ähnlichkeit zu deutschen Wörtern (z. B. *brochure, statue, insect)* oder Wörtern aus anderen Sprachen, z.B. *voice (French: voix; Latin: vox).*

TIPP
Nicht alle Wörter, die im Deutschen und Englischen ähnlich sind, haben auch dieselbe Bedeutung.
Achte daher auf false friends:
handy = praktisch, *nicht* Handy

SF 30 Using a dictionary

Es gibt unterschiedliche Wörterbücher, in denen du nachschlagen kannst. Wenn du die Bedeutung eines unbekannten Wortes nachschlagen willst, dann benutzt du am besten ein zweisprachiges Wörterbuch (Englisch-Deutsch bzw. Deutsch-Englisch). Wenn du mehr Informationen zu englischen Wörtern haben möchtest, etwa Beispielsätze, Definitionen oder Alternativen, dann bietet sich ein einsprachiges Wörterbuch an.

ZWEISPRACHIGE WÖRTERBÜCHER

Die Leitwörter *(running heads)* oben auf der Seite helfen dir, schnell zu finden, was du suchst. Auf der linken Seite steht das erste Stichwort, auf der rechten Seite das letzte Stichwort der Doppelseite.

- *resign* ist das Stichwort *(headword)*. Stichwörter sind alphabetisch geordnet: *r* vor *s*, *ra* vor *re*, *rhe* vor *rhi* usw.
- Die kursiv gedruckten Hinweise helfen dir, die für deinen Text passende Bedeutung zu finden.
- Die Ziffern 1, 2 usw. zeigen, dass ein Stichwort unterschiedliche Bedeutungen haben oder unterschiedlichen Wortarten angehören kann (z. B. Adjektiv, Nomen, Verb).
- Beispielsätze und Redewendungen sind dem Stichwort zugeordnet.
- Unregelmäßige Verbformen, besondere Pluralformen, die Steigerungsformen der Adjektive und ähnliche Hinweise stehen oft in Klammern oder sind kursiv gedruckt.
- Die Lautschrift gibt Auskunft darüber, wie das Wort ausgesprochen und betont wird.

resort

resign /rɪˈzaɪn/
1 BERUF • *als Vorsitzender usw* zurücktreten: ***He resigned from the company.*** Er verließ das Unternehmen.
2 *(job, post)* aufgeben *(Stelle, Posten)*
3 **resign oneself to something** sich mit etwas abfinden

resignation /ˌrezɪɡˈneɪʃn/
1 BERUF • *bei Unternehmen* Kündigung; *von Minister usw* Rücktritt
2 **hand in one's resignation** *von Angestelltem* kündigen; *von Minister usw* sein Amt niederlegen
3 *Gemütszustand* Resignation

resigned /rɪˈzaɪnd/ *(look, sigh)* resigniert

resit¹ /ˌriːˈsɪt/ *Verb* (→ *sit*) *BE (exam)* wiederholen *(Prüfung)*

resit² /ˈriːsɪt/ *Substantiv* • *BE* Wiederholungsprüfung

resolution /ˌrezəˈluːʃn/
1 POLITIK Beschluss, Resolution
2 *bei Problem, Streit* Lösung
3 ≈ *Entschiedenheit* Entschlossenheit

TIPP
Wenn du ein Online-Wörterbuch verwenden möchtest, erkundige dich vorher bei deinem Lehrer/deiner Lehrerin, welche zu empfehlen sind, denn nicht alle sind gleich gut. Fast alle funktionieren aber nach den gleichen Prinzipien wie gedruckte Wörterbücher.

EINSPRACHIGE WÖRTERBÜCHER

Wenn du selbst einen englischen Text schreibst, kannst du ein einsprachiges englisches Wörterbuch zu Hilfe nehmen. Hier findest du mehr über ein englisches Wort heraus als in einem zweisprachigen Wörterbuch:

- Ein einsprachiges Wörterbuch erklärt die Bedeutung eines englischen Wortes auf Englisch. Da manche Wörter mehrere Bedeutungen haben, ist es wichtig, alle Einträge und Beispielsätze zu einem Wort zu lesen und mit deinem englischen Text zu vergleichen, um die korrekte Bedeutung herauszufinden.
- Das Wörterbuch hilft dir, die passende Verbindung mit anderen Wörtern zu finden, z. B. zu Verben, Präpositionen oder in bestimmten feststehenden Wendungen. Das ist nützlich, wenn du selbst einen englischen Text schreiben willst und nach den richtigen Wörtern suchst.

deadly ['dedli] *adj*
1 *able or likely to kill people* {= lethal}: This is no longer a deadly disease.
deadly to The HSN virus is deadly to chickens.
a deadly weapon The new generation of biological weapons is more deadly than ever.
2 *(only before noun)* {= complete}: ***deadly silence*** There was deadly silence after his speech.
a deadly secret Don't tell anyone – this is a deadly secret.
deadly serious *completely serious:* Don't laugh – I am deadly serious!
3 *(informal) very boring*: Many TV programmes are pretty deadly!

SF 31 Ordering and structuring vocabulary

Wenn du einen Text zu einem bestimmten Thema schreiben sollst, ist es nützlich, vorab Vokabeln zu sammeln und zu ordnen, damit dein Text einen abwechslungsreichen Wortschatz hat und sich gut liest. Oft wird auch schon beim Sammeln eine Gliederung des Themas erkennbar. Dadurch merkst du auch schnell, welche Wörter du ggf. noch in einem Wörterbuch nachschlagen musst.

Diese Art, Wortschatz zu sammeln und zu ordnen, hilft dir auch Vokabeln zu lernen oder zu wiederholen und sie zu vernetzen, sodass sie besser in deinem Gedächtnis bleiben.

WORTSCHATZ STRUKTURIEREN

Für das Ordnen von Wortschatz gibt es verschiedene Möglichkeiten. Du solltest unterschiedliche Formen ausprobieren und dann diejenige verwenden, die am besten zu dir oder der Aufgabe passt.

Einige der Formen, die du nutzen kannst, sind:

- Tabellen (tables)
- Diagramme (z. B. tree diagrams)
- Mindmaps

school

people	things	timetable
teachers	...	...
...		

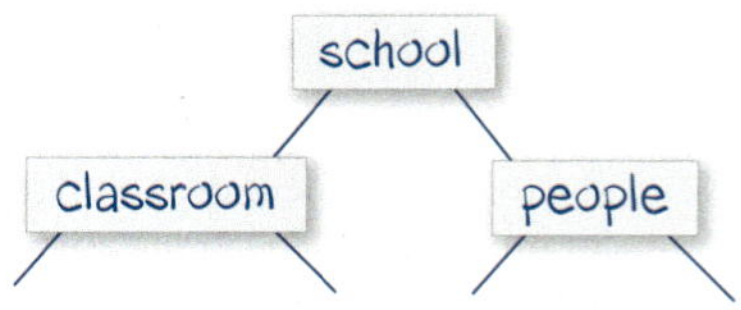

Wenn du Wortschatz zusammenstellst, um damit einen Text zu einem bestimmten Thema zu schreiben, solltest du unbedingt daran denken, dass du für einen guten Text nicht nur Nomen, sondern auch Verben, Adverbien, Adjektive etc. brauchst, sowie Varianten für Ausdrücke, die häufig vorkommen.

WORTSCHATZ LERNEN UND ERWEITERN

Diese Strukturierung eignet sich auch gut, um neue Wörter eines Wortfeldes zu lernen, da sich thematisch zusammenhängende Vokabeln leichter merken lassen. Damit kannst du deinen Wortschatz erweitern.

Eine gute Möglichkeit, thematisch zusammenhängenden Wortschatz zu lernen, ist, aus den Wörtern eines Wortfeldes eine Geschichte zu entwickeln und sie aufzuschreiben und evtl. passend zu illustrieren.

SF 32 Putting a page together

Wenn du eine Seite gestalten möchtest, z. B. für einen Vortrag, einen Blog oder als Folie/Poster für eine Präsentation, können dir folgende Hinweise helfen:

- Sortiere die Informationen, die du vermitteln willst: Was ist wichtig? Was ist ein Unterpunkt? Hast du Beispiele für Thesen/Argumente?
- Gib deinem Produkt eine klare Struktur: Texte haben meist drei Teile (Einleitung, Hauptteil, Schluss), während Folien/Poster häufig aus Aufzählungen wichtiger Punkte bestehen. Beginne für jeden neuen Gedanken einen neuen Absatz bzw. einen neuen Stichpunkt.
- Eine Überschrift verdeutlicht, worum es in deinem Text geht. Sie soll Leser auch neugierig machen auf das, was kommt. Wenn es in deinem Produkt um mehrere Themen/Aspekte eines Themas geht, dann kannst Du für einzelne Abschnitte auch Zwischenüberschriften verwenden. Das gibt dem Ganzen eine klare Struktur und hilft dem Leser, sich schnell zu orientieren.
- Ergänze dein Produkt mit passenden Fotos, Videos, Audios, Statistiken etc. (vergiss nicht anzugeben, woher die Medien stammen). Wenn nicht auf den ersten Blick erkennbar ist, was z.B. ein Bild zeigt, helfen Bildunterschriften.
- Formatiere dein Produkt so, dass es gut lesbar ist. Dabei ist das Medium wichtig – für einen ausgedruckten Handzettel kannst du andere Schriftarten wählen als für einen Text, der am Bildschirm gelesen wird. Für Folien in einer Präsentation oder ein Poster für einen *gallery walk* muss die Schriftgröße größer sein als für einen Ausdruck. Eine große Schriftgröße hilft dir auch, nicht zu viele Punkte auf einer Folie unterzubringen – hier ist weniger mehr.

SF 33 Making and taking notes

Wenn du Informationen oder eigene Gedanken kurz für dich notierst – z.B. als Vorbereitung auf einen eigenen Vortrag oder eine Präsentation –, heißt das im Englischen making notes. Wenn du dir Notizen beim Lesen oder Zuhören machst, heißt das taking notes. Für beide Varianten gelten aber die gleichen Grundsätze.

Step 1: Achte auf keywords, die die wichtigsten Informationen enthalten, um deine Frage/Aufgabe zu beantworten oder den Inhalt eines Textes grob zu verstehen.

Step 2: Notiere nur die wichtigsten Informationen. Verwende Abkürzungen und Symbole, aber achte darauf, dass du ein System hast und immer dieselben verwendest, damit du deine Notizen auch später noch verstehst. Markiere offene Fragen.

Step 3: Geh im Anschluss an das Lesen oder Hören nochmal durch deine Notizen und ergänze evtl. noch fehlende Informationen.

TIPP

Wenn du kein eigenes System von Abkürzungen hast, kannst du diese verwenden:

• the same as	=	• for example	*e.g.*
• not the same as	≠	• important	*!*
• about the same as	≈	• not	*x*
• and	+	• with	*w/*
• becomes/will be	->	• without	*w/o*
• between	*b/w*	• open question	*??*

Grammar File – Inhalt

Seite

GF 1 The tenses Die Zeitformen

1.1 Tense and time

Grammatische Zeitform und wirkliche Zeit

1a *Leon **is enjoying** his stay in Australia.*
1b *Next month, Leon **is flying** home.*

2a *Leon's host family **taught** him to surf.*
2b *Leon would be so happy if his parents **bought** him some surf equipment back home in Germany.*

Wenn man von **„Zeit"** spricht, muss man zwischen **Zeitform *(tense)*** und **wirklicher Zeit *(time)*** unterscheiden.

◄ Die **Zeitform** ist ein grammatischer Begriff.
Die grammatischen Zeitformen können sich auf verschiedene Zeiten in der Wirklichkeit beziehen:
In Satz **1a** bezieht sich die *present progressive tense* auf die Gegenwart, in Satz **1b** auf die Zukunft.
In Satz **2a** bezieht sich die *simple past tense* auf die Vergangenheit, in Satz **2b** auf die Zukunft.

*He **has been** in Australia for almost six months now.*	**present perfect**
Er **ist** jetzt seit fast sechs Monaten in Australien.	**Präsens**
*I'**ll take** the fish, please.*	***will*-future**
Ich **nehme** den Fisch, bitte.	**Präsens**

! Außerdem werden im Englischen und im Deutschen in vergleichbaren Situationen oft unterschiedliche Zeitformen verwendet.

➜ *The simple form and the progressive form: GF 2, pp. 168–169*

1.2 Talking about the present

Über die Gegenwart sprechen

The simple present

Das ***simple present*** wird verwendet,

*At home, Leon **usually gets** the bus to school.*
***On Fridays** his mother **takes** him in the car.*
*He **never cycles** to school because it's too far.*

◄ um über Handlungen und Ereignisse zu sprechen, die **wiederholt, regelmäßig, immer** oder **nie** geschehen. Signalwörter für das *simple present* sind Zeitangaben wie *always, usually, often, every week, on Fridays, never* u.Ä.

*Olivia Wilson and her family **live** in Nottingham.*
*Her mum is Italian, so she **speaks** two languages.*
*She **plays** hockey and **collects** old computer games.*
*Her parents **work** for a computer company.*

◄ um über **Dauerzustände** sowie über **Hobbys** und **Berufe** zu sprechen.

➜ *Unit 1: p. 14, exercise 2*

The present progressive

Das ***present progressive*** wird verwendet,

*What's Mr Bennett **doing**?*
*– He'**s making** a salad.*

Mr Bennett (on the phone): *"I'm busy, Jack. I'**m making** a salad."*

◄ um über Handlungen und Ereignisse zu sprechen, die **jetzt gerade** im Gange sind. Signalwörter für das *present progressive* sind *at the moment, now, just*.

! Die Handlung, um die es geht, kann für einen Augenblick unterbrochen sein, z.B. durch ein Telefonat. Wichtig ist, dass sie noch nicht abgeschlossen ist.

*Olivia has got a holiday job: she'**s working** as a waitress in a small café in Devon. She'**s sharing** a room with another waitress while she's there.*

◄ um über **vorübergehende Zustände** zu sprechen (begrenzter Zeitraum: *while she's there*).

➜ *Unit 1: p. 14, exercise 2*

In English

Talking about the present

Simple present	when something happens regularly, often, always, or never when we talk about something permanent, for example hobbies, jobs, or abilities
Present progressive	when an action or event is in progress and not yet complete

1.3 Talking about the past

Über die Vergangenheit sprechen

The simple past

***Twenty years ago**, Olivia's mother **moved** to England.*
Vor zwanzig Jahren ist Olivias Mutter nach England gezogen / zog Olivias Mutter nach England.

***Last Friday** Olivia's family **flew** to Italy.*

*Yesterday Olivia **went** to town with a friend. First they **looked** round the shops, and Katie **bought** a CD. Then they **tried** on shoes in four shops, but they **didn't buy** any. After that they **had** an ice cream.*

➔ *Unit 1: p. 14, exercise 1 · Unit 4: p. 86, exercises 1, 3*

Das ***simple past*** wird verwendet,

- um über **abgeschlossene** Handlungen und Ereignisse zu sprechen, die zu **einem bestimmten Zeitpunkt in der Vergangenheit** stattfanden. Signalwörter für das *simple past* sind genaue Zeitangaben wie *twenty years ago, last Friday, yesterday, in 2012* u.Ä.
- wenn man über vergangene Ereignisse berichtet oder eine Geschichte erzählt (oft mit *first …, then …, after that …*).

! Im Deutschen steht oft das Perfekt, wo im Englischen das *simple past* stehen muss.

„Früher …" – *used to* + infinitive / *would* + infinitive

*We **used to live** in Manchester.*
Wir wohnten früher in Manchester.
*Manchester United **used to be** my favourite team.*
Früher war Manchester United meine Lieblingsmannschaft.
*I **used to spend** lots of money on sports magazines.*
Ich habe früher immer viel Geld für Sportzeitschriften ausgegeben.

Wenn man beschreiben will, was **früher der Fall war**, aber heute nicht mehr, dann kann man die Konstruktion ***used to* + Infinitiv** verwenden.

*Grandpa **would visit** us every Sunday after church.*
Opa besuchte uns jeden Sonntag nach der Kirche. /
Opa pflegte uns jeden Sonntag nach der Kirche zu besuchen.
*We **would** often **go** for long walks in the woods.*
Wir haben oft lange Spaziergänge im Wald gemacht. /
Wir pflegten lange Spaziergänge im Wald zu machen.

Zum Ausdruck von **früher gewohnheitsmäßig wiederholten Handlungen** wird auch ***would* + *Infinitiv*** verwendet.

The past progressive

*Yesterday at 3.30 Olivia **was walking** home from school. It **was raining**, so lots of people **were hurrying** to the bus stop.*

*Sally **was cycling** home when a dog **ran** out in front of her bike.*
Sally radelte (gerade) nach Hause, als ihr ein Hund vors Fahrrad lief.

➔ *Unit 4: p. 86, exercise 1*

Das ***past progressive*** wird verwendet,

- um über Handlungen und Ereignisse zu sprechen, die **zu einem bestimmten Zeitpunkt in der Vergangenheit** noch im Gange, also **noch nicht abgeschlossen** waren.
- wenn man beschreiben will, was gerade vor sich ging *(she was cycling home)*, als etwas anderes passierte *(a dog ran out in front of her bike)*.

The past perfect (simple)

*When Emily arrived at the diner, her parents **had** already **eaten**.*
Als Emily im Restaurant ankam, hatten ihre Eltern schon gegessen.

*Grandpa **had** already **been** in hospital for a week when we returned from Spain.*
Opa lag schon eine Woche im Krankenhaus, als wir aus Spanien zurückkehrten.

➔ *Unit 4: p. 86, exercise 1*

Das ***past perfect*** wird verwendet,

- um auszudrücken, dass eine Handlung noch **vor einer anderen Handlung in der Vergangenheit** stattgefunden hatte.
- um auszudrücken, dass ein Zustand noch **vor einem Zeitpunkt in der Vergangenheit** begonnen hatte.

The past perfect progressive

➜ CHECK 1: p. 189

NEW

*Olivia was very tired when she arrived home. She **had been studying** for a test all day.*
... Sie hatte den ganzen Tag für einen Test gelernt.

*We **had been playing** tennis for half an hour when it started to rain.*
Wir hatten eine halbe Stunde Tennis gespielt, ...

➜ *Unit 4: p. 86, exercise 3*

Das ***past perfect progressive*** wird verwendet, um auszudrücken, dass eine Handlung vor einem Zeitpunkt in der Vergangenheit begonnen hatte und bis (oder fast bis) zu jenem Zeitpunkt andauerte.

In English

Talking about the past

Simple past	when we want to say or ask when something happened when we talk about things in the past or tell a story
Past progressive	when an action or event was in progress at a particular time in the past
Past perfect	when an action or event had already happened before a time in the past
Past perfect progressive	when an action or event had already begun before a time in the past and had continued up to (or almost up to) that time

1.4 Talking about the past <u>and</u> the present

Über die Vergangenheit <u>und</u> die Gegenwart sprechen

Present perfect und ***present perfect progressive*** haben mit der Vergangenheit und mit der Gegenwart zu tun.

The present perfect (simple)

1 *Matt Damon is great. I**'ve seen** all his films.*
2 *My sister loves books about horses. She**'s read** hundreds of them.*
3 *Mel **has lost** her mobile. Now she can't phone her friends and her mum is angry.*
4 *I**'ve bought** some new jeans, look. They'll go well with my red top.*
5 *Luke **has already done** his Maths homework, but he **hasn't started** his French **yet**.*
6 *I**'ve never been** to Paris. **Have** you **ever been** there? – No, I **haven't**. But I**'ve always wanted** to go.*

Das ***present perfect*** wird verwendet,

◄ um über Handlungen und Ereignisse zu sprechen, die **irgendwann in der Vergangenheit** geschehen sind.

Wie in den Sätzen **3** und **4** hat das Geschehen oft **Auswirkungen auf die Gegenwart oder die Zukunft**.

Ein genauer Zeitpunkt wird nicht genannt. Häufig werden jedoch Adverbien der unbestimmten Zeit wie *already, always, just, not ... yet, often, never* in *present perfect*-Sätzen verwendet – wie in den Sätzen **5** und **6**.

*Leon **has been** a member of his football club **for** ten years now / **since** his sixth birthday.*
Leon ist jetzt seit zehn Jahren / seit seinem sechsten Geburtstag Mitglied in seinem Fußballverein.

◄ um über **Zustände** zu sprechen, die in der Vergangenheit begonnen haben und jetzt noch andauern – oft mit *since* bzw. *for* = deutsch „seit".

! Im Deutschen benutzt man in diesen Fällen meist das Präsens, aber im Englischen **muss** das *present perfect* stehen:
Ich kenne ihn seit ... *I've known him since/for ...*

Zustandsverben sind z.B. *be, have, know, like, hate*.

➜ *Zustandsverben: GF 2.3, p. 169*

„seit ..." – *since / for*

***since* + Zeitpunkt** (wann etwas begann)

*We**'ve had** our dog **since April**.*
... seit April

***for* + Zeitraum** (wie lange etwas andauert)

*We**'ve had** our dog **for three months**.*
... seit drei Monaten

➜ *Unit 1: p. 14, exercise 1*

The present perfect progressive

1 *She's been writing letters all afternoon.*
Sie schreibt (schon) den ganzen Nachmittag Briefe.

2 *My brother **has been playing** the piano since 2013.*
Mein Bruder spielt seit 2013 Klavier.
3 *I've been learning French for three years now.*
Ich lerne jetzt seit drei Jahren Französisch.

Das ***present perfect progressive*** wird verwendet, um auszudrücken, dass eine **Handlung in der Vergangenheit begonnen** hat und jetzt **noch andauert** (auch wenn die Handlung nicht ununterbrochen im Gange war wie etwa in den Sätzen **2** und **3**).

! Auch in diesen Fällen verwenden wir im Deutschen meist das Präsens: *Er spielt seit …*
Aber im Englischen steht das *present perfect progressive*: *He's been playing … since/for …*

In English

Talking about the past and the present

Present perfect	when we want to say that something has happened (not when it happened) when we want to say since when or how long a state has already lasted
Present perfect progressive	when an action or event began in the past and has continued up to (or almost up to) the present

We use ***since*** with **points in time** (when something began).
We use ***for*** with **periods of time** (how long something has been going on).

1.5 Talking about the future

Über die Zukunft sprechen

The *will*-future

CHECK 2: p. 189

Das ***will-future*** wird verwendet,

I'll be 15 next October.
*It **will be** cold and windy, and we **will get** some rain in the afternoon.*

◂ um **Vorhersagen** über die Zukunft zu äußern. Oft geht es dabei um Dinge, die man nicht beeinflussen kann, z.B. das Alter oder das Wetter.

*I suppose Ella **will be** late again as usual.*
Ich nehme an, Ella kommt wie üblich wieder zu spät.

◂ um eine **Vermutung** auszudrücken (oft eingeleitet mit *I suppose, I think, I'm sure, I expect, maybe*).

Unit 3: p. 64, exercise 1

NEW

Just a moment. I'll open the door for you.
Moment. Ich mache Ihnen die Tür auf.

*I **won't tell** anyone what's happened. I promise.*
Ich sage niemandem, was passiert ist. …

◂ wenn man sich **spontan** – also ohne es im Voraus geplant zu haben – zu etwas entschließt. Oft geht es dabei um **Hilfsangebote** oder **Versprechen**.

Unit 3: pp. 68–69, exercises 1–3

The *going to*-future

CHECK 2: p. 189

Das ***going to-future*** wird verwendet,

After school I'm going to study architecture.
Nach der Schule werde ich Architektur studieren / habe ich vor, Architektur zu studieren.

*The Millers **are going to move** to New Zealand.*
Die Millers werden/wollen nach Neuseeland ziehen.

◂ um über **Vorhaben** zu sprechen, zu denen man sich schon vor einiger Zeit entschlossen hat (also über Dinge, die man bereits **geplant** hat).

Unit 3: p. 68, exercise 2

NEW

Look at those clouds. There's going to be a storm.
… Es wird ein Gewitter geben.

Oh dear! Your mother's going to be very angry with us.
… Deine Mutter wird sehr wütend auf uns sein.

◂ um zu betonen, dass man ganz sicher ist, dass etwas gleich geschehen wird (meist gibt es bereits deutliche **Anzeichen** dafür).

Unit 3: p. 64, exercise 2

The present progressive (with future meaning)

We're driving to Scotland next weekend to visit my grandparents.
I'm meeting a friend in town tomorrow at 12.
All my friends are coming to my birthday party on Friday.

➜ *Unit 3: p. 69, exercise 3*

Wenn etwas für die Zukunft **fest verabredet** ist, kann man auch das ***present progressive*** verwenden. Es muss aber deutlich sein, dass es sich um etwas Zukünftiges handelt, z.B. durch eine Zeitangabe *(next weekend, tomorrow, on Sunday)* oder aus dem Zusammenhang.

(Man nennt diese Verwendung des *present progressive* manchmal ***diary future***, weil es dabei oft um Verabredungen geht, die schon im Terminkalender eingetragen sind.)

The simple present (with future meaning)

Our cookery classes start on 2 September.
The film starts at 8 o'clock.
When does the next train to Liverpool leave?
The club meets in an hour, so we'll have to hurry.

Das ***simple present*** mit futurischer Bedeutung wird verwendet, wenn ein zukünftiges Geschehen durch einen **Fahrplan**, ein **Programm** oder Ähnliches genau festgelegt ist. Verben wie ***arrive, leave, go, open, close, start, stop*** werden häufig so verwendet.

(Diese Verwendung des *simple present* wird als ***timetable future*** bezeichnet.)

Wenn man im Englischen über Zukünftiges sprechen will, dann spielen bei der Wahl der richtigen Zeitform die Begriffe ***decision* (Entscheidung, Beschluss), *prediction* (Vorhersage)** und ***arrangement* (Vereinbarung)** eine entscheidende Rolle. Die folgende Tabelle kann dir helfen, die richtige Entscheidung zu treffen.

	will- future	*going to-* future	present progressive	simple present
DECISION (Entscheidung)	spontane Entscheidung	im Voraus geplant		
PREDICTION (Vorhersage)	Vermutungen u. Vorhersagen	betont sichere Vorhersage (Anzeichen vorhanden)		
ARRANGEMENT (Vereinbarung)		seltener, aber nicht falsch	fest verabredet ("diary future")	Fahrplan, Programm ("timetable future")

The future progressive

This time next week my sister will be on her way to Spain – and I'll be doing my maths exam.
Nächste Woche um diese Zeit wird meine Schwester auf dem Weg nach Spanien sein – und ich werde dabei sein, meine Mathe-Prüfung zu machen.

Das ***future progressive*** beschreibt Handlungen und Ereignisse, die **in der Zukunft im Gange sein werden** (noch nicht abgeschlossen sein werden).
Typische Zeitangaben sind *a week today* („heute in einer Woche"), *this time next week* und Ähnliches.

What will you be doing over the next couple of days?

How long will you be staying in Washington?

Will you be staying for dinner?

◂ Das ***future progressive*** wird oft verwendet, um sich höflich nach den Plänen anderer zu erkundigen.

The future perfect

***Next Friday** we **will have finished** all our exams.*
Nächsten Freitag werden wir alle unsere Prüfungen geschafft haben.

*And **by the end of next week** we**'ll have received** our results.*
Und bis Ende nächster Woche werden wir unsere Ergebnisse erhalten haben.

Das ***future perfect*** wird verwendet um auszudrücken, dass etwas **in der Zukunft geschehen oder getan sein wird**.
(Meist wird ein Zeitpunkt genannt – hier: *next Friday; by the end of next week*.)

In English

Talking about the future

***will*-future**	for predictions or assumptions about the future for spontaneous decisions (e.g. offers and promises)
***going to*-future**	for intentions and plans for the future for emphatic predictions (often there are signs of something happening)
Present progressive	when something is definitely planned or arranged for the future ("diary future")
Simple present	for future events that are a fixed part of a timetable, programme, schedule, etc. ("timetable future")
Future progressive	when an action or event will be in progress at a point of time in the future
Future perfect	when an action or event will be complete at a point of time in the future

GF 2 Aspect: the simple form and the progressive form

Aspekt: die einfache Form und die Verlaufsform

2.1 Simple and progressive form in contrast

Einfache Form und Verlaufsform im Vergleich

Tense	Simple form	Progressive form
Present tense	**sing(s)**	**am/are/is singing**
Past tense	**sang**	**was/were singing**
Present perfect	**have/has sung**	**have/has been singing**
Past percfect	**had sung**	**had been singing**
***will*-future**	**will sing**	**will be singing**

Anders als im Deutschen gibt es im Englischen eine **einfache Form** *(simple form)* und eine **Verlaufsform** *(progressive form)* des Verbs.

Mit diesen Formen bringt man zum Ausdruck,
- ob eine Handlung regelmäßig oder wiederholt stattfindet **oder** ob sie sich gerade im Verlauf befindet,
- ob eine Handlung abgeschlossen ist **oder** ob sie noch andauert.

1 *Tom **works** at a garage on Saturdays.* (regelmäßig)
2 *Mr Clark **goes** to work by bike.* (immer, jeden Tag)
3 *Lucy **has written** three letters today.* (sie ist fertig)

◂ Die ***simple form*** wird verwendet
- für regelmäßige/wiederholte Handlungen (**1**)
- für Dauerzustände (wenn etwas immer so ist) (**2**)
- für abgeschlossene Handlungen (**3**).

4 *Tom isn't in. He**'s working**.* (jetzt gerade)
5 *This week Mr Clark **is going** by bus.* (nur diese Woche, denn sein Rad ist kaputt)
6 *Lucy **has been writing** letters all day.* (sie ist noch dabei)

◂ Die ***progressive form*** wird verwendet
- für Handlungen, die gerade im Verlauf sind (**4**)
- für vorübergehende Zustände (wenn etwas nur vorübergehend der Fall ist) (**5**)
- für Handlungen, die noch nicht abgeschlossen sind (**6**).

➜ *Tätigkeits- und Zustandsverben: GF 2.2–2.3, p. 169*

2.2 Activity verbs

➜ CHECK 3: p. 189

Tätigkeitsverben

(in a shop window)	*We **make** the best pizza in town!*
(on the phone)	*Carol **is making** a pizza. Can she call you back?*

*It **gets** dark very early here in winter.*
*At 5 o'clock it **was** already **getting** dark.*

Tätigkeitsverben *(activity verbs)* bezeichnen **Tätigkeiten** *(do, go, make, read, …)* oder **Vorgänge** *(become, get, rain, …)*.

Sie können sowohl in der ***simple form*** als auch in der ***progressive form*** verwendet werden.

2.3 State verbs

➜ CHECK 3: p. 189

Zustandsverben

Zustandsverben *(state verbs)* bezeichnen keine Tätigkeiten oder Vorgänge, sondern **Zustände**. Sie werden in der Regel nur in der ***simple form*** verwendet.

Zu den **Zustandsverben** gehören

- Verben, die **Eigenschaften**, **Besitz** oder **Zugehörigkeit** ausdrücken, z.B. *be, exist, include, seem, sound, mean* („bedeuten"), *cost, need, own, belong, …*
- Verben des **Meinens** und des **Wissens**, z.B. *believe, know, mean* („meinen"), *remember, imagine, realize, recognize, understand, …*
- Verben des **Mögens** und **Wollens**, z.B. *like, love, dislike, hate, mind, prefer, want, …*

*The price **doesn't include** breakfast.*
*Emily **seems** really happy at her new school.*
*Jake's uncle **owns** a nice house in the country.*

***Do** you **believe** their story?*
*I **don't know** the answer to question 5.*
*Anna **didn't understand** what Julie **meant**.*

*Lucy **doesn't like** people who talk a lot.*
*I **don't mind** waiting for you here.*
*We **prefer** brown bread to white bread. It's healthier.*

States and activities

*Julie **has** dark hair.*	**state:**	„haben"
*Julie **is having** a shower.*	**activity:**	„duschen"
*We **were having** fun/a great time.*	**activity:**	„Spaß/eine tolle Zeit haben"
***Do** I **look** silly with my hair like this?*	**state:**	„aussehen"
*I didn't see him. I **wasn't looking**.*	**activity:**	„(hin)schauen, gucken"
*The flowers **smell** wonderful.*	**state:**	„riechen"
*Sophie **is smelling** the roses.*	**activity:**	„*an etwas* riechen"
*The pizza **tastes** good.*	**state:**	„schmecken"
***I'm tasting** the soup now.*	**activity:**	„kosten, probieren"
*I **think** that's a great idea.*	**state:**	„denken, meinen"
*He **was thinking** of moving to Paris.*	**activity:**	„überlegen, nachdenken"

Einige wenige englische Verben können als **Tätigkeits- oder als Zustandsverb** verwendet werden (mit jeweils unterschiedlichen deutschen Entsprechungen).

Als **Zustandsverb** stehen diese Verben immer in der ***simple form***.

Als **Tätigkeitsverb** kommen sie in beiden Formen vor.

Vergleiche die Beispiele im Kasten links.

In English

Activity verbs and state verbs

- **Activity verbs** like *do, make, cook, read, work* can be used in the simple form and in the progressive form:
  *Tom **cooks** lunch every Sunday.* (Tom kocht jeden Sonntag das Mittagessen.)
  *Tom is busy. He**'s cooking** lunch now.* (… Tom kocht gerade das Mittagessen.)
- **State verbs** like *seem, belong, believe, know, like, need, …* are not used in the progressive form:
  *I **don't believe** you.* (**not:** ~~*I'm not believing*~~ *you.*)
- A few verbs are used as state verbs **and** as activity verbs – with different meanings:
  *The soup **tastes** good.* (Die Suppe schmeckt gut.)
  *Quiet now. Grandpa **is tasting** the soup.* (… Opa probiert gerade die Suppe.)

GF 3 The passive Das Passiv

3.1 Active and passive — Aktiv und Passiv

Active ***John Lennon* *wrote* *"Imagine" in 1971.***
John Lennon schrieb „Imagine" im Jahr 1971.

Passive ***"Imagine"* *was written* *in 1971.***
„Imagine" wurde im Jahr 1971 geschrieben.

◂ Beide Sätze beschreiben denselben Sachverhalt, betrachten ihn aber aus unterschiedlichen Blickwinkeln:

Der **Aktivsatz** handelt von John Lennon und informiert uns darüber, dass und wann er das Lied „Imagine" schrieb.

Der ***Passivsatz*** handelt vom Lied „Imagine" und informiert uns über den Zeitpunkt seiner Entstehung.

Active *The manager* ***asked*** ***Ms Jones*** *to work late.*

Passive ***Ms Jones*** ***was asked*** *to work late.*
Ms Jones wurde gebeten, länger zu arbeiten.

Das Passiv kann von Verben gebildet werden, auf die im Aktiv ein Objekt folgt.
Das Subjekt des Passivsatzes entspricht dem Objekt des Aktivsatzes.

Active *The manager* ***paid*** ***her*** *£12 an hour.*

Passive ***She*** ***was paid*** *£12 an hour.*
Ihr wurden £12 die Stunde bezahlt. /
Sie erhielt £12 die Stunde.

◂ Wie dieses Beispiel zeigt, kann das **Subjekt des englischen Passivsatzes** (hier: ***She***) auch einem **deutschen Dativobjekt** (hier: ***Ihr***) entsprechen.
(Siehe dazu auch GF 3.4, The passive of verbs with two objects, p. 171.)

3.2 The passive: use — Das Passiv: Gebrauch

1 *The first goal* ***was scored*** *in the seventh minute.*
… wurde erzielt …

2 *A new sports centre* ***has been opened*** *in Paddington.*
… ist eröffnet worden …

3 *Breakfast* ***is served*** *from 7 to 10.30 am.*
… wird serviert …

4 *The bank robbers* ***have been sentenced*** *to ten years.*
… sind verurteilt worden …

Mit einem **Passivsatz** kann man Handlungen beschreiben, ohne zu sagen, wer die Handlung ausführt.

Oft ist nicht bekannt oder dem Sprecher nicht wichtig, wer die Handlung ausführt (Sätze **1** und **2**), manchmal ist es auch offensichtlich und daher nicht erwähnenswert (Sätze **3** und **4**).

> Yesterday a drunk driver hit a 15-year-old boy in Lichfield Road. The boy was taken to hospital, where he was treated for shock. He is now recovering. The driver was taken to Horton Road police station. He is answering police questions.

Das Passiv findet man oft in Nachrichten, in Zeitungsartikeln (z.B. über Unfälle, Sportereignisse, Verbrechen), in offiziellen Texten, in technischen Beschreibungen und auf Schildern.

Yesterday a drunk driver ***hit*** *a 15-year-old boy … The boy* ***was taken*** *… where he* ***was treated*** *… He* ***is*** *now* ***recovering****. …*

Oft wechselt man zwischen **Aktiv-** und **Passivsätzen**, wenn man mehrere Aussagen über dieselbe Person oder Sache macht.

The driver ***was questioned*** ***by*** *the police.*
Der Fahrer wurde von der Polizei verhört/befragt.

Wenn man in einem Passivsatz „Täter" oder „Verursacher" nennen will, kann man die Präposition ***by*** verwenden.

3.3 The passive: form

Das Passiv: Form

The passive

Simple present	*English **is spoken** in lots of countries.*
Simple past	*The bridge **was completed** in 1998.*
Present perfect	*All the biscuits **have been eaten**.*
Past perfect	*I didn't go to the party because I **hadn't been invited**.*
***going to*-future**	*Look, the lions **are going to be fed** soon.*
***will*-future and modal auxiliaries**	*The last match of the season **will be played** next Friday.* *Mobile phones **should be turned off** during lessons.* *Concert tickets **can be bought** online.*
Future perfect	*I'm sure lots of new planets **will have been discovered** by 2050.*
Present progressive	*Three new blocks of flats **are being built** in King Street.*
Past progressive	*The museum was closed. The rooms **were being painted**.*

Das Passiv bildet man mit einer **Form von *be*** und der **3. Form des Verbs** (Partizip Perfekt, *past participle*).

➜ *Unregelmäßige Verben: S. 264–265*

Bei den *progressive forms* wird das Passiv mit *being* gebildet: *are being built; were being painted*.

*A boy **got hurt** yesterday when he was hit by a car.*

*John's parents **got killed** in a fire when he was 12.*

◄ In informellem Englisch wird statt einer Form von *be* manchmal eine **Form von *get* zur Passivbildung** verwendet, vor allem bei kurzen Vorgängen, die plötzlich und unerwartet eintreten (wie z.B. Unfälle).

3.4 The passive of verbs with two objects

Das Passiv von Verben mit zwei Objekten

	subject	object	object
Active	*The manager promised*	***her***	***a job**.*

Passive ***She*** *(subject) was promised **a job**.*
Ihr *(Dativobjekt)* wurde **eine Stelle** *(Subjekt)* versprochen.

Manche Verben können **zwei Objekte** haben, z.B. *give/promise/send/show **somebody something*** *(**jemandem etwas** geben/versprechen/schicken/zeigen)*.

– **Passivsätze** mit solchen Verben beginnen im Englischen meist mit der **Person**.
Diese Art des Passivs wird ***personal passive*** („persönliches Passiv") genannt.

– Im **Deutschen** kann nur das **direkte Objekt (Sachobjekt)** zum Subjekt des Passivsatzes werden (hier: „eine Stelle"). Die Dativform des Personenobjekts bleibt im Passivsatz erhalten:
„**Ihr** wurde **eine Stelle** versprochen".

***She was paid** a lot of money for her book.*
Ihr wurde eine Menge Geld gezahlt für ihr Buch. /
Sie bekam eine Menge Geld für ihr Buch.

***He was given** the key and went up to his room.*
Ihm wurde der Schlüssel gegeben, ... /
Er bekam den Schlüssel ...

***I've been told** she has lost her job.*
Mir wurde erzählt, dass sie ihre Stelle verloren hat.

◄ Hier findest du weitere Beispiele für das ***personal passive***.
Passivsätze dieser Art sind im Englischen sehr häufig.
Im Deutschen müssen andere Konstruktionen verwendet werden.

In English

The passive

• An **active** sentence describes what somebody (or something) does.	***My uncle*** *designed lots of museums all over England.* (You are talking about your uncle.)
• A **passive** sentence describes what is done or what happens to people or things; often we do not say who does the action. Passive sentences are made with a form of ***be*** + **past participle**.	***Our local museum*** *was designed by a world-famous architect.* (You are talking about your local museum.)
• We find the passive mainly in news reports, official texts, signs, etc. when the 'doer' of the action is not named (because the 'doer' is not known/not important or because it's clear who does the action).	*The boy* ***was taken*** *to hospital, where he* ***was treated*** *for shock.*
• You can use ***by*** if you want to say who does the action.	*We were interrupted* ***by a German couple***.
• In informal English, a form of ***get*** is sometimes used instead of ***be***, especially when something happens suddenly and unexpectedly.	*Three people* ***got killed*** *in the fire.*
• In English, the **indirect object (the 'person object')** of an active sentence can be the subject of a passive sentence. We call this structure the **personal passive**. (This kind of passive sentence is not possible in German.)	Active: *Two Swedes joined* ***us***. Passive: ***We*** *were joined by two Swedes.* (Zwei Schweden schlossen sich **uns** an.) Active: *They offered* ***her*** *a job in Bristol.* Passive: ***She*** *was offered a job in Bristol.* (**Ihr** wurde ein Job im Bristol angeboten.)

GF 4 Modals and their substitutes Modale Hilfsverben und ihre Ersatzverben

4.1 Modal auxiliaries — Modale Hilfsverben

can, may, must, should sind modale Hilfsverben. Sie drücken aus, was jemand tun **kann, darf, muss, soll** usw. Sie werden zusammen mit dem Infinitiv eines Vollverbs verwendet (**1**).
Nur in Kurzantworten können sie allein stehen (**2**).

1 ***Can*** *you* ***play*** *the piano?*
2 *– Yes, I* ***can***. */ No, I* ***can't***.

Weitere Merkmale modaler Hilfsverben:

– Sie haben **nur eine Form**, es gibt also keine Endungen auf *-s*, *-ing* oder *-ed* (3).

3 *She's so good at drawing. She* ***should*** *study art.*

– Frage und Verneinung werden **ohne** *do/does/did* gebildet (4).

4 ***Could*** *you* ***do*** *the exercise? – No, I* ***couldn't***.

– Sie beziehen sich in der Regel auf die Gegenwart oder die Zukunft (5, 6).

5 ***Can*** *we help you in the kitchen, Mum?*
6 *We* ***can*** *play tennis on Saturday if you like.*

4.2 Substitutes — Ersatzverben

Modale Hilfsverben können nicht alle Zeitformen bilden. Daher gibt es zu bestimmten modalen Hilfsverben Ersatzverben mit ähnlicher Bedeutung, von denen man
– den Infinitiv (**1**),
– die *-ing*-Form (**2**),
– alle Zeitformen (**3**, hier: *simple past*)
bilden kann.

1 *I'd love* ***to be able to*** *play the piano.*
Ich würde liebend gern Klavier spielen können.

2 ***Being able to*** *play the piano must be great.*
Es muss großartig sein, Klavier spielen zu können.

3 *We* ***weren't allowed to*** *use dictionaries in the test.*
Wir durften im Test keine Wörterbücher benutzen.

➜ *Unit 2: p. 41, exercise 4*

Sieh dir die Beispielsätze für deutsch **„können"**, **„dürfen"** und **„müssen"** auf der nächsten Seiten an.

„können" – *can / (to) be able to*	*My little brother* **can** */* **is able to** *swim.*	*present:* *can* und *am/is/are able to*
	Tim **could** */* **was able to** *read when he was four.* *I* **could** *smell fire, but I* **couldn't** *see any smoke.*	*past:* *could* und *was/were able to* (*could* steht vor allem in verneinten Sätzen und Fragen und mit Verben der Wahrnehmung wie *smell, see, hear.*)
	I **haven't been able to** *contact him yet.*	*present perfect:* *have/has been able to*
	*I'm taking driving lessons, so next year I***'ll be able to** *drive.*	*will-future:* *will be able to*
„dürfen" – *can, may / (to) be allowed to*	**Can** */* **May** *I have a sleepover on Friday, Mum?* *We* **aren't allowed to** *stay up late in the week.*	*present:* *can, may* und *am/is/are allowed to*
	Under-12s **couldn't** */* **weren't allowed to** *see the film without an adult.*	*past:* *could* und *was/were allowed to*
	*I***'ve** *always* **been allowed to** *have pets.*	*present perfect:* *have/has been allowed to*
	Will *you* **be allowed to** *go to the party on Friday?*	*will-future:* *will be allowed to*
	Jeans **must not** *be worn at this school.* *At my school we***'re not allowed to** *wear jeans.*	! Für **ausdrückliche Verbote** wird *must not (mustn't)* oder *be not allowed to* verwendet.
„müssen" – *must / (to) have to*	Teacher: *You* **must** *work harder, Noah.* *His teacher says Noah* **has to** *work harder.* *I* **needn't** *get up at 6 tomorrow. /* *I* **don't have to** *get up at 6 tomorrow.*	*present:* *must* und *have/has to* – **Verneinung:** *needn't* oder *don't/doesn't have to*
	I **had to** *rewrite my essay.* *We* **didn't have to** *wait long.*	*past:* *had to* – **Verneinung:** *didn't have to*
	Lauren **has had to** *go to the dentist's.*	*present perfect:* *have/has had to*
	You **will have to** *go to the dentist's too if you eat so many sweets.*	*will-future:* *will have to*
	Everyone **needs to** *take a break now and again.* *You* **don't need to** *wait for us.* *I* **didn't need to** *tell her. She already knew it.* **Do** *we* **need** *to book a table?*	◄ Auch das Vollverb *(to) need to* wird verwendet, um zu sagen, dass jemand etwas tun muss oder nicht zu tun braucht.

4.3 Modal auxiliaries – what do they express?

Modale Hilfsverben – was drücken sie aus?

Modale Hilfsverben können ganz unterschiedliche Dinge zum Ausdruck bringen. Mit ***can*** kannst du z.B.
- sagen, dass jemand etwas tun **kann** oder **darf**
- jemanden um etwas **bitten** oder zu etwas **auffordern**
- um **Erlaubnis bitten** oder ein **Verbot aussprechen**

usw.

➔ *Unit 2: pp. 40 – 41, exercises 1 – 4 • p. 46, exercise 3*

Die folgenden Kästen geben dir einen Überblick.

Ability (Fähigkeit)	
I ***can*** *speak French and a little German.*	Ich **kann** Französisch und ein bisschen Deutsch.
They ***could*** *hear someone in the next room.*	Sie **konnten** jemanden im Nebenzimmer hören.

Request (Bitte / Aufforderung)	
Would *you help me to wash the dishes?*	**Würdest** du mir helfen abzuwaschen?
Could *you be quiet, please?*	**Kannst/Könntest** du bitte leise sein?

Permission, prohibition (Erlaubnis, Verbot)	
Can/May *I use your phone, please?*	**Kann/Darf** ich mal dein Telefon benutzen, bitte?
You ***can't*** *take photos in the museum.*	Du **darfst** im Museum nicht fotografieren.
In 1968, children ***could*** *leave school at 15.*	… **konnten/durften** Kinder mit 15 die Schule verlassen.
You ***mustn't*** *tell Julie about the concert. It's a surprise.*	Du **darfst** Julie nichts von dem Konzert erzählen. …

Suggestion (Vorschlag)	
Couldn't *you ask your grandma?*	**Könntest** du nicht deine Oma fragen?
You ***could*** *talk to your teacher.*	Du **könntest** (doch) mit deiner Lehrerin sprechen.
Shall *we eat first and go shopping later?*	**Sollen/Wollen** wir erst essen …?

Offer (Angebot)	
Can/Could *I get you a drink?*	**Kann** ich Ihnen (vielleicht) etwas zu trinken holen?
Would *you like to stay for dinner?*	**Möchten** Sie (nicht) zum Essen bleiben?
Shall *I help you with the dishes?*	**Soll** ich dir beim Abwasch helfen?

Refusal, rejection (Weigerung, Ablehnung)	
My father ***won't*** *let me stay out after ten.*	Mein Vater **will nicht**, dass ich nach zehn noch draußen bin.
I can't get in. The gate ***won't*** *open.*	… Das Tor **will nicht** aufgehen / geht nicht auf.
He knew the answer, but he ***wouldn't*** *tell me.*	…, aber er **wollte** sie mir **nicht** sagen / …, aber er weigerte sich, sie mir zu sagen.

Necessity (Notwendigkeit)	
You ***needn't*** *tell Mel about the concert. She already knows.*	Du **brauchst** Mel **nicht** von dem Konzert zu erzählen. …
I've got a temperature. I ***must*** *stay in bed.*	Ich habe Fieber. Ich **muss** im Bett bleiben.

Obligation, advice (Verpflichtung, Ratschlag)

*Dogs **should** be left outside.*	Hunde **sollten** draußen gelassen werden / draußen bleiben.
*You **should** tell him the truth. / You **ought to** tell him the truth.*	Du **solltest** ihm die Wahrheit sagen.

CHECK 4: p. 190

NEW

„sollen"

*You**'re not supposed to** use mobiles in the theatre. You**'d better** (= had better) turn it off.*
Man **soll** im Theater keine Handys benutzen. Du **solltest** es (lieber) ausschalten.

*I**'d better** go now. It's late.*
*It's cold. You**'d better** not go out.*

*You**'re supposed to** take off your hat when you enter a church.*

*The Carpenters **are supposed to** be very rich.*
*They**'re said to** have six houses.*
Die Carpenters **sollen** sehr reich sein.
Sie **sollen** sechs Häuser haben. / Man sagt, sie hätten sechs Häuser.

*Carrots **are supposed to** be good for your eyes.*

Unit 2: pp. 45–46, exercises 1–4

◄ Auch *had better* und *be supposed to* können für das deutsche „sollen" verwendet werden:

- *had better* ist stärker als *should* und *ought to;* es bringt zum Ausdruck, was jemand in einer bestimmten Situation am besten tun sollte.
- *be supposed to* drückt aus, dass etwas von jemandem erwartet wird bzw. wurde – z. B. weil etwas vereinbart wurde, oder weil Regeln, Traditionen oder Gesetze es verlangen.

◄ *be supposed to* oder *be said to* werden auch verwendet, wenn etwas (angeblich) der Fall sein soll („die Leute sagen", „man sagt").

Possibility, probability, deduction (Möglichkeit, Wahrscheinlichkeit, Schlussfolgerung)

*That **must** be Luke.*	Das **muss** Luke sein.
*– No, it **can't** be Luke. Luke is in Spain.*	– Nein, das **kann nicht** Luke sein. Luke ist in Spanien.
*Where's Dad? – He **could** be at Grandma's.*	… – Er **könnte** bei Oma sein.
*They **may**/**might** still be alive.*	Sie sind **vielleicht** noch am Leben/**könnten** noch am Leben sein.
*Kathy **should** be / **ought to** be here by now.*	Kathy **sollte** jetzt (eigentlich) hier sein.
*There's somebody at the door. – That **will** be Sue.*	Es ist jemand an der Tür. – Das **wird** Sue sein.
*That **can't** have been easy.*	Das **kann nicht** einfach gewesen sein.
*They **must** have fallen asleep.*	Sie **müssen** eingeschlafen sein.

Unit 2: p. 40, exercises 1–2

In English

Modals and their substitutes

- **Modal auxiliaries** (short: **modals**) like *can, could, may, might, must,* etc.

– have only one form	*He may be a bit late.*
– form negatives and questions without *do/does/did*	*I can't hear them. Can you hear them?*
– are followed by an infinitive without *to*	*You should ask your teacher.*
– usually refer to the present or future	*Can I go now? / Can I call you back tomorrow?*
– can express more than one speech function.	***can*** *I can play tennis.* (ability)
	Can I borrow your ruler? (request)
	You can take my bike. (permission)
	That can't be Joe. Joe's in Italy. (possibility)
– cannot form all tenses.	

- **Substitutes** are used to form other tenses:

– *can* („können") – *(to) be able to*	*After a six months, he was able to understand French.*
– *can, may* („dürfen") – *(to) be allowed to*	*We were not allowed to use a dictionary in the test.*
– *must* („müssen") – *(to) have to; (to) need to*	*We had to do extra homework yesterday.*
	I need to get a new pair of trainers.

GF 5 The gerund Das Gerundium

5.1 The gerund as subject and object — Das Gerundium als Subjekt und als Objekt

Subject	Object
Travelling *is fun.*	*I love **travelling**.*
Reisen macht Spaß.	Ich liebe das Reisen. / Ich reise sehr gern.

Wenn die *-ing*-Form eines Verbs die Funktion eines **Nomens** hat, wird sie **Gerundium** *(gerund)* genannt.

Vergleiche: *I love **pop music**.* (*I love* + Nomen)
*I love **travelling**.* (*I love* + *-ing*-Form)

Das Gerundium kann **Subjekt** oder **Objekt** eines Satzes sein.

*I love **playing board games**.*
Ich spiele sehr gern Brettspiele.

Cycling in the rain *can be fun too.*
Radfahren im Regen kann auch Spaß machen. / Im Regen Rad zu fahren kann auch Spaß machen.

◄ Wie ein Verb kann das Gerundium erweitert werden, z.B. durch ein Objekt (hier: *board games*) oder eine Orts- oder Zeitangabe (hier: *in the rain*).

! Beachte:

1 *Nobody **enjoys going** to the dentist's.*
Niemand geht gern zum Zahnarzt.

*I can't **imagine living** in the country.*
Ich kann mir nicht vorstellen, auf dem Land zu leben.

*Tom **suggested going** for an ice cream.*
Tom schlug vor, ein Eis essen zu gehen.

1 Nach einigen Verben kann – anders als im Deutschen – **kein Infinitiv** stehen. Stattdessen muss man ein **Gerundium** verwenden. Also nicht:

~~*I enjoy to go*~~ … / ~~*I can't imagine to live*~~ …

Zu diesen Verben gehören auch:
admit, consider, deny, discuss, dislike fancy, finish, give up, keep, mind miss, practise, regret, risk – *doing sth.*

2 *When it **started** **raining** / **to rain** we all went home.*

*I **hate** / I **don't like** **getting up** / **to get up** when it's still dark.*

2 Nach ***begin/start, continue, hate, like, love, prefer*** kann – bei gleicher Bedeutung – ein Gerundium oder ein *to*-Infinitiv stehen.

3 *My mother **would prefer to move** to a small village, but I **would hate to live** in the country.*

3 Nach ***would like, would love, would hate, would prefer*** kann nur der *to*-Infinitiv stehen.

4 *I'll never **forget meeting** the Queen.*
Ich werde nie vergessen, wie ich … getroffen habe.
*I **forgot to phone** Grandpa. I'm sorry.*
Ich habe vergessen, Opa anzurufen. Es tut mir leid.

*I **remember meeting** her.*
Ich erinnere mich daran, dass ich sie getroffen habe.
*I must **remember to phone** Grandpa.*
Ich muss daran denken (= ich darf nicht vergessen), Opa anzurufen.

*I've **stopped eating** hamburgers.*
Ich habe aufgehört, Hamburger zu essen.
*I **stopped to buy** a hamburger.*
Ich hielt an, um einen Hamburger zu kaufen.

*It's very sour. – **Try using** more sugar.*
… Probier's mal mit mehr Zucker.
*I **tried to kick** the door open and hurt myself.*
Ich versuchte/bemühte mich, die Tür aufzutreten …

4 Nach ***forget, remember, stop, try*** kann entweder ein **Gerundium** oder ein ***to*-Infinitiv** stehen, aber mit **unterschiedlicher Bedeutung**:

– ***forget doing sth.***	vergessen, dass/wie man etwas getan hat
forget to do sth.	vergessen, etwas zu tun
– ***remember doing sth.***	sich daran erinnern, dass/wie man etwas getan hat
remember to do sth.	daran denken (nicht vergessen), etwas zu tun
– ***stop doing sth.***	aufhören, etwas zu tun
stop to do sth.	anhalten, um etwas zu tun
– ***try doing sth.***	etwas (aus)probieren
try to do sth.	versuchen, etwas zu tun

➔ *Unit 4: p. 92, exercises 5–7*

5.2 The gerund after prepositions

Das Gerundium nach Präpositionen

1 *The man left the shop* **without paying**.
… ohne zu bezahlen.

2 *You can save petrol* **by driving** *more slowly.*
… indem man langsamer fährt.

3 *My little brother is* ***afraid of sleeping*** *in the dark.*
… hat Angst davor, im Dunkeln zu schlafen.

4 *What were his* ***reasons for leaving*** *school?*
… seine Gründe dafür, die Schule zu verlassen?

5 *They* ***decided against moving*** *to Italy.*
Sie entschieden sich dagegen, nach Italien zu ziehen.

Wenn auf eine **Präposition** *(about, at, for, in, instead of, of, without, …)* ein **Verb** folgt, dann steht dieses Verb als Gerundium.

◄ Die Präposition kann

- allein stehen (Sätze **1 und 2**) oder
- mit einem anderen Wort fest verbunden sein (Sätze **3 bis 5**).

Im Folgenden findest du eine Reihe von nützlichen Wendungen mit **Präposition + Gerundium**.

Adjektiv + Präposition + Gerundium:

(to) be	***afraid of***	***doing*** *sth.*	Angst haben vor
	excited about		gespannt sein auf; aufgeregt sein wegen
	good/bad at		gut/schlecht sein in; etwas gut/schlecht können
	interested in		interessiert sein an, sich interessieren für
	keen on		begeistert sein von; interessiert sein an
	tired of		genug haben von; etwas über/satt haben

Nomen + Präposition + Gerundium:

the	***chance of***	***doing*** *sth.*	Chance, (günstige) Gelegenheit (zu)
	danger of		Gefahr (zu)
	hope of		Hoffnung (zu/auf)
	idea of		Idee, Gedanke (zu)
	reason for		Grund (für)
	way of		Art und Weise, Weg (zu)

Verb + Präposition + Gerundium:

(to)	***believe in***	***doing*** *sth.*	glauben an
	decide against		sich entscheiden gegen
	dream of/about		träumen von
	look forward to		sich freuen auf
	talk about/of		reden von
	think of		denken an; in Betracht ziehen
	worry about		sich Sorgen machen wegen/um

5.3 The gerund with "its own subject"

Das Gerundium mit „eigenem Subjekt"

1a *Ava can't* ***imagine moving*** *to Wales.*
Ava kann sich nicht vorstellen, nach Wales zu ziehen.

1b *Ava can't* ***imagine her family moving*** *to Wales.*
Ava kann sich nicht vorstellen, dass ihre Familie nach Wales zieht.

◄ In Satz **1b** hat das Gerundium ein „eigenes Subjekt": *moving* bezieht sich auf *her family* (und nicht auf *Ava*, das Subjekt des ganzen Satzes).

2a *Do you* ***mind me leaving*** *early today?*

2b *Do you* ***mind my leaving*** *early today?*
Macht es Ihnen etwas aus, wenn ich heute früher gehe?

◄ Wenn wie in Satz **2a** das Subjekt des Gerundiums ein **Personalpronomen** ist, dann steht es in der Objektform: … ***me*** *leaving* … (nicht: *I*).

Du wirst auch Fälle finden, in denen statt des Personalpronomens ein **Possessivpronomen** steht (Satz **2b**): … ***my*** *leaving* …

In English

The gerund

- An *-ing* form which is used like a noun is called a **gerund**.
- Gerunds can be
  – the **subject** of a sentence: ***Surfing*** */* ***Playing tennis*** *is fun.*
  – the **object** of a sentence: *I love* ***surfing*** */* ***playing tennis****.*
- After some verbs we use a gerund, not an infinitive.
  Examples: ***admit, consider, deny, discuss, dislike, enjoy, fancy, finish, give up, imagine, keep, mind, miss, practise, regret, risk, suggest*** *doing sth.*
- Verbs which follow a **preposition** take the form of a gerund: *Dad gave me some money* ***for cleaning*** *his bike.*
- Gerunds can have **their own subject**: *They're very happy about* ***<u>their son</u> passing*** *the test.*

GF 6 The *to*-infinitive Der Infinitiv mit *to*

6.1 Verb + object + *to*-infinitive — Verb + Objekt + *to*-Infinitiv

Our teacher ***allows*** ***us*** ***to use*** *mobiles.*
... erlaubt uns, Handys zu benutzen.

My sister ***asked*** ***me*** ***not to wear*** *her T-shirts.*
... bat mich, nicht ihre T-Shirts zu tragen.

Pictures can ***help*** ***you*** ***to understand*** *new words.*
Bilder können dir helfen, neue Wörter zu verstehen.

Nach bestimmten Verben kann ein **Objekt** + ***to*-Infinitiv** stehen. Beispiele:
allow/ask/help/invite/teach sb. to do sth.

Im Deutschen steht meist ein Inifinitiv mit „zu“:
jm. erlauben/jn. bitten/jm. helfen/jn. einladen/jm. beibringen, etwas zu tun

The police officer ***told*** ***us*** ***to wait*** *outside.*
... sagte, dass wir draußen warten sollten. /
... forderte uns auf, draußen zu warten.

The hurricane ***caused*** ***the house*** ***to collapse****.*
Der Hurrikan bewirkte, dass das Haus zusammenbrach. /
... verursachte den Zusammenbruch des Hauses.

His parents ***expect/want*** ***him*** ***to be*** *home by ten.*
... erwarten/wollen, dass er um zehn zu Hause ist.

I'd like ***you*** ***to sit*** *down in a circle now.*
Ich möchte, dass ihr euch jetzt im Kreis hinsetzt.

◄ Auch nach den Verben ***cause, expect, tell, want, would like, would love*** kann ein **Objekt** + ***to*-Infinitiv** stehen.

! Nach den entsprechenden deutschen Verben steht meist ein Nebensatz mit „dass“, aber auf die englischen Verben darf **kein *that*-Satz** folgen:

Deutsch: *Ich* ***möchte/erwarte****,* ***dass er uns hilft****.*

Englisch: *I* ***want*** ***him*** */ I* ***expect*** ***him to help us****.*
Nicht: ~~*I want/expect that he ...*~~

6.2 Question word + *to*-infinitive — Fragewort + *to*-Infinitiv

Can you tell me ***how to get*** *to the station?*
Können Sie mir sagen, wie ich zum Bahnhof komme/kommen kann?

I don't know ***what to do****.*
Ich weiß nicht, was ich tun soll.

I need help, but I don't know ***who to ask****.*
Ich brauche Hilfe, aber ich weiß nicht, wen ich fragen kann/soll.

We had no idea ***where to go****.*
Wir hatten keine Ahnung, wohin wir gehen sollten.

Der ***to*-Infinitiv** steht oft nach einem **Fragewort** (*what, who, how, when, where* usw.). Er entspricht in der Regel einem Nebensatz mit modalem Hilfsverb (*can, could, should* usw.).

Vergleiche: *I don't know who to ask.*
I don't know who I can ask/who I should ask.

Die Kombination aus Fragewort und *to*-Infinitiv steht oft nach den Verben *ask, explain, find out, know, show, tell, wonder*.

6.3 The *to*-infinitive instead of a relative clause

CHECK 5: p. 190

Der *to*-Infinitiv anstelle eines Relativsatzes

In den folgenden Fällen entspricht der *to*-Infinitiv einem **Relativsatz**:

*The **first/last (person) to arrive** was Jonathan.*
(The first/last person who arrived …)

*We're **the only shop to offer** this service.*
(… the only shop that offers this service)

*Ava was **the only person/the only one to tell** the truth.*
(… the only person/the only one who told …)

– nach ***the first, the last, the next, the only***

! Nach *the only* muss ein Nomen oder *one/ones* stehen.

*Sophie was **the youngest (girl) to take** part.*
(… the youngest girl who took part)

– nach einem **Superlativ**

*Philip is **the person to ask** about computers.*
*(… the person who you **should** ask …)*

*Luigi's is **the place to go** for a good pizza.*
*(… the place that you **must/should** go to …)*

*I'm looking for **someone to share** a flat with.*
*(… someone who I **can** share a flat with)*

*Lily doesn't know **anybody to play** with.*
*(… anybody who she **can/could** play with)*

*There's **nothing to do** and **nowhere to go**.*
*(… nothing that I **can** do and nowhere that I **can** go)*

– nach einen **Nomen** (besonders häufig nach ***person, place, way***) und nach **Zusammensetzungen mit *some-, any-*** und ***no-*** *(someone, something, anybody, nowhere, …)*

In diesen Fällen entspricht der *to*-Infinitiv einem **Relativsatz mit modalem Hilfsverb**.

Mr Smith is the person to ask
if you have a problem with your electrical wiring.
(*electrical wiring* = elektrische Leitungen)

In English

The *to*-infinitive

The *to*-infinitive is used …

• after **verb** + **object** (e.g. *ask/expect/help/teach/tell/want sb. to do sth.*) ! You mustn't use a *that*-clause after *cause, expect, tell, want, would like, would love*.	*Dad **wants you to help** him.* (not: ~~*Dad wants that you help him*~~.)
• after a question word (instead of a subordinate clause)	*I don't know **what to do**.* *Can you tell me **how to get** to the station?*
• after *the first (person), the last (one), the only one* (instead of a relative clause)	*Sue is always **the first to arrive**.* *He was **the only one to tell** the truth.*
• after superlatives (instead of a relative clause)	*Tom was **the oldest to join** us.*
• after nouns and *someone, anything, nowhere*, etc. (instead of a relative clause)	*That's **the way to do** it!* *Grandpa needs **someone to talk** to.*

GF 7 Indirect speech Indirekte Rede

7.1 Direct and indirect speech — Wörtliche und indirekte Rede

Norah:	*I **love** music. I **go** dancing every Saturday.*	
Direct speech	*Norah says, "I **love** music. I **go** dancing every Saturday."*	◄ In der **direkten Rede** wird **wörtlich** wiedergegeben, was jemand sagt, schreibt oder denkt.
Indirect speech (reporting verb: simple present)	*Norah **says that** she **loves** music, and **that** she **goes** dancing every Saturday.*	◄ In der **indirekten Rede** (*indirect* oder *reported speech*) wird **berichtet**, was jemand sagt, schreibt oder denkt. (Einleitende Verben: *say, tell sb., answer, write, think, …*)
Indirect speech (reporting verb: simple past)	*Norah **said that** she **loved** music, and **that** she **went** dancing every Saturday.*	◄ Wenn das **einleitende Verb im *simple past*** steht (*said, told, wrote* usw.), dann werden die Zeitformen der direkten Rede meist um eine Zeitstufe in die Vergangenheit „zurückverschoben" ***(backshift of tenses)***. Vergleiche: *"I **love** music." – She said she **loved** music.*

Backshift of tenses after a reporting verb in the past

	Direct speech	Indirect speech
present ⟶ past	"I **don't like** musicals." "We**'re** just **having** dinner."	She **told** us she **didn't like** musicals. He **said** they **were** just **having** dinner.
past ⟶ past perfect [1]	"I **arrived** on Friday evening." "Alex **was waiting** for Olivia."	She **said** she **had arrived** on Friday evening. Bobby **said** Alex **had been waiting** for Olivia.
present perfect ⟶ past perfect	"I**'ve seen** that film before."	I **told her** that I **had seen** the film before.
***will*-future ⟶ *would* + infinitive**	"I**'m** sure you**'ll qualify**."	Mr Jones **said** he **was** sure I **would qualify**.
***going to*-future ⟶ *was/were going to* + infinitive**	"We**'re going to fly** to Italy in July."	They **said** they **were going to fly** to Italy in July.
can* ⟶ *could	"You **can use** my laptop."	Her dad **said** she **could use** his laptop.

[1] *Past tense*-Formen der direkten Rede werden in der indirekten Rede oft beibehalten, also nicht ins *past perfect* verändert: *I **arrived** on Friday evening.* ⟶ *She told us she **arrived** on Friday evening.*

*Norah **said** she loved music.*
Norah sagte, dass sie Musik liebt.

! Im Englischen steht vor der indirekten Rede kein Komma, und die Konjunktion *that* („dass") wird oft weggelassen, besonders nach *say, tell, think*.

Direct speech	Norah *"**I** can lend **you my** bike, Ava."*	◄ Wie im Deutschen werden in der indirekten Rede die **Pronomen** und **Possessivbegleiter** angepasst – je nachdem, wer wem berichtet.
(Norah reports)	*I told Ava **I** could lend **her my** bike.*	
(Ava reports)	*Norah said **she** could lend **me her** bike.*	

(On a postcard from Alex)	*I like it a lot **here** in France. I'm flying to Paris **tomorrow** and …*	◄ **Orts- und Zeitangaben** werden in der indirekten Rede aus der Sicht des Berichtenden gewählt. Sie können sich also, je nach Situation, gegenüber der direkten Rede verändern.
His mother (to a friend, a week later)	*He wrote that he liked it a lot **there**, and that he was flying to Paris **the next day**.*	

➜ *Unit 4: pp. 90–91, exercises 1–3*

7.2 Indirect speech: questions

Indirekte Rede: Fragen

with question word

1 *"**Why don't** you **like** musicals?"*
*I **asked** her **why** she **didn't like** musicals.*

2 *"**What's going** on here?"*
*Miss Cleveland **wanted to know what was going** on.*

Auch bei Fragen in der indirekten Rede erfolgt der *backshift of tenses*, wenn das einleitende Verb im *simple past* steht *(asked, wanted to know, wondered)*.

yes/no question

3 *"Do you **want to join** us?"*
*He **asked if** I **wanted to join** them.*

4 *"Are you **going to stay**?"*
*Jake **asked** me **whether** I **was going to stay**.*

◄ Handelt es sich bei der direkten Frage um eine **Frage ohne Fragewort** *(yes/no question)*, dann wird die indirekte Frage mit ***if*** oder ***whether*** (= „ob") eingeleitet.

			S	V	
statement			"We	live	in Hamburg."
direct questions		"Do	you	live	in Hamburg?"
		"Where do	you	live?"	
indirect question	I asked	if	they	lived	in Hamburg.
	I asked	where	they	lived.	

! Die Wortstellung in indirekten Fragen ist wie in Aussagesätzen: **S – V – …**

Anders als in direkten Fragen gibt es **keine Umschreibung mit *do/does/did***.

Direct question *"What **are** you **waiting for**?"*

Indirect question *He asked me what I **was waiting for**.*
…, worauf/auf was ich wartete.

◄ Beachte die **Stellung der Präposition** im Englischen.

➜ *Unit 4: pp. 90 – 91, exercises 1 – 3*

7.3 Indirect speech: requests, commands, advice, suggestions

Indirekte Rede: Bitten, Aufforderungen, Ratschläge, Vorschläge

Bitten, Aufforderungen und **Ratschläge** werden meist durch eine **Infinitivkonstruktion** wiedergegeben:

1 *"Can you look after my bag for a moment?"*
*A man **asked me to look** after his bag for a moment.*
…, einen Moment auf seine Tasche aufzupassen.

◄ Für die Wiedergabe von **Bitten** *(requests)* verwendet man in der Regel ***ask sb. to do sth.*** (bzw. ***ask sb. not to do sth.***). **(1)**

2 *"Don't touch the paintings."*
*The guide **told him not to touch** the paintings.*
… sagte ihm, er solle die Gemälde nicht berühren. / … forderte ihn auf, die Gemälde nicht zu berühren.

3 *He **was told not to touch** the paintings.*
Man sagte ihm, … / Er wurde aufgefordert, …

◄ Für die Wiedergabe von **Aufforderungen** *(commands)* verwendet man gewöhnlich ***tell sb. to do sth.*** (bzw. ***tell sb. not to do sth.***). **(2)**

Oft steht der einleitende Satz mit ***tell*** dabei im Passiv.

➜ *Passiv: GF 3, pp. 170 – 172*

4 *"I would look for a holiday job if I were you."*
*Mr Williams **advised Grace to look** for a holiday job.*
Mr Williams riet Grace, sich einen Ferienjob zu suchen.

◄ Für die Wiedergabe von **Ratschlägen** *(advice)* verwendet man meist ***advise sb. to do sth.*** (bzw. ***advise sb. not to do sth.***). **(4)**

5 *"Let's go for a pizza."*
*Jonathan **suggested going** for a pizza.*
Jonathan schlug vor, eine Pizza essen zu gehen.

"Why don't you look for a holiday job?"
*He **suggested that Grace look** for a holiday job.*
Er schlug vor, dass Grace sich einen Ferienjob sucht.

◄ **Vorschläge** *(suggestions)* werden in der indirekten Rede meist mit ***suggest*** eingeleitet. **(5)**

! Beachte, dass nach ***suggest*** kein *to*-Infinitiv stehen darf:

Also nie: *He ~~suggested to go~~ for a pizza.*
Sondern: *He **suggested going** for a pizza.*
oder: *He **suggested that we go** for a pizza.*
oder: *He **suggested we should go** for a pizza.*

➜ *Unit 4: p. 100, exercises 1 – 3*

In English

Indirect speech

- In **indirect speech**, we report what someone has said or written.
  If the reporting verb is in the past *(said, told,* etc.*)*, there is usually a change of tenses ("backshift"):
  present → past • **past → past perfect** • **present perfect → past perfect**
  going to*-future → *was/were going to* + infinitive** • ***will*-future → *would* + infinitive** • ***can* → *could
- In **indirect questions**, the word order is **S – V – ...**, and *do/does/did* is not used:
  I asked where they lived. | *She wanted to know if we needed anything else.*
- The ***to*-infinitive** is used to report **commands, requests** and **advice**: *tell/ask/advise sb. to do sth.*
  Miss Jones told/asked me to open the window. | *The doctor advised me to eat more fruit.*
- The ***to*-infinitive** cannot be used to report **suggestions**. You can use ***suggest ...ing*** or ***suggest that ...***:
  Miss Bell suggested talking to our parents first / suggested that we (should) talk to our parents first.

GF 8 Conditional sentences Bedingungssätze

Subordinate clause	**Main clause**
If *you give me your number,*	*I'll call you.*
Wenn du mir deine Nummer gibst,	rufe ich dich an.

Bedingungssätze („Wenn ..., dann ...“-Sätze) bestehen aus einem **Hauptsatz** *(main clause)* und einem **Nebensatz** *(subordinate clause)* mit ***if*** („wenn/falls“).

if + present	*will*-future
If I ***miss*** *the bus,*	*I'****ll take*** *a taxi.*

Wenn ich den Bus **verpasse**, **nehme** ich ein Taxi.

If Dan ***misses*** *the bus, he* ***can/should/must take*** *a taxi.*
If you ***miss*** *the bus,* ***take*** *a taxi.*

◄ **Typ 1 („Was ist, wenn ...“-Sätze)**

Diese Bedingungssätze beziehen sich auf die **Gegenwart** oder die **Zukunft**. Sie drücken aus, was unter bestimmten Bedingungen **geschieht/geschehen wird** oder **nicht geschieht/nicht geschehen wird**.

Statt des Futurs mit ***will*** können im Hauptsatz auch die modalen Hilfsverben ***can, should, must*** usw. oder ein **Imperativ** stehen.

if + past	*would* + infinitive
If I ***missed*** *the bus,*	*I'****d*** *(= I* ***would****)* ***take*** *a taxi.*

Wenn ich den Bus **verpasste/verpassen würde**, **würde** ich ein Taxi **nehmen**.

If Dan ***missed*** *the bus, he* ***could/might take*** *a taxi.*

◄ **Typ 2 („Was wäre, wenn ...“-Sätze)**

Auch diese Bedingungssätze beziehen sich auf die **Gegenwart** oder die **Zukunft**. Sie drücken aus, was unter bestimmten Bedingungen **geschehen** oder **nicht geschehen würde**.

Statt ***would*** können im Hauptsatz auch ***could*** oder ***might*** + Infinitiv stehen.

→ *CHECK 6: p. 190*

NEW

if + past perfect	*would have* + past participle
If I ***had missed*** *the bus,*	*I* ***would have taken*** *a taxi.*

Wenn ich den Bus **verpasst hätte**, **hätte** ich ein Taxi **genommen**.

If Dan ***had missed*** *the bus, he* ***could have taken****/ he* ***might have taken*** *a taxi.*

→ *Unit 2: p. 52, exercises 1–3*

◄ **Typ 3 („Was wäre gewesen, wenn ...“-Sätze)**

Diese Bedingungssätze beziehen sich auf die **Vergangenheit**. Sie drücken aus, was unter bestimmten Bedingungen **geschehen oder nicht geschehen wäre**.
Der *if*-Satz nennt eine Bedingung, die **nicht** eingetreten ist *(Ich habe nicht den Bus verpasst)*. Der Sprecher stellt sich nur vor, was geschehen wäre, aber in Wirklichkeit nicht geschehen ist *(Ich hätte ein Taxi genommen)*.

Statt ***would have*** können im Hauptsatz auch ***could have*** oder ***might have*** + *past participle* stehen.

*If I **knew** her better, I **would have asked** her.*
Wenn ich sie besser kennen würde, hätte ich sie gefragt.

*If you**'ve been** here before, you**'ll know** the rules.*
Wenn du schon mal hier warst, dann kennst du (ja) die Regeln.

*If they **left** at seven, they **won't be** here until twelve.*
Wenn sie um sieben losgefahren sind, werden sie nicht vor zwölf hier sein.

◄ Ähnlich wie im Deutschen werden in englischen Bedingungssätzen – je nach Situation – auch andere Kombinationen von Zeitformen verwendet als die auf S. 182 beschriebenen.

Sieh dir die Beispiele und ihre Übersetzungen an.

Wenn wir mit dem Auto gefahren wären, wären wir schon da.

In English

Conditional sentences

- **Type 1** (about the present or the future):
  simple present — ***will*-future or *can/must/should/...* + infinitive**
  *If they **score** another goal, they **will win**.*
  The speaker thinks there is a good chance that they will score another goal. (The match has just begun.)
- **Type 2** (about the present or the future):
  simple past — ***would/could/might* + infinitive**
  *If they **scored** another goal, they **would win**.*
  The speaker thinks it is less probable that they will score another goal. (The match is nearly over.)
- **Type 3** (about the past):
  past perfect — ***would/could/might* + *have* + past participle**
  *If they **had scored** another goal, they **would have won**.*
  The match is over. They didn't score another goal, so they didn't win.
- As in German, there are **mixed types** of conditional sentences in English, depending on the context, e.g.
  *If they **had scored** another goal, they **would be** in the final round now.*
  *If they **have scored** six goals, they surely **must have won** the match.*

GF 9 Relative clauses Relativsätze

9.1 Defining relative clauses — Bestimmende Relativsätze

1 *Do you know the girl **who/that works at the Oxfam shop**?*
... das Mädchen, das im Oxfam-Shop arbeitet?

2 *That's the shop **which/that sells second-hand clothes and books and stuff**.*
... der Laden, der gebrauchte Kleidung und Bücher und so etwas verkauft.

➔ *Unit 1: p. 16, exercise 5*

Bestimmende Relativsätze werden mit den Relativpronomen ***who*** oder ***that*** für **Personen (1)** und ***which*** oder ***that*** für **Dinge (2)** eingeleitet.

Ein bestimmender Relativsatz gibt Informationen, die **zum Verständnis des Satzes notwendig** sind:

Ohne die Relativsätze ... *who/that works at the Oxfam shop* bzw. ... *which/that sells second-hand clothes ...* wüsste man gar nicht, von welchem Mädchen bzw. von welchem Geschäft die Rede ist.

Anders als im Deutschen werden solche Relativsätze nicht durch Kommas abgetrennt.

9.2 Contact clauses

Relativsätze ohne Relativpronomen

1 *Mr Jones is the teacher* ***who I like the most.***
or *Mr Jones is the teacher* ***I like the most.***

2 *These are the photos* ***that Dad took in Wales.***
or *These are the photos* ***Dad took in Wales.***

3 *Who was the man* ***who was talking*** *to Jeremy at the bus stop?*

Wenn das Relativpronomen **Objekt des Relativsatzes** ist, wird es oft weggelassen **(1, 2)**.
Relativsätze ohne Relativpronomen werden ***contact clauses*** genannt.

! Wenn das **Relativpronomen direkt vor dem Verb** steht, ist es **Subjekt** und darf **nicht** weggelassen werden **(3)**.

Vergleiche:
- *… the man* ***who was talking to*** *Jeremy*
  („… der Mann, **der** mit Jeremy gesprochen hat")
- *… the man* ***who Jeremy was talking to*** oder
  … the man ***Jeremy was talking to***
  („… der Mann, mit dem **Jeremy** gesprochen hat")

9.3 Non-defining relative clauses

Nicht bestimmende Relativsätze

Agatha Christie, ***who died in 1976,*** *wrote about 70 detective novels and 17 plays.*

John Lennon, ***whose mother taught him to play the banjo in the 1950s,*** *later became world-famous as a member of the Beatles.*

At 11.35 we landed at Atlanta International, ***which is one of the world's busiest airports.***

Nicht bestimmende Relativsätze kommen hauptsächlich in geschriebenem Englisch vor. Sie geben **Zusatzinformationen**, die man nicht unbedingt braucht, um zu verstehen, von wem oder was die Rede ist: Man versteht den Satz *Agatha Christie wrote about 70 detective novels* auch ohne den Relativsatz *who died in 1976*.

!
- In nicht bestimmenden Relativsätzen darf man das **Relativpronomen nie weglassen**.
- Es können nur die Relativpronomen *who, which* und *whose* verwendet werden – nicht aber *that*.
- Nicht bestimmende Relativsätze werden durch **Kommas** abgetrennt.

9.4 Relative clauses with *which* to refer to a whole clause

Satzbezogene Relativsätze mit *which*

In December 1980, John Lennon was murdered, ***which shocked people all over the world.***
…, was Menschen auf der ganzen Welt schockierte.

Our neighbours helped us to tidy up after the party, ***which I think was very good of them.***
…, was ich sehr nett von ihnen fand.

We're moving to Leeds in the summer, ***which means I'll have to change school.***
…, was bedeutet, dass ich die Schule wechseln muss.

Little Stevie has made dinner for his dad, which is very nice of him.

Relativsätze mit ***which*** können sich auch auf einen ganzen Satz beziehen. Sie kommentieren die Aussage im vorausgehenden Hauptsatz.

Im Deutschen werden solche Relativsätze mit „was" eingeleitet.

Satzbezogene Relativsätze werden durch **Kommas** abgetrennt.

In English

Relative clauses

- A **defining relative clause** gives **necessary** information about the noun that it refers to. You don't use commas with defining relative clauses.	*The man **who answered the phone** was very friendly.*
- You can **only leave out the relative pronoun** when it is the **object** of the relative clause. Relative clauses without a relative pronoun are called ***contact clauses***.	*Don't forget the book **that you borrowed last week**.* → *Don't forget the book **you borrowed last week**.*
- A **non-defining relative clause** gives **extra** information about the noun that it refers to (you can understand the main clause without the information given in the relative clause). You use commas with non-defining relative clauses.	*My friend Jane**, whose dad is English,** is bilingual.*
- Relative clauses with ***which*** can ***refer to the whole main clause***; you use them to make a comment on the main clause.	*Stevie has made dinner for his dad**, which is very nice of him**.*

GF 10 Participles Partizipien

10.1 Participle forms — Formen des Partizips

Present participle: *-ing*

*work → **working***　　*try → **trying***
*dance → **dancing***　　*plan → **planning***

◄ Das **Partizip Präsens** *(present participle)* wird bei allen Verben durch Anhängen von ***-ing*** an den Infinitiv gebildet. Beachte die Besonderheiten bei der Schreibung.

Past participle, regular verbs: *-ed*

*work → **worked***　　*try → **tried***
*dance → **danced***　　*plan → **planned***

◄ Das **Partizip Perfekt** *(past participle)* von **regelmäßigen Verben** bildet man durch Anhängen von ***-ed*** an den Infinitiv.

Past participle, irregular verbs:

*build → **built***　　*grow → **grown***
*make → **made***　　*see → **seen***
*teach → **taught***　　*write → **written***

◄ **Unregelmäßige Verben** haben eigene *past participle*-Formen, die man einzeln lernen muss.

➜ *Unregelmäßige Verben: S. 264–265*

10.2 Participle clauses instead of relative clauses — Partizipialsätze anstelle von Relativsätzen

Relativsätze werden oft zu einem sogenannten **Partizipialsatz** verkürzt.

*The city is always full of people **who are looking for a parking space**.*
→ *… full of people **looking for a parking space**.*
… voller Menschen, die nach einem Parkplatz suchen.

*The man **who was driving the red car** waved at us.*
→ *The man **driving the red car** waved at us.*

◄ Das ***present participle*** entspricht dabei einem Relativpronomen + Verb im **Aktiv**. Vergleiche:
*… people **looking** for a parking space*
*… people **who are looking** for a parking space*

*The Eurovision Song Contest is an international competition **which is watched by millions of people**.*
→ *… competition **watched by millions of people**.*
… Wettbewerb, der … angeschaut wird.

◄ Das ***past participle*** entspricht einem Relativpronomen + Verb im **Passiv**. Vergleiche:
*… competition **watched** by millions of people*
*… competition **which is watched** by millions of people*

➜ *Unit 1: p. 16, exercise 6 • p. 28, exercise 2*

10.3 Verb of perception + object + present participle

Verb der Wahrnehmung + Objekt + Partizip Präsens

	Verb of perception	Object	Present participle	
1 *We*	***heard***	***a baby***	***crying***	.
2 *She*	***saw***	***someone***	***climbing***	*on the roof.*
3 *He*	***watched***	***the band***	***getting***	*ready for the show.*
4 *I*	***noticed***	***two women***	***arguing***	*outside the hotel.*

◄ Auf Verben der Wahrnehmung wie ***feel, hear, listen to, notice, see, smell, spot, watch*** kann ein **Objekt** + **Partizip Präsens** folgen.

Mit solchen Sätzen sagt man, dass man etwas wahrnimmt, das gerade im Gang ist (bzw. war).

1 Wir hörten ein Baby weinen.
2 Sie sah jemanden auf das Dach klettern. / …, wie/dass jemand auf das Dach kletterte.
3 Er beobachtete, wie sich die Band für die Show bereitmachte.
4 Ich bemerkte zwei Frauen, die sich vorm Hotel stritten. / …, dass sich zwei Frauen … stritten.

◄ Im Deutschen steht in diesen Fällen meist ein Infinitiv oder ein Nebensatz mit „wie" oder „dass", manchmal auch ein Relativsatz.

(Wenn man betonen will, dass man ein Geschehen **vollständig – von Anfang bis Ende** – wahrgenommen hat, verwendet man statt des *present participle* einen **Infinitiv**:
*We **saw him grab** the money and **run** away.*
Wir sahen, wie er sich das Geld schnappte und davonlief.)

➔ *Unit 1: p. 16, exercise 7*

NEW

10.4 Participle clauses giving additional information

➔ *CHECK 7: p. 191*

Partizipialsätze zur Angabe von Zusatzinformationen

*It rains a lot here, **sometimes flooding the roads**.*
Hier regnet es viel, und manchmal überschwemmt es (dabei) die Straßen.

*Last Sunday morning, we stayed in bed, **reading and listening to the radio**.*
Letzten Sonntagmorgen sind wir im Bett geblieben und haben gelesen und Radio gehört.

*Charlotte ran down the stairs, **losing a shoe**.*
…, wobei sie einen Schuh verlor.

***Using a knife**, she was able to open the door.*
Indem sie ein Messer benutzte, …

Partizipialsätze mit *present participle* werden oft verwendet, um **Zusatzinformationen** zu geben oder **Begleitumstände** einer Handlung zu beschreiben. (Meist handelt es sich um zeitgleich oder fast zeitgleich stattfindende Handlungen oder Vorgänge.)

Im Deutschen steht meist ein Hauptsatz mit „und", machmal auch ein Nebensatz mit „wobei" oder „indem".

➔ *Unit 1: p. 20, exercises 1–2 · p. 21, exercise 4*

He stood in front of the audience, wishing he was somewhere else.
Er stand vor dem Publikum und wünschte sich, woanders zu sein.

NEW

10.5 Participle clauses instead of adverbial clauses of time

CHECK 8: p. 191

Partizipialsätze anstelle von adverbialen Nebensätzen der Zeit

***When planning** a trip to a foreign country*, start early and ask people who have been there.
Wenn du eine Reise in ein fremdes Land planst, …

***While walking** down the street*, I saw a huge black dog.
Als/Während ich die Straße hinunterging, …

***When asked** why he left school so early*, he answered that he wanted to earn his own money.
Als er gefragt wurde, …

*Always be polite **when asking for information**.*
…, wenn du um Informationen bittest.

Partizipialsätze, die mit *when* oder *while* eingeleitet sind, entsprechen **Nebensätzen der Zeit**.

Das ***present participle*** entspricht dabei wieder einem Verb im **Aktiv** *(while walking = while I was walking)*. Das ***past participle*** entspricht einem Verb im **Passiv** *(when asked = when he was asked)*.

Oft gehen solche Partizipialsätze dem Hauptsatz voran. Sie sind typisch für das geschriebene Englisch.

***Walking** down the street*, I saw a huge black dog.
Als/Während ich die Straße hinunterging, …

***Asked** why he left school so early*, he answered that he wanted to earn his own money.
Als er gefragt wurde, …

◄ Manchmal wird bei Partizipialsätzen anstelle von Nebensätzen der Zeit die Konjunktion weggelassen.

1a *Joe met <u>an old friend</u> **while looking for a job**.*
(= Joe met an old friend while he – Joe – was looking for a job)
…, während er auf der Suche nach einer Stelle war.

1b *Joe met <u>an old friend</u> **looking for a job**.*
(= Joe met an old friend who was looking for a job)
…, der auf der Suche nach einer Stelle war.

➜ *Unit 1: p. 21, exercises 3–4 · p. 28, exercise 2*

! Vorsicht! Wenn der Partizipialsatz auf den Hauptsatz folgt, musst du aufpassen.
Vergleiche die Sätze **1a** und **1b**:

- In **1a** ist es Joe, der eine Stelle suchte.
- In **1b** ist es der Freund, der eine Stelle suchte.

*We saw three seals **while walking** along the beach.*

*We saw three seals **walking** along the beach.*

NEW

10.6 Participle clauses instead of adverbial clauses of reason

CHECK 9: p. 191

Partizipialsätze anstelle von adverbialen Nebensätzen des Grundes

***Feeling** very tired*, I decided to go to bed early.
Weil/Da ich sehr müde war, …

***Being** a doctor*, she knew exactly what to do.
Weil/Da sie Ärztin ist, …

***Warned** by his wife*, the man was able to escape.
Weil er von seiner Frau gewarnt wurde, … /
Von seiner Frau gewarnt, …

➜ *Unit 1: p. 21, exercise 5*

Partizipialsätze können auch **Nebensätzen des Grundes** entsprechen.

! Beachte, dass die Konjunktion *because* nicht in Partizipialsätzen verwendet werden kann. Also nicht:

~~*Because feeling very tired*~~, …
~~*Because being a doctor*~~, …

10.7 Other participle clauses

Andere Partizipialsätze

Although asked ***to stop by the police****, he drove on.*
Obwohl er von der Polizei aufgefordert wurde …

You will have to wait outside ***until asked to enter****.*
…, bis Sie gebeten werden einzutreten.

If posted before 12 o'clock*, the letter should arrive tomorrow.*
Wenn der Brief vor 12 Uhr eingeworfen wird, …

After winning gold*, she decided to resign.*
Nachdem sie die Goldmedaille gewonnen hatte, …

Partizipialsätze können auch durch andere Konjunktionen eingeleitet werden, z.B. durch ***although, until, if, after, before***.

In English

Participles

• You form the **present participle** by adding ***-ing*** to the infinitive. You form the **past participle** by adding ***-ed*** to the infinitive. Irregular verbs have special **past participle** forms.	*(to)* ***dance*** → ***dancing*** *(to)* ***dance*** → ***danced*** *(to)* ***see*** → ***seen*** / *(to)* ***write*** → ***written***
• **Relative clauses** can be **shortened to participle clauses**.	*The man* ***who was driving*** *the red car …* → *The man* ***driving*** *the red car …* *A song* ***which was written*** *by …* → *A song* ***written*** *by …*
• **Verbs of perception** can be followed by an **object + present participle**.	*I* ***felt my heart beating*** *faster.* *Can you* ***hear someone crying****?*
• You can use **present participle clauses** to give **additional information**. In German, we usually use "und" or "wobei" or "indem".	*We stayed in bed,* ***listening to music****.* *He ran out of the house,* ***forgetting his keys****.*
• **Participle clauses** with *when* or *while* can be used instead of **adverbial clauses of time**.	*Try to be friendly* ***when asking for help****.* ***(While) walking down the street****, I met Sue.*
• **Participle clauses** (without a conjunction!) can be used instead of **adverbial clauses of reason**.	***Feeling very tired****, I went to bed early.* ***Being new at his school****, he felt very lonely.*
• **Participle clauses** can also be used instead of other **adverbial clauses**, e.g. conditional clauses or clauses of contrast. Conjunctions often used to introduce these participle clauses are *although, until, if, after, before.*	***Although badly hurt****, he tried to help us.* ***If asked for money****, do not send it!* *Please wait* ***until asked to enter****.*

Check (Aufgaben zur Selbstüberprüfung)

CHECK 1
The past perfect (simple), the past perfect progressive ➜ *Lösungen S. 194*

a) Bilde Sätze im *past perfect progressive* wie in Satz 1.

1 *Mrs Jones was really tired. She (work) in the garden all afternoon.*
She had been working in the garden all afternoon.

2 *Jonathan felt disappointed. He (wait) for Emily for over an hour, but she still hadn't come.*
3 *We (watch) the show for only 20 minutes when it started to rain.*
4 *I didn't know what to say when our teacher asked me because I (not – listen). I (think) of my girlfriend the whole lesson.*

b) *Past perfect (simple)* oder *past perfect progressive*? Vervollständige die Sätze.

*Last night on the way to the cinema, I realized that I (**1** leave)* had left *my money at home. I (**2** look forward) to the film for weeks and I didn't want to miss it, so I got off the bus and ran home. When I arrived, I realized that I (**3** forget) my keys too, so I couldn't get in. I rang the doorbell, but everybody (**4** go) out. So I ran as fast as I could to my friend Jeremy's place. His mother opened the door, but Jeremy wasn't in. He (**5** not – come) home yet. His mother saw that I (**6** run), so she asked me to sit down and gave me a drink. I started playing a game on my phone. I (**7** play) for twenty minutes when Jeremy finally arrived. He lent me some money, and I ran back to the bus stop. When I finally got to the cinema, the film (**8** already – start).*

CHECK 2
The *will*-future, the *going to*-future ➜ *Lösungen S. 194*

a) Was sagt Person B? Vervollständige die Kurzdialoge.

1 **A** *There's somebody at the door.* – **B** *(see)* I'll see who it is.
2 **A** *I can't do this exercise.* – **B** *(help)*
3 **A** *This glass was very expensive.* – **B** *(not drop)*
4 **A** *Olivia mustn't find out.* – **B** *(not tell)*

b) Spontan gefasster Entschluss oder im Voraus geplant?
Vervollständige die Sätze mit der richtigen Verbform – *will-future* oder *going to-future*.

1 *Tea or coffee? – I think I (have) coffee.*
2 *Michael says he (study) art in Berlin.*
3 *Oh no, it's starting to rain. – Don't worry. I (drive) you home.*
4 *There are no buses into town on Sundays, but my father (drive) us.*
5 *The phone is ringing! – OK, I (answer) it.*
6 *Do you have plans for the summer holidays? – Yes, we do. We (spend) two weeks in France.*
7 *Would you like to join us? – Uh … I (think) about it. I (let) you know later, OK?*

CHECK 3
Simple form and progressive form ➜ *Lösungen S. 194*

Simple form oder *progressive form*? Vervollständige die Sätze mit den richtigen Verbformen.
Denk dran: Zustandsverben werden in der Regel nur in der *simple form* verwendet.

1 *(**A** Do you like / **B** Are you liking) my new aftershave? I think it (**C** smells / **D** is smelling) great.*
2 *Caroline (**A** seems / **B** is seeming) to enjoy her training course in London.*
*She told me she (**C** had / **D** was having) a lot of fun.*
3 *It was a great preformance, but not many people (**A** watched / **B** were watching).*
4 *Does anyone know who this watch (**A** belongs to / **B** is belonging to)?*
5 *It says here that the price (**A** includes / **B** is including) a day trip to Brighton.*
6 *Nobody (**A** noticed / **B** was noticing) that he left early.*
*Everybody (**C** looked / **D** was looking) at the people on the stage.*

CHECK 4

German „sollen" ➜ *Lösungen S. 194*

Welche der beiden angegebenen Entsprechungen für das deutsche „sollen" ist korrekt?

1 *Dinner is at six today, so we (**A** had better not / **B** are not supposed to) eat too much now or we won't be hungry.*
2 *Let's go to that new Spanish restaurant. It (**A** should / **B** is supposed to) be very good.*
3 *Some of the guests might not eat meat. We (**A** are supposed to / **B** had better) cook a vegetarian dish.*
4 *You (**A** should / **B** are said to) try gator on a stick when you're in New Orleans.*
*It (**C** is said to / **D** should) be delicious.*
5 *I wouldn't go swimming here. It (**A** is supposed to / **B** should) be very dangerous.*
6 *It's going to rain this afternoon, so you (**A** are said to / **B** had better) take the bus.*
7 *I wonder where Susan is. She (**A** ought to / **B** was supposed to) be here at four. Now it's almost five.*
8 *You (**A** are not supposed to / **B** are not said to) light fires on this campsite.*
*We (**C** are supposed to / **D** had better) use the electric barbecue.*

CHECK 5

The *to*-infinitive instead of a relative clause ➜ *Lösungen S. 194*

a) Sieh dir die Kästen und den Beispielsatz an. Wie ist es in deiner Familie – wer tut die Dinge als Erste(r)/als Letzte(r)/als Einzige(r)? (Du kannst *always, usually, often* usw. ergänzen.)

I		*get up*
My parents	*the first*	*have a shower*
My mother	*the last*	*have breakfast*
My father	*the only one(s)*	*leave home*
My sister		*come home*
My brother		*go to bed*

1 My ... is (usually) the first to get up.
2 I'm (always) ...
3 ...
4 ...
5 ...
6 ...

b) Melinda ist unzufrieden. Aber warum?
Wähle passende Verben aus dem Kasten und vervollständige ihre Sätze wie in Satz 1.

ask · do · give · go · go with · listen to

1 *I'd like to go dancing tonight. The* Funk House *would be the perfect place* to go*, but it's a long way from where I live.*
2 *And there are no buses after 11, so I'd need someone … me a lift back home.*
3 *Jacob would be the person …, but he's away on holiday.*
4 *And I've got nobody … anyway.*
5 *I wish I had some new music …*
6 *I guess it'll be another evening at home with nothing … but watch a film.*

CHECK 6

Conditional sentences, type III ➜ *Lösungen S. 194*

a) Lies die Bedingungssätze 1 – 3 und die Aussagen A – C. Was ist jeweils korrekt – **A**, **B** oder **C**?

1 *If I'd known that the blue shirts were cheaper, I wouldn't have bought a black one.*
A *I bought a blue shirt, and I'm happy with it.*
B *I bought a black shirt, and I'm happy with it.*
C *I bought a black shirt, but I wish I'd bought a blue one.*

2 *If she'd told me about the concert, I would have tried to get a ticket.*
A *She told me about the concert, and I tried to get a ticket.*
B *She told me about the concert, but I didn't try to get a ticket.*
C *She didn't tell me about the concert, so I couldn't try to get a ticket.*

▸▸▸ *continued on p. 191*

3 *Dad wouldn't have allowed me to go camping if he'd known that no adults were going.*
A *Dad allowed me to go camping because he didn't know that no adults were going.*
B *Dad allowed me to go camping although he knew that no adults were going.*
C *Dad didn't allow me to go camping because he knew that no adults were going.*

b) Bilde Bedingungssätze vom Typ 3.

1 *Jason didn't tell her the truth, so Alice broke up with him.*
If Jason had ..., Alice wouldn't ...

2 *"Your handwriting isn't very clear. I can hardly read it." – "Sorry, I did my homework on the bus."*
If I ... on the bus, Mr Jones would/might ... to read it.

CHECK 7

Participle clauses giving additional information

➜ *Lösungen S. 194*

Verwende Partizipialsätze und schreibe die Sätze um wie im Beispiel.

1 *George was walking down King Street. He was talking on his mobile.*
George was walking down King Street, talking on his mobile.

2 *We were standing at the bus stop. We were waiting for the Number 10 bus.*
3 *Amelia was on her way to the station. She was carrying a rucksack and two heavy bags.*
4 *We stood in the queue and waited to buy tickets.*
5 *He used a stone to break the window and climbed into the flat.*

CHECK 8

Participle clauses instead of adverbial clauses of time

➜ *Lösungen S. 194*

Verwende Partizipialsätze mit *while* und schreibe die Sätze um wie im Beispiel.

1 *Jessica walked home from school on Friday afternoon and found a set of keys.*
While walking home from school on Friday afternoon, Jessica found a set of keys.

2 *Ava played tennis and hurt her shoulder.* Ava hurt ...
3 *We sat on the beach and watched the seals on the rocks.* While ..., we watched ...
4 *Noah rode the roller coaster and lost his glasses.* Noah lost ...
5 *Emily was washing the dishes when she cut her finger.* Emily cut ...
6 *He walked through the jungle and was bitten by a snake.* While ..., he ...

CHECK 9

Participle clauses instead of adverbial clauses of reason

➜ *Lösungen S. 194*

Verwende Partizipialsätze und schreibe die Sätze um wie im Beispiel.

1 *Oliver was new in London. That's why he found it very difficult to find his way around.*
Being new in London, Oliver found it very difficult to find his way around.

2 *He didn't know the way to the job centre and got lost.* Not ...
3 *I felt very nervous, so I drove much too slowly in my first driving lesson.*
4 *We didn't have much money, so we went to a cheap restaurant.*
5 *He saw that he had made a mistake, so he said he was sorry.*

Grammatical terms (Grammatische Fachbegriffe)

active ['æktɪv]	Aktiv	*A heavy storm* ***destroyed*** *twelve houses.*
activity verb [æk'tɪvəti vɜːb]	Tätigkeitsverb	*do, go, make, read, repair, ...*
adjective ['ædʒɪktɪv]	Adjektiv (Eigenschaftswort)	*good, new, green, interesting, ...*
adverb ['ædvɜːb]	Adverb	*today, there, outside, very, ...*
adverb of degree [dɪ'griː]	Gradadverb	*very, really, so, quite, almost, a bit, ...*
adverb of frequency ['friːkwənsi]	Häufigkeitsadverb	*always, usually, often, sometimes, never*
adverb of indefinite time [ɪn'defɪnət]	Adverb der unbestimmten Zeit	*already, ever, just, never, before, yet, ...*
adverb of manner ['mænə]	Adverb der Art und Weise	*nicely, happily, quietly, slowly, well, fast, ...*
adverbial clause [æd,vɜːbiəl 'klɔːz]	adverbialer Nebensatz	*I went to bed* ***because I was tired****.*
article ['ɑːtɪkl]	Artikel	*the, a, an*
aspect ['æspekt]	Aspekt	
auxiliary [ɔːg'zɪliəri]	Hilfsverb	*be, have, do; will, can, must, ...*
backshift of tenses ['bækʃɪft]	Rückverschiebung der Zeitformen	*"I'****m*** *tired."* → *She said (that) she* ***was*** *tired.*
command [kə'mɑːnd]	Befehl, Aufforderungssatz	*Open your books. Don't talk.*
comparative [kəm'pærətɪv]	Komparativ (1. Steigerungsform)	*older; more expensive*
comparison [kəm'pærɪsn]	Steigerung	*old – older – oldest;* *expensive – more expensive – most expensive*
compound ['kɒmpaʊnd]	Zusammensetzung	*somebody, anyone, something, ...*
conditional sentence [kən'dɪʃənl]	Bedingungssatz	*If I see Sam, I'll tell him.*
conjunction [kən'dʒʌŋkʃn]	Konjunktion	*and, but, ...; because, when, ...*
contact clause ['kɒntækt klɔːz]	Relativsatz ohne Relativpronomen	*Here's the report* ***I've written****.*
countable noun ['kaʊntəbl]	zählbares Nomen	*girl – girls, car – cars, idea – ideas, ...*
defining relative clause [dɪ'faɪnɪŋ]	bestimmender Relativsatz	*I like teachers* ***who laugh a lot****.*
definite article [,defɪnət‿'ɑːtɪkl]	bestimmter Artikel	*the*
direct speech [,daɪrekt 'spiːtʃ]	direkte Rede	***"I'm tired."***
future perfect [,fjuːtʃə 'pɜːfɪkt]	vollendete Zukunft, Futur II	*On Friday I* ***will have finished*** *my exams.*
future progressive [,fjuːtʃə prə'gresɪv]	Verlaufsform des *will-future*	*How long* ***will*** *you* ***be staying****?*
gerund ['dʒerənd]	Gerundium	*I like* ***dancing****.* ***Dancing*** *is fun.*
***going to*-future** ['fjuːtʃə]	Futur mit *going to*	***I'm going to watch*** *TV tonight.*
***if*-clause** ['ɪf klɔːz]	*if*-Satz, Nebensatz mit *if*	***If I see Jack****, I'll tell him.*
imperative [ɪm'perətɪv]	Imperativ (Befehlsform)	*Open your books. Don't talk.*
indirect speech [,ɪndərekt 'spiːtʃ]	indirekte Rede	*She said (that)* ***she was tired****.*
infinitive [ɪn'fɪnətɪv]	Infinitiv (Grundform des Verbs)	*(to) open, (to) go, ...*
irregular verb [ɪ'regjələ]	unregelmäßiges Verb	*(to) go – went – gone,* *(to) see – saw – seen, ...*
main clause ['meɪn klɔːz]	Hauptsatz	*If I see Jack,* ***I'll tell him****.*
modal auxiliary [,məʊdl‿ɔːg'zɪliəri]	modales Hilfsverb, Modalverb	*can, may, might, needn't, should, must, ...*
negative statement ['negətɪv]	verneinter Aussagesatz	*I don't like oranges.*
non-defining relative clause [dɪ'faɪnɪŋ]	nicht bestimmender Relativsatz	*Drew,* ***who goes to Mobridge-Pollock High School,*** *wants to qualify for the rodeo finals.*
noun [naʊn]	Nomen, Substantiv	*Justin, girl, man, time, name, ...*
object ['ɒbdʒɪkt]	Objekt	*Justin has* ***a new camera****.*
object question	Objektfrage, Frage nach dem Objekt	***Who did*** *Mrs Pascoe* ***invite*** *to tea?*
participle ['pɑːtɪsɪpl]	Partizip	*planning, taking; planned, taken*
participle clause [,pɑːtɪsɪpl 'klɔːz]	Partizipialsatz	*The man* ***waiting at the bus stop*** *is my uncle.*
passive ['pæsɪv]	Passiv	*Twelve houses* ***were destroyed*** *by a storm.*
past participle [,pɑːst 'pɑːtɪsɪpl]	Partizip Perfekt	*checked, phoned, tried, gone, eaten, ...*
past perfect [,pɑːst 'pɜːfɪkt]	*past perfect* (Vorvergangenheit, Plusquamperfekt)	*I* ***had*** *already* ***gone*** *to bed when they arrived.*

past perfect progressive [ˌpɑːstˌpɜːfɪkt prəˈgresɪv]	Verlaufsform des *past perfect*	*He was tired. He **had been working** in the garden for 3 hours.*
past progressive [ˌpɑːst prəˈgresɪv]	Verlaufsform der Vergangenheit	*Olivia **was playing** cards.*
personal passive [ˌpɜːsənl ˈpæsɪv]	persönliches Passiv	*I was offered a job.*
personal pronoun [ˌpɜːsənl ˈprəʊnaʊn]	Personalpronomen (persönliches Fürwort)	*I, you, he, she, it, we, they;* *me, you, him, her, it, us, them*
plural [ˈplʊərəl]	Plural, Mehrzahl	
positive statement [ˈpɒzətɪv]	bejahter Aussagesatz	*I like oranges.*
possessive determiner [pəˌzesɪv dɪˈtɜːmɪnə]	Possessivbegleiter (besitzanzeigender Begleiter)	*my, your, his, her, its, our, their*
possessive form [pəˌzesɪv ˈfɔːm]	s-Genitiv	*Sam's sister, the Blackwells' house, …*
possessive pronoun [pəˌzesɪv ˈprəʊnaʊn]	Possessivpronomen	*mine, yours, his, hers, ours, theirs*
preposition [ˌprepəˈzɪʃn]	Präposition	*after, at, in, into, near, next to, …*
present participle [ˌpreznt ˈpɑːtɪsɪpl]	Partizip Präsens	*checking, phoning, trying, planning, going, …*
present perfect [ˌpreznt ˈpɜːfɪkt]	*present perfect*	*We**'ve made** some scones for you.*
present perfect progressive [ˌpreznt ˌpɜːfɪkt prəˈgresɪv]	Verlaufsform des *present perfect*	*He**'s been watching** TV for hours.*
present progressive [ˌpreznt prəˈgresɪv]	Verlaufsform der Gegenwart	*Olivia **is playing** cards.*
pronoun [ˈprəʊnaʊn]	Pronomen (Fürwort)	
quantifier [ˈkwɒntɪfaɪə]	Mengenangabe	*some, a lot of, many, much, a few, …*
question tag [ˈkwestʃn tæg]	Frageanhängsel	*isn't he?, are you?, can't we?, …*
question word [ˈkwestʃn wɜːd]	Fragewort	*who?, what?, when?, where?, how?, …*
reflexive pronoun [rɪˌfleksɪv ˈprəʊnaʊn]	Reflexivpronomen	*myself, yourself, themselves, …*
regular verb [ˈregjələ]	regelmäßiges Verb	*(to) help – helped, (to) look – looked, …*
relative clause [ˌrelətɪv ˈklɔːz]	Relativsatz	*I like teachers **who laugh a lot**.*
relative pronoun [ˌrelətɪv ˈprəʊnaʊn]	Relativpronomen	*who – which – that*
reported speech [rɪˌpɔːtɪd ˈspiːtʃ]	indirekte Rede	*She said (that) **she was tired**.*
request [rɪˈkwest]	Bitte; Aufforderung	*Can you help me with this?*
short answer [ˌʃɔːt‿ˈɑːnsə]	Kurzantwort	*Yes, I am. / No, we don't. / …*
simple past [ˌsɪmpl ˈpɑːst]	einfache Form der Vergangenheit	*Olivia **played** cards last Friday.*
simple present [ˌsɪmpl ˈpreznt]	einfache Form der Gegenwart	*Olivia **plays** cards every Friday evening.*
singular [ˈsɪŋgjələ]	Singular, Einzahl	
state verb [ˈsteɪt vɜːb]	Zustandsverb	*be, know, like, own, sound, want*
statement [ˈsteɪtmənt]	Aussage(satz)	
subject [ˈsʌbdʒɪkt]	Subjekt	***Justin/He** has a new camera.*
subject question	Subjektfrage, Frage nach dem Subjekt	***Who invited** the Coopers to tea?*
subordinate clause [səˌbɔːdɪnət ˈklɔːz]	Nebensatz	*I like Plymouth **because I like the sea**.*
substitute [ˈsʌbstɪtjuːt]	Ersatzverb (eines Modalverbs)	*be able to, be allowed to, have to*
superlative [suˈpɜːlətɪv]	Superlativ (2. Steigerungsform)	*(the) oldest; (the) most expensive*
tense [tens]	Zeitform	
uncountable noun [ʌnˈkaʊntəbl]	nicht zählbares Nomen	*bread, milk, money, news, work, …*
verb [vɜːb]	**1.** Verb; **2.** Prädikat	*go, help, look, see, …* *Reading **can be** fun.*
verb of perception [pəˈsepʃn]	Verb der Wahrnehmung	*(to) hear, (to) see, (to) notice, (to) smell, …*
***will*-future** [ˈfjuːtʃə]	Futur mit *will*	*I'm sure you**'ll like** the new maths teacher.*
word order [ˈwɜːd‿ˌɔːdə]	Wortstellung	
yes/no question	Entscheidungsfrage	*Are you 14? Do you like oranges?*

Check – Lösungen der Aufgaben zur Selbstüberprüfung

Check 1a) (p. 189)
1 *had been working*
2 *had been waiting*
3 *had been watching*
4 *hadn't been listening … had been thinking*

Check 1b) (p. 189)
1 *had left* – 2 *had been looking forward* – 3 *had forgotten* – 4 *had gone* – 5 *hadn't come* – 6 *had been running* – 7 *had been playing* – 8 *had already started*

Check 2a) (p. 189)
1 *I'll see who it is.*
2 *I'll help you.*
3 *I won't drop it.*
4 *I won't tell her.*

Check 2b) (p. 189)
1 *… – I think* ***I'll*** *have coffee.*
2 *Michael says he****'s going to*** *study art in Berlin.*
3 *… – Don't worry.* ***I'll*** *drive you home.*
4 *…, but my father* ***is going to*** *drive us.*
5 *… – OK,* ***I'll*** *answer it.*
6 *… – Yes, we do. We****'re going to*** *spend two weeks in France.*
7 *… – Uh …* ***I'll*** *think about it.* ***I'll*** *let you know later, OK?*

Check 3 (p. 189)
1 A/C – 2 A/D – 3 B – 4 A – 5 A – 6 A/D

Check 4 (p. 190)
1 A – 2 B – 3 B – 4 A/C – 5 A – 6 B – 7 B – 8 A/D

Check 5a) (p. 190)
… ***is/are the first to*** *get/have/leave/come/go …*
… ***is/are the last to*** *get/have/leave/come/go …*
… ***is/are the only one/ones to*** *get/have/leave/come/go …*

Check 5b) (p. 190)
1 *…* ***the perfect place to go*** *…*
2 *…* ***someone to give me a lift*** *…*
3 *…* ***the person to ask*** *…*
4 *…* ***nobody to go with*** *…*
5 *…* ***some new music to listen to*** *…*
6 *…* ***nothing to do*** *…*

Check 6a) (p. 190)
1 C – 2 C – 3 A

Check 6b) (p. 191)
1 *If Jason* ***had told*** *her the truth, Alice* ***wouldn't have broken up*** *with him.*
2 *If I* ***hadn't done*** *my homework on the bus, Mr Jones* ***would/might have been able*** *to read it.*
3 *If Aidan* ***hadn't been busy****, he* ***would have visited*** *his grandparents.*

Check 7 (p. 191)
1 *George was walking down King Street,* ***talking*** *on his mobile.*
2 *We were standing at the bus stop,* ***waiting*** *for the Number 10 bus.*
3 *Amelia was on her way to the station,* ***carrying*** *a rucksack and two heavy bags.*
4 *We stood in the queue,* ***waiting*** *to buy tickets.*
5 ***Using*** *a stone, he broke the window and climbed into the flat.*

Check 8 (p. 191)
1 ***While walking*** *home from school on Friday afternoon, Jessica found a set of keys.*
2 *Ava hurt her shoulder* ***while playing*** *tennis.*
3 ***While sitting*** *on the beach, we watched the seals on the rocks.*
4 *Noah lost his glasses* ***while riding*** *the roller coaster.*
5 *Emily cut her finger* ***while washing*** *the dishes.*
6 ***While walking*** *through the jungle, he was bitten by a snake.*

Check 9 (p. 191)
1 ***Being new in London,*** *Oliver found it very difficult to find his way around.*
2 ***Not knowing the way to the job centre,*** *he got lost.*
3 ***Feeling very nervous,*** *I drove much too slowly in my first driving lesson.*
4 ***Not having much money,*** *we went to a cheap restaurant.*
5 ***Seeing that he had made a mistake,*** *he said he was sorry.*

Das <u>Vocabulary</u> (S. 195 – 226) enthält alle Wörter und Wendungen deines Englischbuches, die du lernen musst. Sie stehen in der Reihenfolge, in der sie im Buch zum ersten Mal vorkommen.

Hier siehst du, wie das **Vocabulary** aufgebaut ist:

Diese Zahl gibt die **Seite** an, auf der die Wörter zum ersten Mal vorkommen.
pp. 10/11 = Seiten 10 und 11

Die **Lautschrift** zeigt dir, wie ein Wort ausgesprochen wird.
Eine Übersicht über alle **Lautschriftzeichen** findest du auf S. 268.
Die Lautschriftzeichen stehen auch unten auf den **Vocabulary**-Seiten.

pp. 10/11	**region** ['riːdʒən]	Region	! stress: **<u>re</u>gion** ['riːdʒən] Ⓕ la région Ⓛ regio *f*
	tropical ['trɒpɪkl]	tropisch, Tropen-	a ~ rainforest/island/climate/disease Ⓕ tropical, e
	the tropics *(pl)* ['trɒpɪks]	die Tropen	
	poisonous ['pɔɪzənəs]	giftig	Be careful! Snakes can be ~. If you eat ~ plants, you might die.

Eingerückte Wörter lernst du am besten zusammen mit dem vorausgehenden Wort, weil die beiden zusammengehören.

Die Tilde in den Beispielsätzen steht für das neue Wort.
poisonous –
If you eat ~ plants, …
(= … **poisonous** plants)

Part A

p. 12	**quay** [kiː]	Kai	! pronunciation: **quay**
	a **half-hour** ride	eine halbstündige Fahrt	

a half-hour ride, a five-minute walk, …

! Im Englischen steht in Wendungen wie den folgenden das Nomen im Singular:
a **five-minute walk** (*nicht:* **a five-~~minutes~~ walk**)

a **half-hour** ride	eine halbstündige Fahrt	a **ten-kilometre** t…	
a **five-minute** walk	ein fünfminütiger Spaziergang	a **150-kilogram** b…	
a **six-month** stay	ein sechsmonatiger Aufenthalt	a **60-year-old** waiter	ein 60-jähriger Kellner
a **three-week** holiday	ein dreiwöchiger Urlaub	a **24-hour** supermarket	ein Supermarkt, der 24 Stunden geöffnet ist

Das **rote Ausrufezeichen** bedeutet:
Vorsicht, hier macht man leicht Fehler!

	waterfront ['wɔːtəfrʌnt]	Hafenviertel *(oft modernisiert und zum Wohnviertel umgebaut)*	
p. 17	**advantage** [əd'vɑːntɪdʒ]	Vorteil	**advantage** ◄► **disadvantage** [ˌdɪsəd'vɑːntɪdʒ] Not being able to drive can be a **dis~** (Nachteil) when you're looking for a job. Ⓕ l'avantage *(m)*
	hopeful ['həʊpfl]	zuversichtlich, hoffnungsvoll	

hopeful – hopefully
- **hopeful** *(adj)* – It might stop raining, but I'm not very **hopeful**.
- **hopefully** *(adv)* –
  1. We stood on the platform waiting

Diese **Kästen** solltest du dir immer besonders gut ansehen: Hier sind Vokabeln zu einem bestimmten Thema zusammengestellt. Oder du erfährst mehr über ein Wort und wie es verwendet wird.

Dies ist das *„opposite“*-Zeichen („Gegenteil“-Zeichen): **advantage** und **disadvantage** sind *opposites*.

Im **Vocabulary** werden folgende **Abkürzungen** verwendet:

p. = page (Seite) • pp. = pages (Seiten)

sth. = something (etwas) • sb. = somebody (jemand)

jn. = jemanden • jm. = jemandem

pl = *plural* (Mehrzahl) • *adj* = *adjective* • *adv* = *adverb* • *conj* = *conjunction* • *prep* = *preposition*

BE = *British English* • *AE* = *American English* • *AusE* = *Australian English*

infml = *informal* (umgangssprachlich) • *fml* = *formal* (formell, förmlich)

Ⓕ = *verwandtes Wort im Französischen* • Ⓛ = *verwandtes Wort im Lateinischen*

Wenn du **nachschlagen** möchtest, was ein englisches Wort bedeutet oder wie man es ausspricht, dann verwende das **English – German Dictionary** auf den Seiten 227 – 260.

Unit 1 Australia, country and continent

pp. 10/11	**region** ['riːdʒən]	Region	! stress: **<u>re</u>gion** ['riːdʒən] (F) la région (L) regio *f*
	bush [bʊʃ]	Busch, Strauch *(auch: unerschlossenes, „wildes" Land in Australien u. Afrika)*	
	coral ['kɒrəl]	Koralle; Korallen-	! stress: **<u>co</u>ral** ['kɒrəl]
	kangaroo [ˌkæŋɡə'ruː] (*AusE infml:* **roo**)	Känguru	! stress: **kanga<u>roo</u>** [ˌkæŋɡə'ruː]
	the outback ['aʊtbæk]	das Hinterland Australiens	
	spider ['spaɪdə]	Spinne	**spiders** 
	coastal ['kəʊstl]	Küsten-	Plymouth is a ~ town in England.
	exotic [ɪɡ'zɒtɪk]	exotisch	We saw lots of ~ animals at the zoo. (F) exotique
	humid ['hjuːmɪd]	feucht, feuchtwarm	We get a lot of rain here in the summer, so it's often very ~. (F) humide (L) umidus **humid ◄► dry**
	remote [rɪ'məʊt]	abgelegen, abgeschieden	We stayed in a ~ village 60 miles from the nearest town. (L) remotus
	stunning ['stʌnɪŋ]	atemberaubend, überwältigend, umwerfend	= wonderful, amazing, fantastic Don't they look ~ in their wedding clothes? 
	tropical ['trɒpɪkl]	tropisch, Tropen-	a ~ rainforest/island/climate/disease (F) tropical, e
	the tropics *(pl)* ['trɒpɪks]	die Tropen	
	urban ['ɜːbən]	städtisch, Stadt-	**Urban** planners think about the future of towns and cities. (F) urbain, e (L) urbanus
	Aboriginal [ˌæbə'rɪdʒənl]	Aborigine- *(die Ureinwohner/-innen Australiens betreffend)*	~ artists/culture; the ~ population  the **Aboriginal** flag
	camel ['kæml]	Kamel	! stress: **<u>ca</u>mel** ['kæml]
	convict ['kɒnvɪkt]	Sträfling, Strafgefangene(r)	
	koala [kəʊ'ɑːlə]	Koala	 a **koala**
	poisonous ['pɔɪzənəs]	giftig	Be careful! Snakes can be ~. If you eat ~ plants, you might die.
	exchange [ɪks'tʃeɪndʒ]	Austausch	There are some ~ students from France at our school. (F) l'échange *(m)*

Part A

p. 12	**flight** [flaɪt]	Flug	verb: (to) **fly, flew, flown** – noun: **flight** an **in-flight** magazine/meal (Bordmagazin/Bordmahlzeit)

[iː] green · [i] happy · [ɪ] big · [e] red · [æ] cat · [ɑː] class · [ɒ] song · [ɔː] door · [uː] blue · [ʊ] book · [ʌ] mum · [ɜː] girl · [ə] a partner

lively ['laɪvli]	lebendig, lebhaft	My grandma is still very ~ at 75. She goes dancing twice a week.
historical [hɪ'stɒrɪkl]	historisch, geschichtlich	The town's main ~ attraction is a 12th century castle. (F) historique (L) historia, -ae *f*
quarter ['kwɔːtə]	Viertel (*auch:* Stadtviertel)	The student ~ has a lot of pubs and cafés. (F) le quartier
(to) **settle** ['setl]	sich niederlassen, sich ansiedeln	When the Romans **~d** in Britain, they built roads and towns.
trendy ['trendi]	modisch, angesagt, „in"	Everyone is talking about this ~ new restaurant in George Street.
business ['bɪznəs]	Geschäft, Geschäfts-; Unternehmen, Betrieb	**Business** was good. (Die Geschäfte liefen gut.) a ~ trip/lunch (Geschäftsreise/-essen) Mike started his own ~ when he was 17.
district ['dɪstrɪkt]	Gegend, Bezirk, Viertel	There are lots of skyscrapers in Sydney's business ~.
flying fox [ˌflaɪɪŋ 'fɒks]	Flughund	
fox [fɒks]	Fuchs	

a **flying fox**

a **fox**

opera ['ɒprə]	Oper	(F) l'opéra *(m)*
quay [kiː]	Kai	! pronunciation: **quay** ['kiː] (F) le quai
a **half-hour** ride	eine halbstündige Fahrt	

a half-hour ride, a five-minute walk, …

! Im Englischen steht in Wendungen wie den folgenden das **Nomen im Singular**:
a five-minute walk (*nicht:* **a five-~~minutes~~ walk**)

a **five-minute** walk	ein fünfminütiger Spaziergang	a **ten-kilometre** tour	eine Zehn-Kilometer-Tour
a **half-hour** ride	eine halbstündige Fahrt	a **150-kilogram** bear	ein 150 Kilo schwerer Bär
a **six-month** stay	ein sechsmonatiger Aufenthalt	a **60-year-old** waiter	ein 60-jähriger Kellner
a **three-week** holiday	ein dreiwöchiger Urlaub	a **24-hour** supermarket	ein Supermarkt, der 24 Stunden geöffnet ist

waterfront ['wɔːtəfrʌnt]	Hafenviertel *(oft modernisiert und zum Wohnviertel umgebaut)*	
(to) **guide** [gaɪd]	führen	verb: (to) **guide** adj: **guided** – a **guided tour** through the city noun: **guide** 1. Fremdenführer/in; Reiseleiter/in; 2. (*auch:* **guidebook**) Reiseführer
honest ['ɒnɪst]	ehrlich	Be ~ with me! Say what you really think. ! silent "**h**": **honest** ['ɒnɪst] (L) honestus
take (**on** sth.)	Einstellung, Meinung (zu etwas)	What's your ~ **on** this new band?
(to) **catch** a bus/ferry/…	einen Bus/eine Fähre nehmen; einen Bus/eine Fähre (noch) erwischen	Walk to the waterfront and ~ a bus to the city centre. If we run we might still be able to ~ the ferry.
scenic ['siːnɪk]	(landschaftlich) schön	Let's take the ~ coastal route, not the main road.
(to) **transform** [træns'fɔːm]	verwandeln; umwandeln	They're planning to ~ the station into an art gallery. (F) transformer (L) transformare
landmark ['lændmɑːk]	Wahrzeichen	St Paul's Cathedral is one of London's **~s**.
paradise ['pærədaɪs]	Paradies	! stress: **paradise** ['pærədaɪs] (F) le paradis

	bay [beɪ]	Bucht	a beautiful **bay** (F) la baie 
p. 13	**back then**	damals	My grandma was born in 1948. Life was a lot slower **back ~**, she says.
	Aussie ['ɒzi] *(infml)*	Australier/in; australisch	informal for "Australian"

Group nouns

Nomen wie **audience, band, class, family, government, group, team** bezeichnen eine **Gruppe von Menschen**. Sie werden daher **group nouns** (oder **collective nouns**) genannt.

Auch wenn solche **group nouns** im **Singular** verwendet werden, stehen Verben und Pronomen danach oft im **Plural**:

Leon's host **family were** great. **They** quickly made him feel at home.
The **audience are** still cheering although the **band have** already started to put away **their** instruments.
Class 8PW are difficult to teach.

though [ðəʊ]	obwohl	Leon really liked his host family, ~ (= although) it was hard to understand them at first.
barbecue ['bɑːbɪkjuː] *(BE und AusE infml auch:* **barbie**)	Grill; Grillfest, Grillparty	Shall I put some more sausages on the ~? We're having a ~ on Sunday. Would you like to come? 
board [bɔːd] *(kurz für:* **surfboard**)	Surfbrett	
(to) **swallow** ['swɒləʊ]	schlucken; verschlucken	He thought he was going to be sick when he realized that he had **~ed** a spider.
ton [tʌn]	Tonne *(Gewicht)*	It was so hot! We could have sold **~s** of ice cream. (... jede Menge Eis)
private ['praɪvət]	privat	! pronunciation and stress: **private** ['praɪvət] **private** ◄► **public** (F) privé, e (L) privatus, -a, -um
(to) **accept** [ək'sept]	akzeptieren, annehmen	I've asked eight people to our barbecue, and most of them have already **~ed** the invitation. As a child I found it hard to get **~ed** into a group. (F) accepter (L) accipere
talkative ['tɔːkətɪv]	gesprächig	He seemed shy at first, but by the end of the evening he was really ~.
photography [fə'tɒgrəfi]	Fotografie	! stress: **photography** [fə'tɒgrəfi] (F) la photographie
in the end	schließlich, am Ende, zum Schluss	At first no one clapped, but **in the ~** everybody joined in.
(to) **be/get homesick** ['həʊmsɪk]	Heimweh haben/bekommen	*English:* (to) **be homesick** *German:* **Heimweh haben**
Christmas Eve [ˌkrɪsməs‿'iːv]	Heiligabend	
self-confident [ˌself'kɒnfɪdənt] *(kurz auch:* **confident**)	selbstbewusst, (selbst)sicher	She's a **self-confident** student. As a child, I was very shy. Later I became more **confident**. (L) confidere *(vertrauen)*
easy-going [ˌiːzi'gəʊɪŋ]	locker, unbeschwert, gelassen	Most of our teachers are **easy-~**, but Mr Sanders is really strict.
the very first/last/best ...	der/die/das allererste/allerletzte/allerbeste ...	We just managed to catch the ~ **last** tram. You could tell it was his ~ **first** time.

[b] **boat** · [p] **pool** · [d] **dad** · [t] **ten** · [g] **good** · [k] **cat** · [m] **mum** · [n] **no** · [ŋ] **song** · [l] **hello** · [r] **red** · [w] **we** · [j] **you**

p. 14	**sunscreen** ['sʌnskri:n]	Sonnenschutzmittel	Remember to put on ~ before you go out in the sun.
p. 15	**No worries, mate.** ['wʌriz] *(bes. AusE)*	Kein Problem! / Alles OK! / Alles gut!	Thanks very much for helping me. – **No ~, mate.**
	mate [meɪt] *(infml)*	Kumpel, Freund/in	Weekends are a good time to hang out with your **~s**.

p. 17

(to) argue – argument – argumentative

• (to) **argue**	**1.** argumentieren; behaupten **2.** (sich) streiten, (sich) zanken	He tried to **argue** that Shakespeare was German! My brothers **argue** all the time.
• **argument**	**1.** Argument **2.** Streit, Auseinandersetzung	Try to present **arguments** for and against the topic. Sorry about the noise. Our neighbours are having another **argument**.
• **argumentative** [ˌɑ:gju'mentətɪv]	**1.** argumentativ **2.** streitsüchtig	**argumentative writing** (Erörterung, Argumentation) He's a bit **argumentative**. That's why he didn't agree with us.

(to) **brainstorm** ['breɪnstɔ:m]	brainstormen *(so viele Ideen wie möglich sammeln)*	We sat down and **~ed** on how to solve the problem.
(to) **oppose** sth. [ə'pəʊz]	etwas ablehnen, gegen etwas sein	Most people **~d** the plan to build a new road. (to) **support** sth. ◄► (to) **oppose** sth. Ⓛ opponere *(entgegenstellen)*
(to) **state** sth. [steɪt]	etwas äußern, etwas angeben	Try to ~ your opinion in a respectful way. The president **~d** that he would introduce a new law.
abroad [ə'brɔ:d]	im/ins Ausland	My great-grandparents have never been ~. Lots of people like to go ~ on holiday.
in addition to … [ə'dɪʃn]	neben …; außer …; zusätzlich zu …	**In ~ to** the guitar and the piano, he also plays the drums. Ⓛ addere *(hinzufügen)*
personally ['pɜ:sənəli]	persönlich	*English:* **Personally**, I'd rather go by train. *German:* Ich **persönlich** würde lieber mit dem Zug fahren.
(to) **discuss** sth. [dɪ'skʌs]	über etwas diskutieren, etwas besprechen	*English:* (to) **discuss sth.** *German:* **über etwas diskutieren** noun: **discussion** – verb: (to) **discuss sth.**
furthermore [ˌfɜ:ðə'mɔ:]	außerdem, ferner; des Weiteren	The government want to improve our hospitals. **Furthermore**, they have promised to spend more on education.
in my view [vju:]	meiner Ansicht nach, meiner Meinung nach	= in my opinion
On the one hand, … **On the other hand, …**	Einerseits … Andererseits …	**On the one ~,** Australia is close to Asia. **On the other ~,** it has a strong British tradition.
(to) **take a different view**	einen anderen Standpunkt vertreten; anderer Ansicht sein	Most people think it's OK to eat meat, but some **take a different ~**. Some people **took the ~ that** the new skyscraper destroyed the historical skyline. („… waren der Auffassung/Ansicht, dass …")
advantage [əd'vɑ:ntɪdʒ]	Vorteil	**advantage ◄► disadvantage** [ˌdɪsəd'vɑ:ntɪdʒ] Not being able to drive can be a **dis~** (Nachteil) when you're looking for a job. Ⓕ l'avantage *(m)*
comparison [kəm'pærɪsn]	Vergleich	On this website you can **make ~s** between different schools. Ⓕ la comparaison Ⓛ comparare *English:* (to) **make comparisons** *German:* **Vergleiche anstellen; vergleichen**

[f] **f**ather · [v] ri**v**er · [s] **s**ister · [z] plea**s**e · [ʃ] **sh**op · [ʒ] televi**s**ion · [tʃ] **t**eacher · [dʒ] **G**ermany · [θ] **th**anks · [ð] **th**is · [h] **h**ere

	To start with, … / To begin with, …	Erstens …; Zunächst (einmal) …	**To ~ with**, I'd like to point out that …
	Firstly, … ['fɜːstli] **Secondly, …** ['sekəndli] **Thirdly, …** ['θɜːdli]	Erstens … Zweitens … Drittens …	**Firstly**, we have to get something to drink. **Secondly**, we need a DJ. And **thirdly**, …

Part B

pp. 18/19	**reef** [riːf]	Riff	
	(to) **flood** [flʌd]	überfluten, überschwemmen	The rain **~ed** our garden. It looked like a swimming pool. ! pronunciation: **flood** ['flʌd] verb: (to) **flood** – noun: **flood** (Flut; Überschwemmung)
	(to) **be determined to do** sth. [dɪ'tɜːmɪnd]	(fest) entschlossen sein, etwas zu tun	Nothing will stop me: **I'm ~ to** win the race. (L) determinare
	insect ['ɪnsekt]	Insekt	! stress: **insect** ['ɪnsekt] (F) l'insecte *(m)*
	python ['paɪθən]	Python	! pronunciation: **python** ['paɪθən]
	luckily ['lʌkɪli]	glücklicherweise; zum Glück	I dropped a plate yesterday. **Luckily**, it wasn't very expensive.
	(to) **prefer** sth. **(to** sth.) [prɪ'fɜː]	etwas (etwas anderem) vorziehen	My brother **~s** basketball **to** football. (F) préférer (= He likes basketball more than football.) I'd **~ to** stay at home this evening. (Ich würde heute Abend lieber zu Hause bleiben.)
	human ['hjuːmən]	Mensch; menschlich	! **human** = **1.** Mensch – animals and **humans** **2.** menschlich – It's only **human**. (F) humain, e (L) humanus Für das deutsche „Mensch" wird oft auch **human being** verwendet: The earth is much older than **human beings**.
	mainly ['meɪnli]	hauptsächlich, vorwiegend	The hotel was full of tourists, ~ from Germany.
	(to) **provoke** [prə'vəʊk]	provozieren	He's an easy-going guy – it's difficult to ~ him. (F) provoquer (L) provocare
	(to) **injure** sb. ['ɪndʒə]	jn. verletzen	! Bei leichten körperlichen Verletzungen oder wenn Gefühle verletzt werden, wird eher **hurt** verwendet.
	moth [mɒθ]	Nachtfalter; Motte	a **moth** 
	crocodile ['krɒkədaɪl]	Krokodil	! pronunciation and stress: **crocodile** ['krɒkədaɪl]
	(to) **bump into** sb. [bʌmp] *(infml)*	jn. zufällig treffen, jm. zufällig begegnen	In a small town you often **~ into** people you know.
	(to) **snorkel** ['snɔːkl]	schnorcheln	 **snorkelling**
p. 20	**greenhouse** ['griːnhaʊs]	Gewächshaus, Treibhaus	a **greenhouse** 
p. 22	**coastline** ['kəʊstlaɪn]	Küste, Küstenlinie	From the boat we could see the rocky Irish ~.

[iː] green · [i] happy · [ɪ] big · [e] red · [æ] cat · [ɑː] class · [ɒ] song · [ɔː] door · [uː] blue · [ʊ] book · [ʌ] mum · [ɜː] girl · [ə] a partner

dramatic [drə'mætɪk]	dramatisch	I saw a ~ film about a man who escaped from prison. (F) dramatique
facilities *(pl)* [fə'sɪlətiz]	Einrichtungen, Ausstattung, Anlage(n), Angebot(e)	The ~ at the first hotel were much better than the ones in this place! (L) facilis
overcrowded [ˌəʊvə'kraʊdɪd]	überfüllt	~ streets/beaches/classrooms/cities/prisons
rural ['rʊərəl]	ländlich, Land-	**rural ◄► urban** (F) rural, e ◄► urbain, e (L) rus, ruris *n (Land)*
suburban [sə'bɜːbən]	Vorort-, Vorstadt-; vorstädtisch	He walked around the ~ streets taking photos of the houses and gardens. noun: **suburb** ['sʌbɜːb] – adj: **suburban** [sə'bɜːbən]
vast [vɑːst]	riesig	Africa is a ~ continent. It's over 5,000 miles from north to south. **vast ◄► tiny**
inland ['ɪnlænd]	Binnen-; im Landesinneren	Duisburg has the world's largest ~ harbour. **coastal ◄► inland**
mild [maɪld]	mild	a <u>**mild**</u> **climate** ◄► a <u>**tropical**</u> **climate** a <u>**mild**</u> **dish/sauce** ◄► a <u>**hot**</u> **dish/sauce** a <u>**mild**</u> **cheese** ◄► a <u>**strong**</u> **cheese** **!** pronunciation: **mild** [maɪld]
mountainous ['maʊntənəs]	bergig, gebirgig	noun: **mountain** – adj: **mountainous**
old-fashioned [ˌəʊld'fæʃənd]	altmodisch	**old-fashioned ◄► modern, trendy**
flat [flæt]	flach, eben	It's easier to ride a bike in a ~ city like Berlin than in a hilly city like Stuttgart. **mountainous, hilly ◄► flat**
descriptive [dɪ'skrɪptɪv]	beschreibend	verb: (to) **describe** – noun: **description** – adj: **descriptive** (L) describere
collocation [ˌkɒlə'keɪʃn]	Kollokation *(Wörter, die oft zusammen vorkommen)*	words that are often used together, for example • **strong wind** (starker/kräftiger Wind) • **heavy rain** (starker/heftiger Regen) (F) la collocation (L) collocare
p. 23 (to) **disagree (with)** [ˌdɪsə'griː]	anderer Meinung sein (als); nicht übereinstimmen (mit); nicht zustimmen	I'm sorry, but I completely ~ **with** you/**with** that statement. (to) **agree ◄►** (to) **disagree**
rude [ruːd]	unhöflich; unverschämt	I think it's ~ to interrupt when someone else is speaking. **rude ◄► polite** (L) rudis
hurtful ['hɜːtfl]	verletzend	a ~ comment = a comment that hurts/might hurt
nonsense ['nɒnsns]	Unsinn, dummes Zeug	
(to) **share** sth. [ʃeə]	(sich) etwas teilen	(to) **share** a room/a flat I don't ~ his views. (Ich teile seine Ansichten nicht.)
totally ['təʊtəli]	völlig, total	• adv: **totally** (völlig, total) – (F) totalement I **totally** disagree. • adj: **total** (Gesamt-) – (F) total, e the **total** number of pupils at this school
I'm afraid … [ə'freɪd]	Leider …	 **!** **afraid:** **1. I'm afraid of spiders.** (Ich habe Angst …) **2. I'm afraid I can't help you.** (Leider …)

(to) **have a point**	nicht ganz Unrecht haben	You **have a ~** there, but I still think the other arguments are better.
gift voucher ['gɪft vaʊtʃə]	Geschenkgutschein	I got a couple of **gift ~s** for my birthday.

Part C

p. 26

English "so" – German "auch"

Coreen **loves** talking about her culture, and **so do** the other kids. ... und die anderen Kids **auch**.

Mit **so** + **Hilfsverb** + **(Pro-)Nomen** kann man zum Ausdruck bringen, dass etwas **auch** für jemand anders gilt. Weitere Beispiele:

John **is** really clever.	**So is** Joanna.	He **has been** to Australia.	**So has** Joanna.
He**'s got** a great voice.	**So has** Joanna.	He **got** married last year.	**So did** Joanna.
He **can** speak several languages.	**So can** Joanna.	He **would like** to move to Spain.	**So would** Joanna.
He **earns** a lot of money.	**So does** Joanna.		

sort (of) [sɔːt]	Art, Sorte	What ~ of music do you like? Rock? Pop? Jazz?
painting ['peɪntɪŋ]	Gemälde, Bild	verb: **paint** – noun: **painting**
soccer ['sɒkə]	Fußball	! Wie in den USA wird in Australien Fußball eher **soccer** genannt. **Football** ist in beiden Ländern etwas anderes.
(to) **dig (for** sth.**)** [dɪg], **dug, dug** [dʌg]	(nach etwas) graben	**digging a hole** 
opportunity [ˌɒpə'tjuːnəti]	Gelegenheit, Möglichkeit, Chance	I think you'll have better job **opportunities** if you spend a year abroad. (L) opportunus

German "Möglichkeit"

Das deutsche Wort **Möglichkeit** hat mehrere englische Entsprechungen.
Achte darauf, dass du nicht automatisch **possibility** verwendest. Oft sind **opportunity/chance** oder **way** passender:

• **opportunity** oder **chance** entsprechen „Möglichkeit" im Sinne von „Gelegenheit, Chance". (**opportunity** ist etwas förmlicher als **chance**.)	After school, I had the **chance/opportunity** to go to Australia for a year. Dad says he has a better **chance/opportunity** of getting a job if we move to Bristol.
• Wenn „Möglichkeit" im Sinne von „Art und Weise" gemeint ist, kann man **way** verwenden.	We'll have to swim – there's no other **way** to get/of getting to the island.
• Wenn man sagen will, dass etwas möglicherweise der Fall sein könnte (aber es ist nicht sicher, vielleicht sogar unwahrscheinlich!), dann verwendet man **possibility**.	There is a **possibility** of snow in May, but it's not very likely.

work experience *(no pl)* ['wɜːk‿ɪkˌspɪəriəns]	Praktikum; Arbeitserfahrung(en), Praxiserfahrung(en)	Last summer I did some **work ~** at our local supermarket. She has a strong computer background and a lot of **work ~**.
health [helθ]	Gesundheit	
clinic ['klɪnɪk]	Klinik	(F) la clinique
patient ['peɪʃnt]	Patient/in	! pronunciation and stress: **patient** ['peɪʃnt] (L) pati *(leiden)*
p. 27 (to) **debate** sth. [dɪ'beɪt]	über etwas debattieren	We **~d** the topic of bringing mobiles to school. verb: (to) **debate** – noun: **debate** (Debatte)

[b] **boat** · [p] **pool** · [d] **dad** · [t] **ten** · [g] **good** · [k] **cat** · [m] **mum** · [n] **no** · [ŋ] **song** · [l] **hello** · [r] **red** · [w] **we** · [j] **you**

racism ['reɪsɪzm]	Rassismus	! stress: **racism** ['reɪsɪzm] (F) le racisme
racist ['reɪsɪst]	Rassist/in; rassistisch	**racist** ['reɪsɪst] (F) le/la raciste
professional [prə'feʃənl]	professionell, Profi-	(F) professionnel, le (L) profiteri
swan [swɒn]	Schwan	**swans** 
medal ['medl]	Medaille	! stress: **medal** ['medl]
award [ə'wɔːd]	Preis, Auszeichnung	
(to) **stand up (for** sth./sb.**)** [ˌstænd‿'ʌp]	eintreten/sich einsetzen (für etwas/jn.)	It's important to ~ **up for** your rights.
recognition [ˌrekəg'nɪʃn]	Anerkennung	She got an award in ~ of her fight against discrimination. (L) recognoscere *(wiedererkennen)*
stand against sth.	Haltung gegenüber etwas, Widerstand gegen etwas	Martin Luther King is known for his strong ~ **against** discrimination.
(to) **be named** sth.	zu etwas ernannt werden	She **was** ~ sportsperson of the year.
(to) **criticize** sb. **(for)** ['krɪtɪsaɪz]	jn. kritisieren (wegen)	She was **~d for** her article in the school magazine. ! stress: **criticize** ['krɪtɪsaɪz] (F) critiquer
opposing [ə'pəʊzɪŋ]	gegnerisch	the ~ team
ape [eɪp]	Menschenaffe	three **apes** 
row [rəʊ]	Reihe	I don't like sitting in the front ~ in the cinema.
upset [ˌʌp'set]	aufgebracht, gekränkt, mitgenommen	He felt very ~ when the other kids called him names.
victory ['vɪktəri]	Sieg	(F) la victoire (L) victoria
comment ['kɒment]	Bemerkung, Kommentar	(F) le commentaire
innocent ['ɪnəsnt]	unschuldig	I didn't take the money! I'm ~! (F) innocent, e (L) innocens
(to) **put the blame (for** sth.**) on** sb. [bleɪm]	jm. (an etwas) die Schuld geben	My brother always tries to **put the** ~ **on** me when something goes wrong at home.
unfortunately [ʌn'fɔːtʃənətli]	leider, unglücklicherweise	We were planning a barbecue, but ~ it rained. **fortunately** (glücklicherweise) ◄► **unfortunately** (L) fortuna
(to) **bully** sb. ['bʊli]	jn. tyrannisieren, mobben	verb: (to) **bully** – noun: **bully**
appearance [ə'pɪərəns]	Erscheinung(sbild), Aussehen	I was shocked by his ~ – he looked much older than the last time we met. verb: (to) **appear** – noun: **appearance** (F) l'apparence *(f)* (L) apparere
industry ['ɪndəstri]	Industrie	! stress: **industry** ['ɪndəstri] (F) l'industrie *(f)* (L) industria
society [sə'saɪəti]	(die) Gesellschaft	! *No article:* **in (modern) society** **in der (modernen) Gesellschaft** (F) la société (L) societas

[f] father · [v] river · [s] sister · [z] please · [ʃ] shop · [ʒ] television · [tʃ] teacher · [dʒ] Germany · [θ] thanks · [ð] this · [h] here

	incident ['ɪnsɪdənt]	Vorfall, Zwischenfall	The police are still looking into the ~. (F) l'incident *(m)* (L) incidere
	(to) **boo** [bu:]	buhen; ausbuhen	The play was terrible. The audience **~ed** the actors off the stage.
	achievement [ə'tʃi:vmənt]	Errungenschaft, Leistung	Learning to play the guitar isn't easy. It's quite an ~, actually.
p. 29	**series,** *pl* **series** ['sɪəri:z]	(Sende-)Reihe, Serie	It's my favourite ~. I watch it every week. (L) series *f*
	setting ['setɪŋ]	Schauplatz *(Film/Geschichte)*	The ~ of the film is a small village in Cornwall.

Unit 2 Relationships

pp. 34/35	**photographer** [fə'tɒgrəfə]	Fotograf/in	• **photo(graph)** ['fəʊtəʊ, 'fəʊtəgrɑ:f] Foto • (to) **photograph** ['fəʊtəgrɑ:f] fotografieren • **photography** [fə'tɒgrəfi] Fotografie *(Hobby)* • **photographer** [fə'tɒgrəfə] Fotograf/in

Part A

p. 36	**novel** ['nɒvl]	Roman	(L) novus
	I reckon … ['rekən]	Ich schätze …, Ich nehme an …	= I guess …, I think …
	promise ['prɒmɪs]	Versprechen; Verheißung	verb: (to) **promise** – noun: **promise** (L) promittere
	salty ['sɔ:lti]	salzig	noun: **salt** – adj: **salty** (L) sal
	(to) **treat** ['tri:t]	behandeln	verb: (to) **treat** – (F) traiter (L) tractare We should **treat** other people with respect. noun: **treatment** ['tri:tmənt] – (F) le traitement He needed **treatment** on his leg after he fell off his horse.
	haircut ['heəkʌt]	Haarschnitt	Your hair is too long. Go and get a ~. (… lass dir die Haare schneiden.)
	That's fine by me.	Das soll mir recht sein. / Von mir aus gern.	Shall we meet at six? – Sure, **that's ~ by me**. If you want to throw your life away, **that's ~ by me**.
	(to) **vote (for** sb./sth.**)** [vəʊt]	(für jn./etwas) stimmen; wählen, zur Wahl gehen	Who are you going to ~ **for** as band of the year? In most countries you have to be 18 before you can ~. (F) voter (pour qn)
	elections *(pl)* [ɪ'lekʃnz]	Wahlen	**Elections** for President of the United States are held every four years. (F) les élections *(f)* (L) eligere
	subject ['sʌbdʒɪkt], ['sʌbdʒekt]	Thema	I'm reading a book on the ~ of terrorism. (F) le sujet ! **subject** = **1.** Subjekt; **2.** Schulfach; **3.** Thema
	politics ['pɒlətɪks]	Politik	! • Das Wort **politics** ist Singular, trotz des **-s**: **Politics <u>is</u>** interesting for some people, and **<u>it is</u>** boring for others. • stress: **<u>pol</u>itics** ['pɒlətɪks] (F) la politique
	sensitive ['sensətɪv]	empfindlich, sensibel; heikel; einfühlsam, empfindsam	Don't say anything about his big nose: he's very ~ about it. My girlfriend is a good listener and ~ to my feelings.
	issue ['ɪʃu:], ['ɪsju:]	Thema, (Streit-)Frage, Angelegenheit	Pocket money is a sensitive ~ in some families.
	once *(conj)* [wʌns]	sobald, sowie, wenn	! **once** = **1.** *(adv)* einmal – We go there **once** a week. **2.** *(conj)* – **Once** you're finished, we can go.

[i:] green · [i] happy · [ɪ] big · [e] red · [æ] cat · [ɑ:] class · [ɒ] song ·
[ɔ:] door · [u:] blue · [ʊ] book · [ʌ] mum · [3:] girl · [ə] a partner

waste [weɪst]	Verschwendung	noun: **waste** – The meal at that restaurant was awful – a **waste** of time and money. verb: (to) **waste** sth. **(on** sth.**)** – Water is limited. Don't **waste** it.
tree trunk ['tri: trʌŋk] *(oder kurz:* **trunk***)*	Baumstamm	**a tree trunk** (L) truncus 
p. 37 **chin** [tʃɪn]	Kinn	
(to) **tear** [teə], **tore** [tɔ:], **torn** [tɔ:n]	reißen, zerreißen	My jeans **tore** as I climbed over the fence. I was so angry that I **tore** the letter into pieces.
key [ki:]	Taste	
(to) **shake** [ʃeɪk], **shook** [ʃʊk], **shaken** ['ʃeɪkn]	zittern	Look, he's nervous: his hands are **shaking**. **!** (to) **shake** = **1.** schütteln; **2.** zittern
first aid [ˌfɜ:st_'eɪd]	Erste Hilfe	
(to) **breathe** [bri:ð]	atmen	verb: (to) **breathe** [bri:ð] – noun: **breath** [breθ]
skin [skɪn]	Haut	I need some face cream. My ~ is very dry.
cheek [tʃi:k]	Wange	**cheek** **chin** 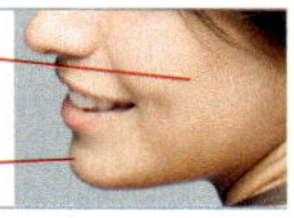
pulse [pʌls]	Puls, Pulsschlag	The doctor took his ~ and blood pressure. (L) pellere
brain [breɪn]	Gehirn	
oxygen ['ɒksɪdʒən]	Sauerstoff	(F) l'oxygène *(m)*
distant ['dɪstənt]	(weit) entfernt, fern	It will take you a long time to get to such a ~ place. The Romans ruled Britain in the ~ past. (L) distare *(entfernt sein)*
(to) **sink** [sɪŋk], **sank** [sæŋk], **sunk** [sʌŋk]	sinken	a **sinking** ship 
intelligent [ɪn'telɪdʒənt]	intelligent	**!** stress: **in<u>tel</u>ligent** [ɪn'telɪdʒənt] (F) intelligent, e (L) intellegere
occasionally [ə'keɪʒnəli]	gelegentlich, ab und zu	We used to see each other a lot but we only meet ~ now. (L) occasio
dreamy ['dri:mi]	verträumt	verb: (to) **dream** – noun: **dream** – adj: **dreamy**
immigrant ['ɪmɪgrənt]	Einwanderer/Einwanderin	**!** stress: **<u>im</u>migrant** ['ɪmɪgrənt] (F) l'immigrant, e / l'immigré, e (L) immigrare
university [ˌju:nɪ'vɜ:səti]	Universität	(F) l'université *(f)* (L) universus

pp. 38/39

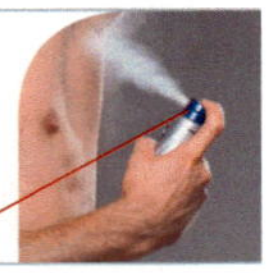

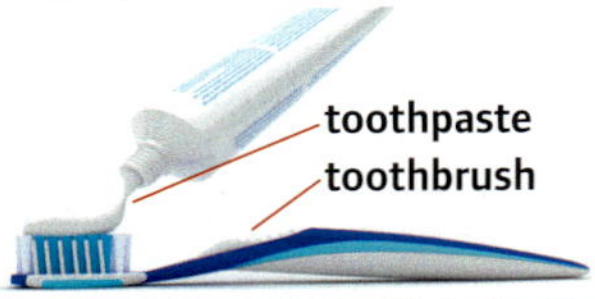

soap [səʊp]	Seife	
deodorant [di'əʊdərənt]	Deodorant	
toothbrush ['tu:θbrʌʃ]	Zahnbürste	
toothpaste ['tu:θpeɪst]	Zahnpasta	
fridge [frɪdʒ]	Kühlschrank	
can [kæn]	Dose	! • In *BE*, the word **can** is always used for drinks. To talk about food, the British usually use **tin**. • In *AE*, **can** is used for both food and drinks.
pretty ['prɪti]	ziemlich	Your new glasses look ~ cool. ! **pretty** = **1.** *(adj)* hübsch; **2.** *(adv)* ziemlich
anyway ['eniweɪ]	trotzdem	

anyway

1. Jedenfalls …	Is her mother American? – I don't really know. But **anyway**, she lives in California now. We'll arrive at 7:35 or 7:45, I'm not sure. **Anyway**, we'll be there before 8.
2. Und überhaupt, …	I don't have the time to go on holiday. **And anyway**, it's too expensive.
3. sowieso	I can give you a lift. I'm going there **anyway**.
4. trotzdem	It was freezing cold, but we went out **anyway**.

familiar [fə'mɪliə]	vertraut	New York's skyline is ~ to people all over the world. I know New York, but I'm not ~ with other American cities. (F) familier, familière (L) familiaris
awkward ['ɔ:kwəd]	peinlich, unangenehm, schwierig	We felt rather ~ when Jake found out we hadn't invited him to the party. It was an ~ question and I had no idea how to answer it.
next door *(adv)* [ˌnekst 'dɔ:]	nebenan	I couldn't sleep. The TV was on all night in the room **next ~**.
muscle ['mʌsl]	Muskel	*English:* He didn't move a **muscle**. (F) le muscle *German:* Er rührte sich nicht.
hand [hænd]	Uhrzeiger	
(to) **mean to do** sth.	etwas tun wollen; die Absicht haben, etwas zu tun	Sorry, I **~t to** phone you, but I forgot. I'm sorry, I didn't **~ to** be rude.
because of *(prep)*	wegen	! • *(conj)* I stayed at home **because** it rained. **weil** es regnete • *(prep)* I stayed at home **because of** the rain. **wegen** des Regens
serious ['sɪəriəs]	ernst; ernsthaft	adj: **serious** – a **serious** illness/problem/… (F) sérieux, se (L) serius adv: **seriously** – **seriously** ill/injured/… (F) sérieusement

	first-person narrative ['nærətɪv]	Ich-Erzählung	(L) narrare
p. 41	**request** [rɪ'kwest]	Bitte, Wunsch	Unfortunately, nobody has reacted to my ~ for help. (L) requirere
	informal [ɪn'fɔːml]	informell; umgangssprachlich	**informal ◄► formal** ['fɔːml] (formell, förmlich) (F) informel, le ◄► formel, le
p. 42	(to) **be attracted to** sb. [ə'træktɪd]	sich zu jm. hingezogen fühlen	I'**m** really ~ **to** boys with blue eyes and a nice smile. (L) attrahere
	(to) **be seeing** sb.	mit jm. zusammen sein	They'**ve been** ~ each other for quite a while now, and next month they're going to get married.
	(to) **fall in love (with** sb.**)**	sich (in jn.) verlieben	*English:* (to) **fall in love with** sb. *German:* sich **in** jn. verlieben
	(to) **date** sb. [deɪt]	mit jm. gehen, mit jm. zusammen sein	Dad **~d** mum for years before they got married.
	(to) **break up (with** sb.**)** [ˌbreɪk_'ʌp]	Schluss machen (mit jm.), sich trennen (von jm.)	Jonathan's parents have **broken** ~ and are getting divorced soon.
	(to) **get to know** sb.	jn. kennenlernen	My parents **got to** ~ each other in high school.
	annoyed (with sb.**/ about** sth.**)** [ə'nɔɪd]	verärgert (über jn./etwas), irritiert	She was ~ **with** him because he was late again. My father often gets ~ **about** the government.
	confused [kən'fjuːzd]	verwirrt	He looked so ~ – he clearly didn't understand you. (F) confus, e (L) confundere
	cross (with sb.**)** [krɒs]	böse, sauer (auf jn.)	Mum was ~ **with** me because I was late.
	frightened ['fraɪtnd]	verängstigt	Don't be ~. Thunder sounds scary but it isn't dangerous.
	hopeful ['həʊpfl]	zuversichtlich, hoffnungsvoll	**hopeful – hopefully** • **hopeful** *(adj)* It might stop raining, but I'm not very **hopeful**. • **hopefully** *(adv)* **1.** We stood on the platform waiting **hopefully** for the train to arrive. (hoffnungsvoll, voller Hoffnung) **2. Hopefully** we'll have good weather for our picnic. (hoffentlich)
	pessimistic [ˌpesɪ'mɪstɪk]	pessimistisch	**optimistic ◄► pessimistic** (F) optimiste ◄► pessimiste
	pleased [pliːzd]	froh, erfreut, zufrieden	I'm really ~ with my new mobile. It's much better than my old one. *English:* **Pleased** to meet you. *German:* Freut mich, Sie kennenzulernen.
	furious (with/at sb.**)** ['fjʊəriəs]	wütend, zornig (auf jn.), wutentbrannt	He was ~ when I told him. I've never seen anyone so angry. (F) furieux, se (L) furor *m*
	heartbroken ['hɑːtbrəʊkən]	todunglücklich, untröstlich	Sally was ~ after her dog died.
	terrified ['terɪfaɪd]	entsetzt	*English:* (to) **be terrified** (of sth.) (F) terrifié, e *German:* **schreckliche Angst** (vor etwas) **haben**
	thrilled [θrɪld]	begeistert	I was ~ when I was offered the leading role in the play.

[f] father · [v] river · [s] sister · [z] please · [ʃ] shop · [ʒ] television · [tʃ] teacher · [dʒ] Germany · [θ] thanks · [ð] this · [h] here

	absolutely ['æbsəluːtli]	völlig, absolut	I wasn't just hungry – I was **absolutely** starving. ! Wenn **absolutely** als zustimmende Entgegnung benutzt wird, liegt die Hauptbetonung auf der 3. Silbe: The show was fantastic, wasn't it? – **Absolutely**! [ˌæbsə'luːtli] (L) absolvere (loslösen)
	ex- [eks]	Ex-; ehemalige(r, s)	my **ex**-boyfriend/girlfriend; London's **ex**-mayor
	male [meɪl]	männlich; männliche Person; Männchen	Most of the workers here are ~. The police are looking for a 40-year-old ~.
	female ['fiːmeɪl]	weiblich; weibliche Person; Weibchen	**Females** often earn less money than males. **male ◄► female**
	acquaintance [ə'kweɪntəns]	Bekannte(r)	I wouldn't say he's a real friend. He's just an ~.
p. 43	(to) **enter** sth. ['entə]	etwas eingeben, eintragen	Please ~ your name on this list. (L) intrare
	password ['pɑːswɜːd]	Passwort	You shouldn't tell other people your ~**s**.
	(to) **update** sth. [ˌʌp'deɪt]	etwas aktualisieren, auf den neuesten Stand bringen	
	status ['steɪtəs]	Status	Philip has just updated his ~. (L) status
	account [ə'kaʊnt]	Account, Konto	You'll need some ID to open a bank ~. How do I change the password of my email ~?

Part B

p. 44	**murder** ['mɜːdə]	Mord	! (to) **murder** (er)morden – **murder** Mord – **murderer** Mörder/in
	(to) **declare** sth. [dɪ'kleə]	etwas erklären, verkünden	He was furious with me and ~**d** that he never wanted to see me again. The United Kingdom ~**d** war on Germany on 3 September 1939. (F) déclarer (L) declarare
	husband ['hʌzbənd]	Ehemann	! ihr Mann = her **husband** (*not:* her ~~man~~)
	wife [waɪf], *pl* **wives** [waɪvz]	Ehefrau	! seine Frau = his **wife** (*not:* his ~~woman~~)
	you **ought to** stop … [ɔːt]	du solltest aufhören, …	Some people say we ~ **to** stop eating meat. (= … we should stop eating meat.)
	diet ['daɪət]	Ernährung(sweise), Speiseplan; Diät	Fruit and vegetables are important for a healthy ~. The doctor said I needed to go on a ~. ! pronunciation and stress: **diet** ['daɪət]
	protein ['prəʊtiːn]	Protein, Eiweiß	! stress: **protein** ['prəʊtiːn]
	healthy ['helθi]	gesund	**healthy ◄► sick, ill**
	(to) **be supposed to do** sth. [sə'pəʊzd]	etwas tun sollen	We**'re not** ~ **to** use our mobiles at school, but some of us do. I haven't heard their new album yet, but it**'s** ~ **to** be really good.
	pasta *(no pl)* ['pæstə]	Nudeln	a plate of **pasta**  *English:* **Pasta is** my favourite food. *German:* **Nudeln sind** mein Lieblingsessen.

[iː] green · [i] happy · [ɪ] big · [e] red · [æ] cat · [ɑː] class · [ɒ] song · [ɔː] door · [uː] blue · [ʊ] book · [ʌ] mum · [ɜː] girl · [ə] a partner

p. 46	**cultural** ['kʌltʃərəl]	kulturell	noun: **culture** – adj: **cultural** ! stress: <u>cul</u>ture, <u>cul</u>tural ['kʌltʃə], ['kʌltʃərəl] (F) culturel, le (L) colere *(pflegen, verehren)*
	communication [kəˌmjuːnɪ'keɪʃn]	Kommunikation, Verständigung	(F) la communication (L) communis *(gemeinsam)*
p. 47	**statistics** *(pl)* [stə'tɪstɪks]	Statistik	**Statistics** show that London's population is continuing to grow. (F) les statistiques
	bar chart ['bɑː tʃɑːt]	Balkendiagramm	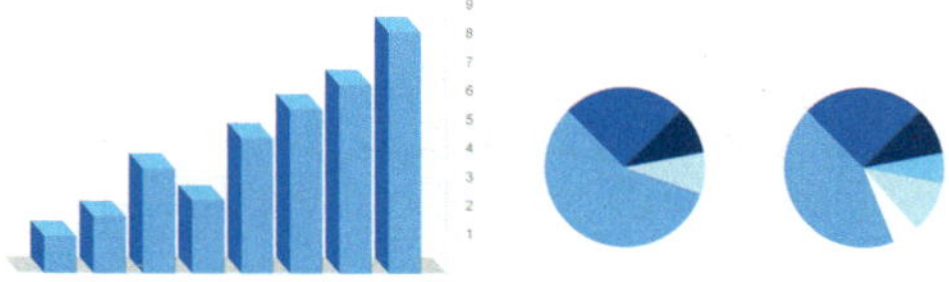 a **bar chart** **pie charts**
	pie chart ['paɪ tʃɑːt]	Tortendiagramm	
	chart [tʃɑːt]	Tabelle, Schaubild	
	average ['ævərɪdʒ]	durchschnittlich; Durchschnitt	The ~ age of students in our year is 16.5. I practise the piano two hours a day **on** ~. (= im Durchschnitt, durchschnittlich)
	length [leŋθ]	Länge; Dauer	The swimming pool has a ~ of 25 metres. I'd say the average ~ of films on DVD is 90 minutes.
	useful ['juːsfl]	nützlich	You'll find this map ~ for finding your way around town. (L) usus
	percentage [pə'sentɪdʒ]	Prozentsatz; prozentualer Anteil	What ~ of your pocket money do you spend on clothes? (F) le pourcentage (L) centum
	chore [tʃɔː]	(Haus-)Arbeit; *(lästige)* Pflicht	What **~s** do you do at home? – I wash the dishes and walk the dog.
	(to) **realize** sth. ['riːəlaɪz]	etwas erkennen; sich einer Sache bewusst werden	When I got home, I **~d** that I had left my bag on the train. (F) réaliser qc
p. 48	**amount (of)** [ə'maʊnt]	Betrag, Menge; Höhe *(von Gehalt, Taschengeld)*	£300? I wouldn't pay that ~ for a pair of jeans. Now add a small ~ **of** salt to the soup.
	(to) **insist on** sth. [ɪn'sɪst]	auf etwas bestehen	I didn't want to go to the Millers but Mum **~ed**. Dad always **~s on** me helping him clean the car. (F) insister (L) insistere
	value ['væljuː]	Wert	Do young people share older people's **~s**? The ~ of our car has gone down by £2000 since I bought it. (F) la valeur (L) valere
	tidy ['taɪdi]	ordentlich, aufgeräumt	
	cash [kæʃ]	Bargeld; *(infml auch:)* Geld	You have to pay ~ in this shop – you can't use a card. *English:* (to) **pay cash** – *German:* **bar bezahlen**
	simply ['sɪmpli]	einfach	adj: **simple** – This is a very **simple** recipe, so you should be able to follow it. adv: **simply** – What are you trying to say? Can you put it more **simply**, please?
	They **run out of** money.	Ihnen geht das Geld aus. / Bei ihnen wird das Geld knapp.	**(to) run out (knapp werden; zu Ende gehen)** • **Time is running out.** (Die Zeit wird knapp.) • **We're running out of time.** (Wir haben keine Zeit mehr.) • **It was so hot that the shops ran out of cold drinks.** (…, dass den Geschäften die kalten Getränke ausgingen.)
	(to) **encourage** sb. [ɪn'kʌrɪdʒ]	jn. ermutigen, jn. ermuntern	My parents **~d** me to go abroad for a year.

	perhaps [pə'hæps]	vielleicht	= maybe
	certain ['sɜːtn]	bestimmte(r, s), gewisse(r, s)	Try to save a ~ amount of money each month. A ~ Mr Davidson called this morning. (L) certus
	habit ['hæbɪt]	(An-)Gewohnheit	something you do regularly: Smoking is a bad ~. (L) habere
p. 49	**agreement** [ə'griːmənt]	Einigung; Vereinbarung	After a long discussion, we finally reached ~. (… haben wir uns schließlich geeinigt.)
	(to) **express** [ɪk'spres]	ausdrücken, zum Ausdruck bringen	"In my opinion", "In my view" and "I think" are useful phrases to ~ your opinion. (L) exprimere
	(to) **stress** [stres]	betonen	noun: **stress** – verb: (to) **stress**
	hen [hen]	Huhn, Henne	
	(to) **agree to differ**	sich darauf einigen, dass man verschiedener Ansicht ist; einsehen, dass man sich nicht einigen kann	The argument could have gone on and on, so we **~d to differ**.
	(to) **remind** sb. [rɪ'maɪnd]	jn. erinnern	Please ~ me that it's Grandma's birthday on Friday. I want to call her. Grandpa always says I ~ him of his sister. ! • **remember sth.** = sich an etwas erinnern Do you **remember** her name? • **remind sb.** = jn. erinnern I mustn't forget. Please **remind** me.

Part C

p. 50	**refugee** [ˌrefju'dʒiː]	Flüchtling	(F) le réfugié, la réfugiée
	youth [juːθ]	Jugend; Jugend-	It's cheaper to stay at a ~ hostel than at a hotel.
	organization [ˌɔːgənaɪ'zeɪʃn]	Organisation	! stress: **organi<u>za</u>tion** [ˌɔːgənaɪ'zeɪʃn] (F) l'organisation *(f)*
	(to) **run** an organization / a business / a hotel / …, **ran, run**	eine Organisation / eine Firma / ein Hotel leiten, führen	My uncle **~s** a motel near New Orleans.
	(to) **publish** ['pʌblɪʃ]	veröffentlichen	The first Harry Potter book was **~ed** in 1997. (F) publier (L) publicus
	friendship ['frendʃɪp]	Freundschaft	
	(to) **fill in a form**	ein Formular ausfüllen	
	distance ['dɪstəns]	Distanz, Entfernung	! stress: **<u>dis</u>tance** ['dɪstəns] (F) la distance (L) distare *(entfernt sein)* *English:* (to) **travel long distances** *German:* weite Strecken fahren/zurücklegen
	transport ['trænspɔːt]	Verkehrsmittel; Transport(wesen)	! stress: **<u>trans</u>port** ['trænspɔːt] (F) le transport (L) trans + portare  different forms of **transport**
	(to) **face** sth. [feɪs]	vor etwas stehen; mit etwas konfrontiert werden *(Problem)*	Jamie, ~ the facts. You'll never be a rock star. As a single parent, you have to ~ problems other parents don't have to deal with. (L) facies

[b] **boat** · [p] **pool** · [d] **dad** · [t] **ten** · [g] **good** · [k] **cat** ·
[m] **mum** · [n] **no** · [ŋ] **song** · [l] **hello** · [r] **red** · [w] **we** · [j] **you**

(to) **fit in** [ˌfɪt‿ˈɪn]	sich einfügen, seinen Platz finden; hineinpassen	At first, I found it difficult to ~ **in** at my new school. There are some students in my sister's class who just don't ~ **in**.
(to) **act** [ækt]	handeln, sich verhalten	When you get older you're expected to ~ more responsibly. Ⓛ agere
(to) **adapt (to** sth.**)** [əˈdæpt]	sich (einer Sache) anpassen	When they moved to India, it took some time to ~ **to** the climate. Ⓕ s'adapter Ⓛ ad + aptare
(to) **get used to** sth. [juːst]	sich an etwas gewöhnen	When we were in England, it was strange to drive on the left, but we soon **got** ~ **to** it. *English:* We **got used to driving** on the left. *German:* Wir **gewöhnten uns daran**, links **zu fahren**. **!** *Nicht verwechseln:* • Did you know that people once **<u>used to drive</u>** on the left in Sweden? (<u>… früher einmal … fuhren</u>) • After a couple of days we **<u>got used to driving</u>** on the left. (<u>… gewöhnten uns daran, … zu fahren</u>)
(to) **end up doing** sth.	schließlich etwas tun	My aunt started her career washing the dishes in a hotel. She **~ed up** owning the place.
responsibility [rɪˌspɒnsəˈbɪləti]	Verantwortung	Having children is a big ~. Ⓕ la responsabilité adj: **responsible** [rɪˈspɒnsəbl] – noun: **responsibility** [rɪˌspɒnsəˈbɪləti]
within [wɪˈðɪn]	innerhalb (von)	Do you think you can finish your project ~ a week? We respect all cultures ~ our community.
advisor [ədˈvaɪzə] (*auch* **adviser**)	Berater/in	verb: (to) **advise** – noun: **1. advice** (Rat); **2. advisor, -ser** (Berater/in)
carer [ˈkeərə]	Betreuer/in	The old man couldn't look after himself any longer and needed a ~.
(to) **be dependent on** sb./sth. [dɪˈpendənt]	von jm./etwas abhängig sein, auf jn./etwas angewiesen sein	Children **are** ~ **on** their parents until they start to earn money. Ⓕ dépendre Ⓛ dependere
(to) **get to do** sth.	etwas tun können/dürfen; die Möglichkeit haben/bekommen, etwas zu tun	I only ~ **to go** to the party tonight if I finish all my homework.
not … anywhere [ˈeniweə]	nirgendwo; nirgendwohin	Where's my key? I can**'t** see it ~. I do**n't** want to go ~. I just want to stay at home. **somewhere** ◄► **not … anywhere**
p. 51 **shop window**	Schaufenster	a **shop window** 
apron [ˈeɪprən]	Schürze	 **aprons**
(to) **be in a hurry** [ˈhʌri]	in Eile sein, es eilig haben	
normally [ˈnɔːməli]	normalerweise; normal	Come for dinner tomorrow. We ~ eat around seven. I tried to act ~, but it was difficult to hide how nervous I was. Ⓕ normal, e – normalement adj: **normal** – adv: **normally**

[f] **father** · [v] **river** · [s] **sister** · [z] **please** · [ʃ] **shop** · [ʒ] **television** ·
[tʃ] **teacher** · [dʒ] **Germany** · [θ] **thanks** · [ð] **this** · [h] **here**

stiff [stɪf]	steif	If you feel ~, you should take a hot shower. The party was a ~ event – everyone just made polite conversation.
including [ɪn'klu:dɪŋ]	einschließlich; darunter (auch)	A lot of famous bands have played here, ~ *Deep Purple* and *Coldplay*. (L) includere *(einschließen)* ! • The price is £48, **including** breakfast. (… **einschließlich** Frühstück.) • Breakfast is **included**. (Frühstück ist **inbegriffen**.)
tandem ['tændəm]	Tandem	a **tandem** 
hub [hʌb]	Mittelpunkt, (Verkehrs-)Knotenpunkt	
handmade [ˌhænd'meɪd]	handgemacht	**Handmade** chocolates are more expensive than ones made in factories.

Unit 3 Big dreams – small steps

pp. 58/59	**army** ['ɑ:mi]	Armee	After he left school, he joined the ~. (F) l'armée *(f)* ! stress: **army** ['ɑ:mi] (L) arma *(die Waffen)*
	athlete ['æθli:t]	Athlet/in, Sportler/in	! stress: **athlete** ['æθli:t] (F) l'athlète *(m, f)*
	global warming [ˌgləʊbl 'wɔ:mɪŋ]	Erderwärmung, Erwärmung der Erdatmosphäre	
	make a difference	etwas bewirken, etwas bewegen	Does voting **make a** ~? What do you think?
	(to) **repair** [rɪ'peə]	reparieren	My bike is broken and needs to be **~ed**. (F) réparer (L) reparare *(wiederherstellen)*
	scientific [ˌsaɪən'tɪfɪk]	(natur)wissenschaftlich	noun: **science** – adj: **scientific** (F) scientifique (L) scientia *(Wissen)*
	skydiving ['skaɪdaɪvɪŋ]	Fallschirmspringen	**skydiving** 
	(to) **achieve** [ə'tʃi:v]	erreichen *(Ziel)*, erzielen *(Resultat)*; zustande bringen	Hmm, this isn't the result we wanted to ~. I've been working all day, but I haven't **~d** much.
	goal [gəʊl]	Ziel	! • ein Ziel erreichen = (to) **achieve a goal** • einen Ort erreichen = (to) **reach a place** / (to) **arrive at a place**
	deadline ['dedlaɪn]	(letzter) Termin	The ~ for this assignment is 1 May.
	(to) **fail (to do** sth.**)** [feɪl]	versagen, scheitern (beim Versuch, etwas zu tun)	I **~ed** to lift the rock: it was just too heavy. (to) **pass a test** ◄► (to) **fail a test** (einen Test nicht bestehen)
	application [ˌæplɪ'keɪʃn]	Bewerbung	*English:* **letter of application** *German:* **Bewerbungsschreiben**
	(to) **apply (for** sth.**)** [ə'plaɪ]	sich (um/für etwas) bewerben	He **applied** for the job, but he didn't get it. I'd love to go to university in Berlin, but I think it's better to ~ to more than one university.

[i:] green · [i] happy · [ɪ] big · [e] red · [æ] cat · [ɑ:] class · [ɒ] song · [ɔ:] door · [u:] blue · [ʊ] book · [ʌ] mum · [ɜ:] girl · [ə] a partner

Part A

p. 60	**excerpt (from)** [ˈeksɜːpt]	Auszug (aus)	This is a short ~ from a long novel. (L) excipere *(herausnehmen)*
	vice- [vaɪs]	Vize-	! pronunciation: **vice** [vaɪs]
	former [ˈfɔːmə]	ehemalige(r, s), frühere(r, s)	Australia is a ~ British colony.
	(to) **be about to do** sth.	im Begriff sein, etwas zu tun; kurz davor sein, etwas zu tun	I was ~ **to go** to bed when the doorbell rang.
	court [kɔːt]	Spielfeld	 a basketball **court**  a tennis **court**
	identical [aɪˈdentɪkl]	identisch	The two versions are very similar but not totally ~. (F) identique
	(to) **shave** [ʃeɪv]	(sich) rasieren	 He's **shaving**.  a **shaved** head (ein kahlgeschorener Kopf)
	(to) **pass** [pɑːs]	abspielen, passen *(Ball)*	I **~ed** to John, who scored the third goal. (F) passer
	the Bible [ˈbaɪbl]	die Bibel	! pronunciation: **the Bible** [ˈbaɪbl]
	religious [rɪˈlɪdʒəs]	religiös	noun: **religion** – adj: **religious** (F) réligieux, réligieuse (L) religio *(Glaube)*
	bald [bɔːld]	kahl, glatzköpfig	
	(to) **tell, told, told**	erkennen, feststellen	Can you ~ the difference between these pictures? They're identical twins. I can never ~ who's who.
	embarrassing [ɪmˈbærəsɪŋ]	peinlich	My mother saw us at the café. – How ~. verb: (to) **embarrass** sb. (jn. in Verlegenheit bringen) – adj: **embarrassing**
p. 61	(to) **fold** [fəʊld]	falten	Take a sheet of paper and ~ it in two. (… und falte es in der Mitte zusammen)
	(to) **match** [mætʃ]	zusammenpassen	Some people say that blue and green don't ~. Grandma was wearing a grey coat with a **~ing** hat.
	fly [flaɪ]	Fliege	a **fly** 
	web [web]	(Spinnen-)Netz	
	(to) **hand** sth. **over** [ˌhænd_ˈəʊvə]	etwas übergeben, aushändigen	What's that behind your back? **Hand** it ~ immediately.
	heat [hiːt]	Hitze, Wärme	adjs: **hot** ◄► **cold** nouns: **heat** ◄► **cold**
	sweat [swet]	Schweiß	! pronunciation: **sweat** [swet]
	neither … nor … [ˈnaɪðə … nɔː, ˈniːðə … nɔː]	weder … noch …	**Neither** Jake ~ Gareth were invited to the party. Only Philip was invited.
	(to) **cheat** [tʃiːt]	schummeln, mogeln; betrügen	Jo failed the test because our teacher found she **~ed**.

	since [sɪns]	da, weil	I won't eat ~ we're going to a restaurant later. ❗ **since** = **1.** seit; **2.** da, weil
	decent ['diːsnt]	anständig	Your skirt is much too short. It's not ~. Ⓛ decens ❗ stress: **decent** ['diːsnt]
	(to) **matter** ['mætə]	von Bedeutung sein, wichtig sein	Do you want to see change in our school? Tell us what you think! Your opinion ~**s**.
	water pipe ['wɔːtə paɪp]	Wasserleitung, Wasserrohr	a **burst water pipe** 
	(to) **burst, burst, burst** [bɜːst]	platzen	
p. 62	**talent** ['tælənt]	Talent	❗ stress: **talent** ['tælənt] Ⓕ le talent
	intelligence [ɪn'telɪdʒəns]	Intelligenz	❗ noun: **intelligence** [ɪn'telɪdʒəns] – adj: **intelligent** [ɪn'telɪdʒənt] Ⓕ l'intelligence *(f)* – intelligent, e Ⓛ intellegere *(begreifen)*
	gift [gɪft]	Geschenk; Gabe	She has a ~ for understanding things very quickly.
	Santa ['sæntə] *(kurz für:* **Santa Claus** ['sæntə klɔːz])	der Weihnachtsmann	Ⓛ sanctus, -a, -um *(heilig)*
	(to) **pick** [pɪk]	wählen, auswählen, aussuchen	(to) choose
	stoplight ['stɒplaɪt] *(AE)*	Ampel	= *BE* traffic light(s)
	character ['kærəktə]	Charakter	❗ stress: **character** ['kærəktə] Ⓕ le caractère
	brave [breɪv]	mutig, tapfer	She was very ~: she jumped into the river and saved the little dog's life. ❗ • ein **mutiges** Kind = a **brave** child • ein **braves** Kind = a **well-behaved** child / a **good** child
	competitive [kəm'petətɪv]	leistungsorientiert, ehrgeizig; Wettkampf-, Leistungs-	Steve is very ~ and always wants to win. This isn't a ~ race – it's just for fun.
	(to) **be crazy about** sth./sb.	verrückt nach etwas/jm. sein	Dad and his friends **are** ~ **about** old motorbikes. They spend an awful lot of money on them.
	loyal ['lɔɪəl]	loyal, treu ergeben	❗ stress: **loyal** ['lɔɪəl] Ⓕ loyal, e
p. 63	**emotion** [ɪ'məʊʃn]	Gefühl, Emotion	❗ stress: **emotion** [ɪ'məʊʃn] Ⓕ l'émotion *(f)*
	sense of humour [ˌsens‿əv 'hjuːmə]	(Sinn für) Humor	*English:* He has **a good sense of humour** / **no sense of humour.** *German:* Er hat **Humor** / **keinen Humor**.
	quality ['kwɒləti]	Eigenschaft, Qualität	What **qualities** does a good teacher need? ❗ stress: **quality** ['kwɒləti] Ⓕ la qualité Ⓛ qualis *(wie beschaffen?)*
	particular [pə'tɪkjələ]	bestimmte(r, s), spezielle(r, s)	Are you looking for a ~ kind of bike? Ⓕ particulier, particulière
	generous ['dʒenərəs]	großzügig	You got a pony? That's very ~ of your parents. Ⓕ généreux, généreuse Ⓛ generosus *(edelmutig)*
	hard-working [ˌhɑːd'wɜːkɪŋ]	fleißig	
	lazy ['leɪzi]	faul	**hard-working** ◄► **lazy**
	mean [miːn]	gemein	Don't be so ~ to your brother. It's not fair.

[b] boat · [p] pool · [d] dad · [t] ten · [g] good · [k] cat · [m] mum · [n] no · [ŋ] song · [l] hello · [r] red · [w] we · [j] you

	tolerant (of) ['tɒlərənt]	tolerant (gegenüber)	I'm very ~ **of** others even if I don't agree with them. ! stress: **tolerant** ['tɒlərənt] (F) tolérant, e (L) tolerare *(ertragen)*
	suffix ['sʌfɪks]	Suffix, Nachsilbe	**prefix** (Vorsilbe) ◄► **suffix** (Nachsilbe) (F) le préfixe ◄► le suffixe
	opposite ['ɒpəzɪt]	entgegengesetzt	That's the wrong way. Let's go in the ~ direction. (L) opponere *(entgegenstellen)*
	(to) **recognize** ['rekəgnaɪz]	erkennen	Oh, it's you! I didn't ~ you: have you been to the hairdresser's? (L) recognoscere *(wiedererkennen)*
p. 64	**prediction** [prɪ'dɪkʃn]	Vorhersage, Voraussage	What is your ~ for the *Bundesliga* this year? Who will win? (L) praedicere *(vorhersagen)*
	category ['kætəgəri]	Kategorie	! stress: **category** ['kætəgəri] (F) la catégorie
	canoeing [kə'nuːɪŋ]	Kanufahren; Kanusport	**canoe**  She's about to go **canoeing**.
	poetry ['pəʊətri]	Lyrik, Dichtung, Poesie	(L) poeta *(Dichter)*

Part B

p. 66	**experiment** [ɪk'sperɪmənt]	Experiment	! stress: **experiment** [ɪk'sperɪmənt] (L) experiri *(erproben)*
	virus ['vaɪrəs], *pl* **viruses** ['vaɪrəsɪz]	Virus	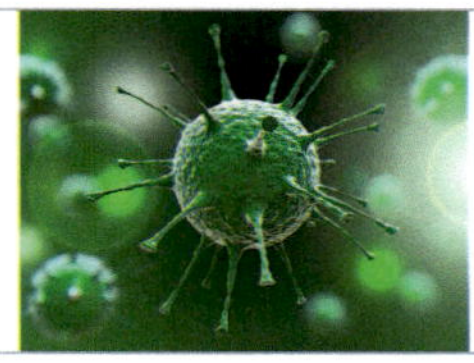 
	(to) **diagnose** ['daɪəgnəʊz]	diagnostizieren	Doctors can't treat a patient until they have **~d** the illness.
	the sooner …, the better …	je eher …, desto besser …	

German "je …, desto …"

The sooner you start, **the sooner** you'll be finished.	Je eher du anfängst, desto eher bist du fertig.
The more you practise, **the better** you'll become.	Je mehr du übst, desto besser wirst du.
The later the evening, **the more beautiful** the guests.	Je später der Abend, desto schöner die Gäste.

refrigeration [rɪˌfrɪdʒə'reɪʃn]	Kühlung	Without ~, meat starts to smell after a few hours. (L) frigidus *(kalt)*
lab [læb] *(kurz für:* **laboratory** [lə'bɒrətri])	Labor	(F) le laboratoire (L) laborare *(arbeiten)*
company ['kʌmpəni]	Firma	My uncle works for an oil ~ in Scotland.
(to) **refuse (to do** sth.) [rɪ'fjuːz]	sich weigern (, etwas zu tun); ablehnen	He **~d** to help his brother although he had problems. She was very proud and **~d** her friend's help. (F) refuser
chemical ['kemɪkl]	Chemikalie	

[f] father · [v] river · [s] sister · [z] please · [ʃ] shop · [ʒ] television · [tʃ] teacher · [dʒ] Germany · [θ] thanks · [ð] this · [h] here

in time (for)	rechtzeitig (zu/für)	If we hurry up, we might get home **in ~ for** the news.
passion ['pæʃn]	Leidenschaft	Music isn't just my hobby - it's my ~! Ⓕ la passion Ⓛ pati *(leiden)*
(to) **develop** [dɪ'veləp]	entwickeln; sich entwickeln	Our company **~s** and sells software. Ⓕ développer The village **~ed** into a town in only ten years.
current ['kʌrənt]	aktuelle(r, s), gegenwärtige(r, s)	This song is the ~ number 1 in the USA. Ⓛ currere *(laufen)*
(to) **submit** sth. **(to)** [səb'mɪt]	etwas einreichen (bei)	Please ~ your report by the end of the week.
fair [feə]	Ausstellung, Messe	
(to) **include** [ɪn'klu:d]	einschließen; beinhalten	Does the trip ~ a tour of the Tower of London? Our group also **~d** three children. (= Zu unserer Gruppe gehörten auch drei Kinder.) Ⓕ inclure Ⓛ includere *(einschließen)*
medicine ['medsn, 'medɪsn]	Medizin; Arznei	! stress: **<u>me</u>dicine** ['medsn, 'medɪsn] Ⓕ la médecine Ⓛ medicina *(Heilkunst, -mittel)*
such as ['sʌtʃ‿əz]	wie etwa	I like ball sports **such** ~ football, basketball or hockey. (= … like football, basketball or hockey)
motivation [ˌməʊtɪ'veɪʃn]	Motivation, Beweggrund	I need to finish my homework but don't feel any ~. Ⓕ la motivation Ⓛ movere *(bewegen)*
p. 67 **mouse** [maʊs], *pl* **mice** [maɪs]	Maus	 a **mouse** Ⓛ mus
evolution [ˌi:və'lu:ʃn]	Evolution	the way life-forms change over generations Ⓕ l'évolution *(f)*
(to) **tackle** sth. ['tækl]	etwas in Angriff nehmen	The government must ~ the problem of racism.
biology [baɪ'ɒlədʒi]	Biologie	! stress: **bi<u>o</u>logy** [baɪ'ɒlədʒi] Ⓕ la biologie
equal ['i:kwəl]	gleich	Do men and women really have ~ rights? Ⓛ aequus, -a, -um *(gleich)*
fur [fɜ:]	Fell; Pelz	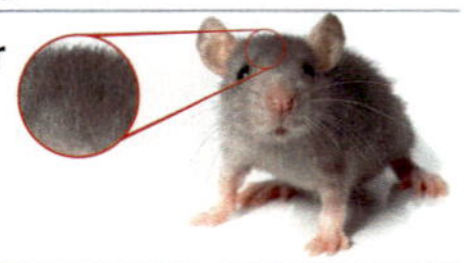
thick [θɪk]	dick	! *German* **dick** = **1. fat** *(person, animal)* **2. thick** *(book, pullover, sauce, skin, wall, …)*
blind alley [ˌblaɪnd‿'æli]	Sackgasse, Irrweg	**blind** = blind • **alley** = Gasse
(to) **have** sth. **done**	etwas machen *(erledigen)* lassen	Your hair looks nice. Did you cut it yourself or did you ~ **it cut**? There's something wrong with our car. We need to ~ **it checked**.
in the long term [tɜ:m]	langfristig, auf lange Sicht	Is buying expensive things cheaper **in the long** ~?
understanding [ˌʌndə'stændɪŋ]	Verständnis	My brother has a good ~ of computers but isn't very good at languages.
principle ['prɪnsəpl]	Prinzip	! stress: **<u>prin</u>ciple** ['prɪnsəpl] Ⓕ le principe
they **do eat** more white mice	sie fressen wirklich mehr weiße Mäuse	

"do/does/did" in positive statements

In bejahten Aussagesätzen im *simple present* und *simple past* kannst du ***do/does/did*** **+ Infinitiv** verwenden, um dem folgenden Verb besonderen Nachdruck zu verleihen. Das Hilfsverb ***do/does/did*** trägt in diesen Fällen die Hauptbetonung.

I **do like** that dress. It **does look** good on you.	Das Kleid gefällt mir wirklich gut. Es steht dir echt gut.
Why don't you help me? You **did promise.**	... Du hast es doch versprochen.
Maybe we're early. – But they **did say** eight o'clock.	... Aber sie haben wirklich acht Uhr gesagt.

	(to) **succeed (in** sth.**)** [sək'si:d]	erfolgreich sein, Erfolg haben (mit etwas, bei etwas)	(to) be successful (at sth.) If you want to ~ in life, you have to make mistakes.
p. 68	(to) **announce** [ə'naʊns]	bekanntgeben, verkünden	The winner will be **~d** tomorrow. verb: (to) **announce** – noun: **announcement** (F) annoncer (L) annuntiare
	spontaneous [spɒn'teɪniəs]	spontan	He hadn't planned to go; it was a ~ decision.
	pirate ['paɪrət]	Pirat/in	! pronunciation: **pirate** ['paɪrət] (F) le/la pirate
p. 69	(to) **focus (on** sth.**)** ['fəʊkəs]	sich (auf etwas) konzentrieren	The text about mice **~ed** on evolution.
p. 70	(to) **search** sth. **for** sth. [sɜ:tʃ]	etwas nach etwas durchsuchen	The police **~ed** the whole flat **for** clues, but they couldn't find any.
	(to) **save** [seɪv]	speichern, sichern *(Daten)*	! **save** = **1.** retten – She **saved** the dog's life. **2.** sparen – **Save** money. Shop at *Cheapster.* **3.** speichern, sichern – I **save** my work every five minutes.
	(to) **limit** sth. **(to)** ['lɪmɪt]	etwas beschränken, begrenzen (auf); etwas einschränken	The audience was **~ed to** 600 people. (F) limiter verb: (to) **limit** – noun: **limit** (L) limes *m (Grenzlinie)*
	carefully ['keəfəli]	sorgfältig, aufmerksam	! **carefully** = **1.** vorsichtig – Drive **carefully**. **2.** sorgfältig, aufmerksam – Listen **carefully**. / Read the description **carefully**.
	(to) **produce** [prə'dju:s]	produzieren, erzeugen, herstellen	Who **~s** more cheese – France or Germany? (F) produire (L) producere *(hervorbringen)*
	source [sɔ:s]	Quelle	I think a book ist better for research than an online ~. (F) la source
	unless [ən'les]	es sei denn; außer (wenn)	You'll fail the test ~ you work harder. (= ... if you don't work harder)
	(to) **quote** [kwəʊt]	zitieren	verb: (to) **quote** – noun: **quotation, quote**
	quotation marks *(pl)* [kwəʊ'teɪʃn mɑ:ks]	Anführungszeichen, -striche	
p. 71	**gesture** ['dʒestʃə]	Geste, Handbewegung	The most common ~ is probably nodding your head. (F) le geste

Part C

p. 72	**mascot** ['mæskət]	Maskottchen	! stress: **mascot** ['mæskət]
	marathon ['mærəθən]	Marathon	(F) le marathon
	(to) **sew** [səʊ], **sewed** [səʊd], **sewn** [səʊn]	nähen	She's **sewing** a button on. (Knopf) ! pronunciation: **sew** [səʊ]

creative [kri'eɪtɪv]	kreativ	! stress: **creative** [kri'eɪtɪv] (F) créatif, créative (L) creare *(schaffen, hervorbringen)*
(to) **rely on** sb./sth. [rɪ'laɪ]	sich auf jn./etwas verlassen	Can I ~ on you to remember to phone me tomorrow?
(to) **contact** sb. ['kɒntækt]	Kontakt zu jm. aufnehmen, sich bei jm. melden	noun: **contact** – verb: (to) **contact** (F) contacter ! stress: **contact** ['kɒntækt] (L) contingere
(to) **damage** ['dæmɪdʒ]	(be)schädigen, schaden	Smoking **~s** your health. (L) damnum The car had hit a tree. It was badly **~d**. *(Schaden)*
trust [trʌst]	Stiftung	The National **Trust** owns many historical buildings in the UK.
(to) **restore** [rɪ'stɔː]	restaurieren, wiederherstellen	He's **restoring** an old chair. (F) restaurer (L) restituere *(wiederherstellen)* 
applicant ['æplɪkənt]	Bewerber/in	There were over 30 **~s** for the job. (L) applicare
CV (curriculum vitae) [ˌsiː 'vi, kəˌrɪkjələm 'viːtaɪ] *(BE)*	Lebenslauf	At the age of 15, your **CV** is probably not very long.
personal ['pɜːsənl]	persönlich	Could we meet? I need to talk about a ~ problem. (F) personnel, le
statement ['steɪtmənt]	Aussage, Erklärung	**personal statement** = Motivationsschreiben *(bei Bewerbungen)*
candidate ['kændɪdət]	Bewerber/in, Kandidat/in	! stress: **candidate** ['kændɪdət] (F) le candidat, la candidate (L) candidatus
date [deɪt]	Datum	(F) la date (L) dare *(geben)*
reverse [rɪ'vɜːs]	umgekehrte(r, s), entgegengesetzte(r, s)	How quickly can you say the alphabet in ~ order? (L) reverti *(zurückkehren)*
term [tɜːm]	Ausdruck, Begriff	
(to) **proofread** sth. ['pruːfriːd], **proofread, proofread** [-red]	etwas Korrektur lesen	Before you send off your application, have it **proofread** by somebody to make sure there are no mistakes in it.
p. 73 **neighbourhood** ['neɪbəhʊd]	Viertel, Gegend, Umgebung; Nachbarschaft	Do you live in a poor or rich ~?
(to) **increase** [ɪn'kriːs]	erhöhen, steigern, vergrößern; (an)steigen, zunehmen	They have **~d** the price of the book to €20. House prices in London have **~d** again. (L) increscere *(anwachsen)*
knowledge *(no pl)* ['nɒlɪdʒ]	Wissen; Kenntnis(se)	Boris has a great ~ of Latin and Greek. verb: (to) **know** [nəʊ] – noun: **knowledge** ['nɒlɪdʒ]
to date	bis heute, bis jetzt	I think his latest book is his best **to ~**.
secondary school ['sekəndri]	weiterführende Schule	
primary school ['praɪməri]	Grundschule	
qualification [ˌkwɒlɪfɪ'keɪʃn]	Qualifikation	What **~s** do you need for this job? (F) la qualification
felt craft ['felt krɑːft]	Filzen	
completion [kəm'pliːʃn]	Abschluss; Fertigstellung	(L) complere *(anfüllen)*
IT [ˌaɪ 'tiː] **(information technology** [tek'nɒlədʒi]**)**	IT (Informationstechnologie)	
Roman ['rəʊmən]	römisch	(F) romain, e (L) Romanus

[b] **boat** · [p] **pool** · [d] **dad** · [t] **ten** · [g] **good** · [k] **cat** ·
[m] **mum** · [n] **no** · [ŋ] **song** · [l] **hello** · [r] **red** · [w] **we** · [j] **you**

Unit 4 It's up to you

pp. 82/83	**It's up to you.**	Du hast die Wahl. / Du entscheidest.	I don't mind if you go or stay: **it's ~ to you**.
	the Antarctic [æn'tɑːktɪk]	die Antarktis	
	(to) **rise up** [ˌraɪz‿'ʌp], **rose** [rəʊz], **risen** ['rɪzn]	sich erheben	The people **rose** ~ against their government.
	collective [kə'lektɪv]	kollektiv, gemeinschaftlich, vereint	Did you all agree? Was it a ~ decision? (L) colligere *(sammeln)*
	(to) **cycle** ['saɪkl]	Rad fahren, mit dem Rad fahren	 **cyclists** in London
	(to) **bring** sth. **about** [ˌbrɪŋ‿ə'baʊt]	etwas hervorrufen, etwas herbeiführen, etwas bewirken	If we all want to be happy, we must **bring** ~ change.
	initiative [ɪ'nɪʃətɪv]	Initiative, Aktion	! stress: **initiative** [ɪ'nɪʃətɪv] (F) l'initiative *(f)* (L) initium *(Beginn)*
	(to) **sign** [saɪn]	unterschreiben	Fill in the form and ~ it, please. (F) signer
	petition [pə'tɪʃn]	Petition, Eingabe, Unterschriftensammlung	! stress: **petition** [pə'tɪʃn] (F) la pétition (L) petere *(zu erreichen suchen)*
	sit-in ['sɪtɪn]	Sit-in, Sitzstreik	
	march [mɑːtʃ]	Marsch, Demonstration	
	(to) **go on strike** [straɪk]	streiken, in den Streik treten	
	(to) **boycott** sth. ['bɔɪkɒt]	etwas boykottieren	! stress: **boycott** ['bɔɪkɒt]
	product ['prɒdʌkt]	Produkt	! verb: (to) **produce** [prə'djuːs] – noun: **product** ['prɒdʌkt] (L) producere (F) le produit

Part A

p. 84	**the United Nations (UN)** [juˌnaɪtɪd 'neɪʃnz]	die Vereinten Nationen	
	conference ['kɒnfrəns]	Konferenz, Kongress	! stress: **conference** ['kɒnfrəns] (F) la conférence (L) conferre *(zusammentragen)*
	(to) **slow** sth. **down**	etwas verlangsamen	(to) **speed up** ◄► (to) **slow down**
	installation [ˌɪnstə'leɪʃn]	Installation	The ~ of new software can take hours.
	(to) **create** [kri'eɪt]	schaffen, erschaffen, kreieren	(F) créer (L) creare
	(to) **project** sth. **(on, onto)** [prə'dʒekt]	etwas projizieren (auf/an)	 She's about to **project** something **onto** the classroom wall. ! verb: (to) **project** [prə'dʒekt] – noun: **project** ['prɒdʒekt] (F) projeter (L) proicere *(vorwerfen)*
p. 85	**all of a sudden** ['sʌdn]	plötzlich	= suddenly
p. 86	**past** [pɑːst]	vergangene(r, s); letzte(r, s)	There were no smartphones in the ~ century. I haven't seen him in the ~ three days.

[f] father · [v] river · [s] sister · [z] please · [ʃ] shop · [ʒ] television · [tʃ] teacher · [dʒ] Germany · [θ] thanks · [ð] this · [h] here

narrative ['nærətɪv]	Erzähl-	• **the narrative tenses** – die Erzähltempora • **first-person narrative** – Ich-Erzählung • **narrator** [nə'reɪtə] – Erzähler/in • **first-person narrator** – Ich-Erzähler/in
in progress ['prəʊgres]	im Gange, im Verlauf	You can't go in, there's a conference **in** ~. (L) progredi *(voranschreiten)*
sight [saɪt]	Anblick	
by the time	wenn, bis	I'll have dinner ready **by the** ~ you get back.
(to) **take a break**	eine Pause machen	We've worked long enough now. Let's **take a** ~.
p. 87 (to) **interpret** sth. [ɪn'tɜːprɪt]	etwas interpretieren, deuten	! stress: **in<u>ter</u>pret** [ɪn'tɜːprɪt] (L) interpres *(Vermittler, Dolmetscher)*
(to) **contain** [kən'teɪn]	enthalten	(F) contenir (L) continere *(zusammenhalten)*
concerned (about) [kən'sɜːnd]	besorgt (über/um)	I'm very ~ **about** Jake. He never looks happy. Everyone should feel ~ **about** global warming.
(to) **depict** sth. [dɪ'pɪkt] *(fml)*	etwas darstellen, abbilden, zeigen	The painting **~s** the artist's mother. (L) pingere *(malen)*
(to) **comment** ['kɒment]	bemerken, sagen; sich äußern, einen Kommentar abgeben	When he saw his mum's new car, he just **~ed** "Nice!". The President refused to ~ on the news. (F) commenter
(to) **analyse** ['ænəlaɪz]	analysieren	! stress: **<u>a</u>nalyse** ['ænəlaɪz]
environmental [ɪnˌvaɪrən'mentl]	Umwelt-	noun: **environment** – adj: **environmental**
political [pə'lɪtɪkl]	politisch	noun: **politics** ['pɒlətɪks] – adj: **political** [pə'lɪtɪkl] (F) politique
(to) **focus on** sth. ['fəʊkəs]	den Blick/die Aufmerksamkeit auf etwas lenken; auf etwas fokussieren	! (to) **focus on** = **1.** sich konzentrieren auf; **2.** den Blick/die Aufmerksamkeit lenken auf
cactus ['kæktəs], *pl* **cactuses** ['kæktəsɪz] *or* **cacti** ['kæktaɪ]	Kaktus	
effective [ɪ'fektɪv]	effektiv, wirkungsvoll	! stress: **ef<u>fec</u>tive** [ɪ'fektɪv] noun: **effect** ((Aus-)Wirkung) – adj: **effective** (L) efficere *(bewirken)*
(to) **make** sb. **do** sth.	jn. dazu bringen, etwas zu tun; jn. zwingen, etwas zu tun	Sad films always ~ me **cry**. I didn't want to go to Uncle Adam's birthday party, but my parents **made** me **go**.

(to) make sb. do sth. – (to) let sb. do sth.

(to) **<u>make</u> sb. do sth.** = jn. dazu bringen/jn. zwingen, etwas zu tun	Mum tried to **make me talk** about my feelings.
(to) **<u>let</u> sb. do sth.** = jn. etwas tun lassen; jm. erlauben, etwas zu tun; zulassen, dass jemand etwas tut	Our teacher **lets us talk** to our neighbours in class.

(to) **come across**	verstanden werden; ankommen, „rüberkommen" *(Botschaft)*	Maybe you meant to be friendly, but the message didn't **come** ~. He doesn't **come** ~ as a very nice person.

Part B

p. 88	(to) **take a stand (on** sth.**)**	Stellung beziehen (zu etwas); ein Zeichen setzen	I'm **taking a** ~ **on** pollution by using cotton bags.
	threat [θret]	Drohung, Bedrohung, Androhung	He said he would beat me up, but it was just an empty ~.
	anonymous [ə'nɒnɪməs]	anonym	! stress: **anonymous** [ə'nɒnɪməs] (F) anonyme
	prime minister [ˌpraɪm 'mɪnɪstə]	Premierminister/in	The British **prime** ~ lives at 10 Downing Street. (F) le premier ministre/la première ministre
	ministry ['mɪnɪstri]	Ministerium	! stress: **ministry** ['mɪnɪstri] (F) le ministère
	slaughter ['slɔːtə]	Schlachtung; Abschlachten	Pigs are often taken to ~ by lorry. Ten thousand soldiers died in the ~.
	anger ['æŋgə]	Wut, Zorn	adj: **angry** – noun: **anger**
	off the coast	vor der Küste	The ship sank two miles ~ **the coast** of Devon.
	cove [kəʊv]	(kleine) Bucht	
	either … or … ['aɪðə], ['iːðə]	entweder … oder …	It's up to you: **either** you stay ~ you leave now.
	alcohol ['ælkəhɒl]	Alkohol	(F) l'alcool *(m)*
	licence *(BE)*, **license** *(AE)* ['laɪsns]	Lizenz, Genehmigung	! stress: **licence** ['laɪsns] (L) licentia *(Erlaubnis)*
	campaign [kæm'peɪn]	Kampagne	• **a campaign for/against** eine Kampagne für/gegen • (to) **campaign for/against** sich einsetzen, kämpfen für/gegen • **campaigner** [kæm'peɪnə] Aktivist/in
	fine [faɪn]	Geldstrafe	My mum got a ~ for driving through a red light.
	owner ['əʊnə]	Besitzer/in, Eigentümer/in	
	meeting ['miːtɪŋ]	Besprechung, Versammlung, Treffen	The drama club **~s** take place every Monday evening.
	councillor ['kaʊnsələ]	Ratsmitglied, (Stadt-, Gemeinde-)Rat/Rätin	(L) concilium *(Versammlung)*
	(to) **deny** [dɪ'naɪ]	bestreiten, abstreiten; leugnen	I don't ~ loving her. But I also don't ~ that she hates me.
	(to) **pass** [pɑːs]	verabschieden, genehmigen *(Gesetz, Antrag)*	The new fishing law will probably be **~ed** tomorrow.

(to) pass

1. *(time)* (to) **pass**	vergehen, vorübergehen	Time **passes** quickly when you're on holiday.
2. (to) **pass sth./sb.**	an etwas/jm. vorbeigehen/-fahren	He **passed us** on his way to the bar, but he didn't say hello.
3. (to) **pass (the ball)**	(den Ball) abspielen	Draxler **passed** to Kimmich, who scored the third goal.
4. (to) **pass a test/an exam**	einen Test/eine Prüfung bestehen	I **passed the exam** and got an "A".
5. (to) **pass a law**	ein Gesetz verabschieden	The new fishing law will probably be **passed** tomorrow.
6. (to) **pass sth. around**	etwas herumgeben, -reichen	These are our holiday photos. I'll **pass them around**.

	(to) **risk** [rɪsk]	riskieren; aufs Spiel setzen	If you drive so fast, you ~ killing yourself. (F) risquer
p. 89	(to) **buy into** sth. *(infml)*	etwas glauben, an etwas glauben	I can't **buy** ~ the idea that old people are boring.
	myth [mɪθ]	Mythos	Is there more milk in white chocolate than in dark chocolate? Or is that just a ~? (F) le mythe

[f] **f**ather · [v] **r**iver · [s] **s**ister · [z] plea**s**e · [ʃ] **sh**op · [ʒ] televi**s**ion · [tʃ] tea**ch**er · [dʒ] **G**ermany · [θ] **th**anks · [ð] **th**is · [h] **h**ere

gender ['dʒendə]	Geschlecht *(als soziales Merkmal)*	There are ~ differences, of course, but men and women should still be equal.
equality [i'kwɒləti]	Gleichheit, Gleichberechtigung	adj: **equal** ['i:kwəl] – noun: **equality** [i'kwɒləti]
reality [ri'æləti]	Realität, Wirklichkeit	! stress: **reality** [ri'æləti] (F) la réalité adj: **real** ['ri:əl] – noun: **reality**
pay [peɪ]	Bezahlung, Lohn	verb: (to) **pay (for)** – noun: **pay**
safety ['seɪfti]	Sicherheit	adj: **safe** – noun: **safety**
accident ['æksɪdənt]	Unfall	There's been an ~. Can someone call the police, please? (F) l'accident *(m)* (L) accidere *(hinfallen; geschehen)*
survey ['sɜ:veɪ]	Umfrage, Untersuchung	We're doing a ~ on pocket money in class.
MP [ˌem'pi:] **(= Member of Parliament)**	Parlamentsmitglied, Abgeordnete(r)	*in Britain:* **MP** (Member of Parliament) *in Germany:* **MdB** (Mitglied des Deutschen Bundestags)
(to) **take action**	etwas unternehmen, tätig werden	We need to ~ **action** and solve this problem.
(to) **admit** [əd'mɪt]	zugeben, (ein)gestehen	After a long discussion I had to ~ that I was wrong. Do you ~ stealing the money? (to) **admit** sth. ◄► (to) **deny** sth. (L) admittere *(zulassen)*
(to) **be to**	*(tun)* werden; sollen	

(to) be to do sth.

Mit **(to) be to + Infinitiv** kann man …

- ausdrücken, dass etwas **offiziell vereinbart** ist:
  The president **is to open** the museum on May 3rd. — Die Präsidentin **wird** das Museum am 3. Mai **eröffnen**.
- **Anweisungen** geben (bzw. die Anweisungen anderer weitergeben):
  OK, you can go to that party. But you**'re to be** back by ten. — … Aber ihr **müsst** um zehn zurück **sein**.
  Dad said we **were to be** back by ten. — Dad hat gesagt, wir **sollen** um zehn zurück **sein**.

solution (to) [sə'lu:ʃn]	Lösung (für) *(Problem; Aufgabe)*	*English:* **the solution to** this problem *German:* **die Lösung für** dieses Problem / **die** Lösung dieses Problems (F) la solution (L) solvere *(lösen)*
certainly ['sɜ:tnli]	sicher(lich), auf jeden Fall	This is a big problem, but we'll ~ find a solution. (F) certainement (L) certus, -a, -um *(sicher)*
(to) **consider** sth. [kən'sɪdə]	etwas bedenken, berücksichtigen; sich mit etwas befassen	Before you start, ~ the following questions: … (L) considerare *(überlegen)*
(to) **consider doing** sth.	erwägen, etwas zu tun; in Betracht ziehen, etwas zu tun	Have you **~ed** applying to a foreign university?
p. 90 **space** [speɪs]	Platz, Raum	I need new shelves. There's no ~ for my books! (F) l'espace *(m)* (L) spatium *(Raum, Zwischenraum)*
(to) **take up** space/time	Raum/Zeit einnehmen, beanspruchen	Your books just ~ **up** too much space. Where can I put my DVDs?
helmet ['helmɪt]	Helm	Never ride your bike without a ~. You risk hurting your head if you have an accident.
(to) **be happy to do** sth.	gern etwas tun; (gern) bereit sein, etwas zu tun	I'd **be** ~ **to** help you if you can't do it alone.

[b] **boat** · [p] **pool** · [d] **dad** · [t] **ten** · [g] **good** · [k] **cat** ·
[m] **mum** · [n] **no** · [ŋ] **song** · [l] **hello** · [r] **red** · [w] **we** · [j] **you**

p. 91	(to) **weaken** ['wi:kən]	schwächen	
	weak [wi:k]	schwach	**weak** ◄► **strong**
	pain [peɪn]	Schmerz(en)	*English:* (to) **be in pain** *German:* **Schmerzen haben**
	(to) **raise your voice** [reɪz]	seine Stimme erheben	Ⓛ vox *(Stimme)*

(to) raise

1. (to) **raise money**	Geld sammeln	The school tried to **raise money** for Children in Need.
2. (to) **raise your voice**	seine Stimme erheben	Don't you **raise your voice** at me!
3. (to) **raise an issue/ a question**	ein Thema zur Sprache bringen; eine Frage aufwerfen/vorbringen	He **raised the** difficult **issue** of the money he had lent us.
4. (to) **raise children**	Kinder auf-/großziehen	I was born and **raised** in England.
5. (to) **raise chicken**	Hühner züchten, halten	Mr Brown **raises** chicken on his farm in Devon.

p. 92	(to) **feel like** sth. / (to) **feel like doing** sth.	Lust auf etwas haben / Lust haben, etwas zu tun	Does anyone **feel** ~ an ice cream? (= ... want an ice cream?) It was so hot, I **felt** ~ **going** for a swim.
	(to) **regret** sth. / (to) **regret doing** sth. [rɪ'gret]	etwas bedauern, bereuen / bedauern, bereuen, etwas getan zu haben	(to) wish that you hadn't done something Jake hates his new bike. He **~s buying** it. (Er bereut, es gekauft zu haben / ..., dass er es gekauft hat.) Ⓕ regretter
	not ... anywhere ['eniweə]	nirgendwo; nirgendwohin	**anywhere** • We did**n't** go **anywhere** this summer. (nirgendwohin) • Did you go **anywhere** last night**?** (irgendwohin?) • I wouldn't want to live **anywhere else**. (irgendwo anders; irgendwo sonst)
	(to) **protest** sth. [prə'test]	gegen etwas protestieren	*English:* (to) **protest against sth.** *or* (to) **protest sth.** *German:* **gegen etwas protestieren** Ⓕ protester (contre)
	after all [ˌɑ:ftər_'ɔ:l]	(schließlich) doch	I know him very well. **After** ~, we've been friends for ten years.
p. 93	**involvement (in)** [ɪn'vɒlvmənt]	Engagement (für); Beteiligung (an)	Ⓛ involvere *(hineinwickeln)*

involvement

involvement	His **involvement** in the peace movement made him famous.	Engagement (für); Beteiligung (an)
(to) **get involved (in)**	She **got involved in** politics because she wanted to change things.	sich engagieren (für, bei); sich beteiligen (an)
(to) **be involved (in)**	We **have been involved in** our local church for 7 years.	beteiligt sein (an); etwas zu tun haben (mit)

senator ['senətə]	Senator/in	
activist ['æktɪvɪst]	Aktivist/in	**!** stress: **<u>ac</u>tivist** ['æktɪvɪst] Ⓕ l'activiste *(m, f)*
activism ['æktɪvɪzəm]	Aktivismus	**<u>ac</u>tivism** ['æktɪvɪzəm] Ⓛ agere *(tun)*
immigration [ˌɪmɪ'greɪʃn]	Einwanderung	Ⓕ l'immigration *(f)* Ⓛ immigrare *(einwandern)*
citizen ['sɪtɪzn]	(Staats-)Bürger/in	Mr Evans has applied to become a German ~. Ⓕ le citoyen, la citoyenne

[f] **f**ather · [v] **r**iver · [s] **s**ister · [z] plea**s**e · [ʃ] **sh**op · [ʒ] televi**s**ion · [tʃ] tea**ch**er · [dʒ] **G**ermany · [θ] **th**anks · [ð] **th**is · [h] **h**ere

	congress ['kɒŋgres]	Kongress	! stress: **congress** ['kɒŋgres] (F) le congrès (L) congredi *(zusammenkommen)*
	democracy [dɪ'mɒkrəsi]	Demokratie	! stress: **democracy** [dɪ'mɒkrəsi] (F) la démocratie
	(to) **demonstrate (for/ against)** ['demənstreɪt]	(für/gegen etwas) demonstrieren	 They're **demonstrating against** war. verb: (to) **demonstrate** ['demənstreɪt] – noun: **demonstration** [ˌdemən'streɪʃn]
	(to) **discriminate against** sb. [dɪ'skrɪmɪneɪt]	jn. diskriminieren, jn. benachteiligen	*English:* (to) **discriminate against sb.** *German:* **jn. diskriminieren** verb: (to) **discriminate against** [dɪ'skrɪmɪneɪt] – noun: **discrimination (against)** [dɪˌskrɪmɪ'neɪʃn]

Part C

p. 96	(to) **be based on** sth. [beɪst]	auf etwas basieren	(F) être basé(e) sur qc
	(to) **escape** sth. [ɪ'skeɪp]	etwas entfliehen, entkommen	He **~d** punishment because he was only 13.
	violence ['vaɪələns]	Gewalt; Gewalttätigkeit	My father says there's too much ~ on TV. (F) la violence (L) violentia
	dawn [dɔːn]	(Morgen-)Dämmerung	The birds wake up and start singing at ~.
	(to) **gather** ['gæðə]	sich versammeln	The head teacher asked all students to ~ in the gym.
	horrible ['hɒrəbl]	grauenhaft, entsetzlich	There's been another ~ accident on the motorway. (F) horrible (L) horribilis *(schrecklich)*
	(to) **struggle** ['strʌgl]	kämpfen, sich wehren	verb: (to) **struggle** – noun: **struggle** (Kampf)
	pyjamas *(pl)* [pə'dʒɑːməz]	Schlafanzug	! Wie die Wörter **trousers, jeans, shorts** ist auch **pyjamas** ein Plural-Wort. Vergleiche: *English:* Where **are** my **pyjamas**? *German:* Wo **ist** …?  a pair of **pyjamas**
	exam [ɪg'zæm]	Prüfung	*English:* (to) **take an exam** *German:* **eine Prüfung ablegen**
	line [laɪn]	(Telefon-)Leitung	(L) linea *(Schnur; Strich)*
	appeal [ə'piːl]	Berufung, Revision	After the ~, he had to go to prison for only a year.
p. 97	**demand (for)** [dɪ'mɑːnd]	Forderung (nach)	a very strong request: **~s** for money
	the Home Office ['həʊm‿ɒfɪs] *(BE)*	das Innenministerium *(in Großbritannien)*	
	department [dɪ'pɑːtmənt]	Abteilung; Fachbereich	Which ~ do you work in? – The production ~.
	playground ['pleɪgraʊnd]	Spielplatz; Schulhof	a **playground** 
	riot ['raɪət]	Aufruhr, Aufstand	The peaceful march soon became a ~.
	civil war [ˌsɪvl 'wɔː]	Bürgerkrieg	(L) civis *m (Bürger)*
	minority [maɪ'nɒrəti]	Minderheit	There are 18 girls and 10 boys in my class. The boys are in the ~. (F) la minorité

[b] **boat** · [p] **pool** · [d] **dad** · [t] **ten** · [g] **good** · [k] **cat** · [m] **mum** · [n] **no** · [ŋ] **song** · [l] **hello** · [r] **red** · [w] **we** · [j] **you**

	(to) **persuade** [pə'sweɪd]	überreden	I didn't want to go at first, but Paul **~d** me that it would be fun. (F) persuader (L) persuadere
	(to) **take notice (of** sth.**)** ['nəʊtɪs]	auf etwas aufmerksam werden, etwas zur Kenntnis nehmen	(L) notare *(bemerken)*
	attention [ə'tenʃn]	Aufmerksamkeit	(F) l'attention *(f)* (L) attentus, -a, -um *(aufmerksam)*

attention

(to) **draw attention to** sth.	How can we **draw attention to** the slaughter of dolphins in Japanese waters? May I **draw your attention to** a few mistakes?	auf etwas aufmerksam machen; die Aufmerksamkeit auf etwas lenken
(to) **attract/catch/grab sb.'s attention**	It was his smile that first **attracted my attention**. He shouted to **grab/catch her attention.**	jemandes Aufmerksamkeit erregen; jemandes Aufmerksamkeit gewinnen
(to) **pay attention (to)**	Stop talking now and **pay attention**. You never **pay attention to** what I'm saying.	aufmerksam sein, aufpassen; zuhören, Beachtung schenken

	case [keɪs]	Fall	"This will be a very difficult ~," the police officer said. (F) le cas (L) casus
	(to) **broadcast, broadcast, broadcast** ['brɔːdkɑːst]	senden, ausstrahlen, übertragen *(Rundfunk, Fernsehen)*	CNN started **~ing** in 1980. *Mr Bean* was first ~ in 1990.
p. 98	**use** [juːs]	Gebrauch, Verwendung; Nutzen	! pronunciation: (to) **use** *(verb)* [juːz] **use** *(noun)* [juːs] (L) usus **use** *(noun)* = **1.** Gebrauch, Verwendung – the **use** of dictionaries **2.** Nutzen – What **use** is Latin today?
	loads (of) [ləʊdz] *(infml)*	eine Menge	= lots of
	though [ðəʊ]	aber; allerdings; jedoch	She was born in France. She isn't French ~. (= … She isn't French, however.) ! Das Adverb **though** steht am Satzende, anders als die deutschen Entsprechungen.
	ability [ə'bɪlɪti]	Fähigkeit, Können	Jonny shows great scientific ~.
	nomadic people [nə'mædɪk]	Nomadenvolk	
	victim ['vɪktɪm]	Opfer	No one should be a ~ of bullying. (F) la victime
	persecution [ˌpɜːsɪ'kjuːʃn]	Verfolgung *(aus religiösen, ethnischen, weltanschaulichen Gründen)*	The ~ of African Americans is still a problem. (F) la persécution (L) persequi *(verfolgen)*
	attempt [ə'tempt]	Versuch	His third ~ was successful. (L) temptare *(versuchen)*
	(to) **forbid** [fə'bɪd], **forbade** [fə'bæd, fə'beɪd], **forbidden** [fə'bɪdn]	verbieten	Smoking in pubs was **forbidden** by the UK government in 2007.
	the Holocaust ['hɒləkɔːst]	der Holocaust *(Massenmord an den Juden in der Zeit des Nationalsozialismus)*	
	widespread ['waɪdspred]	weitverbreitete(r, s)	There is ~ support for this idea in the UK.
p. 100	**intention** [ɪn'tenʃn]	Absicht, Intention	! stress: **in<u>ten</u>tion** [ɪn'tenʃn] (F) l'intention *(f)* (L) intendere *(beabsichtigen)*
p. 101	(to) **refine** [rɪ'faɪn]	verfeinern, verbessern	Try to ~ your search if you can't find what you're looking for.

[f] **f**ather · [v] **r**iver · [s] **s**ister · [z] plea**s**e · [ʃ] **sh**op · [ʒ] televi**s**ion · [tʃ] tea**ch**er · [dʒ] **G**ermany · [θ] **th**anks · [ð] **th**is · [h] **h**ere

(to) **summarize** [ˈsʌməraɪz]	zusammenfassen	Can you ~ the main points of the film?
summary [ˈsʌməri]	Zusammenfassung	What happens in the film? Give me a quick ~.
proof (of) *(no pl)* [pruːf]	Beweis(e) (für)	If you want me to believe you, you need to show me ~. (F) la preuve (L) probare *(prüfen)*
corn *(no pl)* [kɔːn]	*AE:* Mais; *BE:* Korn, Getreide	
crop [krɒp]	(Feld-)Frucht); Ernte	What kinds of **~s** do you grow on this farm?
acre [ˈeɪkə]	*Flächenmaß (= 0,405 Hektar)*	
recently [ˈriːsntli]	vor Kurzem, neulich; in letzter Zeit	I met my old class teacher in London ~. There have been a lot of accidents in our street ~. (F) récemment (L) recens *(frisch, neu)*
shocking [ˈʃɒkɪŋ]	schockierend	**!** I was **shocked** when I heard the news. **schockiert** There was a **shocking** article in the paper yesterday. **schockierend**
(to) **propose** [prəˈpəʊz]	vorschlagen	I ~ we go to London next weekend. (F) proposer (L) proponere
forward [ˈfɔːwəd] (*BE auch:* **forwards**)	vorwärts, nach vorn	He moved ~ to kiss her, but she moved backwards.
a hundred years **from now**	in einhundert Jahren	A week **from now** I'll be in France.
memorable [ˈmemərəbl]	einprägsam; unvergesslich	The song *Hey Jude* has a very ~ chorus. I will never forget that ~ weekend. (L) memor *(eingedenk)*
(to) **suffer (from)** [ˈsʌfə]	leiden (an); erleiden	I often ~ **from** headaches. (= leiden an) He **~ed** a heart attack. (= Er erlitt einen Herzinfarkt.) (F) souffrir (de qc)

[b] **boat** · [p] **pool** · [d] **dad** · [t] **ten** · [g] **good** · [k] **cat** ·
[m] **mum** · [n] **no** · [ŋ] **song** · [l] **hello** · [r] **red** · [w] **we** · [j] **you**

Im English – German Dictionary kannst du nachschlagen, wenn du wissen möchtest, was ein englisches Wort bedeutet, wie man es ausspricht oder wie es geschrieben wird.

Im **Dictionary** werden folgende **Abkürzungen und Symbole** verwendet:

sth. = something (etwas) sb. = somebody (jemand) jn. = jemanden jm. = jemandem
pl = *plural* (Mehrzahl) *infml* = *informal* (umgangssprachlich)
BE = British English *AE* = American English *AusE* = Australian English
° Mit diesem Kringel sind Wörter markiert, die nicht zum Lernwortschatz gehören.

► Der Pfeil weist auf Kästen im **Vocabulary** (S. 195 – 226) hin, in denen du weitere Informationen zu diesem Wort findest.

Die **Fundstellenangaben** zeigen, wo ein Wort zum ersten Mal vorkommt.
I = Band 1; II = Band 2; III = Band 3; IV = Band 4; V 1 (15) = Band 5, Unit 1, Seite 15

Tipps zur Arbeit mit einem Wörterbuch findest du im Skills File auf Seite 159.

1

1960s [ˌnaɪntiːnˈsɪkstiz]: **in the 1960s** in den 60er-Jahren (des 20. Jahrhunderts) IV

A

a [ə]:
1. ein, eine I
2. once a week einmal pro Woche II
°**abandon** [əˈbændən] im Stich lassen
abbreviation [əˌbriːviˈeɪʃn] Abkürzung II
ability [əˈbɪləti] Fähigkeit, Können V 4 (99)
able [ˈeɪbl]: **be able to do sth.** etwas tun können; fähig sein / in der Lage sein, etwas zu tun III
Aboriginal [ˌæbəˈrɪdʒənl] Aborigine- *(die Ureinwohner/- innen Australiens betreffend)* V 1 (10)
about [əˈbaʊt]:
1. about you/... über dich/... I **about yourself** über dich selbst I **It's about ...** Es geht um ... / Es handelt von ... **know about sth.** sich mit etwas auskennen; über etwas Bescheid wissen II **the best thing about ...** das Beste an ... III **What about you?** Und du? / Und was ist mit dir? I **What is the story about?** Wovon handelt die Geschichte? / Worum geht es in der Geschichte? I
2. about 300 ungefähr 300 II
3. be about to do sth. im Begriff sein, etwas zu tun; kurz davor sein, etwas zu tun V 3 (60)
above [əˈbʌv] oben, darüber; über, oberhalb (von) III
°**abridged** [əˈbrɪdʒd] gekürzt
abroad [əˈbrɔːd] im/ins Ausland V 1 (17)
absolutely [ˈæbsəluːtli] völlig, absolut V 2 (42)
accent [ˈæksənt] Akzent III
accept [əkˈsept] akzeptieren, annehmen V 1 (13)
access [ˈækses] Zugang, Zutritt I
accident [ˈæksɪdənt] Unfall V 4 (89)
°**accompany sb./sth.** [əˈkʌmpəni] jn./etwas begleiten
account [əˈkaʊnt] Account, Konto V 2 (43)
°**accumulate sth.** [əˈkjuːmjəleɪt] etwas ansammeln
achieve [əˈtʃiːv] erreichen *(Ziel)*, erzielen *(Resultat)*; zustande bringen V 3 (59)
achievement [əˈtʃiːvmənt] Errungenschaft, Leistung V 1 (27)
acquaintance [əˈkweɪntəns] Bekannte(r) V 4 (42)
acre [ˈeɪkə] Flächenmaß *(= 0,4 Hektar)* V 4 (101)
across [əˈkrɒs]: **across the street** (quer) über die Straße II
act [ækt]:
1. schauspielern II
2. handeln, sich verhalten V 2 (50)
act out [ˌækt‿ˈaʊt] vorspielen I
action [ˈækʃn] Action; Handlung, Tat I **take action** etwas unternehmen, tätig werden V 4 (89)
activism [ˈæktɪvɪzəm] Aktivismus V 4 (93)
activist [ˈæktɪvɪst] Aktivist/in V 4 (93)
activity [ækˈtɪvəti] Aktivität I **free-time activities** Freizeitaktivitäten I
actor [ˈæktə] Schauspieler/in I
actually [ˈæktʃuəli] eigentlich; übrigens; tatsächlich III
°**ad** [æd] *(infml)* (Werbe-)Anzeige
adapt (to sth.) [əˈdæpt] sich (einer Sache) anpassen V 2 (50)
add (to) [æd] hinzufügen, ergänzen, addieren (zu) III
adder [ˈædə] Kreuzotter II
addition [əˈdɪʃn]: **in addition to** neben ...; außer ...; zusätzlich zu ... V 1 (17)
address [əˈdres] Adresse, Anschrift I
adjective [ˈædʒɪktɪv] Adjektiv II
admit [ədˈmɪt] zugeben, (ein)gestehen V 4 (89)
adopted [əˈdɒptɪd] adoptiert, Adoptiv- II
adult [ˈædʌlt]:
1. Erwachsene(r) III
2. erwachsen V 2 (44)
advantage [ədˈvɑːntɪdʒ] Vorteil V 1 (17)
adventure [ədˈventʃə] Abenteuer II
adverb [ˈædvɜːb] Adverb II
advert [ˈædvɜːt] Werbespot, Werbung III
advice *(no pl)* [ədˈvaɪs] Rat, Ratschlag, Ratschläge IV **Take my advice** Hör auf meinen Rat. IV
advise sb. to do sth. [ədˈvaɪz] jm. raten, etwas zu tun IV
advisor [ədˈvaɪzə] *(auch* **adviser***)* Berater/in V 2 (50)
°**affect** [əˈfekt] beeinflussen
°**afford** [əˈfɔːd]: **be able to afford sth.** sich etwas leisten können
°**affordable** [əˈfɔːdəbl] erschwinglich
afraid [əˈfreɪd]: **be afraid (of sth./sb.)** Angst haben (vor etwas/jm.) IV **I'm afraid** Leider ... V 1 (23)
after [ˈɑːftə]:
1. after breakfast nach dem Frühstück I **right after you** gleich nach dir II **after that** danach III
2. nachdem II **just after ...** gleich nachdem ...; kurz nachdem ... II
3. run after sb. hinter jm. herrennen I
4. after all (schließlich) doch V 4 (92)
afternoon [ˌɑːftəˈnuːn] Nachmittag I **in the afternoon** nachmittags, am Nachmittag I **on Saturday afternoon** am Samstagnachmittag I **this afternoon** heute Nachmittag II
again [əˈgen] wieder; noch einmal I **again and again** immer wieder II
against [əˈgenst] gegen I
age [eɪdʒ] Alter I **... is your age ...** ist in deinem Alter; ... ist so alt wie du II
ago [əˈgəʊ]: **two days ago** vor zwei Tagen II

agree [ə'griː] sich einig sein V 2 (49) **agree to differ** sich darauf einigen, dass man verschiedener Ansicht ist; einsehen, dass man sich nicht einigen kann V 2 (49) **agree with sb.** jm. zustimmen I **agree on sth.** sich auf etwas einigen I
agreement [ə'griːmənt] Einigung; Vereinbarung V 2 (49)
aid [eɪd]**: First Aid** Erste Hilfe V 2 (37)
air [eə] Luft II
°**air force** ['eə fɔːs] Luftwaffe
airless ['eələs] stickig IV
airport ['eəpɔːt] Flughafen III
alcohol ['ælkəhɒl] Alkohol V 4 (88)
°**aldermen elections** ['ɔːldəmen e'lekʃnz] Stadtratswahlen *(Ältestenrat)*
alive [ə'laɪv]**: be alive** leben, am Leben sein III
all [ɔːl] alles; alle I **all around her** überall um sie herum III **all of Plymouth** ganz Plymouth, das ganze Plymouth I **all alone** ganz allein II **all day** den ganzen Tag II **all over the city/the world** in der ganzen Stadt / auf der ganzen Welt IV **all the time** die ganze Zeit II **one all** eins zu eins; eins beide III **not … at all** überhaupt nicht(s), gar nicht(s); überhaupt kein/e, gar kein/e IV
allergic (to sth.) [ə'lɜːdʒɪk] allergisch (gegen etwas) IV
alley ['æli] Gasse V 3 (67) **a blind alley** Sackgasse, Irrweg V 3 (67)
alligator ['ælɪgeɪtə] Alligator IV
allow [ə'laʊ] erlauben, zulassen III **be allowed to do sth.** etwas tun dürfen II
all right [ɔːl 'raɪt] okay; in Ordnung I
almost ['ɔːlməʊst] fast, beinahe I
alone [ə'ləʊn] allein II **all alone** ganz allein II
along [ə'lɒŋ]**: along the street / …** die Straße / … entlang I **sing along (with sb.)** (mit jm.) mitsingen III
aloud [ə'laʊd]**: read aloud** laut (vor)lesen II
already [ɔːl'redi] schon, bereits II
also ['ɔːlsəʊ] auch I
°**alternative** [ɔːl'tɜːnətɪv] Alternative
although [ɔːl'ðəʊ] obwohl IV
altogether [ˌɔːltə'geðə] insgesamt, alles in allem III
always ['ɔːlweɪz] immer I
am [ˌeɪ‿'em]**: 4 am** 4 Uhr morgens I
amazing [ə'meɪzɪŋ] erstaunlich, unglaublich III
°**Amethyst python** ['æmɪθɪst ˌpaɪθən] Amethystpython
among [ə'mʌŋ] zwischen, unter (mehreren Personen, Tieren, Dingen) IV
amount (of) [ə'maʊnt] Betrag, Menge, Höhe (von Gehalt, Taschengeld) V 2 (48)
an [æn], [ən] ein, eine I
analyse ['ænəlaɪz] analysieren V 4 (87)
ancestor ['ænsestə] Vorfahr/in III
and [ænd], [ənd] und I
angel ['eɪndʒl] Engel III
anger ['æŋgə] Wut, Zorn V 4 (88)
angry ['æŋgri] wütend I **angry with sb.** wütend, böse auf jn. II
animal ['ænɪml] Tier I
°**animated** ['ænɪmeɪtɪd]**: animated film** Zeichentrickfilm
announce [ə'naʊns] bekanntgeben, verkünden V 3 (68)
announcement [ə'naʊnsmənt] Durchsage, Ansage III
annoyed (with sb./about sth.) [ə'nɔɪd] verärgert (über jn./etwas), irritiert V 2 (42)
°**annual** ['ænjuəl] jährlich, Jahres-
°**annually** ['ænjuəli] jährlich
anonymous [ə'nɒnɪməs] anonym V 4 (88)
another [ə'nʌðə]:
1. ein(e) andere(r, s) I
2. noch ein(e) I
answer ['ɑːnsə]:
1. antworten; beantworten I **answer the phone** ans Telefon gehen II
2. Antwort I
ant [ænt] Ameise I
Antarctic [æn'tɑːktɪk] Antarktis V 4 (82)
anthem ['ænθəm]**: national anthem** Nationalhymne IV
°**anti-** ['æntɪ] Anti-
any ['eni]**: Are there any …?** Gibt es (irgendwelche) …? I **at any time** jederzeit, zu jeder Zeit IV **more than in any other place** mehr als an jedem anderen Ort IV **not … any more** nicht mehr II **There aren't any …** Es gibt keine / Es sind keine … I °**any one thing** jede/irgendeine beliebige Sache
anybody ['enibɒdi]**: anybody?** (irgend)jemand? II **not … anybody** niemand II
anyone ['eniwʌn]**: anyone?** (irgend)jemand? II **not … anyone** niemand II
anything ['eniθɪŋ]**: anything?** (irgend)etwas? II **not … anything** nichts II
anyway ['eniweɪ]:
1. sowieso IV **Anyway, …** Jedenfalls, … / Aber egal, … II **And anyway, …** Und überhaupt, … III
2. trotzdem V 2 (38)
▶ S. 207 anyway
anywhere ['eniweə]**: anywhere?** irgendwohin? V 4 (92) **anywhere else** (irgendwo anders; irgendwo sonst) V 4 (92) **not … anywhere** nirgendwo; nirgendwohin V 2 (50)
apartment [ə'pɑːtmənt] Wohnung II
ape [eɪp] Menschenaffe V 1 (27)
°**apologize (to sb.)** [ə'pɒlədʒaɪz] (jn.) um Verzeihung bitten
appeal [ə'piːl] Berufung, Revision V 4 (97)
appear [ə'pɪə] erscheinen, auftauchen II
appearance [ə'pɪərəns] Erscheinung(sbild), Aussehen V 1 (27)
apple ['æpl] Apfel II
applicant ['æplɪkənt] Bewerber/in V 3 (72)
application [ˌæplɪ'keɪʃn] Bewerbung V 3 (59) **letter of application** Bewerbungsschreiben V 3 (59)
apply (for st.) [ə'plaɪ] sich (um/für etwas) bewerben V 3 (59)
°**appoint sb.** [ə'pɔɪnt] jn. berufen, ernennen
appointment [ə'pɔɪntmənt] Verabredung, Termin I
April ['eɪprəl] April I
apron ['eɪprən] Schürze V 2 (51)
aquarium [ə'kweəriəm] Aquarium; Aquarienhaus I
°**Arabic** ['ærəbɪk] Arabisch; arabisch
architect ['ɑːkɪtekt] Architekt/in III
are [ɑː] bist; sind; seid I **The DVDs are …** Die DVDs kosten … I
area ['eəriə] Bereich; Gebiet, Gegend I
aren't [ɑːnt]**: you aren't …** du bist nicht …; du bist kein/e …; ihr seid nicht …; ihr seid kein/e … I
argue ['ɑːgjuː]:
1. streiten; sich streiten III
2. argumentieren, behaupten V 1 (17)
argument ['ɑːgjumənt]:
1. Streit, Auseinandersetzung III
2. Argument V 1 (17
argumentative [ˌɑːgju'mentətɪv] argumentativ; streitsüchtig V 1 (17) **argumentative writing** Erörterung, Argumentation V 1 (17)
▶ S. 200 (to) argue – argument – argumentative
arm [ɑːm] Arm II **take sb. by the arm** jn. am Arm nehmen II
armchair ['ɑːmtʃeə] Sessel I
army ['ɑːmi] Armee V 3 (59)
around [ə'raʊnd]:
1. **around the library / …** in der Bücherei / … umher I **all around her** überall um sie herum III **look around (the farm)** sich (auf der Farm) umsehen II **walk/run/… around** herumlaufen, umherspazieren / herumrennen, umherrennen II
2. um … herum II **around 6 pm** um 18 Uhr herum, gegen 18 Uhr II
arrange [ə'reɪndʒ] anordnen I
arrest [ə'rest] verhaften, festnehmen IV
arrival [ə'raɪvl] Ankunft III
arrive [ə'raɪv] ankommen, eintreffen I
art [ɑːt] Kunst I
article ['ɑːtɪkl] Artikel II
artist ['ɑːtɪst] Künstler/in II **street artist** Straßenkünstler/in II
°**artistic** [ɑː'tɪstɪk] künstlerisch
°**arvo** ['ɑːvəʊ] *(AusE; infml)* Nachmittag
as [æz], [əz]:
1. als, während II
2. **(not) as big as** (nicht) so groß wie II
3. **as a child** als Kind II **She works as a teacher.** Sie arbeitet als Lehrerin. II
4. **as he said …** Wie er (einmal) sagte … III
5. **as soon as** sobald, sowie III

6. as if als ob III
7. da, weil
ash [æʃ] Asche III **ashes** *(pl)* Asche *(sterbliche Überreste)* III
°**aside** [əˈsaɪd] zur Seite
ask [ɑːsk] fragen I **ask a question** eine Frage stellen I **ask for sth.** um etwas bitten II **ask for directions** nach dem Weg fragen IV **ask sb. the way** jn. nach dem Weg fragen II **ask sb. to do sth.** jemanden bitten, etwas zu tun I
asleep [əˈsliːp]: **be asleep** schlafen II **fall asleep** einschlafen I
°**aspect** [ˈæspekt] Aspekt
assess [əˈses] einschätzen, beurteilen IV
assignment [əˈsaɪnmənt] *(AE)* Hausaufgabe, Hausarbeit IV
assistant [əˈsɪstənt] *(auch* **shop assistant***)* Verkäufer/in II
astronaut [ˈæstrənɔːt] Astronaut/in III
as well [əz ˈwel] auch, ebenso III
°**asylum** [əˈsaɪləm] Asyl
at [æt], [ət] an, bei, in I **at 14 Dean Street** in der Deanstraße 14 I **at any time** jederzeit, zu jeder Zeit IV **at first** zuerst, anfangs, am Anfang II **at Grandma's (house/flat)** bei Oma II **at home** daheim, zu Hause I **at last** endlich, schließlich I **at least** zumindest, wenigstens II **at lunchtime** mittags I **at night** nachts, in der Nacht I **at no time** zu keiner Zeit IV **at school** in der Schule I **at the moment** gerade, im Moment I **at the top (of)** oben, am oberen Ende, an der Spitze (von) II **at the weekend** am Wochenende I
ate [et], [eɪt] *siehe* **eat**
athlete [ˈæθliːt] Athlet/in, Sportler/in V 3 (59)
Atlantic [ətˈlæntɪk]: **the Atlantic (Ocean)** der Atlantik, der Atlantische Ozean III
atmosphere [ˈætməsfɪə] Atmosphäre; Stimmung IV
attack [əˈtæk] angreifen II
attempt [əˈtempt] Versuch V 4 (99)
attend [əˈtend]: **attend a course** einen Kurs besuchen, an einem Kurs teilnehmen IV
attention [əˈtenʃn] Aufmerksamkeit V 4 (98) **attract/catch/grab sb.'s attention** jemandes Aufmerksamkeit erregen; jemandes Aufmerksamkeit gewinnen V 4 (98) **draw attention to sth.** auf etwas aufmerksam machen; die Aufmerksamkeit auf etwas lenken V 4 (98) **pay attention** aufmerksam sein, aufpassen; zuhören, Beachtung schenken V 4 (98)
attic [ˈætɪk] Dachboden I **in the attic** auf dem Dachboden I
attract [əˈtrækt] anziehen, anlocken IV **attract sb.'s attention** jemandes Aufmerksamkeit erregen; jemandes Aufmerksamkeit gewinnen V 4 (98) **be attracted to sb.** sich zu jm. hingezogen fühlen V 2 (42)
attraction [əˈtrækʃn] Attraktion; Anziehungspunkt III
audience [ˈɔːdiəns] Publikum, Zuschauer/innen, Zuhörer/innen II
▶ S. 199 Group nouns
°**audio guide** [ˈɔːdiəʊ gaɪd] Audioguide
audition [ɔːˈdɪʃn] Vorsprechen, Vorsingen, Vorspielen II
August [ˈɔːgəst] August I
aunt [ɑːnt] Tante I
Aussie [ˈɒzi] *(infml)* Australier/in; australisch V 1 (13)
author [ˈɔːθə] Autor/in I
autumn [ˈɔːtəm] Herbst I
available [əˈveɪləbl] erhältlich, verfügbar; erreichbar *(Telefon)* III
avenue [ˈævənjuː] Allee, Boulevard IV
average [ˈævərɪdʒ] durchschnittlich; Durchschnitt V 2 (47)
awake [əˈweɪk] wach III
award [əˈwɔːd] Preis, Auszeichnung V 1 (27)
away [əˈweɪ] weg, fort I
awesome [ˈɔːsəm] *(AE, infml)* klasse, großartig IV
awful [ˈɔːfl] schrecklich, fürchterlich II
awkward [ˈɔːkwəd] peinlich, unangenehm, schwierig V 2 (38)

B

back [bæk]:
1. zurück I **back then** damals V 1 (13)
2. Rücken II
3. from the back of the bus aus dem hinteren Teil des Busses II
°**4. back off** klein beigeben
background [ˈbækgraʊnd] Hintergrund II **background file** *Hintergrundinformation(en)* I
backpack [ˈbækpæk] Rucksack IV
backstage [ˌbækˈsteɪdʒ] hinter der Bühne III
bacon [ˈbeɪkən] Schinkenspeck II
bad [bæd] schlecht, schlimm I **go bad** *(fish, cheese, eggs)* schlecht werden II
Badlands [ˈbædlændz] Ödland IV
badminton [ˈbædmɪntən] Badminton, Federball V 3 (71)
bag [bæg] Tasche, Beutel, Tüte I **school bag** Schultasche I
bagpipes *(pl)* [ˈbægpaɪps] Dudelsack III
bake [beɪk] backen IV
°**balance sth. out** [ˈbæləns] etwas ausbalancieren, etwas ins Gleichgewicht bringen
bald [bɔːld] kahl, glatzköpfig V 3 (60)
ball [bɔːl] Ball I
°**ban sth.** [bæn] etwas verbieten
banana [bəˈnɑːnə] Banane III
band [bænd] Band, (Musik-)Gruppe II
▶ S. 199 Group nouns
bang [bæŋ] Knall III
bank [bæŋk] Bank III °**bank account** Bankkonto
bar [bɑː]:
1. Riegel *(Schokolade, Müsli)*, Tafel *(Schokolade)* III
2. Bar IV
bar chart [ˈbɑː tʃɑːt] Balkendiagramm V 2 (47)
barbecue [ˈbɑːbɪkjuː] *(BE und AusE infml auch:* **barbie***)* Grill; Grillfest, Grillparty V 1 (13)
bare [beə] nackt, bloß *(Hände, Arme, Füße)* III
bark [bɑːk]:
1. bellen I
2. Bellen III
barman [ˈbɑːmən], *pl* **barmen** [ˈbɑːmən] Barkeeper III
barn [bɑːn] Scheune II
based [beɪst]: **be based on sth.** auf etwas basieren V 4 (97)
°**basic** [ˈbeɪsɪk] grundlegend, Grund-
°**basis** [ˈbeɪsɪs] Grundlage
basket [ˈbɑːskɪt] Korb I
basketball [ˈbɑːskɪtbɔːl] Basketball I
bath [bɑːθ] Bad II
bathroom [ˈbɑːθruːm] Badezimmer I
battle [ˈbætl] Schlacht; Kampf II
bay [beɪ] Bucht V 1 (12)
be [bi], **was/were, been:** sein I **be about to do sth.** im Begriff sein, etwas zu tun; kurz davor sein, etwas zu tun V 3 (60) **be to** (tun) werden; sollen V 4 (89) **Dad said we were to be back by ten.** Dad hat gesagt, wir sollen um zehn zurück sein. V 4 (89)
▶ S. 210 (to) be to do sth.
beach [biːtʃ] Strand I
bean [biːn] Bohne IV
bear [beə] Bär I
beard [bɪəd] Bart II
beat [biːt], **beat, beaten** schlagen; besiegen III **beat sb. up** jn. zusammenschlagen IV
beaten [ˈbiːtn] *siehe* **beat**
beautiful [ˈbjuːtɪfl] schön II
became [bɪˈkeɪm] *siehe* **become**
because [bɪˈkɒz] weil I **because of** wegen V 2 (39)
become [bɪˈkʌm], **became, become** werden II
bed [bed] Bett I **bed and breakfast** Frühstückspension; Zimmer mit Frühstück III
bedroom [ˈbedruːm] Schlafzimmer I
beef [biːf] Rindfleisch IV **roast beef** Rinderbraten I
been [biːn]:
1. *siehe* **be**
2. Have you ever been to ...? ... Bist du schon in ... gewesen? II
beep [biːp] piepen II

before [bɪ'fɔː]:
1. bevor I
2. vor I **before school/lessons** vor der Schule *(vor Schulbeginn)* / vorm Unterricht I **before long** schon bald III **before that** davor III
3. (vorher) schon mal II **not/never before** (vorher) noch nie II
4. **the week before** die Woche zuvor; in der Woche davor IV

began [bɪ'gæn] *siehe* **begin**
begin [bɪ'gɪn], **began, begun** beginnen, anfangen II **To begin with, ...** Erstens ...; Zunächst (einmal) ... V 1 (17)
beginning [bɪ'gɪnɪŋ] Anfang, Beginn III **in the beginning** anfangs, zuerst III
begun [bɪ'gʌn] *siehe* **begin**
behave [bɪ'heɪv] sich verhalten, sich benehmen III
behind [bɪ'haɪnd] hinter I **from behind** von hinten II **right behind you** direkt hinter dir, genau hinter dir II
believe [bɪ'liːv] glauben II
bell [bel] Klingel, Glocke I
belong to sb. [bɪ'lɒŋ] jm. gehören; zu jm. gehören IV
below [bɪ'ləʊ] unten, darunter; unter, unterhalb (von) III
°**bench** [bentʃ] (Sitz-)Bank
bend down [bend], **bent, bent** sich hinunterbeugen, sich bücken III
bent [bent] *siehe* **bend**
best [best]: **the best** der/die/das beste; die besten; am besten I **the best thing about ...** das Beste an ... III
better ['betə] besser I **better than ever** besser als je zuvor II **I'd better ... (= I had better ...)** Ich sollte lieber ... IV
between [bɪ'twiːn] zwischen I
Bible ['baɪbl]: **the Bible** die Bibel V 3 (60)
big [bɪg] groß I **big wheel** Riesenrad I **the biggest** der/die/das größte; am größten I
bike [baɪk] Fahrrad I **ride a bike** Fahrrad fahren I **bike path** Radweg V 4 (89)
bilingual [baɪ'lɪŋgwəl] zweisprachig IV
biology [baɪ'ɒlədʒi] Biologie V 3 (67)
bird [bɜːd] Vogel I
birthday ['bɜːθdeɪ] Geburtstag I **My birthday is in May.** Ich habe im Mai Geburtstag. I **My birthday is on 5th May.** Ich habe am 5. May Geburtstag. I **When's your birthday?** Wann hast du Geburtstag? I
biscuit ['bɪskɪt] Keks, Plätzchen I
bit [bɪt]:
1. *siehe* **bite**
2. **a bit** ein bisschen, etwas II
°3. Teil

bite [baɪt]:
1. **(bit, bitten)** beißen I
2. Biss, Bissen III

bitten ['bɪtn] *siehe* **bite**
bitter ['bɪtə] bitter IV
black [blæk] schwarz I
blame [bleɪm]: **put the blame (for sth.) on sb.** jm. (an etwas) die Schuld geben V 1 (27)
°**blank** [blæŋk] ausdruckslos *(Gesicht)*
°**blaze** [bleɪz] lodernde Flamme
blew [bluː] *siehe* **blow**
blind [blaɪnd] blind V 3 (67) **blind alley** Sackgasse, Irrweg V 3 (67)
block [blɒk] (Häuser-, Wohn-)Block IV
blog [blɒg] Blog *(Weblog, digitales Tagebuch)* II
blogger ['blɒgə] Blogger/in III
blond *(bei Frauen oft:* **blonde***)* [blɒnd] blond I
blood [blʌd] Blut III
bloom [bluːm] blühen IV
blow [bləʊ], **blew, blown: blow sth. out** etwas auspusten, ausblasen II **blow (a whistle)** pfeifen *(auf der Trillerpfeife)* III
blown [bləʊn] *siehe* **blow**
blue [bluː] blau I
board [bɔːd]:
1. (Wand-)Tafel I
2. **on board** an Bord III **on board the ship** an Bord des Schiffes III
3. *(kurz für:* **surfboard***)* Surfbrett V 1 (13)
°4. Unterhalt, Verpflegung

boarding school ['bɔːdɪŋ skuːl] Internat II
boat [bəʊt] Boot, Schiff I
body ['bɒdi]:
1. Körper I **part of the body** Körperteil II
2. Leiche III
3. Hauptteil *(eines Textes)* III

boil [bɔɪl] kochen; zum Kochen bringen IV
boo [buː] buhen; ausbuhen V 1 (27)
book [bʊk] Buch I
bookshop ['bʊkʃɒp] Buchladen, Buchhandlung I
°**boomerang** ['buːməræŋ] Bumerang
boot [buːt] Stiefel II
border ['bɔːdə] Grenze III
bored [bɔːd]: **be/feel bored** gelangweilt sein, sich langweilen II
boring ['bɔːrɪŋ] langweilig I
born [bɔːn]: **be born** geboren sein/werden III **I was born in 1998.** Ich bin 1998 geboren. III
borough ['bʌrə], *AE:* ['bɜːrəʊ] (Stadt-)Bezirk IV
borrow sth. (from sb.) ['bɒrəʊ] sich etwas (aus)leihen (vom jm.), etwas entleihen IV
°**botanic** [bə'tænɪk] botanisch
both [bəʊθ] beide II **both ... and ...** sowohl ... als auch ... IV
bottle ['bɒtl] Flasche I
bottom ['bɒtəm]: **at the bottom** unten, am unteren Ende (von) II
bought [bɔːt] *siehe* **buy**
boutique [buː'tiːk] Boutique IV
bow [baʊ] sich verneigen, sich verbeugen II
bowl [bəʊl] Schüssel II
box [bɒks] Kasten, Kiste, Kästchen I **telephone box** Telefonzelle III
boy [bɔɪ] Junge I
boycott sth. ['bɔɪkɒt] etwas boykottieren V 4 (83)
boyfriend ['bɔɪfrend] Freund III
°**bracket** ['brækɪt] Klammer *(in Texten)*
brain [breɪn] Gehirn V 2 (37)
brainstorm ['breɪnstɔːm] brainstormen *(so viele Ideen wie möglich sammeln)* V 1 (17)
brass band [ˌbrɑːs 'bænd] Blaskapelle IV
brave [breɪv] mutig, tapfer V 3 (62)
bread [bred] Brot I
break [breɪk]:
1. Pause I **take a break** eine Pause machen V 4 (86)
2. **(broke, broken)** zerbrechen, kaputt machen I; brechen, kaputt gehen I **break up (with sb.)** Schluss machen (mit jm.), sich trennen (von jm.) V 2 (42)

breakfast ['brekfəst] Frühstück I **have breakfast** frühstücken I **bed and breakfast** Frühstückspension; Zimmer mit Frühstück III
breath [breθ] Atem, Atemzug II **he said ... under his breath** ..., sagte er flüsternd / murmelte er. III
breathe [briːð] atmen V 2 (37)
breeze [briːz] Brise III
bridge [brɪdʒ] Brücke II
briefly ['briːfli] in Kürze, in wenigen Worten IV
bright [braɪt] strahlend, leuchtend, hell I
brilliant ['brɪliənt] glänzend, großartig, genial II
bring [brɪŋ], **brought, brought** (mit-, her)bringen II **bring in** *(hay)* einbringen *(Heu)* II **bring sth. about** etwas hervorrufen, etwas herbeiführen, etwas bewirken V 4 (83)
British ['brɪtɪʃ] britisch I
broadcast ['brɔːdkɑːst], **broadcast, broadcast** senden, ausstrahlen, übertragen (Rundfunk, Fernsehen) V 4 (98)
brochure ['brəʊʃə] Broschüre, Prospekt III
broke [brəʊk] *siehe* **break**
broken [brəʊkən]:
1. *siehe* **break**
2. zerbrochen, kaputt; gebrochen II

brother ['brʌðə] Bruder I
brought [brɔːt] *siehe* **bring**
brown [braʊn] braun I
buck [bʌk] *(infml)* Dollar IV
bucket ['bʌkɪt] Eimer II
buffalo ['bʌfələʊ] *pl* **buffalo, buffaloes** Büffel; Bison IV
°**budget** ['bʌdʒɪt] haushalten
°**bug sb.** [bʌg] jn. ärgern
build [bɪld], **built, built** bauen II
building ['bɪldɪŋ] Gebäude II
built [bɪlt] *siehe* **build**

bully ['bʊli] (Schul-)Tyrann III
bully sb. ['bʊli] jn. tyrannisieren, mobben V 1 (27)
bump into [bʌmp] jn. zufällig treffen, jn. zufällig begegnen V 1 (19)
burger ['bɜːgə] Hamburger II
burn [bɜːn] brennen; verbrennen III
burnt [bɜːnt] verbrannt IV
burst [bɜːst], **burst, burst** platzen V 3 (61) **burst into tears** in Tränen ausbrechen III
bury ['beri] begraben, beerdigen III
bus [bʌs] Bus I **go by bus** mit dem Bus fahren I **get on a bus** (in einen Bus) einsteigen II
bush [bʊʃ] Busch, Strauch *(auch: unerschlossenes, „wildes" Land in Australien u. Afrika)* V 1 (10)
°**bush turkey** [ˌbʊʃ 'tɜːki] Buschhuhn
business ['bɪznəs] Geschäft, Geschäfts-; Unternehmen, Betrieb V 1 (12)
Business was good. Die Geschäfte liefen gut. V 1 (12)
busy ['bɪzi] belebt, geschäftig, hektisch II **be busy** beschäftigt sein; viel zu tun haben I **busy season** Hauptsaison IV
but [bʌt], [bət] aber I
butter ['bʌtə] Butter IV
butterfly ['bʌtəflaɪ] Schmetterling I
buy [baɪ], **bought, bought** kaufen I
buy into sth. *(infml)* (an) etwas glauben V 4 (89)
by [baɪ]:
1. by the sea am Meer I **take sb. by the arm** jn. am Arm nehmen II
2. go by car/bus/... mit dem Auto/Bus/... fahren I
3. by ... von ... II
4. by 8 pm bis (spätestens) 20 Uhr II **by the time** wenn, bis V 4 (86)
5. by the way übrigens III
°**6. By singing, they ...** Indem sie singen, ... / Durch Singen ...
Bye. [baɪ] Tschüs. I

C

cactus ['kæktəs], *pl* **cactuses** ['kæktəsɪz] *or* **cacti** ['kæktaɪ] Kaktus V 4 (87)
café ['kæfeɪ] Café I
cage [keɪdʒ] Käfig I
cake [keɪk] Kuchen I
call [kɔːl]:
1. rufen; anrufen; nennen I **call out the names** die Namen aufrufen II **call sb. names** jn. beschimpfen, jm. Schimpfwörter nachrufen IV
2. *(auch:* **phone call***)* Anruf, Telefonat II
called [kɔːld]: **be called** heißen, genannt werden I
caller ['kɔːlə] Anrufer/in II
calm [kɑːm]:
1. ruhig III
2. calm down sich beruhigen III
calm sb. down jn. beruhigen III
°**camaraderie** [ˌkæmə'rɑːdəri] Kameradschaft, Kamaraderie
came [keɪm] *siehe* **come**
camel ['kæml] Kamel V 1 (10)
camera ['kæmərə] Kamera, Fotoapparat I
cameraman ['kæmrəmæn], *pl* **cameramen** ['kæmrəmen] Kameramann I
°**camp** [kæmp]: **camp out** zelten, im Freien kampieren
campaign [kæm'peɪn]:
1. Kampagne V 4 (88)
2. campaign for/against sich einsetzen, kämpfen für/gegen *(auch im Wahlkampf)* V 4 (88)
campaigner [kæm'peɪnə] Aktivist/in V 4 (88)
campfire ['kæmpfaɪə] Lagerfeuer IV
camping ['kæmpɪŋ] Camping, Zelten II
go camping zelten gehen II
campsite ['kæmpsaɪt] Zeltplatz II
can [kæn]:
1. können I **we cannot** ['kænɒt], **we can't** [kɑːnt] ... wir können nicht ... I
2. Dose V 2 (38)
canal [kə'næl] Kanal III
candidate ['kændɪdət] Bewerber/in, Kandidat/in V 3 (72)
candle ['kændl] Kerze II
canoe [kə'nuː] Kanu V 3 (64)
canoeing [kə'nuːɪŋ] Kanufahren; Kanusport V 3 (64)
canteen [kæn'tiːn] Kantine, (Schul-)Mensa I
canyon ['kænjən] Cañon IV
cap [kæp] Mütze, Kappe II
°**cape** [keɪp] Kap
captain ['kæptɪn] Kapitän/in I
caption ['kæpʃn] Bildunterschrift I
captive ['kæptɪv] Gefangene(r) III
car [kɑː] Auto I **go by car** mit dem Auto fahren I **get in(to) a car** (in ein Auto) einsteigen II
car park ['kɑː pɑːk] Parkplatz IV
caravan ['kærəvæn] Wohnwagen II
card (to) [kɑːd] Karte (an) I
care [keə]: **care about sth.** etwas wichtig nehmen III **I don't care about money.** Geld ist mir egal. III **I really care about animals.** Tiere liegen mir sehr am Herzen. / Tiere sind mir sehr wichtig. III **Who cares?** Na und? / Wen interessiert das? III
career [kə'rɪə] Karriere III
careful ['keəfl]:
1. vorsichtig I
2. sorgfältig, aufmerksam V 3 (70)
carer ['keərə] Betreuer/in V 2 (50)
carnival ['kɑːnɪvl] Karneval, Fasching III
°**Carolina Blue** [ˌkærəlaɪnə 'bluː] *Wappenfarbe der University of North Carolina, Chapel Hill*
carpenter ['kɑːpəntə] Tischler/in, Zimmerer/Zimmerin III
carrot ['kærət] Möhre, Karotte III
carry ['kæri] tragen; befördern III
cart [kɑːt] Karren I
cartoon [kɑː'tuːn] V 4 (87)
carve [kɑːv] meißeln; schnitzen IV
case [keɪs] Fall V 4 (98)
cash [kæʃ] Bargeld; *(infml auch:)* Geld V 2 (48)
cash desk ['kæʃ desk] Kasse *(in Geschäften)* II
°**cash flow** ['kæʃ fləʊ] Cashflow
°**cassowary** [ˌkæsə'weəri] Kasuar *(Laufvogel)*
cast [kɑːst] Besetzung; Mitwirkende *(Theaterstück, Film)* II
casting ['kɑːstɪŋ] Casting *(Auswahlverfahren zur Rollenbesetzung bei Filmen/Theaterstücken)* IV
castle ['kɑːsl] Burg, Schloss I
cat [kæt] Katze I **big cat** Großkatze III
catch [kætʃ], **caught, caught** fangen I **catch a bus/ferry** einen Bus nehmen; einen Bus (noch) erwischen V 1 (12) **catch sb.'s attention** jemandes Aufmerksamkeit erregen; jemandes Aufmerksamkeit gewinnen V 4 (98)
°**I didn't catch that.** Das habe ich nicht verstanden.
catchy ['kætʃi] eingängig *(Melodie, Slogan)* IV
category ['kætəgəri] Kategorie V 3 (64)
cathedral [kə'θiːdrəl] Kathedrale, Dom III
caught [kɔːt] *siehe* **catch**
cause [kɔːz]:
1. Ursache IV
°**2.** Anliegen, Anlass
3. verursachen IV
°**cause** [kɔːz]
cave [keɪv] Höhle II
celebrate ['selɪbreɪt] feiern II
celebration [ˌselɪ'breɪʃn] Feier II
celebrity [sə'lebrəti] Berühmtheit *(berühmte Person)* IV
cell (phone) [sel] *(bes. AE)* Mobiltelefon, Handy IV
Celsius (C) ['selsiəs] Celsius IV
cemetery ['semətri], *AE:* ['semәteri] Friedhof IV
cent [sent] Cent III
centimetre (cm) ['sentɪmiːtə] Zentimeter IV
central ['sentrəl] zentral, Zentral-, Mittel- IV
centre ['sentə] Zentrum; Mitte I
shopping centre Einkaufszentrum II
century ['sentʃəri] Jahrhundert I
ceremony ['serəməni] Zeremonie IV
certain ['sɜːtn] bestimmte(r, s), gewisse(r, s) V 2 (48)
certainly ['sɜːtnli] sicher(lich), auf jeden Fall V 4 (89)
chain [tʃeɪn] Kette I
chair [tʃeə] Stuhl I
challenge ['tʃælɪndʒ]:
1. Herausforderung III

2. challenge sb. (to sth.) jn. herausfordern (zu etwas) III
champion ['tʃæmpiən] Meister/in, Champion II
chance [tʃɑːns] Gelegenheit, Möglichkeit, Chance III
► S. 203 German "Möglichkeit"
change [tʃeɪndʒ]:
1. (ver)ändern; sich (ver)ändern II
2. wechseln, umtauschen *(Geld)* III
3. umsteigen III
4. Wechselgeld II
5. Änderung, Veränderung IV
channel ['tʃænl] Kanal, Sender IV
°**chant** [tʃɑːnt] Gesang, Sprechchor
chaos ['keɪɒs] Chaos I
character ['kærəktə]:
1. Figur, Person *(in Roman, Film, Theaterstück)* I
2. Charakter V 3 (62)
charity ['tʃærəti] Wohlfahrtsorganisation; Wohltätigkeit, wohltätige Zwecke II
chart [tʃɑːt] Tabelle, Schaubild V 2 (47)
chat [tʃæt]:
1. chatten III; plaudern III
2. Chat III
cheap [tʃiːp] billig, preiswert I
cheat [tʃiːt] schummeln, mogeln; betrügen V 3 (61)
check [tʃek]:
1. Überprüfung, Kontrolle I
2. (über)prüfen, kontrollieren I **check sth. out** *(infml)* sich etwas anschauen, anhören; etwas ausprobieren III
checklist ['tʃeklɪst] Checkliste III
cheek [tʃiːk] Wange V 2 (37)
cheer [tʃɪə] jubeln II
cheese [tʃiːz] Käse I
chemical ['kemɪkl] Chemikalie V 3 (66)
chess [tʃes] Schach I
chest [tʃest] Brust, Brustkorb II
chicken ['tʃɪkɪn] Huhn; (Brat-)Hähnchen IV
child [tʃaɪld], *pl* **children** ['tʃɪldrən] Kind I
chin [tʃɪn] Kinn V 2 (37)
chips *(pl)* [tʃɪps] Pommes frites II
chocolate ['tʃɒklət]:
1. Schokolade I
2. Praline II
choice [tʃɔɪs] Wahl; Auswahl IV
choir ['kwaɪə] Chor II
°**chook** [tʃʊk] *(AusE; infml)* Huhn; (Brat-)Hähnchen
choose [tʃuːz], **chose, chosen** aussuchen, (aus)wählen; sich aussuchen I
chore [tʃɔː] (Haus-)Arbeit; (lästige) Pflicht V 2 (47)
chorus ['kɔːrəs] Refrain II
chose [tʃəʊz] *siehe* **choose**
chosen [tʃəʊzn] *siehe* **choose**
Christmas ['krɪsməs] Weihnachten III
Christmas Day 1. Weihnachtstag *(25. Dezember)* III
Christmas Eve [ˌkrɪsməs‿'iːv] Heiligabend V 1 (13)

church [tʃɜːtʃ] Kirche II
°**cigarette** [ˌsɪgə'ret] Zigarette
cinema ['sɪnəmə] Kino I
circle ['sɜːkl] Kreis II
citizen ['sɪtɪzn] (Staats-)Bürger/in V 4 (93)
city ['sɪti] Stadt, Großstadt II
civil [ˌsɪvl]: **civil rights** *(pl)* Bürgerrechte IV **civil war** Bürgerkrieg V 4 (98)
°**civilization** [ˌsɪvəlaɪ'zeɪʃn] Zivilisation
clap [klæp] (Beifall) klatschen II **Clap your hands.** Klatscht in die Hände. II
class [klɑːs] (Schul-)Klasse I °**in class** im Unterricht
► S. 199 Group nouns
classmate ['klɑːsmeɪt] Mitschüler/in, Klassenkamerad/in I
classroom ['klɑːsruːm] Klassenzimmer I
clause [klɔːz]: **main clause** Hauptsatz III
clay [kleɪ] Ton, Lehm III
clean [kliːn]:
1. sauber machen, putzen I
2. sauber II
cleaner ['kliːnə] Reinigungskraft V 3 (72)
°**cleanse** [klenz] säubern
clean-up ['kliːnʌp] Säuberung V 3 (73)
clear [klɪə]:
1. klar, deutlich II
2. räumen; abräumen III
clever ['klevə] klug, schlau I
click [klɪk] klicken IV
cliff [klɪf] Klippe II
climate ['klaɪmət] Klima IV
climb [klaɪm]:
1. klettern; hinaufklettern (auf) II
2. Aufstieg, Anstieg III
clinic ['klɪnɪk] Klinik V 1 (26)
clock [klɒk] (Wand-, Stand-, Turm-)Uhr I
close [kləʊz] schließen II
close (to) [kləʊs] nah, dicht (bei, an) IV
closely ['kləʊsli]: **look closely** genau hinschauen II
closet ['klɒzɪt] Wandschrank *(oft begehbar)* IV
close-up ['kləʊs‿ʌp] Nahaufnahme IV
clothes *(pl)* [kləʊðz] Kleidung, Kleidungsstücke I
cloud [klaʊd] Wolke II
cloudless ['klaʊdləs] wolkenlos IV
cloudy ['klaʊdi] bewölkt II
clown [klaʊn] Clown II
clownish ['klaʊnɪʃ] albern V 3 (60)
club [klʌb] Klub I **join a club** in einen Klub eintreten; sich einem Klub anschließen I
clue [kluː] (Lösungs-)Hinweis; Anhaltspunkt III
coach [kəʊtʃ] Trainer/in IV
coal [kəʊl] Kohle III **coal mine** Kohlebergwerk III
coast [kəʊst] Küste I
coastal ['kəʊstl] Küsten- V 1 (10)
coastline ['kəʊstlaɪn] Küste, Küstenlinie V 1 (22)

coat [kəʊt]:
1. Mantel II
2. Fell III
cocoa ['kəʊkəʊ] Kakao II
coffee ['kɒfi] Kaffee III **make coffee** Kaffee kochen IV
coin [kɔɪn] Münze I
cola ['kəʊlə] Cola I
cold [kəʊld]:
1. kalt I **be cold** frieren I
2. **have a cold** eine Erkältung haben, erkältet sein II:
3. Kälte V 3 (67)
collapse [kə'læps] einstürzen; zusammenbrechen IV
collect [kə'lekt] sammeln I
collective [kə'lektɪv] kollektiv, gemeinschaftlich, vereint V 4 (82)
college ['kɒlɪdʒ] Hochschule IV
collocation [ˌkɒlə'keɪʃn] Kollokation *(Wörter, die oft zusammen vorkommen)* V 1 (22)
colon ['kəʊlən] Doppelpunkt II
°**colonial** [kə'ləʊniəl] kolonial, Kolonial-
°**colonist** ['kɒlənɪst] Siedler/in
°**colonization** [ˌkɒlənaɪ'zeɪʃn] Besiedlung
colony ['kɒləni] Kolonie IV
colour ['kʌlə] Farbe I
coloured ['kʌləd] farbig IV
colourful ['kʌləfl] bunt, farbenfroh IV
column ['kɒləm] Säule III
combine [kəm'baɪn] kombinieren, verbinden IV
come [kʌm], **came, come** kommen I **come across** verstanden werden; ankommen, „rüberkommen" *(Botschaft)* V 4 (87) **come across sth.** stoßen auf etwas, etwas *(zufällig)* treffen III **come down with sth.** etwas bekommen *(Krankheit)*, erkranken an etwas III **come in** hereinkommen I **Come on, Dad.** Na los, Dad! / Komm, Dad! I **come over** herüberkommen (zu/nach), vorbeikommen (bei) III **come up to sb.** auf jn. zukommen IV **come up with sth.** etwas haben, kommen auf etwas *(Idee, Vorschlag)* III
comedian [kə'miːdiən] Komiker/in, Komödiant/in III
comedy ['kɒmədi] Comedyshow, Komödie II
comfortable ['kʌmftəbl] bequem; angenehm IV
comma ['kɒmə] Komma II
comment ['kɒment]:
1. Bemerkung, Kommentar V 1 (27) °**make a comment** sich äußern, einen Kommentar abgeben
2. bemerken, sagen; sich äußern, einen Kommentar abgeben V 4 (87)
°**comment on sth.** etwas kommentieren; sich zu etwas äußern
common ['kɒmən] häufig; weit verbreitet IV **have sth. in common** etwas miteinander gemein haben IV

°**Commons** ['kɒmənz]: **the House of Commons** das Unterhaus
communication [kəˌmjuːnɪ'keɪʃn] Kommunikation, Verständigung V 2 (46)
community [kə'mjuːnəti] Gemeinde; Gemeinschaft III
company ['kʌmpəni] Firma V 3 (66)
compare [kəm'peə] vergleichen IV
comparison [kəm'pærɪsn] Vergleich V 1 (17) **make comparisons** Vergleiche anstellen; vergleichen V 1 (17)
compete in sth. [kəm'piːt] an etwas teilnehmen *(Wettkampf)* III
competition [ˌkɒmpə'tɪʃn] Wettbewerb II
competitive [kəm'petətɪv] leistungsorientiert, ehrgeizig; Wettkampf-, Leistungs- V 3 (62)
complete [kəm'pliːt] komplett, vollständig IV
completely [kəm'pliːtli] völlig, vollkommen IV
completion [kəm'pliːʃn] Abschluss; Fertigstellung V 3 (73)
°**compression** [kəm'preʃn] Komprimierung *(das Zusammenziehen von Lauten)*
computer [kəm'pjuːtə] Computer I
concentrate (on sth.) ['kɒnsntreɪt] sich konzentrieren (auf etwas) III
concerned (about) [kən'sɜːnd] besorgt (über/um) V 4 (87)
concert ['kɒnsət] Konzert II
conclusion [kən'kluːʒn] Schluss(folgerung) III
conditions *(pl)* [kən'dɪʃnz] Verhältnisse, Bedingungen III
conference ['kɒnfrəns] Konferenz, Kongress V 4 (84)
confident ['kɒnfɪdənt] selbstbewusst, (selbst)sicher V 1 (13)
conflict ['kɒnflɪkt] Konflikt, Auseinandersetzung IV
confused [kən'fjuːzd] verwirrt V 2 (42)
congress ['kɒŋgres] Kongress V 4 (93)
connect [kə'nekt] verbinden, verknüpfen III **be connected** verbunden sein II
°**connection** [kə'nekʃn] Verbindung
°**conservative** [kən'sɜːvətɪv] konservativ
consider sth. [kən'sɪdə] etwas bedenken, berücksichtigen; sich mit etwas befassen V 4 (89) **consider doing sth.** erwägen, etwas zu tun; in Betracht ziehen, etwas zu tun V 4 (89)
consonant ['kɒnsənənt] Konsonant, Mitlaut II
°**constitution** [ˌkɒnstɪ'tjuːʃn] Verfassung
contact ['kɒntækt]
1. Kontakt IV **make eye contact** Blickkontakt herstellen IV
2. **contact sb.** Kontakt zu jm. aufnehmen, sich bei jm. melden V 3 (72)
contain [kən'teɪn] enthalten V 4 (87)
° **be contained in** enthalten sein in
°**contemporary** [kən'temprəri] zeitgenössisch
content ['kɒntent] Inhalt III
contest ['kɒntest] Wettbewerb III
context ['kɒntekst] (Satz-, Text-) Zusammenhang, Kontext II
continent ['kɒntɪnənt] Kontinent IV
continue [kən'tɪnjuː]:
1. **continue sth.** etwas fortsetzen III
2. sich fortsetzen, weitergehen III
°**contract** ['kɒntrækt] Vertrag
contrast ['kɒntrɑːst] Kontrast, Gegensatz IV **by contrast** im Gegensatz dazu
°**contrasting** [kən'trɑːstɪŋ] gegensätzlich
conversation [ˌkɒnvə'seɪʃn] Gespräch, Unterhaltung II
convict ['kɒnvɪkt] Sträfling, Strafgefangene(r) V 1 (10)
cook [kʊk]:
1. kochen; zubereiten III
2. Koch, Köchin IV
cookie ['kʊki] *(AE)* Keks IV
cool [kuːl]:
1. cool I
2. kühl II
3. **cool off** sich abkühlen III
coordinator [kəʊ'ɔːdɪneɪtə] Koordinator/in III
copy ['kɒpi]:
1. kopieren, abschreiben I
2. Kopie; Exemplar II
coral ['kɒrəl] Koralle; Korallen- V 1 (10)
corner ['kɔːnə] Ecke I **corner shop** Laden an der Ecke; Tante-Emma-Laden I **on the corner of Church Road and London Road** Church Road, Ecke London Road II
corn *(no pl)* [kɔːn] *AE:* Mais; *BE:* Korn, Getreide V 4 (101)
cornflakes ['kɔːnfleɪks] Cornflakes I
correct [kə'rekt]:
1. richtig, korrekt II
2. korrigieren, verbessern II
°**correction** [kə'rekʃn] Korrektur, Berichtigung
°**correspondent** [ˌkɒrə'spɒndənt] Korrespondent/in
corridor ['kɒrɪdɔː] Gang, Korridor III
cost [kɒst] **(cost, cost)** kosten II
°**costs** *(pl)* [kɒsts] Kosten
costume ['kɒstjuːm] Kostüm, Verkleidung II
cottage ['kɒtɪdʒ] Häuschen, Cottage II
cotton ['kɒtn] Baumwolle IV
cough [kɒf]: **have a cough** Husten haben II
could [kʊd], [kəd]:
1. **he could …** er konnte … I **we couldn't …** ['kʊdnt] wir konnten nicht … I
2. **What could be better?** Was könnte besser sein? II
3. **You could have asked me.** Du hättest mich fragen können. IV
council ['kaʊnsl] Ausschuss; Rat *(Stadtrat, Gemeinderat u.Ä.)* IV
councillor ['kaʊnsələ] Ratsmitglied, (Stadt-, Gemeinde-)Rat/Rätin V 4 (88)
count [kaʊnt] zählen I **count to ten** bis zehn zählen
counter ['kaʊntə]:
1. Theke; Ladentisch IV
2. *(AE, kurz für* **countertop***)* Arbeitsplatte; Küchentheke IV
country ['kʌntri] Land *(Staat)* II
countryside ['kʌntrisaɪd] Landschaft, *(ländliche)* Gegend II
county ['kaʊnti] Grafschaft *(in Großbritannien)* I
couple ['kʌpl]: **a couple** ein Paar; ein paar III
courage ['kʌrɪdʒ] Mut, Courage IV
course [kɔːs] Kurs, Lehrgang I **attend a course** einen Kurs besuchen, an einem Kurs teilnehmen IV
court [kɔːt] Spielfeld V 3 (60)
°**court case** ['kɔːt keɪs] Prozess, Gerichtsverhandlung
courtyard ['kɔːtjɑːd] Innenhof II
cousin ['kʌzn] Cousin, Cousine I
cove [kəʊv] (kleine) Bucht V 4 (88)
cover ['kʌvə]:
1. bedecken, zudecken III
°2. abdecken; behandeln
°3. **inside cover** Umschlaginnenseite
cow [kaʊ] Kuh II
°**CPR** [ˌsiːpiː'ɑː] *(cardiopulmonary resuscitation)* Herz-Lungen-Wiederbelebung
crab [kræb] Krebs I
°**crack** [kræk]: **crack a joke** einen Witz reißen **crack a window** ein Fenster einen Spalt öffnen
cranberry ['krænbəri] Preiselbeere IV
crash [kræʃ]:
1. crashen II
2. **crash into sth.** *(Flugzeug)* in etwas stürzen; *(Auto)* gegen etwas fahren IV
3. abstürzen *(Flugzeug; Computer)* IV
crazy ['kreɪzi] verrückt IV **be crazy about sb./sth.** verrückt nach etwas/jm. sein V 3 (62)
cream [kriːm] Sahne I
create [kri'eɪt] schaffen, erschaffen, kreieren V 4 (84)
creative [kri'eɪtɪv] kreativ V 3 (72)
°**creek** [kriːk] Bach
°**creep** [kriːp]: **creep by** vorbei-, voran-kriechen **creep up** sich langsam erheben
crib sheet ['krɪb ʃiːt] *(infml)* Spickzettel, Merkzettel II
cricket ['krɪkɪt] Cricket I
°**criss-crossed** ['krɪskrɒst] durchkreuzt
°**criterion** [kraɪ'tɪəriən], *pl* **criteria** [kraɪ'tɪəriə] Kriterium
criticize sb. (for) ['krɪtɪsaɪz] jn. kritisieren (wegen) V 1 (27)
crocodile ['krɒkədaɪl] Krokodil V 1 (19)
crop [krɒp] (Feld-)Frucht); Ernte V 4 (101)
cross [krɒs]:
1. überqueren; sich kreuzen II:

2. **cross (with sb.)** böse, sauer (auf jn.) V 2 (42)
°**crossover** ['krɒsəʊvə] Crossover *(schneller Handwechsel beim Dribbeln)*
crossword ['krɒswɜːd] Kreuzworträtsel III
crowd [kraʊd] (Menschen-)Menge II
crowded ['kraʊdɪd] voller Menschen; überfüllt III
crown [kraʊn]:
1. Krone II
2. krönen IV
cruel ['kruːl] grausam III
cruise [kruːz] Kreuzfahrt, Schiffsreise, Bootsfahrt III
crush [krʌʃ] zerquetschen, zerdrücken IV
cry [kraɪ] schreien; weinen II
cue [kjuː] Stichwort, Signal *(Theater)* III
cultural ['kʌltʃərəl] kulturell V 2 (46)
culture ['kʌltʃə] Kultur III
cup [kʌp]: **a cup of tea** eine Tasse Tee I **World Cup** Weltmeisterschaft III
cupboard ['kʌbəd] Schrank I
curious ['kjʊəriəs] wissbegierig, neugierig III
°**curled up** [ˌkɜːld‿'ʌp] zusammengerollt
currency ['kʌrənsi] Währung III
current ['kʌrənt] aktuelle(r, s), gegenwärtige(r, s) V 3 (66)
curry ['kʌri] Curry(gericht) III
cut [kʌt], **cut, cut** schneiden II **Cut!** Schnitt! *(beim Filmen)* II **be cut off from sth.** von etwas abgeschnitten/abgetrennt sein IV
cute [kjuːt] niedlich, süß IV
CV (curriculum vitae) [ˌsiː 'viː], [kəˌrɪkjələm 'viːtaɪ] Lebenslauf V 3 (72)
cycle ['saɪkl] Rad fahren, mit dem Rad fahren V 4 (82) **cycle path** Radweg V 4 (89)
cyclist ['saɪklɪst] Radfahrer/in V 4 (82)
°**cyclone** ['saɪkləʊn] Zyklon, Wirbelsturm

D

dad [dæd] Papa, Vati I
°**daft** [dɑːft] albern
dairy products *(pl)* ['deəri prɒdʌkts] Milchprodukte, Molkereiprodukte IV
dam [dæm] Damm, Staudamm IV
damage ['dæmɪdʒ] (be)schädigen, schaden V 3 (72)
dance [dɑːns]:
1. tanzen I
2. Tanz II
dance floor ['dɑːns flɔː] Tanzfläche II
dancer ['dɑːnsə] Tänzer/in II
danger ['deɪndʒə] Gefahr II
dangerous ['deɪndʒərəs] gefährlich I
dark [dɑːk]:
1. dunkel I
2. Dunkelheit III
darkness ['dɑːknəs] Dunkelheit, Finsternis III
darling ['dɑːlɪŋ] Schatz, Liebling III
date [deɪt]:
1. Datum V 3 (72) **to date** bis heute, bis jetzt V 3 (73)
2. **date sb.** mit jm. gehen, mit jm. zusammen sein V 2 (42)
daughter ['dɔːtə] Tochter II
dawn [dɔːn] (Morgen-)Dämmerung V 4 (97)
day [deɪ] Tag I **all day** den ganzen Tag II **day of the week** Wochentag I **get/have a day off** einen Tag frei bekommen/haben III **go on day trips** Tagesausflüge machen II
dead [ded] tot I
deadline ['dedlaɪn] (letzter) Termin V 3 (58)
°**deal** [diːl] Geschäft
dear [dɪə]:
1. **Oh dear!** Oje! II
2. **dear** liebe(r, s) II
death [deθ] Tod III °**death penalty** Todesstrafe
debate [dɪ'beɪt]:
1. Debatte, Diskussion V 1 (27)
2. **debate sth.** über etwas debattieren V 1 (27)
°**decade** ['dekeɪd] Jahrzehnt
December [dɪ'sembə] Dezember I
decent ['diːsnt] anständig V 3 (61)
decide [dɪ'saɪd] beschließen, sich entscheiden II
decision [dɪ'sɪʒn] Entscheidung III
deck [dek] Deck, Terrasse I
declare sth. [dɪ'kleə] etwas erklären, verkünden V 2 (44)
dedicated ['dedɪkeɪtɪd]: **be dedicated to** gewidmet sein *(einer Sache/Person)* IV
deep [diːp] tief II
deer [dɪə], *pl* **deer** Reh, Hirsch II
defend [dɪ'fend]: **defend sb./sth. (against sb./sth.)** jn./etwas verteidigen (gegen jn./etwas) II
°**definition** [ˌdefɪ'nɪʃn] Definition, Begriffserklärung
degree [dɪ'griː] Grad IV
delicious [dɪ'lɪʃəs] köstlich, lecker II
delivery [dɪ'lɪvəri] Vortragsweise IV
demand (for) [dɪ'mɑːnd] Forderung (nach) V 4 (98)
democracy [dɪ'mɒkrəsi] Demokratie V 4 (93)
°**Democrat** ['deməkræt]: **the Democrats** die Demokraten *(US-Partei)*
°**democratic** [ˌdemə'krætɪk] demokratisch
demonstrate (for/against) ['demənstreɪt] (für/gegen etwas) demonstrieren V 4 (93)
demonstration [ˌdemən'streɪʃn] Demonstration, Vorführung II
°**demonstrator** ['demənstreɪtə] Demonstrant/in
°**denim capris** *(pl)* [ˌdenɪm kə'priːz] Caprihose, Dreiviertel-Hose aus Jeansstoff
dentist ['dentɪst] Zahnarzt/-ärztin II
deny [dɪ'naɪ] bestreiten, abstreiten; leugnen V 4 (88)
deodorant [di'əʊdərənt] Deodorant V 2 (37)
department [dɪ'pɑːtmənt] Abteilung; Fachbereich V 4 (98)
dependent [dɪ'pendənt]: **be dependent on sb./sth.** von jm./etwas abhängig sein, auf jn./etwas angewiesen sein V 2 (50)
depict sth. [dɪ'pɪkt] *(fml)* etwas darstellen, abbilden, zeigen V 4 (87)
°**deport sb.** [dɪ'pɔːt] jn. abschieben
describe sth. (to sb.) [dɪ'skraɪb] (jm.) etwas beschreiben II
description [dɪ'skrɪpʃn] Beschreibung III
descriptive [dɪ'skrɪptɪv] beschreibend V 1 (22)
desert ['dezət] Wüste IV
design [dɪ'zaɪn]:
1. entwerfen, konstruieren, entwickeln III
2. Design; Gestaltung; Konstruktion III **design and technology** Design und Technik I
°**designate** ['dezɪgneɪt] erklären
designer [dɪ'zaɪnə] Designer/in II
desk [desk] Schreibtisch I
dessert [dɪ'zɜːt] Nachtisch, Nachspeise I
destroy [dɪ'strɔɪ] zerstören II
detail ['diːteɪl] Detail, Einzelheit III
determined [dɪ'tɜːmɪnd]: **be determined to do sth.** (fest) entschlossen sein, etwas zu tun V 1 (18)
develop [dɪ'veləp] entwickeln; sich entwickeln V 3 (66)
diagnose ['daɪəgnəʊz] diagnostizieren V 3 (66)
diagram ['daɪəgræm] Diagramm IV
°**dialect** ['daɪəlekt] Dialekt
dialogue ['daɪəlɒg] Dialog II
diary ['daɪəri] Tagebuch; Kalender I
dictionary ['dɪkʃənri] alphabetisches Wörterverzeichnis, Wörterbuch I
did [dɪd]:
1. *siehe* **do**
2. **They did say eight o'clock.** Sie haben wirklich acht Uhr gesagt. V 3 (67) **You did promise.** Du hast es doch versprochen. V 3 (67)
°**didgeridoo** [ˌdɪdʒəri'duː] Didgeridoo *(Holzblasinstrument)*
die [daɪ] sterben I
diet ['daɪət] Ernährung(sweise), Speiseplan; Diät V 2 (44)
difference ['dɪfrəns] Unterschied IV **make a difference** etwas bewirken, etwas bewegen V 3 (59)
different ['dɪfrənt] verschieden; anders I **it was no different** es war nicht anders III
difficult ['dɪfɪkəlt] schwierig, schwer III

dig (for sth.) [dɪg], **dug, dug** (nach etwas) graben V 1 (26)
dignified ['dɪgnɪfaɪd] würdevoll, würdig IV
diner ['daɪnə] *(AE) (kleines, preiswertes)* Restaurant IV
dining room ['daɪnɪŋ ruːm] Esszimmer I
dinner ['dɪnə] Abendessen, Abendbrot I **have dinner** zu Abend essen I
direct [də'rekt], [daɪ'rekt] direkt III
directions *(pl)* [də'rekʃənz] Wegbeschreibung(en) IV **ask for directions** nach dem Weg fragen IV **give sb. directions (to)** jm. den Weg beschreiben (zu/nach) IV
director [də'rektə]:
1. Leiter/in III
2. Regisseur/in II
dirty ['dɜːti] schmutzig II
disadvantage [ˌdɪsəd'vɑːntɪdʒ] Nachteil V 1 (17)
disagree (with) [ˌdɪsə'griː] anderer Meinung sein (als); nicht übereinstimmen (mit); nicht zustimmen V 1 (23)
disappear [ˌdɪsə'pɪə] verschwinden II
disappointed (with) [ˌdɪsə'pɔɪntɪd] enttäuscht (von) IV
disco ['dɪskəʊ] Disko II
discover [dɪ'skʌvə] entdecken; herausfinden IV
discovery [dɪ'skʌvəri] Entdeckung IV
discriminate against sb. [dɪ'skrɪmɪneɪt] jn. diskriminieren, jn. benachteiligen V 4 (93)
discrimination (against) [dɪˌskrɪmɪ'neɪʃn] Diskriminierung (von) IV
discuss sth. [dɪ'skʌs] über etwas diskutieren, etwas besprechen V 1 (17)
discussion [dɪ'skʌʃn] Diskussion III
disease [dɪ'ziːz] *(ansteckende)* Krankheit III
disgusting [dɪs'gʌstɪŋ] ekelhaft, widerlich IV
dish [dɪʃ]:
1. Gericht (Speise) IV
2. **dishes** *(pl)*: **clear the dishes** das Geschirr abräumen III **wash the dishes** das Geschirr abwaschen, spülen II
dishonest [dɪs'ɒnɪst] unehrlich V 3 (63)
dislike [dɪs'laɪk] nicht mögen, nicht leiden können III
dislikes [dɪs'laɪks]: **likes and dislikes** *(pl)* Vorlieben und Abneigungen I
disrespectful [ˌdɪsrɪ'spektfl] respektlos V 3 (63)
distance ['dɪstəns] Distanz, Entfernung V 2 (50)
distant ['dɪstənt] (weit) entfernt, fern V 2 (37)
district ['dɪstrɪkt] Gegend, Bezirk, Viertel V 1 (12)
ditch [dɪtʃ] Graben III
dive in [daɪv‿'ɪn] *(mit dem Kopf voran)* hineinspringen III

divide (into) [dɪ'vaɪd] (sich) teilen (in), (sich) aufteilen (in) IV
divorced [dɪ'vɔːst] geschieden I
dizzy ['dɪzi] schwindlig III
do [duː], **did, done** machen, tun I **do sport** Sport treiben I **Don't go.** Geh nicht. I **he doesn't have time** er hat keine Zeit I **It does look good on you.** Es steht dir echt gut. V 3 (67) **they do eat more** sie essen wirklich mehr V 3 (67)
▶ S. 218 "do/does/did" in positive statements
doctor ['dɒktə] Arzt/Ärztin, Doktor II
documentary [ˌdɒkju'mentri] Dokumentarfilm IV
dog [dɒg] Hund I **walk the dog** mit dem Hund rausgehen, den Hund ausführen III
dollar ['dɒlə] Dollar IV
dolphin ['dɒlfɪn] Delfin III
done [dʌn] *siehe* **do**
door [dɔː] Tür I
doorbell ['dɔːbel] Türklingel II
dorsal fin [ˌdɔːsl 'fɪn] Rückenflosse III
°**dot** [dɒt] Pünktchen
double ['dʌbl] Doppel- I °**do a double-take** stutzen; zweimal hinschauen müssen
down [daʊn] hinunter, herunter; nach unten I **down there** dort unten II **up and down** auf und ab; rauf und runter I °**get sb. down** jn. runterziehen, jn. deprimieren
downhill [ˌdaʊn'hɪl] bergab III
downstairs [ˌdaʊn'steəz] unten; nach unten *(im Haus)* I
downstream [ˌdaʊn'striːm] flussabwärts III
downtown ['daʊntaʊn]: **in downtown New Orleans** *(AE)* im Zentrum von New Orleans IV
draft [drɑːft] Entwurf II
drama ['drɑːmə] Schauspiel; darstellende Kunst II
dramatic [drə'mætɪk] dramatisch V 1 (22)
drank [dræŋk] *siehe* **drink**
draw [drɔː], **drew, drawn** zeichnen I **draw attention to sth.** auf etwas aufmerksam machen; die Aufmerksamkeit auf etwas lenken V 4 (98)
drawing ['drɔːɪŋ] Zeichnung I
drawn [drɔːn] *siehe* **draw**
°**dreads** *(pl)* [dredz] Rastalocken
dream [driːm]:
1. Traum I
2. träumen V 2 (37)
dreamy ['driːmi] verträumt V 2 (37)
dress [dres] Kleid I
dress up [ˌdres‿'ʌp]:
1. sich verkleiden II
2. sich schick anziehen II
drew [druː] *siehe* **draw**
°**drift around** [ˌdrɪft‿ə'raʊnd] umhertreiben *(im Wasser)*

drink [drɪŋk]:
1. **(drank, drunk)** trinken I **drinking fountain** *(bes. BE)* Trinkbrunnen
2. Getränk I
drive [draɪv], **drove, driven** *(mit dem Auto)* fahren II **driver's license** *(AE)*; **driving licence** *(BE)* Führerschein, Fahrerlaubnis IV
driven ['drɪvn] *siehe* **drive**
drop [drɒp] fallen III **drop sth.** etwas fallen lassen II
drought [draʊt] Dürre, Trockenheit IV
drove [drəʊv] *siehe* **drive**
drown [draʊn] ertrinken III
drum [drʌm] Trommel I **drums** *(pl)* Schlagzeug I **play the drums** Schlagzeug spielen I
drummer ['drʌmə] Trommler/in; Schlagzeuger/in III
drunk [drʌŋk] *siehe* **drink**
dry [draɪ] trocken III
dug [dʌg] *siehe* **dig**
°**Duke** [djuːk] *Duke University in Durham, North Carolina*
°**dunk** [dʌŋk] den Ball in den Korb von oberhalb stopfen *(Basketball)*
during ['djʊərɪŋ] während III
dust [dʌst] Staub IV
dusty ['dʌsti] staubig IV
DVD [ˌdiːviː'diː] DVD I

E

each [iːtʃ] jeder, jede, jedes (einzelne) II
each other [iːtʃ‿'ʌðə] sich (gegenseitig), einander III
ear [ɪə] Ohr I
early ['ɜːli] früh I
earn [ɜːn] verdienen *(Geld)* III
earphones *(pl)* ['ɪəfəʊnz] Ohrhörer, Kopfhörer II
earring ['ɪərɪŋ] Ohrring IV
earth [ɜːθ] Erde *(der Planet)* II **on earth** auf der Erde II
east [iːst] Osten; nach Osten; östlich III
eastbound ['iːstbaʊnd] Richtung Osten III
Easter ['iːstə] Ostern III
eastern ['iːstən] östlich, Ost- III
easy ['iːzi] leicht, einfach I
easy-going [ˌiːzi'gəʊɪŋ] locker, unbeschwert, gelassen V 1 (13)
eat [iːt], **ate, eaten** essen I
eaten ['iːtn] *siehe* **eat**
°**echo** ['ekəʊ]:
1. Echo
2. **echo sth.** etwas wiederholen
ecology [i'kɒlədʒi] Ökologie IV
°**economy** [ɪ'kɒnəmi] (Volks-)Wirtschaft
edge [edʒ] Rand, Kante III
edit ['edɪt] bearbeiten; schneiden *(Film, Video)* I
editor ['edɪtə] Redakteur/in; Herausgeber/in III

education [ˌedʒu'keɪʃn] (Schul-, Aus-) Bildung; Erziehung III
effect [ɪ'fekt] (Aus-)Wirkung (auf) IV
effective [ɪ'fektɪv] effektiv, wirkungsvoll V 4 (87)
e.g. [ˌiː 'dʒiː] z.B. (zum Beispiel) II
egg [eg] Ei II
eight [eɪt] acht I
either ['aɪðə], ['iːðə]: **not … either** auch nicht II **either … or …** entweder … oder … V 4 (88)
°**elders** *(pl)* ['eldəz] Ältere
°**elect sb.** [ɪ'lekt] jn. ins Amt wählen
elections *(pl)* [ɪ'lekʃnz] Wahlen V 2 (36)
electronic [ɪˌlek'trɒnɪk] elektronisch III
element ['elɪmənt] Element III
elephant ['elɪfənt] Elefant I
elevator ['elɪveɪtə] *(bes. AE)* Fahrstuhl, Aufzug, Lift IV
eleven [ɪ'levn] elf I
else [els]: **anything else** sonst noch etwas III **everybody else** alle anderen; sonst jeder III **no one else** niemand anders; niemand sonst III **someone else** jemand anders III ° **somewhere else** anderswo **what else?** was (sonst) noch? III **who else?** wer (sonst) noch? III
email ['iːmeɪl] E-Mail I
embarrass sb. [ɪm'bærəs] jn. in Verlegenheit bringen V 3 (60)
embarrassing [ɪm'bærəsɪŋ] peinlich V 3 (60)
emergency [ɪ'mɜːdʒənsi] Notfall, Not- IV
emigrate ['emɪgreɪt] auswandern, emigrieren III
emotion [ɪ'məʊʃn] Gefühl, Emotion V 3 (63)
emotional [ɪ'məʊʃənl] emotional; gefühlsbetont IV
°**employer** [ɪm'plɔɪə] Arbeitgeber/in
empty ['empti] leer III
encore ['ɒŋkɔː] Zugabe II
°**encounter** [ɪn'kaʊntə] Begegnung
encourage [ɪn'kʌrɪdʒ] ermutigen V 2 (48)
end [end]:
1. Ende, Schluss I **in the end** schließlich, am Ende, zum Schluss V 1 (13)
2. enden; beenden III **end up doing sth.** schließlich etwas tun V 2 (50)
ending ['endɪŋ] Ende, (Ab-)Schluss II
endless ['endləs] endlos IV
enemy ['enəmi] Feind/in II
energy ['enədʒi] Energie, Kraft III
engine ['endʒɪn] Motor, Maschine IV
engineer [ˌendʒɪ'nɪə] Ingenieur/in III
English ['ɪŋglɪʃ] Englisch; englisch I **in English** auf Englisch I
enjoy [ɪn'dʒɔɪ] genießen III **Enjoy yourself.** Viel Spaß! / Amüsiere dich gut! III
enough [ɪ'nʌf] genug I
enter ['entə]:
1. betreten, hineingehen in II
2. enter sth. etwas eingeben, eintragen V 2 (43)
entertainment [ˌentə'teɪnmənt] Unterhaltung III
°**entire** [ɪn'taɪə] ganze(r, s)
entry ['entri]:
1. Eintrag, Eintragung *(im Tagebuch, Wörterbuch)* II
2. Eintritt, Zutritt III
environment [ɪn'vaɪrənmənt] Umwelt IV
environmental [ɪnˌvaɪrən'mentl] Umwelt- V 4 (87)
°**episode** ['epɪsəʊd] Episode
equal ['iːkwəl] gleich(gestellt) V 3 (67)
equality [i'kwɒləti] Gleichheit, Gleichberechtigung V 4 (89)
equipment *(no pl)* [ɪ'kwɪpmənt] Ausrüstung III
escape [ɪ'skeɪp]:
1. fliehen III **escape sth.** etwas entfliehen, entkommen V 4 (97)
2. Flucht III
°**esky** ['eski] *(AusE; infml)* Kühlbox
especially [ɪ'speʃli] besonders, vor allem III
°**established** [ɪ'stæblɪʃt] etabliert, gängig
°**estimate** ['estɪmeɪt] (ein)schätzen
etc. (et cetera) [et'setərə] usw. (und so weiter) II
EU, the [ˌiː 'juː] die Europäische Union III
euro ['jʊərəʊ] Euro III
Europe ['jʊərəp] Europa III
European Union, the [ˌjʊərəpiːən 'juːniən] die Europäische Union III
eurozone ['jʊərəʊzəʊn] Eurozone III
evacuate [ɪ'vækjueɪt] evakuieren IV
°**evaluate** [ɪ'væljueɪt] bewerten, einschätzen
°**evaluation** [ɪˌvælju'eɪʃn] Bewertung, Beurteilung
even ['iːvn] sogar II **not even** (noch) nicht einmal II **even if** selbst wenn II **even though** auch wenn; obwohl IV
evening ['iːvnɪŋ] Abend I **in the evening** abends, am Abend I **this evening** heute Abend II
event [ɪ'vent] Ereignis II
eventful [ɪ'ventfl] ereignisreich IV
ever ['evə] jemals II **better than ever** besser als je zuvor II **for ever** (für) immer; ewig II ° **Ever since …** Von dem Tag an, an dem …
every day/colour/boat ['evri] jeder Tag / jede Farbe / jedes Boot I
everybody ['evribɒdi] jeder; alle I
everyday ['evrideɪ] Alltags- I
everyone ['evriwʌn] jeder; alle I
everything ['evriθɪŋ] alles II
everywhere ['evriweə] überall II
evolution [ˌiːvə'luːʃn] Evolution V 3 (67)
ex- [eks] Ex-; ehemalige(r, s) V 2 (42)
exact [ɪg'zækt] genau III
exactly [ɪg'zæktli] genau III
exam [ɪg'zæm] Prüfung V 4 (97) **take an exam** eine Prüfung ablegen V 4 (97)
°**examine** [ɪg'zæmɪn] prüfen
example [ɪg'zɑːmpl] Beispiel II
excellent ['eksələnt] ausgezeichnet, hervorragend IV
except [ɪk'sept] außer, bis auf II
excerpt (from) ['eksɜːpt] Auszug (aus) V 3 (60)
exchange [ɪks'tʃeɪndʒ] Austausch, Austausch- V 1 (11)
excited [ɪk'saɪtɪd] aufgeregt, gespannt I
exciting [ɪk'saɪtɪŋ] aufregend, spannend I
exclamation mark [ˌekskla'meɪʃn mɑːk] Ausrufezeichen II
Excuse me, … [ɪk'skjuːz miː] Entschuldigung, … / Entschuldigen Sie, … II
excused [ɪk'skjuːzd] entschuldigt IV
exercise ['eksəsaɪz] Aufgabe, Übung I
exercise book ['eksəsaɪz bʊk] Schulheft, Übungsheft I
exotic [ɪg'zɒtɪk] exotisch V 1 (10)
expect [ɪk'spekt] erwarten III
°**expenses** *(pl)* [ɪk'spensɪs] Kosten, Ausgaben
expensive [ɪk'spensɪv] teuer I
experience [ɪk'spɪəriəns]:
1. Erfahrung(en) III
°**2.** Erlebnis
3. erfahren, erleben IV
experienced [ɪk'spɪəriənst] erfahren V 1 (16)
experiment [ɪk'sperɪmənt] Experiment V 3 (66)
expert ['ekspɜːt] Experte/Expertin IV
explain sth. to sb. [ɪk'spleɪn] jm. etwas erklären, erläutern I
explanation [ˌeksplə'neɪʃn] Erklärung IV
explore [ɪk'splɔː] erkunden, erforschen III
export ['ekspɔːt] Export, Ausfuhr III
express [ɪk'spres] ausdrücken, zum Ausdruck bringen V 2 (49)
expression [ɪk'spreʃn] Ausdruck III
extra ['ekstrə] zusätzlich IV
°**extract** ['ekstrækt] Auszug
extraordinary [ɪk'strɔːdnri] außergewöhnlich III
extremely [ɪk'striːmli] äußerst, höchst IV
eye [aɪ] Auge I

F

°**F** [ef] ungenügend *(Schulnote)*
face [feɪs]:
1. Gesicht I
2. face sth. vor etwas stehen; mit etwas konfrontiert werden *(Problem)* V 2 (50)
facial expression [ˌfeɪʃl‿ɪk'spreʃn] Gesichtsausdruck, Mimik III

facilities *(pl)* [fə'sɪlətiz] Einrichtungen, Ausstattung, Anlage(n), Angebot(e) V 1 (22)
fact [fækt] Tatsache, Fakt III **in fact** eigentlich, in Wirklichkeit III
factory ['fæktri] Fabrik IV
Fahrenheit (F) ['færənhaɪt] Fahrenheit IV
fail [feɪl]: **fail (to do sth.)** versagen, scheitern (beim Versuch, etwas zu tun) V 3 (58) **fail (a test)** nicht bestehen *(Test, Prüfung)*; durchfallen IV
faint [feɪnt]: **I'm feeling faint.** Mir ist schwindelig. IV
fair [feə]:
1. fair, gerecht I
2. Ausstellung, Messe V 3 (66)
fairly ['feəli] ziemlich IV
fall [fɔːl], **fell, fallen** fallen, stürzen; hinfallen I **fall asleep** einschlafen I **fall in love (with sb.)** sich (in jn.) verlieben V 2 (42)
fallen ['fɔːlən] *siehe* **fall**
false [fɔːls] falsch III
familiar [fə'mɪliə] vertraut V 2 (38)
family ['fæməli] Familie I **a family of four** eine vierköpfige Familie III **the Bell family** (die) Familie Bell I **family tree** (Familien-)Stammbaum I **host family** Gastfamilie II
► S. 199 Group nouns
famine ['fæmɪn] Hungersnot III
famous (for) ['feɪməs] berühmt (für, wegen) II
fan [fæn] Fan, Anhänger/in I
fancy sth. ['fænsi] *(infml)* Lust auf / zu etwas haben IV
fantastic [fæn'tæstɪk] fantastisch I
far [fɑː] weit (entfernt) I **so far** bis jetzt; bis hierher II
°**faraway** ['fɑːrəweɪ] fern
farm [fɑːm] Bauernhof, Farm I
farmer ['fɑːmə] Bauer/Bäuerin, Landwirt/in I
farmhouse ['fɑːmhaʊs] Bauernhaus III
fashion ['fæʃn] Mode II
fast [fɑːst]:
1. schnell I **be fast** vorgehen *(Uhr)* III
°2. **be fast asleep** tief/fest schlafen
fat [fæt] dick, fett I
father ['fɑːðə] Vater I
fault [fɔːlt] Schuld, Fehler III
favourite ['feɪvərɪt]: **my favourite animal** mein Lieblingstier I
February ['februəri] Februar I
fed [fed] *siehe* **feed**
°**federal** ['fedərəl] Bundes-
feed [fiːd], **fed, fed** füttern I **feeding time** Fütterungszeit I **feed on sth.** sich von etwas ernähren V 1 (19)
feedback *(no pl)* ['fiːdbæk] Rückmeldung, Feedback III
feel [fiːl], **felt, felt** fühlen; sich fühlen I; sich anfühlen III **feel like (doing) sth.** Lust auf etwas haben / Lust haben, etwas zu tun V 4 (92) **I feel sick.** Mir ist schlecht. II **I don't feel well** Ich fühle mich nicht gut. / Mir geht's nicht gut. II
feeling ['fiːlɪŋ] Gefühl I
°**fees** *(pl)* [fiːz] Gebühren
feet [fiːt] *Plural von* **foot** II
fell [fel] *siehe* **fall**
°**fellow** ['feləʊ] Kamerad/in **fellows** *(pl)* Mitmenschen; Kollegen/-innen
felt [felt] *siehe* **feel**
felt craft ['felt krɑːft] Filzen V 3 (73)
felt pen [felt 'pen] Filzstift II
female ['fiːmeɪl] weiblich; weibliche Person; Weibchen V 4 (42)
fence [fens] Zaun II
ferry ['feri] Fähre I
festival ['festɪvl] Fest, Festival II
few [fjuː]: **a few** ein paar, einige II
field [fiːld] Feld, Acker, Weide II
fight [faɪt]:
1. **(fought, fought)** kämpfen I **fight sb.** jn. bekämpfen II
2. Kampf, Schlägerei III
fighter ['faɪtə] Kämpfer/in II
figure ['fɪgə]:
1. Zahl, Ziffer III
2. Figur, Gestalt III
°**figure** ['fɪgə] glauben, annehmen
file [faɪl]: **background file** *Hintergrundinformation(en)* I **grammar file** *Zusammenfassung der Grammatik jeder Unit* I **skills file** *Übersicht über Lern- und Arbeitstechniken* I
fill [fɪl] füllen III **fill in a form** ein Formular ausfüllen V 2 (50)
film [fɪlm]:
1. filmen I
2. Film I
°**film-maker** ['fɪlmˌmeɪkə] Filmemacher/in
filthy ['fɪlθi] schmutzig, dreckig IV
fin [fɪn] Flosse III **dorsal fin** Rückenflosse III
final ['faɪnl]:
1. Finale, Endspiel I
2. letzte(r, s), End- III
finally ['faɪnəli] endlich, schließlich III
find [faɪnd], **found, found** finden I **Find someone who …** Finde jemanden, der … I **find sth. out** etwas herausfinden II
fine [faɪn]:
1. fein II **Fine, thanks.** Gut, danke. I **That's fine by me.** Das soll mir recht sein. / Von mir aus gern. V 2 (36)
2. Geldstrafe V 4 (88)
finger ['fɪŋgə] Finger II
finish ['fɪnɪʃ]:
1. enden I
2. **finish sth**. etwas beenden; mit etwas fertig werden/sein I **We're finished.** Wir sind fertig. I
°3. Ende
fire ['faɪə] Feuer II
fire department ['faɪə dɪˌpɑːtmənt] *(AE)* Feuerwehr IV
firefighter ['faɪəfaɪtə] Feuerwehrmann/-frau IV
fireplace ['faɪəpleɪs] Kamin II
°**firepower** ['faɪəpaʊə] Feuerkraft
firework ['faɪəwɜːk] Feuerwerkskörper II **fireworks** *(pl)* Feuerwerk II
first [fɜːst] zuerst, als Erstes I **at first** zuerst, anfangs, am Anfang II **first name** Vorname IV **the first day** der erste Tag I **First Aid** Erste Hilfe V 2 (37) **first-person narrative** Ich-Erzählung V 4 (86) **first-person narrator** Ich-Erzähler/in V 4 (86)
Firstly, … ['fɜːstli] Erstens … V 1 (17)
fish [fɪʃ]:
1. *pl* **fish** Fisch I
2. fischen, angeln V 2 (41) **fish sth. out** etwas herausfischen III
fishing ['fɪʃɪŋ]:
1. Fischerei III
2. **go fishing** angeln; angeln gehen IV
°3. **fishing gear** Angelausrüstung
fit in [ˌfɪt_'ɪn] sich einfügen, seinen Platz finden; hineinpassen V 2 (50)
five [faɪv] fünf I
flag [flæg] Fahne, Flagge II
flame [fleɪm] Flamme IV
flash [flæʃ]:
1. Lichtblitz II **a flash of lightning** ein Blitz II
2. **flash (through sb.'s mind)** jm. durch den Kopf schießen IV °**flash a smile** ein Lächeln aufblitzen lassen
flashmob ['flæʃmɒb] V 4 (82)
flat [flæt]:
1. Wohnung I
2. flach, eben V 1 (22)
°**flaunt sth.** [flɔːnt] etwas zur Schau stellen, mit etwas protzen
flew [fluː] *siehe* **fly**
flight [flaɪt] Flug V 1 (12)
flood [flʌd]:
1. überfluten, überschwemmen V 1 (18)
2. Flut, Überschwemmung V 1 (18)
floodlight ['flʌdlaɪt] Flutlicht(lampe) IV
floor [flɔː]:
1. Fußboden I
2. Stock(werk) II
flour ['flaʊə] Mehl IV
flow [fləʊ] fließen IV
flower ['flaʊə] Blume; Blüte II
flown [fləʊn] *siehe* **fly**
fly [flaɪ]:
1. Fliege V 3 (61)
2. **(flew, flown)** fliegen II
flying fox [ˌflaɪɪŋ 'fɒks] Flughund V 1 (12)
focus ['fəʊkəs]:
1. **focus (on sth.)** sich (auf etwas) konzentrieren V 3 (69)
2. **focus on sth.** den Blick/die Aufmerksamkeit auf etwas lenken; auf etwas fokussieren V 4 (87)
fold [fəʊld] falten V 3 (61)
folk [fəʊk] *(pl, infml)* Leute III

follow ['fɒləʊ] folgen I **Follow me.** Folg(t) mir. I
food [fu:d] Essen; Lebensmittel; Futter I
°**fool sb.** [fu:l] jn. zum Narren halten, jn. hereinlegen
foot [fʊt], *pl* **feet** [fi:t]:
1. Fuß II
2. Fuß *(Längenmaß; ca. 30 cm)* IV
football ['fʊtbɔ:l] Fußball I
°**footbridge** ['fʊtbrɪdʒ] Fußgängerbrücke
footprint ['fʊtprɪnt] Fußabdruck II
footstep ['fʊtstep] Schritt IV
for [fɔ:], [fə] für I **for ever** (für) immer; ewig II **for example** zum Beispiel II **for hours/weeks/...** seit Stunden/Wochen/... III **for miles** meilenweit II **for the first time** zum ersten Mal III **What's for lunch?** Was gibt es zum Mittagessen? I **What's for homework?** Was haben wir als Hausaufgabe auf? I
forbade [fə'bæd], [fə'beɪd] *siehe* **forbid**
forbid [fə'bɪd], **forbade, forbidden** verbieten V 4 (99)
forbidden [fə'bɪdn] *siehe* **forbid**
force [fɔ:s]:
1. **force sb. to do sth.** jn. zwingen, etwas zu tun; jn. dazu bringen, etwas zu tun IV
°2. **in force** in Kraft
foreground ['fɔ:graʊnd] Vordergrund II
foreign ['fɒrən] fremd, ausländisch IV
foreign language Fremdsprache IV
forest ['fɒrɪst] Wald II
forever [fər'evə] (für) immer; ewig IV
forget [fə'get], **forgot, forgotten** vergessen I
forgot [fə'gɒt] *siehe* **forget**
forgotten [fə'gɒtn] *siehe* **forget**
fork [fɔ:k] Gabel II
form [fɔ:m]:
1. Form I
2. bilden, formen III
3. Formular V 2 (50)
formal ['fɔ:ml] formell, förmlich V 2 (41)
former ['fɔ:mə] ehemalige(r, s), frühere(r, s) V 3 (60)
fortunately ['fɔ:tʃənətli] glücklicherweise V 1 (27)
forward ['fɔ:wəd] *(BE auch:* **forwards***)* vorwärts, nach vorn V 4 (101) **look forward to sth.** sich auf etwas freuen II
fought [fɔ:t] *siehe* **fight**
foul [faʊl] Foul III
found [faʊnd]:
1. *siehe* **find**
2. gründen III
fountain ['faʊntən]: **water fountain** *(bes. AE)*; **drinking fountain** *(bes. BE)* Trinkbrunnen IV
four [fɔ:] vier I **a family of four** eine vierköpfige Familie III
fox [fɒks] Fuchs V 1 (12)
free [fri:]:
1. frei I **free time** Freizeit, freie Zeit I **free-time activities** Freizeitaktivitäten I **free kick** Freistoß III
2. kostenlos II
freeze [fri:z], **froze, frozen** (ge)frieren; zufrieren; einfrieren IV **It's freezing.** Es ist sehr kalt. IV
French [frentʃ] Französisch I
fresh [freʃ] frisch II
Friday ['fraɪdeɪ] Freitag I
fridge [frɪdʒ] Kühlschrank V 2 (38)
friend ['frend] Freund/in I
friendly ['frendli] freundlich I
friendship ['frendʃɪp] Freundschaft V 2 (50)
fries *(pl)* [fraɪz] Pommes frites II
°**friggin'** [ˌfrɪgɪŋ]: **He's friggin' dead!** *(infml)* Er ist tot, verdammt!
frightened ['fraɪtnd] verängstigt V 2 (42)
frog [frɒg] Frosch I
from [frɒm], [frəm] aus, von I **from ... to ...** von ... bis ... I **a hundred years from now** in einhundert Jahren V 4 (101)
front [frʌnt]:
1. Vorderseite I
2. **in front of** vor *(räumlich)*
3. **to the front** nach vorne II
4. Front V 2 (44)
frown [fraʊn] die Stirn runzeln II
froze [frəʊz] *siehe* **freeze**
frozen ['frəʊzn]:
1. *siehe* **freeze**
2. tiefgekühlt IV
fruit [fru:t] Obst, Früchte; Frucht I
fruit salad Obstsalat I
fry [fraɪ] braten *(in der Pfanne)* IV
frying pan ['fraɪɪŋ pæn] Bratpfanne IV
full (of) [fʊl] voll II **full sentence** ganzer Satz II
full stop [ˌfʊl 'stɒp] Punkt II
fumes *(pl)* [fju:mz] Dämpfe, Abgase, Schwaden IV
fun [fʌn] Spaß I **have fun** Spaß haben, sich amüsieren I **make fun of sb./sth.** sich über jn./etwas lustig machen III **That sounds fun.** Das klingt nach Spaß. I **Was it fun?** Hat es Spaß gemacht? I
funeral ['fju:nərəl] Trauerfeier III
funny ['fʌni] witzig, komisch I
fun park ['fʌn pɑ:k] Vergnügungspark II
fur [fɜ:] Fell; Pelz V 3 (67)
furious (with/at sb.) ['fjʊəriəs] wütend, zornig (auf jn.), wutentbrannt V 2 (42)
furniture *(no pl)* ['fɜ:nɪtʃə] Möbel III
The furniture is new. Die Möbel sind neu. III **a piece of furniture** ein Möbel(stück) III
further ['fɜ:ðə] weiter II
furthermore [ˌfɜ:ðə'mɔ:] außerdem, ferner; des Weiteren V 1 (17)
furthest ['fɜ:ðɪst] am weitesten II
future ['fju:tʃə]:
1. Zukunft II
2. zukünftige(r, s) II

G

gallery ['gæləri] Galerie III
gallop ['gæləp]:
1. Galopp IV
2. galoppieren IV
game [geɪm] Spiel I
garage ['gærɑ:ʒ], ['gærɪdʒ] Garage I
garbage ['gɑ:bɪdʒ] *(AE)* Müll, Abfall IV
garden ['gɑ:dn] Garten I
gardener ['gɑ:dnə] Gärtner/in IV
gardening ['gɑ:dnɪŋ] Gärtnern, Gartenarbeit I
garlic ['gɑ:lɪk] Knoblauch IV
gate [geɪt] Tor, Pforte, Gatter II
gather ['gæðə] sich versammeln V 4 (97)
gave [geɪv] *siehe* **give**
gaze [geɪz] blicken, starren IV
gel [dʒel] Gel II
gender ['dʒendə] Geschlecht *(als soziale Merkmal)* V 4 (89)
°**general** ['dʒenrəl] allgemeine(r, s)
generation [ˌdʒenə'reɪʃn] Generation IV
generous ['dʒenərəs] großzügig V 3 (63)
gently ['dʒentli] behutsam, sanft III
geography [dʒi'ɒgrəfi] Geografie I
German ['dʒɜ:mən] Deutsch; deutsch I
in German auf Deutsch I
gesture ['dʒestʃə] Geste, Handbewegung V 3 (71)
get [get], **got, got**:
1. bekommen I **Did you get it?** *(infml)* Hast du es mitbekommen/verstanden? I **get paid** Geld bekommen III **get sth.** (sich) etwas besorgen, (sich) etwas holen II
2. gelangen, (hin)kommen I **get in touch (with sb.)** (mit jm.) Kontakt aufnehmen; sich (mit jm.) in Verbindung setzen II **get in(to) a car** in ein Auto einsteigen II **get into trouble** in Schwierigkeiten geraten, Ärger kriegen III **get on a bus/train/plane** in einen Bus/Zug, in ein Flugzeug einsteigen II **get off a bus/boat** aus einem Bus/Boot aussteigen I **get out of a car** aus einem Auto aussteigen II **get to know sb.** jn. kennenlernen V 2 (42)
3. **get on** vorankommen, zurechtkommen II
4. **get up** aufstehen I
5. **get angry/cold/...** wütend/kalt/... werden I **get ready (for)** sich fertig machen (für), sich vorbereiten (auf) II
ghost [gəʊst] Geist, Gespenst I
giant ['dʒaɪənt]:
1. Riese III
2. riesig, Riesen- IV
gift [gɪft] Geschenk; Gabe V 3 (62) **gift voucher** Geschenkgutschein V 1 (23)
giraffe [dʒə'rɑ:f] Giraffe I
girl [gɜ:l] Mädchen I
girlfriend ['gɜ:lfrend] Freundin III
give [gɪv], **gave, given:** geben I **give a talk (about)** einen Vortrag / eine

Fede halten (über) I **give sb. a lift** jn. mitnehmen II **give sb. a hug** jn. umarmen II **give up** aufgeben III **give sb. a hard time** jn. fertig machen, jm. einheizen III **give sb. directions (to)** jm. den Weg beschreiben (zu/nach) IV
given ['gɪvn] *siehe* **give**
glad [glæd] froh, dankbar III
°**glance** [glɑːns]: **sneak glances** einen schnellen Blick werfen
glass [glɑːs] Glas II **a glass of water** ein Glas Wasser II
glasses *(pl)* ['glɑːsɪz] (eine) Brille II
global ['gləʊbl] global V 3 (59) **global warming** Erderwärmung, Erwärmung der Erdatmosphäre V 3 (59)
glove [glʌv] Handschuh II
glue [gluː] Klebstoff I
glue stick ['gluː stɪk] Klebestift I
glum [glʌm] niedergeschlagen IV
go [gəʊ]:
1. **(went, gone)** gehen; fahren I **go by** *(time)* vergehen, vorübergehen *(Zeit)* II **go down** untergehen *(Sonne)* I **go for a walk** spazieren gehen, einen Spaziergang machen I **go green/hard/...** grün/hart/... werden II **go in** hineingehen II **go on** 1. weiterreden, fortfahren; weitermachen I 2. im Gang sein; andauern III **go on day trips** Tagesausflüge machen II **go red** rot werden, erröten II **go together** zusammenpassen, zueinander passen III **go with sth.** zu etwas gehören, zu etwas passen I **Here we go.** Los geht's. / Jetzt geht's los. I **I'm going to sing a song.** Ich werde ein Lied singen. / Ich habe vor ein Lied zu singen. II
2. **Have a go.** Versuch's mal. I
goal [gəʊl]:
1. Tor *(Sport)* III **goal net** Tornetz III **goalkeeper** ['gəʊlkiːpə] Torwart, Torfrau III
2. Ziel V 3 (58)
°**goanna** [gəʊ'ænə] Waran
goat [gəʊt] Ziege II
God [gɒd] Gott III
go-kart ['gəʊ kɑːt] Gokart II
gold [gəʊld]:
1. Gold I
2. golden, Gold- II
golden ['gəʊldən] golden IV
gone [gɒn] *siehe* **go** **be gone** weg sein, nicht (mehr) da sein III
good [gʊd]:
1. gut I **be good at kung fu** gut sein in Kung-Fu; gut Kung-Fu können I **Good luck!** Viel Glück! I **Good morning.** Guten Morgen. I
2. brav II
Goodbye. [ˌgʊd'baɪ] Auf Wiedersehen. I
good-looking [ˌgʊd'lʊkɪŋ] gutaussehend II
goods *(pl)* [gʊdz] Waren, Güter I
°**gorgeous** ['gɔːdʒəs] hinreißend, prachtvoll
got [gɒt]:
1. *siehe* **get**
2. **Have you got ...?** Haben Sie ...? / Hast du ...? / Habt ihr ...? II
govern ['gʌvən] regieren IV
government ['gʌvənmənt] Regierung III
▶ S. 199 Group nouns
°**Governor** ['gʌvənə] Gouverneur/in
grab [græb] schnappen, packen III **grab sb.'s attention** jemandes Aufmerksamkeit erregen; jemandes Aufmerksamkeit gewinnen V 4 (98)
grade [greɪd]:
1. *(AE)* Jahrgangsstufe, Klasse IV
2. *(bes. AE)* (Schul-)Note, Zensur IV
graffiti [grə'fiːti] Graffiti IV
gram (g) [græm] Gramm II
grammar file ['græmə ˌfaɪl] *Zusammenfassung der Grammatik* I
°**grand** [grænd] groß
grandfather ['grænfɑːðə] Großvater I
grandma ['grænmɑː] Oma I **at Grandma's (house/flat)** bei Oma II
grandmother ['grænmʌðə] Großmutter I
grandpa ['grænpɑː] Opa I
grandparents *(pl)* ['grænpeərənts] Großeltern I
granite ['grænɪt] Granit IV
graphics *(pl)* ['græfɪks] Grafiken IV
grass [grɑːs] Gras; Rasen II
grave [greɪv] Grab II
gravestone ['greɪvstəʊn] Grabstein III
great [greɪt] großartig I
great-grandfather [ˌgreɪt'grænfɑːðə] Urgroßvater IV
great-grandmother [ˌgreɪt'grænmʌðə] Urgroßmutter IV
green [griːn] grün I
greenhouse ['griːnhaʊs] Gewächshaus, Treibhaus V 1 (20)
grew [gruː] *siehe* **grow**
grey *(BE)* / **gray** *(AE)* [greɪ] grau I
groan [grəʊn]:
1. Stöhnen II
2. stöhnen II
ground [graʊnd]:
1. (Erd-)Boden II
2. **ground sb.** jm. Hausarrest/Ausgehverbot erteilen III
grounds *(pl)* [graʊndz] Gelände IV
group (of) [gruːp] Gruppe I
▶ S. 199 Group nouns
grow [grəʊ], **grew, grown:**
1. anbauen, anpflanzen I
2. wachsen II
3. **grow up** [ˌgrəʊ‿'ʌp] erwachsen werden; aufwachsen III
grown [grəʊn] *siehe* **grow**
grown up [ˌgrəʊn‿'ʌp] erwachsen V 1 (26)
guard [gɑːd]:
1. Wachposten, Wache II
2. bewachen III
guess [ges] raten, erraten, schätzen I **Guess what, Dad ...** Stell dir vor, Papa ... / Weißt du was, Papa ... I **I guess ...** Ich nehme an, ... / Ich denke, ... IV
guest [gest] Gast III
°**guidance service** ['gaɪdəns] Beratungsservice
guide [gaɪd]:
1. Fremdenführer/in; Reiseleiter/in II
2. Reiseführer V 1 (12)
3. führen V 1 (12) **guided tour** Führung V 1 (12)
guidebook ['gaɪdbʊk] Reiseführer III
guinea pig ['gɪni pɪg] Meerschweinchen I
guitar [gɪ'tɑː] Gitarre I **play the guitar** Gitarre spielen I
guy [gaɪ] Typ, Kerl IV **guys** *(pl)* Leute IV
gym [dʒɪm]:
1. Turnhalle I
2. Fitnessstudio IV
gymnastics [dʒɪm'næstɪks] Gymnastik, Turnen I

H

habit ['hæbɪt] (An-)Gewohnheit V 2 (48) °**get in the saving habit** sich das Sparen angewöhnen
hack [hæk] hacken V 2 (43)
hacker [hækə] Hacker/in V 4 (88)
habitat ['hæbɪtæt] Lebensraum III
had [hæd] *siehe* **have**
hair [heə] Haar, Haare I
haircut ['heəkʌt] Haarschnitt V 2 (36)
hairdresser ['heədresə] Friseur/in III
half [hɑːf], *pl* **halves** [hɑːvz]:
1. Hälfte IV **half past ten** halb elf (10.30 / 22.30) I **one and a half** eineinhalb IV
2. Halbzeit I **at half-time** zur Halbzeit III
3. **a half-hour ride** eine halbstündige Fahrt V 1 (12)
▶ S. 198 a half-hour ride ...
hall [hɔːl]: **town hall** Rathaus II
hamburger ['hæmbɜːgə] Hamburger II
hammer ['hæmə]:
1. Hammer III
2. hämmern III
hamster ['hæmstə] Hamster II
hand [hænd]:
1. Hand I **Clap your hands.** Klatscht in die Hände. II **on the one hand, on the other hand** Einerseits ... Andererseits ... V 1 (17) **put your hand up** sich melden III
2. **hand sth. in** etwas abgeben; etwas einreichen II **hand sth. over** etwas übergeben, aushändigen V 3 (61)
3. Uhrzeiger V 2 (39)
°**handcuff sb.** ['hændkʌf] jn. in Handschellen anlegen
°**handle sth.** ['hændl] etwas erledigen

handmade [ˌhænd'meɪd] handgemacht V 2 (51)
handout ['hændaʊt] Handout, Handzettel III
hang [hæŋ], **hung, hung:** hängen II **hang out** [ˌhæŋ‿'aʊt] *(infml)* hängen, abhängen, rumhängen IV
happen (to) ['hæpən] geschehen, passieren (mit) II
happy ['hæpi] glücklich, froh I **be happy to do sth.** gern etwas tun; (gern) bereit sein, etwas zu tun V 4 (90)
harbour ['hɑːbə] Hafen I
hard [hɑːd] schwer, schwierig; hart I **give sb. a hard time** jn. fertig machen, jm. einheizen; III **go hard** *(bread)* hart werden II
hardly ['hɑːdli] kaum IV
hard-working [ˌhɑːd'wɜːkɪŋ] fleißig V 3 (63)
harmonica [hɑː'mɒnɪkə] Mundharmonika IV
has [hæz]: **he/she has** er/sie hat I
hat [hæt] Hut II
hate [heɪt] hassen III
have [hæv], [həv], **had, had** haben I **Have a go.** Versuch's mal. I **have breakfast** frühstücken I **have lunch/dinner** zu Mittag/Abend essen I **have fun** Spaß haben, sich amüsieren I **have sth. done** etwas machen (erledigen) lassen V 3 (67) **have to do** tun müssen I **I'll have a tea/...** Ich nehme einen Tee/... *(beim Essen, im Restaurant)* II **May I have a word with you?** Kann ich Sie kurz sprechen? II
have got [hæv 'gɒt], [həv 'gɒt], **had, had** haben II **Have you got ...?** Hast du ...? II
hay [heɪ] Heu II
he [hiː] er I
head [hed]
1. Kopf I °**head of state** Staatsoberhaupt
2. head for sth. auf etwas zusteuern/zugehen/zufahren III °**head off (to ...)** sich auf den Weg (nach/zu ...) machen
headache ['hedeɪk]: **have a headache** Kopfschmerzen haben II
heading ['hedɪŋ] Überschrift IV
head teacher [ˌhed 'tiːtʃə] Schulleiter/in III
headword ['hedwɜːd] Stichwort *(im Wörterbuch)* III
health [helθ] Gesundheit V 1 (26)
healthy ['helθi] gesund V 2 (45)
hear [hɪə], **heard, heard** hören I
heard [hɜːd] *siehe* **hear**
heart [hɑːt] Herz II **My heart goes out to ...** Ich fühle mit ... / Mein Mitgefühl gilt ... IV
heartbroken ['hɑːtbrəʊkən] todunglücklich, untröstlich V 2 (42)
heartless ['hɑːtləs] herzlos IV
heat [hiːt] Hitze, Wärme V 3 (61) °**take the heat** den Kopf hinhalten
heather ['heðə] Heide(kraut) III
heaven ['hevn] Himmel *(im religiösen Sinn)* III
heavy ['hevi] schwer *(von Gewicht)* II **heavy rain** starker Regen, heftiger Regen II
held [held] *siehe* **hold**
helicopter ['helɪkɒptə] Hubschrauber, Helikopter IV
hell [hel] Hölle III
Hello. [hə'ləʊ] Hallo. / Guten Tag. I
helmet ['helmɪt] Helm V 4 (90)
help [help]:
1. Hilfe I
2. helfen I **Help yourself.** Greif zu! / Bedien dich! III
helper ['helpə] Helfer/in II
helpful ['helpfl] hilfreich IV
hen [hen] Huhn, Henne V 2 (49)
her [hɜː], [hə]:
1. ihr, ihre I **her best friend** ihr bester Freund / ihre beste Freundin I
2. sie; ihr I
herb [hɜːb] (Gewürz-)Kraut IV
here [hɪə] hier; hierher I **Here we go.** Los geht's. / Jetzt geht's los. I **Here you are.** Bitte sehr. / Hier bitte. II **near here** (hier) in der Nähe I **over here** hier herüber II **up here** hier oben; nach hier oben II
hero ['hɪərəʊ], *pl* **heroes** Held/in III
hers [hɜːz] ihrer, ihre, ihrs II
herself [hɜː'self] sich III
°**hesitation** [ˌhezɪ'teɪʃn] Zögern
hid [hɪd] *siehe* **hide**
hidden ['hɪdn] *siehe* **hide**
hide [haɪd], **hid, hidden** (sich) verstecken I
high [haɪ] hoch I
highland ['haɪlənd]: **the Highlands** *(pl)* das schottische Hochland III
highlight ['haɪlaɪt] hervorheben, markieren *(mit Textmarker)* II
high school ['haɪ skuːl] *(USA)* Schule für 14- bis 18-Jährige IV
°**highway** ['haɪweɪ] *(AusE)* Autobahn
hill [hɪl] Hügel I
him [hɪm] ihn; ihm I
himself [hɪm'self] sich III **He did it himself.** Er hat es selbst gemacht. IV **The director himself welcomed us.** Der Regisseur selbst hieß uns willkommen. IV
hip [hɪp] Hüfte III
°**hire sb.** ['haɪə] jn. einstellen, engagieren
his [hɪz]:
1. his friend sein Freund / seine Freundin I
2. seiner, seine, seins II
hiss [hɪs] zischen II
°**historic** [hɪ'stɒrɪk] historisch *(geschichtlich bedeutsam)*
historical [hɪ'stɒrɪkl] historisch, geschichtlich V 1 (12)
history ['hɪstri] Geschichte I **natural history** Naturkunde III
hit [hɪt], **hit, hit:**
1. prallen, stoßen gegen I
2. schlagen II
3. treffen II
hobby ['hɒbi] Hobby I
hold [həʊld], **held, held** halten I **Hold on a minute.** Bleib / Bleiben Sie am Apparat. *(am Telefon)* II **hold onto sth.** sich an etwas festhalten III
hole [həʊl] Loch II
holiday ['hɒlədeɪ] Urlaub II **be on holiday** in Urlaub sein II **go on holiday** in Urlaub fahren II
holidays *(pl)* ['hɒlədeɪz] Ferien I
°**holler** ['hɒlə] brüllen, schreien
the Holocaust ['hɒləkɔːst] der Holocaust *(Massenmord an den Juden in der Zeit des Nationalsozialismus)* V 4 (99)
home [həʊm] Heim, Zuhause I **at home** daheim, zu Hause I **be home to ...** Heimat sein für etwas; etwas beheimaten III **come/go home** nach Hause kommen/gehen I **the Home Office** *(BE)* das Innenministerium *(in Großbritannien)* V 4 (98)
homeless ['həʊmləs] obdachlos IV
homesick ['həʊmsɪk]: **be/get homesick** Heimweh haben/bekommen V 1 (13)
hometown [ˌhəʊm'taʊn] Heimatstadt I
homework ['həʊmwɜːk] Hausaufgabe(n) I **Do your homework.** Mach deine Hausaufgaben. I **What's for homework?** Was haben wir als Hausaufgabe auf? I
honest ['ɒnɪst] ehrlich V 1 (12)
honesty ['ɒnəsti] Ehrlichkeit V 3 (63)
honey ['hʌni] Honig; *(infml, als Anrede:)* Schatz, Schätzchen IV
honk [hɒŋk] hupen IV
honour ['ɒnə] Ehre II
hook [hʊk]:
1. Haken IV
2. an den Haken / an die Angel bekommen IV
hope [həʊp]:
1. Hoffnung IV
2. hoffen I
hopeful ['həʊpfl] zuversichtlich, hoffnungsvoll V 2 (42)
hopefully ['həʊpfəli] hoffnungsvoll, voller Hoffnung; hoffentlich V 2 (42)
▶ S. 208 hopeful – hopefully
horn [hɔːn] Horn III
horrible ['hɒrəbl] grauenhaft, entsetzlich V 4 (97)
horror ['hɒrə]: **in horror** entsetzt III
horse [hɔːs] Pferd I **on horseback** ['hɔːsbæk] zu Pferd IV
hospital ['hɒspɪtl] Krankenhaus II
host [həʊst]
1. host family Gastfamilie II
°**2. a host of ...** eine Menge ...
hostel ['hɒstl] Herberge, Wohnheim III

hostess ['həʊstəs] Gastgeberin *(in USA auch: Frau, die in einem Restaurant die Gäste in Empfang nimmt)* IV
hot [hɒt]**:**
1 heiß I
2 scharf (gewürzt) IV
hotel [həʊ'tel] Hotel II
hour ['aʊə] Stunde I **a half-hour ride** eine halbstündige Fahrt V 1 (12) **an hour** pro Stunde III **a one-hour concert** ein einstündiges Konzert III
house [haʊs] Haus I
household ['haʊshəʊld] Haushalt; haushalts… V 2 (47)
°**housing advisor** ['haʊzɪŋ‿əd,vaɪzə] Berater/in in Wohnungsfragen
how [haʊ] wie I **How are you?** Wie geht's? / Wie geht es dir/euch? I **How do you know (about …)?** Woher weißt/kennst du …? III **How do you like it?** Wie findest du es (sie/ihn)? / Wie gefällt es (sie/er) dir? I **How many?** Wie viele? I **How much?** Wie viel? I **How much are / is …?** Was kosten / kostet …? I **How old are you?** Wie alt bist du? I **how to do sth.** wie man etwas macht / machen kann / machen soll III
however [haʊ'evə] aber; allerdings; jedoch IV
hub [hʌb] Mittelpunkt, (Verkehrs-)Knotenpunkt V 2 (51)
°**huddled up** [,hʌdld‿'ʌp] zusammengekauert
hug [hʌg]**:**
1. jn. umarmen II
2. **give sb. a hug** jn. umarmen II
huge [hjuːdʒ] riesig, sehr groß III
°**hum** [hʌm] brummen *(TV)*
human ['hjuːmən] Mensch; menschlich V 1 (19) **human being** Mensch V 1 (19)
humid ['hjuːmɪd] feucht, feuchtwarm V 1 (10)
humour ['hjuːmə]**: sense of humour** (Sinn für) Humor V 3 (63)
hundred [hʌndrəd]**: a/one hundred** einhundert I
hung [hʌŋ] *siehe* **hang**
hungry ['hʌŋgri]**: be hungry** hungrig sein, Hunger haben I
hunt [hʌnt] jagen IV
hurricane ['hʌrɪkən] Hurrikan, Orkan IV
hurry ['hʌri]**:**
1. eilen; sich beeilen II **hurry up** sich beeilen I
2. **be in a hurry** in Eile sein, es eilig haben V 2 (51)
hurt [hɜːt]**, hurt, hurt:** schmerzen, wehtun; verletzen II
hurtful ['hɜːtfl] verletzend V 1 (23)
husband ['hʌzbənd] Ehemann V 2 (44)
°**hut** [hʌt] Hütte
hyphen ['haɪfən] Bindestrich II

I

I [aɪ] ich I **I'm from Plymouth.** Ich bin/komme aus Plymouth. I **I'm two years old.** Ich bin zwei Jahre alt. I
ice [aɪs] Eis II
ice cream [,aɪs 'kriːm] (Speise-)Eis I
iced tea [,aɪst 'tiː] Eistee II
ICT [,aɪ siː 'tiː] Informations- und Kommunikationstechnologie I
ID [,aɪ 'diː] Ausweis IV **ID card** Personalausweis III
idea [aɪ'dɪə] Idee; Vorstellung I
identical [aɪ'dentɪkl] identisch V 3 (60)
identify [aɪ'dentɪfaɪ]**: identify sb./sth. (by sth.)** jn./etwas identifizieren (anhand von etwas) III
°**identity** [aɪ'dentəti] Identität
if [ɪf]**:**
1. wenn, falls II **even if** selbst wenn II **if-clause** Nebensatz mit *if* III
2. ob III
3. **as if** als ob III
°**ignore** [ɪg'nɔː] ignorieren
ill [ɪl] krank II
illegal [ɪ'liːgl] illegal, ungesetzlich IV
illness ['ɪlnəs] Krankheit III
image ['ɪmɪdʒ] Bild, Abbild; Vorstellung IV
imagine sth. [ɪ'mædʒɪn] sich etwas vorstellen I
°**imbecile** ['ɪmbəsiːl] Schwachkopf
immediately [ɪ'miːdiətli] sofort III
immigrant ['ɪmɪgrənt] Einwanderer/Einwanderin V 2 (37)
immigration [,ɪmɪ'greɪʃn] Einwanderung V 4 (93)
impatience [ɪm'peɪʃns] Ungeduld V 3 (63)
impatient [ɪm'peɪʃnt] ungeduldig IV
imperfect [ɪm'pɜːfɪkt] unvollkommen, mangelhaft IV
impolite [,ɪmpə'laɪt] unhöflich III
important [ɪm'pɔːtnt] wichtig I
impossible [ɪm'pɒsəbl] unmöglich II
impractical [ɪm'præktɪkl] unpraktisch IV
impression [ɪm'preʃn] Eindruck III
improbable [ɪm'prɒbəbl] unwahrscheinlich IV
improve [ɪm'pruːv] verbessern; sich verbessern III
°**improvement** [ɪm'pruːvmənt] Verbesserung
in [ɪn] in I **be in** zu Hause sein II **come in** hereinkommen I **in 1580** im Jahr 1580 I **in a loud voice** mit lauter Stimme II **in front of** vor *(räumlich)* I **in German** auf Deutsch I **in the afternoon** nachmittags, am Nachmittag I **in the attic** auf dem Dachboden I **in the evening** abends, am Abend I **in the morning** morgens, vormittags, am Morgen/Vormittag I **in the photo** auf dem Foto I **in the world** auf der Welt II
inch [ɪntʃ] Zoll *(Längenmaß; 2,54 cm)* IV
incident ['ɪnsɪdənt] Vorfall, Zwischenfall V 1 (27)
include [ɪn'kluːd] einschließen; beinhalten V 3 (66) **Our group also included three children.** Zu unserer Gruppe gehörten auch drei Kinder. V 3 (66)
including [ɪn'kluːdɪŋ] einschließlich; darunter (auch) V 2 (51)
incorrect [,ɪnkə'rekt] falsch, fehlerhaft IV
increase [ɪn'kriːs] erhöhen, steigern, vergrößern; (an)steigen, zunehmen V 3 (73)
°**independent** [,ɪndɪ'pendənt] unabhängig
Indian ['ɪndiən] Inder/in; indisch II
indirect [,ɪndə'rekt], [,ɪndaɪ'rekt] III
indoor ['ɪndɔː] Innen-; Hallen- IV
industry ['ɪndəstri] Industrie V 1 (27)
inexpensive [,ɪnɪk'spensɪv] preiswert, günstig IV
infinitive [ɪn'fɪnətɪv] Infinitiv III
in-flight magazine/meal ['ɪn,flaɪt] Bordmagazin/-mahlzeit V 1 (12)
informal [ɪn'fɔːml] informell; umgangssprachlich V 2 (41)
information (about/on) *(no pl)* [,ɪnfə'meɪʃn] Information(en) (über) I **Information and Communications Technology** Informations- und Kommunikationstechnologie I
°**infrastructure** ['ɪnfrəstrʌktʃə] Infrastruktur
ingredient [ɪn'griːdiənt] Zutat IV
initiative [ɪ'nɪʃətɪv] Initiative, Aktion V 4 (83)
injure ['ɪndʒə] jn. verletzen V 1 (19)
inland ['ɪnlænd] Binnen-; im Landesinneren V 1 (22)
innocent ['ɪnəsnt] unschuldig V 1 (27)
insect ['ɪnsekt] Insekt V 1 (18)
inside [,ɪn'saɪd]**:**
1. drinnen; nach drinnen I
2. die Innenseite; das Innere III
3. **inside sth.** innerhalb von etwas II
°4. **inside cover** Umschlaginnenseite
insist on sth. [ɪn'sɪst] auf etwas bestehen V 2 (48)
installation [,ɪnstə'leɪʃn] Installation V 4 (84)
instead [ɪn'sted] stattdessen II **instead of** [ɪn'sted‿əv] anstelle von, statt III
°**institution** [,ɪnstɪ'tjuːʃn] Einrichtung
instrument ['ɪnstrəmənt] Instrument I
insult (to) ['ɪnsʌlt] Beleidigung (für) IV
insulted [ɪn'sʌltɪd] beleidigt IV
intelligence [ɪn'telɪdʒəns] Intelligenz V 3 (62)
intelligent [ɪn'telɪdʒənt] intelligent V 2 (37)
intention [ɪn'tenʃn] Absicht, Intention V 4 (100)
interaction [,ɪntər'ækʃn] Interaktion, Umgang III

interest ['ɪntrəst]:
1. Interesse V 2 (50)
2. interessieren III
interested ['ɪntrəstɪd]: **be interested (in)** sich interessieren (für), interessiert sein (an) II
interesting ['ɪntrəstɪŋ] interessant I
international [ˌɪntə'næʃnəl] international III
interpret sth. [ɪn'tɜːprɪt] etwas interpretieren, deuten V 4 (87)
interrupt [ˌɪntə'rʌpt] unterbrechen II
interview ['ɪntəvjuː]:
1. Interview II; Vorstellungsgespräch V 3 (76)
2. interviewen, befragen I
interviewer ['ɪntəvjuːə] Leiter/in des Vorstellungsgesprächs V 3 (76)
into ['ɪntʊ]:
1. into the kitchen in die Küche (hinein) I
2. be into sth. *(infml)* etwas mögen, auf etwas stehen III **° get into sth.** sich auf etwas einlassen; sich einer Sache anpassen
intolerant [ɪn'tɒlərənt] intolerant V 3 (63)
introduce [ˌɪntrə'djuːs]:
1. (etwas Neues) einführen IV
2. introduce sth./sb. (to sb.) etwas/jn. (jm.) vorstellen II
introduction [ˌɪntrə'dʌkʃn] Einleitung, Einführung III
invade (a country) [ɪn'veɪd] (in ein Land) einmarschieren II
invent [ɪn'vent] erfinden III
investigate [ɪn'vestɪgeɪt] *(polizeilich)* untersuchen; ermitteln IV
invitation (to) [ˌɪnvɪ'teɪʃn] Einladung (zu, nach) I
invite sb. (to) [ɪn'vaɪt] jn. einladen (zu, nach) II
involvement (in) [ɪn'vɒlvmənt] Engagement (für); Beteiligung (an) V 4 (93)
involved [ɪn'vɒlvd]: **be involved (in)** beteiligt sein (an); etwas zu tun haben (mit) V 4 (93) **get involved (in)** sich engagieren (für, bei); sich beteiligen (an) V 4 (93)
► S. 224 involvement
irregular [ɪ'regjələ] unregelmäßig II
irresponsible [ˌɪrɪ'spɒnsəbl] unverantwortlich; verantwortungslos IV
is [ɪz]: **Is it Monday?** Ist es Montag? I **Is that you?** Bist du's? / Bist du das? I **The book is ...** Das Buch kostet ... I
island ['aɪlənd] Insel I
isle [aɪl] (kleine) Insel, Eiland III
isn't ['ɪznt]: **he/she/it isn't (= is not)** er/sie/es ist nicht ... I
issue ['ɪʃuː], ['ɪsjuː] Thema, (Streit-)Frage, Angelegenheit V 2 (36)
it [ɪt] er, sie, es I
IT (information technology) [ˌaɪ 'tiː] IT (Informationstechnologie) V 3 (73)
it's ... (= it is) [ɪts] er/sie/es ist ... I
itself [ɪt'self] sich III **The room itself was OK, ...** Das Zimmer selbst war in Ordnung, ... IV
its name [ɪts] sein Name / ihr Name I

J

jacket ['dʒækɪt] Jacke II
jam [dʒæm] Marmelade I
January ['dʒænjuəri] Januar I
jazz [dʒæz] Jazz IV
jealous ['dʒeləs] neidisch (auf); eifersüchtig (auf) III
jealousy ['dʒeləsi] Eifersucht, Neid V 3 (63)
jeans *(pl)* [dʒiːnz] Jeans I
jeep [dʒiːp] Jeep III
°jeer [dʒɪə] höhnische Bemerkung
jewellery *(BE)* **/ jewelry** *(AE) (no pl)* ['dʒuːəlri] Schmuck IV
jewels *(pl)* ['dʒuːəlz] Juwelen III
jigsaw ['dʒɪgsɔː] Puzzle II
job [dʒɒb]:
1. Job, (Arbeits-)Stelle I
2. Aufgabe II
join [dʒɔɪn]:
1. join a club in einen Klub eintreten; sich einem Klub anschließen I
2. join in (sth.) (bei etwas) mitmachen III
joke [dʒəʊk] Witz I **° crack a joke** einen Witz reißen
journey ['dʒɜːni] Reise, Fahrt II
judo ['dʒuːdəʊ] Judo I
juggle sth. ['dʒʌgl] mit etwas jonglieren II
juggler ['dʒʌglə] Jongleur/in II
juice [dʒuːs] Saft II
July [dʒu'laɪ] Juli I
jump [dʒʌmp]:
1. springen I **jump up** aufspringen, hochspringen II
2. Sprung I
°jumper ['dʒʌmpə] Sprungwurf *(Basketball)*
junction ['dʒʌŋkʃn] (Straßen-)Kreuzung III
June [dʒuːn] Juni I
just [dʒʌst]:
1. (einfach) nur, bloß I
2. gerade (eben), soeben II **just after ...** gleich nachdem ...; kurz nachdem ... II **just then** genau in dem Moment; gerade dann II
3. just like genau wie ... II

K

°kaleidoscope [kə'laɪdəskəʊp] Kaleidoskop
kangaroo *(infml* **roo***)* [ˌkæŋgə'ruː] Känguru V 1 (10)
kayak ['kaɪæk] Kajak III
keen [kiːn]: **be keen on doing sth.** wild darauf sein, etwas zu tun IV **be keen on sth.** wild auf etwas sein IV
keep [kiːp], **kept, kept:**
1. aufheben; aufsparen; aufbewahren III
2. keep doing sth. etwas immer wieder / weiter tun; etwas ständig tun III
3. halten; erhalten IV **keep to sth.** sich an etwas halten *(Plan, Zeitlimit)* IV **keep sth. up** etwas aufrechterhalten, etwas fortsetzen IV **keep sth. warm/alive** etwas warm halten; etwas am Leben (er)halten IV
kept [kept] *siehe* **keep**
key [kiː]:
1. Schlüssel II
2. Taste V 2 (37)
3. Schlüssel- II
keyword ['kiːwɜːd] Schlüsselwort I
kick [kɪk]:
1. treten III
2. free kick Freistoß III
kid [kɪd] Kind I
kill [kɪl] töten II
kilogram, kilo (kg) ['kɪləgræm], ['kiːləʊ] Kilogramm, Kilo I
kilometre (km) ['kɪləmiːtə], [kɪ'lɒmɪtə] Kilometer I **square kilometre** Quadratkilometer II
kind [kaɪnd]:
1. a kind of ... eine Art (von) ... I
2. freundlich, nett II
kinda ['kaɪndə] *(infml,* = **kind of***)* irgendwie IV
kindness ['kaɪndnəs] Freundlichkeit, Güte V 3 (63)
king [kɪŋ] König II
kingdom ['kɪŋdəm] Königreich III
kiss [kɪs] küssen; sich küssen II
kit [kɪt] Ausrüstung I
kitchen ['kɪtʃɪn] Küche I **kitchen island** Koch-, Kücheninsel V 2 (51)
°kitesurfing ['kaɪtsɜːfɪŋ] Kitesurfen
knee [niː] Knie II
kneel [niːl], **knelt, knelt** knien II
knelt [nelt] *siehe* **kneel**
knew [njuː] *siehe* **know**
knife [naɪf], *pl* **knives** [naɪvz] Messer II
knight [naɪt] Ritter II
knock (on sth.) [nɒk] (an)klopfen (an etwas) III
know [nəʊ], **knew, known** wissen; kennen I **get to know sb.** jn. kennenlernen V 2 (42) **I don't know.** Ich weiß (es) nicht. I **know about sth.** sich mit etwas auskennen; über etwas Bescheid wissen II **..., you know.** ..., weißt du. I
knowledge *(no pl)* ['nɒlɪdʒ] Wissen; Kenntnis(se) V 3 (73)
known [nəʊn] *siehe* **know**
koala [kəʊ'ɑːlə] Koala V 1 (10)
kung fu [ˌkʌŋ 'fuː] Kung Fu I
°Kurdish ['kɜːdɪʃ] kurdisch

L

lab [læb] *(kurz für* **laboratory** [lə'bɒrətri]*)* Labor V 3 (66)
°**Labour** ['leɪbə] die Labour-Partei
label ['leɪbl]:
1. beschriften; etikettieren II
2. Beschriftung; Schild, Etikett II
Ladies and gentlemen [ˌleɪdiz_ən 'dʒentlmən] Meine Damen und Herren / Sehr geehrte Damen und Herren IV
lain [leɪn] *siehe* **lie**
lake [leɪk] (Binnen-)See I
lamb [læm] Lamm II
lamp [læmp] Lampe I
land [lænd]:
1. landen, an Land gehen II
2. Land II
landmark ['lændmɑːk] Wahrzeichen V 1 (12)
landscape ['lændskeɪp] Landschaft IV
language ['læŋgwɪdʒ] Sprache I
laptop ['læptɒp] Laptop III
large [lɑːdʒ] groß II
last [lɑːst]:
1. **last Friday** letzten Freitag I **last year's …** das … vom letzten Jahr II
2. **at last** endlich, schließlich I
late [leɪt] spät I **You're late.** Du bist spät dran. / Du bist zu spät. I **stay up late** lang aufbleiben II **the latest** das Neueste IV
later ['leɪtə] später I
laugh [lɑːf] lachen I **laugh at sb./sth.** über jn./etwas lachen; jn. auslachen II
laughter ['lɑːftə] Gelächter III
°**laundry** ['lɔːndri] (schmutzige) Wäsche
law [lɔː] Gesetz IV
lawn [lɔːn] Rasen IV
lay [leɪ] *siehe* **lie**
layout ['leɪaʊt] Layout, Gestaltung III
laziness ['leɪzinəs] Faulheit V 3 (63)
lazy ['leɪzi] faul V 3 (63)
lead [liːd], **led, led** führen, leiten III
leader ['liːdə] Leiter/in III
lean [liːn] sich lehnen; sich beugen IV
learn [lɜːn]:
1. lernen I
2. erfahren IV
least [liːst]: **at least** zumindest, wenigstens II °**not in the least bit** nicht im Geringsten
leather ['leðə] Leder IV
leave [liːv], **left, left:**
1. verlassen; zurücklassen I
2. lassen II **leave a message** eine Nachricht hinterlassen II **leave sth.** etwas übrig lassen II **leave sth. out** etwas weglassen, auslassen V 2 (40)
3. (weg)gehen; abfahren II
led [led] *siehe* **lead**
left [left]:
1. *siehe* **leave**
2. linke(r, s); (nach) links II **on the left** links/auf der linken Seite II
3. **be left** übrig sein III
leg [leg] Bein I
legal ['liːgl] legal IV
legend ['ledʒənd] Legende, Sage II
legendary ['ledʒəndri] legendär, berühmt IV
°**legislature** ['ledʒɪsleɪtʃə] Legislative
lemon ['lemən] Zitrone IV
lend [lend], **lent, lent** jm. etwas leihen IV
length [leŋθ] Länge; Dauer V 2 (47)
lent [lent] *siehe* **leave**
lentil ['lentl] Linse *(Gemüse)* IV
less (than) [les] weniger (als) III
lesson ['lesn] (Unterrichts-)Stunde I **before lessons** vorm Unterricht I
let [let], **let, let** lassen I **Let me show you …** Lass mich dir … zeigen. I **Let's …** Lass uns … I **Let's go to England.** Lass uns nach England gehen/fahren. I
▶ S. 221 (to) make sb. do sth. – (to) let sb. do sth.
letter ['letə]:
1. Brief I **letter of application** Bewerbungsschreiben V 3 (59)
2. Buchstabe I
°**level** ['levl] Niveau, Ebene
liberty ['lɪbəti] Freiheit IV
library ['laɪbrəri] Bibliothek, Bücherei I
licence ['laɪsns] *(AE:* **license***)* Lizenz, Genehmigung V 4 (88) **driving licence** *(BE)*, **driver's license** *(AE)* Führerschein, Fahrerlaubnis IV °**licence holder/license holder** Lizenzinhaber/in
lie [laɪ], **lay, lain** liegen II **lie down** sich hinlegen III
life [laɪf], *pl* **lives** [laɪvz] Leben I
life jacket ['laɪf dʒækɪt] Schwimmweste I
°**lifestyle** ['laɪfstaɪl] Lebensstil
lift [lɪft]:
1. *(bes. BE)* Mitfahrgelegenheit II **give sb. a lift** jn. mitnehmen II
2. Fahrstuhl, Aufzug III
light [laɪt]:
1. Licht I **traffic light** (Verkehrs-) Ampel *(oft auch:* **traffic lights** *(pl))* III
2. **(lit, lit)** anzünden II **light up** aufleuchten IV **light sth. up** etwas erhellen *(aufleuchten lassen)* II
3. **light green/blue/…** hellgrün/-blau/… IV
lightning *(no pl)* ['laɪtnɪŋ] Blitz II **a flash of lightning** ein Blitz II
like [laɪk]:
1. mögen, gernhaben I **I like …** Ich mag … I **I'd like …** Ich hätte gern … / Ich möchte … I **I'd like to go** Ich möchte gehen / Ich würde gern gehen I **I'd like you to be/do …** Ich möchte, dass du … bist/tust. IV
2. **like boys** wie Jungen I **just like** genau wie … II **like that** so *(auf diese Weise)* I **like this** so II **What's she like?** Wie ist sie (so)? I **What was it like?** Wie war es? II
3. *(infml)* als ob III
4. **He was like: "Stop!"** *(infml)* Und er so: „Stop!" III
likes and dislikes *(pl)* [ˌlaɪks_ən 'dɪslaɪks] Vorlieben und Abneigungen I
limit ['lɪmɪt]:
1. Begrenzung, Beschränkung, Limit IV
2. **limit sth. (to)** etwas beschränken, begrenzen (auf); etwas einschränken V 3 (70)
limited ['lɪmɪtɪd] beschränkt, begrenzt IV
limousine [ˌlɪmə'ziːn], ['lɪməziːn] Luxuslimousine, Straßenkreuzer IV
line [laɪn]:
1. Zeile I
2. (U-Bahn-)Linie III
3. Reihe III *(AE)* Schlange, Reihe *(wartender Menschen)* IV **stand/wait in line** *(AE)* Schlange stehen, sich anstellen IV
4. Leine, (Angel-)Schnur IV
5. (Telefon-)Leitung V 4 (97)
°**lined up** [ˌlaɪnd_'ʌp] aufgereiht
link ['lɪŋk]:
1. verbinden, verknüpfen III **linking word** Bindewort III
°2. Link *(Internet)*
lion ['laɪən] Löwe I
lip [lɪp] Lippe II
list [lɪst]:
1. Liste I
2. auflisten III
listen ['lɪsn] zuhören, horchen I **listen to sb.** jm. zuhören I **listen to sth.** sich etwas anhören I
listener ['lɪsənə] Zuhörer/in II
lit [lɪt] *siehe* **light**
literature ['lɪtrətʃə] Literatur IV
litter bin ['lɪtə bɪn] Abfalleimer II
little ['lɪtl]:
1. klein I
2. **a little** ein bisschen, ein wenig, etwas IV
live [lɪv] leben; wohnen I
liveliness ['laɪvlinəs] Lebhaftigkeit, Munterkeit V 3 (63)
lively ['laɪvli] lebendig, lebhaft V 1 (12)
living room ['lɪvɪŋ ruːm] Wohnzimmer I
loads (of) [ləʊdz] *(infml)* eine Menge V 4 (99)
local ['ləʊkl] örtlich, Lokal-; am/vom Ort; einheimisch III
location [ləʊ'keɪʃn] Position, Standort III
locker ['lɒkə] Schließfach, Spind IV
log in/out [lɒg] sich ein-/ausloggen V 2 (43)
lonely ['ləʊnli] einsam I
long [lɒŋ] lang I **(the) longest …** der/die/das längste …; am längsten II **not (…) any longer** nicht länger; nicht mehr IV

long shot ['lɒŋ ʃɒt] Totale, Totalaufnahme IV
look [lʊk]:
1. schauen I **Look, ...** Sieh / Schau mal, ... **look after sb.** auf jn. aufpassen; sich um jn. kümmern II **look at** anschauen, ansehen I **look for sth.** etwas suchen I **look forward to sth.** sich auf etwas freuen II **look happy** glücklich aussehen I **look into sth.** etwas untersuchen, prüfen III **Look out!** Achtung! Aufgepasst! III **look out for sb./sth.** nach jm./etwas Ausschau halten IV **look sth. up** etwas nachschlagen III **look up** hochsehen, aufschauen II
2. **have a look** nachschauen **have a look at sth.** einen Blick auf etwas werfen III
°**lord** ['lɔːd]: **the House of Lords** das Oberhaus
lorry ['lɒri] Lastwagen, LKW IV
lose [luːz], **lost, lost** verlieren II
loser ['luːzə] Verlierer/in IV
lost [lɒst] *siehe* **lose** °**get lost** sich verlaufen
lot [lɒt]: **a lot** viel I **That helped us a lot.** Das hat uns sehr geholfen. I **lots of ...** viel ..., viele ... I
loud [laʊd] laut I **in a loud voice** mit lauter Stimme II
loudspeaker [ˌlaʊd'spiːkə] Lautsprecher; Megaphon III
love [lʌv]:
1. lieben, sehr mögen I **I'd love to ...** Ich würde sehr gern ... II
2. **Love, ...** Alles Liebe, ... *(Briefschluss)* II
lovely ['lʌvli] schön, hübsch, herrlich, entzückend II
loyal ['lɔɪəl] loyal, treu ergeben V 3 (62)
luck [lʌk]: **Good luck!** Viel Glück! I
luckily ['lʌkɪli] glücklicherweise; zum Glück V 1 (19)
lucky ['lʌki]: **be lucky** Glück haben II **Lucky you.** Du Glückspilz. II
°**lump** [lʌmp] Klumpen
lunch [lʌntʃ] Mittagessen I **have lunch** zu Mittag essen I **What's for lunch?** Was gibt es zum Mittagessen? I
lunchtime ['lʌntʃtaɪm] Mittagszeit I **at lunchtime** mittags I
lynx [lɪŋks], *pl* **lynx** *or* **lynxes** Luchs III

M

°**m** *Abkürzung für* **million** *und* **metre**
°**macaroon** [ˌmækə'ruːn] Makrone
mad [mæd] verrückt I **go mad** verrückt werden
made [meɪd]:
1. *siehe* **make**
2. **be made of sth.** aus etwas (gemacht) sein II
magazine [ˌmægə'ziːn] Zeitschrift I
magic ['mædʒɪk] magisch, Zauber- II
magical ['mædʒɪkl] zauberhaft, wundervoll; magisch III
mail [meɪl] E-Mail II
main [meɪn] Haupt- II **main clause** Hauptsatz III
mainly ['meɪnli] hauptsächlich, vorwiegend V 1 (19)
make [meɪk], **made, made**: machen; herstellen I °**make a comment** sich äußern, einen Kommentar abgeben **make a wish** sich etwas wünschen I **make friends** Freunde finden I **make fun of sb./sth.** sich über jn./etwas lustig machen III **make sb. do sth.** jn. dazu bringen, etwas zu tun; jn. zwingen, etwas zu tun V 4 (87)
▶ S. 221 (to) make sb. do sth. – (to) let sb. do sth.
make sb. sth. jn. zu etwas machen II **make sth. into sth.** etwas in etwas umwandeln IV **make sth. up** sich etwas ausdenken III **make sure that ...** sich vergewissern, dass ...; darauf achten, dass ...; dafür sorgen, dass ... II **make tea / coffee / soup** Tee/Kaffee/Suppe kochen
make-up ['meɪk‿ʌp] Make-up II
malaria [mə'leəriə] Malaria III
male [meɪl] männlich; männliche Person; Männchen V 4 (42)
mall [mɔːl] (großes) Einkaufszentrum I
mammal ['mæml] Säugetier III
man [mæn], *pl* **men** [men] Mann I
manage sth. ['mænɪdʒ] etwas schaffen; etwas zustande bringen III
management ['mænɪdʒmənt]: **time management** Zeitmanagement, Zeiteinteilung V 3 (66)
manager ['mænɪdʒə]:
1. Trainer/in *(von Sportmannschaften)* III
2. Manager/in V 4 (92)
°**mangrove** ['mængrəʊv] Mangrovenbaum
man-made [ˌmæn'meɪd] künstlich, Kunst- IV
many ['meni] viele I **How many?** Wie viele? I
map [mæp] Landkarte; Stadtplan I **on the map** auf der Landkarte; auf dem Stadtplan I
marathon ['mærəθən] Marathon V 3 (72)
March [mɑːtʃ] März I
march [mɑːtʃ] Marsch, Demonstration V 4 (83)
Mardi Gras [ˌmɑːdi 'grɑː] Faschingsdienstag *(auch: die Karnevalsfeiern in New Orleans)* IV
marine [mə'riːn]:
1. Meeres- IV
°2. Marineinfanterist/in, Soldat/in bei der Marine
mark [mɑːk]:
1. markieren II **mark sth. up** etwas markieren, kennzeichnen II
2. **stress mark** Betonungszeichen III
3. *(BE)* (Schul-)Note, Zensur IV
market ['mɑːkɪt] Markt I
°**marriage** ['mærɪdʒ] Ehe **same-sex marriage** gleichgeschlechtliche Ehe
married (to) ['mærɪd] verheiratet (mit) I
marry sb. ['mæri] jn. heiraten III
mascot ['mæskət] Maskottchen V 3 (72)
mask [mɑːsk] Maske III
master ['mɑːstə] Meister/in I
match [mætʃ]:
1. Spiel, Wettkampf, Match I
°2. **match sth. (to sth.)** etwas (zu etwas) zuordnen
°3. **match sth.** sich mit etwas messen; an etwas herankommen
match [mætʃ] zusammenpassen V 3 (61)
matching ['mætʃɪŋ] passende(r, s) V 3 (61)
mate [meɪt] Kumpel, Freund/in V 1 (15)
material [mə'tɪəriəl] Material, Stoff III
maths [mæθs] Mathematik I
matter ['mætə] von Bedeutung sein, wichtig sein V 3 (61)
matter ['mætə]: **What's the matter?** Was ist denn? / Was ist los? I
May [meɪ] Mai I
may [meɪ] dürfen II **May I have a word with you?** Kann ich Sie kurz sprechen? II **they may be ...** sie sind vielleicht ... III
maybe ['meɪbi] vielleicht I
mayor [meə] Bürgermeister/in II
me [miː] mich; mir I **Me too.** Ich auch. I
meal [miːl] Mahlzeit, Essen III
mean [miːn], **meant, meant**:
1. bedeuten II
2. meinen II **mean to do sth.** etwas tun wollen; die Absicht haben, etwas zu tun V 2 (39)
3. gemein V 3 (63)
meaning ['miːnɪŋ] Bedeutung II
meanness ['miːnnəs] Gemeinheit V 3 (63)
meant [ment] *siehe* **mean**
°**measles** ['miːzlz] Masern
meat [miːt] Fleisch I
medal ['medl] Medaille V 1 (27)
media *(pl)* ['miːdiə]: **social media** soziale Medien III
mediation [ˌmiːdi'eɪʃn] Sprachmittlung, Mediation I
medicine ['medsn, 'medɪsn] Medizin; Arznei V 3 (66)
medium ['miːdiəm] mittelgroß; mittel- IV **medium shot** Halbtotale IV
meet [miːt], **met, met**:
1. treffen; kennenlernen I **Nice to meet you.** Freut mich, dich/euch/Sie kennenzulernen. I
2. sich treffen I
meeting ['miːtɪŋ] Besprechung, Versammlung, Treffen V 4 (88)
°**melody** ['melədi] Melodie
melt [melt] schmelzen II
member ['membə] Mitglied III
memorable ['memərəbl] einprägsam; unvergesslich V 4 (101)

memorial [mə'mɔːriəl] Denkmal; Gedenk- III
memory ['meməri]:
1. Erinnerung II
2. Gedächtnis IV
men [men] *Plural von* **man** I
°**mental** ['mentl] *(infml)* verrückt
°**mention** ['menʃn] erwähnen
menu ['menjuː] Speisekarte IV
°**merchandise** ['mɜːtʃəndaɪs] Werbeartikel *(Poster, T-Shirts usw.)*
message ['mesɪdʒ]:
1. Nachricht II **text message** SMS II
2. Botschaft, Aussage III
messenger ['mesɪndʒə] Bote/Botin IV
met [met] *siehe* **meet**
metal ['metl] Metall; Metall- IV
°**metaphor** ['metəfə] Metapher, bildlicher Ausdruck
°**method** ['meθəd] Methode
metre ['miːtə] Meter I
microphone ['maɪkrəfəʊn] Mikrofon IV
middle ['mɪdl] Mitte I **in the middle** in der Mitte I
midnight ['mɪdnaɪt] Mitternacht I
might [maɪt]: **it might be the other side** es könnte die andere Seite sein III
mild [maɪld] mild V 1 (22)
mile [maɪl] Meile *(ca. 1,6 km)* II **for miles** meilenweit II
milk [mɪlk] Milch I
million ['mɪljən] Million II
mind [maɪnd]:
1. Verstand, Sinn, Geist IV
change your mind seine Meinung ändern IV **read sb.'s mind** jemandes Gedanken lesen III
2. etwas dagegen haben III **I don't mind helping.** Es macht mir nichts aus zu helfen.
°**mind map** ['maɪnd mæp] Mindmap
mine [maɪn]:
1. meiner, meine, meins II
2. Bergwerk, Mine III **coal mine** Kohlebergwerk III
3. Mine II
4. abbauen III
°**minerals** *(pl)* ['mɪnərəlz] Mineralien
minibus ['mɪnibʌs] Kleinbus I
°**minimum wage** [ˌmɪnɪməm 'weɪdʒ] Mindestlohn
ministry ['mɪnɪstri] Ministerium V 4 (88)
minority [maɪ'nɒrəti] Minderheit V 4 (98)
minute ['mɪnɪt] Minute I **a five-minute walk** ein fünfminütiger Spaziergang V 1 (12)
► S. 198 a half-hour ride …
a 30-minute ride eine 30-minütige Fahrt III **wait a minute** Warte einen Moment. / Moment mal. I
miracle ['mɪrəkl] Wunder IV
mirror ['mɪrə] Spiegel II
miss [mɪs]:
1. verpassen I
2. vermissen III

Miss [mɪs]: **Miss Bell** Frau Bell *(übliche Anrede von Lehrerinnen)* I
missing ['mɪsɪŋ] verschollen, vermisst III **the missing words** die fehlenden Wörter I **be missing** fehlen II
mist [mɪst] (leichter) Nebel, Dunst(schleier) II
mistake [mɪ'steɪk] Fehler II **make a mistake** einen Fehler machen II
°**mix** [mɪks]: **mix sth. up** etwas gründlich mischen **mixed-race** gemischtrassig
°**mob** [mɒb] Gruppe *(Kängurus)*
mobile (phone) [ˌməʊbaɪl 'fəʊn] Mobiltelefon, Handy I
model ['mɒdl]:
1. Model II
2. Modell III
modern ['mɒdən] modern III
°**module** ['mɒdjuːl] Modul, Baustein
moment ['məʊmənt] Moment I **at the moment** gerade, im Moment I
°**monarchy** ['mɒnəki] Monarchie
Monday ['mʌndeɪ] Montag I
money ['mʌni] Geld I
monitor ['mɒnɪtə] nachverfolgen; überwachen III
monkey ['mʌŋki] Affe I
monster ['mɒnstə] Monster I
month [mʌnθ] Monat I **a six-month stay** ein sechsmonatiger Aufenthalt V 1 (12)
► S. 198 a half-hour ride …
monument (to) ['mɒnjumənt] Denkmal, Monument (für / zum Gedenken an) III
mood [muːd] Laune, Stimmung IV **be in a bad/good mood** schlechte/gute Laune haben IV
moon [muːn] Mond I **at full moon** bei Vollmond II
moonless ['muːnləs] mondlos IV
moonlight ['muːnlaɪt] Mondlicht III
moor [mɔː], [mʊə] Hochmoor II
mop [mɒp]:
1. Wischmopp III
2. wischen *(Fußboden)* III
moral ['mɒrəl] Lehre, Moral IV
more [mɔː] mehr I **more beautiful (than)** schöner (als) II **one more photo** noch ein Foto; ein weiteres Foto II
morning ['mɔːnɪŋ] Morgen, Vormittag I **Good morning.** Guten Morgen. I **in the morning** morgens, vormittags, am Morgen/Vormittag I **tomorrow morning** morgen früh, morgen Vormittag II
mosque [mɒsk] Moschee III
most [məʊst]: **most people** die meisten Menschen II **most of them** die meisten von ihnen II **(the) most beautiful** der/die/das schönste …; am schönsten II
motel [məʊ'tel] Motel *(Hotel mit Zimmern und Garagen an einer Autostraße)* IV

moth [mɒθ] Nachtfalter, Motte V 1 (19)
mother ['mʌðə] Mutter I
motion ['məʊʃn]: **slow motion** Zeitlupe III
motivation [ˌməʊtɪ'veɪʃn] Motivation, Beweggrund V 3 (66)
motorbike ['məʊtəbaɪk] Motorrad III
mountain ['maʊntən] Berg II
mountainous ['maʊntənəs] bergig, gebirgig V 1 (22)
mouse [maʊs], *pl* **mice** [maɪs] Maus V 3 (67)
mouth [maʊθ] Mund; Maul I
move [muːv]:
1. bewegen; sich bewegen I
2. **move (to)** umziehen (nach) II **move house/flat** umziehen IV **move in** einziehen II **move into a house** einziehen in ein Haus… II **move on to sth.** zu etwas übergehen IV
3. Zug *(bei Brettspielen)* IV
movement ['muːvmənt] Bewegung III
movie ['muːvi] Film III
movie theater ['muːvi θɪətə] *(AE)* Kino IV
°**mozzie** ['mɒzi] *(AusE; infml)* Mücke, Moskito
MP (= Member of Parliament) [ˌem'piː] Parlamentsmitglied, Abgeordnete(r) V 4 (89)
mph (miles per hour) [ˌem piː‿'eɪtʃ] Meilen pro Stunde IV
MP3 player [ˌem piː 'θriː ˌpleɪə] MP3-Spieler I
Mr Schwarz ['mɪstə] Herr Schwarz I *(AE:* **Mr.***)* IV
Mrs Schwarz ['mɪsɪz] Frau Schwarz I *(AE:* **Mrs.***)* IV
Ms Miller [mɪz], [məz] Frau Miller *(AE:* **Ms.***)* IV
much [mʌtʃ] viel I **How much …?** Wie viel …? I **How much are …?** Was kosten …? I **How much is …?** Was kostet …? I
mud [mʌd] Schlamm, Matsch II
mug [mʌg]: **a mug (of)** ein Becher II
mum [mʌm] Mama, Mutti I
murder ['mɜːdə] morden, ermorden IV
murder ['mɜːdə] Mord V 2 (44)
murderer ['mɜːdərə] Mörder/in V 2 (44)
muscle ['mʌsl] Muskel V 2 (39)
museum [mju'ziːəm] Museum I
mushroom ['mʌʃrʊm], ['mʌʃruːm] Pilz IV
music ['mjuːzɪk] Musik I
musical ['mjuːzɪkl] Musical II
musician [mju'zɪʃn] Musiker/in III
must [mʌst] müssen II **you mustn't do it** ['mʌsnt] du darfst es nicht tun II **He must have been asleep.** Er muss geschlafen haben. IV
my [maɪ] mein/e I **My birthday is in May.** Ich habe im Mai Geburtstag. I **My birthday is on 5th August.** Ich habe am 5. August Geburtstag. I **My name is …** Ich heiße … I

myself [maɪ'self] mich, mir III
myth [mɪθ] Mythos V 4 (89)

N

°**naive** [naɪ'i:v] naiv, unkritisch
name [neɪm]:
1. Name I **My name is ...** Ich heiße ... I **What's your name?** Wie heißt du? / Wie heißt ihr? I **call sb. names** jn. beschimpfen, jm. Schimpfwörter nachrufen IV **first name** Vorname IV
2. (be)nennen III **be named sth.** zu etwas ernannt werden V 1 (27)
°**napping** ['næpɪŋ]: **a dog caught napping** ein Hund, der beim Schlafen erwischt wird
narrative ['nærətɪv] Erzähl- V 4 (86) **the narrative tenses** die Erzähltempora V 4 (86)
narrator [nə'reɪtə] Erzähler/in V 4 (86)
narrow ['nærəʊ] schmal, eng II
nation ['neɪʃn] Nation, Volk III
national ['næʃnəl] national, National- III **national anthem** Nationalhymne IV
native ['neɪtɪv]: **Native American** amerikanischer Ureinwohner/in IV °**native people** *(pl)* Einheimische
native speaker [ˌneɪtɪv 'spi:kə] Muttersprachler/in IV
natural ['nætʃrəl] natürlich III **natural history** Naturkunde III **natural world** (Welt der) Natur III
°**navigate** ['nævɪgeɪt] navigieren; sich zurechtfinden in
navy ['neɪvi] Marine I
°**NBA** [en bi 'eɪ] (= **National Basketball Association**), *US-Basketballverband*
near [nɪə] in der Nähe von, nahe (bei) I **near here** (hier) in der Nähe I
nearby ['nɪəbaɪ] in der Nähe IV **a nearby town** eine nahegelegene Stadt II
nearly ['nɪəli] fast, beinahe III
necessary ['nesəsəri] notwendig III
neck [nek] Hals II
need [ni:d]:
1. brauchen, benötigen I **need to do sth.** etwas tun müssen II **you needn't do it** ['ni:dnt] du musst es nicht tun II **You needn't have made a cake.** Du hättest keinen Kuchen zu machen brauchen. IV
°2. **needs and wants** Bedürfnisse und Wünsche
negative ['negətɪv] negativ IV
neighbour ['neɪbə] Nachbar/in II
neighbourhood ['neɪbəhʊd] Viertel, Gegend, Umgebung; Nachbarschaft V 3 (73)
neither ['naɪðə], ['ni:ðə] **me neither** Ich auch nicht. III **neither ... nor ...** weder ... noch ... V 3 (61)
nervous ['nɜ:vəs] nervös, aufgeregt II
net [net] Netz III **goal net** Tornetz III
°**network** ['netwɜ:k] Netzwerk
neutral ['nju:trəl] neutral IV
never ['nevə] nie, niemals I
new [nju:] neu I
news *(no pl)* [nju:z]:
1. Nachrichten I
2. Neuigkeiten II
newspaper ['nju:zpeɪpə] Zeitung; *(kurz auch:* **paper***)* IV
New Year's Eve [ˌnju: jɪəz‿'i:v] Silvester II
next [nekst]:
1. **next year's ...** das ... vom nächsten Jahr II **the next question** die nächste Frage I
2. als Nächstes III
3. **next to** ['nekst tʊ] neben II **next door** nebenan V 2 (38)
nice [naɪs] nett, schön I **Nice to meet you.** Freut mich, dich/euch/Sie kennenzulernen. I
night [naɪt] Nacht I **at night** nachts, in der Nacht I
nil [nɪl] null, Null III
nine [naɪn] neun I
no [nəʊ]:
1. nein I **No, that's wrong.** Nein, das ist falsch. / Nein, das stimmt nicht. I
2. kein, keine I **at no time** zu keiner Zeit IV **it was no different** es war nicht anders III **No way!** Auf keinen Fall! / Kommt nicht in Frage! III
nobody ['nəʊbədi] niemand I
nod [nɒd] nicken II
noise [nɔɪz] Geräusch; Lärm III
noisy ['nɔɪzi] laut, lärmend, voller Lärm II
nomadic [nə'mædɪk]: **nomadic people** Nomadenvolk V 4 (99)
none (of) [nʌn] keine(r, s) (von ...) III
nonsense ['nɒnsns] Unsinn, dummes Zeug V 1 (23) **noon** [nu:n] Mittag IV
no one ['nəʊ wʌn] niemand I
°**Nope.** [nəʊp] *(infml)* Nein.
normal ['nɔ:məl] normal III
normally ['nɔ:məli] normalerweise V 2 (51)
north [nɔ:θ] Norden; nach Norden; nördlich III **northbound** ['nɔ:θbaʊnd] Richtung Norden III **north-east** [ˌnɔ:θ‿'i:st] Nordosten; nach Nordosten; nordöstlich III **northern** ['nɔ:ðən] nördlich, Nord- III **north-west** [ˌnɔ:θ'west] Nordwesten; nach Nordwesten; nordwestlich III
nose [nəʊz] Nase I
°**nostril** ['nɒstrəl] Nasenloch
not [nɒt] nicht I **he/she/it is not** er/sie/es ist nicht ... I **not till three** erst um drei, nicht vor drei II **not ... yet** noch nicht I **not ... at all** überhaupt nicht(s), gar nicht(s); überhaupt kein/e, gar kein/e IV
note [nəʊt]:
1. Notiz, Mitteilung I **make notes (on/about sth.)** (sich) Notizen machen (über/zu etwas) *(zur Vorbereitung)* II **take notes (on/about sth.)** (sich) Notizen machen (über/zu etwas) *(beim Lesen oder Zuhören)* II
2. Note *(Musik)* III
nothing ['nʌθɪŋ] (gar) nichts I
notice ['nəʊtɪs]:
1. merken, bemerken IV
2. **take notice (of sth.)** auf etwas aufmerksam werden, etwas zur Kenntnis nehmen V 4 (98)
noun [naʊn] Nomen, Substantiv III
novel ['nɒvl] Roman V 2 (36)
November [nəʊ'vembə] November I
now [naʊ] nun, jetzt I **Now that ...** Jetzt, wo ... / Nun, da ... III **right now** jetzt gerade II
nowhere ['nəʊweə] nirgendwo; nirgendwohin III **out of nowhere** (wie) aus dem Nichts III
number ['nʌmbə] Zahl, Nummer, Ziffer I; Anzahl III
nut [nʌt] Nuss IV

O

o [əʊ] Null *(in Telefonnummern)* I
object ['ɒbdʒɪkt], ['ɒbdʒekt] Objekt II; Gegenstand IV
observation deck [ˌɒbzə'veɪʃn dek] Aussichtsplattform IV
occasion [ə'keɪʒn] Anlass, Ereignis IV
occasionally [ə'keɪʒnəli] gelegentlich, ab und zu V 2 (37)
ocean ['əʊʃn] Ozean I
o'clock [ə'klɒk]: **at 1 o'clock** um 1 Uhr / um 13 Uhr I
October [ɒk'təʊbə] Oktober I
of [ɒv], [əv] von I
of course [əv 'kɔ:s] natürlich, selbstverständlich I
off [ɒf]: **Off you go now.** Ab mit euch jetzt! / Los mit euch jetzt! III **be off** aus(geschaltet) sein *(Radio, Licht usw.)* III **fall off a bike** vom Fahrrad herunterfallen III **get/have a day off** einen Tag frei bekommen/haben III **off the coast** vor der Küste V 4 (88) **run off** wegrennen III
offensive [ə'fensɪv] beleidigend, Anstoß erregend IV
offer ['ɒfə] anbieten II
office ['ɒfɪs] Büro III **ticket office** Fahrkartenschalter; Kasse *(für den Verkauf von Eintrittskarten)* III
official [ə'fɪʃl]
1. amtlich, Amts- III
2. Beamte(r), Beamtin III
often ['ɒfn], ['ɒftən] oft I
oh [əʊ]: **Oh, it's you.** Ach, du bist es. I
oil [ɔɪl] Öl III
old [əʊld] alt I **in the old days** früher (einmal) III

old-fashioned [ˌəʊld'fæʃənd] altmodisch V 1 (22)
°**Olympic Games** *(pl)* [əˌlɪmpɪk 'geɪmz] Olympische Spiele
on [ɒn] auf I **be on** eingeschaltet sein, an sein *(Radio, Licht usw.)*; laufen, übertragen werden *(Programm, Sendung)* III **on earth** auf der Erde II **on Monday** am Montag I **on Monday afternoon** am Montagnachmittag I **on the phone** am Telefon II **on the plane** im Flugzeug II **on the radio** im Radio I **on top of each other** übereinander, aufeinander III **on TV** im Fernsehen III **walk/run/... on** weitergehen/-laufen/... II
once [wʌns]:
1. einmal II **once a week/year** einmal pro Woche/Jahr II
°2. einst, früher einmal
once [wʌns] sobald, sowie, wenn V 2 (36)
one [wʌn] eins I **a one-hour concert** ein einstündiges Konzert III **one all** eins zu eins; eins beide III **one by one** einzeln; einer nach dem anderen II **one night/day** eines Nachts/Tages II **one-syllable** einsilbige(r, s) II **a white one** ein weißer / eine weiße / ein weißes II **the blue one** der/die/das blaue IV **the ones in Bourbon Street** die in Bourbon Street IV **this one** diese(r, s) II **two black ones** zwei schwarze II **Which one?** Welche(r, s)? II **You know which one.** Du weißt, welche(r, s). IV
onion ['ʌnjənz] Zwiebel IV
online [ˌɒn'laɪn] online II
only ['əʊnli]:
1. nur, bloß I **the only ...** der/die/das einzige ...; die einzigen... II
2. erst I
onto ['ɒntʊ] auf (... hinauf) I
open ['əʊpən]:
1. öffnen, aufmachen I; sich öffnen I **opening times** *(pl)* Öffnungszeiten III
2. geöffnet, offen I
opener ['əʊpənə] Aufmacher; Einleitungssatz V 4 (101)
opera ['ɒprə] Oper V 1 (12)
°**operate** ['ɒpəreɪt] agieren, operieren, tätig sein
opinion [ə'pɪnjən] Meinung III **in my opinion** meiner Meinung nach III
°**opinion poll** [pəʊl] Meinungsumfrage
opportunity [ˌɒpə'tju:nəti] Gelegenheit, Möglichkeit, Chance V 1 (26)
► S. 203 German "Möglichkeit"
oppose sth. [ə'pəʊz] etwas ablehnen, gegen etwas sein V 1 (17)
opposing [ə'pəʊzɪŋ] gegnerisch V 1 (27)
opposite ['ɒpəzɪt]:
1. gegenüber (von) II
2. Gegenteil IV
3. entgegengesetzt V 3 (63)
°**oppression** [ə'preʃn] Unterdrückung
optimistic [ˌɒptɪ'mɪstɪk] optimistisch IV
or [ɔ:] oder I
°**oral** ['ɔ:rəl] mündlich
orange ['ɒrɪndʒ]:
1. orange I
2. Orange, Apfelsine I
order ['ɔ:də]:
1. Reihenfolge I
2. bestellen II
3. ordnen III
organization [ˌɔ:gənaɪ'zeɪʃn] Organisation V 2 (50)
organize ['ɔ:gənaɪz] organisieren; ordnen III
other ['ʌðə] andere(r, s) I
°**otherwise** ['ʌðəwaɪz] sonst; anderweitig, auf andere Weise
otter ['ɒtə] Otter II
ought [ɔ:t]: **you ought to stop ...** du solltest aufhören, ... V 2 (44)
our ['aʊə] unser/e I
ours ['aʊəz] unserer, unsere, unseres II
ourselves [ɑ:'selvz], [aʊə'selvz] uns III **We painted the room ourselves.** Wir haben das Zimmer selbst gestrichen. IV
out ['aʊt]:
1. heraus, hinaus, nach draußen II **out and about** unterwegs II
2. **be out** nicht zu Hause sein, nicht da sein II
3. **out of ...** ['aʊt‿əv] aus ... (heraus/hinaus) I
outback, the ['aʊtbæk] das Hinterland Australiens V 1 (10)
outdoor ['aʊtdɔ:] Außen-, im Freien II
outline ['aʊtlaɪn] Gliederung IV
outside [ˌaʊt'saɪd]:
1. draußen; nach draußen I **outside the house** vor dem Haus, außerhalb vom Haus II
2. die Außenseite; das Äußere III
oval ['əʊvl] oval IV
oven ['ʌvn] Backofen IV
over ['əʊvə]:
1. über I **run over (to)** hinüberrennen (zu/nach) II **over to ...** hinüber zu/nach ... I **over here** hier herüber II **over there** da drüben, dort drüben II
2. **over 4 years** über 4 Jahre; mehr als 4 Jahre I
3. **be over** vorbei / zu Ende sein I
overcrowded [ˌəʊvə'kraʊdɪd] überfüllt V 1 (22)
°**override sth.** [ˌəʊvə'raɪd] etwas außer Kraft setzen; sich über etwas hinwegsetzen
°**overview** ['əʊvəvju:] Überblick
own [əʊn]:
1. besitzen II
2. **my own room/...** mein eigenes Zimmer/... II
3. **on my/your/their/... own** allein II
owner ['əʊnə] Besitzer/in, Eigentümer/in V 4 (88)
oxygen ['ɒksɪdʒən] Sauerstoff V 2 (37)
°**Oz** [ɒz] *(infml)* Australien

P

p [pi:] *Abkürzung für „pence", „penny"* I
pack [pæk] packen III
packet ['pækɪt] Packung, Päckchen II
page [peɪdʒ] Seite I **What page are we on?** Auf welcher Seite sind wir? I
paid [peɪd]:
1. *siehe* **pay**
2. **get paid** Geld bekommen III
pain [peɪn] Schmerz(en) V 4 (91) **be in pain** Schmerzen haben V 4 (91)
paint [peɪnt] (an)streichen; (an)malen II
painted ['peɪntɪd] bemalt, angemalt II
painter ['peɪntə] Maler/in III
painting ['peɪntɪŋ] Gemälde, Malerei V 1 (26)
pair [peə]: **a pair (of)** ein Paar II
°**pair sth.** [peə] ein Paar machen aus etwas
palace ['pæləs] Palast, Schloss III
palm tree ['pɑ:m tri:] Palme IV
°**pamphlet** ['pæmflət] Flugblatt, Merkblatt, Pamphlet
pancake ['pænkeɪk] Pfannkuchen II
panic ['pænɪk], **panicked, panicked** in Panik geraten III
pants *(pl)* [pænts] *(AE)* Hose IV
paper ['peɪpə]:
1. Zeitung I
2. Papier I
parade [pə'reɪd] Parade, Umzug II
paradise ['pærədaɪs] Paradies V 1 (12)
paragraph ['pærəgrɑ:f] Absatz *(in einem Text)* I
paraphrase ['pærəfreɪz] umschreiben, anders ausdrücken IV
parents *(pl)* ['peərənts] Eltern I
park [pɑ:k]:
1. Park I **parking lot** *(AE)* Parkplatz IV **parking space** Parkplatz, Parklücke IV
2. parken III
parliament ['pɑ:ləmənt] Parlament III
parsley ['pɑ:sli] Petersilie IV
part [pɑ:t]:
1. Teil I **part of speech** Wortart III **part of the body** Körperteil II **take part in sth.** an etwas teilnehmen II
2. Rolle IV
°**participate (in)** [pɑ:'tɪsɪpeɪt] sich beteiligen (an)
particular [pə'tɪkjələ] bestimmte(r, s), spezielle(r, s) V 3 (63)
partner ['pɑ:tnə] Partner/in I
party ['pɑ:ti]:
1. Party I
2. feiern, Party machen IV
°3. Partei
pass [pɑ:s]:
1. vergehen, vorübergehen *(Zeit)* III
2. **pass sth./sb.** an etwas/jm. vorbeigehen/vorbeifahren II
3. **pass sth. around** etwas herumgeben, herumreichen II °**pass sth.**

on etwas weitergeben
4. pass (a test) bestehen *(Test, Prüfung)* IV
5. abspielen, passen *(Ball)* V 3 (60)
6. verabschieden, genehmigen *(Gesetz, Antrag)* V 4 (88)
► S. 222 (to) pass
passion ['pæʃn] Leidenschaft V 3 (66)
passport ['pɑːspɔːt] (Reise-)Pass III
password ['pɑːswɜːd] Passwort V 2 (43)
past [pɑːst]:
1. Vergangenheit I
2. half past ten halb elf (10.30 / 22.30) I **quarter past ten** Viertel nach zehn (10.15 / 22.15) I
3. vorbei (an), vorüber (an) II
past [pɑːst] vergangene(r, s); letzte(r, s) V 4 (86)
pasta *(no pl)* ['pæstə] Nudeln V 2 (44)
pat [pæt] tätscheln IV **pat sb. on the head** jm. den Kopf tätscheln IV
path [pɑːθ] Pfad, Weg II **bike path** Radweg V 4 (89)
patience ['peɪʃns] Geduld V 3 (63)
patient ['peɪʃnt] geduldig IV
patient ['peɪʃnt] Patient/in V 1 (26)
patriotism ['peɪtriətɪzəm] Patriotismus IV
pattern ['pætn] Muster IV
pause [pɔːz] innehalten, pausieren; eine Pause einlegen II
pavement ['peɪvmənt] Gehweg, Bürgersteig III
paw [pɔː] Pfote, Tatze II
pay [peɪ]:
1. (paid, paid) bezahlen **pay for sth.** etwas bezahlen II **get paid** Geld bekommen III **pay attention** aufmerksam sein, aufpassen; zuhören, Beachtung schenken V 4 (98) **° pay off** sich rentieren, sich auszahlen:
2. Bezahlung, Lohn V 4 (89)
PE [ˌpiː‿'iː] Sportunterricht, Turnen I
peace [piːs] Friede, Frieden III
peaceful ['piːsfl] friedlich; friedfertig II
pedestrian [pə'destriən] Fußgänger/in III **pedestrian zone** Fußgängerzone II
pen [pen] Kugelschreiber, Stift, Füller I
°penalty ['penəlti] Strafe
pence [pens] Pence *(Plural von* **penny***)* I
pencil ['pensl] Bleistift I
pencil case ['pensl keɪs] Federmäppchen I
people ['piːpl]:
1. *(Singular)* Volk III
2. *(Plural)* Leute, Menschen I
pepper ['pepə]:
1. Pfeffer I
2. Paprika(schote) IV
per [pə, pɜː] pro IV **percent, per cent** [pə'sent] Prozent IV
percentage [pə'sentɪdʒ] Prozentsatz; prozentualer Anteil V 2 (47)
perfect ['pɜːfɪkt] perfekt, ideal I
°perfect [pə'fekt] perfektionieren, vervollkommnen
perform [pə'fɔːm] auftreten *(Künstler/in)* III
performance [pə'fɔːməns] Aufführung, Vorstellung, Auftritt IV
performer [pə'fɔːmə] Künstler/in III
perhaps [pə'hæps] vielleicht V 2 (48)
period ['pɪəriəd] *(bes. AE)* Unterrichtsstunde, Schulstunde IV
permission [pə'mɪʃn] Erlaubnis IV
permit ['pɜːmɪt] Genehmigung, Erlaubnis(schein) IV
persecution [ˌpɜːsɪ'kjuːʃn] Verfolgung *(aus religiösen, ethnischen, weltanschaulichen Gründen)* V 4 (99)
person ['pɜːsn] Person I
personal ['pɜːsənl] persönlich V 3 (72)
personal statement Motivationsschreiben V 3 (72)
personally ['pɜːsənəli] persönlich V 1 (17)
°perspective [pə'spektɪv] Perspektive
persuade [pə'sweɪd] überreden V 4 (98)
pessimistic [ˌpesɪ'mɪstɪk] pessimistisch V 2 (42)
pet [pet] Haustier III
petition [pə'tɪʃn] Petition, Eingabe, Unterschriftensammlung V 4 (83)
°phenomenal [fə'nɒmɪnl] phänomenal, überragend
phone [fəʊn]:
1. Telefon I **answer the phone** ans Telefon gehen II **on the phone** am Telefon II
2. phone sb. jn. anrufen II
phone call ['fəʊn kɔːl] *(kurz auch:* **call***)* Anruf; Telefongespräch II
photo ['fəʊtəʊ] Foto I **in the photo** auf dem Foto I **take photos** fotografieren, Fotos machen I
photograph ['fəʊtəgrɑːf]:
1. fotografieren III
2. Foto(grafie) V 1 (20)
photographer [fə'tɒgrəfə] Fotograf/in V 2 (34)
photography [fə'tɒgrəfi] Fotografie V 1 (13)
phrase [freɪz] Ausdruck, (Rede-)Wendung I
Physical Education [ˌfɪzɪkl‿ˌedʒu'keɪʃn] Sportunterricht, Turnen I
piano [pi'ænəʊ] Klavier, Piano I **play the piano** Klavier spielen I
pick [pɪk] wählen, auswählen, aussuchen V 3 (62) **pick on sb.** auf jm. herumhacken III **pick sb. up** jn. abholen II **pick sth. up** etwas aufheben *(vom Boden)*, etwas hochheben II
picnic ['pɪknɪk] Picknick I
picture ['pɪktʃə] Bild I **in the picture** auf dem Bild I
pie [paɪ] Obstkuchen; Pastete IV
pie chart ['paɪ tʃɑːt] Tortendiagramm V 2 (47)
piece (of) [piːs] ein Stück … III
pig [pɪg] Schwein I
°piggy bank ['pɪgi bæŋk] Sparschwein
pigeon ['pɪdʒɪn] (Stadt-)Taube IV
pile [paɪl] Stapel, Haufen IV
°pinball machine ['pɪnbɔːl məʃiːn] Flipper(automat)
pink [pɪŋk] pink, rosa I
pipe [paɪp]:
1. Pfeife III
2. water pipe Wasserleitung, Wasserrohr V 3 (61)
pirate ['paɪrət] Pirat/in V 3 (68)
pitch [pɪtʃ] (Sport-)Platz, Spielfeld III
pity ['pɪti]: **It was a pity that …** Es war schade, dass … III **take pity on sb.** Mitleid mit jm. haben ; sich jemandes erbarmen IV
pizza ['piːtsə] Pizza I
place [pleɪs] Ort, Platz, Stelle I **be in place** im Einsatz sein; vor Ort sein IV **in second place** auf dem zweiten Platz; an zweiter Stelle III **take place** stattfinden III
plan [plæn]:
1. Plan I
2. planen II
plane [pleɪn] Flugzeug II **get on a plane** in ein Flugzeug einsteigen II **on the plane** im Flugzeug II
planet ['plænɪt] Planet I
plant [plɑːnt]:
1. Pflanze II
2. pflanzen II
plantation [plɑːn'teɪʃn] Plantage III
plaster ['plɑːstə] (Heft-)Pflaster II
plastic ['plæstɪk] Plastik, Kunststoff II
plate [pleɪt] **a plate of …** ein Teller … I
platform ['plætfɔːm]:
1. Plattform III
2. Bahnsteig, Gleis III
play [pleɪ]:
1. spielen I **play the drums / the guitar / the piano** Schlagzeug/Gitarre/Klavier spielen I
2. abspielen *(CD, DVD)* I
3. Theaterstück I
player ['pleɪə] Spieler/in I
playground ['pleɪgraʊnd] Spielplatz; Schulhof V 4 (98)
please [pliːz] bitte I
pleased [pliːzd] froh, erfreut, zufrieden V 2 (42) **Pleased to meet you.** Freut mich, Sie kennenzulernen. V 2 (42)
pm: 4 pm [ˌpiː‿'em] 4 Uhr nachmittags / 16 Uhr I
pocket ['pɒkɪt] Tasche *(Manteltasche, Hosentasche usw.)* II **pocket money** Taschengeld V 2 (44)
poem ['pəʊɪm] Gedicht II
poetry ['pəʊətri] Lyrik, Dichtung, Poesie V 3 (64)
point [pɔɪnt]:
1. Punkt I **point: 1.6 (one point six)** 1,6 (eins Komma sechs) III **point of view (on sth.)** Standpunkt (in/über/zu etwas) III **from my point**

of view aus meiner Sicht III **have a point** nicht ganz Unrecht haben V 1 (23)
2. point to sth. auf etwas zeigen, deuten I **point sth. at sb.** etwas auf jn. richten I **point sth. out (to sb.)** (jn.) auf etwas hinweisen III

poisonous ['pɔɪzənəs] giftig V 1 (10)

police *(pl)* [pə'li:s] Polizei III **police officer** Polizist/in I **police station** Polizeiwache, -revier III **The police are on their way.** Die Polizei ist auf dem Weg. III

policeman [pə'li:smən] Polizist I

policewoman [pə'li:swʊmən] Polizistin III

°**policy** ['pɒləsi] Politik, politische Linie, Strategie, Vorgehensweise

polite [pə'laɪt] höflich III

politeness [pə'laɪtnəs] Höflichkeit V 3 (63)

political [pə'lɪtɪkl] politisch V 4 (87)

politics ['pɒlətɪks] Politik V 2 (36)

°**poll** [pəʊl] Umfrage

pollution [pə'lu:ʃn] (Umwelt-) Verschmutzung III

°**Pom** [pɒm] *(AusE; infml)* Brite/Britin

pony ['pəʊni] Pony II

pool [pu:l] Schwimmbad, Schwimmbecken I

poor [pɔ:], [pʊə] arm I

popular (with) ['pɒpjələ] populär, beliebt (bei) III

population [ˌpɒpju'leɪʃn] Bevölkerung, Einwohner(zahl) III

porch [pɔ:tʃ] *(AE)* Veranda; *(BE)* Vorbau, Vordach IV

pork [pɔ:k] Schweinefleisch IV

position [pə'zɪʃn] Platz, Position III

positive ['pɒzətɪv] positiv IV

°**possession** [pə'zeʃn]: **take possession of sth.** Besitz ergreifen von etwas; etwas in Besitz nehmen

possibility [ˌpɒsə'bɪləti] Möglichkeit V 1 (26)
▶ S. 203 German "Möglichkeit"

possible ['pɒsəbl] möglich IV

°**possum** ['pɒsəm] Opossum

post [pəʊst]:
1. Posting *(auf Blog)*, Blog-Eintrag III
2. posten, bekanntgeben V 1 (18) **post sth.** etwas posten V 2 (43)

postcard ['pəʊstkɑ:d] Postkarte II

posted ['pəʊstɪd]: **Stay posted!** Bleib(t) auf dem Laufenden! IV

poster ['pəʊstə] Poster I

post office ['pəʊst_ɒfɪs] Postamt II

pot [pɒt] Gefäß; Topf III

potato [pə'teɪtəʊ], *pl* **potatoes** Kartoffel I

°**potential** [pə'tenʃl] Potential

pound [paʊnd] Pfund *(britische Währung)* I

pour [pɔ:] gießen II

°**poverty** ['pɒvəti] Armut

powder ['paʊdə] Pulver IV

power ['paʊə] Energie, Strom; Kraft, Stärke; Macht IV

powerful ['paʊəfl] mächtig, kräftig, stark IV

practical ['præktɪkl] praktisch III

practice ['præktɪs]:
1. Übung I **it takes practice** es erfordert Übung IV
2. *(AE)* üben, trainieren *(= BE* **practise***)* IV

practise ['præktɪs] *(BE)* üben, trainieren I

prairie ['preəri] Prärie, Grasland IV

°**pranked** [præŋkt] angeschmiert

pray [preɪ] beten IV

prayer [preə] Gebet IV

predator ['predətə] Raubtier III

prediction [prɪ'dɪkʃn] Vorhersage, Voraussage V 3 (64)

prefer sth. (to sth.) [prɪ'fɜ:] etwas (etwas anderem) vorziehen V 1 (19)

prefix ['pri:fɪks] Präfix, Vorsilbe IV

prejudice (against) ['predʒudɪs] Vorurteil (gegen), Voreingenommenheit (gegenüber) IV

°**preparation** [ˌprepə'reɪʃn] Vorbereitung

prepare sth. [prɪ'peə]:
1. etwas vorbereiten I
2. etwas zubereiten IV

present ['preznt]:
1. Geschenk I
2. Gegenwart II

present sth. (to sb.) [prɪ'zent] (jm.) etwas präsentieren, vorstellen II

presentation [ˌprezn'teɪʃn] Präsentation, Vorstellung II

°**present-day** [ˌpreznt'deɪ] heutige(r, s)

°**presenter** [prɪ'zentə] Moderator/in

president ['prezɪdənt] Präsident/in III

press [pres] drücken III

pressure ['preʃə] Druck IV °**pressure group** Interessenverband

pretend [prɪ'tend] so tun, als ob III

pretty ['prɪti]:
1. hübsch II
2. *(adv)* ziemlich V 2 (38)

prevent [prɪ'vent] etwas verhindern IV

price [praɪs] (Kauf-)Preis I

pride (in sth.) [praɪd] Stolz (auf etwas) IV

primary school ['praɪməri] Grundschule V 3 (73)

°**primaries** *(pl)* ['praɪməriz] US-Vorwahlen

prime minister [ˌpraɪm 'mɪnɪstə] Premierminister/in V 4 (88)

prince [prɪns] Prinz II

princess [ˌprɪn'ses], ['prɪnses] Prinzessin II

principal ['prɪnsəpl] *(bes. AE)* Schulleiter/in IV

principle ['prɪnsəpl] Prinzip V 3 (67)

print [prɪnt] Druck; Print- IV

prison ['prɪzn] Gefängnis I

private ['praɪvət] privat V 1 (13)

prize [praɪz] Preis, Gewinn II

probable ['prɒbəbl] wahrscheinlich III

probably ['prɒbəbli] wahrscheinlich II

problem ['prɒbləm] Problem I

process ['prəʊses] Prozess, Vorgang IV

produce [prə'dju:s] produzieren, erzeugen, herstellen V 3 (70)

produce [prə'dju:s] produzieren, erzeugen, herstellen V 4 (83)

product ['prɒdʌkt] Produkt V 4 (83) **dairy products** Milchprodukte, Molkereiprodukte IV

professional [prə'feʃənl] professionell, Profi- V 1 (27)

profile ['prəʊfaɪl] Profil; Beschreibung, Porträt I

program ['prəʊgræm]:
1. *(AE)* Programm; (Fernseh-/Radio-) Sendung IV
2. (Computer-)Programm IV
3. programmieren IV

programme ['prəʊgræm] *(BE)* Programm *(auch im Theater usw.)*; (Radio-, Fernseh-)Sendung I

progress ['prəʊgres]: **in progress** im Gange, im Verlauf V 4 (86)

project ['prɒdʒekt] Projekt II

project sth. (on, onto) [prə'dʒekt] etwas projizieren (auf/an) V 4 (84)

promise ['prɒmɪs]:
1. versprechen II
2. Versprechen; Verheißung V 2 (36)

promote sth. [prə'məʊt] Werbung machen für etwas III

pronounce [prə'naʊns] aussprechen IV

pronunciation [prəˌnʌnsi'eɪʃn] Aussprache I

proof (of) *(no pl)* [pru:f] Beweis(e) V 4 (101)

proofread sth. ['pru:fri:d], **proofread** ['pru:fred], **proofread** ['pru:fred] etwas Korrektur lesen V 3 (72)

property ['prɒpəti] Eigentum IV

°**proportional** [prə'pɔ:ʃənl] proportional; *(Wahlsystem)* Verhältnis-

propose [prə'pəʊz] vorschlagen V 4 (101)

protect sb./sth. (from sb./sth.) [prə'tekt] jn./etwas (be)schützen (vor jm./etwas) III

protein ['prəʊti:n] Protein, Eiweiß V 2 (44)

protest ['prəʊtest] Protest III

protest [prə'test] protestieren III **protest (against) sth.** gegen etwas protestieren V 4 (92)

protester [prə'testə] Demonstrant/in IV

proud (of) [praʊd] stolz (auf) III

provoke [prə'vəʊk] provozieren V 1 (19)

pub [pʌb] Kneipe, Lokal III

public ['pʌblɪk] öffentliche(r, s) IV

publish ['pʌblɪʃ] veröffentlichen V 2 (50)

pull [pʊl] ziehen I **pull sth. out** etwas herausziehen II

pullover ['pʊləʊvə] Pullover II

pulse [pʌls] Puls, Pulsschlag V 2 (37)

pumpkin ['pʌmpkɪn] Kürbis IV

punctuation [ˌpʌŋktʃu'eɪʃn] Zeichensetzung II
punishment ['pʌnɪʃmənt] Bestrafung, Strafe III
puppet ['pʌpɪt] Marionette, Handpuppe II
purple ['pɜːpl] violett, lila I
push [pʊʃ] drücken, schieben, stoßen I
put [pʊt], **put, put** legen, stellen, *(etwas wohin)* tun I **put out (a fire)** (ein Feuer) löschen IV ° **put sb. through (to sb.)** jn. (mit jm.) verbinden **put sth. down** etwas hinlegen III **put sth. on** etwas anziehen *(Kleidung)*; etwas aufsetzen *(Hut, Helm)* II **put your hand up** sich melden III
pyjamas *(pl)* [pə'dʒɑːməz] Schlafanzug V 4 (97)
python ['paɪθən] Python V 1 (19)

Q

qualification [ˌkwɒlɪfɪ'keɪʃn] Qualifikation V 3 (73)
qualify ['kwɒlɪfaɪ] sich qualifizieren IV
quality ['kwɒləti] Eigenschaft, Qualität V 3 (63)
quarter ['kwɔːtə] **quarter past ten** Viertel nach zehn (10.15 / 22.15) I **quarter to eleven** Viertel vor elf (10.45 / 22.45) I
quarter ['kwɔːtə] Viertel *(auch:* Stadtviertel*)* V 1 (12)
quay [kiː] Kai V 1 (12)
queen [kwiːn] Königin II
question ['kwestʃən] Frage I **question mark** Fragezeichen II
queue [kjuː]:
1. Schlange stehen, sich anstellen II
2. Schlange, Reihe *(wartender Menschen)* III
quick [kwɪk] schnell II
quiet ['kwaɪət] ruhig, still, leise I
quite [kwaɪt] ziemlich; völlig, ganz III
quiz [kwɪz] Quiz, Ratespiel I
quotation [kwəʊ'teɪʃn] Zitat IV **quotation marks** *(pl)* Anführungszeichen, -striche V 3 (70)
quote [kwəʊt]:
1. zitieren V 3 (70)
2. *(infml)* Zitat IV

R

rabbit ['ræbɪt] Kaninchen I
race [reɪs]:
1. Rennen, (Wett-)Lauf II
2. rasen III
racism ['reɪsɪzm] Rassismus V 1 (27)
racist ['reɪsɪst] Rassist/in; rassistisch V 1 (27)
radio ['reɪdiəʊ] Radio I **on the radio** im Radio I
railing ['reɪlɪŋ] Geländer IV
railroad ['reɪlrəʊd] *(AE)* Eisenbahn IV
railway ['reɪlweɪ] Eisenbahn IV
rain [reɪn]:
1. Regen II **heavy rain** starker Regen, heftiger Regen II
2. regnen II
rainbow ['reɪnbəʊ] Regenbogen III
raincoat ['reɪnkəʊt] Regenmantel II
rainforest ['reɪnfɒrɪst] Regenwald II
rainless ['reɪnləs] regenfrei, niederschlagsfrei IV
rainy ['reɪni] regnerisch II
raise [reɪz]: **raise a question** eine Frage aufwerfen/vorbringen V 4 (91) **raise an issue** ein Thema zur Sprache bringen V 4 (91) **raise chicken** Hühner züchten, halten V 4 (91) **raise children** Kinder auf-/großziehen V 4 (91) **raise money (for sth.)** Geld sammeln (für etwas) II **raise your voice** seine Stimme erheben V 4 (91)
▶ S. 224 (to) raise
°**rake** [reɪk] rechen, harken
rally ['ræli] Rallye II
ran [ræn] *siehe* **run**
rang [ræŋ] *siehe* **ring**
rat [ræt] Ratte I
°**rate** [reɪt] einschätzen
raven ['reɪvn] Rabe III
reach [riːtʃ] erreichen III **reach over** die Hand ausstrecken III
react (to) [ri'kt] reagieren (auf) III
reaction (to) [ri'ækʃn] Reaktion (auf) IV
read [riːd], **read** [red], **read** [red] lesen I **read sb.'s mind** jemandes Gedanken lesen III °**The message reads: ...** Die Botschaft lautet: ...
reader ['riːdə] Leser/in II
ready ['redi] bereit, fertig I
real ['riːəl] echt, wirklich II **real fast** *(AE, infml)* echt schnell IV
reality [ri'æləti] Realität, Wirklichkeit V 4 (89)
realize sth. ['riːəlaɪz] etwas erkennen; sich einer Sache bewusst werden V 2 (47)
really ['rɪəli] echt, wirklich I
reason ['riːzn]:
1. Grund, Begründung II **for this reason** aus diesem Grund IV
°2. vernünftig reden
rebuild [ˌriː'bɪld] wiederaufbauen IV
rebuilt [ˌriː'bɪlt] *siehe* **rebuild**
recent ['riːsnt]: **in recent years/months/...** in den letzten Jahren/Monaten/... IV
recently ['riːsntli] vor Kurzem, neulich; in letzter Zeit V 4 (101)
receptionist [rɪ'sepʃənɪst] Empfangschef/in IV
recipe ['resəpi] (Koch-)Rezept II
reckon ['rekən]: **I reckon** Ich schätze ..., Ich nehme an ... V 2 (36)
°**reclaim** [rɪ'kleɪm] zurückfordern
recognition [ˌrekəg'nɪʃn] Anerkennung V 1 (27)
recognize ['rekəgnaɪz] erkennen V 3 (63)
recommend sth. (to sb.) [ˌrekə'mend] (jm.) etwas empfehlen IV
record [rɪ'kɔːd] aufzeichnen *(Musik, Daten)*; dokumentieren *(Daten)* III
recorder [rɪ'kɔːdə] Blockflöte II
red [red] rot I **go red** rot werden, erröten II
reef [riːf] Riff V 1 (18)
refer to sth. [rɪ'fɜː] auf etwas verweisen, etwas erwähnen; sich auf etwas beziehen IV
referee [ˌrefə'riː] Schiedsrichter/in III
°**referendum** [ˌrefə'rendəm] Volksentscheid, Referendum
refine [rɪ'faɪn] verfeinern, verbessern V 4 (101)
refrigeration [rɪˌfrɪdʒə'reɪʃn] Kühlung V 3 (66)
refugee [ˌrefju'dʒiː] Flüchtling V 2 (50)
refuse (to do sth.) [rɪ'fjuːz] sich weigern (, etwas zu tun); ablehnen V 3 (66)
°**regardless (of)** [rɪ'gɑːdləs] ungeachtet
region ['riːdʒən] Region V 1 (10)
regional ['riːdʒənl] regional III
register ['redʒɪstə]:
1. Klassenbuch; Register, Verzeichnis IV
°2. sich registrieren
regret [rɪ'gret]: **regret sth.** etwas bedauern, bereuen V 4 (92) **regret doing sth.** bedauern, bereuen, etwas getan zu haben V 4 (92)
regular ['regjələ] regelmäßig II
rehearsal [rɪ'hɜːsl] Probe *(Theater)* III
°**reject** [rɪ'dʒekt] abweisen, zurückweisen
°**relate to** [rɪ'leɪt] sich beziehen auf, Bezug haben auf
relations *(pl)* [rɪ'leɪʃnz] Beziehungen IV
relationship [rɪ'leɪʃnʃɪp] Beziehung, Verhältnis IV
relax [rɪ'læks] sich entspannen, sich ausruhen III
relaxed [rɪ'lækst] entspannt IV
relaxing [rɪ'læksɪŋ] erholsam, entspannend V 1 (12)
relevant (to sth.) ['reləvənt] relevant, wichtig (für etwas) IV
°**reliable** [rɪ'laɪəbl] zuverlässig
°**relieved** [rɪ'liːvd] erleichtert
religion [rɪ'lɪdʒən] Religion I
religious [rɪ'lɪdʒəs] religiös V 3 (60)
rely on sb./sth. [rɪ'laɪ] sich auf jn./etwas verlassen V 3 (72)
°**remain** [rɪ'meɪn] bleiben, verbleiben
remember sth. [rɪ'membə]:
1. sich an etwas erinnern I
2. an etwas denken; sich etwas merken III
remind sb. [rɪ'maɪnd] jn. erinnern V 2 (49)
remote [rɪ'məʊt] abgelegen, abgeschieden V 1 (10)
remote (control) [rɪˌməʊt kən'trəʊl] Fernbedienung III

repair [rɪˈpeə] reparieren V 3 (59)
repeat [rɪˈpiːt] wiederholen II
reply (to) [rɪˈplaɪ] antworten (auf); erwidern, entgegnen III
report [rɪˈpɔːt]:
1. Bericht, Reportage II
2. berichten IV
reporter [rɪˈpɔːtə] Reporter/in IV
°**represent** [ˌreprɪˈzent]: **be represented** vertreten sein
°**Representative** [ˌreprɪˈzentətɪv] *(USA)* Abgeordnete(r) im Repräsentantenhaus
republic [rɪˈpʌblɪk] Republik III
°**Republican** [rɪˈpʌblɪkən]: **the Republicans** *(pl)* die Republikaner *(US-Partei)*
request [rɪˈkwest] Bitte, Wunsch V 2 (41)
rescue [ˈreskjuː] retten II
research [ˈriːsɜːtʃ] Recherche, Forschung(en) III
reservation [ˌrezəˈveɪʃn] Reservat, Reservation IV
reserve [rɪˈzɜːv]:
1. reservieren, buchen III
2. Schutzgebiet, Reservat IV
resident [ˈrezɪdənt] Bewohner/in, Anwohner/in IV
°**resist** [rɪˈzɪst] Widerstand leisten
respect [rɪˈspekt] Respekt, Achtung III
respectful [rɪˈspektfl] respektvoll IV
°**response** [rɪˈspɒns] Antwort, Reaktion
responsibility [rɪˌspɒnsəˈbɪləti] Verantwortung V 2 (50)
responsible [rɪˈspɒnsəbl] verantwortlich II
rest [rest]:
1. ruhen, sich ausruhen III
2. Rest III
restaurant [ˈrestrɒnt] Restaurant III
restful [ˈrestfl] ruhig, erholsam IV
restore [rɪˈstɔː] restaurieren, wiederherstellen V 3 (72)
restroom [ˈrestruːm] *(AE)* (öffentliche) Toilette, WC IV
result [rɪˈzʌlt] Ergebnis, Resultat III
return [rɪˈtɜːn]
1. zurückkehren IV
°2. **in return** als Gegenleistung
reveal [rɪˈviːl] offenbaren, preisgeben, verraten IV
reverse [rɪˈvɜːs] umgekehrte(r, s), entgegengesetzte(r, s) V 3 (72)
revise [rɪˈvaɪz] überarbeiten; *(Lernstoff)* wiederholen III
revision [rɪˈvɪʒn] Wiederholung *(des Lernstoffs)* II
°**rewrite** [ˌriːˈraɪt] neu schreiben, umarbeiten
rhyme [raɪm] Reim; Vers I
rhythm [ˈrɪðəm] Rhythmus III
rice [raɪs] Reis IV
rich [rɪtʃ] reich I
ridden [ˈrɪdn] *siehe* **ride**
ride [raɪd]:
1. Fahrt I; Ritt, Ausritt III; *(bes. AE)* Mitfahrgelegenheit IV
2. **(rode, ridden)** reiten; (Rad) fahren II **ride a bike** Fahrrad fahren I
rider [ˈraɪdə] Reiter/in IV
riding [ˈraɪdɪŋ] Reiten I
right [raɪt]:
1. Recht IV **civil rights** *(pl)* Bürgerrechte IV
2. richtig I **sb. is right** jemand hat Recht I **…, right?** …, nicht wahr? II ° **She'll be right.** *(AusE; infml) etwa:* Alles wird gut sein. **Yes, that's right.** Ja, das ist richtig. / Ja, das stimmt. I
3. rechte(r, s); (nach) rechts II **on the right** rechts/auf der rechten Seite II
4. **right after you** gleich nach dir II **right behind you** direkt hinter dir, genau hinter dir II
ring [rɪŋ]:
1. **(rang, rung)** klingeln, läuten II
2. Ring II
riot [ˈraɪət] Aufruhr, Aufstand V 4 (98)
°**rip sth. off** [ˌrɪp‿ˈɒf] etwas abreißen
rise up [ˌraɪz‿ˈʌp], **rose, risen:**
1. aufragen, emporragen *(Berge, Säulen, Türme, …)* III
2. sich erheben V 4 (82)
risen [ˈrɪzn] *siehe* **rise up**
risk [rɪsk] riskieren; aufs Spiel setzen V 4 (88)
river [ˈrɪvə] Fluss I
road [rəʊd] Straße I **at 8 Beach Road** in der Beach Road 8 I **in Beach Road** in der Beach Road I
roar [rɔː] brüllen III
roar [rɔː] tosen, dröhnen IV
roast [rəʊst] braten *(im Backofen)* IV **roast beef** Rinderbraten I **roast potatoes** *(pl) im Backofen in Fett gebackene Kartoffeln* I
rock [rɒk]:
1. Fels, Felsen I
2. **rock (music)** Rockmusik II
°**rock-bottom** [ˌrɒkˈbɒtm] Nullpunkt, Tiefpunkt
rocky [ˈrɒki] felsig, steinig II
rode [rəʊd] *siehe* **ride**
rodeo [ˈrəʊdiəʊ] Rodeo IV
role [rəʊl] Rolle *(in einem Theaterstück, Film)* II
role-play [ˈrəʊlpleɪ] Rollenspiel IV
roll [rəʊl] rollen II
roller coaster [ˈrəʊlə kəʊstə] Achterbahn IV
Roman [ˈrəʊmən] römisch V 3 (73)
roof [ruːf] Dach II
room [ruːm]:
1. Zimmer, Raum I
2. Platz III
rope [rəʊp] Seil III
rose [rəʊz]:
1. Rose IV
2. *siehe* **rise**
°**rosella** [rəʊˈzelə] Rosellasittich
rough [rʌf] stürmisch, rau *(See)* III
round [raʊnd]:
1. rund IV
2. **round the world** um die Welt II **round here** hier in der Gegend III
°3. Runde
roundabout [ˈraʊndəbaʊt] Kreisverkehr II
°**rouse** [raʊz] wecken
route [ruːt] Strecke, Route III
°**routine** [ruːˈtiːn] Routine, Prozedur
row [rəʊ] Reihe V 1 (27)
royal [ˈrɔɪəl] königlich II
rubber [ˈrʌbə] Radiergummi I
rubbish [ˈrʌbɪʃ] Müll, Abfall II **rubbish bin** Mülltonne, Abfalleimer IV
rucksack [ˈrʌksæk] Rucksack I
rude [ruːd] unhöflich; unverschämt V 1 (23)
rudeness [ˈruːdnəs] (grobe) Unhöflichkeit V 3 (63)
rugby [ˈrʌgbi] Rugby V 1 (13)
ruin [ˈruːɪn] Ruine II
rule [ruːl] Regel, Vorschrift II
ruler [ˈruːlə] Lineal I
run [rʌn], **ran, run** rennen, laufen I **run an organization/a business/a hotel** eine Organisation / eine Firma / ein Hotel leiten, führen V 2 (50) **run after sb.** hinter jm. herrennen I **run around** herumrennen, umherrennen II **run into sb.** *(infml)* jn. zufällig treffen IV **run off** wegrennen III **run on** weiterlaufen II **run over (to)** (zu/nach …) hinüberrennen II **they run out of money** ihnen geht das Geld aus V 2 (48)
► S. 210 (to) run out
rung [rʌŋ] *siehe* **ring** II
runner [ˈrʌnə] Läufer/in II
rural [ˈrʊərəl] ländlich, Land- V 1 (22)

S

sacred [ˈseɪkrɪd] heilig IV
sad [sæd] traurig I
safari [səˈfɑːri] Safari IV
safe [seɪf] sicher, in Sicherheit IV
safety [ˈseɪfti] Sicherheit V 4 (89)
said [sed] *siehe* **say**
sail [seɪl] segeln II **go sailing** segeln; segeln gehen I **sailing boat** Segelboot I
sailor [ˈseɪlə] Seemann, Matrose, Matrosin III
salad [ˈsæləd] Salat *(als Gericht oder Beilage)* I **fruit salad** Obstsalat I
°**sales** *(pl)* [seɪlz] Verkäufe
salt [sɔːlt] Salz IV
salty [ˈsɔːlti] salzig V 2 (36)
samba [ˈsæmbə] Samba I
same [seɪm]: **the same as …** der-/die-/dasselbe wie … I ° **same-sex marriage** gleichgeschlechtliche Ehe
sand [sænd] Sand I
sandcastle [ˈsændkɑːsl] Sandburg V 1 (19)

sandwich ['sænwɪtʃ], ['sænwɪdʒ] Sandwich, (zusammengeklapptes) belegtes Brot I
sandy ['sændi] sandig V 1 (10) sang [sæŋ] *siehe* **sing**
sank *siehe* **sink**
Santa (Claus) ['sæntə klɔːz] der Weihnachtsmann V 3 (62)
sat [sæt] *siehe* **sit**
Saturday ['sætədeɪ] Samstag, Sonnabend I
sauce [sɔːs] Soße IV
saucepan ['sɔːspən] Kochtopf, Stieltopf IV
sausage ['sɒsɪdʒ] Wurst, Würstchen IV
save [seɪv]:
1. retten I
2. sichern; speichern V 3 (70)
3. sparen V 3 (70) °**get in the saving habit** sich das Sparen angewöhnen
saw [sɔː] *siehe* **see**
say [seɪ], **said, said** sagen I **Say hello to … for me.** Grüß … von mir. II
saying ['seɪɪŋ] Sprichwort, Redensart IV
°**scale** [skeɪl] Skala, Spektrum
scan sth. (for sth.) [skæn] etwas (nach etwas) absuchen III **scan a text** einen Text schnell nach bestimmten Wörtern/Informationen absuchen II
scare sb. [skeə] jn. erschrecken; jm. Angst machen III
scared [skeəd] verängstigt II
scarf [skɑːf], *pl* **scarves** [skɑːvz] Schal III
scary ['skeəri] unheimlich, gruselig I
scene [siːn] Szene I °**set the scene for sth.** in etwas einführen; die Ausgangslage für etwas beschreiben
scenic ['siːnɪk] (landschaftlich) schön V 1 (12)
schedule ['ʃedjuːl], ['skedjuːl,] (Zeit-)Plan, Programm III
°**scholarship** ['skɒləʃɪp] Stipendium
school [skuːl] Schule I **at school** in der Schule I **before school** vor der Schule *(vor Schulbeginn)* I **in front of the school** vor der Schule *(vor dem Schulgebäude)* I **school bag** Schultasche I
science ['saɪəns] Naturwissenschaft I
scientific [ˌsaɪən'tɪfɪk] (natur)wissenschaftlich V 3 (59)
scientist ['saɪəntɪst] Naturwissenschaftler/in III
scone [skɒn], [skəʊn] *kleines rundes Milchbrötchen, leicht süß* I
score [skɔː]:
1. einen Treffer erzielen, ein Tor schießen I
2. Spielstand; Punktestand III **What's the score?** Wie steht es? III
scream [skriːm]:
1. schreien II
2. Schrei III
screen [skriːn] Bildschirm II
script [skrɪpt] Drehbuch; Manuskript IV
sculpture ['skʌlptʃə] Skulptur IV
sea [siː] Meer I
seagull ['siːgʌl] Möwe I
seal [siːl] Robbe I
search [sɜːtʃ]:
1. Durchsuchung; Suche (nach) IV
2. **search sth. for sth.** etwas nach etwas durchsuchen V 3 (70)
seasick ['siːsɪk] seekrank III
season ['siːzn]:
1. Jahreszeit; Saison IV **busy season** Hauptsaison IV
2. *(bes. AE)* Staffel *(einer Fernsehserie)* IV
seat [siːt] Sitz, Platz II
°**seated** ['siːtɪd] sitzend
second ['sekənd]:
1. zweite(r, s) I **second biggest** zweitgrößte(r, s) II
2. Sekunde II
Secondly, … ['sekəndli] Zweitens … V 1 (17)
secondary school ['sekəndri] weiterführende Schule V 3 (73)
security [sɪ'kjʊərəti] Sicherheit, Sicherheits- IV
see [siː], **saw, seen** sehen; besuchen I; *(Arzt)* aufsuchen II **I see.** Aha! / Verstehe. III **See you.** Bis gleich. / Bis bald. I **…, you see.** …, weißt du. II **be seeing sb.** mit jm. zusammen sein V 2 (42)
seed [siːd] Samen IV
seem (to be/do) [siːm] (zu sein/zu tun) scheinen III
seen [siːn] *siehe* **see**
segregation [ˌsegrɪ'geɪʃn] Trennung *(nach Hautfarbe, Religion oder Geschlecht)* IV
°**select** [sɪ'lekt] (aus)wählen
self-confidence [ˌself'kɒnfɪdəns] Selbstbewusstsein V 3 (63)
self-confident [ˌself'kɒnfɪdənt] *(kurz auch:* **confident***)* selbstbewusst, (selbst)sicher V 1 (13)
sell [sel], **sold, sold** verkaufen I
°**Senate** ['senət] Senat
senator ['senətə] Senator/in V 4 (93)
send [send], **sent, sent** schicken, senden I
sense [sens]: **sense of humour** (Sinn für) Humor V 3 (63) °**make sense** plausibel klingen
sensitive ['sensətɪv] empfindlich, sensibel; heikel; einfühlsam, empfindsam V 2 (36)
sent [sent] *siehe* **send**
sentence ['sentəns] Satz I **full sentence** ganzer Satz II **topic sentence** Satz, der in das Thema eines Absatzes einführt III
separate ['seprət] getrennt, separat, eigen IV
separately ['seprətli] einzeln, separat IV
September [sep'tembə] September I
series ['sɪəriːz], **pl series** (Sende-)Reihe, Serie V 1 (29)
serious ['sɪəriəs] ernst; ernsthaft V 2 (39)
seriously ['sɪəriəsli] ernsthaft, ernstlich V 2 (39)
service ['sɜːvɪs]:
1. Dienst, Service IV
2. Gottesdienst III
session ['seʃn] Sitzung, Einheit IV
set [set]:
1. Satz, Set II
2. **set sth. up (set, set)** etwas errichten, aufbauen; etwas arrangieren IV °**set the scene for sth.** in etwas einführen; die Ausgangslage für etwas beschreiben
setting ['setɪŋ] Schauplatz (Film/Geschichte) V 1 (29) °**settings** *(pl)* Einstellungen
settle ['setl] sich niederlassen, sich ansiedeln V 1 (12)
settler ['setlə] Siedler/in IV
seven ['sevn] sieben I
several ['sevrəl] mehrere, verschiedene III
sew [səʊ], **sewed, sewn** nähen V 3 (72)
sewed [səʊd] *siehe* **sew**
sewn [səʊn] *siehe* **sew**
shadow ['ʃædəʊ] Schatten II
shake [ʃeɪk], **shook, shaken** schütteln II; zittern V 2 (37)
shaken [ʃeɪkn] *siehe* **shake**
shall [ʃæl]: **Shall I …?** Soll ich …? III
shape [ʃeɪp]:
1. Form, Gestalt III **Those glasses are an interesting shape.** Die Brille hat eine interessante Form. III
°2. gestalten, formen
share [ʃeə] (sich) etwas teilen V 1 (23) °**share in sth.** an etwas beteiligt sein
shark [ʃɑːk] Hai I
sharp [ʃɑːp] scharf IV
sharpener ['ʃɑːpnə] Anspitzer I
shave [ʃeɪv] (sich) rasieren V 3 (60)
she [ʃiː] sie I
sheep [ʃiːp], *pl* **sheep** Schaf II
sheepdog ['ʃiːpdɒg] Hütehund III
sheet [ʃiːt] Blatt, Bogen (Papier) IV
shelf [ʃelf], *pl* **shelves** [ʃelvz] Regal I
shell [ʃel] Muschel(schale) IV
shepherd ['ʃepəd] Schäfer/in, Schafhirte/-hirtin III
°**shimmer** ['ʃɪmə] Schimmer
shine [ʃaɪn], **shone, shone** scheinen *(Sonne)* III
shiny ['ʃaɪni] glänzend IV
ship [ʃɪp] Schiff I
shirt [ʃɜːt] Hemd II; Trikot III
shocked [ʃɒkt] schockiert, entsetzt II
shocking ['ʃɒkɪŋ] schockierend V 4 (101)
shoe [ʃuː] Schuh I
shone *BE:* [ʃɒn], *AE:* [ʃəʊn] *siehe* **shine**
shook [ʃʊk] *siehe* **shake**
shoot [ʃuːt], **shot, shot** schießen; erschießen IV
°**shooting guard** ['ʃuːtɪŋ gɑːd] Aufbauspieler/in der hinteren Angriffsreihe *(Basketball)*

shop [ʃɒp]:
1. Laden I **corner shop** Laden an der Ecke; Tante-Emma-Laden I **shop assistant** Verkäufer/in II **shop window** Schaufenster V 2 (51)
2. einkaufen II
shopper ['ʃɒpə] (Ein-)Käufer/in II
shopping ['ʃɒpɪŋ]: **do the/some shopping** einkaufen gehen; Einkäufe erledigen II **go shopping** einkaufen gehen I **shopping centre** Einkaufszentrum II **shopping mall** (großes) Einkaufszentrum I
shore [ʃɔː] Ufer, Strand II
short [ʃɔːt] kurz I
shorts *(pl)* [ʃɔːts] Shorts, kurze Hose I
shot [ʃɒt]:
1. Aufnahme, Foto; (Film) Einstellung, Szene IV **medium shot** Halbtotale IV
2. *siehe* **shoot**
should [ʃʊd], [ʃəd]: **You should ...** Du solltest ... / Ihr solltet ... / Sie sollten ... II **You shouldn't have swum there.** Du hättest dort nicht schwimmen sollen. IV
shoulder ['ʃəʊldə] Schulter II
shout [ʃaʊt] schreien, rufen I
show [ʃəʊ]:
1. **(showed, shown)** zeigen I
2. Show, Vorstellung II
shower ['ʃaʊə] Dusche III **have a shower** (sich) duschen III
shown [ʃəʊn] *siehe* **show**
°**showoff** ['ʃəʊɒf] Angeber/in
shrimp [ʃrɪmp] Garnele IV
shrub [ʃrʌb] Strauch, Busch IV
shy [ʃaɪ] schüchtern, scheu II
sick [sɪk] krank I **be sick** sich übergeben II **I feel sick.** Mir ist schlecht. II **I'm going to be sick.** Ich muss mich übergeben. II
side [saɪd] Seite II
°**sidestep sb.** ['saɪdstep] jm. ausweichen; jn. ausspielen
sidewalk ['saɪdwɔːk] *(AE)* Gehweg, Bürgersteig IV
sigh [saɪ] seufzen III
sight [saɪt] Anblick V 4 (86)
sighting ['saɪtɪŋ] Sichtung III
sights *(pl)* [saɪts] Sehenswürdigkeiten I
sightseeing ['saɪtsiːɪŋ] Sightseeing; das Besichtigen von Sehenswürdigkeiten IV
sign [saɪn]:
1. Schild; Zeichen I **no sign of ...** keine Spur von ... III
2. unterschreiben V 4 (83)
°**signature** ['sɪgnətʃə] Unterschrift
silence ['saɪləns] Stille; Schweigen IV
silent ['saɪlənt] still, leise III
silently ['saɪləntli] lautlos; schweigend III
silky ['sɪlki] seidig I
silly ['sɪli]:
1. albern; blöd I
2. Dummerchen I

similar (to sth./sb.) ['sɪmələ] (etwas/jm.) ähnlich II
simply ['sɪmpli] einfach V 2 (48)
since [sɪns]:
1. **since 10 o'clock / last week** seit 10 Uhr / letzter Woche III
2. da, weil V 3 (61)
sing [sɪŋ], **sang, sung** singen I **sing along (with sb.)** (mit jm.) mitsingen III
singer ['sɪŋə] Sänger/in II
single ['sɪŋgl]:
1. ledig, alleinstehend I
°2. ungeteilt
sink [sɪŋk, sæŋk, sʌŋk], **sank, sunk** sinken V 2 (37) °2. versenken
°**sir** [sɜː] Sir *(höfliche Anrede, z. B. für Kunden, Vorgesetzte oder Lehrer)*
siren ['saɪrən] Sirene III
sister ['sɪstə] Schwester I
sit [sɪt], **sat, sat** sitzen; sich setzen I **sit down** sich hinsetzen I **sit up** sich aufsetzen III
sitcom ['sɪtkɒm] Situationskomödie IV
°**site** [saɪt] Website
sit-in ['sɪtɪn] Sit-in, Sitzstreik V 4 (83)
situation [ˌsɪtʃu'eɪʃn] Situation III
six [sɪks] sechs I
size [saɪz] Größe II **What size tea would you like?** Wie groß soll der/dein Tee sein? II
skates [skeɪts] Inlineskates I
skating ['skeɪtɪŋ] Inlineskaten, Rollschuhlaufen I
skill [skɪl] Fertigkeit II **skills file** *Übersicht über Lern- und Arbeitstechniken* I **study skills** *Lern- und Arbeitstechniken* I
skim [skɪm]: **skim a text** einen Text überfliegen *(um den Inhalt grob zu erfassen)* IV
skin [skɪn] Haut V 2 (37)
skirt [skɜːt] Rock II
sky [skaɪ] Himmel II
skydiving ['skaɪdaɪvɪŋ] Fallschirmspringen V 3 (59)
skyline ['skaɪlaɪn] Skyline; Horizont III
skyscraper ['skaɪskreɪpə] Wolkenkratzer IV
slap [slæp] knallen, klatschen IV
°**slasher** ['slæʃə] *(Basketball) Spieler/in mit Zug zum Korb*
slaughter ['slɔːtə] Schlachtung; Abschlachten V 4 (88)
slave [sleɪv] Sklave, Sklavin III
slavery ['sleɪvəri] Sklaverei III
sleep [sliːp]:
1. **(slept, slept)** schlafen I
2. Schlaf III **sleeping bag** Schlafsack V 2 (37)
sleepless ['sliːpləs] schlaflos IV
sleepover ['sliːpəʊvə] Schlafparty I
°**slender** ['slendə] schmal
slept [slept] *siehe* **sleep**
°**slick** [slɪk]: **a slick shot** ein raffinierter/gekonnter Wurf
°**slip** [slɪp] schlüpfen

slippery ['slɪpəri] rutschig, glatt III
slogan ['sləʊgn] Slogan, Werbespruch V 2 (44)
slow [sləʊ]:
1. langsam I **be slow** nachgehen *(Uhr)* III **slow motion** Zeitlupe III
2. **slow sth. down** etwas verlangsamen V 4 (84) °**Slow down.** Langsam!
small [smɔːl] klein I **small talk** Smalltalk *(spontan geführtes Gespräch in umgangssprachlichem Ton)* III
°**smallpox** ['smɔːlpɒks] Pocken
smartphone ['smɑːtfəʊn] Smartphone V 2 (44)
smell [smel] riechen I **smell sth.** an etwas riechen I **smell good** gut riechen II
smile [smaɪl]:
1. lächeln I **smile at sb.** jn. anlächeln I
2. Lächeln III
smiley ['smaɪli] Smiley I
smoke [sməʊk] rauchen III
smuggle ['smʌgl] schmuggeln I
smuggler ['smʌglə] Schmuggler/in I
smuggling ['smʌglɪŋ] der Schmuggel, das Schmuggeln I
snack [snæk] Snack, Imbiss I
snake [sneɪk] Schlange I
°**sneaks** *(pl)* [sniːks] *(auch:* **sneakers***)* Turnschuhe
°**sneak** [sniːk]: **sneak glances** einen schnellen Blick werfen
°**sneaky** ['sniːki] raffiniert
sneeze [sniːz] niesen I
snorkel ['snɔːkl] schnorcheln V 1 (19)
snow [snəʊ] Schnee II
so [səʊ]:
1. also; deshalb, daher I
2. **so cool/nice** so cool/nett I **so far** bis jetzt; bis hierher II
3. **So?** Und? / Na und? I
4. **so that / so** sodass, damit II
5. auch V 1 (26)I
► S. 203 English "so" – German "auch"
soap [səʊp] Seife V 2 (37)
soccer ['sɒkə] Fußball V 1 (26)
social ['səʊʃl] sozial, Sozial-, gesellschaftlich IV **social media** *(pl)* soziale Medien III **social studies** Gemeinschaftskunde, Sozialkunde, Politische Bildung IV
society [sə'saɪəti] (die) Gesellschaft V 1 (27)
sock [sɒk] Socke II
sofa ['səʊfə] Sofa I
soft [sɒft] weich I **in a soft voice** sanft II
softly ['sɒftli] sanft III **she sang softly** sie sang leise II
sold [səʊld] *siehe* **sell**
soldier ['səʊldʒə] Soldat/in III
solo ['səʊləʊ] Solo- II
solution (to) [sə'luːʃn] Lösung (für) *(Problem; Aufgabe)* V 4 (89)
solve [sɒlv] lösen III

some [sʌm] einige, ein paar; etwas I **° some 50,000 people** etwa 50.000 Menschen
somebody ['sʌmbədi] jemand I
someone ['sʌmwʌn] jemand I
something ['sʌmθɪŋ] etwas I
sometimes ['sʌmtaɪmz] manchmal I
somewhere ['sʌmweə] irgendwo, irgendwohin IV **° somewhere else** anderswo
son [sʌn] Sohn II
song [sɒŋ] Lied, Song I
°**songline** ['sɒŋlaɪn] Traumpfad
soon [su:n] bald I
sore [sɔ:] wund II **have a sore throat** Halsschmerzen haben II
sorry ['sɒri]: **(I'm) sorry.** Tut mir leid. / Entschuldigung. I **I'm sorry about ...** Es tut mir leid wegen ... I **Sorry?** Wie bitte? IV
sort (of) [sɔ:t] Art, Sorte V 1 (26)
sound [saʊnd]:
1. klingen, sich anhören I
2. Geräusch; Klang I
soup [su:p] Suppe I **make soup** Suppe kochen IV
sour ['saʊə] sauer, säuerlich IV
source [sɔ:s] Quelle V 3 (70)
south [saʊθ] Süden; nach Süden; südlich III **southbound** ['saʊθbaʊnd] Richtung Süden III **south-east** [ˌsaʊθ‿'i:st] Südosten; nach Südosten; südöstlich III **southern** ['sʌðən] südlich, Süd- III **south-west** [ˌsaʊθ'west] Südwesten; nach Südwesten; südwestlich III
souvenir [ˌsu:və'nɪə] Andenken, Souvenir II
space [speɪs] Platz, Raum V 4 (90) **take up space/time** Raum/Zeit einnehmen, beanspruchen V 4 (90)
spaghetti [spə'geti] Spagetti I
°**spam** [spæm] Frühstücksfleisch
Spanish ['spænɪʃ] spanisch II
°**spare ribs** *(pl)* [speə 'rɪbz] Spareribs *(gegrillte Schweinerippchen)*
speak [spi:k], **spoke, spoken** sprechen I; reden II **speak to sb.** mit jm. sprechen II **speak out** den Mund aufmachen; sich (kritisch) äußern IV
speaker ['spi:kə] Sprecher/in I; Redner/in II
°**speakerphone** ['spi:kəfəʊn] Telefon mit Freisprechanlage
special ['speʃl] besondere(r, s) II **What's special about it?** Was ist das Besondere daran? IV
°**specific** [spə'sɪfɪk] spezifisch
°**speckled** ['spekld] gesprenkelt
speech [spi:tʃ] *(offizielle)* Rede II **part of speech** Wortart III **° speech bubble** Sprechblase
speed [spi:d] Geschwindigkeit III
speed up [ˌspi:d‿'ʌp] beschleunigen, schneller werden IV
spell [spel] buchstabieren I
spelling ['spelɪŋ] Rechtschreibung; Schreibweise III
spend [spend], **spent, spent: spend time (on)** Zeit verbringen (mit) **spend money (on)** Geld ausgeben (für) III
spent [spent] *siehe* **spend**
spice [spaɪs] Gewürz IV
spicy ['spaɪsi] würzig, pikant IV
spider ['spaɪdə] Spinne V 1 (10)
spin around [ˌspɪn‿ə'raʊnd], **spun, spun** sich (im Kreis) drehen; herumwirbeln III
spinach ['spɪnɪtʃ] Spinat IV
°**spiritual** ['spɪrɪtʃuəl] spirituell
splash sb. [splæʃ] jn. nass spritzen III
split screen [splɪt 'skri:n] geteilter Bildschirm; Bildschirm(auf)teilung III
spoke [spəʊk] *siehe* **speak**
spoken ['spəʊkn] *siehe* **speak**
°**sponsorship** ['spɒnsəʃɪp] Förderung
spontaneous [spɒn'teɪniəs] spontan V 3 (68)
spoon [spu:n] Löffel II
sport [spɔ:t] Sport; Sportart I **do sport** Sport treiben I
sportsperson ['spɔ:tspɜ:sn] Sportler/in III
spot [spɒt]:
1. Fleck, Punkt I
2. **spot sb./sth.** jn./etwas entdecken, erblicken IV
spray [spreɪ] (be)sprühen, sprayen IV
spread [spred], **spread, spread** (sich) ausbreiten, verbreiten III
spring [sprɪŋ]:
1. Frühling I
°2. Quelle
spun [spʌn] *siehe* **spin**
square [skweə]:
1. Platz (in der Stadt) IV
2. quadratisch; Quadrat- IV **square kilometre, sq km** Quadratkilometer II
squeeze [skwi:z] drücken IV
stadium ['steɪdiəm] Stadion III
stage [steɪdʒ] Bühne II
stairs *(pl)* [steəz] Treppe; Treppenstufen II
stall [stɔ:l] (Markt-)Stand II
stamp [stæmp] Stempel II
stand [stænd], **stood, stood** stehen; sich (hin)stellen II **stand up** aufstehen III **I can't stand ...** Ich kann ... nicht ausstehen/ertragen. IV **stand against sth.** Haltung gegenüber etwas, Widerstand gegen etwas V 1 (27) **stand up (for sth./sb.)** eintreten/sich einsetzen (für etwas/jn.) V 1 (27) **° stand for election** sich zur Wahl stellen; kandidieren **take a stand (on sth.)** Stellung beziehen (zu etwas); ein Zeichen setzen V 4 (88)
standard ['stændəd] Standard; Standard- III
star [stɑ:]:
1. (Film-, Pop-)Star I
2. Stern III
stare (at sb./sth.) [steə] (jn./etwas an) starren III
start [stɑ:t] anfangen, beginnen I **To start with, ...** Erstens ...; Zunächst (einmal) ... V 1 (17)
starving ['stɑ:vɪŋ]: **be starving** einen Riesenhunger haben III
state [steɪt] Staat III **° head of state** Staatsoberhaupt
state sth. [steɪt] etwas äußern, etwas angeben V 1 (17)
statement ['steɪtmənt] Aussage, Erklärung V 3 (72)
station ['steɪʃn]:
1. Bahnhof II
°2. *(AusE)* Rinder- oder Schaf(zucht) farm, Ranch
statistics *(pl)* [stə'tɪstɪks] Statistik V 2 (47)
statue ['stætʃu:] Statue IV
status ['steɪtəs] Status V 2 (43)
stay [steɪ]:
1. bleiben I; *(vorübergehend)* wohnen, übernachten III **stay in touch (with sb.)** (mit jm.) Kontakt halten; (mit jm.) in Verbindung bleiben II **stay up late** lang aufbleiben II **Stay posted!** Bleib(t) auf dem Laufenden! IV
2. Aufenthalt IV
steal [sti:l], **stole, stolen** stehlen III
steep [sti:p] steil III
steer [stɪə] steuern, lenken I
steering wheel ['stɪərɪŋ wi:l] Lenkrad IV
step [step]:
1. Schritt I
2. Stufe III
stew [stju:] Eintopf IV
stick [stɪk]:
1. Stock III
2. **(stuck, stuck) stick sth. into sth.** etwas in etwas stechen, stecken II
sticky ['stɪki] klebrig II
stiff [stɪf] steif V 2 (51)
still [stɪl]:
1. (immer) noch I
2. trotzdem, dennoch II
°**still** [stɪl] Standbild
°**stink** [stɪŋk], **stank, stunk** stinken
stole [stəʊl] *siehe* **steal**
stolen ['stəʊlən] *siehe* **steal**
stomach ['stʌmək] Magen II
stone [stəʊn] Stein II
stood [stʊd] *siehe* **stand**
stop [stɒp]:
1. anhalten, stoppen I **Stop it!** *(infml)* Hör auf (damit)! / Lass das! II
2. Halt; Station, Haltestelle II
stoplight ['stɒplaɪt] *(AE)* Ampel V 3 (62)
store [stɔ:] *(bes. AE)* Laden, Geschäft IV
storey ['stɔ:ri] Stock, Stockwerk, Etage IV
storm [stɔ:m] Sturm, Unwetter, Gewitter II

story ['stɔːri]:
1. Geschichte, Erzählung I
2. *(AE)* Stock, Stockwerk, Etage IV
°**storyboard** ['stɔːribɔːd] Storyboard *(aus Einzelbildern bestehende Abfolge eines Films)*
storyteller ['stɔːritelə] Geschichtenerzähler/in IV
storytelling ['stɔːritelɪŋ] (das) Geschichtenerzählen IV
straight [streɪt]:
1. direkt, geradewegs IV **straight on** geradeaus weiter II
2. ehrlich
strange [streɪndʒ] seltsam, komisch I
stranger ['streɪndʒə] Fremde(r), Unbekannte(r) IV
°**strategy** ['strætədʒi] Strategie, Taktik
strawberry ['strɔːbəri] Erdbeere II
stream [striːm] Bach III
street [striːt] Straße I **at 14 Dean Street** in der Deanstraße 14 **in Dean Street** in der Dean Street I **street artist** Straßenkünstler/in II
streetcar ['striːtkɑː] *(AE)* Straßenbahn IV
strength [streŋθ] Stärke, Kraft IV
stress [stres]:
1. Betonung III **stress mark** Betonungszeichen III
2. betonen V 2 (49)
stretch [stretʃ] sich dehnen, sich strecken IV
strict [strɪkt] streng IV
strike [straɪk]:
1. Streik V 4 (83) **go on strike** streiken, in den Streik treten V 4 (83)
°**2. third strike** dritter (Regel-)Verstoß
string [strɪŋ] Saite IV
strong [strɒŋ] stark, kräftig II
structure ['strʌktʃə]:
1. strukturieren, gliedern III
2. Struktur, Gliederung IV
struggle ['strʌgl]:
1. kämpfen, sich wehren V 4 (97)
2. Kampf V 4 (97)
°**strut** [strʌt] stolzieren
stuck [stʌk] *siehe* **stick**
student ['stjuːdənt] Schüler/in; Student/in I
studio ['stjuːdiəʊ] Studio I
study ['stʌdi] studieren; untersuchen, beobachten; lernen III **study skills** *Lern- und Arbeitstechniken* I **study poster** Lernposter II
stuff [stʌf] Zeug, Kram III
stunning ['stʌnɪŋ] atemberaubend, überwältigend, umwerfend V 1 (10)
stupid ['stjuːpɪd] dumm, blöd III
°**stutter step** ['stʌtə step] ein schneller Verzögerungs- oder Trippelschritt zur Verwirrung des Gegners *(Basketball)*
style [staɪl] Stil IV
sub-clause ['sʌbklɔːz] Nebensatz I
sub-heading ['sʌbˌhedɪŋ] Zwischenüberschrift; Kapitelüberschrift IV
subject ['sʌbdʒɪkt], ['sʌbdʒekt]:
1. Schulfach I
2. Subjekt II
3. Thema V 2 (36)
submit sth. (to) [səb'mɪt] etwas einreichen (bei) V 3 (66)
°**substitute teacher** ['sʌbstɪtjuːt] Vertretungslehrer/in
subtitle ['sʌbtaɪtl] Untertitel I
suburb ['sʌbɜːb] Vorort IV
suburban [sə'bɜːbən] Vorort-, Vorstadt-; vorstädtisch V 1 (22)
subway ['sʌbweɪ] *(AE)* U-Bahn IV
succeed (in sth.) [sək'siːd] erfolgreich sein, Erfolg haben (mit etwas, bei etwas) V 3 (67)
success [sək'ses] Erfolg III
successful [sək'sesfl] erfolgreich IV
such [sʌtʃ]: **such a** so ein/e …; solch ein/e … III **such as** wie etwa V 3 (66)
sudden ['sʌdn]: **all of a sudden** plötzlich V 4 (85)
suddenly ['sʌdnli] plötzlich, auf einmal I
suffer (from) ['sʌfə] leiden (an); erleiden V 4 (101)
°**suffering** ['sʌfərɪŋ] Leiden
suffix ['sʌfɪks] Suffix, Nachsilbe V 3 (63)
sugar ['ʃʊgə] Zucker IV
suggest sth. (to sb.) [sə'dʒest] (jm.) etwas vorschlagen III **Dad suggested that we go to the cinema.** Papa schlug vor, ins Kino zu gehen. III
suggestion [sə'dʒestʃən] Vorschlag IV
suit [suːt] Anzug III
sum sth. up [ˌsʌm_'ʌp] etwas zusammenfassen IV **To sum up, …** Zusammenfassend: … IV
summarize ['sʌməraɪz] zusammenfassen V 4 (101)
summary ['sʌməri] Zusammenfassung V 4 (101)
summer ['sʌmə] Sommer I
summit ['sʌmɪt] Gipfel III
sun [sʌn] Sonne I
Sunday ['sʌndeɪ] Sonntag I
°**sundown** ['sʌndaʊn] Sonnenuntergang
sung [sʌŋ] *siehe* **sing**
sunglasses *(pl)* ['sʌnglɑːsɪz] (eine) Sonnenbrille II
sunk *siehe* **sink**
sunny ['sʌni] sonnig II
sunscreen ['sʌnskriːn] Sonnenschutzmittel V 1 (14)
sunset ['sʌnset] Sonnenuntergang IV
sunshine ['sʌnʃaɪn] Sonnenschein III
support [sə'pɔːt]:
1. unterstützen IV
2. Unterstützung IV
°**supporter** [sə'pɔːtə] Unterstützer/in, Befürworter/in
supposed [sə'pəʊzd]: **be supposed to do sth.** etwas tun sollen V 2 (46)
°**Supreme Court** [suˌpriːm 'kɔːt] Oberster Gerichtshof
sure [ʃʊə], [ʃɔː] sicher II **make sure that …** sich vergewissern, dass …; darauf achten, dass …; dafür sorgen, dass … II
surf [sɜːf] surfen V 1 (12)
surface ['sɜːfɪs] Oberfläche III
surfboard [sɜːfbɔːd] Surfbrett V 1 (13)
surprise [sə'praɪz] Überraschung II **in surprise** voller Überraschung IV
surprised [sə'praɪzd] überrascht I
surprising [sə'praɪzɪŋ] überraschend IV
survey ['sɜːveɪ] Umfrage, Untersuchung V 4 (89)
survive [sə'vaɪv] überleben III
°**suspend sb.** [sə'spend] jn. suspendieren, vom Unterricht ausschließen
swallow ['swɒləʊ] schlucken; verschlucken V 1 (13)
swam [swæm] *siehe* **swim**
swamp [swɒmp] Sumpf IV
swan [swɒn] Schwan V 1 (27)
°**swap** [swɒp] tauschen
sweat [swet] Schweiß V 3 (61)
sweet [swiːt] süß II **sweet potato** Süßkartoffel IV
sweets *(pl)* [swiːts] Süßigkeiten II
swim [swɪm], **swam, swum** schwimmen I
swim [swɪm] Bad V 1 (12)
swimmer ['swɪmə] Schwimmer/in I
swimming pool ['swɪmɪŋ puːl] Schwimmbad, Schwimmbecken I
switch [swɪtʃ] wechseln IV
sword [sɔːd] Schwert I
swum [swʌm] *siehe* **swim**
syllable ['sɪləbl] Silbe II **one-/two-syllable** ein-/zweisilbig II
symbol ['sɪmbl] Symbol II
°**symbolize** ['sɪmbəlaɪz] symbolisieren, sinnbildlich darstellen
synonym ['sɪnənɪm] Synonym *(bedeutungsgleiches Wort)* IV
system ['sɪstəm] System IV

T

table ['teɪbl]:
1. Tisch I **table tennis** Tischtennis II
2. Tabelle I
tackle sth. ['tækl] etwas in Angriff nehmen V 3 (67)
°**tactic** ['tæktɪk] Taktik
take [teɪk]:
1. (took, taken) nehmen, mitnehmen; (weg-, hin)bringen I; *(Zeit)* brauchen; dauern II **take action** etwas unternehmen, tätig werden V 4 (89) **take a break** eine Pause machen V 4 (86) **take a different view** einen anderen Standpunkt vertreten; anderer Ansicht sein V 1 (17) **take a stand (on sth.)** Stellung beziehen (zu etwas); ein Zeichen setzen V 4 (88) **take an exam** eine Prüfung ablegen V 4 (97) **take a walk**

spazieren gehen, einen Spaziergang machen IV **take care of sth.** sich (gut) um etwas kümmern; sorgfältig mit etwas umgehen IV **° Take it easy.** Immer mit der Ruhe! **take notes (on/about sth.)** (sich) Notizen machen (über/zu etwas) *(beim Lesen oder Zuhören)* II **take notice (of sth.)** auf etwas aufmerksam werden, etwas zur Kenntnis nehmen V 4 (98) **take part in sth.** an etwas teilnehmen II **take photos** fotografieren, Fotos machen I **take pity on sb.** Mitleid mit jm. haben ; sich jemandes erbarmen IV **take place** stattfinden III **take sth. off** etwas ausziehen *(Kleidung)*; etwas absetzen *(Hut, Helm)* II **° take the heat** den Kopf hinhalten **take the view that** der Auffassung sein, dass / der Ansicht sein, dass V 1 (17) **°take turns (to do sth.)** sich abwechseln (etwas zu tun) **take up space/ time** Raum/Zeit einnehmen, beanspruchen V 4 (90)
2. Einstellung, Take *(beim Film)* IV
take (on sth.) Einstellung, Meinung (zu etwas) V 1 (12)

takeaway ['teɪkəweɪ] *Restaurant/Imbissgeschäft, das auch Essen zum Mitnehmen verkauft; Essen zum Mitnehmen* II
taken ['teɪkən] *siehe* **take**
talent ['tælənt] Talent V 3 (62)
talented ['tæləntɪd] begabt, talentiert II
talk [tɔːk]:
1. Vortrag, Referat, Rede I **give a talk (about)** einen Vortrag / eine Rede halten (über) I
2. talk (to) reden (mit), sich unterhalten (mit) I **talking** sprechend IV
talkative ['tɔːkətɪv] gesprächig V 1 (13)
tall [tɔːl] groß *(Person)*; hoch *(Gebäude, Baum)* II
tandem ['tændəm] Tandem V 2 (51)
tap [tæp]:
1. tippen, *(vorsichtig)* klopfen II
2. *(leichtes)* Klopfen III
°target ['tɑːgɪt] Zielscheibe
task [tɑːsk] Aufgabe I
taste [teɪst]:
1. schmecken I
2. Geschmack IV
tasteful ['teɪstfl] geschmackvoll IV
tasty ['teɪsti] lecker II
taught [tɔːt] *siehe* **teach**
tax [tæks] (die) Steuer IV
taxi ['tæksi] Taxi II
taxpayer ['tækspeɪə] Steuerzahler/in IV
tea [tiː]:
1. Tee I **make tea** Tee kochen IV
2. *leichte Nachmittags- oder Abendmahlzeit* II
teach [tiːtʃ], **taught, taught** unterrichten, lehren III **teach sb. to do sth.** jm. etwas beibringen, etwas zu tun III
teacher ['tiːtʃə] Lehrer/in I
team [tiːm] Team, Mannschaft I
► S. 199 Group nouns
°teamwork ['tiːmwɜːk] Teamwork
tear [tɪə] Träne II
tear [teə], **tore, torn** reißen, zerreißen V 2 (37) **tear sth. down** etwas abreißen IV
teaspoon ['tiːspuːn] Teelöffel II
technique [tek'niːk] Technik, Methode IV
teen [tiːn] Teenager/in IV
teeth [tiːθ] *Plural von* **tooth**
telephone ['telɪfəʊn] Telefon I
telephone box Telefonzelle III
tell [tel], **told, told:** erkennen, feststellen V 3 (60) **tell sb. about sth.** jm. von etwas erzählen; jm. über etwas berichten I **° tell sb. apart** jn. auseinanderhalten **tell sb. the way (to ...)** jm. den Weg (nach ...) beschreiben II **tell sb. (not) to do sth.** jn. auffordern, etwas (nicht) zu tun; jm. sagen, dass er/sie etwas (nicht) tun soll III
temperature ['temprətʃə] Temperatur, Fieber II **have a temperature** Fieber haben II
ten [ten] zehn I
tennis ['tenɪs] Tennis I **table tennis** Tischtennis II
tense [tens] *(grammatische)* Zeit, Tempus III
tension ['tenʃn] Spannung, Anspannung III
tent [tent] Zelt II
term [tɜːm]:
1. Trimester II **in the long term** langfristig, auf lange Sicht V 3 (67)
2. Ausdruck, Begriff V 3 (72)
terrible ['terəbl] schrecklich, furchtbar II
terrified ['terɪfaɪd]: entsetzt
be terrified (of sth.) schreckliche Angst (vor etwas) haben V 2 (42)
territory ['terətri] Revier, Territorium III
°terrorism ['terərɪzm] Terrorismus
terrorist ['terərɪst] terroristische(r, s); Terrorist/in IV
test ['test]:
1. Test, (Klassen-)Arbeit III
2. testen, prüfen III
°testimonial [ˌtestɪ'məʊniəl] Erfahrungsbericht
text [tekst]:
1. Text I
2. *(auch* **text message***)* SMS II
3. text sb. jm. eine SMS schicken I
than [ðæn], [ðən]: **bigger than** größer als II
thank sb. [θæŋk] jm. danken III
Thank you. Danke. I **Thank you for listening.** Danke, dass ihr zugehört habt. / Danke für eure Aufmerksamkeit. II
thanks ['θæŋks] Danke. I **thanks to Maya** dank Maya II
Thanksgiving [θæŋks'gɪvɪŋ] Erntedankfest *(amerikanischer Feiertag am 4. Donnerstag im November)* IV
that [ðæt], [ðət]:
1. it shows that ... es zeigt, dass ... I
2. that group die Gruppe (dort), jene Gruppe I
3. that's das ist I
4. der/die/das; die *(Relativpronomen)* II
5. that's why deshalb, darum II
the [ðə] der, die, das; die I **the (sooner) ... the (better) ...** je eher ..., desto besser ... V 3 (66)
► S. 216 German "je ..., desto ..."
theatre ['θɪətə] Theater II
their [ðeə] ihr I **their first day** ihr erster Tag I
theirs [ðeəz] ihrer, ihre, ihrs II
them [ðem], [ðəm]:
1. sie; ihnen I
2. ihn oder sie (= **him or her**) IV
theme [θiːm] Thema II
themselves [ðəm'selvz] sich III
then [ðen] dann I **back then** damals V 1 (13) **just then** genau in dem Moment; gerade dann II
there [ðeə] da, dort; dahin, dorthin I **down there** dort unten II **over there** da drüben, dort drüben II **There are ...** Es sind/gibt ... I **There's ...** Es ist/gibt ... I
thermometer [θə'mɒmɪtə] Thermometer II
these [ðiːz] diese, die (hier) I
they [ðeɪ]:
1. sie *(Plural)* I
2. er oder sie (= **he or she**) IV
thick [θɪk] dick V 3 (67)
thief [θiːf], *pl* **thieves** [θiːvz] Dieb/in I
thing [θɪŋ] Sache, Ding, Gegenstand I
think [θɪŋk], **thought, thought** denken, glauben I **think of sth.** sich etwas ausdenken; an etwas denken I
third [θɜːd] dritte(r, s) I **third biggest** drittgrößte(r, s) II
Thirdly, ... ['θɜːdli] Drittens ... V 1 (17)
thirsty ['θɜːsti]: **be thirsty** durstig sein, Durst haben I
this [ðɪs]:
1. This is ... Dies ist ... / Das ist ... I
2. this place/break/subject dieser Ort / diese Pause / dieses Fach I **this time** dieses Mal II **this afternoon/ evening/...** heute Nachmittag/Abend/ ... II **this year's ...** das diesjährige ... II
those [ðəʊz] die ... dort; jene ... I
though [ðəʊ] obwohl V 1 (13)
though [ðəʊ] aber; allerdings; jedoch V 4 (99)
thought [θɔːt]:
1. Gedanke III **give some thought to sth.** über etwas nachdenken; sich über etwas Gedanken machen V 4 (87)
2. *siehe* **think**

thousand ['θaʊznd] Tausend, tausend III
threat [θret] Drohung, Bedrohung, Androhung V 4 (88)
three [θriː] drei I
threw [θruː] *siehe* **throw**
thrilled [θrɪld] begeistert V 2 (42)
throat [θrəʊt] Hals, Kehle II **have a sore throat** Halsschmerzen haben II
through [θruː] durch I
throw [θrəʊ]:
1. **(threw, thrown)** werfen I;
°2. **free throw** Freiwurf *(Basketball)*
thrown [θrəʊn] *siehe* **throw**
thunder ['θʌndə] Donner II
Thursday ['θɜːzdeɪ] Donnerstag I
ticket ['tɪkɪt] Eintrittskarte I; Fahrkarte I **ticket office** Fahrkartenschalter; Kasse *(für den Verkauf von Eintrittskarten)* III
tidy ['taɪdi] ordentlich, aufgeräumt V 2 (48)
°**tight** [taɪt] *(infml)* stylisch
tighten ['taɪtn] spannen, festziehen, nachziehen IV
till [tɪl]: **till 1 o'clock** bis 1 Uhr I **not till three** erst um drei, nicht vor drei II
time [taɪm]:
1 Zeit; Uhrzeit I **at any time** jederzeit, zu jeder Zeit IV **at no time** zu keiner Zeit IV **at one time** zur selben Zeit, gleichzeitig III **by the time** wenn, bis V 4 (86) **in time (for)** rechtzeitig (zu/für) V 3 (66) **over time** mit der Zeit, im Lauf der Zeit V 3 (67) **take up time** Raum/Zeit einnehmen, beanspruchen V 4 (90) **What time is it?** Wie spät ist es? I
2 Mal II **this time** dieses Mal II
°**timekeeper** ['taɪmkiːpə] *(Arbeitszeit)* Zeitnehmer/in, Zeitkontrolleur/in
timer ['taɪmə] Zeitmesser IV
timetable ['taɪmteɪbl]:
1. Stundenplan I
2. Fahrplan III
tin [tɪn] Dose II
tinned [tɪnd] Dosen-; in Dosen IV
tiny ['taɪni] winzig IV
tip [tɪp] Tipp I
tired ['taɪəd] müde I **be tired of sth.** genug von etwas haben; etwas satt haben III
title ['taɪtl] Titel, Überschrift I
to [tu], [tə]:
1. zu, nach I **count to ten** bis zehn zählen **from … to …** von … bis … I **to the front** nach vorne II
2. **Nice to meet you.** Freut mich, dich/euch/Sie kennenzulernen. I
3. **quarter to eleven** Viertel vor elf (10.45 / 22.45) I
4. um zu II
toast [təʊst] Toast(brot) III
today [tə'deɪ] heute I
toe [təʊ] Zeh II
tofu ['təʊfuː] Tofu V 2 (44)
together [tə'geðə] zusammen I

toilet ['tɔɪlət] Toilette I
told [təʊld] *siehe* **tell**
tolerance ['tɒlərəns] Toleranz V 3 (63)
tolerant ['tɒlərənt] tolerant (gegenüber) V 3 (63)
tomato [tə'mɑːtəʊ] Tomate II
tomorrow [tə'mɒrəʊ] morgen II **tomorrow morning** morgen früh, morgen Vormittag II
ton [tʌn] Tonne (Gewicht) V 1 (13) **a ton of …** jede Menge … V 1 (13)
tongue [tʌŋ] Zunge II
tongue-twister ['tʌŋˌtwɪstə] Zungenbrecher II
tonight [tə'naɪt] heute Nacht, heute Abend III
too [tuː]:
1. auch I
2. **too late/cold/big/…** zu spät/kalt/groß/… I
took [tʊk] *siehe* **take**
tooth [tuːθ], *pl* **teeth** [tiːθ] Zahn II
toothache ['tuːθeɪk]: **have a toothache** Zahnschmerzen haben II
toothbrush ['tuːθbrʌʃ] Zahnbürste V 2 (37)
toothpaste ['tuːθpeɪst] Zahnpasta V 2 (37)
top [tɒp]:
1. Spitze II **at the top (of)** oben, am oberen Ende, an der Spitze (von) II **on top of each other** übereinander, aufeinander III
2. Spitzen-, oberste(r, s) I
3. Top, Oberteil I
topic ['tɒpɪk] Thema, Themengebiet II **topic sentence** Satz, der in das Thema eines Absatzes einführt III
torch [tɔːtʃ]:
1. Taschenlampe II
2. Fackel II
tore [tɔː] *siehe* **tear**
torn [tɔːn] *siehe* **tear**
tortoise ['tɔːtəs] (Land-)Schildkröte III
total ['təʊtl]: **a total of …** eine Gesamtsumme von …; insgesamt III
totally ['təʊtəli] völlig, total V 1 (23)
touch [tʌtʃ]:
1. berühren, anfassen I
2. **get in touch (with sb.)** (mit jm.) Kontakt aufnehmen; sich (mit jm.) in Verbindung setzen II **stay in touch (with sb.)** (mit jm.) Kontakt halten; (mit jm.) in Verbindung bleiben II
tough [tʌf] (knall)hart, schwierig III
tour (of) ['tʊər] Rundgang, Rundfahrt, Reise (durch) I
tourist ['tʊərɪst] Tourist/in I
towards [tə'wɔːdz]: **towards the station / John** auf den Bahnhof / John zu, in Richtung Bahnhof / John III
tower ['taʊə] Turm I
town [taʊn] Stadt I **town hall** Rathaus II
toy [tɔɪ] Spielzeug I

track [træk]:
1. (Bahn-)Gleis IV
2. (Feld-)Weg, Pfad IV
tractor ['træktə] Traktor II
trade [treɪd]:
1. Handel III
°2. **trade (with)** Handel treiben (mit)
tradition [trə'dɪʃn] Tradition IV
traditional [trə'dɪʃənl] traditionell II
traffic ['træfɪk] Verkehr III **traffic light** (Verkehrs-)Ampel *(oft auch:* **traffic lights** *(pl)*) III
trail [treɪl] Weg, Pfad III
train [treɪn]:
1. Zug II **get on a train** in einen Zug einsteigen II
2. trainieren II
trainer ['treɪnə] Turnschuh I
training ['treɪnɪŋ] Training(sstunde) I
°**trait** [treɪt] Characterzug
tram [træm] Straßenbahn IV
trance [trɑːns], *AE:* [træns] Trance IV
transform [træns'fɔːm] verwandeln; umwandeln V 1 (12)
translate [træns'leɪt] übersetzen II
translator [træns'leɪtə] Übersetzer/in V 2 (50)
translation [træns'leɪʃn] Übersetzung III
transparency [træns'pærənsi] Folie *(für Projektor)* III
transport ['trænspɔːt] Verkehrsmittel; Transport(wesen) V 2 (50)
trash can ['træʃ kæn] *(AE)* Mülltonne, Abfalleimer IV
travel ['trævl] reisen I
traveller ['trævələ] Reisende(r) I
tread [tred], **trod, trodden: tread on sb.'s toes** jm. auf die Füße/Zehen treten *(auch im übertragenen Sinne)* III
treat ['triːt] behandeln V 2 (36)
treatment ['triːtmənt] Behandlung V 2 (36)
tree [triː] Baum I
tree trunk ['triː trʌŋk] Baumstamm V 2 (36)
trendy ['trendi] modisch, angesagt, „in" V 1 (12)
trials *(pl)* ['traɪəlz] Turnier, Wettkampf III
triangle ['traɪæŋgl] Dreieck III
triangular [traɪ'æŋgjələ] dreieckig IV
tribe [traɪb] (Volks-)Stamm IV
trick [trɪk] Kunststück, Trick II
°**tricky** ['trɪki] verzwickt, heikel
trip [trɪp] Ausflug; Reise I **go on day trips** Tagesausflüge machen II
°**triple** ['trɪpl] dreimal
trod [trɒd] *siehe* **tread**
trodden [trɒdn] *siehe* **tread**
trophy ['trəʊfi] Pokal; Trophäe I
tropical ['trɒpɪkl] tropisch, Tropen- V 1 (10)
tropics, the *(pl)* ['trɒpɪks] die Tropen V 1 (10)

trouble ['trʌbl]: **be in trouble** in Schwierigkeiten sein; Ärger kriegen I **get into trouble** in Schwierigkeiten geraten, Ärger kriegen III
trousers *(pl)* ['traʊzəz] Hose II
truck [trʌk] Lastwagen, LKW IV
true [truː] wahr I
trunk [trʌŋk] Baumstamm V 2 (36)
trust [trʌst] Stiftung V 3 (72)
truth [truːθ] Wahrheit II
try [traɪ]:
1. (aus)probieren; versuchen I
2. Versuch III
T-shirt ['tiːʃɜːt] T-Shirt I
tube [tjuːb]: **the Tube** die U-Bahn *(in London)* III **on the Tube** in der U-Bahn III
tuck [tʌk] stecken, klemmen IV
Tuesday ['tjuːzdeɪ] Dienstag I
tulip ['tjuːlɪp] Tulpe II
tune [tjuːn] stimmen *(Instrument)* IV
tunnel ['tʌnl] Tunnel II
turkey ['tɜːki] Pute, Truthahn IV
turn [tɜːn]:
1. **(It's) my turn.** Ich bin dran / an der Reihe. I °**take turns** sich abwechseln *(etwas zu tun)*
2. sich umdrehen III **turn around** sich umdrehen; wenden, umdrehen I **turn round** sich umdrehen III **turn to sb.** sich jm. zuwenden; sich an jn. wenden II
3. **turn sth. down** etwas leiser stellen III **turn sth. off** etwas ausschalten II **turn sth. on** etwas einschalten I **turn sth. up** etwas lauter stellen III
4. **turn left/right** (nach) links/rechts abbiegen II
5. **turn red/cold** rot/kalt werden III
tutor sb. ['tjuːtə] jn. unterrichten, jm. Stunden geben IV
TV [ˌtiː'viː] Fernsehen, Fernsehgerät I **on TV** im Fernsehen III
twelve [twelv] zwölf I
twice [twaɪs] zweimal II
twins *(pl)* [twɪnz] Zwillinge I
two [tuː] zwei I **two-syllable** zweisilbig II
typical (of) ['tɪpɪkl] typisch (für) IV

U

UK [ˌjuː 'keɪ]: **the UK** das Vereinigte Königreich III
umbrella [ʌm'brelə] Regenschirm I
uncle ['ʌŋkl] Onkel I
uncomfortable [ʌn'kʌmftəbl] unbequem IV
under ['ʌndə] unter I
underground [ˌʌndə'graʊnd] unterirdisch, unter der Erde III **the underground** die U-Bahn III
underline [ˌʌndə'laɪn] unterstreichen II
understand [ˌʌndə'stænd], **understood, understood** verstehen I
understanding [ˌʌndə'stændɪŋ] Verständnis V 3 (67)
understood [ˌʌndə'stʊd] *siehe* **understand**
unemotional [ˌʌnɪ'məʊʃənl] gefühllos, emotionslos V 3 (63)
unexcused [ˌʌnɪk'skjuːzd] unentschuldigt IV
unexpected [ˌʌnɪk'spektɪd] unerwartet V 1 (19)
unfair [ʌn'feə] unfair, ungerecht III
unfortunately [ʌn'fɔːtʃənətli] leider, unglücklicherweise V 1 (27)
unfriendly [ʌn'frendli] unfreundlich IV
unhappy [ʌn'hæpi] unglücklich II
uniform ['juːnɪfɔːm] Uniform I
uninteresting [ʌn'ɪntrəstɪŋ] uninteressant IV
unit ['juːnɪt] Kapitel, Lektion I
united [ju'naɪtɪd] vereinigt III **the United Kingdom** das Vereinigte Königreich III **the United Nations (UN)** die Vereinten Nationen V 4 (84)
university [ˌjuːnɪ'vɜːsəti] Universität V 2 (37)
unkind [ˌʌn'kaɪnd] unfreundlich, wenig nett, herzlos V 3 (63)
unless [ən'les] es sei denn; außer (wenn) V 3 (70)
°**unlike** [ˌʌn'laɪk] anders als; im Gegensatz zu
unlucky [ʌn'lʌki]: **be unlucky** Pech haben IV
unnecessary [ʌn'nesəsəri] unnötig IV
unpack [ˌʌn'pæk] auspacken III
unpopular [ʌn'pɒpjələ] unbeliebt IV
unstoppable [ʌn'stɒpəbl] unaufhaltsam, unaufhaltbar IV
until [ən'tɪl] bis II **not until** erst, nicht vor III
unusual [ʌn'juːʒuəl] ungewöhnlich III
up [ʌp] hinauf, herauf; (nach) oben I **up and down** auf und ab; rauf und runter I **up here** hier oben; nach hier oben II **up to** bis (zu) II **What's up?** Was gibt's? / Was ist los? III **It's up to you.** Du hast die Wahl. / Du entscheidest. V 4 (82) ° **up by sixteen** mit sechzehn Punkten vorn
update sth. [ˌʌp'deɪt] etwas aktualisieren, auf den neuesten Stand bringen V 2 (43)
uphill [ˌʌp'hɪl] bergauf III
upset [ˌʌp'set] aufgebracht, gekränkt, mitgenommen V 1 (27)
upstairs [ˌʌp'steəz] oben; nach oben *(im Haus)* I
upstream [ˌʌp'striːm] flussaufwärts III
urban ['ɜːbən] städtisch, Stadt- V 1 (10)
us [ʌs], [əs] uns I
use [juːs] Gebrauch, Verwendung; Nutzen V 4 (98)
use [juːz] benutzen, verwenden I
used to ['juːst tə]:
1. **where the towers used to be** wo die Türme früher waren/standen IV
2. **get used to sth.** sich an etwas gewöhnen V 2 (50)
useful ['juːsfl] nützlich V 2 (47)
usual ['juːʒuəl] gewöhnlich, üblich III
usually ['juːʒuəli] meistens, normalerweise, gewöhnlich I

V

vacation [və'keɪʃn] *(AE)* Urlaub IV
valley ['væli] Tal II
value ['væljuː] Wert V 2 (48)
van [væn] Transporter, Lieferwagen III
vast [vɑːst] riesig V 1 (22)
vegan ['viːgən] vegan V 3 (64)
vegetables *(pl)* ['vedʒtəblz] Gemüse I
vegetarian [ˌvedʒə'teəriən]:
1. Vegetarier/in II
2. vegetarisch II
verb [vɜːb] Verb III
verse [vɜːs] Vers, Strophe II
very ['veri]:
1. sehr I
2. **at the very beginning** ganz am Anfang V 4 (101) **the very first/last/best ...** der/die/das allererste/allerletzte/allerbeste ... V 1 (13)
°3. **this very subject** genau dieses Thema
vice- [vaɪs] Vize- V 3 (60)
victim ['vɪktɪm] Opfer V 4 (99)
victory ['vɪktəri] Sieg V 1 (27)
video ['vɪdiəʊ] Video I
video camera ['vɪdiəʊ ˌkæmərə] Videokamera I
view (of) [vjuː] Aussicht, Blick (auf) II **point of view (on sth.)** Standpunkt (in/über/zu etwas) III **in my view** meiner Ansicht nach, meiner Meinung nach V 1 (17) **take a different view** einen anderen Standpunkt vertreten; anderer Ansicht sein V 1 (17) **take the view that** der Auffassung sein, dass / der Ansicht sein, dass V 1 (17)
°**viewer** ['vjuːə] Zuschauer/in
village ['vɪlɪdʒ] Dorf I
violence ['vaɪələns] Gewalt; Gewalttätigkeit V 4 (97)
VIP [ˌviː‿aɪ 'piː] **(very important person)** Prominente(r) IV
viral ['vaɪrəl]: **go viral** sich wie ein Virus ausbreiten / sich wie ein Lauffeuer verbreiten IV
virus ['vaɪrəs], *pl* **viruses** ['vaɪrəsɪz] Virus V 3 (66)
visa ['viːzə] Visum III
visit ['vɪzɪt]:
1. besuchen I
2. Besuch I
visitor ['vɪzɪtə] Besucher/in, Gast II
°**vital** ['vaɪtl] (lebens)wichtig

vocabulary [və'kæbjələri] Vokabelverzeichnis, Wörterverzeichnis I
voice [vɔɪs] Stimme I **in a loud voice** mit lauter Stimme II
volleyball ['vɒlibɔːl] Volleyball I
volunteer [ˌvɒlən'tɪə]:
1. sich freiwillig melden; freiwillig/ehrenamtlich arbeiten *(unbezahlt)* III
2. Freiwillige(r), Ehrenamtliche(r) III
vote [vəʊt]:
1. **vote (for)** (für jn./etwas) stimmen; wählen, zur Wahl gehen V 2 (36)
°2. Abstimmung **hold a vote** eine Abstimmung durchführen
°**voter** ['vəʊtə] Wähler/in
voucher ['vaʊtʃə]: **gift voucher** Geschenkgutschein V 1 (23)
vowel ['vaʊəl] Vokal, Selbstlaut II

W

°**wage** [weɪdʒ] Lohn
waist [weɪst] Taille II
wait (for) [weɪt] warten (auf) I **wait a minute** Warte einen Moment. / Moment mal. I **I can't wait to see …** Ich kann es kaum erwarten, … zu sehen II
waiter ['weɪtə] Kellner IV
waitress ['weɪtrəs] Kellnerin IV
wake up [ˌweɪk_'ʌp], **woke, woken**:
1. aufwachen I
2. **wake sb. up** jn. (auf)wecken II
walk [wɔːk]:
1. Spaziergang I **go for a walk** spazieren gehen, einen Spaziergang machen I **take a walk** *(bes. AE)* spazieren gehen, einen Spaziergang machen IV
2. (zu Fuß) gehen I **walk around** herumlaufen, umherspazieren II **walk on** weitergehen II **walk the dog** mit dem Hund rausgehen, den Hund ausführen III
°**walkabout** ['wɔːkəˌbaʊt] *(AusE; infml)* Wanderung **go walkabout** wandern
°**walkway** ['wɔːkweɪ] Fußweg, Spazierweg
wall [wɔːl] Mauer; Wand II
wander ['wɒndə] herumlaufen; herumirren II
want [wɒnt]: **want sth.** etwas (haben) wollen I **want to do sth.** etwas tun wollen I
war [wɔː] Krieg III
warm [wɔːm] warm I
warning ['wɔːnɪŋ] Warnung III
was [wɒz], [wəz]:
1. *siehe* **be**
2. **I wish I was there.** Ich wünschte, ich wäre da. II
wash [wɒʃ] waschen, wischen III **wash the dishes** *(pl)* das Geschirr abwaschen, spülen II °**washed up (on a beach)** angeschwemmt

waste [weɪst]:
1. Verschwendung V 2 (36):
2. **waste sth. (on sth.)** etwas (für etwas) verschwenden V 2 (36)
watch [wɒtʃ]:
1. Armbanduhr I
2. sich etwas anschauen; beobachten I **watch TV** fernsehen I **Watch out!** Pass auf! / Vorsicht! I **watch out for sth./sb.** nach jm./etwas Ausschau halten IV
°**watchdog** ['wɒtʃdɒg] Wächter/in, Aufpasser/in
water ['wɔːtə] Wasser I **water fountain** *(bes. AE)* Trinkbrunnen IV **waters** *(pl)* Gewässer V 1 (19) **water pipe** Wasserleitung, Wasserrohr V 3 (61)
waterfall ['wɔːtəfɔːl] Wasserfall II
waterfront ['wɔːtəfrʌnt] Hafenviertel *(oft modernisiert und zum Wohnviertel umgebaut)* V 1 (12)
wave [weɪv] Welle II
way [weɪ]:
1. Weg I **ask sb. the way** jn. nach dem Weg fragen II **No way!** Auf keinen Fall! / Kommt nicht in Frage! III **on the way to …** auf dem Weg zu/nach … I **tell sb. the way (to …)** jm. den Weg (nach …) beschreiben II **this/that way** hier entlang/dort entlang; in die Richtung II
2. Art und Weise III **in an interesting way** auf eine interessante Art und Weise III **in this way** auf diese Weise III **the way he …** die Art und Weise, wie er … III **in some/many ways** in mancher/vielerlei Hinsicht III **way of life** Lebensweise, Lebensart IV
we [wiː] wir I
weak [wiːk] schwach V 4 (91)
weaken ['wiːkən] schwächen V 4 (91)
°**weakness** ['wiːknəs] Schwäche
wear [weə], **wore, worn** tragen *(Kleidung)* I
°**weapon** ['wepən] Waffe
weather ['weðə] Wetter II
web [web] (Spinnen-)Netz V 3 (61)
website ['websaɪt] Website I
wedding ['wedɪŋ] Hochzeit, Trauung IV
Wednesday ['wenzdeɪ] Mittwoch I
wee [wiː] *(Scottish, infml)* klein III
week [wiːk] Woche I **a three-week holiday** ein dreiwöchiger Urlaub III
► S. 198 a half-hour ride …
weekday ['wiːkdeɪ] Wochentag, Werktag IV
weekend [ˌwiːk'end] Wochenende I **at the weekend** am Wochenende I **on the weekend** *(AE)* am Wochenende IV
weigh [weɪ] wiegen I
weird [wɪəd] seltsam, komisch III
weirdo ['wɪədəʊ] *(infml)* Spinner/in IV
welcome sb. (to) ['welkəm] jn. begrüßen (in), jn. willkommen heißen (in) III **Welcome to Plymouth.** Willkommen in Plymouth. I

well [wel]:
1. gut II; *(gesundheitlich)* gesund II **I don't feel well** Ich fühle mich nicht gut. / Mir geht's nicht gut. II) **well-behaved** brav V 3 (62
2. **Well, …** Nun, … / Also, … / Na ja, … I
well-known [ˌwel'nəʊn], ['welˌnəʊn] bekannt, wohlbekannt III
Welsh [welʃ] Walisisch; walisisch III
went [went] *siehe* **go**
were [wɜː], [wə] *siehe* **be**
west [west] Westen; nach Westen; westlich III **westbound** ['westbaʊnd] Richtung Westen III **western** ['westən] westlich, West- III **western** ['westən] westlich, West- III
wet [wet] nass I
°**wetsuit** ['wetsuːt] Taucheranzug
whale [weɪl] Wal I
°**wharf** [wɔːf] Kai, Pier
what? [wɒt] was? I **What about you?** Und du/ihr? / Und was ist mit dir/euch? I **What about …?** Wie wäre es mit …? II **What colour …?** Welche Farbe …? I **What is the story about?** Wovon handelt die Geschichte? Worum geht es in der Geschichte? I **What programmes …?** Welche Programme …? / Welche Art von Programmen …? I **What size tea would you like?** Wie groß soll der/dein Tee sein? II **What time is it?** Wie spät ist es? I **What's your name?** Wie heißt du? I **What's she like?** Wie ist sie? / Wie ist sie so? I **What's up?** Was gibt's? / Was ist los? III **I don't know what to do.** Ich weiß nicht, was ich tun soll. III
whatever [wɒt'evə] was (auch) immer III
wheel [wiːl]
1. Rad IV
2. *(kurz für* **steering wheel***)* Lenkrad IV
3. **big wheel** Riesenrad I
4. **wheels** *(pl, infml)* fahrbarer Untersatz IV
when [wen]:
1. wenn I
2. als I
3. **when?** wann? I
whenever [ˌwen'evə] wann (auch) immer; egal, wann III
where? [weə] wo? / wohin? / woher? I **We had no idea where to go.** Wir hatten keine Ahnung, wohin wir gehen sollten. III
wherever [weər'evə] wo (auch) immer III
whether ['weðə] ob IV
which [wɪtʃ]:
1. **which?** welche(r, s)? I
2. der/die/das; die *(Relativpronomen)* II
while [waɪl]:
1. während II

2. eine Weile, einige Zeit III **for a while** eine Weile, eine Zeit lang III
whisper ['wɪspə] flüstern II
whistle ['wɪsl]:
1. pfeifen II
2. (Triller-)Pfeife III **blow a whistle** pfeifen (auf der Trillerpfeife) III
3. Pfiff III
white [waɪt] weiß I
whiteboard ['waɪtbɔːd] Whiteboard, Weißwandtafel III
who [huː]:
1. Who is there? Wer ist da? I **Who did you tell?** Wem hast du es erzählt? II **Who does he know?** Wen kennt er? II **I don't know who to ask.** Ich weiß nicht, wen ich fragen kann/soll. III
2. der/die/das; die *(Relativpronomen)* II
whoever [huː'evə] wer (auch) immer III
whole [həʊl] ganze(r, s), gesamte(r, s) II
whose [huːz]:
1. whose? wessen? II
2. the men whose homes ... die Männer, deren Wohnungen ... IV
why [waɪ] warum I **that's why** deshalb, darum II **Why not try ...?** Warum probierst du nicht ...? / Warum probieren wir nicht ...? IV
wide [waɪd] weit; breit III
widespread ['waɪdspred] weitverbreitete(r, s) V 4 (99)
wife [waɪf], *pl* **wives** [waɪvz] Ehefrau V 2 (44)
wild [waɪld] wild II
wildfire ['waɪldfaɪə] Waldbrand, Buschbrand IV
wildlife ['waɪldlaɪf] Tierwelt, frei lebende Tiere IV
will [wɪl]: **we'll miss the girls (= we will miss the girls)** wir werden die Mädchen verpassen II **I'll have a tea.** Ich nehme einen Tee. *(beim Essen, im Restaurant)* II
win [wɪn], **won, won** gewinnen I
° **win sb. over** jn. für sich gewinnen, jn. überzeugen
wind [wɪnd] Wind II
window ['wɪndəʊ] Fenster I ° **crack a window** ein Fenster einen Spalt öffnen
windy ['wɪndi] windig II
wing [wɪŋ] Flügel III
winner ['wɪnə] Gewinner/in, Sieger/in I
winter ['wɪntə] Winter I
wise [waɪz] weise II
wish [wɪʃ]:
1. Wunsch I **make a wish** sich etwas wünschen I
2. wünschen II **I wish I was there.** Ich wünschte, ich wäre da. II
°**witchetty grub** ['wɪtʃəti grʌb] Witchetty-Made
with [wɪð]:
1. mit I
2. bei I
within [wɪ'ðɪn] innerhalb (von) V 2 (50)
without [wɪ'ðaʊt] ohne I
woke [wəʊk] *siehe* **wake**
woken [wəʊkən] *siehe* **wake**
woman ['wʊmən], *pl* **women** ['wɪmɪn] Frau I
won [wʌn] *siehe* **win**
wonder ['wʌndə]:
1. sich fragen, gern wissen wollen III
2. Wunder IV **No wonder ...** Kein Wunder ... IV
wonderful ['wʌndəfəl] wunderbar IV
won't [wəʊnt]: **she won't come (= she will not come)** sie wird nicht kommen II
wood [wʊd] Holz II
wooden ['wʊdn] hölzern; Holz- III
°**wool** [wʊl] Wolle
word [wɜːd] Wort I **May I have a word with you?** Kann ich Sie kurz sprechen? II **word order** Wortstellung I
wordbank ['wɜːdˌbæŋk] „Wortspeicher" I
wore [wɔː] *siehe* **wear**
work [wɜːk]:
1. arbeiten I **work sth. out** etwas herausbekommen, herausarbeiten V 3 (67)
2. Arbeit I **work of art** Kunstwerk IV **work experience** Praktikum; Arbeitserfahrung(en), Praxiserfahrung(en) V 1 (26)
3. funktionieren III
workbook ['wɜːkbʊk] Arbeitsheft I
worker ['wɜːkə] Arbeiter/in II
worksheet ['wɜːkʃiːt] Arbeitsblatt II
workshop ['wɜːkʃɒp] Werkstatt III; Workshop, Lehrgang II
worktop ['wɜːktɒp] Arbeitsplatte; Küchentheke IV
world [wɜːld] Welt II **in the world** auf der Welt II **natural world** (Welt der) Natur III **World Cup** Weltmeisterschaft III
worm [wɜːm] Wurm I
worn [wɔːn] *siehe* **wear**
worried ['wʌrid] besorgt, beunruhigt I
worry (about) ['wʌri] sich Sorgen machen (wegen, um) II **No worries.** Kein Problem! / Alles OK! / Alles gut! V 1 (15)
worse [wɜːs] schlechter, schlimmer II
worst [wɜːst] der/die/das schlechteste/schlimmste ...; am schlechtesten/schlimmsten II
worth [wɜːθ] wert III
would [wʊd]: **I would choose Sam** ich würde Sam wählen II **What would you like to eat?** Was möchtest du essen? I **I'd (= I would) like ...** Ich möchte ... I **I would have screamed.** Ich hätte geschrien. IV
write [raɪt], **wrote, written** schreiben I **write sth. down** etwas aufschreiben II
writer ['raɪtə] Schreiber/in III; Schriftsteller/in III
written ['rɪtn] *siehe* **write**
wrong [rɒŋ]:
1. falsch, verkehrt I **go wrong** schiefgehen IV **No, that's wrong.** Nein, das stimmt nicht. I
2. sb. is wrong jemand irrt sich; jemand hat Unrecht I
3. What's wrong with you? Was fehlt dir?; Was ist los mit dir? II
wrote [rəʊt] *siehe* **write**

Y

yacht [jɒt] Jacht III
year [jɪə]:
1. Jahr I **last/next year's ...** das ... vom letzten/nächsten Jahr II **this year's ...** das diesjährige ... II
2. Jahrgang(sstufe) I
yellow ['jeləʊ] gelb I
yes [jes] ja I **Yes, that's right.** Ja, das ist richtig. / Ja, das stimmt. I
yesterday ['jestədeɪ] gestern I
yet [jet]: **not ... yet** noch nicht I **Have you ... yet?** Hast du schon ...? II
yoga ['jəʊgə] Yoga I
yoghurt ['jɒgət] Joghurt I
you [juː]:
1. du; Sie; ihr; dir; dich; euch; Ihnen I
2. man III
young [jʌŋ] jung I
your [jɔː], [jə] dein/e; euer/eure; Ihr/Ihre I
yours [jɔːz] deiner, deine, deins; eurer, eure, eures II ° **Yours sincerely** [sɪn'sɪəli] Mit freundlichen Grüßen
yourself [jɔː'self] dich, dir; sich (bei „Sie") III **about yourself** über dich selbst I **Enjoy yourself.** Viel Spaß! / Amüsiere dich gut! III **Help yourself.** Greif zu! / Bedien dich! III **Did you cook it yourself?** Hast du es selbst gekocht? IV
yourselves [jɔː'selvz] euch; sich *(bei „Sie")* III
youth [juːθ] Jugend; Jugend- V 2 (50)
yummy ['jʌmi] *(infml)* lecker I

Z

zone [zəʊn]: **pedestrian zone** Fußgängerzone II
zombie ['zɒmbi] Zombie V 2 (44)
zoo [zuː] Zoo I

Place names

Alice Springs [ˌælɪs 'sprɪŋz]
Atlanta [ət'lænta]
Auckland ['ɔ:klənd]
Barron Gorge [ˌbærən 'gɔ:dʒ]
Berlin [bɜ:'lɪn]
Cairns [keənz]
Canberra ['kænbərə]
Cape Tribulation [ˌkeɪp trɪbju'leɪʃn]
Cardiff ['kɑ:dɪf]
Casuarina [ˌkæzjuə'ri:nə]
Circular Quay [ˌsɜ:kjʊlə 'ki:]
Connecticut [kə'netɪkət]
the Daintree ['deɪntri:]
Darwin ['dɑ:wɪn]
Drumchapel ['drʌmtʃæpl]
Gibson Desert [ˌgɪbsn 'dezət]
Great Barrier Reef [ˌgreɪt 'bæriə ri:f]
Harrogate ['hærəgət]
Harvard ['hɑ:vəd]
Hathaway ['hæθəweɪ]
Kintore ['kɪntɔ:]
Lancashire ['læŋkəʃə]
Manly [mænli]
Melbourne ['melbən], [melbɔ:n]
Mindli ['mɪndli]
Morecambe ['mɔ:kəm]
Ohio [əʊ'haɪəʊ]
Palo Canyon [ˌpæləʊ 'kænjən]
Paris ['pærɪs]
Perth [pɜ:θ]
Princeton ['prɪnstən]
Queensland ['kwi:nzlənd]
Rapid Creek [ˌræpɪd 'kri:k]
Royal Botanic Gardens [bə'tænɪk]
Sydney ['sɪdni]
Tasmania [tæz'meɪniə]
Timor Sea ['ti:mɔ:]
Woolloomooloo [ˌwʊləmə'lu:]

First names

Aaron ['ærən]
Alicia [ə'li:ʃə]
Amy ['eɪmi]
Ange [ændʒ]
Bruce [bru:s]
Cathy ['kæθi]
Colm [kɒlm]
Cooper ['ku:pə]
Coreen [kə'ri:n]
David ['deɪvɪd]
Duncan ['dʌŋkn]
Elvira [el'vɪərə]
Graham ['greɪəm]
Juan [hwɑ:n]
Kirsty ['kɜ:sti]
Kwame ['kwɑ:meɪ], [kweɪm]
Kyanna [ki'ænə]
Layla ['leɪlə]
Liza ['laɪzə]
Logan ['ləʊgn]
Merryn ['merɪn]
Nic [nɪk]
Nick [nɪk]
Noah ['nəʊə]
Olivia [ə'lɪviə]
Ozzie ['ɒzi]
Samuel ['sæmjuəl]
Taylor ['teɪlə]
Titus ['taɪtəs]
Wes [wes]
Yuma ['ju:mə]
Zoe ['zəʊi]

Family names

Alexander [ˌælɪg'zɑ:ndə]
Barton ['bɑ:tn]
Bazemore ['beɪzmɔ:]
Beckett ['bekɪt]
Cohen ['kəʊɪn]
Faulkner ['fɔ:lknə]
Fermer ['fɜ:mə]
Freeman ['fri:mən]
Girvan ['gɜ:vən]
Goodes [gʊdz]
Hallisey ['hæləsi]
Jacob ['dʒeɪkəb]
Jessop ['dʒesəp]
Lee [li:]
Lewis ['lu:ɪs]
McCabe [mə'keɪb]
McCaughrean [mə'kɔ:kreɪn]
Somerset ['sʌməset]

Other names

Delaney [dɪ'leɪni]
Gujingga [gu:'dʒɪŋgə]
Pintupi [pɪn'tu:pi]
Roma *(pl)* ['rɒmə]
Rosella [rə'selə]
vivid (VividSydney) ['vɪvɪd]

Countries and continents

Country/Continent	Adjective	Person	People
*Marco is from **Italy**.*	*Pizza is **Italian**.*	*Marco is **an Italian**.*	***The Italians** invented pizza.*
Afghanistan [æf'gænɪstæn]	Afghan ['æfgæn]	an Afghan	the Afghans
Africa ['æfrɪkə] *Afrika*	African ['æfrɪkən]	an African	the Africans
Asia ['eɪʒə, 'eɪʃə] *Asien*	Asian ['eɪʃn, 'eɪʒn]	an Asian	the Asians
Australia [ɒ'streɪliə] *Australien*	Australian [ɒ'streɪliən]	an Australian	the Australians
Austria ['ɒstriə] *Österreich*	Austrian ['ɒstriən]	an Austrian	the Austrians
Belarus [ˌbelə'ruːs] *Weißrussland*	Belarusian [ˌbelə'ruːsiən]	a Belarusian	the Belarusians
Belgium ['beldʒəm] *Belgien*	Belgian ['beldʒən]	a Belgian	the Belgians
Bosnia and Herzegovina ['bɒzniə ən ˌhɜːtsəgə'viːnə] *Bosnien und Herzegowina*	Bosnian ['bɒzniən]; Herzegovinian [ˌhɜːtsəgə'vɪniən]	a Bosnian; a Herzegovinian	the Bosnians; the Herzegovinians
Canada ['kænədə] *Kanada*	Canadian [kə'neɪdiən]	a Canadian	the Canadians
China ['tʃaɪnə]	Chinese [ˌtʃaɪ'niːz]	a Chinese	the Chinese
Croatia [krəʊ'eɪʃə] *Kroatien*	Croatian [krəʊ'eɪʃn]	a Croatian	the Croatians
the **Czech Republic** [ˌtʃek rɪ'pʌblɪk] *Tschechien, die Tschechische Republik*	Czech [tʃek]	a Czech	the Czechs
Denmark ['denmɑːk] *Dänemark*	Danish ['deɪnɪʃ]	a Dane [deɪn]	the Danes
Egypt ['iːdʒɪpt] *Ägypten*	Egyptian [i'dʒɪpʃən]	an Egyptian	the Egyptians
England ['ɪŋglənd]	English ['ɪŋglɪʃ]	an Englishman / -woman	the English
Estonia [e'stəʊniə] *Estland*	Estonian [e'stəʊniən]	an Estonian	the Estonians
Europe ['jʊərəp] *Europa*	European [ˌjʊərə'piːən]	a European	the Europeans
Finland ['fɪnlənd] *Finnland*	Finnish ['fɪnɪʃ]	a Finn [fɪn]	the Finns
France [frɑːns] *Frankreich*	French [frentʃ]	a Frenchman / -woman	the French
Germany ['dʒɜːməni] *Deutschland*	German ['dʒɜːmən]	a German	the Germans
(Great) Britain ['brɪtn] *Großbritannien*	British ['brɪtɪʃ]	a Briton ['brɪtn]	the British
Greece [griːs] *Griechenland*	Greek [griːk]	a Greek	the Greeks
Guinea ['gɪni]	Guinean ['gɪniən]	a Guinean	the Guineans
Hungary ['hʌŋgəri] *Ungarn*	Hungarian [hʌŋ'geəriən]	a Hungarian	the Hungarians
Iceland ['aɪslənd] *Island*	Icelandic [aɪs'lændɪk]	an Icelander ['aɪsləndə]	the Icelanders
India ['ɪndiə] *Indien*	Indian ['ɪndiən]	an Indian	the Indians
Ireland ['aɪələnd] *Irland*	Irish ['aɪrɪʃ]	an Irishman / -woman	the Irish
Italy ['ɪtəli] *Italien*	Italian [ɪ'tæliən]	an Italian	the Italians
Kosovo ['kɒsəvəʊ]	Kosovan ['kɒsəvən]	a Kosovan	the Kosovans
Latvia ['lætviə] *Lettland*	Latvian ['lætviən]	a Latvian	the Latvians
Lithuania [ˌlɪθju'eɪniə] *Litauen*	Lithuanian [ˌlɪθju'eɪniə]	a Lithuanian	the Lithuanians
Luxembourg ['lʌksəmbɜːg] *Luxemburg*	Luxembourg	a Luxembourger ['lʌksəmbɜːgə]	the Luxembourgers

Country/Continent	Adjective	Person	People
*Marco is from **Italy**.*	*Pizza is **Italian**.*	*Marco is **an Italian**.*	***The Italians** invented pizza.*
Macedonia [ˌmæsəˈdəʊniə] *Mazedonien*	Macedonian [ˌmæsəˈdəʊniən]	a Macedonian	the Macedonians
Malta [ˈmɔːltə]	Maltese [mɔːlˈtiːz]	a Maltese	the Maltese
Moldova [mɒlˈdəʊvə] *Moldawien*	Moldovan [mɒlˈdəʊvən]	a Moldovan	the Moldovans
Montenegro [ˌmɒntɪˈniːgrəʊ] *Montenegro*	Montenegrin [ˌmɒntɪˈniːgrɪn]	a Montenegrin	the Montenegrins
Namibia [nəˈmɪbiə]	Namibian	a Namibian	the Namibians
the **Netherlands** [ˈneðələndz] *die Niederlande*	Dutch [dʌtʃ]	a Dutchman / a Dutchwoman	the Dutch
New Zealand [ˌnjuː ˈziːlənd] *Neuseeland*	New Zealand	a New Zealander	the New Zealanders
Northern Ireland [ˌnɔːðən‿ˈaɪələnd] *Nordirland*	Northern Irish [ˌnɔːðən‿ˈaɪrɪʃ]	a Northern Irishman / a Northern Irishwoman	the Northern Irish
Norway [ˈnɔːweɪ] *Norwegen*	Norwegian [nɔːˈwiːdʒən]	a Norwegian	the Norwegians
Pakistan [ˌpækɪstæn]	Pakistani	a Pakistani	the Pakistanis
Poland [ˈpəʊlənd] *Polen*	Polish [ˈpəʊlɪʃ]	a Pole [pəʊl]	the Poles
Portugal [ˈpɔːtʃʊgl]	Portuguese [ˌpɔːtʃuˈgiːz]	a Portuguese	the Portuguese
Romania [ruˈmeɪniə] *Rumänien*	Romanian [ruˈmeɪniən]	a Romanian	the Romanians
Russia [ˈrʌʃə] *Russland*	Russian [ˈrʌʃn]	a Russian	the Russians
Scotland [ˈskɒtlənd] *Schottland*	Scottish [ˈskɒtɪʃ]	a Scot [skɒt]; a Scotsman / a Scotswoman	the Scots, the Scottish
Serbia [ˈsɜːbiə] *Serbien*	Serbian [ˈsɜːbiən]	a Serbian	the Serbians
Slovakia [sləʊˈvækiə] *die Slowakei*	Slovak [ˈsləʊvæk]	a Slovak	the Slovaks
Slovenia [sləʊˈviːniə] *Slowenien*	Slovenian [sləʊˈviːniən]	a Slovenian	the Slovenians
South Africa [ˌsaʊθ‿ˈæfrɪkən]	South African	a South African	the South Africans
South America [ˌsaʊθ‿əˈmerɪkə] *Südamerika*	South American [ˌsaʊθ‿əˈmerɪkən]	a South American	the South Americans
Spain [speɪn] *Spanien*	Spanish [ˈspænɪʃ]	a Spaniard [ˈspænɪəd]	the Spanish
Sweden [ˈswiːdn] *Schweden*	Swedish [ˈswiːdɪʃ]	a Swede [swiːd]	the Swedes
Switzerland [ˈswɪtsələnd] *die Schweiz*	Swiss [swɪs]	a Swiss	the Swiss
Syria [ˈsɪriə] *Syrien*	Syrian [ˈsɪriən]	a Syrian	the Syrians
Turkey [ˈtɜːki] *die Türkei*	Turkish [ˈtɜːkɪʃ]	a Turk [tɜːk]	the Turks
Ukraine [juːˈkreɪn] *die Ukraine*	Ukrainian [juːˈkreɪniən]	a Ukrainian	the Ukrainians
the **United Kingdom** [juˌnaɪtɪd ˈkɪŋdəm] *das Vereinigte Königreich*	British [ˈbrɪtɪʃ]	a Briton [ˈbrɪtn]	the British
the **United States of America** [juˌnaɪtɪd ˌsteɪts‿əv‿əˈmerɪkə] *die Vereinigten Staaten von Amerika*	American [əˈmerɪkən]	an American	the Americans
Vietnam [ˌviːetˈnæm]	Vietnamese [viːˌetnəˈmiːz]	a Vietnamese	the Vietnamese
Wales [weɪlz]	Welsh [welʃ]	a Welshman/-woman	the Welsh

Irregular verbs

infinitive	simple past	past participle	
(to) **be**	**was; were**	**been**	sein
(to) **beat**	**beat**	**beaten**	schlagen; besiegen
(to) **become**	**became**	**become**	werden
(to) **begin**	**began**	**begun**	beginnen, anfangen
(to) **bend**	**bent**	**bent**	sich bücken, sich beugen
(to) **bite** [aɪ]	**bit** [ɪ]	**bitten** [ɪ]	beißen
(to) **blow sth. out**	**blew**	**blown**	etwas auspusten, ausblasen
(to) **break** [eɪ]	**broke**	**broken**	brechen; zerbrechen
(to) **bring**	**brought**	**brought**	(mit-, her)bringen
(to) **broadcast**	**broadcast**	**broadcast**	senden, ausstrahlen, übertragen *(Rundfunk, Fernsehen)*
(to) **build**	**built**	**built**	bauen
(to) **burst**	**burst**	**burst**	platzen
(to) **buy**	**bought**	**bought**	kaufen
(to) **catch**	**caught**	**caught**	fangen
(to) **choose** [uː]	**chose** [əʊ]	**chosen** [əʊ]	aussuchen, (aus)wählen; sich aussuchen
(to) **come**	**came**	**come**	kommen
(to) **cost**	**cost**	**cost**	kosten
(to) **cut**	**cut**	**cut**	schneiden
(to) **dig**	**dug**	**dug**	graben
(to) **do**	**did**	**done** [ʌ]	tun, machen
(to) **draw**	**drew**	**drawn**	zeichnen
(to) **drive** [aɪ]	**drove** [əʊ]	**driven** [ɪ]	(mit dem Auto) fahren
(to) **drink**	**drank**	**drunk**	trinken
(to) **eat**	**ate** [et, eɪt]	**eaten**	essen
(to) **fall**	**fell**	**fallen**	fallen, stürzen; hinfallen
(to) **feed**	**fed**	**fed**	füttern
(to) **feel**	**felt**	**felt**	fühlen; sich fühlen
(to) **fight**	**fought**	**fought**	(be)kämpfen
(to) **find**	**found**	**found**	finden
(to) **fly**	**flew**	**flown**	fliegen
(to) **forbid**	**forbade**	**forbidden**	verbieten
(to) **forget**	**forgot**	**forgotten**	vergessen
(to) **freeze**	**froze**	**frozen**	(ge)frieren; zufrieren; einfrieren
(to) **get**	**got**	**got**	bekommen; holen; werden; gelangen
(to) **give**	**gave**	**given**	geben
(to) **go**	**went**	**gone** [ɒ]	gehen
(to) **grow**	**grew**	**grown**	wachsen; anbauen, anpflanzen
(to) **hang**	**hung**	**hung**	hängen
(to) **have**	**had**	**had**	haben
(to) **hear** [ɪə]	**heard** [ɜː]	**heard** [ɜː]	hören
(to) **hide** [aɪ]	**hid** [ɪ]	**hidden** [ɪ]	verstecken; sich verstecken
(to) **hit**	**hit**	**hit**	schlagen
(to) **hold**	**held**	**held**	halten
(to) **hurt**	**hurt**	**hurt**	schmerzen, wehtun; verletzen
(to) **keep**	**kept**	**kept**	behalten; aufheben, aufsparen; aufbewahren
(to) **kneel** [niːl]	**knelt** [nelt]	**knelt** [nelt]	knien
(to) **know** [nəʊ]	**knew** [njuː]	**known** [nəʊn]	wissen; kennen
(to) **lead** [iː]	**led**	**led**	führen, leiten
(to) **leave** [iː]	**left**	**left**	(weg)gehen; abfahren; (zurück)lassen; verlassen

infinitive	simple past	past participle	
(to) **lend sb. sth.**	**lent**	**lent**	jm. etwas leihen
(to) **let**	**let**	**let**	lassen
(to) **lie**	**lay**	**lain**	liegen
(to) **light** [aɪ]	**lit** [ɪ]	**lit** [ɪ]	anzünden
(to) **lose** [uː]	**lost** [ɒ]	**lost** [ɒ]	verlieren
(to) **make**	**made**	**made**	machen; herstellen
(to) **mean** [iː]	**meant** [e]	**meant** [e]	bedeuten; meinen
(to) **meet** [iː]	**met** [e]	**met**	treffen; sich treffen; kennenlernen
(to) **pay**	**paid**	**paid**	bezahlen
(to) **put**	**put**	**put**	(etwas wohin) tun, legen, stellen
(to) **read** [iː]	**read** [e]	**read** [e]	lesen
(to) **ride** [aɪ]	**rode**	**ridden** [ɪ]	reiten; (Rad) fahren
(to) **ring**	**rang**	**rung**	klingeln, läuten
(to) **rise up** [aɪ]	**rose**	**risen** [ɪ]	aufragen, emporragen; sich erheben
(to) **run**	**ran**	**run**	rennen, laufen
(to) **say** [eɪ]	**said** [e]	**said** [e]	sagen
(to) **see**	**saw**	**seen**	sehen
(to) **sell**	**sold**	**sold**	verkaufen
(to) **send**	**sent**	**sent**	schicken, senden
(to) **set sth. up**	**set**	**set**	etwas errichten, aufbauen; etwas arrangieren
(to) **sew** [əʊ]	**sewed** [əʊ]	**sewn** [əʊ]	nähen
(to) **shake**	**shook**	**shaken**	schütteln; zittern
(to) **shine**	**shone** [*BE:* ɒ, *AE:* əʊ]	**shone** [ɒ, əʊ]	scheinen *(Sonne)*
(to) **shoot** [uː]	**shot** [ɒ]	**shot** [ɒ]	schießen; erschießen
(to) **sing**	**sang**	**sung**	singen
(to) **sink**	**sank**	**sunk**	sinken
(to) **sit**	**sat**	**sat**	sitzen; sich setzen
(to) **sleep**	**slept**	**slept**	schlafen
(to) **speak** [iː]	**spoke**	**spoken**	sprechen
(to) **spend**	**spent**	**spent**	*(Zeit)* verbringen; *(Geld)* ausgeben
(to) **spin around**	**spun**	**spun**	sich (im Kreis) drehen; herumwirbeln
(to) **spread** [e]	**spread** [e]	**spread** [e]	ausbreiten, verbreiten; sich ausbreiten, verbreiten
(to) **stand**	**stood**	**stood**	stehen; sich (hin)stellen
(to) **steal**	**stole**	**stolen**	stehlen
(to) **stick**	**stuck**	**stuck**	stechen, stecken
(to) **swim**	**swam**	**swum**	schwimmen
(to) **take**	**took**	**taken**	(mit)nehmen; (weg-, hin)bringen; dauern
(to) **teach**	**taught**	**taught**	unterrichten, lehren
(to) **tear** [teə]	**tore**	**torn**	reißen, zerreißen
(to) **tell**	**told**	**told**	erzählen, berichten
(to) **think**	**thought**	**thought**	denken, glauben
(to) **throw**	**threw**	**thrown**	werfen
(to) **tread** [e]	**trod**	**trodden**	treten
(to) **understand**	**understood**	**understood**	verstehen
(to) **wake up**	**woke up**	**woken up**	aufwachen; (auf)wecken
(to) **wear** [eə]	**wore** [ɔː]	**worn** [ɔː]	tragen *(Kleidung)*
(to) **win**	**won** [ʌ]	**won** [ʌ]	gewinnen
(to) **write**	**wrote**	**written**	schreiben

Early finisher solutions

Which place in Sydney?

p. 122

1 Sydney Harbour National Park 2 Sydney Opera House 3 Woolloomooloo

Photo captions

p. 122

1 JUMPING 2 LAUGHING 3 BURNING 4 CLIMBING 5 FLYING

The place in Sydney is Manly.

Whose tent?

p. 123

Tent numbers

1 Cara; Gary; 3 Amy; 4 Bob; 5 Hal; 6 Eddy; 7 Fiona; 8 Isabel; 9 Doris

Which sports?

p. 123

1 SOCCER 2 VOLLEYBALL 3 TENNIS 4 JUDO 5 BASKETBALL
6 CRICKET 7 GYMNASTICS 8 SWIMMING

The other sport is CANOEING.

Australian sign language

p. 124

Suggestions

2 There are trains crossing down the road. You should drive carefully or you could crash into one.
3 There are cassowaries in this area. You should watch out or you might kill one.
4 Kangaroos could cross the road for the next 86 kilometres. If you drive too fast, you could hit one.
5 The road is not just for cars. Don't go too close to people on bikes because they might get scared.
6 There are koalas in this area. Drive slowly or you might not be able to stop in time.
7 Camels can be found this area. You should be very careful as they could damage your car.
8 There may be sharks in the water. Be very careful if you go swimming, as they could attack you.

Find the food

p. 124

1 CHICKEN SANDWICH 2 CHOCOLATE SAUCE 3 POTATO SALAD 4 PASTA, SPAGHETTI
5 APPLE JUICE, WATER 6 CORNFLAKES, SUGAR 7 SAUSAGE, MEAT 8 DAIRY, YOGHURT

Sayings about money

p. 125

1 grow (d) 2 hand (c) 3 burn (f) 4 leg (b) 5 song (a) 6 mouth (e)

Tina's advice for teens

p. 125

1 c 2 a 3 e 4 b

Cartoon captions

p. 126

Opposites: dishonest, unkind, impatient, impolite , impractical, disrespectful, intolerant
Captions (suggestions): 1 An unkind cat, 2 An impolite lady, 3 A dishonest referee, 4 A disrespectful dog, 5 an impatient man

Change one letter

p. 126

1 CHEAT, 2 WISE, 3 TEXT, 4 ADVERT, 5 MATCH, 6 TEETH,
7 SIGHTS, 8 PASS, 9 SWEAT, 10 STAGE, 11 STEP

Hidden word: Text message

Check the corrections

p. 127

announcement: wrong word (*advert, advertisement*); years: wrong expression *(years old)*
am: grammar *(have been)*; english: spelling *(English)*; since: wrong word *(for)*; many: grammar *(a lot of)*; childrens: spelling *(children)*; neighbours: punctuation *(neighbour's or neighbours')*; hobbys: spelling *(hobbies)*; aktivities: spelling *(activities)*; hear: grammar *(hearing)*; sincerly: spelling *(sincerely)*

practise, skills, working and well are all correct.

Colour phrases

p. 127

1 E (white Christmas); 2 F (green light) 3 A (black sheep) 4 B (white, ghost)
5 C (red card) 6 D (green fingers)

An airport incident

p. 128

There paragraphs should be in this order: 1 D, 2 F, 3 B, 4 C, 5 A, 6 E

Cartoon captions

p. 128

There are many possible captions. Here are some ideas:

1. "My promise holds – until Friday." or "Why do some people think I'm dishonest?" ...
2. Penguins: "Well, we don't need to worry about global warming, do we?" or Polar bear: "Oh no, my ice cream is melting." ...
3. "Who says the world is getting hotter?" or "You can do a lot with solar energy." ...

Definitions

p. 129

1 protest, 2 government, 3 demonstration, 4 election, 5 strike, 6 campaign, 7 vote, 8 parliament
The hidden word is petition.
Possible definition: a request in writing made by people to the government

Presentation tips

p. 129

1, 20 Make eye contact
4, 15 End with a bang
5, 21 Practise as often as you can
6, 12 Smile at your audience
8, 2 Use a strong opener
9, 7 Don't read out a script
10, 3 Arrive early
11, 22 Don't speak too fast
13, 19 all equipment
16, 24 Keep it simple
17, 14 Use notes
23, 18 Face your audience

English sounds

[iː] green, he, sea
[i] happy, monkey
[ɪ] big, in, expensive
[e] red, yes, again, breakfast
[æ] cat, animal, apple, black
[ɑː] class, ask, car, park
[ɒ] song, on, dog, what
[ɔː] door, or, ball, four, morning
[uː] blue, ruler, too, two, you
[ʊ] book, good, pullover
[ʌ] mum, bus, colour
[ɜː] girl, early, her, work, T-shirt
[ə] a partner, again, today

[eɪ] name, eight, play, great
[aɪ] time, right, my, I
[ɔɪ] boy, toilet, noise
[əʊ] old, no, road, yellow
[aʊ] town, now, house
[ɪə] here, year, idea
[eə] where, pair, share, their
[ʊə] tour

[b] boat, table, verb
[p] pool, paper, shop
[d] dad, window, good
[t] ten, letter, at
[g] good, again, bag
[k] cat, kitchen, back
[m] mum, man, remember
[n] no, one, ten
[ŋ] song, young, uncle, thanks
[l] hello, like, old, small
[r] red, ruler, friend, sorry
[w] we, where, one
[j] you, yes, uniform
[f] family, after, laugh
[v] river, very, seven, have
[s] sister, poster, yes
[z] please, zoo, quiz, his, music
[ʃ] shop, station, English
[ʒ] television, usually
[tʃ] teacher, child, watch
[dʒ] Germany, job, project, orange
[θ] thanks, three, bathroom
[ð] the, this, father, with
[h] here, who, behind
[x] loch

Am besten kannst du dir die Aussprache der einzelnen Lautzeichen einprägen, wenn du dir zu jedem Zeichen ein einfaches Wort merkst – das [iː] ist der **green**-Laut, das [eɪ] ist der **name**-Laut usw.

False friends

! Leider gibt es einige Wörter, die im Englischen und Deutschen ähnlich klingen oder aussehen, aber eine ganz andere Bedeutung haben.
Hier sind einige Beispiele für *false friends*:

English	German	German	English
also	= auch	also	= **so; Well …**
bald	= glatzköpfig	bald	= **soon**
become	= werden	bekommen	= **get**
brave	= mutig	brav	= **good, well-behaved**
boot	= Stiefel	Boot	= **boat**
build	= bauen	bilden	= **make, form**
chips	= Pommes frites	Kartoffelchips	= **crisps**
fire	= Feuer	Feier	= **celebration**
gift	= Geschenk	Gift	= **poison**
grade	= Klasse, Jahrgangsstufe	Grad	= **degree**
kind	= freundlich	Kind	= **child**
handy	= praktisch	Handy	= **mobile**
listen	= zuhören	Listen	= **lists**
map	= Landkarte	Mappe	= **folder**
mist	= Nebel	Mist *(Unsinn)*	= **rubbish**
mode	= Methode	Mode	= **fashion**
Roman	= römisch	Roman	= **novel**
snake	= Schlange	Schnecke	= **snail**
stay	= bleiben	stehen	= **stand**
where	= wo	wer	= **who**
while	= während	weil	= **because**

English G Access uses the same special vocabulary *('Operatoren')* that is used in standard tests.
Make sure you understand what you need to do when you read one of the verbs below.

The task says	German	Example
ANFORDERUNGSBEREICH I (Comprehension)		
Complete/Finish sth.	Vervollständige etwas.	*Use the words in brackets to complete the sentences. Finish three sentences in a different way.*
Describe sth.	Beschreibe etwas.	*Describe the atmosphere in the park.*
Imagine.	Stelle dir vor.	*Imagine you live in New York.*
List things.	Liste/ Führe Sachen auf.	*List the reasons the two writers give.*
Look sth. up.	Schlage etwas nach.	*Look up the words in a dictionary.*
Make notes (on/about sth.).	Mach (dir) Notizen (über/zu etwas) (zur Vorbereitung)	*Make notes on what you see in the photos.*
Match sth.	Ordne etwas zu.	*Match the definitions to the pictures.*
Scan a text (for sth.).	Suche einen Text (nach etwas) ab.	*Scan the article for these numbers.*
Skim a text.	Überfliege einen Text (um den Inhalt grob zu erfassen)	*Go to page 177. Skim the three texts there and decide which one you should read.*
Structure sth.	Strukturiere etwas.	*Structure the vocabulary in the box.*
Sum (sth.) up.	Fass (etwas) zusammen.	*Sum up the main points of your presentation.*
Take notes (on/about sth.).	Mach (dir) Notizen (über/zu etwas) (beim Lesen oder Zuhören)	*Listen to the woman and take notes on what she tells you.*
Work sth. out.	Finde etwas heraus.	*In each situation, there is something you can't hear. Work out from the context what it is.*
Write *(+ text type)*	Schreibe *(+ Texttyp)*.	*Choose five words from box 1 and write sentences with them.*
ANFORDERUNGSBEREICH I/II (Comprehension/Analysis)		
Present sth.	Stelle etwas vor.	*Discuss your ideas and present them to the class.*
Report sth. (to sb.)	Berichte (jm.) (von) etwas.	*Report your ideas to the class.*
ANFORDERUNGSBEREICH II (Analysis)		
Check sth.	Prüfe etwas.	*Check that you have all the special vocabulary you need.*
Compare two things.	Vergleiche zwei Sachen.	*Compare your tables and correct them if necessary.*
Decide.	Entscheide dich.	*Decide if the people in the dialogues speak British or American English.*
Explain sth.	Erkläre etwas.	*Explain what decision she has made and why.*
Give reasons for sth.	Begründe etwas.	*Give reasons for your answer.*
ANFORDERUNGSBEREICH III (Discussion and comment)		
Agree on sth.	Einigt euch auf etwas.	*Use a placemat to agree on five places to visit.*
Assess sth.	Beurteile etwas.	*Use the feedback sheet to assess each other's report.*
Comment on sth.	Kommentiere etwas.	*Comment on what went wrong.*
Discuss sth.	Diskutiert über etwas / Besprecht etwas.	*Discuss your alternative titles and choose the best one.*
Give (sb.) feedback.	*Gib (jm.) Feedback/Rückmeldung.*	*Take notes on your partner's talk and give them feedback.*
Share sth. (with sb.)	*Teile etwas (mit jm.)*	*Share your ideas and give each other feedback.*

Quellenverzeichnis

Titelbild

Skyline (M): **Shutterstock**/Wouter Tolenaars, Oper (M): **F1online**

Illustrationen

Doreen Arnold, Berlin (S. 160); **Tobias Dahmen**, Utrecht/ **www.tobidahmen.de** (S. 23; S. 40; S. 49 unten; S. 68; S. 69; S. 90); **Carlos Borrell Eiköter**, Berlin (U2); **Michael Fleischmann**, Waldegg (S. 164 unten; S. 171; S. 173; S. 177; S. 179; S. 183; S. 184; S. 186; S. 187); **Eric Gira**, Berlin (S. 12; S. 53; S. 57; S. 101 Smiley; S. 123; S. 157); **M. B. Schulz**, Düsseldorf (S. 14; S. 16; S. 41; S. 45; S. 114; S. 163; S. 164 oben; S. 166)

Fotos

action press (S. 18 unten links: NEWSPIX; S. 19 oben links: REX FEATURES LTD; S. 72 links: REX FEATURES LTD. LONDON EC1R 5D); **ACTV** (S. 29); **akg-images** (S. 26 oben: Horizons); **Dean Atta** (S. 107: Hussina Raja, 2015); **Bridgeman Art Library** (S. 34 (1)); **Cartoonbank**, The New Yorker Collection (S. 87 (A): Mick Stevens, (B): Sam Gross); **CartoonStock**, Bath (S. 49 oben: Jim Sizemore; S. 63: Mike Flanagan) **ClipDealer** (S. 30 (A): Steffi Weiß; S. 64 (E), S. 118 (E): Axel Bueckert; S. 67 2. von links: © www.isselee.com); **Coffee Crank Cooperative** (S. 83); **Corbis** (S. 27: Steve Christo/Steve Christo Photography; S. 28 unten: Giansanti-Langevin-Orban/Sygma; S. 30 (C): Maria Nguyen/ Demotix); **Bonnie Glänzer** (S. 140; S. 144); **Crooked Letter Films**, New York (S. 152); **ddp images** (S. 6 unten (u. S. 94 unten li.): INTERTOPICS/Empics/Yui Mok; S. 94 unten links (u. S. 6 unten): INTERTOPICS/Empics/Yui Mok; S. 109: Camera Press/Wattie Cheung; S. 112 rechts: ZUMA); **Picture-Alliance** (S. 18 Mitte li. u. Mitte re.: dpa; S. 69 oben: SZ Photo; S. 95 oben: AP Photo, Mitte: empics, unten: AP Photo; S. 102 unten links: Miro May); **F1online** (S. 19 unten links: Carol Buchanan); **Philip Fleischhauer** (S. 13: Uwe Tröger); **Fotolia** (S. 6 oben (u. S. 58): stockphoto-graf; S. 10 (E): bennymarty, (F): Szilard Szasz-Toth; S. 11 (G): aussieanouk; S. 18 oben: BlueOrange Studio; S. 20 (A): Rita Kochmarjova, (D): Robert Kneschke, (E): mOai99; S. 44: zia_shusha; S. 58 (u. S. 6 oben): stockphoto-graf; S. 59: stockpics; S. 64 (A): Nightman1965; S. 64 (B): zsv3207, (C): tlovely4, (F): anyaberkut; S. 67 2. von rechts: yevgeniy11; S. 77: wikornr; S. 89 unten: kurapatka; S. 100: kharhan; S. 115 (A): Rita Kochmarjova, (D): Robert Kneschke, (E): mOai99; S. 118 (A): Nightman1965, (B): zsv3207, (C): tlovely4, (F): anyaberkut; S. 122 (4): aussieanouk, (5): DirkR; S. 122 oben: Christopher Meder; S. 124 (2) u. (4) u. (7): mastersky, (3): Rafael Ben-Ari, (6): Andrew Bayda, (8): Sondem, unten: WavebreakMediaMicro; S. 126 (1): oxanaart, (2): John Takai, (3): CurvaBezier, (4): zooco, (5): yaistantine; S. 128 links: olegan, Mitte: Kakigori Studio, rechts: jemastock; S. 146 unten: www.miriamdoerr.com; S. 154: pressmaster; S. 196 oben: Henrik Larsson; S. 205 2. von unten: Coka); **GlowImages** (S. 34 (A): BlendRF; S. 35 (6): CulturaRF); **Google, Inc.**, Screenshot der Redaktion (S. 70); **Greenwich Free Press** (S. 66: Leslie Yager); **Houghton Mifflin Harcourt** (S. 60); **Image Source** (S. 35 (B): Brock Jones); **imago** (S. 91: Bettina Strenske; S. 102 unten rechts: Christian Ditsch; S. 113: United Archives International); **interfilm** (S. 43 Walter Woodman & Patrick Cederberg/ interfilm Berlin Management GmbH; S. 71 oben: Aviary/ Corrie Chen; S. 99); **INTERFOTO** (S. 30 (D): LatitudeStock/ JeffGoodman; S. 112 links: SuperStock); **Refugee Youth** (S. 50); **JR** (S. 84); **laif** (S. 85: Frank Heuer); **LOOK-foto** (S. 18 unten rechts: Karl Johaentges; S. 19 oben rechts: Konrad Wothe); **Murdo MacLeod** (S. 32: Copyright Murdo MacLeod, no syndication, no redistribution, Murdo Macleod's repro fees apply sgealbadh. Commed) **mauritius images** (S. 4 oben: (u. S. 11 (D): imagebroker.com; S. 10 (A): Alamy Stock Photo/Andy Selinge; S. 11 (C), (D): imagebroker.com; S. 12 oben: Alamy Stock Photo/tbkmedia.de; S. 26 unten links: Alamy Stock Photo/Bill Bachman; S. 30 (B): Alamy Stock Photo/Tim Graham; S. 35 (C): Alamy/Catchlight Visual Services; S. 36: Alamy/Ryan Jorgensen; S. 94 unten rechts: Alamy/Anthony Collins; S. 146 oben: Alamy/Picture Partners); **Cecile Niemitz-Rossant**, Berlin (S. 54 unten); **PantherMedia** (S. 34 (3): Sergej Seemann); **Photoshot** (S. 26 unten Mitte: NHPA); **Rockfinch** (S. 76: Claire Cunningham); **Reuters** (S. 82: Pichi Chuang; S. 89 oben: Kevork Djansezian); **Sapna Richter**, Berlin (S. 28 oben; S. 31; S. 54; S. 55; S. 102 alle oben; S. 103 alle; S. 132 alle; S. 147; S. 155; S. 156 oben); **ROLAND Rechtsschutz-Versicherungs-AG** (S. 130; S. 135); **Scottish Government**/Union, 2009 (S. 56); **Shutterstock** (S. 4 unten (u. S. 35 (5)); S. 8/9: Ipatov; S. 11 (B): FiledIMAGE; S. 12 unten: Leah-Anne Thompson; S. 15: Gordon Bell; S. 19 unten rechts: mark higgins; S. 20 (B): Olga Rosi, (C): Aleksey Sagitov, (F): NatUlrich; S. 26 unten rechts: Gianna Stadelmyer; S. 34 (2): 1000 Words; S. 35 (4): noolwlee, (5) (u. S. 4 unten): mooinblack; S. 64 (D): PHOTO FUN; S. 65 oben: Monkey Business Images, unten: aceshot1; S. 67 links: Eric Isselee, Mitte: Alexander Ishchenko, rechts: kontur-vid; S. 72 rechts: Volker Muether; S. 78: Kichigin; S. 88 oben: NeydtStock; S. 88 unten: SpeedKingz; S. 92: emka74; S. 94 oben: Joseph Sohm; S. 101 Hund: N K; S. 101 Obama: Action Sports Photography; S. 104: jlarrumbe; S. 110 oben: Dubova, Mitte: Smirnof, unten: Undrey; S. 111 oben: Irina Ippolitova, unten: Rus Limon; S. 112 2. von links: Everett Historical, 2. von rechts: Peter Probst; S. 115 (B): Olga Rosi, (C): Aleksey Sagitov, (F): NatUlrich; S. 118 (D): PHOTO FUN; S. 122 Utzon's building: Constantin Stanciu, wooden building: Olga Kashubin, (1): Loralya, (2): SHADOWMAC PHOTOGRAPHY, (3): Federherz; S. 124 (1): FooTToo; S. 124 (5): Mr Privacy; S. 137: sarahdesign; S. 138: AVAVA; S. 156 unten: Cartoonresource; S. 167: phloxii; S. 196 2. von oben: Phil Date; S. 196 2. von unten: e X p o s e; S. 196 unten: jeep2499; S. 197 links: tagstiles.com - S.Gruene, rechts: Miroslav Hlavko; S. 198 oben: Ruth Lawton, unten: stockcreations; S. 200 oben: Melinda Fawver, Mitte: Dudarev Mikhail, unten: a40757; S. 201: withGod; S. 202: Grandpa; S. 203 oben: Bildagentur Zoonar GmbH, unten links: Nagel Photography, unten Mitte: Eric Isselee, unten rechts: andamanec; S. 205 oben: Dmitry Naumov, Klaviertastatur: DVARG,Schlüssel: Ensuper, Tastatur: Claudio Divizia, Telefon: withGod, unten: blambca; S. 206 oben links: sumire8, oben rechts: BlueSkyImageq, Mitte: Jovanovic Dejan, unten: Fotovika; S. 208: Timolina; S. 209: Ico Maker; S. 210: browndogstudios; S. 211 oben: Rudchenko Liliia, unten: Kasa_s; S. 212 oben: theblackfatcat; S. 212 unten: Mauricio Graiki; S. 213 Mitte links: Goodluz, Mitte rechts: fototip, oben links: Joseph Sohm, oben rechts: Domenic Gareri, unten: irin-k; S. 214: IanRedding; S. 215 oben: sianc, unten links: Crevis, unten rechts: nanami7; S. 216 beide: kontur-vid; S. 217: esolla; S. 218: Josep Curto; S. 219 oben: Bikeworldtravel, unten: racorn; S. 220 oben: softRobot, unten: Bernadette Heath; S. 224 oben: Evgenii Bobrov, Mitte: The Last Word, unten: Vladimir Nenezic; S. 226 links: Maks Narodenko, rechts: 5 second Studio); **Yidumduma** (S. 24; S. 25); **Über den Tellerrand kochen GmbH**, Berlin (S. 51)

Liedtexte

S. 109 *Roar*. Lukasz Gottwald, Max Martin, Henry Walter, Bonnie McKee © Published by Cirkut Breaker LLC, Kascz Money Publishing, Prescription Songs LLC and MXM (ASCAP). Administered by Kobalt Music Publishing Limited and Kobalt Songs Music Publishing (ASCAP); Songs of Pulse Recording/When I'm rich you'll be my bitch - ImagemMusic GmbH, Berlin / NeueWelt Musikverlag GmbH, Hamburg; **S. 110-111** *Seven Years*. Text: Brown, Christopher Steven/ Forchhammer, Lukas/Forrest, Stefan/JENSEN, MORTEN RISTORP/Labrel, David, James/Pilegaard, Morten (c) Copyright Big Dreams Aps/Fuck you Dave/Halla! Halla! Publishing/Late 80's Music/Stefmusic/Then we take the world/Thou art the hunger/WB Music Corp/Westside Independent Music Publishing; LLC; Warner Bros Inc / Neue Welt Musikverlag GmbH, Hamburg

Texte

S. 36-38 Excerpts from *Coast to Coast* by David Fermer, Cornelsen Verlag GmbH, 2016; **S. 32-33** Experience: *I am 16 and live alone in the wilderness.* As told to Joan McFadden. Copyright Guardian News & Media Ltd 2017. Fotograf: MURDOPHOTO.COM; **S. 48** *Solving the pocket money problem* from Merryn Somerset-Webb, Channel 4, London, 2 July 2013; **S. 91** *Raise your voice*. ROLAND Rechtsschutz-Versicherungs-AG; **S. 96-98** *GLASGOW GIRLS* © 2012 by David Greig. All rights whatsoever in this play are strictly reserved and application for performance etc., must be made before rehearsal to Casarotto Ramsay & Associates Ltd., 7-12 Noel Street, London W1F 8GQ (rights@casarotto.co.uk). No performance may be given unless a licence has been obtained; **S. 108** *Veggie Panini* from "More Than Friends: Poems from Him and Her" by Sara Holbrook and Allan Wolf. Copyright © 2008 Sara Holbrook and Allan Wolf. Published by WordSong, an imprint of Boyds Mills Press. Reprinted by permission; **S. 108** *Taking one for the team* from "Weird? (Me, Too!) Let's Be Friends" by Sara Holbrook. Copyright © 2011 by Sara Holbrook. Published by WordSong, an imprint of Boyds Mills Press. Reprinted by permission; **S. 78-80** Excerpt from *The White Darkness* by Geraldine McCaughrean, Oxford University Press 2005; **S. 104-106** *In the outback*. Excerpt from "A Prayer for Blue Delaney" by Kirsty Murray, Cornelsen Verlag 2005

√ Choose criteria[1] for your feedback.

✎ Add other criteria you need, e.g. for feedback on a story.

TEXT | PRESENTATION

	CONTENT
√	You covered the important points in the task.
√	The information was interesting/new.
√	You gave examples/details.
√	You gave your opinion.
√	You gave arguments for your opinion.
✎	*Your story had a plot.*[2]
	You described the characters.
	…

TEXT

	STRUCTURE
√	Your introduction said what the text is about.
√	You used paragraphs.
√	Each paragraph had a new idea.
√	You had a conclusion.
✎	…

	LANGUAGE
√	You used different adjectives and adverbs.
√	You joined sentences with linking words.
√	You used special vocabulary for the topic.
√	Your spelling was correct.
√	Your grammar was correct.
✎	…

PRESENTATION

	STRUCTURE
√	You introduced the topic.
√	Your presentation had a clear structure.
√	You showed your main points on a poster/…
√	You summed up at the end.
√	You invited us to ask questions.
✎	…

	DELIVERY
√	You seemed relaxed.
√	You made eye contact.
√	You used notes.
√	You spoke clearly.
√	You explained your pictures.
✎	…

	GROUP PRESENTATION
√	You each took on responsibility.
√	You all supported each other.
√	Each presenter introduced their contribution[3].
√	The different contributions were relevant to the topic.
√	The different contributions fitted together.
✎	…

[1] **criteria** *(pl)* [kraɪˈtɪəriə] Kriterien [2] **plot** [plɒt] Handlung [3] **contribution** [ˌkɒntrɪˈbjuːʃn] Beitrag